The Edward Said Reader

Edward W. Said is University Professor of English and Comparative Literature at Columbia University. He is the author of twenty books, including *Orientalism,* which was nominated for a National Book Critics Circle Award, *Culture and Imperialism,* and a memoir, *Out of Place.*

ALSO BY EDWARD SAID

Joseph Conrad and the Fiction of Autobiography

Beginnings: Intention and Method

Orientalism

The Question of Palestine

Literature and Society (editor)

Covering Islam

The World, the Text, and the Critic

After the Last Sky (with Jean Mohr)

Blaming the Victims

Musical Elaborations

Culture and Imperialism

The Politics of Dispossession

Representations of the Intellectual

Peace and Its Discontents

The Pen and the Sword

Entre guerre et paix

Out of Place

The End of the Peace Process

THE EDWARD SAID READER

THE *Edward Said* READER

EDITED BY

Moustafa Bayoumi

AND

Andrew Rubin

VINTAGE BOOKS

A DIVISION OF RANDOM HOUSE, INC.

NEW YORK

A VINTAGE BOOKS ORIGINAL, SEPTEMBER 2000

 Published in the United States by Vintage Books, a division of Random House, Inc., New York, and simultaneously in Canada by Random House of Canada Limited, Toronto.

Library of Congress Cataloging-in-Publication Data
The Edward Said reader / edited by
Moustafa Bayoumi and Andrew Rubin.
New York : Vintage Books, 2000.
I. Bayoumi, Moustafa. II. Rubin, Andrew.
Includes bibliographical references.
IBSN: 0-375-70936-3
00-34947
CIP

Book design by Rebecca Aidlin

www.vintagebooks.com

Printed in the United States of America
10 9 8 7 6 5 4 3 2 1

ACKNOWLEDGMENTS

The editors wish to thank Dr. Zaineb Istrabadi, Jin Auh, Diana Secker Larson, Shelley Wanger, and, most of all, Edward W. Said for making this publication possible.

CONTENTS

INTRODUCTION

Moustafa Bayoumi and Andrew Rubin

In early September 1991 Edward Said traveled to London to attend a conference he had organized. Taking place on the eve of the Madrid Peace Conference, the event was made up of Palestinian intellectuals and activists who heeded Said's call for joining together in a position of strength to counter the weakness of the Palestinian situation after the Gulf War. It turned out to be a conference of disappointments for Said, full of "the endless repetition of well-known arguments."[1] Midway through it, Said telephoned his wife in New York and asked for the results of his annual physical, as he was concerned about his cholesterol. The cholesterol was fine, his wife told him, but she added that he should call his doctor when he returned to New York. There was something in the hesitation of her voice, Said recalls, that made him call Dr. Hazzi immediately. It was there, in a stolen moment between debates, that Said discovered that he had leukemia.

Edward Said has the uncanny ability to find himself on the losing side of time. The tragic convergences of this story—while fighting for the disappearing voice of his people he learns he has the fight for his own life ahead of him—seem the stuff of Shakespeare. But Said is no Othello, full of destructive self-pity. His self-made role has been to challenge authority, not to assume it, although his intellect and accomplishments have been nothing less than magisterial.

Anti-dynastic, rigorous, erudite, polemical, and always driven by a quest for secular justice, Said's contribution is the clear vision and moral energy to turn catastrophe into ethical challenge and scholarship into intellectual obligation. This means, of course, that he is often on the wrong side of power, challenging the status quo and our critical conscience in a world divided by conflict and driven by arrogant oppression. It is this quality of speaking out on the side of the oppressed that puts Said in the long tradition of engaged intellectuals, people like Jean-Paul Sartre, Simone de Beauvoir, Angela Davis, Frantz Fanon, Noam Chomsky, C. L. R James, James Baldwin, Malcolm X, and Huda Shaarawi—those who seek, as Marx once noted, not just to interpret the world, but to change it. Said's commitments to his people, to his scholarship, and to his own talents have made him arguably the most important intellectual of the latter half of the twentieth century.

Like many intellectuals of the turbulent twentieth century, Said has had to reckon with his life as an exile, and the pain of exile has been a grounding philosophy to all his work. Born to a wealthy Palestinian family in Jerusalem in 1935, Said—like the vast majority of Palestinians—was displaced and dispossessed of his home and homeland by the cataclysmic events of 1948. He eventually moved to the United States in 1951, but to live in exile is to exist somehow in an embattled relationship with time. Said's dissonances with the temporal, however, do not remain on the philosophical level. Tirelessly on the side of the weak and the forgotten, he has become the primary spokesperson in the West for the Palestinians, crafting books and articles, appearing regularly on television and radio, lecturing an American and Western public on the injustices inflicted on them.

This exposure comes with a price. Said is routinely vilified in much of the popular press. He has been dubbed a "professor of terror," and "Arafat's man in New York." His Columbia University office has been ransacked, he has received numerous death threats, and the New York City Police Department once considered his life in enough peril to install a "panic button" in his apartment. Yet he remains wedded to his principles and unseduced by authority. In September 1993, when the White House called Said and asked him attend the signing ceremony for the Oslo agreements (which he opposed for several reasons, including the fact that the agreements said nothing about the forgotten majority of Palestinians who now reside outside of Gaza and the West Bank), Said declined, telling them the day should be known as a Palistinian "day of mourning."

This impulse to bring to light truths that powerful forces either obscure, suppress, or distort can be found not only in Said's work as a Palestinian activist but in almost all of his work, from his literary and music criticism to his political pieces. *Orientalism,* his 1978 book on the Western representations of the Muslim Middle East, forced a major rethinking of the workings of culture precisely because it argued that political ideas of domination and colonization can find their strength and justification in the production of cultural knowledge. At a time when most American literary scholarship was engaged in highly specialized, esoteric textual practices to discover "universal truths," *Orientalism* forced academics of all kinds to reevaluate the political nature and consequences of their work in the ensuing storm. *The Question of Palestine,* a highly learned and polemical work, harnessed this same drive to reveal how European colonialism, Zionism, and American geopolitics have all systematically excluded and dispossessed Palestinians from their homeland and dehumanized them to the point where they were almost prevented from representing their existence. In *Culture and Imperialism,* Said elucidated a more general relationship between imperial ideology and the workings of culture and argued that even the small world drawn by the treasured literary icon Jane Austen is deeply imbricated in the material facts of European colonialism.

What has occupied much of Said's energies has been the role and vocation of the intellectual. Europe's study of the Orient was, after all, for Said an "intellectual" (as well as a human) failure.[2] In *The World, the Text, and the Critic,* Said argues that "criticism must think of itself as life-enhancing and constitutively opposed to every form of tyranny, domination, and abuse; its social goals are noncoercive knowledge produced in the interests of human freedom," and he posits that the most useful adjective to be joined to criticism would be *oppositional*.[3] In another essay ("Opponents, Audiences, Constituencies, and Community") he advocates that "the politics of interpretation demand a dialectical response from a critical consciousness [a repeating phrase in Said's work] worthy of its name. Instead of noninterference and specialization, there must be *interference,* crossing of borders and obstacles, a determined attempt to generalize exactly at those points where generalizations seem impossible to make."[4] And in *Representations of the Intellectual,* he again puts forth the idea that "[l]east of all should an intellectual be there to make his/her audiences feel good; the whole point [to being an intellectual] is to be embarrassing, contrary, even unpleasant."[5] For Said, his life has been a commitment to two things: an incorruptible, unassailable belief in the dignity of all people and human justice for everyone, and a lifelong pursuit in the rigors of scholarship to excavate, uncover, review, and interpret all facets of human experience, particularly those that are overlooked by any structure of authority. With these commitments, Said's oppositional stance becomes not merely a radical posture but a manner of living.

Said's deliberate opposition to authority needs to be considered in connection with his meditations on exile. "It is a part of morality not to be at home in one's home," wrote the German philosopher Theodor Adorno,[6] and Said's own ethics derive in significant part precisely from this sense of "homelessness." Living as an exile and thus in an ambivalent relationship with two cultures often at odds with each other (American and Arab), Said has often described how he feels not quite at home in either one. Yet rather than lament this condition of displacement, as many in the twentieth century have done, Said offers a qualified celebration of the possibilities it affords. "Most people are principally aware of one culture, one setting, one home; exiles are aware of at least two, and this plurality of vision give rise to an awareness of simultaneous dimensions, an awareness that—to borrow a phrase from music—is contrapuntal. . . . There is a unique pleasure in this sort of apprehension, especially if the exile is conscious of other contrapuntal juxtapositions that diminish orthodox judgment and elevate appreciative sympathy. There is also a particular sense of achievement in acting as if one were at home wherever one happens to be."[7]

Out of displacement and discomfort, Said weaves an approach to the major questions of our era that is neither self-indulgent nor self-pitying. There is no silence or cunning involved in Said's exile; instead there is the cultivation of a critical consciousness and, perhaps, as Mary McCarthy has described exile, "an oscillation between melancholy and euphoria."[8] Said's exile has enabled him to see his surroundings slightly askew of those at home in them. "Even if one is not an actual immigrant or expatriate," Said tells us, "it is still possible to think as one, to imagine and investigate in spite of barriers, and always to move away from the centralizing authorities towards the margins, where you see things that are usually lost on minds that have never traveled beyond the conventional and the comfortable." If alienation from exile was the paradigmatic mode of the first part of the century, Said's "pleasures of exile" offer a way to think beyond alienation and embrace creativity and critique.

Noam Chomsky has described Said's intellectual contribution in this manner: "His scholarly work has been devoted to unraveling mythologies about ourselves and our interpretation of others, reshaping our perceptions of what the rest of the world is and what we are. The second is the harder task; nothing's harder than looking into the mirror." Chomsky, himself a veteran of the media wars, continues: "Edward's in an ambivalent position in relation to the media and mainstream culture: his contributions are recognized, yet he's the target of constant vilification. It comes with the turf if you separate yourself from the dominant culture."[9]

What Chomsky describes is, in one way, a possible irony of Said's work. Despite the criticism that he incurs and the provocative issues he forces his audiences to confront, Said has achieved a remarkable level of influence and recognition. He holds one of the eight University Professorships at Columbia University (University Professor is the highest rank possible for faculty at Columbia). He has published twenty books, which have been translated into thirty-one languages. Over two hundred universities around the world have heard him lecture, and he has delivered prestigious lecture series such as the Reith Lectures for the BBC, the Empson Lectures at Cambridge University, the René Wellek Memorial Lectures at the University of California-Irvine, the Henry Stafford Little Lecture at Princeton University, the T. B. Davie Academic Freedom Lecture at the University of Cape Town in South Africa, a series of lectures of the Collège de France, and many others. He is a member of the American Academy of Arts and Sciences, the Royal Society of Literature, and an Honorary member of King's College, Cambridge. He has been a member of the Executive Board of PEN, is a member of the Council on Foreign Relations, and was president of the Modern Language Association (1999). He has been awarded numerous honorary doctorates, from institutions of higher learning including the University of Chicago, Jawaharlal Nehru University in India, Bir Zeit University in the West Bank, the University of Michigan, the American University in Cairo, and the National University of Ireland. He is also the music critic for the *Nation*.

In addressing this apparent contradiction—the success of an

oppositional critic—it is important to recognize first of all that despite his status, Said is routinely vilified and dismissed by certain segments of the population (particularly for his continued advocacy of the Palestinian cause). More important, however, Said's reception is instructive for what it reveals about intellectual labor and about the possibilities of a just future for all. "There is no such thing as a private intellectual," Said explains in *Representations of the Intellectual,* "since the moment you set down words and then publish them you have entered a public world. Nor is there only a public intellectual, someone who exists just as a figurehead or spokesperson or symbol of a cause, movement, or position. There is always the personal inflection and the private sensibility, and those give meaning to what is being said or written."[10] Said's own manner of "personal inflection," his passionate yet reasoned intellect, his erudite yet democratic spirit, his elegance of prose and presentation, have in important ways contributed to the reception of his intellectual beliefs in justice and coexistence in an increasingly fractured world.

Of even greater significance, however, is that the integrity of the work, committed to the universal application of basic human rights, is globally appreciated. Our overwhelming need to hear and read someone like Edward Said is a double-sided signifier. On the one hand, it reveals that the dominant ways of political power continue to deny basic human rights to people everywhere. Around the world, people feel the need for ideas that can challenge and usurp the triumphalist thinking of Eurocentric colonialism or the defensive reactions of nativist ideologies. This desire to engage with Said—by Indonesians and Parisians, from the Irish to the Iroquois—is perhaps felt even more so today, as bland pronouncements of globalization often mean little more than extending the military and economic reach of the United States, and the confusing reactions to global power fall prey to simple "us" versus "them" dichotomies. Forever wedded to the possibilities of mutual coexistence and universal recognition, Said's thought has helped many think their way through the minefields not only of the Palestinian struggle, but also of many other such conflicts the world over. On the other hand, the fact that Said has built such a large readership is itself indicative not only of the power of his ideas but also of the future possibilities for justice and dignity contained therein.

. . .

Edward Said was born in November 1935 in his family's two-story home in Talbiyah, a section of West Jerusalem inhabited at the time almost exclusively by Palestinian Christians. He would be the eldest son in a family of four sisters. Having lost an earlier child shortly after childbirth in Cairo, Said's mother was determined that her next be born in Jerusalem, and the Saids, living mainly in Cairo at the time, journeyed back to Jerusalem that summer and waited for their son's birth in his uncle and aunt's house. The itinerant lifestyle that would mark Said's later life, both as a Palestinian living in exile and as a world renowned intellectual, was established for Edward even before he was born.

Said's father, Wadie, a Jerusalemite, had moved to Cairo in 1929 to establish the Standard Stationary Company, the Egyptian branch of the Palestine Educational Company, a concern founded by Boulos Said, Wadie's cousin and the husband to his sister Nabiha. In 1932 Wadie married Edward's mother Hilda Musa, born in Nazareth, who had earlier been a gifted young student at the American School for Girls in Beirut (her mother was Lebanese). Said's father was a strict, almost Victorian man who believed in the value of an education and uncritically in the worth of the United States. He was made up of "an absolute, unarguable paradox, repression and liberation opening on to each other."[11] Said's relationship with his mother, full of tender mercies and filial devotion, was marked by the need to seek her affections, where he often found a nurturing repose, and the fear that these same affections could be capriciously withdrawn. He calls her "my closest and most intimate companion for the first twenty-five years of my life,"[12] and although his father unfailingly supported Said's artistic hunger—by providing him with piano lessons from the age of six, opera visits, a rich library—it was through his mother that the young Edward began to cultivate his aesthetic sensibility. Mother and son read *Hamlet* together in the front reception room of their Cairo apartment when the young Edward was only nine years old.

Interestingly, both parents had a historic connection to the United States. Hilda Said's father, who was a Baptist minister in Nazareth, had studied for a time in Texas. Said's father, who had been urged to leave Palestine by his father to avoid conscription in the Ottoman army, had sojourned to the United States in 1911 after a brief six-month stint in Liverpool. From Liverpool, he and a Palestinian friend took jobs on an American passenger liner as stewards, later disembarking in New York without valid papers. Eventually, he became a salesman for ARCO, a Cleveland paint company, studied at Case Western Reserve University, and upon hearing that the Canadians were sending a battalion "to fight the Turks in Palestine"[13] during World War I, he crossed the border and enlisted. When he found out that no such battalion existed, he deserted and crossed back to the United States, where he joined the American Expeditionary Force. Based first in Georgia, Wadie Said was then sent to France to fight for the Americans. After the war, he returned to Cleveland and established his own paint company. Upon the urgings of his mother who wanted him nearby, he returned to Palestine in 1920 as an American citizen.

Despite her father's history with the United States and her husband's citizenship, Hilda Said never assumed American citizenship. After 1948, her citizenship as a stateless Palestinian presented numerous problems for the Saids. Told that she would have to reside in the United States for two years to acquire citizenship, she refused, and only after 1956, with the help of the Lebanese ambassador to Egypt, did she obtain a Lebanese passport. Twenty years later, with the outbreak of the Lebanese civil war, even this passport created problems. Having come to the United States on a visitor's visa to receive treatment for breast cancer, she overstayed the official date, and despite the fact that she was hospitalized and comatose, the Immigration and Naturalization Service began deportation proceedings against her. The case was thrown out by an angry judge who rebuked the INS for its insensitivity.

As was common at the time for families of means, the Saids traveled often and easily between the different countries of the region. Cairo was the place of the family business, Jerusalem the center of family and relatives, and a Lebanese mountain village, Dhour el-Shweir, was the site of annual summer vacations. In Cairo, Said received a strict and unhappy colonial education, first at the Gezira Preparatory School (GPS), where there were no Egyptian teachers. He describes the colonial atmosphere of GPS as "one of unquestioned assent framed with hateful servility by teachers and students alike."[14] The family was now living in Zamalek, a Cairo neighborhood that was at the time a "colonial outpost whose tone was set by Europeans with whom we had little or no contact: we built our own world within it." Before 1947, the Saids were virtually alone in Cairo, joined only by Said's maternal aunt and, later, his grandmother.

In 1946, Said graduated to the Cairo School for American Children (CSAC; 1946–49). This school offered a more relaxed and democratic environment than GPS did, but still here Said felt alienated from his American and English classmates, never experiencing "a pleasurable moment of camaraderie," as he recalls in his memoir.[15] In 1947 the Saids moved back to Jerusalem for the bulk of that year, and Said was enrolled in his father's alma mater, St. George's School. Jerusalem was a tense city by this time, but Edward had lived a largely isolated and sheltered life and had little sense of the increasing gravity of the situation around him. The Saids remained in Jerusalem until December 1947, when they returned to Cairo. By March 1948, every member of his extended family had been driven out of the city by the war, and the Saids narrowly escaped. It would be forty-five years before he would set foot in Jerusalem again.

Back in Cairo, a twelve-year-old, somewhat bewildered Said watched "the sadness and destitution in the faces and lives of people I had formerly known as ordinary middle-class people in Palestine, but I couldn't really comprehend the tragedy that had befallen them nor could I piece together all the different narrative fragments to understand what had really happened in Palestine."[16] Said's aunt Nabiha, "a woman of almost superhuman energy and charity,"[17] moved to Egypt after the *nakba* (catastrophe) and began her own dedicated campaign to alleviate the sufferings of Palestinian refugees in Egypt. Said has written often and movingly about her efforts, from which he learned to understand "the desolations of being without a country or a place to return to, of being unprotected by any national authority or institutions."[18] He also seemed to draw valuable lessons of empathy and commitment from her work. Nabiha tirelessly received destitute Palestinians who enlisted her aid, pressed every friend and acquaintance she knew to place lost refugees in their offices or schools, and traveled to the squalid slums and distributed medicines and food. For her work, she earned the title "Mother of Palestine" from many of the people she assisted.

On the whole, however, Said continued to live a relatively cloistered life as a young teenager, and he survived his schooling through compliance to authority, with little sense of who he was except a nagging feeling of being always out of place. After finishing CSAC in 1949, he went to Victoria College in Cairo, a prestigious but cheerless colonial school where Arabic was outlawed and English mores and institutions were strenuously taught and reinforced.

In 1951 Said was sent to the United States, where he was enrolled at Mount Hermon, a puritanical New England boarding school. It was there that Said first encountered teachers who broadened his intellectual curiosity and helped him rediscover his passion for the piano. By the end of his two years there, he had become a pianist of note, and academically he was one of the top two students in his class. Despite his successes, however, Said still felt himself an outsider in this environment, and his feelings were confirmed when he was denied any role in the graduation ceremonies. Accepted to both Princeton and Harvard, Said began at Princeton the next year.

Oppressed by the rigid club system, Said despised the oligarchic nature of Princeton in the 1950s, though writing about it now he observes: "a new faculty, the deemphasis of the wretched clubs, and of course, the presence of women and minorities have transformed [Princeton] from the provincial, small-minded college I attended between 1953 and 1957 into a genuine university."[19] Two professors, however, did have a profound influence on Said, notably the literary critic R. P. Blackmur (whose work on close, explicatory reading would influence much of Said's writing, particularly on literature and music), and the philosophy professor Arthur Szathmary, whose critical point of view was passed on to Said. At Princeton, Said was finally exposed to the pleasures of academic rigor as opposed to rote learning, and after graduating Phi Beta Kappa he received a scholarship for graduate study at Harvard, which he deferred for one year.

That year was spent mostly in Cairo, and it proved a difficult time for his father's business as Gamal Abdul Nasser of Egypt embarked on his campaign of "Arab socialism." Eventually the family business was sold to the Nasser government, and the family, squeezed by their resident alien status in Nasser's Egypt, packed and moved to Lebanon. Said returned to the United States to spend the next five years at Harvard, working on a dissertation on Joseph Conrad under the supervision of Harry Levin and Monroe Engel, and, when in Cairo, continuing to study piano under Ignace Tiegerman. During his Harvard years, Said's political life remained dormant as he immersed himself in being a graduate student of literature. In 1959 a family friend of the Saids, Farid Haddad, "a profoundly political man"[20] and a medical doctor in Cairo who had worked closely with Said's aunt Nabiha, was jailed, beaten, and killed by the Egyptian security forces for his dedicated activity in the Egyptian Communist Party. Said was—and continues to be—deeply affected by the murder: "Farid's life and death have been an underground motif in my life for four decades now, not all of them periods of awareness or of active political struggle."[21] He would later dedicate *The Question of Palestine* to Farid Haddad (and to the Palestinian poet Rashid Hussein). After completing his dissertation, in 1963, Said accepted a position as an instructor at Columbia University and has lived in New York ever since. His prodigious intellectual life was about to begin.

Said's first book, *Joseph Conrad and the Fiction of Autobiography* (1966), was a fastidious, methodical investigation of the interplay between Conrad's fiction and his correspondence. If it reveals anything about Said and his predicament, it does so in purely abstract and existential terms centered on the condition of Conrad's alienation. As a young literary scholar teaching at Columbia University in the 1960s—where he was surrounded by figures like Lionel Trilling and F.W. Dupee—Said had placed himself in an environment that presented few reminders of his past and his identity. In 1967 all that would change.

The Arab-Israeli war shattered and dashed Palestinian hopes of returning home. Within seven days in 1967 Israel defeated the armies of Egypt, Syria, and Jordan and went on to occupy the West Bank, Gaza, the Golan Heights, and the Sinai Peninsula. As Said recalled in *Out of Place,* the 1967 war "seemed to embody *the* dislocation that subsumed all the other losses, the disappeared worlds of my youth, the unpolitical years of my education, the assumption of disengaged teaching at Columbia . . . I was no longer the same person after 1967; the shock of that war drove me back to where it had all started."[22] It was out of the experience of 1967, as a Palestinian living in the United States, that Said conceived the central theme of *Orientalism.* "The Arab Portrayed," which he wrote in 1968 at the behest of Ibrahim Abu-Lughod, attacked the way Arabs were portrayed in the media as only sheikhs or terrorists. For the first time, Said expressed an interest in the politics of cultural representation; he wrote: "If the Arab occupies space enough for attention it is a negative value. He is seen as a disrupter of Israel's and the West's existence, or . . . as a surmountable obstacle to Israel's creation in 1948. Palestine was imagined as an empty desert waiting to burst into bloom, its inhabitants inconsequential nomads possessing no stable claim to the land and therefore no cultural permanence."[23]

The war also made Said reconnect with friends and relatives in the Palestinian political community in Amman and Beirut. "I began to feel that what happened in the Arab World concerned me personally and could no longer be accepted with a passive political disengagement," he wrote.[24] In 1969 he met with Kamal Nasser, a distant relative and poet who served as a Palestinian official spokesperson until an Israeli hit squad assassinated him in Beirut in 1973. Said began meeting diplomats from the United Nations in New York as his circle of associates expanded. He had been planning a book on Jonathan Swift, but his attention shifted to another idea that formed the basis for his second book, *Beginnings*. "*Beginnings* was really a project of reaction to a crisis which caused me to rethink what I was doing, and try to make more connections in my life between things that had been either suppressed, or denied, or hidden," Said recalled. "It was the product of the 1967 War."

For Said, *Beginnings* was an attempt to work through the conditions of his political awakening in literary terms. In the high modernist novels of Joseph Conrad, Marcel Proust, and Thomas Mann, he saw that beginnings were crucial to understanding how certain individuals (or narrators) negotiated authority, the power of tradition, the constraints and dictates of convention, and above all, the limits of narrative form. As Hayden White observed, *Beginnings* was a political allegory,[25] an almost introspective work that abstractly engaged the problem of how to *begin* to grasp the relationship between the past and the circumstances and exigencies of the present.

The eighteenth-century Italian philologist Giambiatisa Vico gave *Beginnings* its political and philosophical coherence. Vico's importance remained for Said almost as unshakably symbolic as Conrad's. In *Beginnings,* Said called Vico "a prototypical modern thinker" who "perceives beginning as an activity requiring the writer to maintain an unstraying obligation to practical reality and sympathetic imagination in equally strong parts."[26] Vico represented a method of situating and unfolding the literary work of art in all its worldly, secular relations. Furthermore, he challenged the specialization and sequestering of knowledge. "Vico's *New Science*," Said wrote, "is everywhere a reminder that scholars hide, overlook, or mistreat the gross physical evidences of human activity, including their own."[27]

Said took Vico's *New Science* to heart. By the early 1970s, he became increasingly more active and engaged as a public intellectual. He began writing for a wider audience in English, Arabic, and French. He wrote op-eds on Palestine for *The New York Times, Newsweek,* and *Le Monde diplomatique*. His reputation as an engaged Palestinian intellectual was beginning to emerge. In an editorial for *The New York Times,* Said declared, "the Jews are not a chosen people, but Jews and Arabs together, one as oppressor and the other as oppressed, have chosen each other for a struggle whose roots seem to go deeper with each year, and whose future seems less thinkable and resolvable each year. Neither people can develop without the other there, harassing, taunting, fighting. . . . Each is the other."[28] In 1975 he testified before the U.S. Congressional Subcommittee on International Relations: "Imagine to yourselves," he told the committee chaired by Representative Lee Hamilton, "that by some malicious irony you found yourselves declared foreigners in your own country. This is the essence of the Palestinian's fate during the twentieth century."[29]

In 1976, two years prior to the publication of *Orientalism,* Said won Columbia University's Lionel Trilling Award for *Beginnings,* and a year later he was promoted to Parr Professor of English and Comparative Literature. Said's presence and visibility in the United States was seen as indispensable to the Palestine National Council (PNC). In 1977 Said, along with his friend Ibrahim Abu-Lughod, was elected to the PNC as an independent, choosing not to ally himself with any of the member parties. Over the fourteen years that he was a member, Said attended fewer than six PNC meetings, and he took orders from nobody, according to Shafiq al-Hout, a long-time friend and member of the executive council of the PLO.

According to Said, his membership in the PNC was largely "an act of solidarity," allowing him to assert his Palestinian identity to act politically on behalf of Palestinian self-determination.[30]

On sabbatical leave at Stanford University from 1975 to 1976, Said returned to the question he raised in "The Arab Portrayed" and completed *Orientalism.* If *Beginnings* dealt with questions of authority and power in terms of literary debates about language and narrative, *Orientalism* engaged the themes of knowledge and power in much more explicit ways. It examined an array of nineteenth-century French and British novelists, poets, politicians, philologists, historians, travelers, and imperial administrators. Together, their writings made up a discipline (Orientalism) by which European culture produced and managed the "Orient." Their writings expressed "a will . . . not only to understand what [was] non-European, but also to control and manipulate what was manifestly different."[31] They formed a medium that constituted power and through which power was exercised.

The contemporary Orientalist guild and its defenders responded fiercely to Said's polemic. Leon Wieseltier wrote that *Orientalism* issued "little more than abject canards of Arab propaganda."[32] In a riposte published in *The New York Review of Books,* Bernard Lewis accused Said of "poisoning" the field of "Oriental" studies. Calling Said "reckless," "arbitrary," "insouciant," and "outrageous," Lewis recounted how Said, along with other Arab, Muslim, and Marxist critics, had "polluted" the word "Orientalism." Said, Lewis argued, had attempted to denigrate the work of well-intentioned, disinterested Orientalists; he had politicized an innocent scholarship.[33] Yet the shrill protests from Said's critics revealed less about Said's work than about the critics' own hypocrisy. Veiled in language of "scholarship" and "objectivity," their indignation was, as Talal Asad put it, "an indication of the Orientalist attitudes that Said himself had described."[34] Said pointed out that Lewis had merely "delivered ahistorical and willful political assertions in the form of scholarly argument, a practice thoroughly in keeping with the least creditable aspects of old-fashioned colonialist Orientalism."[35]

By the late 1970s, Said's work was beginning to gain acceptance and acclaim from a wider public. In 1979 *Orientalism* was runner-up in the "Criticism" category for the National Book Critics Circle Award. Said wrote a number of articles for *Time* magazine and several more op-eds for *The New York Times* that year in which he popularized many of the themes that he had discussed in *Orientalism* and related them to the Palestinian question. In 1979 he published his book *The Question of Palestine,* departing from traditional literary scholarship and into a more political, cultural, and historical investigation of Palestinian dispossession. If *Orientalism* defined the theories of imperialism at the level of representation, *The Question of Palestine* delved into the brute practices of the various colonialisms that the Palestinians have endured. American publishers found *The Question of Palestine* too provocative to publish. Beacon Press and Pantheon rejected the manuscript. Furthermore, many Palestinians took issue with Said's support for a two-state solution. When a Beirut publisher offered to bring the book out in Arabic, it asked Said to remove his criticism of Syria and Saudi Arabia. Said refused, and although the book was published in Israel, it still has not appeared in Arabic.

In 1979 Times Books published *The Question of Palestine,* and the next year Vintage Books brought out the paperback of this major work. Said suggested in *The Question of Palestine* that the political impasse between Zionism and the Palestinians was historically and culturally grounded in an unwillingness on the part of Zionism to recognize the realities and experiences of the Palestinians. "An iron circle of inhumanity" circumscribed them both. Although most Palestinians "fully realize that Israeli Jewish people . . . are a concrete reality," Said argued, Israel's repudiation of the existence of Palestinians prevented a resolution of the conflict. Said thus supported a two-state solution, a position that openly opposed PLO politics, although many in the PLO also realized this option was a greater possibility than liberating historical Palestine. Indeed, by 1980 Israel directly controlled large portions of the West Bank and Gaza, enforcing and justifying its military authority on colonial grounds—a dubious extension of the 1936 Emergency Regulation Act that the British had adopted to suppress Arab labor strikes. Zionism's vision thus rested on England's colonial legacy. Said wrote: "In joining the general Western enthusiasm for overseas territorial acquisition, Zionism *never* spoke of itself unambiguously as a Jewish liberation movement, but rather as a Jewish movement for colonial settlement in the Orient."[36]

In 1979 Said began writing *Covering Islam,* the third book in the

Orientalism trilogy. The United States was in grips of the "hostage crisis," after Iranian students seized the American embassy in Teheran on November 4, 1979, and demanded that the United States turn over Mohammed Reza Shah Pahlevi for trial. Hardly a day went by that the media didn't give special coverage to the "revival of Islam." Said broadened the *Orientalism* argument to expose the underlying ethnocentric assumptions of the view that "Islam" was a homogeneous and monolithic threat to U.S. hegemony. He advocated that reporters and critics develop a sense of internationalism and "worldliness" to grasp the events in Iran in the greater context of U.S. involvement in the overthrow of Mossedegh and the brutality of the U.S.-trained Iranian secret police known as SAVAK.

At the same time that Said was engaged with international affairs, he continued to devote a lot of his attention to the state of the literary profession. In essays such as "Traveling Theory," "Reflections on American 'Left' Literary Criticism," and others that made up his sixth book, *The World, the Text, and the Critic,* Said assailed a different kind of provincialism and unworldliness that he saw threatening the study and interpretation of literature. He perceived that a great deal of literary theory was provincial in its connection to a cult of professionalism that transformed scholars into myopic specialists. He urged academics "to break out of the disciplinary ghettoes in which . . . [they] have been confined."[37] Even among the post-structuralists—whom he originally admired—he lamented the cultivation of "corrosive irony." Of the influential literary critic Paul de Man, Said wrote: "De Man is always interested in showing that when critics or poets believe themselves to be stating something, they are really revealing . . . the impossible premises of stating anything at all, the so-called aporias of thought to which de Man believes all great literature always returns."[38] Leftist criticism faired no better in his judgment: "We argue in theory for what in practice we never do, and we do the same kind of thing with regard to what we oppose."[39] For Said, it was imperative that literary criticism not lose sight of its own conditions in the world and the political circumstances that demanded critical attention.

The Israeli invasion of Lebanon in 1982 deeply troubled Said, who feared for the safety of his own family and relatives there. That summer, Israel relentlessly bombarded Beirut from the air and from the sea, with cluster bombs, vacuum bombs, phosphorous rockets, and mortars.[40] On the evening of September 16, 1982, with prior knowledge and support of the Israeli Defense Forces, Christian Phalangist militias massacred 2,062 Palestinians and Lebanese at the Sabra and Shatila refugee camps in Lebanon.[41] The attack was a coordinated part of Israel's invasion. Yet few in the West raised concern about Israel's attack. "How is it," Said asked in "Permission to Narrate," an article published in the *London Review of Books*, "that the premises on which Western support for Israel is based are still maintained even though the reality, the facts, cannot possibly bear these premises out?"[42] By labeling Palestinians as terrorists, Said answered, Israel and the West had systematically suppressed the reality of the Palestinian experience of dispossession. In the *Raritan Quarterly*, Richard Poirier reiterated Said's charge: "Feelings about the victims of the siege [on Beirut] could not . . . be attached to an idea for the creation of a Palestinian homeland, since . . . no such idea has yet managed to find an enabling vocabulary within what is considered 'reasonable' political discourse in the . . . [United States]."[43] In *Le Monde diplomatique*, Israeli journalist Amnon Kapeliouk offered proof that the goal of Israeli policy in the mid-1970s was to undermine Palestinian nationalism by defining its main expression—the PLO—as terrorist. "The better," Said wrote, "to be able to ignore [Palestinians'] undeniable claims to Israel."[44]

As Said recognized, it was becoming increasingly important to represent Palestinian experience in all its facets. In the spring of 1984 this exigency acquired a renewed urgency: Harper and Row published Joan Peters's *From Time Immemorial*, a compendium of historical fabrications that incredibly sought to deny the historical existence of Palestinians. Despite its reliance on spurious and contrived evidence, the work received widespread acclaim. Barbara Tuchman, Elie Wiesel, Saul Bellow, Theodor White, and other prominent authors praised the book. Few reviewers in the United States questioned the book's veracity. It was Norman Finklestein, then a graduate student at Princeton University, however, who exposed the book as a complete hoax.[45] Said wrote in *The Nation*, "To read Peters and her supporters is for Palestinians to experience an extended act of ethnocide carried out by pseudoscholarship. Tom Sawyer attends his own funeral as a kind of lark, whereas we are being threatened with death before being permitted birth."[46]

If Palestinians existed at all in the imagination of the West, they were represented "not so much a people as a call to arms."[47] In an effort to demystify everyday Palestinian life, Said, who was serving as a consultant for the United Nations International Conference on the Question of Palestine (ICQP), proposed a UN exhibition of Swiss photographer Jean Mohr's work, which presented the daily reality of the Palestinian experience. Said viewed the purpose of the exhibition as to "deny the habitually simple, even harmful representations of Palestinians, and to replace them with something more capable of capturing the complex reality of their experience."[48] Although the United Nations approved of the photographs, it found Said's accompanying captions "controversial" and decided to permit the exhibit only if Said's captions were removed. A number of Arab states, it seemed, had disagreed with Mohr and Said's intentions. "Palestine to them was useful to a point—for attacking Israel, for railing against Zionism, imperialism, and the United States. . . . Beyond that point," Said wrote, "when it came to the urgent needs of Palestinians as a people, or to the deplorable conditions in which many Palestinians live in Arab countries as well as Israel, lines had to be drawn."[49] Together the photographs and captions were published in *After the Last Sky* (1986), Said's first major autobiographical work.

In *After the Last Sky,* Said dwelled on the themes of loss and exile, echoing the themes expressed in his first book on Joseph Conrad. Exile was an existential reality for Said who, as a member of PNC, was prohibited from visiting Israel. "Our truest reality," he wrote, "is expressed in the way we [Palestinians] cross over from one place to another. We are migrants and perhaps hybrids, in but not of any situation in which we find ourselves. This is the deepest continuity of our lives as a nation in exile and constantly on the move."[50] Said's work acquired a more mournful tone as he considered exile a symbolically powerful, yet tragic condition. In "Reflections on Exile," he observed, "exile is strangely compelling to think about but terrible to experience. . . . [I]t is life outside habitual order. It is nomadic, decentered, contrapuntal; . . . no sooner does one get accustomed to it than its unsettling force erupts anew."[51]

In the face of loss and exile, Said devoted more and more of his energies to writing about music, which had always for him had the Proustian capacity to recover lost time and place. A talented pianist,

Said began writing a music column for *The Nation* magazine in 1987. Of all the performers he reviewed, he had the highest regard for the pianist Glenn Gould, whose technical and intellectual majesty recalled Said's interest in Vico and Auerbach's philological method. "[A]s you listen to [Gould's] music," Said wrote in *Vanity Fair*, "you feel as if you are watching a tightly packed, dense work being unfolded, resolved almost, into a set of intertwined links held together not by two hands but by ten fingers, each responsive to all the others, as well as to the two hands and the one mind really back of everything."[52] His work on music continued. In 1989 Said delivered the prestigious Wellek Library Lectures at University of California, Irvine, in which he accompanied his talk with his own performance on the piano. The result, in printed form, was *Musical Elaborations* (1991), which further extended his reflections on the place of music in society.

Said's reflections on Gould's contrapuntal technique had far-reaching implications for his cultural and literary criticism. In *Culture and Imperialism* (1993), he adapted a musical term for literary criticism, arguing that literary works should be considered *contrapuntally*. By contrapuntal criticism Said meant that European culture needs to be read in relation to its geographic and spatial relations to empire as well as in counterpoint to the works the colonized themselves produced in response to colonial domination. In his widely debated chapter "Jane Austen and Empire," for example, Said argued that "we should . . . regard the geographical division of the world—after all significant in *Mansfield Park*—as not neutral, but as politically charged, beseeching the attention and elucidation its considerable proportions require. The question is not only how to understand and with what to connect Austen's morality and its social basis, but what to *read* of it."

Almost without exception, reviewers of *Culture and Imperialism* focused on "Jane Austen and Empire." *The New York Times*, *The London Review of Books*, *The Nation*, and *Dissent* all published articles that emphasized Said's criticism of *Mansfield Park*.[53] In *The Nation*, John Leonard wrote: "See Jane sit in the poise and order of Mansfield Park, not much bothering her pretty head about the fact that harmonious 'social space,' Sir Thomas Bertram's country estate, is sustained by slave labor."[54] Said's argument was that Austen's vision of Fanny Price's moral improvement rested on the estate's dependency on its slave holdings in Antigua, largely absent from the groomed and ordered grounds of Mansfield Park. Many critics misunderstood Said's argument. Irving Howe, for example, saw Said's essay as an attack on Austen's status as a novelist. Yet Said was not demeaning Austen's literary value; he was urging readers to develop a critical awareness of the European novel's relations to the colonial enterprises and imperial projects of the nineteenth and twentieth centuries.

By the early 1990s, Said's reputation had assumed international proportions, through both his eloquent pleas for justice for the Palestinians and the innovative humanistic scholarship he was producing. *Orientalism* had been translated into French, German, Spanish, Catalan, Arabic, Persian, Turkish, Japanese, Korean, and Swedish. The work had an enormously wide-ranging impact in the humanities and social sciences. An entire field of postcolonial studies was beginning to develop around Said's work. While a younger generation of scholars were actively pursuing the critiques of culture and power found in Said's work, Said himself was making a greater effort to situate the Palestinian struggle in relation to other national liberation movements around the world—in Vietnam, Algeria, Latin America, the Caribbean, Ireland, and South Africa. This effort to look critically and comparatively at other colonial resistance movements represented Said's own expanding vision of the relevance of his work both as a Palestinian exile and as an engaged scholar. *Culture and Imperialism,* a work seeking to discover "the general relationship between culture and empire," was Said's attempt to theorize this comparative outlook culturally and systematically.

The 1991 Gulf War confirmed for Said the extent to which American intellectuals had abandoned their responsibility to criticize and expose the abuses of American power abroad. In an interview published after the war, Said roared, "The intellectual community doesn't operate according to principles and doesn't consider itself bound by responsibilities toward the common weal. . . . The large body of American intellectuals is basically provincial, drawn only by virtue of expertise."[55] Increasingly, the necessity of the nonaligned intellectual to pursue scholarship away from the corruptions of authority and the abuses of professionalism came to figure importantly in his written work. In September 1991, Said resigned from the PNC. Although he cited his recently diagnosed leukemia as the reason for his departure, his decision had in fact been sealed by the Palestinian leadership's support of Saddam Hussein during the Gulf War. In 1992 Said returned to Palestine for the first time in forty-five years.

His illness did not deter him from his commitments and his passions. In the face of the diagnosis, he struggled even more intensively and actively as he became aware of the ebb of his life. In 1992 he was promoted to University Professor, the highest rank of professorship at Columbia University. He continued to teach and write, in spite of the debilitating side effects of the chemotherapy and radiation treatments. In 1993 he delivered the prestigious Reith Lectures for the BBC and seized the opportunity to emphasize the importance of independent critical activity: "Despite the abuse and vilification that any outspoken supporter of Palestinian rights and self-determination earns for himself or herself, the truth deserves to be spoken, represented by an unafraid and compassionate intellectual. . . . The great euphoria produced by . . . [the Oslo Accords] . . . obscured the fact that far from guaranteeing Palestinian rights, the documents in effect guaranteed the prolongation of Israeli control over the Occupied Territories. To criticize this means in effect taking a position against 'hope' and 'peace.'"[56]

From the beginning, Said saw through the pomp of the Oslo Accords between the PLO and the Israeli government. For a long time, he remained the only major critic of the Accords, their process, and their signatories. Negotiated in secret in 1993, the agreements were, in Said's words, the equivalent of the Palestinian "Treaty of Versailles." They made no mention of the end of the Israeli occupation and conceded Israel ultimate authority over the majority of the West Bank and Gaza. Even in the zones of Palestinian control, the Palestinians were granted no meaningful sovereignty. "There was Clinton," Said declared, "like a Roman emperor bringing two vassal kings to his imperial court and making them shake hands in front of him."[57]

The agreement amounted to an effort by Arafat to preserve the PLO and Arafat's own authority, which had been profoundly weakened by the PLO's support of Iraq during the Gulf War. Said called on Arafat to resign, only to have the Palestinian authority respond with a ban (still in effect) on his books. Said continued his caustic criticism, largely through his biweekly columns in *Al-Hayat* and *Al-Ahram Weekly*. The pieces were tough and uncompromising in their demands for clear vision and justice, stating that if peace were to have any substantive meaning, it could not be brought about under duress. For Said, the history of imperially administered partitions in India, Pakistan, Cyprus, and Ireland was the source of violence, not a solution to it. Observing that Oslo amounted to little more than an enforced policy of demographic separation between two peoples whose lives were inextricably intertwined, Said, in a 1999 article in the *New York Times Magazine*,[58] called for the establishment of a binational Israeli-Palestinian state. He argued that real and lasting peace was possible only if the terms of citizenship were made inclusive, democratic, and not based on principles of racial or religious difference.

To that end, Said drew upon his musical interests to encourage a common understanding between Israelis and Palestinians. In January 1999 he organized a performance by the celebrated Israeli pianist and conductor Daniel Barenboim at Bir Zeit University. Barenboim and he had become close friends in the early 1990s, partly through their deep appreciation of music and partly through their experience of 1967. The two had collaborated before. In 1998 Said wrote a new libretto replacing the spoken dialogue for Beethoven's opera *Fidelio*, and Barenboim conducted the work at the Chicago Symphony. Barenboim's performance of Beethoven's "Pathetique" and Opus 109 at Bir Zeit deeply stirred the audience.

In the meantime, while passionately pursuing redemptive cultural exchanges, Said, aware that he had entered the last phase of his life, continued to work quietly on a memoir, a work he had begun in 1994. In September 1999, *Out of Place: A Memoir*, a "subjective chronicle of an essentially lost or forgotten world, that of my early life," appeared. In 1999 Said also assumed the presidency of the Modern Languages Association. Despite his leukemia (which, after experimental therapy in the summer of 1998, went into remission but is slowly creeping back), he continues to teach, write, play music, lecture, advocate, opine, argue, research, and live with the same indefatigable energy as ever.

. . .

To squeeze the life's work of a major intellectual as prodigious and prolific as Edward Said into the pages of a single volume is no easy task. The sum total of the work defies easy condensation, and each selection bears more commentary than we can provide here. Nevertheless, *The Edward Said Reader* is an attempt to offer readers the opportunity to view the remarkable scope, the critical rhythms, the intellectual affinities, and the sheer strength of Said's criticism in his role as an internationally renowned literary critic and as a passionately engaged public intellectual. Drawing on material from Edward Said's books to date—beginning with his 1966 revised doctoral dissertation *Joseph Conrad and the Fiction of Autobiography* and working through to his 1999 memoir *Out of Place*—we have been guided by a belief that a single, easily accessible book that spans Said's career will be as useful to the new reader seeking to understand what Saidian criticism is all about as it will be to the scholar searching for Said's own genealogical foundations and historical development."[59]

The Edward Said Reader is divided into three major sections and an interview: "Beginnings," "*Orientalism* and After," and "Late Styles." "Beginnings" draws the arc of Said's early investigations, both in literary criticism and in his burgeoning Palestinian interventions. The early Said is forever attached to Conrad and fully invested in all the literary and philosophical trends of his time and seeking to make them his own. "*Orientalism* and After" acknowledges the tremendous impact that work had on both the life and the work of Said and on the humanities in general. Said's tone changes to that of the fully engaged intellectual, often angry, frequently profound, and always fabulously erudite. In "Late Styles" Said meditates more on the life of the intellectual, on the relationship between music and culture, on politics and commitment, and on his own life after having been diagnosed with leukemia. The book concludes with an interview we conducted with Edward Said in the summer of 1999.

There is no one else like Edward Said. His critical interventions have forced Western culture not only to confront its views of the non-European world but also to seriously assess its own ideas of itself. He has expanded the literatures and paradigms of literary study while maintaining a dedicated attachment to European literature and its aesthetics. Without the eloquence and energy of Edward Said, the situations and aspirations of the Palestinian people likely would have remained shielded from the West, buried under acres of stereotypes and histories of oppression. And his commitment to seeking justice for everyone has not lessened the searing bite of his pen when he inveighs against the falsities of the contemporary peace process or the corruptions of the Palestinian Authority.

Our own contact with Edward Said began when we read him as undergraduates, long before we were his graduate students at Columbia University, but it is through this association that we came to study under him. Ultimately, what we find in the broad variety of works we present here is an affirmation of the intellectual vocation, an unwavering belief that the rigors of intellectual thought and the courage to speak one's convictions will lead one down the incorruptible road to discovering and demanding equal justice for all. A teacher can bestow no finer lesson to his students.

PART I

Beginnings

I

The Claims of Individuality

(1966)

"Over the years," Said wrote, "I have found myself writing about Conrad like a *cantus firmus,* a steady groundbass to much that I have experienced."[1] There was much in Conrad's life with which Said identified. Conrad had grown up under the shadow of imperial occupation; he had left his native homeland during his adolescence, and he had found himself eventually living and writing in a Western European culture in which he felt neither fully at ease nor at home.

Published in 1966, *Joseph Conrad and the Fiction of Autobiography* was Said's first book, a revision of his dissertation, which he wrote at Harvard University under the direction of Monroe Engel and Harry Levin. It was, as Said wrote, "a phenomenological exploration of Conrad's consciousness." The book drew on the literary criticism of what was known as the Geneva School, a group of literary critics centered on Georges Poulet, Jean Rousset, and Jean Starobinski. Espousing a view of literature and criticism based on the philosophies of Husserl and Merleau-Ponty, the Geneva critics held that literary works were embodiments of authorial consciousness. As J. Hillis Miller wrote, the Geneva critics saw literary criticism as the "consciousness of consciousness."

In *Joseph Conrad and the Fiction of Autobiography,* Said undertook the colossal task of examining eight volumes of Conrad's letters so as to reconstruct Conrad's conception of his own identity, as an accomplished writer, as an émigré, and as a Pole. Yet if Said read Conrad's letters to understand the vicissitudes of Conrad's life, he also saw his prose as the self-conscious expressions of a writer whose relationship to the English language and culture was never entirely stable.

Although the critic F. R. Leavis considered Conrad's prose to be marred by imprecise diction and insufficient grasp of idiosyncratic English, Said viewed Conrad's relationship to the English language as an expression of Conrad's experience of exile. For Said, Conrad's writing conveyed an "aura of dislocation, instability and strangeness." "No one," Said later wrote, "could represent the fate of lostness and disorientation better than [Conrad] did, and no one was more ironic about the effort of trying to replace that condition with arrangements and accommodations."

On November 1, 1906, having received an affectionately inscribed copy of *The Mirror of the Sea* from Conrad, Henry James wrote to his odd Anglo-Polish colleague: "No one has *known*—for intellectual use—the things you know, and you have as artist of the whole matter, an authority that no one has approached."[2] Conrad could scarcely have wished for more eloquent tribute to the mastery with which, in the little book of sea sketches, he had consciously mediated claims of memory and artifice. *The Mirror of the Sea,* however, was an agreeable item fashioned by Conrad out of what James called "the prodigy of your past experience." To the casual observer—which James was not—Conrad's experience was largely a matter of ships and foreign ports, seas and storms; that, anyway, was what *The Mirror of the Sea* seemed to be about. Yet to Conrad, and to his fellow expatriate James speaking from a shared community of "afflicted existence," experience was a spiritual struggle filling what Flaubert had called the long patience of artistic life. When in *The Mirror* Conrad covered his deeply felt experience with a surface that showed very little of what his life had really cost him, he was acting like Almayer, one of his characters, who in erasing his daughter's footsteps in the sand was denying the pain she had caused him.

Even in the best of Conrad's fiction there is very often a distracting surface of overrhetorical, melodramatic prose that critics like F. R. Leavis, sensitive to the precise and most efficient use of language, have severely disparaged. Yet it is not enough, I think, to criticize these imprecisions as the effusions of a writer calling attention to himself. On the contrary, Conrad was hiding himself within rhetoric, using it for his personal needs without considering the niceties of tone and style that later writers have wished he had had. He was a self-conscious foreigner writing of obscure experiences in an alien language, and he was only too aware of this. Thus his extravagant or chatty prose—when it is most noticeable—is the groping of an uncertain Anglo-Pole for the least awkward, most "stylistic" mode of expression. It is also the easiest way to conceal the embarrassments and the difficulties of an overwhelmingly untidy existence as a French-speaking, self-exiled, extremely articulate Pole, who had been a sailor and was now, for reasons not quite clear to him, a writer of so-called adventure stories. Conrad's prose is not the unearned prolixity of a careless writer, but rather the concrete and particular result of his immense struggle with himself. If at times he is too adjectival, it is because he failed to find a better way of making his experience clear. That failure is, in his earliest works, the true theme of his fiction. He had failed, in the putting down of words, to rescue meaning from his undisciplined experience. Nor had he rescued himself from the difficulties of his life: this is why his letters, where all of these problems are explicitly treated, are necessary to a full understanding of his fiction.

Pain and intense effort are the profound keynotes of Conrad's spiritual history, and his letters attest to this. There is good reason for recalling Newman's impassioned reminder in the *Apologia* that any autobiographical document (and a letter is certainly that) is not only a chronicle of states of mind, but also an attempt to render the individual energy of one's life. That energy has been urgently apparent, and pressing for attention ever since the publication in 1927 of Jean-Aubry's *Joseph Conrad, Life and Letters.*

The abundant difficulties with which the letters teem are, nevertheless, the difficulties of Conrad's spiritual life, so that critics are almost forced to associate the problems of his life with the problems of his fiction; the task here, different but related, is to see how the letters relate first to the man and then to his work. Each letter is an exercise of Conrad's individuality as it connects his present with his past by forging a new link of self-awareness. Taken in their available entirety, Conrad's letters present a slowly unfolding discovery of his mind, his temperament, his character—a discovery, in short, that is Conrad's spiritual history as written by Conrad himself.

The accurate grasp of someone else's deepest concerns is never an easy matter. But even in the case of a writer like Conrad, whose self-concern was so intense, it is possible to view his letters in the essential, even simple, terms of their internal disposition. To cite "pain" and "effort" as hallmarks of Conrad's experience, for example, reveals little specifically of the man other than that he allowed himself repeated encounters with what caused pain and required effort. Yet there is a way of picturing Conrad in a characteristic and consistent stance or attitude of being, which enables us to perceive just what it was he was struggling against, and this way is to apply Richard Curle's wise observation that Conrad "was absorbed . . . in the whole mechanism of existence."[3] In these terms not only is it possible to apprehend the degree and kind of Conrad's pain and effort, but one can also discover the immediate reasons for them. Granted, of course, that Curle's phrase is perhaps unintentionally wise, and granted that the letters are informal and personal rather than formal or systematic, a peculiar kind of "absorption" is everywhere apparent in Conrad's letters, particularly since the existence to which he was committed was so manifestly enduring in its trials. For Conrad's absorption, as I understand it, was that he consciously felt a large measure of unrestful submission to the complexities of life, on the one hand and, on the other, that he remained interested in the submission not as a *fait accompli* but as a constantly renewed act of living, as a *condition humanisée* and not as a *condition humaine.* "The whole mechanism of existence" further explains Conrad's preoccupations by allowing him the assumption that life itself was the total of a series of particular occurrences. Certain of these occurrences, and especially those concerning his own welfare, were connected and informed by a mechanical and perverse inevitability; nothing like cosmic optimism could be attributed to the structures of such events. He was, he felt, simply a man tortured by a finite number of intolerably fixed situations to which he seemed to return everlastingly, and this very fact had a curious pull on him. The dynamics of these persisting situations are what gripped Conrad almost from the beginning of his recorded writings to their end. And it is both the situations themselves and the way they unfold (their metaphorical expression) that the letters record in prodigious detail.

There is more to be said about this haunting phrase, "the whole mechanism of existence." From Conrad's point of view—for the phrase has sympathetic echoes in the letters—it is a statement about a certain kind of conscious psychology. At first sight it is reminiscent of eighteenth-century mechanistic psychology, say of Hartley's theory of association and elementary determinism. To the contemporary mind, however, the phrase appeals easily to the commonplaces of the Freudian or Jungian psychologies, to the "mechanism" of the unconscious, to the complexes, myths, archetypes, and rituals in which each individual is somehow implicated. Yet, in his remarkable study, *The Emotions: Outline of a Theory*, Jean-Paul Sartre points up the inherent contradiction in a psychology confined to the unconscious. He writes there: "It is the profound contradiction of all psychoanalysis to introduce *both* a bond of causality and a bond of comprehension between the phenomena which it studies. These two types of connection are incompatible."[4] Sartre's distinction between causality and comprehension is a useful way of remarking that an analysis of a hypothetical *cause* does not logically make the *effect* comprehensible. If the unconscious can be said ultimately to determine the conscious—and this point is not at issue—we are hardly closer to comprehending the conscious as it presents itself to us. The literary critic is, I think, most interested in comprehension, because the critical act is first of all an act of comprehension: a particular comprehension of the written work, and not of its origins in a general theory of the unconscious. Comprehension, furthermore, is a phenomenon of consciousness, and it is in the openness of the conscious mind that critic and writer meet to engage in the act of knowing and being aware of an experience. Only that engagement, made in the interests of literary and historical fidelity, can prevent Conrad's remark "I am living a nightmare" from being accepted (or dismissed) as a hyperbolic effusion, instead of as an authentic and intense fact of experience.

As a writer, Conrad's job was to make intellectual use of what he had known, and "use," in this Jamesian employment of the term, means rendering, making overt. It would not, furthermore, be over-interpreting James's compliment if I emphasize that Conrad recognized the difference between the rendering of personal experience for public consumption on one side and, on the other, for the eyes of a few close friends. Now it is precisely with this process of making experience overt and intelligible for the benefit of his intimates that Conrad's letters, and consequently my discussion, are concerned. First of all we should investigate the *idiom* of Conrad's rendering of his experience: the words and the images he chose to express himself. In philosophical terms, this study attempts a phenomenological exploration of Conrad's consciousness, so that the kind of mind he had, both in its distinction and energy, will become apparent. The great value of the letters, therefore, is that they make such a study possible by disclosing the background of speculation and insight that strengthens the fiction.[5]

When "knowing" and "knowing for intellectual use" are spoken of in the same breath, when what is being described and the idiom of that description are taken together as an indissoluble unity, Conrad himself emerges from the letters as a significantly developing intellectual and spiritual reality. The mechanisms of existence he describes and his way of describing them are Conrad's very own. At his most rhetorical (and surely in this the letters often surpass the works) there is a discoverable mind working habitually, though perhaps with less energy than usual. Far more often the flurries of "big" words he uses—such as *life, the incomprehensible, the soul*—carry with them the proud muscularity of the European tradition of empirical morality, for the important recurring touchstone here is Conrad's sense of *vécu:* he has lived what he describes. Often he will bring the ceaseless activity of his mind to a kind of brief nervous stop, in much the same way that a man presenting a detailed argument stops because he needs to reflect, to take stock of what he has said. Then the movement of his thought resumes. Conrad saw in certain fiction, for example, the quality of an understated simplicity whose deeper recesses, like his own during those summary stops that fill the letters, cover a vital mechanism of lived knowledge. Yet he was bothered by the elegance of a rich narrative that went forward so smoothly and at the same time withheld its inner workings. No wonder that Maupassant was a discouraging master: "I am afraid I am too much under the influence of Maupassant. I have studied *Pierre et Jean*—thought, method, and everything—with the deepest discouragement. It seems to be nothing at all, but the mechanics are so complex that they make me tear out my hair. You want to weep with rage in reading it. That's a fact!"[6]

Despite the rhetoric, however, and the pauses it creates, to speak of Conrad's spiritual and intellectual reality is also to recognize a long, remarkable continuity in his abiding concerns. For this continuity, eminently Conrad's own, is precisely his emerging individuality, and this is the measure of his absorption in, and knowledge of, the mechanisms of existence. Conrad's individuality resides in a continuous exposure of his sense of himself to a sense of what is not himself: he set himself, lumpish and problematic, against the dynamic, fluid processes of life. Because of this, then, the great human appeal and distinction of Conrad's life is the dramatic spirit of partnership, however uneasy or indecorous, his life exemplifies, a partnership between himself and the external world. I am speaking of the full exposition of his soul to the vast panorama of existence it has discerned outside itself. He had the courage to risk a full confrontation with what, most of the time, seemed to him to be a threatening and unpleasant world. Moreover, the outcome of this dialectic is an experiencing of existential reality at that deepest level of alternative and potentiality which is the true life of the mind. Now the vocabulary and rhetoric of this experience (which I have called its idiom) is what the letters provide us with to such a degree that we are able to discover the contours of Conrad's mind as it engages itself in a partnership with existence. For "exposure" of the mind and soul has its literary paradigm: it is a habitual verbal exercise (hence, *idiom*) whose purpose is to arbitrate the relations between a problematic subject and a dynamic object. The more distinguished a mind, the greater need there is that this habitual exercise be disciplined, regulated by serious and satisfying moral norms that derive from one's personal experience. Basically, of course, I am equating distinction of mind with individuality of mind. There can be little doubt that Conrad had such a mind, and the problem of discipline is one that caused him deep concern as both man and artist.

All of this is, I think, as it should be. Because Conrad could, in his finest essay, praise James as the "historian of fine consciences"[7] and acknowledge him as his master, Conrad himself had to know what it meant to write the history of conscience, to record the growth of the faculty that grants one a moral awareness of conduct. And where but in his own mind could his apprenticeship have taken place? For, he wrote in the James essay,

> action in its essence, the creative art of a writer of fiction may be compared to rescue work carried out in darkness against cross gusts of wind swaying the action of a great multitude. It is rescue work, this snatching of vanishing phases of turbulence, disguised in fair words, out of the native obscurity into a light where the struggling forms may be seen, seized upon, endowed with the only possible form of permanence in this world of relative values—the permanence of memory. And the multitude feels it obscurely too; since the demand of the individual to the artist is, in effect, the cry, "Take me out of myself!" meaning really, out of my perishable activity . . . But everything is relative, and the light of consciousness is only enduring, merely the most enduring of the things of this earth, imperishable only as against the short-lived work of our industrious hands.[8]

It was the winning of a "sense of truth, of necessity—before all, of conduct," for the characters of his fiction that the writer literally possessed his subject—the history of conscience. The task was even more difficult when the writer's values themselves had to be rescued from a "native obscurity" too dark and confused for easy acceptance. The real adventure of Conrad's life is the effort to rescue significance and value in their "struggling forms" from within his own existence. Just as he had to rescue his experience for the satisfaction of his consciousness, to believe that he had put down the important parts of the truth as he saw it, so also his critic has to relive that rescue, without heroism, alas, but with equal determination.

Conrad does not make the task easy, of course. His combination of evasion with a seemingly artless candor in his autobiographical pronouncements poses intricate problems for the student of his fiction. His bent for the revisional, sometimes petulant interpretation of his life needs, for the moment, only the briefest recall. There is one story told by R. L. Megroz concerning an interchange between Conrad and his wife: "On one of his naughty days he said that the Black Mate was his first work, and when I [Jessie] said, 'No, *Almayer's Folly* was the first thing you ever did,' he burst out: 'If I like to say *The Black Mate* was my first work, I shall say so.'"[9] The often willful inaccuracy of Conrad's memory about his works and life—of which this is almost certainly an example—is too persistent a habit to be glossed over. He chose to consider the facts of his life as an historian, according to Huizinga, considers his subject, as if the actual facts are not yet determined. Huizinga writes:

> The historian . . . must always maintain towards his subject an indeterminist point of view. He must constantly put himself at a point in the past at which the known factors still seem to permit different outcomes. If he speaks of Salamis, then it must be as if the Persians might still win; if he speaks of the *coup d'état* of Brumaire, then it must remain to be seen if Bonaparte will be ignominiously repulsed. Only by continually recognizing that possibilities are unlimited can the historian do justice to the fulness of life.[10]

The link of self-awareness forged by Conrad in each letter (of which I spoke earlier) in reality describes the spiritual act of comprehension he performed as he viewed his own being in the past in connection with his being in the present. The indeterminist viewpoint to which Huizinga refers is a constant feature of Conrad's recollection of his past and, necessarily, a function of that harassed insecurity which spurs the novelist-historian to execute judgment. Between Conrad's life, then, and his fiction there exists much the same relation as between the two divisions (past and present) of his life. The critic's job is to seek out the common denominator of the two sets of relations. As Conrad's history of his past is to his present, so his historical being as a man is to his fiction. And the only way the relation can be articulated is, as I said earlier, to identify certain dynamic movements or structures of experience (mechanisms) that emerge from the letters. In one of his earliest works, *History and*

Class Consciousness, Georg Lukács has described structures similar to these: Lucien Goldmann calls them *significant dynamic structures*, because they maintain a context by which every human act preserves an individual's past evolution as well as the inner tendencies that drive him toward the future.[11] But the Marxist conclusion, class consciousness, does not suit the bias of this study. Because I am more concerned with the individual, I shall concentrate on the exigencies of Conrad's personal situation.

Conrad's stake in the structures of experience he had created was absolutely crucial, since it was rooted in the human desire to make a character of and for himself. Character is what enables the individual to make his way through the world, the faculty of rational self-possession that regulates the exchange between the world and the self; the more cogent the identity, the more certain a course of action. One of the curious facts of history is that it is the compulsive man of action who feels the need for character more strongly than the man who is only on the verge of action. T. E. Lawrence, Conrad's notorious near-contemporary, has been described by R. P. Blackmur as a man capable only of creating a personality for himself: his failure to forge a character, Blackmur argues, is the secret of his life and writing.[12] Conrad's predicament was, I think, not unlike Lawrence's: he, too, was a man of action urgently in need of a role to play so that he could locate himself solidly in existence. But whereas Lawrence failed, Conrad succeeded (although at immense cost). This is another aspect of Conrad's life of adventure. To Conrad it seemed as if he had to *rescue himself*, and, not surprisingly, this is one of the themes of his short fiction. Marlow and Falk, to take two examples, are faced with the terrible dilemma of either allowing themselves to vanish into "native obscurity" or, equally oppressive, undertaking to save themselves by the compromising deceit of egoism: nothingness on one side or shameful pride on the other. That is, either one loses one's sense of identity and thereby seems to vanish into the chaotic, undifferentiated, and anonymous flux of passing time, or one asserts oneself so strongly as to become a hard and monstrous egoist.

It is important, therefore, to distinguish the dominant mode of Conrad's structures of experience: quite simply, it can be called their radical either/or posture. By this I mean a habitual view of experience that allows *either* a surrender to chaos *or* a comparably frightful surrender to egoistic order. There is no middle way, and there is no other method of putting the issues. Either one allows that meaningless chaos is the hopeless restriction upon human behavior, or one must admit that order and significance depend only upon man's will to live at all costs. This, of course, is the Schopenhauerian dilemma, Conrad's solutions always had one end in view—the achievement of character—and his fiction is a vital reflection of his developing character. The mechanisms of existence discernible in the letters are Conrad's portrayal of himself in the process of living. They are sections of a long drama in which the arrangements of setting, act, and actor are Conrad's consciousness of himself in the struggle toward the equilibrium of character.

from *Joseph Conrad and the Fiction of Autobiography*

2

The Palestinian Experience

(1968–1969)

First published in Europe in 1970 (and reprinted in *The Politics of Dispossession*), "The Palestinian Experience" is one of Said's earliest exercises in political analysis and reportage. Said has written in other places that he was almost completely apolitical in his work and life until the June 1967 war, but the destruction of the war left the Arab world—and him—shattered. "For the first time since I had left to come to the United States, I was emotionally reclaimed by the Arab World in general and by Palestine in particular," he writes.[1] This dawning consciousness of both the plight of his people and of his own identity within that collective world would lead him to marshal his talents to the best of his abilities and to become, with time, the most important spokesperson the Palestinian cause has had.

"The Palestinian Experience" is an interesting example of Said's early writings for several reasons. First, we can immediately recognize the candid style of addressing a reader on both a personal and a political level simultaneously. Said would use this same method of narrating politics—of involving the reader in suppressed stories, hidden histories and autobiographical moments—many times over the years, and most splendidly in his *After the Last Sky*. There is an urgent political need for such narration in the Palestinian situation. To testify to the very existence of the Palestinians as a people (and as people), with a history, a culture, and a right to self-determination, was a radical and unsettling move for a culture that denied them all this, even refusing them the opportunity to represent themselves.

Second, despite its slightly awkward prose, reticent tone, and sometimes clumsy terminology ("Palestinianism"), "The Palestinian Experience" shows how remarkably consistent Said has been in his political and moral vision from the very outset. Palestinian history is asserted as being multiracial and multireligious from the get go. No exclusivism can be found here; rather we see that the same drive for coexistence that propels much of Said's later writings is already present. Yet the recognition that Palestinian suffering has been at the hands of those who suffered in the Holocaust, a point Said would later develop into a major essay ("Zionism from the Standpoint of Its Victims"), can also be found here, along with the indignation that the American liberal establishment refuses to recognize the Palestinians' plight. Said excoriates the failures of nationalism—both Arab and Israeli—without losing the argument for Palestinian self-determination. His brief analyses of Western cultural figures such as T. E. Lawrence prefigure the argument in *Orientalism*.

Finally, what is perhaps most remarkable about this essay is that by detailing the slow emergence of an indigenous, Palestinian resistance movement through the device of analysis and personal experience, "The Palestinian Experience" is in fact narrating to us Said's own emergence as an engaged Palestinian intellectual.

Anyone who has tried seriously to examine the contemporary Near East is frequently tempted to conclude that the project is unmanageable. Every sort of distraction gets in the way;

after a time, a distraction seems as inherent a necessity as an essential. Yet if one believes that the crux of the Near East today is the conflict between Israel and a dispersed, or occupied, population of Palestinian Arabs, then a clearer view of that problem becomes possible. For the major distraction to any scrutiny of the region has been *everyone's* unwillingness to allow for a Palestinian presence. This has been no less true of the Palestinians themselves, than it has of the other Arabs, or of Israel. My thesis is that since 1967 the confusions have somewhat diminished because the Palestinians have had to recognize this truth, and have gradually begun to act upon it. This recognition is the source of what I call Palestinianism: a political movement that is being built out of a reassertion of Palestine's multiracial and multireligious history. The aim of Palestinianism is the full integration of the Arab Palestinian with lands and, more importantly with political processes that for twenty-one years have either systematically excluded him or made him a more and more intractable prisoner.

It seems to me to be a useless dodge to assert—as most anti-Palestinian polemics do—that the Palestinian popular resistance to the exclusions of Zionism is simply a version of Arab anti-Semitism, or still another threat of genocide against the Jews. I have felt that the best way to disprove this view would be to put the Palestinian experience to the reader on both a personal and a public level. Each, I think, is as honest as I could make it, and that has required an approach to Palestinianism by a passage through other Arab countries, notably Lebanon and Egypt. By a happy coincidence both countries have been familiar to the Western reader, accessible to me, and logical geographic and ideological ways of getting to Palestinianism and to its temporary headquarters in Jordan. Another virtue of the approach is that it helps to reduce the difficulty of writing about the Palestinian experience in a language not properly its own. For by moving to the Palestinian through the screens that have surrounded him and are now unsettled by him, even as he continues in exile, an English transcription of the process dramatizes the real difficulties of peripherality, silence, and displacement that the Palestinian has suffered. Palestinianism then is an effort at repatriation, but the present stage of the Palestinian experience (as this essay tries to show) is a problematic early transition for *being* in exile to *becoming* a Palestinian once again.

. . .

Two of the oldest beach facilities in Beirut are called Saint Simon and Saint Michel; they are also known together in Arabic by a different name, *Al-Ganah'*, that does not approximate a translation of their French titles. To this peculiar cohabitation of French and Arabic, tolerated by everyone without much attention, was recently added a third beach establishment adjacent to the other two: Saint Picot. In June 1969, when I was in Beirut, the new place and its name assumed a powerful symbolic value for me, as did all the *discordia concors* that makes up Beirut. Clearly someone had assumed that "Saint" meant "beach," and since Georges Picot was still a name to be reckoned with, what better conjunction than Saint Picot. But then the contradictions and ironies multiply without control. Lebanon was in the midst of its worst internal crisis in many years, a crisis whose dimensions, depending on whom you talked to, seemed at once definitively critical and endlessly analyzeable. The fact was that only a caretaker government held office since no cabinet could be formed. One supervening reason for this state of affairs was the lack of a workable definition of Lebanon's sovereignty: an undetermined number of Palestinian *fedayin* were encamped in the South (next to the Israeli border), and although "accepted" as Arab brothers engaged in a legitimate struggle against Israel, the presence of these men had in some very fundamental way unsettled Lebanon's identity, if not its remarkable economy. Yet they remained, the crisis continued, as did Lebanon's suspense for many weeks. Beirut contained this paralyzing collision of views, just as it has contained, indeed exposed and incarnated, almost every contradiction of the Arab Near East. Thus in a small way the endowment of Picot's name (to which the Arabs have no reason to be grateful) with sainthood, and the entitlement of a Lebanese beach to so oddly decorated a European name, was a reflection of the cabinet crisis, of reverberations that came from Syrian, Jordanian, Israeli, Egyptian, American, and Russian unrest, but above all, of Beirut's unique status as a place of natural entry from the West onto the confusing modern topography of the Arab world.

Engaged in the astonishing variety of history the Lebanese is used to finding himself split several ways, most of them contradictory and, as I have been suggesting, utterly Lebanese in the nearfreakishness of their resolution. (I use Beirut and Lebanon interchangeably, despite an inevitable slurring of nuances. There are enough nuances to be taken account of, however, without worrying too much about these.) What is Lebanese is the public and direct availability for daily use of these contradictions in so tiny a country. They *are* Lebanon, and have been for at least a century. The order of Lebanon is how miraculously it accommodates everything, and how its citizens can stand the accommodations that might cripple everyone else. To live in Beirut means, among other things, having the choice of doing, feeling, thinking, speaking, and even being, the following, in a huge assortment of possible combinations: Christian (Protestant, Maronite, Greek Orthodox, Melchite, Roman Catholic, etc.), Moslem (Sunnite or Shiite), Druze, Armenian, Jewish, French, American, British, Arab, Kurdish, Phoenecian, part of pan-Islamism, part of Arab nationalism, tribal, cosmopolitan, Nasserite, communist, socialist, capitalist, hedonist, puritan, rich, poor or neither, involved in the Arab struggle against Israel (i.e., for the *fedayin,* for the Israeli airport attack as a sign of involvement), disengaged from the Arab struggle against Israel (i.e., against the *fedayin,* for the airport attack insofar as it demonstrated Lebanon's peaceful position by the absence of any resistance given the raiders), and so on. The poverty of labels like left-wing and right-wing is immediately apparent.

Lebanon then has stood for accommodation, tolerance and, especially, representation. It is no accident, for example, that such disparities as the ideas of Arab nationalism, the renaissance of Arabic as a modern language, the foundations of the Egyptian press, the living possibility and continuity of the good life and commercial entrepreneurism (at least for the twentieth-century Arab) originated in Lebanon. Yet the crisis of 1969 developed out of the wealth of what was represented in the country and the lack of suitable Lebanese instruments, for once, to extract the best possible combination for Lebanon's destiny. For if past, present, and future are all readily negotiable with most interests, as I felt they were in Beirut, then crisis ensues. Call it equilibrium, and it still remains critical. As I saw it, Beirut was a victim of its openness and its true cultural virtuosity, as well as of the absence of an articulable foundation upon which to draw.

By comparison Damascus was scarcely visible at all. An accident of personal history made it impossible for me to visit the city: no Americans are permitted there, and since I had American citizenship, despite my birth in Jerusalem into a Jerusalem Arab family, I could not even drive through Syria on my way to Amman. As the plane to Amman flew over Damascus, the city's appearance from the air confirmed my impression of it as the most impenetrable Arab city I had ever known. It seemed gorged on its hermetic involutions. The Syrian regime, which tangled the rhetorical mysteries of Baath politics with the secret intricacies of Aliwite religion, had closed the country off and turned away the flavor of its life from the observer.

Everything about Amman, whose central position for the Palestinian has been strengthened since June 1967, testifies to austerity and *Ersatz.* Scarcely a town before 1948, its helter-skelter growth has made it a city by default. Many refugee camps surround it of course, but unlike Beirut, whatever internationalism Amman possesses remains only in a lingering sense of British discipline one encounters here and there. The streets are hopelessly crowded with pedestrians and cars, although a kind of martial informality pervades all activity. At first, I kept asking myself and others which people were Palestinians and which were Jordanians. The number of men in uniforms or green fatigues prompted my questions, but a few hours after arrival I gave up asking. By then it had become evident to me that in spite of its Hashemite throne, all of Jordan had become a temporary substitute for Arab Palestine. So far as I could tell—and this was certainly true for me—no one really felt at home in Amman, and yet no Palestinian could feel more at home anywhere else now. Aside from a few places on the hills where rather commonly despised *parvenus* had built ostentatious villas, Amman is a city carrying the single-minded Palestinian energy. No particularly apparent heroism or self-conscious cause mongering are in the air: both Amman's setting and its means are too daylit in their poverty to permit these futile games. The city has a bustling commercial life, but an impressive dedication to Arab Palestine overrides even that. In Amman, one cannot escape the necessity of that cause (and this accounts for the city's austerity): *everyone,* you feel, has been touched in a concrete way by "the Palestinian question." Cafés, television, movies, social gatherings—all these amenities are permanently subordinated to an overwhelmingly powerful experience.

In Amman today two ways of life enclose all the other ways, which finally connect the main two. These two are being a refugee in a camp and being an active member of one of the resistance groups. It is difficult to remember, as one visits the refugee camps, that such places, with their mean rows of neat, ugly tents, are not there to be visited, nor even to impress one in a sentimental way with their poverty and squalor. Each camp is an absolute minimum, where a communal life can be led just because refugees believe that they need continue in this confining fashion *only until* they can return to their place of origin. A Palestinian UNRWA official with whom I chatted said that what never failed to amaze him was how the refugees simply hung on. He had difficulty describing the quality of the refugee's life, and I noticed how anxious he was to avoid the word "passivity." He went on to say that although each camp contained about 35,000 people there was no crime to report, no "immorality," no social unrest. I saw that what he was doing—since he himself was also a refugee—was protecting the camp-dwellers, or rather protecting their right to be as they were, for the time being: I took this as I think he wanted it taken, that the duration of a refugee's life in the camp was a moral fact with unspoken meaning, attested to by some deep faculty of knowing endurance, and a faith that being a refugee would end at the right time.

Women and children were very much in evidence, but hardly any men or young boys. If they are not engaged as day laborers in the Ghor (the valley between Amman and the river) they belong to one of the guerrilla groups, the boys to the *Ashbal* (cubs) whose regimen includes a standard education and military training. There are almost daily air attacks (about which little is heard in the U.S.A.) by the Israelis over the fertile Ghor. The pretext of these raids is military targets, but their achievement is the destruction of crops and of the few inhabited villages left. Yet life there, like that of the camps, goes on because there is some evidence that hope is not entirely baseless. I talked with three Fatah men who had just returned from a raid; five of the original party were killed, but the three who came back had expected a loss of this magnitude. They all had wives and mothers in the camps. Now they also have dead or living comrades and relatives on the West Bank: this investment has made a difference, and no amount of tiresome cant about being refugees who won't settle with, or won't be settled by, the other Arabs, or being "pawns" or "footballs" or "terrorists," can alter it for them.

The other Arab cities are, of course, touched by the experience of the past twenty years, but none today so urgently enlivens that experience as Amman. This has not always been true since 1948; but it is true now, for reasons that have to do with each Arab country. I shall return to those reasons shortly. To the Palestinian Arab the Jordanian border with Israel is *the* border: the closest one spiritually, the one travelled across most painfully, the one that most fully characterizes the displacement and the proximity of its cause. Therefore, as a place Amman has become a terminal with no other *raison d'être* than temporarily to preserve displacement; beyond the city, physically and in consciousness, are a desert and extinction. In Amman the Palestinian either stays on as best he can, or he repatriates himself from it as a guerrilla. He has really stopped thinking about Kuwait, or Beirut, or Cairo. He has only himself to consider now, and what he discovers, by whatever technique he uses, is how he is a Palestinian—or rather, how he has already become a Palestinian again and what this must mean for him. For the most recent arrivals in Amman it has been a necessity, and this necessity has galvanized the residents who have been there since 1948. What has emerged, in short, is Palestinianism.

States of the popular soul are, I know, almost impossible to examine scientifically, even discursively. It is no false modesty on my part, for example, to feel that what I am now writing is at too far a remove from the ongoing fortunes of Palestinianism. The realities of the Palestinian experience are both complex and elusive, so much so as to escape the descriptive order of what must appear to be a series of afterthoughts. But this recognition, which I certainly make, is an exact analogy of a significant new aspect of the Palestinian experience. The discontinuity between writing *about,* let us say, and the direct experience of which the writing tries to treat, is like the essential condition for the Palestinian's transformed consciousness. Just as he can see that Amman is not Jerusalem, Beirut not Amman, Cairo not Amman—hitherto interchangeable parts of a collective Arab dream, strung together like identical beads on a string—he can now know that being a Palestinian includes, but does not reconcile, being in Amman *and* being under military occupation in Jerusalem, Gaza, Nablus, or Jericho. Yet what he feels as discontinuity is no longer a void which he had previously tried to forget—by going to Beirut, or coming to the United States. That void had been an inert gap that stood for the absence of any real encounter with Israel.

For there has been one major encounter between the Palestinians and Israel since June 1967, an encounter that aptly concentrated and thereby symbolized the possibility of popular resistance to a political enemy (despite a whole prior series of sporadic guerrilla operations, which had lacked coherence). That was the battle of Karameh in March 1968. At that moment, when an invading Israeli force was *met* by a local one defending what it could no longer afford to give up, at that moment the void changed into a direct experience of true political discontinuity: the actual face-to-face enmity between Zionism and Palestinianism. This conflict thus became an event, not simply a news release doctored to fit a wildly polemical broadcast.

All occurrences become events after they occur. In part, events are mythic, but like all effective myths they record an important aspect of a real experience. An event like the battle of Karameh was a decisive moment which, for the Palestinians, was suited to be a certain demarcation between what came before it and what came after it. At Karameh—unlike the West Bank village of Al-Sammu, which Israel had razed unopposed—the opponents were clearly pitted against each other. A regular Israeli force moved against an irregular Palestinian one, and the latter answered with a refusal merely to push off and let Karameh (a village built by refugees: hence its significance) be destroyed; by refusing, it stayed to become a truly popular activation of a conflict that had formerly been left to the Arabs at large. Thus Karameh divides the Palestinian experience into a *before* that had refused an encounter, which meant accepting a retrospective fiat declared against the Palestinian Arab past, and an *after* that finds the Palestinian standing in, becoming, fighting to dramatize, the disjunction of his history in Palestine before 1948 with his history at the peripheries since 1948. In this sense then a void, felt by every Palestinian, has been altered by an event into a discontinuity. And the difference between void and discontinuity is crucial: one is inert absence, the other is disconnection that requires re-connection.

The odds against a re-connection of the displaced Palestinian with his land and with his subjugated compatriot are severe indeed, and the battle has only just begun. Israel's stated policy has been categorically to deny the reality of a Palestinian people, but such a policy is thoroughly consonant with the Zionist vision since Herzl. Nevertheless morale is probably higher amongst West Bank Arabs than it is outside, because on the West Bank at least one is an inhabitant (albeit a third-class citizen), whereas outside, the Palestinian is excruciatingly aware of how thin his existence has been during the past twenty-one years. A better way of saying this is that the displaced Palestinian has had his human prerogative, i.e., the right to object to his exile, suffering, loss, death, taken from him in his political struggle. His oppressor has been a political enemy surfeited with this prerogative. But whereas the very most has been made out of Jewish suffering, the very least has been made out of Palestinian Arab suffering. For example, the diplomatic haggling between Israel and the Arab states is always depicted by Israel and its supporters as a quarrel between "Jews" who want peace and a place of their own at last, and "Arabs" who will not let them have either. That Israel has been more than a match for a whole world of Arabs, or that it is presently inflated to three times its original size or, most important, that Palestinian Arabs, who have suffered incalculable miseries for the sake of Western anti-Semitism, really do exist, have existed, and will continue to exist as part of Israel's extravagant cost—about these things very little is heard, apart from the usual unctuous complaints about injustice, the lack of reason, and the necessity of peace.

It is becoming more and more certain to the Palestinian that Israel in its present state of thriving militarism has no need of peace. If it does want peace that would be because the Israelis wanted some rest from the strain on their economy or on their "image." Most Palestinians fear large-scale sell-outs by the Arab states, themselves tired out by the uneven struggle. It is due to this fear that relations between the *fedayin* and the Arab governments are so problematic: each suspects that the other's interest will suffer, as it must of course. Another danger is that the Palestinian organizations will allow themselves to become enmeshed in local Arab conflicts. Yet from the larger world the Palestinian expects (and is getting) attention, but no more than that. He has no benefits to gain from Western good-thinkers who sympathize so effortlessly with the Vietnamese peasant, the American black, or the Latin American laborer. And this only because he is an "Arab" who is opposed by the "Jew." To live in America, for example, and to know this truth is especially painful. For here the emotional residue of what has been a singularly dirty chapter in world history, from no matter whose side it is studied, has been turned against the Arab. Even the word "Arab" works quite easily as an insult. From the Final Solution, to American unwillingness to permit European Jews entry to the United States, to Lord Moyne's murder, to the sordid role of the British, to the Lavon affair, to Sirhan's assassination of Robert Kennedy (which was stripped of its political significance by the press), to Bernadotte's murder by the Stern Gang: the tracks are messy, yet scarcely recognizable in, for instance, *Commentary's* clean pages.

Insofar as my personal experience is admissible in evidence, I can try to substantiate a few of these thoughts. In 1948 I was twelve, a student at an English school in Cairo. Aside from my immediate family, most of my other relatives were in Palestine. For one reason or another they were to resettle themselves either in Jordan, Egypt, or Lebanon: a few remained in Israel. My closest friend at the time was a Jewish boy who had a Spanish passport. I remember him telling me that autumn how shameful it was that six countries were pitted against one; the appeal, I believed, was to my sporting instinct developed at cricket and soccer games. I said nothing, but I felt badly. On similar occasions many years later I also said nothing (actually I said I was from Lebanon, which was as cowardly as saying nothing since it meant saying something that was intended to be deliberately not provocative). I was born in Jerusalem, so was my father, his father, and so on; my mother was born in Nazareth. These facts were rarely mentioned. I earned my degrees, I became a professor, I wrote books and articles on European literature. And, as the jolts of Near Eastern politics dictated, I occasionally saw my family on vacations: sometimes in Egypt, in Jordan, finally in Lebanon. In 1967 I was "from" Lebanon.

That did me no good during that awful week in June. I was an Arab, and we—"you" to most of my embarrassed friends—were being whipped. I wrote one or two eloquent letters to the *Times,* but these were not published, and with a few other Arabs had sessions of group-think that were really group therapy; then I began compulsively to clip things out of papers and magazines. A year and a half later, out of those smoldering extracts and with a dose of self-pity, I wrote an essay called "The Arab Portrayed" in which I lamented and documented the ways in which the Arab, in contrast to the Israeli, had been depicted in America. This vulgar demotion, as I called it, was what made American accounts of the June War so unfair and so disgraceful an example of anti-Arabism. Yet what I was also saying, almost without realizing it, was that a too-integral nationalism, which the Arab himself purported to embody, had failed him as much as it had failed even the Israelis, who in the months after June 1967 were robbed of "Arab" recognition. In the meantime I continued with my own work, and the "Arabs" with theirs.

By Arab work I mean the way in which, *grosso modo,* the Arab countries set about their national existence as a result of the June War (of course I am being impressionistic). Much of the very recent work done by the Arabs has been reductive. This is not entirely bad and, to my mind, it has been necessary. Arab independence was, and in some cases still is, a Western construction. I am not a political scientist nor a social psychologist, but what I am trying to articulate is my sense that Arab independence was not so much earned but granted in forms that suited the former colonizers. One becomes especially conscious of this in, to take a classic case, *The Seven Pillars of Wisdom,* where it is gradually revealed that Lawrence's triumph was in having used the Arabs' vague national aspiration as the stuff out of which *his* chivalric-medieval-romantic dream could be carved. Even if Lawrence and the Arabs both awakened to the dream's betrayal, it has taken the Arabs a longer time to rid themselves of its haunting effects. Therefore the nationalism of independence, when finally left to itself, was in part borrowed, grandiose, aimless, self-serving, relatively authentic—but fairly inexpensive. The reductive process has been costly, for there has been a realization of these inadequacies, and an attempt to decompose Arab nationalism into discreter units finely sensitive to the true cost of real independence. In most Arab countries today (Egypt, Syria, Iraq, and Lebanon in particular) the reduction has taken the form of left-wing critique amongst many, but by no means all, thinkers: thus it could be shown that the traditional class structure of those societies has yet to undergo revolutionary change.

This may be true, but lurking in everyone's mind is the massive fact of Israel's presence, and the costs of that presence have still to be fully felt universally. Hence the accentuated importance of the Palestinian today, for he is being pragmatically forced to create his identity in accordance with real impingements upon it.

I remarked above that one working psychological change since 1967 was that Amman and Jordan had become more central to the whole Palestinian question than ever before. The reason for this refocusing is not only because the Palestinian has made the change, but also—let it be admitted—because of a general feeling in other Arab countries that Palestine had neither served, nor been adequately served by, actions taken in the interests of Arab nationalism. I don't want to dwell on this too much because, like my comments on Arab independence, at best I am making general, rather presumptuous speculations about some very complicated movements in the Arab world at large (from which I have conveniently excluded Libya, Sudan, Algeria, Tunis, and Morocco); besides, things are in too much flux to do more than suggest reasons tentatively. First, of course, was the military defeat, as well as the humiliating difference between the exhuberance of prediction and the aftermath of rout. For no matter how correct the moral stand it could not be detached from the methods of its implementation and expression, and those were shown to be disastrously wanting. Second, it became apparent that Arab nationalism was far from unitary; the creed was fed by many subsidiary ideologies, and therefore assumed differing roles. Abdallah Laroui's book, *L'Idéologie arabe contemporaine,* is an excellent recent account both of what makes up Arab nationalism, as well as its differences from other Third World movements. I need not go over what he has discussed so well.

On what seemed Arab nationalism's most unanimous argument, opposition to Israel, there could never be real thought since, as Sartre and Cecil Hourani have both observed, one cannot truly oppose what one neither knows nor confronts. The hiatus that prevented Arab unity was Israel, and this the Arabs collectively proclaimed; but a hiatus, like any other rupture, cannot be dealt with by not dealing with it. By this I mean that the problem of Israel always remained on *the other side,* literally and figuratively, of what the Arabs collectively did. Israel was always being *left to* the realm of generality (in which, not surprisingly, Arab nationalism also operated) where it was hoped that Zionism could be treated as an interruption to be ignored, or drowned out by a general concert of voices and action. This concert then was the job of Arabism, just as on other levels it was the job of the army, of the ministries of information, of the Arab League, in sum, of the Arab Nation. Since Israel was the Other, which of course it still is, it was felt that *other agencies* would take care of it on behalf of *us*. One always felt involved in the sentiments of anti-Zionism, whereas the action always seemed to be taken by proxy, at some distance from the sentiments. That sort of cleavage, then, is what 1967 exposed.

It was as an understandable reaction to the devastations of the June War that in Egypt, to take the principle case in point, open-minded intellectuals recognized the limitations of the prewar psychology by rediscovering the limits of their own national interests. The expedition to Yemen had further irritated their awareness. In refusing to be deluded by proclamations that the June War was only a setback, these intellectuals saw that what one of them called "nationalitarianism" did Egypt itself a disservice. One perhaps minor but fascinating development out of this view was a renewed interest in works like Hussein Fawzi's brilliant *Sinbad Misri (An Egyptian Sinbad)* which had originally appeared in 1961, subtitled "Voyages Over the Vast Spaces of History." Quite the most original work produced in Egypt over the past twenty years, Fawzi's book took for its theme the absolute coherence of *Egypt's* history, from the pharaohs to the modern period.

Although the book's theme was not a new one, the assured subtlety of his thought enabled Fawzi to construct a series of historical tableaux in which a specifically Egyptian kind of history developed which, he argued, showed Egypt's people to be "makers of civilization." The implicit point here, made explicitly by other Egyptian intellectuals like Lewis Awad, was that Egypt had its own mission, quite apart from an Arab one, to fulfill, and that did not *primarily* include violence. Israel's occupation of Sinai has unfortunately vitiated the argument somewhat.

There were comparable redefinitions of the relationship between Arabism and local nationalism taking place, in different forms of course and not always as standard left-wing critiques, in the other Arab countries. However I do not wish to imply that such reassessments had never taken place before; they have been taking place all along—witness the earlier work of Constantine Zurayck, Ra'if Khouri, Ibrahim Amer, and Salama Musa, to mention a few examples at random. It is just that the present redefinitions possess a cumulative thrust that has sharpened and extended the horizon of national self-knowledge. Like the Lebanese cabinet stalemate of 1969, the recent redefinitions and self-criticisms can be understood in psychological terms as what Erik Erikson has called identity crisis, although certainly I am aware that analogies between individual and collective identities are dangerous to make. Another risk is that Erikson's use of his own concept is so finely ingenious as to make gross adaptations like mine seem clumsy and hopelessly far-fetched. Still there is something to be gained, I believe, from applying the following description by Erikson to the post-1967 period:

> I have called the major crisis of adolescence the identity crisis; it occurs in that period of the life cycle when each youth must forge for himself some central perspective and direction, some working unity, out of the effective remnants of his childhood and the hopes of his anticipated adulthood; he must detect some meaningful resemblance between what he has come to see in himself and what his sharpened awareness tells him others judge and expect him to be. This sounds dangerously like common sense; like all health, however, it is a matter of course only to those who possess it, and appears as a most complex achievement to those who have tasted its absence. Only in ill health does one realize the intricacy of the body; and only in a crisis, individual or historical, does it become obvious what a sensitive combination of interrelated factors the human personality is—a combination of capacities created in the distant past and of opportunities divined in the present; a combination of totally unconscious preconditions developed in individual growth and of social conditions created and recreated in the precarious interplay of generations. In some young people, in some classes, at some periods in history, this crisis will be minimal; in other people, classes, and periods, the crisis will be clearly marked off as a critical period, a kind of "second birth," apt to be aggravated either by widespread neuroticisms or by pervasive ideological unrest.[2]

"Adolescence" must not at all be understood as implying condescension towards a recent history that has so obviously been painful: this is why the present identity crisis is not minimal, but a matter of profound moment. What is crucial to Erikson's definition is awareness of the crisis on the part of those undergoing it—and this, I think, is the new situation amongst those who together make up the vanguard of the Arab mind today. Whereas Jacques Berque, in some minds the most brilliant Western thinker about the Arabs, had deliberately called the first chapter of his book on the Arabs "The Disruption of Traditional Man," the notion was not commonly recognized to be true, and thereby acted upon, by Arabs themselves.

The identity crisis solicits above all a recognition of disruption. And to have this recognition one needs a very clear idea that something has been left behind in order that a new development based on a stronger identity might become possible. I speculate once again when I suggest that what is now being left behind is the Arab-Islamic idea of reality, staggeringly complex no doubt, but based, as Berque argues so cogently, on the plenitude of the present. Hitherto the Arab genius had taken the world as fullness and simultaneity; thus, there was no unconscious, no latency that was not immediately accessible to vision, belief, tradition, and especially, language. Any change in that sort of order can only be a mixed blessing that disturbs confidence, yet in the context of Arab national independence (which roughly coincided with the inception and growth of Zionism) the phase to 1948 was a period of youth and adolescence, of initiation into a new history. After 1967 came the slow realization of what that really meant.

It is useful to compare the course of Arab nationalism with that of Jewish nationalism in order to indicate the traumas involved in the change I have just been discussing. Near the beginning of this century both nationalisms seem to have been phenomena of projection, like all emerging national ideologies. Each had its aims, its plans for realizations, and its philosophical and rhetorical styles. The Arab version has been studied and restudied at great length in works like George Antonious's *The Arab Awakening* and Albert Hourani's *Arabic Thought in the Liberal Age*. What 1967 climaxed for the Arabs, however, was a gradual attenuation of their projection; and it seemed to them that Zionism—no longer an idea but a state that sprawled over much of their territory—had realized its original projections. Neither side, each occupied with its own problems, was charitably aware of hardships suffered by the other. For the Arab then it seemed that quite without him a foreign growth had spread in his midst, forcing him to attenuate his vision from pan-Arabism to collective as well as individual defeat, displacement, loss. To him the Israeli had asked for and received the world's backing in a well-planned project of dissemination and growth. Yet the current emergence of the Palestinian movement is not only, I think, a sign of the diminished vision of Arab nationalism, but also a hopeful sign that the contrast between Arab and Jewish nationalism has been muted. In having to respond to the claims of Palestinians Zionism must itself undergo the attenuation it had forced on the Arabs at large, and if there is any future reconciliation between Jewish nationalists and the Palestinians it must be as a result of this reversal of trends.

It can also be said that during the years up to and including 1967 it never did the Arabs much good to believe that absolute right was on their side. I do not mean by this that Zionism was something to be tolerated passively, but rather that the elevation of a political conflict into a framework of cosmic morality had two noticeably damaging effects. In the first place, it made the Arabs rely on the self-convincing moral force of their arguments which, as I said above, isolated the Israelis and insulated the Arabs from the essentially *political* nature of the conflict. Emotion and rhetoric can never be wholly divorced from politics (this is particularly true, as I shall remark a little later, in so fraught a region as Palestine) but it is when they are employed as a substitute for politics that they do most harm. Worst of all they play directly into the hands of a political argument whose greatest strength is its apparent aloofness from history and politics: and this is the second damaging effect. For Zionism, or Jewish nationalism, has prospered on arguments and actions either *for or against* its exclusivity, whether as positive good or, from the Arab side, as negative evil.

This is not as paradoxical as it may seem. Zionism is historically incommensurate with any sort of liberalism so long as Zionism is believed by its supporters to be identical with, or at least a logical extension of, Judaism as a religion of secular exclusion and non-assimilation. This is not to say that every Zionist is a Herzl or a Jabotinsky or a Dayan; Buber, Magnes, and in America, I. F. Stone had argued for some sort of dilution of the extremist view. In the main, however, the moderates have not fared well. The dialectic of polar opposition has been too strong for them. With every apparent consolidation of its national existence Israel seems more and more to represent not only the *place apart* of Judaism but also the concentrated actions of Judaism. And Judaism, in two dimensions, each, commonsensically, incompatible with the other; the universal (timeless) and the secular (temporal). Thus Israel can make claims for its historical presence based on its timeless attachment to a place, and supports its universalism by absolutely rejecting, with tangible military force, any other historical or temporal (in this case Arab Palestinian) counterclaims. I do not think it is unfair either to the Israelis or to the Arabs to say that both contributed, each in his own way, to this maelstrom of exclusions. The Arab has acceded to that aspect of Judaism which, as Arthur Koestler put it in *The Trial of the Dinosaur,* "unlike any other [religion], is racially discriminating, nationally segregative, socially tension-creating." In his refusal to deal with Israel at all, the Arab simply enforced the self-segregating tendency in Judaism, for which Israel assumed secular responsibility.

The obvious bearing of the Jewish experience in World War II on present-day Zionism cannot be overestimated. Yet even there, as Hannah Arendt, for one, sensitively exposed the issues in her *Eichmann in Jerusalem,* problems for the non-Israeli Jew, especially for the notoriously conservative American Zionist, persist. It is not my task to consider here the ambiguities of being a Zionist, remaining in America, and thinking of the Arab solely as Israel's opponent, beyond remarking how American Zionism symbolizes the vast range of the Zionist projection and, conversely, the attenuation of Arabism: both nationalisms have reached their furthest extremities. Yet because of the Palestinian resurgence the conflict has been compressed into its most economical local form in the present confrontation between the conquering Israeli and the resisting Palestinian. For all its difficulty and violence this form of conflict strikes me as being more clear, and more hopeful, than the morass of thought which seeks to drag in every conceivable confusion. Nevertheless, many doubtless imponderable forces also intersect at the essential node of the conflict. These range from overtly bumbling great power competition to, equally irrational and perhaps even more compelling, the subliminal forces of primitive religious emotion, mythic racism, and ideological originality of the worst sort. For it must never be forgotten—and this may be the clue to the entire imbroglio—that Palestine carries the heaviest weight of competing monotheistic totalitarianism of any spot on earth. While it may be dangerously optimistic to pretend that a reconciliation of supernatural arguments can take place in a natural setting, there is some encouragement in remembering that until 1948 Palestine seems simultaneously to have given birth to interconnected ideas of the One *and* the Many, of the individual *and* the community.

Since 1948 the Arab Palestinian has had to endure a political living death, and whatever he now experiences in the way of vitality is because since 1967 he has begun to revitalize his thought just to avoid total extinction, and because the dreams of Arabism have broken on his acutely exposed situation. The two reasons are different sides of the same coin. The main characteristics of the Arab Palestinian's life since 1948 had been his peripherality, his isolation, and his silence—all of those are conditions of displacement and loss. (It cannot fail to escape the Palestinian's notice, by the way, how much his experience begins to resemble that of the Diaspora Jew.) Peripherality, like the other two characteristics I've mentioned, is not tolerable past the point where displacement (not being where you ought to be) means not being any place else really, not being able to stand at the center of your destiny, feeling that all your prerogatives have been usurped. If you cede your initiatives to a larger entity, and if you tie your fortunes to others', you are apt to be awakened from this passivity when you discover that your priorities have been disordered. Like every other Mediterranean, the way Maurice Le Lannou describes him, the Palestinian belongs first to his village, land, and tribe, then second, and with many misgivings, to the vaster group. When after 1967 it became apparent that the first fact of the Palestinian's life was Israeli occupation, the second his dispersion amongst the other Arabs, and only third, his Arabism, the priorities had righted themselves. Peripherality took on a close literal meaning, and was intolerable.

Political silence, in the case of the Palestinian, has meant not knowing to whom or for what to talk, and therefore talking with different voices, none of them his own. The silence was broken under the new, more oppressive occupation of 1967. Here too the priorities emerged more clearly: the Palestinian must first address the Israeli, now as a rebellious prisoner speaking to his guard, or as a challenge to a coercive presence. It is the Arabs inside occupied Palestine whose restiveness, at least as far as the outside world is concerned, has made pre-1967 silence seem inauthentic. A whole range of Palestinian speech has erupted, all originating at the proper source—Arabs under occupation in Palestine—and thereby channelled out to the world. Call them rumors, myths, para-literature, propaganda, or whatever: they replace the silence with what is now only a substitute political voice (just as Amman is a substitute political center), but which at least derives from an objective, because directly experienced, condition of imposed silence. This essay of mine, I feel, because it is in English partakes both of the peripherality and of the paradoxical silence that I have been trying to describe.

The Palestinian's isolation has been a disorientation more than anything else. Or so it now appears. Previously a classless "refugee," since 1967 he has become a political consciousness with nothing to lose but his refugeedom; that isn't much of a possession, and it is his only political possession at present. The attenuation of the Arab project, or the demythification of the Arab potential, has left the Palestinian with his original starting point, as Gerard Manley Hopkins phrased it, being "a lonely began": the fact that he is a deracinated refugee from Palestine. Karameh presented the refugee with a new alternative, the chance to root peripherality, isolation, and silence in resisting action. If once it made the Palestinian generally angry and resentful that neither the Arabs, the Israelis, nor the rest of the world fully grasped his predicament, such organizations as the Popular Front for the Liberation of Palestine, al-Fatah, and even the Institute for Palestine Studies in Beirut are his way of grasping himself and his predicament alone.

Before discussing the meaning of the Palestinian movement more fully, it may be worthwhile to comment briefly on two sympathetic sources of outside interest in the Palestinian issue. One is the so-called realistic view, which is held by some Zionists and many non-Zionists as well. In this view the word "tragedy" turns up with cloying frequency. Thus, runs the argument, while the Jews have an undeniable right to what they have so laboriously earned, it is a tragedy that a million and a half Arabs, innocent of European anti-Semitism, have had to be one of the costs of the enterprise. Such is the material of tragedy, but life must go on. Reason, and negotiation, ought now to prevail. The trouble with this argument is that, no less than Four Power settlement, it is an imposition of an occidental aesthetic model on what is in large measure a non-occidental political situation. Tragedy, as Jaspers put it bluntly in another connection, is not enough. It would be just as silly to try to convince a refugee living in a tent outside Amman that he is the daily victim of a tragedy, as it would be to tell an Israeli that he is a tragic hero. Tragedy is not a Semitic idea, much less a universal one. Moreover, the tragic vision is a static one, unsuited to the dynamics of political action currently enacted and lived through. If there was a tragedy, it was part of the common Semitic past in its sufferings at the hands of the West: the Jews in World War II, the Arabs in Palestine evicted by the power of Western-backed Zionism. The reality of Palestine remains, however, and that requires action, not tragic suffering.

The second source of sympathy is from the international radical Left. Although wishing to accept that sympathy, the Palestinians—myself included—suggest a number of reservations. One is that the Left argues the case against Israel too much from the outside, whereas what is needed is a corrective from the inside of the situation. It might have been possible to show how Israel was originally a creation of Western colonialism (as Maxime Rodinson has done with such telling effect), yet it does not alter the fact that there is such a thing as Israeli imperialism and that is now affecting all Palestinians more directly than Western colonialism. The latter, to Israel's immediate credit and to its ultimate disadvantage, has had the function of helping the Israelis remain in the curiously skewed position of assuming territorially sovereign status as well as a historically and politically aloof and repressive position whenever it came to the Arab inhabitants of Palestine. To the Palestinian, what matters now is the troubling immediacy of the Israeli presence, not the contradictions inherent in European and American colonialism.

Another aspect of the Left argument that disquiets me (I can't speak for anyone besides myself) is what bothered me when I quoted Erikson so tentatively, or when I disavowed the tragic view. I simply have no way of knowing how political analyses developed in the West ultimately apply elsewhere. There is, for example, an Israeli Left, just as there is an Arab Left: they are still opposed on more direct grounds than theoretical ones. I have no answer to this problem, and I raise it only as a symptom of difficulties with any so-called internationalist overview, whether political, psychological, or aesthetic. Finally, no Palestinian can forget three things about the Left. First, that it was Russia and its satellites that went along with the United States in the Partition Plans and in UN creation of Israel in 1948. Second, that there is an alarming symmetry in the manner by which the Left has recently joined or replaced anti-Semitic supporters (who were a source of endless trouble) of the Arabs against Israel. Third, that the new Palestinian ideology owes next to nothing to the Western Left which, bogged down in its dynastic worries and conflicts over racism and/or conflicts and/or its own internationalism, had little to contribute to the Palestinian during the 1967 War.

The present phase of the Palestinian experience is in trying to sharpen the experience by keeping it pertinent to *Palestine,* thereby liberating Palestine, actually and intellectually, from the segregations and the confusions that have captured it for so long. All sorts of difficulties tamper with this effort, Israel most of all. Every Jewish Zionist I have either read, heard, or spoken to, whether he is an Israeli or an American, adheres to a notion whose common denominator is that Israel must remain as it is now is in order to safeguard the Jewish *rhythm of life,* a phrase that presumably serves to camouflage the wide social discrepancies between the European, the Oriental, the Orthodox, and the secular Jews in Israel. This, I gather, makes sense to many Jews: I can't tell. For a Palestinian, it is difficult to accept the rhythm-of-life view except as one of two things. Either the phrase stands for a fear that the Holocaust could be repeated, which makes of Israel (after twenty-one years of much-vaunted independence) what the English would call a funk-hole for every still-dispersed Jew. Or the phrase is an argument for preserving Israel from having to face the no less real truth that the Jewish rhythm has supplanted a more inclusive one, the Palestinian, which has and would allow Christian, Moslem, and Jew to live in counterpoint with each other.

Probably the most serious psychological obstacle preventing close and fair political scrutiny of Palestinianism is, as I said above, the heavy emotional pressure of the Holocaust. To this pressure every civilized man must of course submit, so long as it does not inhibit anyone's political rights, particularly those of people who are absolutely dissociable from what has been an entirely European complicity. It cannot be emphasized enough, I think, that no Arab feels any of the sort of guilt or shame that every Westerner (apparently) feels, or is impelled to show he is feeling, for that horrible chapter in history. For a Palestinian Arab, therefore, it is not taboo: to speak of "Jews" in connection with Israel and its supporters, to make comparisons between the Israeli and the German occupations, to excoriate journalism that reports Jewish suffering but ignores, or discounts, Israel's razing of Arab homes and villages, Israeli napalm bombing, Israeli torture of Palestinian resistance fighters and civilians, Israel's deliberate attempt to obliterate the Palestinian Arab, Israel's use of its understanding of "Arab psychology" to offend the Arab's human status, Israel's callous use of Jewish suffering to blackmail Christians and Moslems by toying with "plans" for Jerusalem—and so on.

The Palestinian organizations active today have Palestinianism in common. They do not project too far ahead of plans somehow to open Palestine to all Palestinians. Despite Israeli disclaimers, their penetration into occupied territory and the surprisingly tough resistance of the Arab residents in those territories are keeping the possibility of Palestine very alive. During a period of a few weeks this past spring al-Fatah claimed 168 raids within Israel: this is a considerable toll on Arabs and Jews, but given the self-defeating Israeli inflexibility, it is not a senseless toll. If Jews are to stay, the Palestinians argue fairly, then Christians and Moslems must be allowed the same, equal privilege. Interestingly, past tension between Arab Christians and Moslems has been surmounted among the Palestinians. Christians sit on the Fatah Executive Committee, and the leader of the Popular Front is a Christian. While in Amman I spoke with a clergyman who had been active in West Bank resistance—he had been imprisoned by the Israelis, abused, then deported; to him, the Moslems and the Christians in the village were exactly alike in their interests and in their enemy. But the plight of Arabs in occupied Palestine is morally awful. To believe in a democratic, progressive, multi-confessional Palestine and yet to be forced to live "cooperatively" under Israeli domination is a condition not borne easily. Only the merchant class, never particularly admirable, has found life not so bad, cooperating with whomever has seemed most profitable to it.

As to methods for achieving Palestine, they are shrouded in circumstances as yet not fully known. The essential point is that the goal has to be won from the ground up. It might mean—if Israel were to expand still further—the turning of many more Arabs (Jordanians, Lebanese, Syrians, for example) into "Palestinians." The present regimes everywhere in the Arab world are in a state of tricky balance, but for the moment the Palestinians anxiously avoid involving themselves too deeply in the mire of Arab politics. Most Arab leaders presently can win a measure of popular favor, and much-needed glamour, by openly consulting with Yasir Arafat. For example, al-Fatah still plays its part independently of Nasser, Hussein, or the Syrians. To what extent this can continue, and to what extent the Americans and the Russians are (or will be) involved in Palestinian affairs are hard questions to answer. What matters most is that the Palestinian has made of his dismal experience an important political weapon for his purposes, and so long as it remains his own, developed as it is out of attachments to his native land, the cost will not have been too high.

from *The Politics of Dispossession*

3

Molestation and Authority in Narrative Fiction

(1971)

Published in 1971 in a collection of essays edited by J. Hillis Miller,[1] "Molestation and Authority in Narrative Fiction" was the first of several essays in which Said seriously engages the problem of authority in works of literary fiction, an issue that would find full expression later in *Orientalism*. Lengthened and revised as Chapter 3 of *Beginnings* (1975), it was also among one of the first essays wherein Said juxtaposed the European novel to developments in Arab literature. Although Said would rethink many of the original claims he put forward in "Molestation and Authority," the essay marked for Said a methodological shift from the phenomenological criticism of Georges Poulet, Jean Rousset, and Merleau-Ponty to the narrative theory of the structuralists like Tsvetan Todorov and Roland Barthes.

Throughout Said's earliest critical work—in his book on Conrad, for example, and his reviews for journals and magazines such as the *Partisan Review* and *The Nation*,[2] Said showed a keen interest in the work of the Geneva School, a movement of literary critics centered on the work of George Poulet, Jean Rousset, and Jean Starobinski, among others. Espousing a view of literature and criticism based on the phenomenological writings of philosophers Husserl and Merleau-Ponty, the Geneva critics held that literary works were embodiments of authorial consciousness. Until the mid-1960s, the Geneva School thus offered literary critics a secular and serious philosophical alternative to the southern agrarian and spiritual undertones that had come to characterize many of the threads of the American New Criticism of the postdepression and postwar era.

Yet by 1966, the emergence of French structuralism had challenged many of the suppositions of phenomenological criticism. In *Tristes Tropiques,* the anthropologist Claude Lévi-Strauss charged that phenomenological criticism had "promoted private preoccupations to the rank of philosophical problems." Merleau-Ponty, whose *Phenomenology of Perception* had inspired the Geneva School, had also conceded that much of phenomenological criticism was in fact solipsistic. Structuralism thus became, in the words of Said's mentor Harry Levin, "the Alexandrianism of our time." Said wrote: "The structuralists were like men who [stood] at the beginning of a new era and at the twilight of an old one."

Yet neither current of criticism entirely appealed to Said. Phenomenological critics such George Poulet had failed to account not only for the "brute temporal sequence" of an author's production, but also for the authors' "shaping of the works into independent formal texts."[3] And the structuralists, in their somewhat crusading drive to isolate the general structures of human activity, had, Said claimed, domesticated the human subject to the tyranny of system. "A major criticism of the structuralists," he wrote, "is that the moving force of life and behavior . . . has been, in their work, totally domesticated by system."[4]

Literary criticism, as Said had come to know it, was thus in crisis, and *Beginnings,* Said's second book, was his attempt to assimilate and adapt many of the insights of phenomenological criticism to methods of a structuralist interpretation of narrative form.

In its fully developed form as the great classical novel, from Defoe to Dickens and Balzac, narrative prose fiction is by no means a type of literature common to all traditions. Even in those traditions of which it is a part, the novel has had a limited life. This, I think, is an important fact. It may not tell us what the novel is, but it can help us to understand what needs the novel has filled and what effects it has produced among readers, societies, and traditions in which the genre is significant. Let me limit myself to a brief example that illustrates some of what I mean. Modern Arabic literature includes novels, but they are almost entirely of this century. There is no tradition out of which these modern works developed; basically at some point writers in Arabic became aware of European novels and began to write works like them. Obviously it is not that simple; nevertheless, it is significant that the desire to create an alternative world, to modify or augment the real world through the act of writing (which is one motive underlying the novelistic tradition in the West) is inimical to the Islamic world-view. The Prophet is he who has *completed* a world-view; thus the word *heresy* in Arabic is synonymous with the verb "to innovate" or "to begin." Islam views the world as a plenum, capable of neither diminishment nor amplification. Consequently, stories like those in *The Arabian Nights* are ornamental, variations on the world, not completions of it; neither are they lessons, structures, extensions, or totalities designed to illustrate either the author's prowess in representation, the education of a character, or ways in which the world can be viewed and changed.

Thus even autobiography as a genre scarcely exists in Arabic literature. When it is to be found, the result is wholly special. One of the finest and most famous books in modern Arabic letters is Taha Hussein's three-part autobiography *Al-Ayam* (sometimes translated as *Stream of Days*), of which the first part (1929) is the most interesting. It describes the author's boyhood in an Egyptian village early in the century. At the time he wrote the book, Hussein was already a learned man of letters and ex-Azharite whose later European education wrought in him a unique fusion between the traditional Islamic and occidental cultures. Hussein's achievements as a scholar, however, do not explain a remarkable feature of *Al-Ayam*. For almost every childhood occurrence narrated by Hussein is in some way connected with the Koran—not as a body of doctrine, but as a presence or fact of everyday life. Thus the boy's greatest ambition is to memorize the Koran; his father is happy when he does his recitation well and angry when he does not; his friends are all fellow learners; and so on and on. The book's narrative style bears no resemblance to Koranic Arabic, so there is no question of imitation and hence of addition as in the Christian tradition. Rather one's impression is that life is mediated by the Koran, informed by it; a gesture or an episode or a feeling in the boy's life is inevitably reduced (always in an interesting way) back to a relationship to the Koran. In other words, no action can depart from the Koran; rather each action confirms the already completed presence of the Koran and, consequently, human existence.

Examples like this make it apparent that a central purpose of the Western novel is to enable the writer to represent characters and societies more or less freely in development. Characters and societies so represented grow and move in the novel because they mirror a process of engenderment or beginning and growth possible and permissible for the mind to imagine. Novels, therefore, are aesthetic objects that fill gaps in an incomplete world: they satisfy a human urge to add to reality by portraying (fictional) characters in which one can believe. Novels are much more than that, of course. Nevertheless, I should like now to consider the institution of narrative prose fiction as a kind of appetite that writers develop for modifying reality—as if from the beginning—as a desire to create a new or beginning fictional entity while accepting the consequences of that desire.

Every novel is at the same time a form of discovery and also a way of accommodating discovery, if not to a social norm, then to a specialized "novelistic" reading process. As Harry Levin has said, the novel is an institution, wholly differentiated from the more generalized idea of "fiction," to which even the most unusual and *novel* experiences are admitted as functions.[5] Every novelist has taken the genre as both an enabling condition and a restraint upon his inventiveness. Both these factors are time- and culture-bound, but how exactly they are bound has yet fully to be studied. My thesis is that invention and restraint—or as I shall call them, "authority" and "molestation," respectively—ultimately have *conserved* the novel because novelists have construed them together as *beginning* conditions, not as conditions for limitlessly expansive fictional invention. Thus the novel represents a beginning of a very precisely finite sort insofar as what may ensue from that beginning. In this respect the classical novel has been a far more conservative and more precisely constraining beginning than would otherwise be expected of a genre so explicitly committed to fabulation. Alain Robbe-Grillet makes this point in his polemic attacking outdated conceptions of the novel, "Sur quelques notions périmées" (1957),[6] an essay that accurately notes just how severe and timebound are critical constraints upon the form.

By my two terms, *authority* and *molestation,* I wish to indicate the kind of perspective I am now adopting. *Authority* suggests to me a constellation of linked meanings: not only, as the OED tells us, "a power to enforce obedience," or "a derived or delegated power," or "a power to influence action," or "a power to inspire belief," or "a person whose opinion is accepted"; not only those, but a connection as well with *author*—that is, a person who originates or gives existence to something, a begetter, beginner, father, or ancestor, a person also who sets forth written statements. There is still another cluster of meanings: *author* is tied to the past participle *auctus* of the verb *augere;* therefore *auctor,* according to Eric Partridge, is literally an increaser and thus a founder.[7] *Auctoritas* is production, invention, cause, in addition to meaning a right of possession. Finally, it means continuance, or a causing to continue. Taken together these meanings are all grounded in the following notions: (1) that of the power of an individual to initiate, institute, establish—in short, to begin; (2) that this power and its product are an increase over what has been there previously; (3) that the individual wielding this power controls its issue and what is derived therefrom; (4) that authority maintains the continuity of its course. All four of these abstractions can be used to describe the way in which narrative fiction asserts itself psychologically and aesthetically through the technical efforts of the novelist. Thus in the written statement, beginning or inauguration, augmentation by extension, possession and continuity stand for the word *authority.*

Now, *molestation* is a word I shall use to describe the bother and responsibility of all these powers and efforts. By that I mean that no novelist has ever been unaware that his authority, regardless of how complete, or the authority of a narrator, is a sham. Molestation, then, is a consciousness of one's duplicity, one's confinement to a fictive, scriptive realm, whether one is a character or a novelist. And molestation occurs when novelists and critics traditionally remind themselves of how the novel is always subject to a comparison with reality and thereby found to be illusion. Or again, molestation is central to a character's experience of disillusionment during the course of a novel. To speak of authority in narrative prose fiction is also inevitably to speak of the molestations that accompany it.

Authority and its molestations are at the root of the fictional process; at least this is the enabling relationship that most fiction itself renders. Later we shall examine some reasons why this is so. But the problematic of novelistic fiction from the early eighteenth century on is how narrative institutes, alongside the world of common discourse, another discourse whose beginning is important—indeed, crucial—to it, located as it is in the responsibility taken for it by the begetting writer/speaker. Yet this fictional progenitor is bound by the fact that he is always at a remove from a truly fundamental role. It is no accident, I think, that James and Conrad, those exceptionally reflective autumnal craftsmen of fiction, made this tantalizing distance from a radical beginning the theme of much of their best work. *Heart of Darkness* explores beginnings paradoxically through a series of obscuring narrative frames; borne from one narrative level to another, Marlow's African adventure gains its power from the uniqueness, the strangeness, of its persistence in those levels, not unequivocally from the strangeness of the experience itself. The heart of the matter—Kurtz's experience—is posited outside Marlow's discourse, which leaves us to investigate, if we can, the speaker's authority. By the end of the tale we are aware of something that Marlow has given birth to that eludes empirical verification, even as it rests most securely upon the fact that Marlow has delivered it. Here, in most of its senses, authority is involved, except that we are required to accept that authority as never final. There is derivation, begetting, continuity, augmentation—and also a nagging, molesting awareness that beyond these there is something still more authentic, beside which fiction is secondary.

No writer before Freud and Nietzsche to my knowledge has so obsessively investigated some of these notions as Kierkegaard, whose meditations examine more than a century of fictional authority. To read *The Point of View for My Work as an Author* (written in 1848; published 1859) simply as commentary on his own work is to rob it of its most useful insights. For there Kierkegaard probes what is fundamental to all writing (preeminently fiction and personal discourse) in the center of which is the relationship between a focal character whose voice for the reader is authoritative and the nature of the authorship such a voice entails. It is of a kind with the relationship between Isabel Archer, for example, the movement of whose consciousness the reader attends to very carefully, and the type of writing James had to practice in order to produce her. Behind both is the generative authority that as secular critics we characterize as "imaginative," but which Kierkegaard the Christian called "divine governance" (*Styrelse*). The role of such governance is described only after Kierkegaard lays out the principles that have distinguished his work. He has been writing two sorts of books, he says: aesthetic and religious. The former sort seems to contradict the more obviously urgent religious works, but Kierkegaard wants it understood that the aesthetic books have been designed, in manner at least, to deal with serious questions in a mode suitable to the frivolity of his contemporaries. Taken alone, then, the aesthetic works would be confusing, not to say hopelessly lacking in seriousness. But viewed as necessary preparations for the directly religious works, his aesthetic writings become indirect, ironic communications of higher truths.

Here we have the characteristic Kierkegaardian figure of repetition. The aesthetic works are what he calls a dialectical reduplication of the truth: "For as a woman's coyness has a reference to the true lover and yields when he appears, so, too, dialectical reduplication has a reference to true seriousness."[8] There is a strict connection between aesthetic and religious, one that binds them together in bonds of necessity: the religious is a prior, more important truth given in secondary, ironic and dissembling forms. The aesthetic works do not occur in a void, even though it appears otherwise, so striking is the freedom of their expression. We must remember, therefore, that "there is a difference between writing on a blank sheet of paper and bringing to light by the application of a caustic fluid a text which is hidden under another text."[9] The aesthetic hides or signals the religious, just as Socrates' comic personality conceals the deepest seriousness. We accept the indirect mode, which seems to nullify the truth in order that the truth might emerge more fully later. This is, says Kierkegaard, a teleological suspension practiced so that the truth may become truer.

Kierkegaard's authorship is a deliberately composite one; and the patron of his enterprise is Socrates, to whom he devoted his master's thesis, *The Concept of Irony.* What always interests Kierkegaard is the difficulty of speaking directly to an unresponsive audience about matters for which silence is the most suitable expression. The difficulty, however, reflects as much on the author's weakness as it does on that of his audience. In an extremely long footnote to a phrase in chapter 3 of *The Point of View,* Kierkegaard argues that his total authorship is a superfluity only because he has depended on God and has been a weak human being; otherwise his work would have come to grips with the human situation and "would have been interrelated with the instant and the effective in the instant."[10] So in his aesthetic works Kierkegaard is the strong author whose mode conceals the true weakness vis-à-vis God which the religious author was at pains to reveal. The aesthetic, then, is an ironic double, a dialectical reduplication, of a religious truth. The human author augments and is strong, whereas with regard to the divine he is weak; the divine causes his work to stand apart and to appear to be superfluous to the here and now.

One aspect of authorship, then, is its contingent authority, its ability to initiate or build structures whose absolute authority is radically nil, but whose contingent authority is a quite satisfactory transitory alternative to the absolute truth. Therefore, the difference between Abraham's true authority in Kierkegaard's *Fear and Trembling* and the narrator's contingent authority is that Abraham is silent, whereas the narrator universalizes in language; the point is that any absolute truth cannot be expressed in words, for only diminished, flawed versions of the truth are available to language. This is as much as to say that *fiction alone speaks or is written*—for truth has no need of words—*and that all voices are assumed ones.* The importance of Kierkegaard's formulations is that he is particularly adept in describing the tactics of his authorship, with its recourse to revealing pseudonyms, and that he is more generally accurate in describing the tactics of writing that commit the author self-consciously to using an assumed voice. This voice sounds certain because it apparently (or in fact) *intentionally* determines its own way and validates its pronouncements by acceptable and sometimes dramatic means. Thus Kierkegaard, calling himself Johannes de Silentio in order ironically to remind us how far his words are from Abraham's silence and truth, writes the following mock disclaimer in *Fear and Trembling:*

> The present writer is nothing of a philosopher; he is, *poetice et eleganter,* an amateur writer who neither writes the System nor *promises* of the System, who neither subscribes to the System nor ascribes anything to it. He writes because for him it is a luxury which becomes the more agreeable and more evident, the fewer there are who buy and read what he writes.[11]

Yet the assumed voice's authority is a usurped one, for behind the voice is the truth, somehow and always unapprehendable, irreducible to words, and perhaps even unattractive, to which the voice remains subservient in an entirely interesting way. (It is perhaps worth suggesting here that the novel is the aesthetic form of servitude: no other genre so completely renders the meaning of *secondariness.*) Here again Kierkegaard is very subtle. The relationship between truth and its artistic version is dialectical, not strictly mimetic—by which I mean that Kierkegaard permits the aesthetic a maximum freedom without losing an awareness of the aesthetic's rewording of the religious, without forgetting its precarious status. In other words, we are to understand the dialectical connection as making ironic the convincing pretensions of the aesthetic.

Any novelistic narrative has for an immediate referent the act of speaking or writing: "I speak . . . ," or "It is spoken . . . ," or "He speaks. . . ." Beyond that, of course, the narrative is not obliged to be "real" except in the formal ways analyzed at great length in such works as Wayne Booth's *Rhetoric of Fiction.*[12] Kierkegaard's insistence upon the inventiveness and freedom of the aesthetic (i.e., the fictional) mode emphasizes how narratives do more than simply and generally repeat reality: they create another sense altogether by repeating, by making repetition itself the very form of novelty. Thus, as Gilles Deleuze has shown, such intentional repetition opposes the laws of nature and the moral law, goes beyond good and evil, and stands against the generality of habit and the particularity of memory. Moreover, such intentional repetition "appears as the *logos* of the solitary, the singular, the *logos* of the private thinker."[13] The actuality of the narrative process is repetition, it is true, but it is not the repetition of backward but of *forward* recollection. Kierkegaard links repetition with the essence of creation, not of slavish transcription:

> If God himself had not willed repetition, the world would never have come into existence. He would either have followed the light plans of hope, or He would have recalled it all and conserved it in recollection. This He did not do, therefore the world endures, and it endures for the fact that it is a repetition. Repetition is reality, and it is the seriousness of life.[14]

Kierkegaard everywhere insists on the individuality of the aesthetic repeating voice. It is neither abstract nor vaguely communal. In an important passage in *The Concept of Irony* he discusses the most distinctive feature of the ironic, aesthetic voice:

> But the outstanding feature of irony . . . is the subjective freedom which at every moment has within its power the possibility of a beginning and is not generated from previous conditions. There is something seductive about every beginning because the subject is still free, and this is the satisfaction the ironist longs for. At such moments actuality loses its validity for him; he is free and above it.[15]

What the ironic voice goes on to create is a "usurped totality" of progression based on a seductive beginning. Insofar as an author begins to write at all he is ironic, since for him, too, there is a deceptive, subjective freedom at the outset. The distance that separates him from actuality is a function of his personality—which, Kierkegaard says, "is at least momentarily incommensurable with actuality"[16]—and, we might add, of his continuing, augmenting authority. But we must never forget the abiding truth, from which the author departs in search of his new fulfillment.

Kierkegaard's analysis of authorship exposes the uneasiness and vacillation with which narrative fiction begins and from which it develops. If we suspend for a moment our lifelong familiarity with fiction and try not to take the existence of novels for granted, we will see that the seminal beginning conception of narrative fiction depends simultaneously upon three special conditions. The first of these is that there must be some strong sense of doubt that the authority of any single voice, or group of voices, is sufficient unto itself. In the community formed among reader, author, and character, each desires the company of another voice. Each hears in the other the seductive beginning of a new life, an alternative to his own; and yet each grows progressively aware of an authenticity systematically betrayed during the course of the partnership—the novelistic character feels this most of all. Our interest in Dorothea Brooke in *Middlemarch* rests on our perception of her expectations of some life different from the one she presently leads; impelled by those expectations, she becomes another person in her marriage to Dr. Casaubon. What she leaves behind during that unhappy episode she later recovers in a form tempered by the experience of self-deception. Initially dissatisfied with herself, she doubles her life by adding a new one to it. She does this by the authority of her personality, yet her travails are no less the result of that molesting authority. So too for Eliot, who creates Dorothea in the enactment of her (Eliot's) will to be another. Similarly the reader, who allows Dorothea the benefit of his doubt about his isolated self.

The inaugural act of usurpation once performed—because of pleasure taken in a free beginning, because of a desire to reduplicate, to repeat life in a more accessible form—there follows consolidation of the initial gain by various means. One is by the accumulation of prerogatives. Notice how skillfully this is done by Huck Finn at the opening of his narrative, as he asserts his right to tell us *his* version of things:

> You don't know about me without you have read a book by the name of *Adventures of Tom Sawyer*, but that ain't no matter. That book was made by Mr. Mark Twain and he told the truth, mainly. There was things which he stretched, but mainly he told the truth. That is nothing. I never seen anybody but lied one time or another.[17]

Other means include strengthening one's belief in one's project, cultivating psychological arrangements, and placing useful as well as frightening things in convenient locations.

In the chapter in *Capital* entitled "The Secret of Primitive Accumulation," Marx traces the growth of capitalist society from the dissolution of feudal society in terms that deserve mention here: he claims that once the individual has "escaped from the regime of the guilds, their rules for apprenticeship and journeymen, and the impediments of their labour regulations," he becomes a free-seller of himself, and thereby a producer firsthand.[18] Of course, Marx adds, this is really just another form of enslavement, for man has been robbed of his personal means of production: he therefore creates others, alternative to his own, and then falls prey to the illusion that he has free labor power. The real power is elsewhere, but the illusion persists that the individual is in control of his life as he generates values and prerogatives suitable to his condition. This is perfectly consonant with what Pip does in *Great Expectations*. Self-created, he labors to be a free gentleman leading a gentleman's life while in fact he is enslaved by an outcast who has himself been victimized by society. By his schemes Pip grants himself the right to manners, thoughts, and actions that dispose of life with grand ease. It is with the exposure of the falseness of these schemes, as well as with the actual successes he manages, that the novel is concerned.

The systematic reinforcement of illusions, which Marx and Engels treated earlier in *The German Ideology*, underlies Pip's course in *Great Expectations*. His progress up the social scale is supported by every character in the novel, so committed is everyone (Joe Gargery included)—in thought, at least—to an ideology that equates money with privilege, morality, and worth. Although the novel itself licenses Pip's expectations, it also mercilessly undercuts them, mainly by showing that these expectations are inherently self-limiting. That is, Pip can neither hold expectations nor realize them without a patron who makes them possible. Thus Pip's freedom is dependent upon an unnamed patron who requires visits to Jaggers, who requires that no questions be asked, and so on. The more Pip believes he is acting on his own, the more tightly he is drawn into an intricate web of circumstances that weighs him down completely; the plot's progressive revelation of accidents connecting the principal characters is Dickens's method of countering Pip's ideology of free upward progress. For Marx, the equivalent of Dickens's plot is history, which progressively reveals how one or another "freedom" is in fact a function of class interest and alliances and not really freedom at all: hence the illusion of free labor-power that allows the worker to think he can do as he pleases, whereas in fact he dangles on strings pulled by others.

The second special condition for generating narrative fiction is that the truth—whatever that may be—can only be approached indirectly, by means of a mediation that, paradoxically, because of its falseness makes the truth truer. In this context, a truer truth is one arrived at by a process of elimination: alternatives similar to the truth are shed one by one. The elevation of truth-resembling fiction to preeminence becomes a habitual practice when fiction comes to be considered the trial of truth by error. In trying to account for this rationale we enter a realm of speculation to which the best guide is Vico. In *The New Science,* Vico focuses his inquiries on a point of original juncture of three primal elements: human identity, human history, and human language. Since these are also the components with which the novel must begin its work, each of which it in turn individualizes, the correspondence between Vico and the engenderment of a novel is worth examining. Let us keep in mind, first of all, that in the center of a novel is the character who, unlike his counterpart in the classical drama, is not conceded at the very outset to be a known figure. Tom Jones, Clarissa, Robinson Crusoe, Tristram Shandy, Ahab, Julien Sorel, Frederic Moreau, Stavrogin—all these are figures deliberately and specifically original, however much they are generally of one type or another; they are not Oedipus or Agamemnon, for whose portrayal the dramatist relies upon a common mythic past, or upon a community of socially invested values and symbols. A novel's protagonist may resemble a known character, but the filiation is an indirect one. Whatever we recognize in the novelistic character we do at another level of much less prominence—that is, at the level of private authority.

Authority, says Vico, comes from *auctor,* which "certainly comes from *autos* (*proprius* or *suus ipsius*)"; thus the word's original meaning is "property." Property is dependent upon human will and upon choice; therefore, it is axiomatic for Vico that "philology observes the authority of human choice, whence comes consciousness of the certain." So the study of language recovers the conscious choices by which man established his identity and his authority: language preserves the traces of these choices, which a philologist can then decipher. Opposed to philology is philosophy, "which contemplates reason, whence comes knowledge of the true."[19] Note the demarcation: on the one hand, language, authority, and certain identity, on the other hand, the true. Certainty pertains to poetic creation (and its understanding to philology), for creation does its work in three forms of authority: divine, human, and natural. By this Vico means that human history is made by man in three stages of mythologized power, three phases of locating human interests and forming agencies to maintain them. In the divine phase, the gods fix the giants by chaining the latter to earth (*terrore defixi*): whatever man fears he divides into a subduing and a subdued power. Thus Jove and the chained giants. In the second or human phase, the giants, who have been wandering the earth, learn to control their bodies, thereby exercising will. They inhabit caves, and settle there, domesticated. Finally, after a long period of settlement, they become lords of dominion, occupation, and possession. A third division occurs: there are *gentes majores,* or the founders and originators of families, on the one hand, and the people over whom they rule on the other hand.[20]

Vico's term for this succession of periods, "poetic history," designates not so much a "real" sequence as a retrospective construction. What the construction describes, however, is real enough, even if its figures are highly metaphorical. It is the institution of a humanized milieu, populated with beings and maintained by an authority that conserves itself while slowly being reduced from grandiose powers to more and more sharply differentiated functions—just as, for example, in *Mansfield Park* Fanny apprehensively enters the wealthy environment of her aunt's house, then slowly comes to understand and live with it enough to disapprove of her cousins' mistreatment of its spirit. The pivotal moment in Vico's sequence is the Flood, or great rupture, an event that separates man's history into two distinct types that thereafter flow concurrently: sacred history and gentile history. Of the first Vico has little to say, except that it is in a sort of permanent rapport with God. The second is mankind's, an alternative to the first: it is the "new" life sought by Julien Sorel, or the one created perforce by Crusoe. Like Kierkegaard, Vico sees things in a double perspective, aesthetic and religious. And like Kierkegaard's writing, his is more fluent, more at home in the former than in the latter. The important point is that both men see that the aesthetic (or poetic) requires a reconstructive *technique* (since it is an order of repetition), that it gives rise to a special manner of being and to a universe of distinctions, while always remaining conscious of its alternative status. What is most interesting about this alternative consciousness is that it is a valid and even necessary institution of life despite the relative subservience of its position, which we may call aesthetic and ironic with Kierkegaard, or poetic and fictional with Vico.

The third special condition for the generation of novelistic fiction is an extraordinary fear of the void that antedates private authority. This, I think, is one of the less well-noted themes of the novel which extends at least as far back as *Robinson Crusoe*. For in the shipwreck that casts him into his island wilderness, Crusoe is "born," with extinction always threatening afterward, and with his new-gained and constantly experienced authority over his domain providing the safeguard of his continuing existence. A whole range of principal characters in fiction are based upon the same premise: orphans, outcasts, parvenus, emanations, solitaries, and deranged types whose background is either rejected, mysterious, or unknown. Sterne's fascination with Tristram's birth toys with the seemingly limitless hovering between nullity and existence that is central to the novelistic conception of character and to its representation in language. Were it not for a rejection of the anonymous void, both Ishmael and Pip, for example, would be unthinkable. Ishmael pointedly tells us that his narrative of shipboard existence is a substitute for the philosophical flourish with which Cato threw himself upon his sword. And the bond between the character's novelistic life and the death from which he is stayed while he lasts before us is querulously summed up in *The Nigger of the Narcissus* by James Wait, who announces, "I must live till I die."

I said parenthetically above that the novel is a literary form of secondariness; here we can refine this generality to say that the novel makes, procreates, a certain secondary and alternative life possible for heroes who are otherwise lost in society. In a sense, the novel's attitude as a formal institution toward its *dramatis personae* is that of a chiding father who has endowed his children with a patrimony and an abode he himself cannot really ever relinquish. In being the author—and notice how this applies equally to the writer/author, the novel-father/author and the character/author—one engages oneself in a whole process of filiation not easily escaped. In this (as in so much else) *Don Quixote* is exemplary.

There is the Cervantes-Sidi Hamete-Quixote relationship. There is the Amadis-Quixote relationship, there is the astonishingly fertile link between Quixote and Panza—now one, now the other rears his partner in the furthering and fathering forth of illusion; and there is, as every novelist and historian of the novel avers, *Don Quixote* itself as parent novel. James Wait's "I must live till I die" is an alternative way of saying that as a novelistic character he must live in that abode, in the family of men (the crew) which is taken by the novelist to be the stuff of fiction and which is, so far as the plot is concerned, inherited from life and from the life of novels, therefrom to be fashioned into a line of succession. This line and this sense of heritage, it seems to me, stands at the absolute center of the classical novel; and yet how interestingly secondary, how intentionally flawed and derived a line it is. I shall return to it presently.

In using Marx, Kierkegaard, and Vico to point up requisite conditions for fiction I have tried to parallel their thought with the novel's ground in human experience. Thus the philosopher or historian belongs in his work to a common mode of conceiving experience of which another version is the novel. I refer, of course, to such common themes as succession, sequence, derivation, portrayal, and alternation, to say nothing of authority itself. Here we may remark the similarities between thought that produces philosophical works, for instance, and thought that produces novels. Yet the difference is no less crucial. It is a difference in degree. The difference between Kierkegaard's anthropology of authority and, say, Pip's in *Great Expectations* is that Pip is *more* of an augmenter, continuer, and originator, both because Dickens willed it so and because that is Pip's essence as a character. As to the productive impulse that has such staying power that is not commonly diverted into either philosophy or history (Tolstoi is an exception), we can look ahead briefly to Freud for an explanation.

In any of the reconstructive techniques, whether history, philosophy, or personal narrative, the objective, according to Freud, is both to create alternatives to a confusing reality and to minimize the pain of experience. In other words, the project is an economic one. Yet insofar as it is also a repetitive procedure it has to do with instincts leading the mind over ground already traveled. Some instincts are life-promoting, others return one to the primal unity of death. The novelistic character gains his fictional authority, as we saw, in the desire to escape death; therefore, the narrative process endures so long as that essentially procreative will persists. Yet because a character's real beginning takes place in the avoidance of the anonymity of pure negation—and this is nowhere more beautifully described than in the first and last volumes of Proust's novel—there is a simultaneous pressure exerted upon him by that which he is always resisting. The demystification, the decreation or education, of illusions, which is the novel's central theme—and, paradoxically, its own alternate theme—is thus an enactment of the character's increasing molestation by a truer process pushing him to an ending that resembles his beginning in the midst of negation. The sheer length of the classical novel can almost be accounted for by the desire to initiate and promote a reduplication of life and, at the same time, to allow for a convincing portrayal of how that sort of life leads inevitably to the revelation of a merely borrowed authority. The element that contains as well as symbolizes the whole enterprise is, as recent critics have shown, the language of temporal duration.[21]

But whether we depict the narrative in temporal or strictly verbal terms, the important thing is that one must understand narrative as wholly qualified by the extremely complex authority of its presentation. Pip, Dorothea, and Isabel (in *The Portrait of a Lady*) are flawed by their illusions, by a skewing of their vision of themselves and of others. Yet all three of them *move:* out of them rises, from them *begins,* a sense of motion and of change that engages our serious interest as readers. For Pip's illusions there are, as an unforgettable counterpoise, Miss Havisham's solitary paralysis: whereas he generates a life for himself whose falseness is more and more manifest, she does next to nothing, memorialized in the sarcophagus of Satis House. Late in the novel he tells her accusingly, "You let me go on"; what is enough for her is only the beginning for Pip. And Dorothea's affections and aspirations contrast sharply with Dr. Casaubon's frigid personality, symbolized by his unfinished, locked-up manuscript. Lastly, James contrasts Isabel's flights with Osmond's perfect retreat at Roccanera, the one whose manner is that of a beautiful projector, the other the creature of a prison from which all humanity has been excluded. Within a novel, then, the principle of authority provides a motion always attempting to steer clear of obstacles that emerge to inhibit, maim, or destroy it utterly.

In historical novels of the early nineteenth century there are figures of authority to whom the protagonists are subordinate. Cardinal Borromeo in *I Promessi Sposi* and the King in *Quentin Durward,* to mention only two examples, each serves within the novel as a reminder of the limits to a character's secular power, limits that are vestiges of the "real," historical world, the truer realm, which persist into the fiction. Yet the function of each will become incorporated into the character's increasing self-consciousness of his weakness in the world, in the same way that the Marshalsea Prison in *Little Dorrit* is still more a psychological molestation of poor Mr. Dorrit when he is free than even it was in reality. The incorporation of reality into the great realistic novels of the mid-nineteenth century is performed by converting figures of secular authority into forms of sociomaterial resistance faced by the protagonists. If these forms are not imaginatively represented by cities—as in the Paris of Balzac and Flaubert, Dickens's London, and so forth—they are nevertheless felt by such figures as the Underground Man to be the generally hostile outer reality.

Such exterior circumstances exist at the level of plot. I want now to return to the authoritative character as the novel's conceptual matrix. Sometimes, as in Goethe's *Wahlverwandtschaften* or Laclos's *Liaisons dangereuses,* the fiction is sustained by pairs whose destiny is always intertwined. Edward, Ottilie, and Charlotte produce Goethe's story through a complex series of partnerships whose permanence is practically ontological in terms of the novel's existence; similarly Valmont and Merteuil, whose schemes together are the veritable abstract without which the plot could not be. Richardson's Clarissa, in comparison, is an example of private authority resisting interventions, yet beseeching Lovelace's interventions by the deep attractiveness of her inviolate privacy. In the case of Pip—which I want to analyze in some detail—we have a remarkably economical individual character. From Pip, Dickens is able to derive a very diverse range of originating circumstances (circumstances that give rise to an entire world), which taken as a group provide a perfect example of the authoritative or authorizing fictional consciousness. The more remarkable is this economy when we realize that Dickens makes use of every traditional narrative device—development, climax, linear plot sequence, physical setting, realistic accuracy of detail—together with a thoroughly imaginative method of using them, in so complete a way that even James and Eliot cannot match him. *Great Expectations* reposes upon Dickens's portrayal of Pip as at once the novel's condition for being, the novel's action, and the character in it: this gives the notions of authority and molestation I have been discussing an archetypal form. The first-person narration adds to the purity of Dickens's achievement.

Pip's name, he tells us at the outset, is the sort of beginning sign for the identity he is left with after he mixes and shortens his given name Philip Pirrip, words no longer meaningful to him but inherited by him "on the authority" of his parents' tombstones and by his sister's command. He lives, then, as an alternative being: as an orphan without real parents and as a harassed surrogate son of a much older sister. Throughout the novel the initial division will be perpetuated. On the other hand, there is Pip's natural, true genealogy that is banished from the novel at the outset, but which makes its appearance fitfully through Joe, Biddy, and the new little Pip who springs up near the novel's end. The fact that Joe Gargery is like a father to him, though in fact being his brother-in-law, makes Pip's alienation from the family continuity all the more poignant. On the other hand, the second branch in the novel's order is a substitute family, which has its roots in the unpleasant household of Mrs. Joe. Once established by Dickens, this order recurs throughout, with Pip going from one incarnation of it to another. This is the novel's most insistent pattern of narrative organization: how Pip situates himself at and affiliates himself with the center of several family groups, families whose authority he challenges by trying to institute his own through the great expectations that finally destroy him. Each family is revealed successively to belong within the sphere of another, more dominant, prior one. Miss Havisham and Estella's circle later admits Jaggers, then Magwitch, then Molly and Compeyson. And after each revelation Pip finds himself a little more self-implicated and a little less central. Each discovery informs him that his beginning has been preceded by compromises that emerge, one after the other, to wound him.

In this sequence of discoveries Dickens allows Pip, even though he seems occasionally to be fortunate, to see how there is a necessary connection between himself and prison and crime. Those fearful things are real enough, as are, too, the harshness of his childhood, the schemes of Magwitch and Miss Havisham (his alternate parents), and the bankruptcy to which he arrives later on. Set against this theme is the motif of reassembling unpleasant fragments—for nothing is given whole to Pip, or to anyone else—into new, fabricated units. A brief sojourn at Miss Havisham's is transformed by Pip into an extraordinary adventure which, despite Joe's solemn warnings, he will repeat again and again. The ironical significance of Pip's constructions is accentuated by Wemmick's house, that fantastic melange of remnants fabricated into a mock-medieval castle by the man's irrepressible desire to create a better life at Falworth—and also by Wopsle's acting, for which Shakespeare is only a beginning excuse for a rather free improvisation. These, like Pip, are *bricoleurs,* who, "brought up by hand," by fits and starts, assert their authority over the threats of unpleasant dispersion.[22] The image of a fabricating hand and its cognates is carried over into almost every corner of the novel: for example, chains are filed through, a release effected, and the hands retied in a different manner. Pip is linked by strong hands with Magwitch's and with Miss Havisham's compensatory impulses and, through Estella, with Molly's exceptionally powerful hands. After his breakdown, Pip finds himself reposing like a baby in Joe's paternal arms.

The basic scheme I have been describing is the cycle of birth and death. Pip's origin as a novelistic character is rooted in the death of his parents. By his wish to make up for that long series of graves and tombstones he creates a way for himself; and yet, over the novel's duration, Pip finds one route after another blocked, only to force open another. Like Isabel and Dorothea, Pip as a character is conceived as excess, wanting more, trying to be more than in fact he is. The augmentations are finally all rooted in the death from which he springs, and to which he returns in the end. Only by then a new, more authentic dispensation has been bred, which finally yields up a new little Pip:

> For eleven years I had not seen Joe nor Biddy with my bodily eyes—though they had both been often before my fancy in the East—when, upon an evening in December, an hour or two after dark, I laid my hand softly on the latch of the old kitchen door. I touched it so softly that I was not heard, and I looked in unseen. There, smoking his pipe in the old place by the kitchen firelight, as hale and as strong as ever, though a little grey, sat Joe; and there, fenced into the

> corner with Joe's leg, and sitting on my own little stool looking at the fire, was—I again!
>
> "We giv' him the name of Pip for your sake, dear old chap," said Joe, delighted when I took another stool by the child's side (but I did *not* rumple his hair), "and we hoped he might grow a bit like you, and we think he do."[23]

Between them, the two Pips cover an expanse whose poles are true life, on the one hand, and novelistic life on the other. Both Dickens in *Great Expectations* and Flaubert in *Madame Bovary* use money to signify the protagonists' transitory power to shore up their authority to dream and even for a while to be something they cannot long remain being. Catherine, the aged farmworker, little Pip, Joe and Biddy—these are the inarticulate, abiding natures that money cannot touch nor illusion tempt.

Together little Pip and old Pip are Dickens's way of aligning the molestations of truth against an imperious authority badly in need of restraint. That Dickens makes the alignment explicitly only near the novel's end is a sign of how, relatively late in his novelistic career, he had come to see the problem of authority as rooted in the self and therefore to be checked primarily also by the self: hence little Pip appears only to *confirm* Pip's transgression, his subsequent education, and his irremediable alienation from the family of man. One indication of Dickens's later acute understanding of the self's way with itself is that in *Great Expectations* Pip undergoes the experiences of mystification and demystification on his own, *within himself;* whereas in *Martin Chuzzlewit* two estranged Martins, one young and one old, educate one another into a family embrace. In the later novel Dickens represents the harsher principles of authority—that at bottom the self wants its own way, unshared, and that its awakening to truth entails a still more unpleasant alienation from others—which in the earlier novel he had divided between a pair of misunderstanding, willful relatives. The self's authority splits apart again later in the century—for example, in *The Picture of Dorian Gray,* in *The Strange Case of Dr. Jekyll and Mr. Hyde*, and, later still, in "The Secret Sharer." In all three of these works, however, the alter ego is a hidden reminder of the primary self's unstable authority. Jekyll's sense of "the fortress of identity" includes as well a recognition that the fortress has hideous, molesting foundations. Dickens refused to embody these recognitions *outside* the individual, as would Wilde, Stevenson, and Conrad: it is imperative in Dickens's view that such an individual as Pip should become the architect equally of his expectations and of their destruction. Doubtless he saw Pip's predicament as one communally shared and even abetted. But nowhere is there any excuse for Pip—neither orphanhood, nor poverty, nor circumstance—that can reduce the deliberateness of his choices, his individual responsibility, and his often venal compromises with reality, all of which return finally to burden him:

> That I had a fever and was avoided, that I suffered greatly, that I often lost my reason, that the time seemed interminable, that I confounded impossible existences with my own identity; that I was a brick in the house wall, and yet entreating to be released from the giddy place where the builders had set me; that I was a steel beam of a vast engine, clashing and whirling over a gulf, and yet that I implored in my own person to have the engine stopped, and my part in it hammered off; that I passed through these phases of disease, I know of my own remembrance, and did in some sort know at the time.[24]

Here the severe repetitiveness of his realizations and their insistent parallelism appear to Pip as the actual material of a reality from which he has hitherto hidden himself. After such knowledge he can only be "a weak helpless creature" and thankful for the Gargery family's solicitude; but he remains an orphan.

Yet Pip's history begins with the loss of a family and—no less important—with a favor performed out of fear. Pip's act of terrified charity is the germ of his later experience; so far as the plot is concerned, it is the author of his history and, of course, of his troubles. One might be perhaps too rash to say that in its bases at least, Pip's act, with its extended consequences, is an aesthetic dialectical reduplication, even an ironic one, of the charity we associate with Christ's ministry and agony. And yet, directly or not, novels too reflect the ethos of the Christian West. The original instance of divine errancy, the Incarnation, transformed God into man, an alternative being—the record of that mystery is given in language that only approximates the deed.

So, we might say, novels represent that process and its record at many removes, and after many secular transformations. The beginning attribution of authority to a character by a writer; the implementation of that authority in a narrative form, and the burdens and difficulties admitted as a result—all these are ways by which the almost numinous communal institutions of language accept and conserve the imprint of an individual force. This is why the novel is an institutionalization of the intention to begin. If in the end this institution chastens the individual, it is because he needs to be reminded that private authority is part of an integral truth that it nevertheless cannot fully imitate. The authority of any single piece of fiction repeats that insight, for invariably the central consciousness of a novel is found wanting in the wholeness which we normally associate with truth. Each piece of fiction, therefore, excludes a larger truth than it contains, even though it is the novelist's task to make his readers see active relationships among various orders of reality or truth both inside and outside the text.

from *Beginnings: Intention and Method*

PART II

Orientalism *and After*

4

Orientalism

(1978)

No other book of Edward Said's has enjoyed the attention of *Orientalism.* Since its publication in the United States in 1978, it has been translated into more than twenty-five languages with still more translations in progress. It has been the subject of countless conferences and impassioned debates. Perhaps more than any work of late twentieth-century criticism, it has transformed the study of literature and culture.

Yet for all of its success, *Orientalism* initially had difficulty finding a major publisher. Some publishing houses did not consider the book's idea groundbreaking; still others were unwilling to back a book whose politics were at odds with the mainstream's view of Palestinians, Arabs, and Israel. Of the few publishers that expressed an early interest in it, the University of California Press offered Said a paltry $250 advance for the book. Eventually, however, Pantheon, renowned for publishing the works of radical critics like Noam Chomsky and Michel Foucault, sent *Orientalism* to press in late 1977.

Orientalism's impact surprised both publishers and even Said himself. For the topic of Orientalism—Europe's representations of the East—was not totally new; other scholars had addressed the subject before. In 1953 Raymond Schwab wrote *Le Renaissance orientale* (a fastidiously detailed study of Europe's nineteenth-century experience of the Orient); a decade later, Anwar Abdel Malek wrote an influential article

"Orientalism in Crisis" (a Marxist interpretation of Europe's representation of the "East"). In 1969 V. G. Kiernan wrote *The Lords of the Human Kind* (a history of European colonization).[1]

But *Orientalism* differed markedly from its predecessors. It brought together the philosophies of Michel Foucault and Antonio Gramsci to challenge the authority of Western knowledge of—and power over—the Orient. It examined an array of nineteenth-century French and British novelists, poets, politicians, philologists, historians, travelers, and imperial administrators: the voyages and travel narratives of nineteenth-century French authors such as Chateaubriand, Lamartine, Nerval, and Flaubert; the Indian journalism of Karl Marx; the writings of the first modern Orientalist Sylvestre de Sacy and of the French nineteenth-century philologist Ernest Renan; the adventure tales of Richard Burton and T. E. Lawrence; the speeches of Alfred Balfour; and the cables of British colonial governors in Egypt like Lord Cromer.

Drawing on the work of Michel Foucault, Said viewed this ensemble of writing on the Orient as a discourse. Together the writings of Renan, Flaubert, T. E. Lawrence, and others composed a discipline by which European culture managed and produced the "Orient." Their writings expressed "a will . . . not only to understand what [was] non-European, but also to control and manipulate what was manifestly different."[2]

Yet if Foucault offered Said a means of describing the relationship between knowledge and power over the Orient, Antonio Gramsci's concept of hegemony provided a way of explaining how the influence of certain ideas about the "Orient" prevailed over others. The extensive influence of a particular idea, Gramsci argued, operated not through the brute application of force in nontotalitarian societies, but by consent—a tacit, unwritten agreement often passed off as conventional wisdom or common sense. Hegemony, Said explained, was how Orientalism could remain an indefatigable cultural and political force in the Western media's representations of Palestinians, Arabs, and Muslims.

Yet Gramsci's writings suggested more to Said than the idea of hegemony; Gramsci offered him a way of conceptualizing his own predicament. The best and most effective critiques, wrote Gramsci, begin when writers understand themselves as products of the historical process, a process that leaves its traces without necessarily leaving an inventory of them.[3] *Orientalism* was thus Said's own account, his own inventory, of "the infinite traces" that decades of dispossession and exile inflicted on him and other "Oriental" subjects.

Among the traces deposited by the years of dispossession was Said's experience of the June 1967 Arab-Israel War. As Said recounted in the documentary film *In Search of Palestine* (1998),[4] the Arab defeat in 1967 had magnified his sense of national loss. Israel had come to occupy the West Bank and Gaza. In his early essay "The Arab Portrayed" (1968), written in the aftermath of the war, Said penned what later became the central theme of *Orientalism:*

> If the Arab occupies space enough for attention, it is a negative value. He is seen as a disrupter of Israel's and the West's existence, or . . . as a surmountable obstacle to Israel's creation in 1948. Palestine was imagined as an empty desert waiting to burst into bloom, its inhabitants inconsequential nomads possessing no stable claim to the land and therefore no cultural permanence.[5]

Orientalism was thus "a history of personal loss and national disintegration," as he later wrote.[6] Its aim was to "liberate intellectuals from the shackles of systems of thought like Orientalism."[7]

The apprentices of modern-day Orientalism responded fiercely. Leon Wieseltier, ironically one of Said's former students, wrote that *Orientalism* issued "little more than abject canards of Arab propaganda."[8] In a riposte published in *The New York Review of Books,* Bernard Lewis accused Said of "poisoning" the field of "Oriental" studies. Calling Said "reckless," "arbitrary," "insouciant," and "outrageous," Lewis recounted how Said, along with other Arab, Muslim, and Marxist critics, had "polluted" the word "Orientalism." Said, Lewis argued, had attempted to denigrate the work of well-intentioned, disinterested Orientalists; he had politicized an innocent scholarship.[9]

Yet the shrill protests from Said's critics revealed less about Said's work than it did about their own hypocrisy. Veiled in language of "scholarship" and "objectivity," their indignation was, as one reviewer put it, "an indication of the Orientalist attitudes that Said himself had described."[10] Lewis merely "delivered ahistorical and willful political assertions in the form of scholarly argument, a practice thoroughly in keeping with the least creditable aspects of old-fashioned colonialist Orientalism," Said responded.[11]

International publishers soon took notice. Within two years of its publication and a year after its debut in England (1979), numerous translations began to appear. In 1980 Editions du Seuil published the French edition with a introduction by the French-Bulgarian literary critic Tzvetan Todorov. In the same year, Kamul Abu Deeb, the Syrian poet and critic, published an innovative translation in Arabic. Translations in German, Turkish, and Persian soon followed. The Spanish and Catalan editions were published in 1991. There were translations in Japanese and Swedish in 1993, as well as others in Serbo-Croatian, Dutch, Polish, Portuguese, Korean, Greek, and most recently Vietnamese and Hebrew.

Yet *Orientalism*'s real significance lay not in its

international acclaim, but in its method. After *Orientalism,* scholars in the humanities and the social sciences could no longer ignore questions of difference and the politics of representation. Art history, anthropology, history, political science, sociology, philosophy, and literary studies were all forced to confront its vision of culture.

"In a Borgesian way," Said wrote in his afterword to the 1995 edition, "*Orientalism* has become several different books." For some scholars and intellectuals, the book was read as a defense of Islam. Others found in the work the possibility of "writing back," of giving voice to their experiences silenced by the cultural hegemony of the West. Native Americans, Africans, Asians, Latin Americans, and other colonized peoples and oppressed groups located in *Orientalism* a method to challenge a chronic tendency of the West to deny, suppress, and distort their cultures and histories. In the academy, this challenge has come to be known as postcolonial studies. *Orientalism* was seditious in its effects.[12]

INTRODUCTION TO ORIENTALISM

On a visit to Beirut during the terrible civil war of 1975–1976 a French journalist wrote regretfully of the gutted downtown area that "it had once seemed to belong to . . . the Orient of Chateaubriand and Nerval."[13] He was right about the place, of course, especially so far as a European was concerned. The Orient was almost a European invention, and had been since antiquity a place of romance, exotic beings, haunting memories and landscapes, remarkable experiences. Now it was disappearing; in a sense it had happened, its time was over. Perhaps it seemed irrelevant that Orientals themselves had something at stake in the process, that even in the time of Chateaubriand and Nerval Orientals had lived there, and that now it was they who were suffering; the main thing for the European visitor was a European representation of the Orient and its contemporary fate, both of which had a privileged communal significance for the journalist and his French readers.

Americans will not feel quite the same about the Orient, which for them is much more likely to be associated very differently with the Far East (China and Japan, mainly). Unlike the Americans, the French and the British—less so the Germans, Russians, Spanish, Portuguese, Italians, and Swiss—have had a long tradition of what I shall be calling *Orientalism,* a way of coming to terms with the Orient that is based on the Orient's special place in European Western experience. The Orient is not only adjacent to Europe; it is also the place of Europe's greatest and richest and oldest colonies, the source of its civilizations and languages, its cultural contestant, and one of its deepest and most recurring images of the Other. In addition, the Orient has helped to define Europe (or the West) as its contrasting image, idea, personality, experience. Yet none of this Orient is merely imaginative. The Orient is an integral part of European *material* civilization and culture. Orientalism expresses and represents that part culturally and even ideologically as a mode of discourse with supporting institutions, vocabulary, scholarship, imagery, doctrines, even colonial bureaucracies and colonial styles. In contrast, the American understanding of the Orient will seem considerably less dense, although our recent Japanese, Korean, and Indochinese adventures ought now to be creating a more sober, more realistic "Oriental" awareness. Moreover, the vastly expanded American political and economic role in the Near East (the Middle East) makes great claims on our understanding of that Orient.

It will be clear to the reader that by Orientalism I mean several things, all of them interdependent. The most readily accepted designation for Orientalism is an academic one, and indeed the label still serves in a number of academic institutions. Anyone who teaches, writes about, or researches the Orient—and this applies whether the person is an anthropologist, sociologist, historian, or philologist—either in its specific or its general aspects, is an Orientalist, and what he or she does is Orientalism. Compared with *Oriental studies* or *area studies,* it is true that the term *Orientalism* is less preferred by specialists today, both because it is too vague and general and because it connotes the high-handed executive attitude of nineteenth-century and early-twentieth-century European colonialism. Nevertheless books are written and congresses held with "the Orient" as their main focus, with the Orientalist in his new or old guise as their main authority. The point is that even if it does not survive as it once did, Orientalism lives on academically through its doctrines and theses about the Orient and the Oriental.

Related to this academic tradition, whose fortunes, transmigrations, specializations, and transmissions are in part the subject of this study, is a more general meaning for Orientalism. Orientalism is a style of thought based upon an ontological and epistemological distinction made between "the Orient" and (most of the time) "the Occident." Thus a very large mass of writers, among whom are poets, novelists, philosophers, political theorists, economists, and imperial administrators, have accepted the basic distinction between East and West as the starting point for elaborate theories, epics, novels, social descriptions, and political accounts concerning the Orient, its people, customs, "mind," destiny, and so on. *This* Orientalism can accommodate Aeschylus, say, and Victor Hugo, Dante and Karl Marx. A little later I shall deal with the methodological problems one encounters in so broadly construed a "field" as this.

The interchange between the academic and the more or less imaginative meanings of Orientalism is a constant one, and since the late eighteenth century there has been a considerable, quite disciplined—perhaps even regulated—traffic between the two. Here I come to the third meaning of Orientalism, which is something more historically and materially defined than either of the other two. Taking the late eighteenth century as a very roughly defined starting point Orientalism can be discussed and analyzed as the corporate institution for dealing with the Orient—dealing with it by making statements about it, authorizing views of it, describing it, by teaching it, settling it, ruling over it: in short, Orientalism as a Western style for dominating, restructuring, and having authority over the Orient. I have found it useful here to employ Michel Foucault's notion of a discourse, as described by him in *The Archaeology of Knowledge* and in *Discipline and Punish,* to identify Orientalism. My contention is that without examining Orientalism as a discourse one cannot possibly understand the enormously systematic discipline by which European culture was able to manage—and even produce—the Orient politically, sociologically, militarily, ideologically, scientifically, and imaginatively during the post-Enlightenment period. Moreover, so authoritative a position did Orientalism have that I believe no one writing, thinking, or acting on the Orient could do so without taking account of the limitations on thought and action imposed by Orientalism. In brief, because of Orientalism the Orient was not (and is not) a free subject of thought or action. This is not to say that Orientalism unilaterally determines what can be said about the Orient, but that it is the whole network of interests inevitably brought to bear on (and therefore always involved in) any occasion when that peculiar entity "the Orient" is in question. How this happens is what this book tries to demonstrate. It also tries to show that European culture gained in strength and identity by setting itself off against the Orient as a sort of surrogate and even underground self.

Historically and culturally there is a quantitative as well as a qualitative difference between the Franco-British involvement in the Orient and—until the period of American ascendancy after World War II—the involvement of every other European and Atlantic power. To speak of Orientalism therefore is to speak mainly, although not exclusively, of a British and French cultural enterprise, a project whose dimensions take in such disparate realms as the imagination itself, the whole of India and the Levant, the Biblical texts and the Biblical lands, the spice trade, colonial armies and a long tradition of colonial administrators, a formidable scholarly corpus, innumerable Oriental "experts" and "hands," an Oriental professorate, a complex array of "Oriental" ideas (Oriental despotism, Oriental splendor, cruelty, sensuality), many Eastern sects, philosophies, and wisdoms domesticated for local European use—the list can be extended more or less indefinitely. My point is that Orientalism derives from a particular closeness experienced between Britain and France and the Orient, which until the early nineteenth century had really meant only India and the Bible lands. From the beginning of the nineteenth century until the end of World War II France and Britain dominated the Orient and Orientalism; since World War II America has dominated the Orient, and approaches it as France and Britain once did. Out of that closeness, whose dynamic is enormously productive even if it always demonstrates the comparatively greater strength of the Occident (British, French, or American), comes the large body of texts I call Orientalist.

II

I have begun with the assumption that the Orient is not an inert fact of nature. It is not merely *there,* just as the Occident itself is not just *there* either. We must take seriously Vico's great observation that men make their own history, that what they can know is what they have made, and extend it to geography: as both geographical and cultural entities—to say nothing of historical entities—such locales, regions, geographical sectors as "Orient" and "Occident" are man-made. Therefore as much as the West itself, the Orient is an idea that has a history and a tradition of thought, imagery, and vocabulary that have given it reality and presence in and for the West. The two geographical entities thus support and to an extent reflect each other.

Having said that, one must go on to state a number of reasonable qualifications. In the first place, it would be wrong to conclude that the Orient was *essentially* an idea, or a creation with no corresponding reality. When Disraeli said in his novel *Tancred* that the East was a career, he meant that to be interested in the East was something bright young Westerners would find to be an all-consuming passion; he should not be interpreted as saying that the East was *only* a career for Westerners. There were—and are—cultures and nations whose location is in the East, and their lives, histories, and customs have a brute reality obviously greater than anything that could be said about them in the West. About that fact this study of Orientalism has very little to contribute, except to acknowledge it tacitly. But the phenomenon of Orientalism as I study it here deals principally, not with a correspondence between Orientalism and Orient, but with the internal consistency of Orientalism and its ideas about the Orient (the East as career) despite or beyond any correspondence, or lack thereof, with a "real" Orient. My point is that Disraeli's statement about the East refers mainly to that created consistency, that regular constellation of ideas as the preeminent thing about the Orient, and not to its mere being, as Wallace Stevens's phrase has it.

A second qualification is that ideas, cultures, and histories cannot seriously be understood or studied without their force, or more precisely their configurations of power, also being studied. To believe that the Orient was created—or, as I call it, "Orientalized"—and to believe that such things happen simply as a necessity of the imagination, is to be disingenuous. The relationship between Occident and Orient is a relationship of power, of domination, of varying degrees of a complex hegemony, and is quite accurately indicated in the title of K. M. Panikkar's classic *Asia and Western Dominance.*[14] The Orient was Orientalized not only because it was discovered to be "Oriental" in all those ways considered commonplace by an average nineteenth-century European, but also because it *could be*—that is, submitted to being—*made* Oriental. There is very little consent to be found, for example, in the fact that Flaubert's encounter with an Egyptian courtesan produced a widely influential model of the Oriental woman; she never spoke of herself, she never represented her emotions, presence, or history. *He* spoke for and represented her. He was foreign, comparatively wealthy, male, and these were historical facts of domination that allowed him not only to possess Kuchuk Hanem physically but to speak for her and tell his readers in what way she was "typically Oriental." My argument is that Flaubert's situation of strength in relation to Kuchuk Hanem was not an isolated instance. It fairly stands for the pattern of relative strength between East and West, and the discourse about the Orient that it enabled.

This brings us to a third qualification. One ought never to assume that the structure of Orientalism is nothing more than a structure of lies or of myths which, were the truth about them to be told, would simply blow away. I myself believe that Orientalism is more particularly valuable as a sign of European-Atlantic power over the Orient than it is as a veridic discourse about the Orient (which is what, in its academic or scholarly form, it claims to be). Nevertheless, what we must respect and try to grasp is the sheer knitted-together strength of Orientalist discourse, its very close ties to the enabling socio-economic and political institutions, and its redoubtable durability. After all, any system of ideas that can remain unchanged as teachable wisdom (in academies, books, congresses, universities, foreign-service institutes) from the period of Ernest Renan in the late 1840s until the present in the United States must be something more formidable than a mere collection of lies. Orientalism, therefore, is not an airy European fantasy about the Orient, but a created body of theory and practice in which, for many generations, there has been a considerable material investment. Continued investment made Orientalism, as a system of knowledge about the Orient, an accepted grid for filtering through the Orient into Western consciousness, just as that same investment multiplied—indeed, made truly productive—the statements proliferating out from Orientalism into the general culture.

Gramsci has made the useful analytic distinction between civil and political society in which the former is made up of voluntary (or at least rational and noncoercive) affiliations like schools, families, and unions, the latter of state institutions (the army, the police, the central bureaucracy) whose role in the polity is direct domination. Culture, of course, is to be found operating within civil society, where the influence of ideas, of institutions, and of other persons works not through domination but by what Gramsci calls consent. In any society not totalitarian, then, certain cultural forms predominate over others, just as certain ideas are more influential than others; the form of this cultural leadership is what Gramsci has identified as *hegemony*, an indispensable concept for any understanding of cultural life in the industrial West. It is hegemony, or rather the result of cultural hegemony at work, that gives Orientalism the durability and the strength I have been speaking about so far. Orientalism is never far from what Denys Hay has called the idea of Europe,[15] a collective notion identifying "us" Europeans as against all "those" non-Europeans, and indeed it can be argued that the major component in European culture is precisely what made that culture hegemonic both in and outside Europe: the idea of European identity as a superior one in comparison with all the non-European peoples and cultures. There is in addition the hegemony of European ideas about the Orient, themselves reiterating European superiority over Oriental backwardness, usually overriding the possibility that a more independent, or more skeptical, thinker might have had different views on the matter.

In a quite constant way, Orientalism depends for its strategy on this flexible *positional* superiority, which puts the Westerner in a whole series of possible relationships with the Orient without ever losing him the relative upper hand. And why should it have been otherwise, especially during the period of extraordinary European ascendancy from the late Renaissance to the present? The scientist, the scholar, the missionary, the trader, or the soldier was in, or thought about, the Orient because he *could be there*, or could think about it, with very little resistance on the Orient's part. Under the general heading of knowledge of the Orient, and within the umbrella of Western hegemony over the Orient during the period from the end of the eighteenth century, there emerged a complex Orient suitable for study in the academy, for display in the museum, for reconstruction in the colonial office, for theoretical illustration in anthropological, biological, linguistic, racial, and historical theses about mankind and the universe, for instances of economic and sociological theories of development, revolution, cultural personality, national or religious character. Additionally, the imaginative examination of things Oriental was based more or less exclusively upon a sovereign Western consciousness out of whose unchallenged centrality an Oriental world emerged, first according to general ideas about who or what was an Oriental, then according to a detailed logic governed not simply by empirical reality but by a battery of desires, repressions, investments, and projections. If we can point to great Orientalist works of genuine scholarship like Silvestre de Sacy's *Chrestomathie arabe* or Edward William Lane's *Account of the Manners and Customs of the Modern Egyptians,* we need also to note that Renan's and Gobineau's racial ideas came out of the same impulse, as did a great many Victorian pornographic novels (see the analysis by Steven Marcus of "The Lustful Turk"[16]).

And yet, one must repeatedly ask oneself whether what matters in Orientalism is the general group of ideas overriding the mass of material—about which who could deny that they were shot through with doctrines of European superiority, various kinds of racism, imperialism, and the like, dogmatic views of "the Oriental" as a kind of ideal and unchanging abstraction?—or the much more varied work produced by almost uncountable individual writers, whom one would take up as individual instances of authors dealing with the Orient. In a sense the two alternatives, general and particular, are really two perspectives on the same material: in both instances one would have to deal with pioneers in the field like William Jones, with great artists like Nerval or Flaubert. And why would it not be possible to employ both perspectives together, or one after the other?

Isn't there an obvious danger of distortion (of precisely the kind that academic Orientalism has always been prone to) if either too general or too specific a level of description is maintained systematically?

My two fears are distortion and inaccuracy, or rather the kind of inaccuracy produced by too dogmatic a generality and too positivistic a localized focus. In trying to deal with these problems I have tried to deal with three main aspects of my own contemporary reality that seem to me to point the way out of the methodological or perspectival difficulties I have been discussing, difficulties that might force one, in the first instance, into writing a coarse polemic on so unacceptably general a level of description as not to be worth the effort, or in the second instance, into writing so detailed and atomistic a series of analyses as to lose all track of the general lines of force informing the field, giving it its special cogency. How then to recognize individuality and to reconcile it with its intelligent, and by no means passive or merely dictatorial, general and hegemonic context?

III

It is very easy to argue that knowledge about Shakespeare or Wordsworth is not political whereas knowledge about contemporary China or the Soviet Union is. My own formal and professional designation is that of "humanist," a title which indicates the humanities as my field and therefore the unlikely eventuality that there might be anything political about what I do in that field. Of course, all these labels and terms are quite unnuanced as I use them here, but the general truth of what I am pointing to is, I think, widely held. One reason for saying that a humanist who writes about Wordsworth, or an editor whose specialty is Keats, is not involved in anything political is that what he does seems to have no direct political effect upon reality in the everyday sense. A scholar whose field is Soviet economics works in a highly charged area where there is much government interest, and what he might produce in the way of studies or proposals will be taken up by policymakers, government officials, institutional economists, intelligence experts. The distinction between "humanists" and persons whose work has policy implications, or political significance, can be broadened further by saying that the former's ideological color is a matter of incidental importance to politics (although possibly of great moment to his colleagues in the field, who may object to his Stalinism or fascism or too easy liberalism), whereas the ideology of the latter is woven directly into his material—indeed, economics, politics, and sociology in the modern academy are ideological sciences—and therefore taken for granted as being "political."

Nevertheless the determining impingement on most knowledge produced in the contemporary West (and here I speak mainly about the United States) is that it be nonpolitical, that is, scholarly, academic, impartial, above partisan or small-minded doctrinal belief. One can have no quarrel with such an ambition in theory, perhaps, but in practice the reality is much more problematic. No one has ever devised a method for detaching the scholar from the circumstances of life, from the fact of his involvement (conscious or unconscious) with a class, a set of beliefs, a social position, or from the mere activity of being a member of a society. These continue to bear on what he does professionally, even though naturally enough his research and its fruits do attempt to reach a level of relative freedom from the inhibitions and the restrictions of brute, everyday reality. For there is such a thing as knowledge that is less, rather than more, partial than the individual (with his entangling and distracting life circumstances) who produces it. Yet this knowledge is not therefore automatically nonpolitical.

What I am interested in doing now is suggesting how the general liberal consensus that "true" knowledge is fundamentally nonpolitical (and conversely, that overtly political knowledge is not "true" knowledge) obscures the highly if obscurely organized political circumstances obtaining when knowledge is produced. No one is helped in understanding this today when the adjective "political" is used as a label to discredit any work for daring to violate the protocol of pretended suprapolitical objectivity. We may say, first, that civil society recognizes a gradation of political importance in the various fields of knowledge. To some extent the political importance given a field comes from the possibility of its direct translation into economic terms; but to a greater extent political importance comes from the closeness of a field to ascertainable sources of power in political society. Thus an economic study of long-term Soviet energy potential and its effect on military capability is likely to be commissioned by the Defense Department, and thereafter to acquire a kind of political status impossible for a study of Tolstoi's early fiction financed in part by a foundation. Yet both works belong in what civil society acknowledges to be a similar field, Russian studies, even though one work may be done by a very conservative economist, the other by a radical literary historian. My point here is that "Russia" as a general subject matter has political priority over nicer distinctions such as "economics" and "literary history," because political society in Gramsci's sense reaches into such realms of civil society as the academy and saturates them with significance of direct concern to it.

I do not want to press all this any further on general theoretical grounds: it seems to me that the value and credibility of my case can be demonstrated by being much more specific, in the way, for example, Noam Chomsky has studied the instrumental connection between the Vietnam War and the notion of objective scholarship as it was applied to cover state-sponsored military research.[17] Now because Britain, France and recently the United States are imperial powers, their political societies impart to their civil societies a sense of urgency, a direct political infusion as it were, where and whenever matters pertaining to their imperial interests abroad are concerned. I doubt that it is controversial, for example, to say that an Englishman in India or Egypt in the later nineteenth century took an interest in those countries that was never far from their status in his mind as British colonies. To say this may seem quite different from saying that all academic knowledge about India and Egypt is somehow tinged and impressed with, violated by, the gross political fact—and yet *that is what I am saying* in this study of Orientalism. For if it is true that no production of knowledge in the human sciences can ever ignore or disclaim its author's involvement as a human subject in his own circumstances, then it must also be true that for a European or American studying the Orient there can be no disclaiming the main circumstances of *his* actuality: that he comes up against the Orient as a European or American first, as an individual second. And to be a European or an American in such a situation is by no means an inert fact. It meant and means being aware, however dimly, that one belongs to a power with definite interests in the Orient, and more important, that one belongs to a part of the earth with a definite history of involvement in the Orient almost since the time of Homer.

Put in this way, these political actualities are still too undefined and general to be really interesting. Anyone would agree to them without necessarily agreeing also that they mattered very much, for instance, to Flaubert as he wrote *Salammbô,* or to H. A. R. Gibb as he wrote *Modern Trends in Islam.* The trouble is that there is too great a distance between the big dominating fact, as I have described it, and the details of everyday life that govern the minute discipline of a novel or a scholarly text as each is being written. Yet if we eliminate from the start any notion that "big" facts like imperial domination can be applied mechanically and deterministically to such complex matters as culture and ideas, then we will begin to approach an interesting kind of study. My idea is that European and then American interest in the Orient was political according to some of the obvious historical accounts of it that I have given here, but that it was the culture that created that interest, that acted dynamically along with brute political, economic, and military rationales to make the Orient the varied and complicated place that it obviously was in the field I call Orientalism.

Therefore, Orientalism is not a mere political subject matter or field that is reflected passively by culture, scholarship, or institutions; nor is it a large and diffuse collection of texts about the Orient; nor is it representative and expressive of some nefarious "Western" imperialist plot to hold down the "Oriental" world. It is rather a *distribution* of geopolitical awareness into aesthetic, scholarly, economic, sociological, historical, and philological texts; it is an *elaboration* not only of a basic geographical distinction (the world is made up of two unequal halves, Orient and Occident) but also of a whole series of "interests" which, by such means as scholarly discovery, philological reconstruction, psychological analysis, landscape and sociological description, it not only creates but also maintains; it *is,* rather than expresses, a certain *will* or *intention* to understand, in some cases to control, manipulate, even to incorporate, what is a manifestly different (or alternative and novel) world; it is, above all, a discourse that is by no means in direct, corresponding relationship with political power in the raw, but rather is produced and exists in an uneven exchange with various kinds of power, shaped to a degree by the exchange with power political (as with a colonial or imperial establishment), power intellectual (as with reigning sciences like comparative linguistics or anatomy, or any of the modern policy sciences), power cultural (as with orthodoxies and canons of taste, texts, values), power moral (as with ideas about what "we" do and what "they" cannot do or understand as "we" do). Indeed, my real argument is that Orientalism is—and does not simply represent—a considerable dimension of modern political-intellectual culture, and as such has less to do with the Orient than it does with "our" world.

Because Orientalism is a cultural and a political fact, then, it does not exist in some archival vacuum; quite the contrary, I think it can be shown that what is thought, said, or even done about the Orient follows (perhaps occurs within) certain distinct and intellectually knowable lines. Here too a considerable degree of nuance and elaboration can be seen working as between the broad superstructural pressures and the details of composition, the facts of textuality. Most humanistic scholars are, I think, perfectly happy with the notion that texts exist in contexts, that there is such a thing as intertextuality, that the pressures of conventions, predecessors, and rhetorical styles limit what Walter Benjamin once called the "overtaxing of the productive person in the name of . . . the principle of 'creativity,'" in which the poet is believed on his own, and out of his pure mind, to have brought forth his work.[18] Yet there is a reluctance to allow that political, institutional, and ideological constraints act in the same manner on the individual author. A humanist will believe it to be an interesting fact to any interpreter of Balzac that he was influenced in the *Comédie humaine* by the conflict between Geoffroy Saint-Hilaire and Cuvier, but the same sort of pressure on Balzac of deeply reactionary monarchism is felt in some vague way to demean his literary "genius" and therefore to be less worth serious study. Similarly—as Harry Bracken has been tirelessly showing—philosophers will conduct their discussions of Locke, Hume, and empiricism without ever taking into account that there is an explicit connection in these classic writers between their "philosophic" doctrines and racial theory, justifications of slavery, or arguments for colonial exploitation.[19] These are common enough ways by which contemporary scholarship keeps itself pure.

Perhaps it is true that most attempts to rub culture's nose in the mud of politics have been crudely iconoclastic; perhaps also the social interpretation of literature in my own field has simply not kept up with the enormous technical advances in detailed textual analysis. But there is no getting away from the fact that literary studies in general, and American Marxist theorists in particular, have avoided the effort of seriously bridging the gap between the superstructural and the base levels in textual, historical scholarship; on another occasion I have gone so far as to say that the literary-cultural establishment as a whole has declared the serious study of imperialism and culture off limits.[20] For Orientalism brings one up directly against that question—that is, to realizing that political imperialism governs an entire field of study, imagination, and scholarly institutions—in such a way as to make its avoidance an intellectual and historical impossibility. Yet there will always remain the perennial escape mechanism of saying that a literary scholar and a philosopher, for example, are trained in literature and philosophy respectively, not in politics or ideological analysis. In other words, the specialist argument can work quite effectively to block the larger and, in my opinion, the more intellectually serious perspective.

Here it seems to me there is a simple two-part answer to be given, at least so far as the study of imperialism and culture (or Orientalism) is concerned. In the first place, nearly every nineteenth-century writer (and the same is true enough of writers in earlier periods) was extraordinarily well aware of the fact of empire: this is a subject not very well studied, but it will not take a modern Victorian specialist long to admit that liberal cultural heroes like John Stuart Mill, Arnold, Carlyle, Newman, Macaulay, Ruskin, George Eliot, and even Dickens had definite views on race and imperialism, which are quite easily to be found at work in their writing. So even a specialist must deal with the knowledge that Mill, for example, made it clear in *On Liberty* and *Representative Government* that his views there could not be applied to India (he was an India Office functionary for a good deal of his life, after all) because the Indians were civilizationally, if not racially, inferior. The same kind of paradox is to be found in Marx. In the second place, to believe that politics in the form of imperialism bears upon the production of literature, scholarship, social theory, and history writing is by no means equivalent to saying that culture is therefore a demeaned or denigrated thing. Quite the contrary: my whole point is to say that we can better understand the persistence and the durability of saturating hegemonic systems like culture when we realize that their internal constraints upon writers and thinkers were *productive*, not unilaterally inhibiting. It is this idea that Gramsci, certainly, and Foucault and Raymond Williams in their very different ways have been trying to illustrate. Even one or two pages by Williams on "the uses of the Empire" in *The Long Revolution* tell us more about nineteenth-century cultural richness than many volumes of hermetic textual analyses.[21]

Therefore I study Orientalism as a dynamic exchange between individual authors and the large political concerns shaped by the three great empires—British, French, American—in whose intellectual and imaginative territory the writing was produced. What interests me most as a scholar is not the gross political verity but the detail, as indeed what interests us in someone like Lane or Flaubert or Renan is not the (to him) indisputable truth that Occidentals are superior to Orientals, but the profoundly worked over and modulated evidence of his detailed work within the very wide space opened up by that truth. One need only remember that Lane's *Manners and Customs of the Modern Egyptians* is a classic of historical and anthropological observation because of its style, its enormously intelligent and brilliant details, not because of its simple reflection of racial superiority, to understand what I am saying here.

The kind of political questions raised by Orientalism, then, are as follows: What other sorts of intellectual, aesthetic, scholarly, and cultural energies went into the making of an imperialist tradition like the Orientalist one? How did philology, lexicography, history, biology, political and economic theory, novel-writing, and lyric poetry come to the service of Orientalism's broadly imperialist view of the world? What changes, modulations, refinements, even revolutions take place within Orientalism? What is the meaning of originality, of continuity, of individuality, in this context? How does Orientalism transmit or reproduce itself from one epoch to another? In fine, how can we treat the cultural, historical phenomenon of Orientalism as a kind of *willed human work*—not of mere unconditioned ratiocination—in all its historical complexity, detail, and worth without at the same time losing sight of the alliance between cultural work, political tendencies, the state, and the specific realities of domination? Governed by such concerns a humanistic study can responsibly address itself to politics *and* culture. But this is not to say that such a study establishes a hard-and-fast rule about the relationship between knowledge and politics. My argument is that each humanistic investigation must formulate the nature of that connection in the specific context of the study, the subject matter, and its historical circumstances.

In a previous book I gave a good deal of thought and analysis to the methodological importance for work in the human sciences of finding and formulating a first step, a point of departure, a beginning principle.[22] A major lesson I learned and tried to present was that there is no such thing as a merely given, or simply available, starting point: beginnings have to be made for each project in such a way as to *enable* what follows from them. Nowhere in my experience has the difficulty of this lesson been more consciously lived (with what success—or failure—I cannot really say) than in this study of Orientalism. The idea of beginning, indeed the act of beginning, necessarily involves an act of delimitation by which something is cut out of a great mass of material, separated from the mass, and made to stand for, as well as be, a starting point, a beginning; for the student of texts one such notion of inaugural delimitation is Louis Althusser's idea of the *problematic,* a specific determinate unity of a text, or group of texts, which is something given rise to by analysis.[23] Yet in the case of Orientalism (as opposed to the case of Marx's texts, which is what Althusser studies) there is not simply the problem of finding a point of departure, or problematic, but also the question of designating which texts, authors, and periods are the ones best suited for study.

It has seemed to me foolish to attempt an encyclopedic narrative history of Orientalism, first of all because if my guiding principle was to be "the European idea of the Orient" there would be virtually no limit to the material I would have had to deal with; second, because the narrative model itself did not suit my descriptive and political interests; third, because in such books as Raymond Schwab's *La Renaissance orientale,* Johann Fück's *Die Arabischen Studien in Europa bis in den Anfang des 20. Jahrhunderts,* and more recently, Dorothee Metlitzki's *The Matter of Araby in Medieval England*[24] there already exist encyclopedic works on certain aspects of the European-Oriental encounter such as make the critic's job, in the general political and intellectual context I sketched above, a different one.

There still remained the problem of cutting down a very fat archive to manageable dimensions, and more important, outlining something in the nature of an intellectual order within that group of texts without at the same time following a mindlessly chronological order. My starting point therefore has been the British, French, and American experience of the Orient taken as a unit, what made that experience possible by way of historical and intellectual background, what the quality and character of the experience has been. For reasons I shall discuss presently I limited that already limited (but still inordinately large) set of questions to the Anglo-French-American experience of the Arabs and Islam, which for almost a thousand years together stood for the Orient. Immediately upon doing that, a large part of the Orient seemed to have been eliminated—India, Japan, China, and other sections of the Far East—not because these regions were not important (they obviously have been) but because one could discuss Europe's experience of the Near Orient, or of Islam, apart from its experience of the Far Orient. Yet at certain moments of that general European history of interest in the East, particular parts of the Orient like Egypt, Syria, and Arabia cannot be discussed without also studying Europe's involvement in the more distant parts, of which Persia and India are the most important; a notable case in point is the connection between Egypt and India so far as eighteenth- and nineteenth-century Britain was concerned. Similarly the French role in deciphering the Zend-Avesta, the pre-eminence of Paris as a center of Sanskrit studies during the first decade of the nineteenth century, the fact that Napoleon's interest in the Orient was contingent upon his sense of the British role in India: all these Far Eastern interests directly influenced French interest in the Near East, Islam, and the Arabs.

Britain and France dominated the Eastern Mediterranean from about the end of the seventeenth century on. Yet my discussion of that domination and systematic interest does not do justice to (*a*) the important contributions of Orientalism of Germany, Italy, Russia, Spain, and Portugal and (*b*) the fact that one of the important impulses toward the study of the Orient in the eighteenth century was the revolution in Biblical studies stimulated by such variously interesting pioneers as Bishop Lowth, Eichhorn, Herder, and Michaelis. In the first place, I had to focus rigorously upon the British-French and later the American material because it seemed inescapably true not only that Britain or France were the pioneer nations in the Orient and in Oriental studies, but that these vanguard positions were held by virtue of the two greatest colonial networks in pre-twentieth-century history; the American Oriental position since World War II has fit—I think, quite self-consciously—in the places excavated by the two earlier European powers. Then too, I believe that the sheer quality, consistency, and mass of British, French, and American writing on the Orient lifts it above the doubtless crucial work done in Germany, Italy, Russia, and elsewhere. But I think it is also true that the major steps in Oriental scholarship were first taken in either Britain or France, then elaborated upon by Germans. Silvestre de Sacy, for example, was not only the first modern and institutional European Orientalist, who worked on Islam, Arabic literature, the Druze religion, and Sassanid Persia; he was also the teacher of Champollion and of Franz Bopp, the founder of German comparative linguistics. A similar claim of priority and subsequent pre-eminence can be made for William Jones and Edward William Lane.

In the second place—and here the failings of my study of Orientalism are amply made up for—there has been some important recent work on the background in Biblical scholarship to the rise of what I have called modern Orientalism. The best and the most illuminatingly relevant is E. S. Shaffer's impressive *"Kubla Khan" and The Fall of Jerusalem,*[25] an indispensable study of the origins of Romanticism, and of the intellectual activity underpinning a great deal of what goes on in Coleridge, Browning, and George Eliot. To some degree Shaffer's work refines upon the outlines provided in Schwab, by articulating the material of relevance to be found in the German Biblical scholars and using that material to read, in an intelligent and always interesting way, the work of three major British writers. Yet what is missing in the book is some sense of the political as well as ideological edge given the Oriental material by the British and French writers I am principally concerned with; in addition, unlike Shaffer I attempt to elucidate subsequent developments in academic as well as literary Orientalism that bear on the connection between British and French Orientalism on the one hand and the rise of an explicitly colonial-minded imperialism on the other. Then too, I wish to show how all these earlier matters are reproduced more or less in American Orientalism after the Second World War.

Nevertheless there is a possibly misleading aspect to my study, where, aside from an occasional reference, I do not exhaustively discuss the German developments after the inaugural period dominated by Sacy. Any work that seeks to provide an understanding of academic Orientalism and pays little attention to scholars like Steinthal, Müller, Becker, Goldziher, Brockelmann, Nöldeke—to mention only a handful—needs to be reproached, and I freely reproach myself. I particularly regret not taking more account of the great scientific prestige that accrued to German scholarship by the middle of the nineteenth century, whose neglect was made into a denunciation of insular British scholars by George Eliot. I have in mind Eliot's unforgettable portrait of Mr. Casaubon in *Middlemarch*. One reason Casaubon cannot finish his Key to All Mythologies is, according to his young cousin Will Ladislaw, that he is unacquainted with German scholarship. For not only has Casaubon chosen a subject "as changing as chemistry: new discoveries are constantly making new points of view": he is undertaking a job similar to a refutation of Paracelsus because "he is not an Orientalist, you know."[26]

Eliot was not wrong in implying that by about 1830, which is when *Middlemarch* is set, German scholarship had fully attained its European pre-eminence. Yet at no time in German scholarship during the first two-thirds of the nineteenth century could a close partnership have developed between Orientalists and a protracted, sustained *national* interest in the Orient. There was nothing in Germany to correspond to the Anglo-French presence in India, the Levant, North Africa. Moreover, the German Orient was almost exclusively a scholarly, or at least a classical, Orient: it was made the subject of lyrics, fantasies, and even novels, but it was never actual, the way Egypt and Syria were actual for Chateaubriand, Lane, Lamartine, Burton, Disraeli, or Nerval. There is some significance in the fact that the two most renowned German works on the Orient, Goethe's *Westöstlicher Diwan* and Friedrich Schlegel's *Über die Sprache und Weisheit der Indier*, were based respectively on a Rhine journey and on hours spent in Paris libraries. What German Oriental scholarship did was to refine and elaborate techniques whose application was to texts, myths, ideas, and languages almost literally gathered from the Orient by imperial Britain and France.

Yet what German Orientalism had in common with Anglo-French

and later American Orientalism was a kind of intellectual *authority* over the Orient within Western culture. This authority must in large part be the subject of any description of Orientalism, and it is so in this study. Even the name *Orientalism* suggests a serious, perhaps ponderous style of expertise; when I apply it to modern American social scientists (since they do not call themselves Orientalists, my use of the word is anomalous), it is to draw attention to the way Middle East experts can still draw on the vestiges of Orientalism's intellectual position in nineteenth-century Europe.

There is nothing mysterious or natural about authority. It is formed, irradiated, disseminated; it is instrumental, it is persuasive; it has status, it establishes canons of taste and value; it is virtually indistinguishable from certain ideas it dignifies as true, and from traditions, perceptions, and judgments it forms, transmits, reproduces. Above all, authority can, indeed must, be analyzed. All these attributes of authority apply to Orientalism, and much of what I do in this study is to describe both the historical authority in and the personal authorities of Orientalism.

My principal methodological devices for studying authority here are what can be called *strategic location,* which is a way of describing the author's position in a text with regard to the Oriental material he writes about, and *strategic formation,* which is a way of analyzing the relationship between texts and the way in which groups of texts, types of texts, even textual genres, acquire mass, density, and referential power among themselves and thereafter in the culture at large. I use the notion of strategy simply to identify the problem every writer on the Orient has faced: how to get hold of it, how to approach it, how not to be defeated or overwhelmed by its sublimity, its scope, its awful dimensions. Everyone who writes about the Orient must locate himself vis-à-vis the Orient; translated into his text, this location includes the kind of narrative voice he adopts, the type of structure he builds, the kinds of images, themes, motifs that circulate in his text—all of which add up to deliberate ways of addressing the reader, containing the Orient, and finally, representing it or speaking in its behalf. None of this takes place in the abstract, however. Every writer on the Orient (and this is true even of Homer) assumes more Oriental precedent, some previous knowledge of the Orient, to which he refers and on which he relies. Additionally, each work on the Orient *affiliates* itself with other works, with audiences, with institutions, with the Orient itself. The ensemble of relationships between works, audiences, and some particular aspects of the Orient therefore constitutes an analyzable formation—for example, that of philological studies, of anthologies of extracts from Oriental literature, of travel books, of Oriental fantasies—whose presence in time, in discourse, in institutions (schools, libraries, foreign services) gives it strength and authority.

It is clear, I hope, that my concern with authority does not entail analysis of what lies hidden in the Orientalist text, but analysis rather of the text's surface, its exteriority to what it describes. I do not think that this idea can be overemphasized. Orientalism is premised upon exteriority, that is, on the fact that the Orientalist, poet or scholar, makes the Orient speak, describes the Orient, renders its mysteries plain for and to the West. He is never concerned with the Orient except as the first cause of what he says. What he says and writes, by virtue of the fact that it is said or written, is meant to indicate that the Orientalist is outside the Orient, both as an existential and as a moral fact. The principal product of this exteriority is of course representation: as early as Aeschylus's play *The Persians* the Orient is transformed from a very far distant and often threatening Otherness into figures that are relatively familiar (in Aeschylus's case, grieving Asiatic women). The dramatic immediacy of representation in *The Persians* obscures the fact that the audience is watching a highly artificial enactment of what a non-Oriental has made into a symbol for the whole Orient. My analysis of the Orientalist text therefore places emphasis on the evidence, which is by no means invisible, for such representations *as representations,* not as "natural" depictions of the Orient. This evidence is found just as prominently in the so-called truthful text (histories, philological analyses, political treatises) as in the avowedly artistic (i.e., openly imaginative) text. The things to look at are style, figures of speech, setting, narrative devices, historical and social circumstances, *not* the correctness of the representation nor its fidelity to some great original. The exteriority of the representation is always governed by some version of the truism that if the Orient could represent itself, it would; since it cannot, the representation does the job, for the West, and *faute de mieux,* for the poor Orient. "Sie können sich nicht vertreten, sie müssen vertreten werden," as Marx wrote in *The Eighteenth Brumaire of Louis Bonaparte.*

Another reason for insisting upon exteriority is that I believe it needs to be made clear about cultural discourse and exchange within a culture that what is commonly circulated by it is not "truth" but representations. It hardly needs to be demonstrated again that language itself is a highly organized and encoded system, which employs many devices to express, indicate, exchange messages and information, represent, and so forth. In any instance of at least written language, there is no such thing as a delivered presence, but a *re-presence,* or a representation. The value, efficacy, strength, apparent veracity of a written statement about the Orient therefore relies very little, and cannot instrumentally depend, on the Orient as such. On the contrary, the written statement is a presence to the reader by virtue of its having excluded, displaced, made supererogatory any such *real thing* as "the Orient." Thus all of Orientalism stands forth and away from the Orient: that Orientalism makes sense at all depends more on the West than on the Orient, and this sense is directly indebted to various Western techniques of representation that make the Orient visible, clear, "there" in discourse about it. And these representations rely upon institutions, traditions, conventions, agreed-upon codes of understanding for their effects, not upon a distant and amorphous Orient.

The difference between representations of the Orient before the last third of the eighteenth century and those after it (that is, those belonging to what I call modern Orientalism) is that the range of representation expanded enormously in the later period. It is true that after William Jones and Anquetil-Duperron, and after Napoleon's Egyptian expedition, Europe came to know the Orient more scientifically, to live in it with greater authority and discipline than ever before. But what mattered to Europe was the expanded scope and the much greater refinement given its techniques for receiving the Orient. When around the turn of the eighteenth century the Orient definitively revealed the age of its languages—thus outdating Hebrew's divine pedigree—it was a group of Europeans who made the discovery, passed it on to other scholars, and preserved the discovery in the new science of Indo-European philology. A new powerful science for viewing the linguistic Orient was born, and with it, as Foucault has shown in *The Order of Things,* a whole web of related scientific interests. Similarly William Beckford, Byron, Goethe, and Hugo restructured the Orient by their art and made its colors, lights, and people visible through their images, rhythms, and motifs. At most, the "real" Orient provoked a writer to his vision; it very rarely guided it.

Orientalism responded more to the culture that produced it than to its putative object, which was also produced by the West. Thus the history of Orientalism has both an internal consistency and a highly articulated set of relationships to the dominant culture surrounding it. My analyses consequently try to show the field's shape and internal organization, its pioneers, patriarchal authorities, canonical texts, doxological ideas, exemplary figures, its followers, elaborators, and new authorities; I try also to explain how Orientalism borrowed and was frequently informed by "strong" ideas, doctrines, and trends ruling the culture. Thus there was (and is) a linguistic Orient, a Freudian Orient, a Spenglerian Orient, a Darwinian Orient, a racist Orient—and so on. Yet never has there been such a thing as a pure, or unconditional, Orient; similarly, never has there been a nonmaterial form of Orientalism, much less something so innocent as an "idea" of the Orient. In this underlying conviction and in its ensuing methodological consequences do I differ from scholars who study the history of ideas. For the emphases and the executive form, above all the material effectiveness, of statements made by Orientalist discourse are possible in ways that any hermetic history of ideas tends completely to scant. Without those emphases and that material effectiveness Orientalism would be just another idea, whereas it is and was much more than that. Therefore I set out to examine not only scholarly works but also works of literature, political tracts, journalistic texts, travel books, religious and philological studies. In other words, my hybrid perspective is broadly historical and "anthropological," given that I believe all texts to be worldly and circumstantial in (of course) ways that vary from genre to genre, and from historical period to historical period.

Yet unlike Michel Foucault, to whose work I am greatly indebted, I do believe in the determining imprint of individual writers upon the otherwise anonymous collective body of texts constituting a discursive formation like Orientalism. The unity of the large ensemble of texts I analyze is due in part to the fact that they frequently refer to each other: Orientalism is after all a system for citing works and authors. Edward William Lane's *Manners and Customs of the Modern Egyptians* was read and cited by such diverse figures as Nerval,

Flaubert, and Richard Burton. He was an authority whose use was an imperative for anyone writing or thinking about the Orient, not just about Egypt: when Nerval borrows passages verbatim from *Modern Egyptians* it is to use Lane's authority to assist him in describing village scenes in Syria, not Egypt. Lane's authority and the opportunities provided for citing him discriminately as well as indiscriminately were there because Orientalism could give his text the kind of distributive currency that he acquired. There is no way, however, of understanding Lane's currency without also understanding the peculiar features of *his* text; this is equally true of Renan, Sacy, Lamartine, Schlegel, and a group of other influential writers. Foucault believes that in general the individual text or author counts for very little; empirically, in the case of Orientalism (and perhaps nowhere else) I find this not to be so. Accordingly my analyses employ close textual readings whose goal is to reveal the dialectic between individual text or writer and the complex collective formation to which his work is a contribution.

In the *Prison Notebooks* Gramsci says: "The starting-point of critical elaboration is the consciousness of what one really is, and is 'knowing thyself' as a product of the historical process to date, which has deposited in you an infinity of traces, without leaving an inventory." The only available English translation inexplicably leaves Gramsci's comment at that, whereas in fact Gramsci's Italian text concludes by adding, "therefore it is imperative at the outset to compile such an inventory."[27]

Much of the personal investment in this study derives from my awareness of being an "Oriental" as a child growing up in two British colonies. All of my education, in those colonies (Palestine and Egypt) and in the United States, has been Western, and yet that deep early awareness has persisted. In many ways my study of Orientalism has been an attempt to inventory the traces upon me, the Oriental subject, of the culture whose domination has been so powerful a factor in the life of all Orientals. This is why for me the Islamic Orient has had to be the center of attention. Whether what I have achieved is the inventory prescribed by Gramsci is not for me to judge, although I have felt it important to be conscious of trying to produce one. Along the way, as severely and as rationally as I have been able, I have tried to maintain a critical consciousness, as well as employing those instruments of historical, humanistic, and cultural research of which my education has made me the fortunate beneficiary. In none of that, however, have I ever lost hold of the cultural reality of, the personal involvement in having been constituted as, "an Oriental."

The historical circumstances making such a study possible are fairly complex, and I can only list them schematically here. Anyone resident in the West since the 1950s, particularly in the United States, will have lived through an era of extraordinary turbulence in the relations of East and West. No one will have failed to note how "East" has always signified danger and threat during this period, even as it has meant the traditional Orient as well as Russia. In the universities a growing establishment of area-studies programs and institutes has made the scholarly study of the Orient a branch of national policy. Public affairs in this country include a healthy interest in the Orient, as much for its strategic and economic importance as for its traditional exoticism. If the world has become immediately accessible to a Western citizen living in the electronic age, the Orient too has drawn nearer to him, and is now less a myth perhaps than a place crisscrossed by Western, especially American, interests.

One aspect of the electronic, postmodern world is that there has been a reinforcement of the stereotypes by which the Orient is viewed. Television, the films, and all the media's resources have forced information into more and more standardized molds. So far as the Orient is concerned, standardization and cultural stereotyping have intensified the hold of the nineteenth-century academic and imaginative demonology of "the mysterious Orient." This is nowhere more true than in the ways by which the Near East is grasped. Three things have contributed to making even the simplest perceptions of the Arabs and Islam into a highly politicized, almost raucous matter: one, the history of popular anti-Arab and anti-Islamic prejudice in the West, which is immediately reflected in the history of Orientalism; two, the struggle between the Arabs and Israeli Zionism, and its effects upon American Jews as well as upon both the liberal culture and the population at large; three, the almost total absence of any cultural position making it possible either to identify with or dispassionately to discuss the Arabs or Islam. Furthermore, it hardly needs saying that because the Middle East is now so identified with Great Power politics, oil economics, and the simple-minded dichotomy of freedom-loving, democratic Israel and evil, totalitarian, and terroristic Arabs, the chances of anything like a clear view of what one talks about in talking about the Near East are depressingly small.

My own experiences of these matters are in part what made me write this book. The life of an Arab Palestinian in the West, particularly in America, is disheartening. There exists here an almost unanimous consensus that politically he does not exist, and when it is allowed that he does, it is either as a nuisance or as an Oriental. The web of racism, cultural stereotypes, political imperialism, dehumanizing ideology holding in the Arab or the Muslim is very strong indeed, and it is this web which every Palestinian has come to feel as his uniquely punishing destiny. It has made matters worse for him to remark that no person academically involved with the Near East—no Orientalist, that is—has ever in the United States culturally and politically identified himself wholeheartedly with the Arabs; certainly there have been identifications on some level, but they have never taken an "acceptable" form as has liberal American identification with Zionism, and all too frequently they have been radically flawed by their association either with discredited political and economic interests (oil-company and State Department Arabists, for example) or with religion.

The nexus of knowledge and power creating "the Oriental" and in a sense obliterating him as a human being is therefore not for me an exclusively academic matter. Yet it is an *intellectual* matter of some very obvious importance. I have been able to put to use my humanistic and political concerns for the analysis and description of a very worldly matter, the rise, development, and consolidation of Orientalism. Too often literature and culture are presumed to be politically, even historically innocent; it has regularly seemed otherwise to me, and certainly my study of Orientalism has convinced me (and I hope will convince my literary colleagues) that society and literary culture can only be understood and studied together. In addition, and by an almost inescapable logic, I have found myself writing the history of a strange, secret sharer of Western anti-Semitism. That anti-Semitism and, as I have discussed it in its Islamic branch, Orientalism resemble each other very closely is a historical, cultural, and political truth that needs only to be mentioned to an Arab Palestinian for its irony to be perfectly understood. But what I should like also to have contributed here is a better understanding of the way cultural domination has operated. If this stimulates a new kind of dealing with the Orient, indeed if it eliminates the "Orient" and "Occident" altogether, then we shall have advanced a little in the process of what Raymond Williams has called the "unlearning" of "the inherent dominative mode."[28]

THE SCOPE OF ORIENTALISM

PROJECTS

It is necessary to examine the more flamboyant operational successes of Orientalism if only to judge how exactly wrong (and how totally opposite to the truth) was the grandly menacing idea expressed by Michelet, that "the Orient advances, invincible, fatal to the gods of light by the charm of its dreams, by the magic of its *chiaroscuro*."[29] Cultural, material, and intellectual relations between Europe and the Orient have gone through innumerable phases, even though the line between East and West has made a certain constant impression upon Europe. Yet in general it was the West that moved upon the East, not vice versa. *Orientalism* is the generic term that I have been employing to describe the Western approach to the Orient; Orientalism is the discipline by which the Orient was (and is) approached systematically, as a topic of learning, discovery, and practice. But in addition I have been using the word to designate that collection of dreams, images, and vocabularies available to anyone who has tried to talk about what lies east of the dividing line. These two aspects of Orientalism are not incongruent, since by use of them both Europe could advance securely and unmetaphorically upon the Orient. Here I should like principally to consider material evidence of this advance.

Islam excepted, the Orient for Europe was until the nineteenth century a domain with a continuous history of unchallenged Western dominance. This is patently true of the British experience in India, the Portuguese experience in the East Indies, China, and

Japan, and the French and Italian experiences in various regions of the Orient. There were occasional instances of native intransigence to disturb the idyll, as when in 1638–1639 a group of Japanese Christians threw the Portuguese out of the area; by and large, however, only the Arab and Islamic Orient presented Europe with an unresolved challenge on the political, intellectual, and for a time, economic levels. For much of its history, then, Orientalism carries within it the stamp of a problematic European attitude towards Islam, and it is this acutely sensitive aspect of Orientalism around which my interest in this study turns.

Doubtless Islam was a real provocation in many ways. It lay uneasily close to Christianity, geographically and culturally. It drew on the Judeo-Hellenic traditions, it borrowed creatively from Christianity, it could boast of unrivaled military and political successes. Nor was this all. The Islamic lands sit adjacent to and even on top of the Biblical lands; moreover, the heart of the Islamic domain has always been the region closest to Europe, what has been called the Near Orient or Near East. Arabic and Hebrew are Semitic languages, and together they dispose and redispose of material that is urgently important to Christianity. From the end of the seventh century until the battle of Lepanto in 1571, Islam in either its Arab, Ottoman, or North African and Spanish form dominated or effectively threatened European Christianity. That Islam outstripped and outshone Rome cannot have been absent from the mind of any European past or present. Even Gibbon was no exception, as is evident in the following passage from the *Decline and Fall:*

> In the victorious days of the Roman republic it had been the aim of the senate to confine their councils and legions to a single war, and completely to suppress a first enemy before they provoked the hostilities of a second. These timid maxims of policy were disdained by the magnanimity or enthusiasm of the Arabian caliphs. With the same vigour and success they invaded the successors of Augustus and Artaxerxes; and the rival monarchies at the same instant became the prey of an enemy whom they had so long been accustomed to despise. In the ten years of the administration of Omar, the Saracens reduced to his obedience thirty-six thousand cities or castles, destroyed four thousand churches or temples of the unbelievers, and edified fourteen hundred moschs for the exercise of the religion

> of Mohammed. One hundred years after his flight from Mecca the arms and reign of his successors extended from India to the Atlantic Ocean, over the various and distant provinces.[30]

When the term *Orient* was not simply a synonym for the Asiatic East as a whole, or taken as generally denoting the distant and exotic, it was most rigorously understood as applying to the Islamic Orient. This "militant" Orient came to stand for what Henri Baudet has called "the Asiatic tidal wave."[31] Certainly this was the case in Europe through the middle of the eighteenth century, the point at which repositories of "Oriental" knowledge like d'Herbelot's *Bibliothèque orientale* stop meaning primarily Islam, the Arabs, or the Ottomans. Until that time cultural memory gave understandable prominence to such relatively distant events as the fall of Constantinople, the Crusades, and the conquest of Sicily and Spain, but if these signified the menacing Orient they did not at the same time efface what remained of Asia.

For there was always India, where, after Portugal pioneered the first bases of European presence in the early sixteenth century, Europe, and primarily England after a long period (from 1600 to 1758) of essentially commercial activity, dominated politically as an occupying force. Yet India itself never provided an indigenous threat to Europe. Rather it was because native authority crumbled there and opened the land to inter-European rivalry and to outright European political control that the Indian Orient could be treated by Europe with such proprietary hauteur—never with the sense of danger reserved for Islam.[32] Nevertheless, between this hauteur and anything like accurate positive knowledge there existed a vast disparity. D'Herbelot's entries for Indo-Persian subjects in the *Bibliothèque* were all based on Islamic sources, and it is true to say that until the early nineteenth century "Oriental languages" was considered a synonym for "Semitic languages." The Oriental renaissance of which Quinet spoke served the function of expanding some fairly narrow limits, in which Islam was the catchall Oriental example.[33] Sanskrit, Indian religion, and Indian history did not acquire the status of scientific knowledge until after Sir William Jones's efforts in the late eighteenth century, and even Jones's interest in India came to him by way of his prior interest in and knowledge of Islam.

It is not surprising, then, that the first major work of Oriental scholarship after d'Herbelot's *Bibliothèque* was Simon Ockley's *History of the Saracens,* whose first volume appeared in 1708. A recent historian of Orientalism has opined that Ockley's attitude towards the Muslims—that to them is owed what was first known by philosophy by European Christians—"shocked painfully" his European audience. For not only did Ockley make this Islamic pre-eminence clear in his work; he also "gave Europe its first authentic and substantial taste of the Arab viewpoint touching the wars with Byzantium and Persia."[34] However, Ockley was careful to dissociate himself with the infectious influence of Islam, and unlike his colleague William Whiston (Newton's successor at Cambridge), he always made it clear that Islam was an outrageous heresy. For his Islamic enthusiasm, on the other hand, Whiston was expelled from Cambridge in 1709.

Access to Indian (Oriental) riches had always to be made by first crossing the Islamic provinces and by withstanding the dangerous effect of Islam as a system of quasi-Arian belief. And at least for the larger segment of the eighteenth century, Britain and France were successful. The Ottoman Empire had long since settled into a (for Europe) comfortable senescence, to be inscribed in the nineteenth century as the "Eastern Question." Britain and France fought each other in India between 1744 and 1748 and again between 1756 and 1763, until, in 1769, the British emerged in practical economic and political control of the subcontinent. What was more inevitable than that Napoleon should choose to harass Britain's Oriental empire by first intercepting its Islamic throughway, Egypt?

Although it was almost immediately preceded by at least two major Orientalist projects, Napoleon's invasion of Egypt in 1798 and his foray into Syria have had by far the greater consequence for the modern history of Orientalism. Before Napoleon only two efforts (both by scholars) had been made to invade the Orient by stripping it of its veils and also by going beyond the comparative shelter of the Biblical Orient. The first was by Abraham-Hyacinthe Anquetil-Duperron (1731–1805), an eccentric theoretician of egalitarianism, a man who managed in his head to reconcile Jansenism with orthodox Catholicism and Brahmanism, and who traveled to Asia in order to prove the actual primitive existence of a Chosen People and of the Biblical genealogies. Instead he overshot his early goal and traveled as far east as Surat, there to find a cache of Avestan texts, there also to complete his translation of the Avesta. Raymond Schwab has said of the mysterious Avestan fragment that set Anquetil off on his voyages that whereas "the scholars looked at the famous fragment of Oxford and then returned to their studies, Anquetil looked, and then went to India." Schwab also remarks that Anquetil and Voltaire, though temperamentally and ideologically at hopeless odds with each other, had a similar interest in the Orient and the Bible, "the one to make the Bible more indisputable, the other to make it more unbelievable." Ironically, Anquetil's Avesta translations served Voltaire's purposes, since Anquetil's discoveries "soon led to criticism of the very [Biblical] texts which had hitherto been considered to be revealed texts." The net effect of Anquetil's expedition is well described by Schwab:

> In 1759, Anquetil finished his translation of the *Avesta* at Surat; in 1786 that of the *Upanishads* in Paris—he had dug a channel between the hemispheres of human genius, correcting and expanding the old humanism of the Mediterranean basin. Less than fifty years earlier, his compatriots were asked what it was like to be Persian, when he taught them how to compare the monuments of the Persians to those of the Greeks. Before him, one looked for information on the remote past of our planet exclusively among the great Latin, Greek, Jewish, and Arabic writers. The Bible was regarded as a lonely rock, an aerolite. A universe in writing was available, but scarcely anyone seemed to suspect the immensity of those unknown lands. The realization began with his translation of the *Avesta,* and reached dizzying heights owing to the exploration in Central Asia of the languages that multiplied after Babel. Into our schools, up to that time limited to the narrow Greco-Latin heritage of the Renaissance [of which much had been transmitted to Europe by Islam], he interjected a vision of innumerable civilizations from ages past, of an infinity of literatures; moreover the few European provinces were not the only places to have left their mark in history.[35]

For the first time, the Orient was revealed to Europe in the materiality of its texts, languages, and civilizations. Also for the first time, Asia acquired a precise intellectual and historical dimension with which to buttress the myths of its geographic distance and vastness. By one of those inevitable contracting compensations for a sudden cultural expansion, Anquetil's Oriental labors were succeeded by William Jones's, the second of the pre-Napoleonic projects I mentioned above. Whereas Anquetil opened large vistas, Jones closed them down, codifying, tabulating, comparing. Before he left England for India in 1783, Jones was already a master of Arabic, Hebrew, and Persian. These seemed perhaps the least of his accomplishments: he was also a poet, a jurist, a polyhistor, a classicist, and an indefatigable scholar whose powers would recommend him to such as Benjamin Franklin, Edmund Burke, William Pitt, and Samuel Johnson. In due course he was appointed to "an honorable and profitable place in the Indies," and immediately upon his arrival there to take up a post with the East India Company began the course of personal study that was to gather in, to rope off, to domesticate the Orient and thereby turn it into a province of European learning. For his personal work, entitled "Objects of Enquiry During My Residence in Asia" he enumerated among the topics of his investigation "the Laws of the Hindus and Mohammedans, Modern Politics and Geography of Hindustan, Best Mode of Governing Bengal, Arithmetic and Geometry, and Mixed Sciences of the Asiaticks, Medicine, Chemistry, Surgery, and Anatomy of the Indians, Natural Productions of India, Poetry, Rhetoric and Morality of Asia, Music of the Eastern Nations, Trade, Manufacture, Agriculture, and Commerce of India," and so forth. On August 17, 1787, he wrote unassumingly to Lord Althorp that "it is my ambition to know *India* better than any other European ever knew it." Here is where Balfour in 1910 could find the first adumbration of his claim as an Englishman to know the Orient more and better than anyone else.

Jones's official work was the law, an occupation with symbolic significance for the history of Orientalism. Seven years before Jones arrived in India, Warren Hastings had decided that Indians were to be ruled by their own laws, a more enterprising project than it appears at first glance since the Sanskrit code of laws existed then for practical use only in a Persian translation, and no Englishman at that time knew Sanskrit well enough to consult the original texts. A company official, Charles Wilkins, first mastered Sanskrit, then began to translate the *Institutes* of Manu; in this labor he was soon to be assisted by Jones. (Wilkins, incidentally, was the first translator of the Bhagavad-Gita.) In January 1784 Jones convened the inaugural meeting of the Asiatic Society of Bengal, which was to be for India what the Royal Society was for England. As first president of the society and as magistrate, Jones acquired the effective knowledge of the Orient and of Orientals that was later to make him the undisputed founder (the phrase is A. J. Arberry's) of Orientalism. To rule and to learn, then to compare Orient with Occident: these were Jones's goals, which, with an irresistible impulse always to codify, to subdue the infinite variety of the Orient to "a complete digest" of laws, figures, customs, and works, he is believed to have achieved. His most famous pronouncement indicates the extent to which modern Orientalism, even in its philosophical beginnings, was a comparative discipline having for its principal goal the grounding of the European languages in a distant, and harmless, Oriental source:

> The *Sanscrit* language, whatever be its antiquity, is of a wonderful structure; more perfect than the *Greek,* more copious than the *Latin,* and more exquisitely refined than either, yet bearing to both of them a stronger affinity, both in the roots of verbs and in the forms of grammar, than could possibly have been produced by accident; so strong indeed, that no philologer could examine them all three without believing them to have sprung from some common source.[36]

Many of the early English Orientalists in India were, like Jones, legal scholars, or else, interestingly enough, they were medical men with strong missionary leanings. So far as one can tell, most of them were imbued with the dual purpose of investigating "the sciences and the arts of Asia, with the hope of facilitating ameliorations there and of advancing knowledge and improving the arts at home":[37] so the common Orientalist goal was stated in the *Centenary Volume* of the Royal Asiatic Society founded in 1823 by Henry Thomas Colebrooke. In their dealings with the modern Orientals, the early professional Orientalists like Jones had only two roles to fulfill, yet we cannot today fault them for strictures placed on their humanity by the official *Occidental* character of their presence in the Orient. They were either judges or they were doctors. Even Edgar Quinet, writing more metaphysically than realistically, was dimly aware of this therapeutic relationship. "L'Asie a les prophètes," he said in *Le Génie des religions;* "L'Europe a les docteurs."[38] Proper knowledge of the Orient proceeded from a thorough study of the classical texts, and only after that to an application of those texts to the modern Orient. Faced with the obvious decrepitude and political impotence of the modern Oriental, the European Orientalist found it his duty to rescue some portion of a lost, past classical Oriental grandeur in order to "facilitate ameliorations" in the present Orient. What the European took from the classical Oriental past was a vision (and thousands of facts and artifacts) which only he could employ to the best advantage; to the modern Oriental he gave facilitation and amelioration—and, too, the benefit of his judgment as to what was best for the modern Orient.

It was characteristic of all Orientalist projects before Napoleon's that very little could be done in advance of the project to prepare for its success. Anquetil and Jones, for example, learned what they did about the Orient only after they got there. They were confronting, as it were, the whole Orient, and only after a while and after considerable improvising could they whittle it down to a smaller province. Napoleon, on the other hand, wanted nothing less than to take the whole of Egypt, and his advance preparations were of unparalleled magnitude and thoroughness. Even so, these preparations were almost fanatically schematic and—if I may use the word—textual, which are features that will bear some analysis here. Three things above all else seem to have been in Napoleon's mind as he readied himself while in Italy in 1797 for his next military move. First, aside from the still threatening power of England, his military successes that had culminated in the Treaty of Campo Formio left him no other place to turn for additional glory than the East. Moreover, Talleyrand had recently animadverted on "les avantages à retirer de colonies nouvelles dans les circonstances présentes," and this notion, along with the appealing prospect of hurting Britain, drew him eastwards. Secondly, Napoleon had been attracted to the Orient since his adolescence; his youthful manuscripts, for example, contain a summary he made of Marigny's *Histoire des Arabes,* and it is evident from all of his writing and conversation that he was steeped, as Jean Thiry has put it, in the memories and glories that were attached to Alexander's Orient generally and to Egypt in particular.[39] Thus the idea of reconquering Egypt as a new Alexander proposed itself to him, allied with the additional benefit of acquiring a new Islamic colony at England's expense. Thirdly, Napoleon considered Egypt a likely project precisely because he knew it tactically, strategically, historically, and—not to be underestimated—textually, that is, as something one read about and knew through the writings of recent as well as classical European authorities. The point in all this is that for Napoleon Egypt was a project that acquired reality in his mind, and later in his preparations for its conquest, through experiences that belong to the realm of ideas and myths culled from texts, not empirical reality. His plans for Egypt therefore became the first in a long series of European encounters with the Orient in which the Orientalist's special expertise was put directly to functional colonial use; for at the crucial instant when an Orientalist had to decide whether his loyalties and sympathies lay with the Orient or with the conquering West, he always chose the latter, from Napoleon's time on. As for the emperor himself, he saw the Orient only as it had been encoded first by classical texts and then by Orientalist experts, whose vision, based on classical texts, seemed a useful substitute for any actual encounter with the real Orient.

Napoleon's enlistment of several dozen "savants" for his Egyptian Expedition is too well known to require detail here. His idea was to build a sort of living archive for the expedition, in the form of studies conducted on all topics by the members of the Institut d'Égypte, which he founded. What is perhaps less well known is Napoleon's prior reliance upon the work of the Comte de Volney, a French traveler whose *Voyage en Égypte et en Syrie* appeared in two volumes in 1787. Aside from a short personal preface informing the reader that the sudden acquisition of some money (his inheritance) made it possible for him to take the trip east in 1783, Volney's *Voyage* is an almost oppressively impersonal document. Volney evidently saw himself as a scientist, whose job it was always to record the "état" of something he saw. The climax of the *Voyage* occurs in the second volume, an account of Islam as a religion.[40] Volney's views were canonically hostile to Islam as a religion and as a system of political institutions; nevertheless Napoleon found this work and Volney's *Considérations sur la guerre actuel de Turcs* (1788) of particular importance. For Volney after all was a canny Frenchman, and—like Chateaubriand and Lamartine a quarter-century after him—he eyed the Near Orient as a likely place for the realization of French colonial ambition. What Napoleon profited from in Volney was the enumeration, in ascending order of difficulty, of the obstacles to be faced in the Orient by any French expeditionary force.

Napoleon refers explicitly to Volney in his reflections on the Egyptian expedition, the *Campagnes d'Égypte et de Syrie, 1798–1799,* which he dictated to General Bertrand on Saint Helena. Volney, he said, considered that there were three barriers to French hegemony in the Orient and that any French force would therefore have to fight three wars: one against England, a second against the Ottoman Porte, and a third, the most difficult, against the Muslims.[41] Volney's assessment was both shrewd and hard to fault since it was clear to Napoleon, as it would be to anyone who read Volney, that his *Voyage* and the *Considérations* were effective texts to be used by any European wishing to win in the Orient. In other words, Volney's work constituted a handbook for attenuating the human shock a European might feel as he directly experienced the Orient: Read the books, seems to have been Volney's thesis, and far from being disoriented by the Orient, you will compel it to you.

Napoleon took Volney almost literally, but in a characteristically subtle way. From the first moment that the Armée d'Égypte appeared on the Egyptian horizon, every effort was made to convince the Muslims that "nous sommes les vrais musulmans," as Bonaparte's proclamation of July 2, 1798, put it to the people of Alexandria.[42] Equipped with a team of Orientalists (and sitting on board a flagship called the *Orient*), Napoleon used Egyptian enmity toward the Mamelukes and appeals to the revolutionary idea of equal opportunity for all to wage a uniquely benign and selective war against Islam. What more than anything impressed the first Arab chronicler of the expedition, Abd-al-Rahman al-Jabarti, was Napoleon's use of scholars to manage his contacts with the natives—that and the impact of watching a modern European intellectual establishment at close quarters.[43] Napoleon tried everywhere to prove that he was fighting *for* Islam; everything he said was translated into Koranic Arabic, just as the French army was urged by its command always to remember the Islamic sensibility. (Compare, in this regard, Napoleon's tactics in Egypt with the tactics of the *Requerimiento,* a document drawn up in 1513—in Spanish—by the Spaniards to be read aloud to the Indians: "We shall take you and your wives and your children, and shall make slaves of them, and as such sell and dispose of them as their Highnesses [the King and Queen of Spain] may command; and we shall take away your goods, and shall do you all the mischief and damage that we can, as to vassals who do not obey," etc. etc.[44]) When it seemed obvious to Napoleon that his force was too small to impose itself on the Egyptians, he then tried to make the local imams, cadis, muftis, and ulemas interpret the Koran in favor of the Grande Armée. To this end, the sixty ulemas who taught at the Azhar were invited to his quarters, given full military honors, and then allowed to be flattered by Napoleon's admiration for Islam and Mohammed and by his obvious veneration for the Koran, with which he seemed perfectly familiar. This worked, and soon the population of Cairo seemed to have lost its distrust of the occupiers.[45] Napoleon later gave his deputy Kleber strict instructions after he left always to administer Egypt through the Orientalists and the religious Islamic leaders whom they could win over; any other politics was too expensive and foolish.[46] Hugo thought that he grasped the tactful glory of Napoleon's Oriental expedition in his poem "Lui":

Au Nil je le retrouve encore.
L'Égypte resplendit des feux de son aurore;
Son astre impérial se lève à l'orient.

Vainqueur, enthousiaste, éclatant de prestiges,
Prodige, il étonna la terre des prodiges.
Les vieux scheiks vénéraient l'émir jeune et prudent;
Le peuple redoutait ses armes inouïes;
Sublime, il apparut aux tribes éblouies
Comme un Mahomet d'occident.[47]

(By the Nile, I find him once again.
Egypt shines with the fires of his dawn;
His imperial orb rises in the Orient.

Victor, enthusiast, bursting with achievements,
Prodigious, he stunned the land of prodigies.
The old sheikhs venerated the young and prudent emir.
The people dreaded his unprecedented arms;
Sublime, he appeared to the dazzled tribes
Like a Mahomet of the Occident.)

Such a triumph could only have been prepared *before* a military expedition, perhaps only by someone who had no prior experience of the Orient except what books and scholars told him. The idea of taking along a full-scale academy is very much an aspect of this textual attitude to the Orient. And this attitude in turn was bolstered by specific Revolutionary decrees (particularly the one of 10 Germinal An III—March 30, 1793—establishing an *école publique* in the Bibliothèque nationale to teach Arabic, Turkish, and Persian)[48] whose object was the rationalist one of dispelling mystery and institutionalizing even the most recondite knowledge. Thus many of Napoleon's Orientalist translators were students of Silvestre de Sacy, who, beginning in June 1796, was the first and only teacher of Arabic at the École publique des langues orientales. Sacy later became the teacher of nearly every major Orientalist in Europe, where his students dominated the field for about three-quarters of a century. Many of them were politically useful, in the ways that several had been to Napoleon in Egypt.

But dealings with the Muslims were only a part of Napoleon's project to dominate Egypt. The other part was to render it completely open, to make it totally accessible to European scrutiny. From being a land of obscurity and a part of the Orient hitherto known at second hand through the exploits of earlier travelers, scholars, and conquerors, Egypt was to become a department of French learning. Here too the textual and schematic attitudes are evident. The Institut, with its teams of chemists, historians, biologists, archaeologists, surgeons, and antiquarians, was the learned division of the army. Its job was no less aggressive: to put Egypt into modern French; and unlike the Abbé Le Mascrier's 1735 *Description de l'Égypte,* Napoleon's was to be a universal undertaking. Almost from the first moments of the occupation Napoleon saw to it that the Institut began its meetings, its experiments—its fact-finding mission, as we would call it today. Most important, everything said, seen, and studied was to be recorded, and indeed was recorded in that great collective appropriation of one country by another, the *Description de l'Égypte,* published in twenty-three enormous volumes between 1809 and 1828.[49]

The *Description*'s uniqueness is not only in its size, or even in the intelligence of its contributors, but in its attitude to its subject matter, and it is this attitude that makes it of great interest for the study of modern Orientalist projects. The first few pages of its *préface historique*, written by Jean-Baptiste-Joseph Fourier, the Institut's secretary, make it clear that in "doing" Egypt the scholars were also grappling directly with a kind of unadulterated cultural, geographical, and historical significance. Egypt was the focal point of the relationships between Africa and Asia, between Europe and the East, between memory and actuality.

> Placed between Africa and Asia, and communicating easily with Europe, Egypt occupies the center of the ancient continent. This country presents only great memories; it is the homeland of the arts and conserves innumerable monuments; its principal temples and the palaces inhabited by its kings still exist, even though its least ancient edifices had already been built by the time of the Trojan War. Homer, Lycurgus, Solon, Pythagoras, and Plato all went to Egypt to study the sciences, religion, and the laws. Alexander founded an opulent city there, which for a long time enjoyed commercial supremacy and which witnessed Pompey, Caesar, Mark Antony, and Augustus deciding between them the fate of Rome and that of the entire world. It is therefore proper for this country to attract the attention of illustrious princes who rule the destiny of nations.
>
> No considerable power was ever amassed by any nation, whether in the West or in Asia, that did not also turn that nation toward Egypt, which was regarded in some measure as its natural lot.[50]

Because Egypt was saturated with meaning for the arts, sciences, and government, its role was to be the stage on which actions of a world-historical importance would take place. By taking Egypt, then, a modern power would naturally demonstrate its strength and justify history; Egypt's own destiny was to be annexed, to Europe preferably. In addition, this power would also enter a history whose common element was defined by figures no less great than Homer, Alexander, Caesar, Plato, Solon, and Pythagoras, who graced the Orient with their prior presence there. The Orient, in short, existed as a set of values attached, not to its modern realities, but to a series of valorized contacts it had had with a distant European past. This is a pure example of the textual, schematic attitude I have been referring to.

Fourier continues similarly for over a hundred pages (each page, incidentally, is a square meter in size, as if the project and the size of the page had been thought of as possessing comparable scale). Out of the free-floating past, however, he must justify the Napoleonic expedition as something that needed to be undertaken when it happened. The dramatic perspective is never abandoned. Conscious of his European audience and of the Oriental figures he was manipulating, he writes:

> One remembers the impression made on the whole of Europe by the astounding news that the French were in the Orient. . . . This great project was meditated in silence, and was prepared with such activity and secrecy that the worried vigilance of our enemies was deceived; only at the moment that it happened did they learn that it had been conceived, undertaken, and carried out successfully.

So dramatic a *coup de théâtre* had its advantages for the Orient as well:

> This country, which has transmitted its knowledge to so many nations, is today plunged into barbarism.

Only a hero could bring all these factors together, which is what Fourier now describes:

> Napoleon appreciated the influence that this event would have on the relations between Europe, the Orient, and Africa, on Mediterranean shipping, and on Asia's destiny. . . . Napoleon wanted to offer a useful European example to the Orient, and finally also to make the inhabitants' lives more pleasant, as well as to procure for them all the advantages of a perfected civilization.
>
> None of this would be possible without a continuous application to the project of the arts and sciences.[51]

To restore a region from its present barbarism to its former classical greatness; to instruct (for its own benefit) the Orient in the ways of the modern West; to subordinate or underplay military power in order to aggrandize the project of glorious knowledge acquired in the process of political domination of the Orient; to formulate the

Orient, to give it shape, identity, definition with full recognition of its place in memory, its importance to imperial strategy, and its "natural" role as an appendage to Europe; to dignify all the knowledge collected during colonial occupation with the title "contribution to modern learning" when the natives had neither been consulted nor treated as anything except as pretexts for a text whose usefulness was not to the natives; to feel oneself as a European in command, almost at will, of Oriental history, time, and geography; to institute new areas of specialization; to establish new disciplines; to divide, deploy, schematize, tabulate, index, and record everything in sight (and out of sight); to make out of every observable detail a generalization and out of every generalization an immutable law about the Oriental nature, temperament, mentality, custom, or type; and, above all, to transmute living reality into the stuffs of texts, to possess (or think one possesses) actuality mainly because nothing in the Orient seems to resist one's powers: these are the features of Orientalist projection entirely realized in the *Description de l'Égypte,* itself enabled and reinforced by Napoleon's wholly Orientalist engulfment of Egypt by the instruments of Western knowledge and power. Thus Fourier concludes his preface by announcing that history will remember how "Égypte fut le théâtre de sa [Napoleon's] gloire, et préserve de l'oubli toutes les circonstances de cet évènement extraordinaire."[52]

The *Description* thereby displaces Egyptian or Oriental history as a history possessing its own coherence, identity, and sense. Instead, history as recorded in the *Description* supplants Egyptian or Oriental history by identifying itself directly and immediately with world history, a euphemism for European history. To save an event from oblivion is in the Orientalist's mind the equivalent of turning the Orient into a theater for his representations of the Orient: this is almost exactly what Fourier says. Moreover, the sheer power of having described the Orient in modern Occidental terms lifts the Orient from the realms of silent obscurity where it has lain neglected (except for the inchoate murmurings of a vast but undefined sense of its own past) into the clarity of modern European science. There this new Orient figures as—for instance, in Geoffroy Saint-Hilaire's biological theses in the *Description*—the confirmation of laws of zoological specialization formulated by Buffon.[53] Or it serves as a "contraste frapante avec les habitudes des nations Européennes,"[54] in which the "bizarre jouissances" of Orientals serve to highlight the sobriety and rationality of Occidental habits. Or, to cite one more use for the Orient, equivalents of those Oriental physiological characteristics that made possible the successful embalming of bodies are sought for in European bodies, so that chevaliers fallen on the field of honor can be preserved as lifelike relics of Napoleon's great Oriental campaign.[55]

Yet the military failure of Napoleon's occupation of Egypt did not also destroy the fertility of its over-all projection for Egypt or the rest of the Orient. Quite literally, the occupation gave birth to the entire modern experience of the Orient as interpreted from within the universe of discourse founded by Napoleon in Egypt, whose agencies of domination and dissemination included the Institut and the *Description*. The idea, as it has been characterized by Charles-Roux, was that Egypt "restored to prosperity, regenerated by wise and enlightened administration . . . would shed its civilizing rays upon all its Oriental neighbors."[56] True, the other European powers would seek to compete in this mission, none more than England. But what would happen as a continuing legacy of the common Occidental mission to the Orient—despite inter-European squabbling, indecent competition, or outright war—would be the creation of new projects, new visions, new enterprises combining additional parts of the old Orient with the conquering European spirit. After Napoleon, then, the very language of Orientalism changed radically. Its descriptive realism was upgraded and became not merely a style of representation but a language, indeed a means of *creation*. Along with the *langues mères*, as those forgotten dormant sources for the modern European demotics were entitled by Antoine Fabre d'Olivet, the Orient was reconstructed, reassembled, crafted, in short, *born* out of the Orientalists' efforts. The *Description* became the master type of all further efforts to bring the Orient closer to Europe, thereafter to absorb it entirely and—centrally important—to cancel, or at least subdue and reduce, its strangeness and, in the case of Islam, its hostility. For the Islamic Orient would henceforth appear as a category denoting the Orientalists' power and not the Islamic people as humans nor their history as history.

Thus out of the Napoleonic expedition there issued a whole series of textual children, from Chateaubriand's *Itinéraire* to Lamartine's *Voyage en Orient* to Flaubert's *Salammbô*, and in the same tradition, Lane's *Manners and Customs of the Modern Egyptians* and Richard Burton's *Personal Narrative of a Pilgrimage to al-Madinah and Meccah*. What binds them together is not only their common background in Oriental legend and experience but also their learned reliance on the Orient as a kind of womb out of which they were brought forth. If paradoxically these creations turned out to be highly stylized simulacra, elaborately wrought imitations of what a live Orient might be thought to look like, that by no means detracts either from the strength of their imaginative conception or from the strength of European mastery of the Orient, whose prototypes respectively were Cagliostro, the great European impersonator of the Orient, and Napoleon, its first modern conqueror.

Artistic or textual work was not the only product of the Napoleonic expedition. There were, in addition and certainly more influential, the scientific project, whose chief instance is Ernest Renan's *Système comparé et histoire générale des langues sémitiques*, completed in 1848 for—neatly enough—the Prix Volney, and the geopolitical project, of which Ferdinand de Lesseps's Suez Canal and England's occupation of Egypt in 1882 are prime instances. The difference between the two is not only in manifest scale but also in quality of Orientalist conviction. Renan truly believed that he had re-created the Orient, as it really was, in his work. De Lesseps, on the other hand, always was somewhat awed by the newness his project had released out of the old Orient, and this sense communicated itself to everyone for whom the opening of the canal in 1869 was no ordinary event. In his *Excursionist and Tourist Advertiser* for July 1, 1869, Thomas Cook's enthusiasm carries on de Lesseps's:

> On November the 17th, the greatest engineering feat of the present century is to have its success celebrated by a magnificent inauguration fête, at which nearly every European royal family will have its special representative. Truly the occasion will be an exceptional one. The formation of a line of water communication between Europe and the East, has been the thought of centuries, occupying in turn the minds of Greeks, Roman, Saxon and Gaul, but it was not until within the last few years that modern civilization began seriously to set about emulating the labours of the ancient Pharaohs, who, many centuries since, constructed a canal between the two seas, traces of which remain to this day. . . . Everything connected with [the mod-

> ern] works are on the most gigantic scale, and a perusal of a little pamphlet, descriptive of the undertaking, from the pen of the Chevalier de St. Stoess, impresses us most forcibly with the genius of the great Master-mind—M. Ferdinand de Lesseps—to whose perseverance, calm daring and foresight, the dream of ages has at last become a real and tangible fact . . . the project for bringing more closely together the countries of the West and the East, and thus uniting the civilizations of different epochs.[57]

The combination of old ideas with new methods, the bringing together of cultures whose relations to the nineteenth century were different, the genuine imposition of the power of modern technology and intellectual will upon formerly stable and divided geographical entities like East and West: this is what Cook perceives and what, in his journals, speeches, prospectuses, and letters, de Lesseps advertises.

Genealogically, Ferdinand's start was auspicious. Mathieu de Lesseps, his father, had come to Egypt with Napoleon and remained there (as "unofficial French representative," Marlowe says[58]) for four years after the French evacuated it in 1801. Many of Ferdinand's later writings refer back to Napoleon's own interest in digging a canal, which, because he had been misinformed by experts, he never thought was a realizable goal. Infected by the erratic history of canal projects that included French schemes entertained by Richelieu and the Saint-Simonians, de Lesseps returned to Egypt in 1854, there to embark on the undertaking that was eventually completed fifteen years later. He had no real engineering background. Only a tremendous faith in his near-divine skills as builder, mover, and creator kept him going; as his diplomatic and financial talents gained him Egyptian and European support, he seems to have acquired the necessary knowledge to carry matters to completion. More useful, perhaps, he learned how to plant his potential contributors in the world-historical theater and make them see what his "pensée morale," as he called his project, really meant. "Vous envisagez," he told them in 1860, "les immenses services que le rapprochement de l'occident et de l'orient doit rendre à la civilization et au développement de la richesse générale. Le monde attend de vous un grand progrès et vous voulez répondre à l'attente du monde."[59] In accordance with such notions the name of the investment company formed by de Lesseps in 1858 was a charged one and reflected the grandiose plans he cherished: the Compagnie universelle. In 1862 the Académie française offered a prize for an epic on the canal. Bornier, the winner, delivered himself of such hyperbole as the following, none of it fundamentally contradicting de Lesseps's picture of what he was up to:

> *Au travail! Ouvriers que notre France envoie,*
> *Tracez, pour l'univers, cette nouvelle voie!*
> *Vos pères, les héros, sont venus jusqu'ici;*
> *Soyez ferme comme aux intrepides,*
> *Comme eux vous combattez aux pieds des pyramides,*
> *Et leurs quatre mille ans vous contemplent aussi!*
>
> *Oui, c'est pour l'univers! Pour l'Asie et l'Europe,*
> *Pour ces climats lointain que la nuit enveloppe,*
> *Pour le Chinois perfide et l'Indien demi-nu;*
> *Pour les peuples heureux, libres, humains et braves,*
> *Pour les peuples méchants, pour les peuples esclaves,*
> *Pour ceux à qui le Christ est encore inconnu.*[60]

De Lesseps was nowhere more eloquent and resourceful than when he was called upon to justify the enormous expense in money and men the canal would require. He could pour out statistics to enchant any ear; he would quote Herodotus and maritime statistics with equal fluency. In his journal entries for 1864 he cited with approbation Casimir Leconte's observation that an eccentric life would develop significant originality in men, and from originality would come great and unusual exploits.[61] Such exploits were their own justification. Despite its immemorial pedigree of failures, its outrageous cost, its astounding ambitions for altering the way Europe would handle the Orient, the canal was worth the effort. It was a project uniquely able to override the objections of those who were consulted and, in improving the Orient as a whole, to do what scheming Egyptians, perfidious Chinese, and half-naked Indians could never have done for themselves.

The opening ceremonies in November 1869 were an occasion which, no less than the whole history of de Lesseps's machinations, perfectly embodied his ideas. For years his speeches, letters, and pamphlets were laden with a vividly energetic and theatrical vocabulary. In the pursuit of success, he could be found saying of himself (always in the first person plural), we created, fought, disposed, achieved, acted, recognized, persevered, advanced; nothing, he repeated on many occasions, could stop us, nothing was impossible, nothing mattered finally except the realization of "le résultat final, le grand but," which he had conceived, defined, and finally executed. As the papal envoy to the ceremonies spoke on November 16 to the assembled dignitaries, his speech strove desperately to match the intellectual and imaginative spectacle offered by de Lesseps's canal:

> Il est permis d'affirmer que l'heure qui vient de sonner est non seulement une des plus solennelles de ce siècle, mais encore une des plus grandes et des plus décisives qu'ait vues l'humanité, depuis qu'elle a une histoire ci-bas. Ce lieu, où confinent—sans désormais y toucher—l'Afrique et l'Asie, cette grande fête du genre humain, cette assistance auguste et cosmopolite, toutes les races du globe, tous les drapeaux, tous les pavillions, flottant joyeusement sous ce ciel radieux et immense, la croix debout et respectée de tous en face du croissant, que de merveilles, que de contrastes saississants, que de rêves réputés chimériques devenus de palpables réalités! et, dans cet assemblage de tant de prodiges, que de sujets de réflexions pour le penseur, que de joies dans l'heure présente et, dans les perspectives de l'avenir, que de glorieuses espérances! . . .
>
> Les deux extrémités du globe se rapprochent; en se rapprochant, elles se reconnaissent; en se reconnaissant, tous les hommes, enfants d'un seul et même Dieu, éprouvent le tressaillement joyeux de leur mutuelle fraternité! O Occident! O Orient! rapprochez, regardez, reconnaissez, saluez, étreignez-vous! . . .
>
> Mais derrière le phénomène matériel, le regard du penseur découvre des horizons plus vastes que les espaces mésurables, les horizons sans bornes où mouvent les plus hautes destinées, les plus glorieuses conquêtes, les plus immortelles certitudes du genre humain. . . .
>
> [Dieu] que votre souffle divin plane sur ces eaux! Qu'il y passe et repasse, de l'Occident à l'Orient, de l'Orient à l'Occident! O Dieu! Servez vous de cette voie pour rapprocher les hommes les uns des autres![62]

The whole world seemed crowded in to render homage to a scheme that God could only bless and make use of himself. Old distinctions and inhibitions were dissolved: the Cross faced down the Crescent, the West had come to the Orient never to leave it (until, in July 1956, Gamal Abdel Nasser would activate Egypt's taking over of the canal by pronouncing the name of de Lesseps).

In the Suez Canal idea we see the logical conclusion of Orientalist thought and, more interesting, of Orientalist effort. To the West, Asia had once represented silent distance and alienation; Islam was militant hostility to European Christianity. To overcome such redoubtable constants the Orient needed first to be known, then invaded and possessed, then re-created by scholars, soldiers, and judges who disinterred forgotten languages, histories, races, and cultures in order to posit them—beyond the modern Oriental's ken—as the true classical Orient that could be used to judge and rule the modern Orient. The obscurity faded to be replaced by hothouse entities; the Orient was a scholar's word, signifying what modern Europe had recently made of the still peculiar East. De Lesseps and his canal finally destroyed the Orient's distance, its cloistered intimacy *away* from the West, its perdurable exoticism. Just as a land barrier could be transmuted into a liquid artery, so too the Orient was transubstantiated from resistant hostility into obliging, and submissive, partnership. After de Lesseps no one could speak of the Orient as belonging to another world, strictly speaking. There was only "our" world, "one" world bound together because the Suez Canal had frustrated those last provincials who still believed in the difference between worlds. Thereafter the notion of "Oriental" is an administrative or executive one, and it is subordinate to demographic, economic, and sociological factors. For imperialists like Balfour, or for anti-imperialists like J. A. Hobson, the Oriental, like the African, is a member of a subject race and not exclusively an inhabitant of a geographical area. De Lesseps had melted away the Orient's geographical identity by (almost literally) dragging the Orient into the West and finally dispelling the threat of Islam. New categories and experiences, including the imperialist ones, would emerge, and in time Orientalism would adapt itself to them, but not without some difficulty.

from *Orientalism*

5

Zionism from the Standpoint of Its Victims

(1979)

When Edward Said completed *The Question of Palestine* in 1978, publishers found it too provocative to publish. Beacon Press and Pantheon Books rejected the manuscript. When a Beirut publisher offered to bring the book out in Arabic, it asked Said to remove his criticism of Syria and Saudi Arabia. Said refused. Eventually, Time Books published it in 1979.

Said's investigation of the history and ideology of Zionism raised hackles from different quarters. Some Jewish critics, such as Robert Wistrich, protested the connections Said made between Zionism and European colonialism. As Said wrote, "There is an unmistakable coincidence between the experiences of Arab Palestinians at the hands of Zionism and the experiences of those black, yellow, and brown people who were described as inferior and subhuman by nineteenth-century imperialists." If Zionist critics tried to disavow the imperial legacies of Zionism, many Palestinians thought that Said had conceded too much. In effect, "Zionism from the Standpoint of Its Victims" considered the fact that the Palestinians, as "the victims of victims," have become a crucial part of Zionism's history. Said argued that they must be acknowledged within this history just as no Palestinian can ignore Zionism.

In 1978, such an approach was linked closely to strategies of "mutual recognition" and "two-state solutions" of the conflict between Palestinians and Israel. As Eqbal Ahmad observed in his review in *The Nation,* Said was the first Palestinian of any prominence "to argue for the necessity of a full-scale political encounter between Jews and Palestinians."[1] Said explains: "[J]ust as no Jew in the last hundred years or so has been untouched by Zionism, so too no Palestinian has been unmarked by it." Said warns, "Yet it must not be forgotten, that the Palestinian was not simply a function of Zionism. His life, culture, and politics have their own dynamic and ultimately their own authenticity."

I

Zionism and the Attitudes of European Colonialism

Every idea or system of ideas exists *somewhere,* is mixed in with historical circumstances, is part of what one may very simply call "reality." One of the enduring attributes of self-serving idealism, however, is the notion that ideas are just ideas, and that they exist only in the realm of ideas. The tendency to view ideas as pertaining only to a world of abstractions increases among people for whom an idea is essentially perfect, good, uncontaminated by human desire or will. Such a view also applies when the ideas are considered to be evil, absolutely perfect in their evil, and so forth. When an idea has become effective—that is, when its value has been proved in reality by its widespread acceptance—some revision of it will of course seem to be necessary, since the idea must be viewed as having taken on some of the characteristics of brute reality. Thus it is frequently argued that such an idea as Zionism, for all its political tribulations and the struggles on its behalf, is at bottom an *unchanging* idea that expresses the yearning for Jewish political and religious self-determination—for Jewish national selfhood—to be exercised on the promised land. Because Zionism seems to have culminated in the creation of the state of Israel, it is also argued that the historical realization of the idea confirms its unchanging essence and, no less important, the means used for its realization. Very little is said about what Zionism entailed for non-Jews who happened to have encountered it; for that matter, nothing is said about where (outside Jewish history) it took place, and from what in the historical context of nineteenth-century Europe Zionism drew its force. To the Palestinian, for whom Zionism was somebody else's idea imported into Palestine and for which in a very concrete way he or she was made to pay and suffer, these forgotten things about Zionism are the very things that are centrally important.

In short, effective political ideas like Zionism need to be examined historically in two ways: (1) *genealogically* in order that their provenance, their kinship and descent, their affiliation both with other ideas and with political institutions may be demonstrated; (2) as practical systems for *accumulation* (of power, land, ideological legitimacy) and *displacement* (of people, other ideas, prior legitimacy). Present political and cultural actualities make such an examination extraordinarily difficult, as much because Zionism in the postindustrial West has acquired for itself an almost unchallenged hegemony in liberal "establishment" discourse, as because in keeping with one of its central ideological characteristics, Zionism has hidden, or caused to disappear, the literal historical ground of its growth, its political cost to the native inhabitants of Palestine, and its militantly oppressive discriminations between Jews and non-Jews.

Consider as a startling instance of what I mean, the symbolism of Menachem Begin, a former head of the Irgun terror organization, in whose part are numerous (and frequently admitted) acts of cold-blooded murder, being honored as Israeli premier at Northwestern University in May 1978 with a doctorate of laws *honoris causa;* a leader whose army a scant month before had created 300,000 new refugees in South Lebanon, who spoke constantly of "Judea and Samaria" as "rightful" parts of the Jewish state (claims made on the basis of the Old Testament and without so much as a reference to the land's actual inhabitants); and all this without—on the part of the press or the intellectual community—one sign of comprehension that Menachem Begin's honored position came about literally at the expense of Palestinian Arab silence in the Western "marketplace of ideas," that the entire historical duration of a Jewish state in Palestine prior to 1948 was a sixty-year period two millennia ago, that the dispersion of the Palestinians was not a fact of nature but a result of specific force and strategies. The concealment by Zionism of its own history has by now therefore become institutionalized, and not only in Israel. To bring out its history as in a sense it was exacted from Palestine and the Palestinians, these victims on whose suppression Zionism and Israel have depended, is thus a specific intellectual/political task in the present context of discussion about "a comprehensive peace" in the Middle East.

The special, one might even call it the privileged, place in this discussion of the United States is impressive, for all sorts of reasons. In no other country, except Israel, is Zionism enshrined as an unquestioned good, and in no other country is there so strong a conjuncture of powerful institutions and interests—the press, the liberal intelligentsia, the military-industrial complex, the academic community, labor unions—for whom [. . .] uncritical support of Israel and Zionism enhances their domestic as well as international standing. Although there has recently been some modulation in this remarkable consensus—due to the influence of Arab oil, the emergence of countervailing conservative states allied to the United States (Saudi Arabia, Egypt), the redoubtable political and military visibility of the Palestinian people and their representatives the PLO—the prevailing pro-Israeli bias persists. For not only does it have deep cultural roots in the West generally and the United States in particular, but its *negative, interdictory* character vis-à-vis the *whole* historical reality is systematic.

Yet there is no getting around the formidable historical reality that in trying to deal with what Zionism has suppressed about the Palestinian people, one also abuts the entire disastrous problem of anti-Semitism on the one hand, and on the other, the complex interrelationship between the Palestinians and the Arab states. Anyone who watched the spring 1978 NBC presentation of *Holocaust* was aware that at least part of the program was intended as a justification for Zionism—even while at about the same time Israeli troops in Lebanon produced devastation, thousands of civilian casualties, and untold suffering of a sort likened by a few courageous reporters to the U.S. devastation of Vietnam (see, for example, H. D. S. Greenway, "Vietnam-style Raids Gut South Lebanon: Israel Leaves a Path of Destruction," *Washington Post,* March 25, 1978). Similarly, the furor created by the package deal in early 1978 as a result of which U.S. war planes were sold to Israel, Egypt, and Saudi Arabia made the predicament of Arab liberation interlocking with right-wing Arab regimes even more acute. The task of criticism, or, to put it another way, the role of the critical consciousness in such cases is to be able to make distinctions, to produce differences where at present there are none. To write critically about Zionism in Palestine has therefore never meant, and does not mean now, being anti-Semitic; conversely, the struggle for Palestinian rights and self-determination does not mean support for the Saudi royal family, nor for the antiquated and oppressive state structures of most of the Arab nations.

One must admit, however, that all liberals and even most "radicals" have been unable to overcome the Zionist habit of equating anti-Zionism with anti-Semitism. Any well-meaning person can thus oppose South African or American racism and at the same time tacitly support Zionist racial discrimination against non-Jews in Palestine. The almost total absence of any handily available historical knowledge from non-Zionist sources, the dissemination by the media of malicious simplifications (e.g., Jews vs. Arabs), the cynical opportunism of various Zionist pressure groups, the tendency endemic to university intellectuals uncritically to repeat cant phrases and political clichés (this is the role Gramsci assigned to traditional intellectuals, that of being "experts in legitimation"), the fear of treading upon the highly sensitive terrain of what Jews did to *their* victims, in an age of genocidal extermination of Jews—all this contributes to the dulling, regulated enforcement of almost unanimous support for Israel. But, as I. F. Stone recently noted, this unanimity exceeds even the Zionism of most Israelis.[2]

On the other hand, it would be totally unjust to neglect the power of Zionism as an idea for Jews, or to minimize the complex internal debates characterizing Zionism, its true meaning, its messianic destiny, etc. Even to speak about this subject, much less than attempting to "define" Zionism, is for an Arab quite a difficult matter, but it must honestly be looked at. Let me use myself as an example. Most of my education, and certainly all of my basic intellectual formation, are Western; in what I have read, in what I write about, even in what I do politically, I am profoundly influenced by mainstream Western attitudes toward the history of the Jews, anti-Semitism, the destruction of European Jewry. Unlike most other Arab intellectuals, the majority of whom obviously have not had my kind of background, I have been directly exposed to those aspects of Jewish history and experience that have mattered singularly for Jews and for Western non-Jews reading and thinking about Jewish history. I know as well as any educated Western non-Jew can know, what anti-Semitism has meant for the Jews, especially in this century. Consequently I can understand the intertwined terror and the exultation out of which Zionism has been nourished, and I think I can at least grasp the meaning of Israel for Jews, and even for the enlightened Western liberal. And yet, because I am an Arab Palestinian, I can also see and feel other things—and it is these things that complicate matters considerably, that cause me also to focus on Zionism's *other* aspects. The result is, I think, worth describing, not because what I think is crucial, but because it is useful to see the same phenomenon in two complementary ways, not normally associated with each other.

One can begin with a literary example: George Eliot's last novel, *Daniel Deronda* (1876). The unusual thing about the book is that its main subject is Zionism, although the novel's principal themes are recognizable to anyone who has read Eliiot's earlier fiction. Seen in the context of Eliot's general interest in idealism and spiritual yearning, Zionism for her was one in a series of worldly projects for the nineteenth-century mind still committed to hopes for a secular religious community. In her earlier books, Eliot had studied a variety of enthusiasms, all of them replacements for organized religion, all of them attractive to persons who would have been Saint Teresa had they lived during a period of coherent faith. The reference to Saint Teresa was originally made by Eliot in *Middlemarch*, an earlier novel of hers; in using it to describe the novel's heroine, Dorothea Brooke, Eliot had intended to compliment her own visionary and moral energy, sustained despite the absence in the modern world of certain assurances for faith and knowledge. Dorothea emerges at the end of *Middlemarch* as a chastened woman, forced to concede her grand visions of a "fulfilled" life in return for a relatively modest domestic success as a wife and mother. It is this considerably diminished view of things that *Daniel Deronda*, and Zionism in particular, revise upward: toward a genuinely hopeful socioreligious project in which individual energies can be merged and identified with a collective national vision, the whole emanating out of Judaism.

The novel's plot alternates between the presentation of a bitter comedy of manners involving a surprisingly rootless segment of the British upper bourgeoisie, and the gradual revelation to Daniel Deronda—an exotic young man whose parentage is unknown but who is the ward of Sir Hugo Mallinger, a British aristocrat—of his Jewish identity and, when he becomes the spiritual disciple of Mordecai Ezra Cohen, his Jewish destiny. At the end of the novel, Daniel marries Mirah, Mordecai's sister, and commits himself to fulfilling Mordecai's hopes for the future of the Jews. Mordecai dies as the young pair get married, although it is clear well before his death that his Zionist ideas have been passed on to Daniel, so much so that among the newlyweds' "splendid wedding-gifts" is "a complete equipment for travel" provided by Sir Hugo and Lady Mallinger. For Daniel and his wife will be traveling to Palestine, presumably to set the great Zionist plan in motion.

The crucial thing about the way Zionism is presented in the novel is that its backdrop is a generalized condition of homelessness. Not only the Jews, but even the well-born Englishmen and women in the novel are portrayed as wandering and alienated beings. If the novel's poorer English people (for example, Mrs. Davilow and her daughters) seem always to be moving from one rented house to another, the wealthy aristocrats are no less cut off from some permanent home. Thus Eliot uses the plight of the Jews to make a universal statement about the nineteenth century's need for a home, given the spiritual and psychological rootlessness reflected in her characters' almost ontological physical restlessness. Her interest in Zionism therefore can be traced to her reflection, made early in the novel, that

> a human life, I think, should be well rooted in some spot of a native land, where it may get the love of tender kindship for the face of the earth, for the labours men go forth to, for the sounds and accents

> that haunt it, for whatever will give that early home a familiar, unmistakable difference amidst the future widening of knowledge.[3]

To find the "early home" means to find the place where originally one was *at home*, a task to be undertaken more or less interchangeably by individuals and by "people." It becomes historically appropriate therefore that those individuals and that "people" best suited to the task are Jews. Only the Jews as a people (and consequently as individuals) have retained both a sense of their original home in Zion and an acute, always contemporary, feeling of loss. Despite the prevalence of anti-Semitism everywhere, the Jews are a reproach to the Gentiles who have long since forsaken the "observance" of any civilizing communal belief. Thus Mordecai puts these sentiments positively as a definite program for today's Jews:

> They [the Gentiles] scorn our people's ignorant observance; but the most accursed ignorance is that which has no observance—sunk to the cunning greed of the fox, to which all law is no more than a trap or the cry of the worrying hound. There is a degradation deep down below the memory that has withered into superstition. In the multitudes of the ignorant on three continents who observe our rites and make the confession of the divine Unity, the soul of Judaism is not dead. Revive the organic centre: let the unity of Israel which has made the growth and form of its religion be an outward reality. Looking towards a land and a polity, our dispersed people in all the ends of the earth may share the dignity of a national life which has a voice among the peoples of the East and the West—which will plant the wisdom and skill of our race so that it may be, as of old, a medium of transmission and understanding. Let that come to pass, and the living warmth will spread to the weak extremities of Israel, and superstition will not vanish, not in the lawlessness of the renegade, but in the illumination of great facts which will widen feeling, and make all knowledge alive as the young offspring of beloved memories.[4]

"The illumination of great facts which widen feeling" is a typical phrase for Eliot, and there is no doubt that her approbation for her Zionists derives from her belief that they were a group almost exactly expressing her own grand ideas about an expanded life of feelings. Yet if there is a felt reality about "the peoples of the West," there is no such reality for the "peoples of the East." They are named, it is true, but are no more substantial than a phrase. The few references to the East in *Daniel Deronda* are always to England's Indian colonies, for whose people—as people having wishes, values, aspirations—Eliot expresses the complete indifference of absolute silence. Of the fact that Zion will be "planted" in the East, Eliot takes no very detailed account; it is as if the phrase "the people of the East and the West" covers what will, territorially at least, be a neutral inaugural reality. In turn, that reality will be replaced by a permanent accomplishment when the newly founded state becomes the "medium of transmission and understanding." For how could Eliot imagine that even Eastern people would object to such grand benefits for all?

There is, however, a disturbing insistence on these matters when Mordecai continues his speech. For him, Zionism means that "our race takes on again the character of a nationality . . . a labour which shall be a worthy fruit of the long anguish whereby our fathers maintained their separateness, refusing the ease of falsehood." Zionism is to be a dramatic lesson for mankind. But what ought to catch the reader's attention about the way Mordecai illustrates his thesis is his depiction of the land:

> [The Jews] have wealth enough *to redeem the soil from debauched and paupered conquerors;* they have the skill of the statesman to devise, the tongue of the operator to persuade. And is there no prophet or poet among us to make the ears of Christian Europe tingle with shame at the hideous obloquy of Christian strife *which the Turk gazes at* [the reference here is to the long history of European disputes about the Holy Land] *as at the fighting of beasts to which he has lent an arena?* There is a store of wisdom among us *to found a new Jewish polity, grand, simple, just like the old*—a republic where there is equality of protection, an equality which shone like a star on the forehead of our ancient community, *and gave it more than the brightness of Western freedom amid the despotisms of the East.* Then our race shall have an organic centre, a heart and brain to watch and guide and execute; *the outraged Jew shall have a defence in the court of nations,* as the outraged Englishman or American. And the world

> will gain as Israel gains. For there will be a community in the van of the East which carries the culture and the sympathies of every great nation in its bosom; *there will be a land set for a halting-place of enmities, a neutral ground for the East as Belgium is for the West.* Difficulties? I know there are difficulties. But let the spirit of sublime achievement move in the great among our people, and the work will begin. [Emphasis added][5]

The land itself is characterized in two separate ways. On the one hand, it is associated with debauched and paupered conquerors, an arena lent by the Turk to fighting beasts, a part of the despotic East; on the other, with "the brightness of Western freedom," with nations like England and America, with the idea of neutrality (Belgium). In short, with a degraded and unworthy East and a noble, enlightened West. The bridge between those warring representatives of East and West will be Zionism.

Interestingly, Eliot cannot sustain her admiration of Zionism except by seeing it as a method for transforming the East into the West. This is not to say that she does not have sympathy for Zionism and for the Jews themselves: she obviously does. But there is a whole area of Jewish experience, lying somewhere between longing for a homeland (which everyone, including the Gentile, feels) and actually getting it, that she is dim about. Otherwise she is quite capable of seeing that Zionism can easily be accommodated to several varieties of Western (as opposed to Eastern) thought, principal among them the idea that the East is degraded, that it needs reconstruction according to enlightened Western notions about politics, that any reconstructed portion of the East can with small reservations become as "English as England" to its new inhabitants. Underlying all this, however, is the total absence of any thought about the actual inhabitants of the East, Palestine in particular. They are irrelevant both to the Zionists in *Daniel Deronda* and to the English characters. Brightness, freedom, and redemption—key matters for Eliot—are to be restricted to Europeans and the Jews, who are themselves European prototypes so far as colonizing the East is concerned. There is a remarkable failure when it comes to taking anything non-European into consideration although curiously all of Eliot's descriptions of Jews stress their exotic, "Eastern" aspects. Humanity and sympathy, it seems, are not endowments of anything but an Occidental mentality; to look for them in the despotic East, much less find them, is to waste one's time.

Two points need to be made immediately. One is that Eliot is no different from other European apostles of sympathy, humanity, and understanding for whom noble sentiments were either left behind in Europe, or made programmatically inapplicable outside Europe. There are the chastening examples of John Stuart Mill and Karl Marx (both of whom I have discussed in *Orientalism*),[6] two thinkers known doctrinally to be opponents of injustice and oppression. Yet both of them seemed to have believed that such ideas as liberty, representative government, and individual happiness must not be applied in the Orient for reasons that today we would call racist. The fact is that nineteenth-century European culture was racist with a greater or lesser degree of virulence depending on the individual: The French writer Ernest Renan, for instance, was an outright anti-Semite; Eliot was indifferent to races who could not be assimilated to European ideas.

Here we come to the second point. Eliot's account of Zionism in *Daniel Deronda* was intended as a sort of assenting Gentile response to prevalent Jewish-Zionist currents; the novel therefore serves as an indication of how much in Zionism was legitimated and indeed valorized by Gentile European thought. On one important issue there was complete agreement between the Gentile and Jewish versions of Zionism: their view of the Holy Land as essentially empty of inhabitants, not because there were no inhabitants—there were, and they were frequently described in numerous travel accounts, in novels like Benjamin Disrael's *Tancred*, even in the various nineteenth-century Baedekers—but because their status as sovereign and human inhabitants was systematically denied. While it may be possible to differentiate between Jewish and Gentile Zionists on this point (they ignored the Arab inhabitants for different reasons), the Palestinian Arab was ignored nonetheless. That is what needs emphasis: the extent to which the roots of Jewish *and* Gentile Zionism are in the culture of high liberal-capitalism, and how the work of its vanguard liberals like George Eliot reinforced, perhaps also completed, that culture's less attractive tendencies.

None of what I have so far said applies adequately to what Zionism meant for Jews or what it represented as an advanced idea for enthusiastic non-Jews; it applies exclusively to those less fortunate beings who happened to be living on the land, people of whom no notice was taken. What has too long been forgotten is that while important European thinkers considered the desirable and later the probable fate of Palestine, the land was being tilled, villages and towns built and lived in by thousands of natives who believed that it was *their* homeland. In the meantime their actual physical being was ignored; later it became a troublesome detail. Strikingly, therefore, Eliot sounds very much like Moses Hess, an early Zionist idealist who in his *Rome and Jerusalem* (1862) uses the same theoretical language to be given to Mordecai:

> What we have to do at present for the regeneration of the Jewish nation is, first, to keep alive the hope of the political rebirth of our people, and, next, to reawaken that hope where it slumbers. When political conditions in the Orient shape themselves so as to permit the organization of a beginning of the restoration of the Jewish state, this beginning will express itself in the founding of Jewish colonies in the land of their ancestors, to which enterprise France will undoubtedly lend a hand. France, beloved friend, is the savior who will restore our people to its place in universal history. Just as we once searched in the West for a road to India, and incidentally discovered a new world, so will our lost fatherland be rediscovered on the road to India and China that is now being built in the Orient.[7]

Hess continues his paean to France (since every Zionist saw one or another of the imperial powers as patron) by quoting at some length from Ernest Laharanne's *The New Eastern Question*, from which Hess draws the following passage for his peroration:

> "A great calling is reserved for the Jews: to be a living channel of communication between three continents. You shall be the bearers of civilization to peoples who are still inexperienced and their teachers in the European sciences, to which your race has contributed so much. You shall be the mediators between Europe and far Asia, opening the roads that lead to India and China—those unknown regions which must ultimately be thrown open to civilisation. You will come to the land of your fathers decorated with the crown of

> age-long martyrdom, and there, finally, you will be completely healed from all your ills! Your capital will again bring the wide stretches of barren land under cultivation; your labor and industry will once more turn the ancient soil into fruitful valleys, reclaiming it from the encroaching sands of the desert, and the world will again pay its homage to the oldest of peoples."[8]

Between them, Hess and Eliot concur that Zionism is to be carried out by the Jews with the assistance of major European powers; that Zionism will restore "a lost fatherland," and in so doing mediate between the various civilizations; that present-day Palestine was in need of cultivation, civilization, reconstitution; that Zionism would finally bring enlightenment and progress where at present there was neither. The three ideas that depended on one another in Hess and Eliot—and later in almost every Zionist thinker or ideologue—are (a) the nonexistent Arab inhabitants, (b) the complementary Western-Jewish attitude to an "empty" territory, and (c) the restorative Zionist project, which would repeat by rebuilding a vanished Jewish state and combine it with modern elements like disciplined, separate colonies, a special agency for land acquisition, etc. Of course, none of these ideas would have any force were it not for the additional fact of their being addressed to, shaped for, and out of an *international* (i.e., non-Oriental and hence European) context. This context was the reality, not only because of the ethnocentric rationale governing the whole project, but also because of the overwhelming facts of Diaspora realities and imperialist hegemony over the entire gamut of European culture. It needs to be remarked, however, that Zionism (like the view of America as an empty land held by Puritans) was a colonial vision unlike that of most other nineteenth-century European powers, for whom the natives of outlying territories were *included* in the redemptive *mission civilisatrice.*

From the earliest phases of its modern evolution until it culminated in the creation of Israel, Zionism appealed to a European audience for whom the classification of overseas territories and natives into various uneven classes was canonical and "natural." That is why, for example, every single state or movement in the formerly colonized territories of Africa and Asia today identifies with, fully supports, and understands the Palestinian struggle. In many instances—as I hope to show presently—there is an unmistakable coincidence between the experiences of Arab Palestinians at the hands of Zionism and the experiences of those black, yellow, and brown people who were described as inferior and subhuman by nineteenth-century imperialists. For although it coincided with an era of the most virulent Western anti-Semitism, Zionism also coincided with the period of unparalleled European territorial acquisition in Africa and Asia, and it was as part of this general movement of acquisition and occupation that Zionism was launched initially by Theodor Herzl. During the latter part of the greatest period in European colonial expansion, Zionism also made its crucial first moves along the way to getting what has now become a sizeable Asiatic territory. And it is important to remember that in joining the general Western enthusiasm for overseas territorial acquisition, Zionism *never* spoke of itself unambiguously as a Jewish liberation movement, but rather as a Jewish movement for colonial settlement in the Orient. To those Palestinian victims that Zionism displaced, it *cannot have meant anything by way of sufficient cause* that Jews were victims of European anti-Semitism and, given Israel's continued oppression of Palestinians, few Palestinians are able to see beyond their reality, namely, that once victims themselves, Occidental Jews in Israel have become oppressors (of Palestinian Arabs and Oriental Jews).

These are not intended to be backward-looking historical observations, for in a very vital way they explain and even determine much of what now happens in the Middle East. The fact that no sizeable segment of the Israeli population has as yet been able to confront the terrible social and political injustice done the native Palestinians is an indication of how deeply ingrained are the (by now) anomalous imperialist perspectives basic to Zionism, its view of the world, its sense of an inferior native Other. The fact also that no Palestinian, regardless of his political stripe, has been able to reconcile himself to Zionism suggests the extent to which, for the Palestinian, Zionism has appeared to be an uncompromisingly exclusionary, discriminatory, colonialist praxis. So powerful, and so unhesitatingly followed, has been the radical Zionist distinction between privileged Jews in Palestine and unprivileged non-Jews there, that nothing else has emerged, no perception of suffering human existence has escaped from the two camps created thereby.[9]

As a result, it has been impossible for Jews to understand the human tragedy caused the Arab Palestinians by Zionism; and it has been impossible for Arab Palestinians to see in Zionism anything except an ideology and a practice keeping them, and Israeli Jews, imprisoned. But in order to break down the iron circle of inhumanity, we must see how it was forged, and there it is ideas and culture themselves that play the major role.

Consider Herzl. If it was the Dreyfus Affair that first brought him to Jewish consciousness, it was the idea of overseas colonial settlement for the Jews that came to him at roughly the same time as an antidote for anti-Semitism. The idea itself was current at the end of the nineteenth century, even as an idea for Jews. Herzl's first significant contact was Baron Maurice de Hirsch, a wealthy philanthropist who had for some time been behind the Jewish Colonization Association for helping Eastern Jews to emigrate to Argentina and Brazil. Later, Herzl thought generally about South America, then about Africa as places for establishing a Jewish colony. Both areas were widely acceptable as places for European colonialism, and that Herzl's mind followed along the orthodox imperialist track of his period is perhaps understandable. The impressive thing, however, is the degree to which Herzl had absorbed and internalized the imperialist perspective on "natives" and their "territory."[10]

There could have been no doubt whatever in Herzl's mind that Palestine in the late nineteenth century was peopled. True, it was under Ottoman administration (and therefore already a colony), but it had been the subject of numerous travel accounts, most of them famous, by Lamartine, Chateaubriand, Flaubert, and others. Yet even if he had not read these authors, Herzl as a journalist must surely have looked at a Baedeker to ascertain that Palestine was indeed inhabited by (in the 1880s) 650,000 mostly Arab people. This did not stop him from regarding their presence as manageable in ways that, in his diary, he spelled out with a rather chilling prescience for what later took place. The mass of poor natives were to be expropriated and, he added, "both the expropriation and the removal of the poor must be carried out discreetly and circumspectly." This was to be done by "spirit[ing] the penniless population across the border by procuring employment for it in the transit countries, while denying it any employment in our own country."

With uncannily accurate cynicism, Herzl predicted that the small class of large landowners could be "had for a price"—as indeed they were. The whole scheme for displacing the native population of Palestine far outstripped any of the then current plans for taking over vast reaches of Africa. As Demond Stewart aptly says:

> Herzl seems to have foreseen that in going further than any colonialist had so far gone in Africa, he would, temporarily, alienate civilised opinion. "At first, incidentally," he writes on the pages describing "involuntary expropriation," "people will avoid us. We are in bad odor. By the time the reshaping of world opinion in our favor has been completed, we shall be firmly established in our country, no longer fearing the influx of foreigners, and receiving our visitors with aristocratic benevolence and proud amiability."
>
> This was not a prospect to charm a peon in Argentina or a fellah in Palestine. But Herzl did not intend his Diary for immediate publication.[11]

One need not wholly accept the conspiratorial tone of these comments (whether Herzl's or Stewart's) to grant that world opinion has not been, until during the sixties and seventies when the Palestinians forced their presence on world politics, very much concerned with the expropriation of Palestine. I said earlier that in this regard the major Zionist achievement was getting international legitimization for its own accomplishments, thereby making the Palestinian cost of these accomplishments seem to be irrelevant. But it is clear from Herzl's thinking that that could not have been done unless there was a prior European inclination to view the natives as irrelevant *to begin with.* That is, those natives already fit a more or less acceptable classificatory grid, which made them sui generis inferior to Western or white men—and it is this grid that Zionists like Herzl appropriated, domesticating it from the general culture of their time to the unique needs of a developing Jewish nationalism. One needs to repeat that what in Zionism served the no doubt justified ends of Jewish tradition, saving the Jews as a people from homelessness and anti-Semitism and restoring them to nationhood, also collaborated with those aspects of the dominant Western culture (in which Zionism institutionally lived) making it possible for Europeans to view non-Europeans as inferior, marginal, and irrelevant. For the Palestinian Arab, therefore, it is the collaboration that has counted, not by any means the good done to Jews. The Arab has been on the receiving end not of benign Zionism—which has been restricted to Jews—but of an essentially discriminatory and powerful culture, of which, in Palestine, Zionism has been the agent.

Here I must digress to say that the great difficulty today of writing about what has happened to the Arab Palestinian as a result of Zionism, is that Zionism has had a large number of successes. There is no doubt in my mind, for example, that most Jews do regard Zionism and Israel as urgently important facts for Jewish life, particularly because of what happened to the Jews in this century. Then too, Israel has some remarkable political and cultural achievements to its credit, quite apart from its spectacular military successes until recently. Most important, Israel is a subject about which, on the whole, one can feel positive with less reservations than the ones experienced in thinking about the Arabs, who are outlandish, strange, hostile Orientals after all; surely that is an obvious fact to anyone living in the West. Together these successes of Zionism have produced a prevailing view of the question of Palestine that almost totally favors the victor, and takes hardly any account of the victim.

Yet what did the victim feel as he watched the Zionists arriving in Palestine? What does he think as he watches Zionism described today? Where does he look in Zionism's history to locate its roots, and the origins of its practices toward him? These are the questions that are never asked—and they are precisely the ones that I am trying to raise, as well as answer, here in this examination of the links between Zionism and European imperialism. My interest is in trying to record the effects of Zionism on its victims, and these effects can only be studied genealogically in the framework provided by imperialism, even during the nineteenth century when Zionism was still an idea and not a state called Israel. For the Palestinian now who writes critically to see what his or her history has meant, and who tries—as I am now trying—to see what Zionism has been for the Palestinians, Antonio Gramsci's observation is relevant, that "the consciousness of what one really is . . . is 'knowing thyself' as a product of the historical process to date which has deposited in you an infinity of traces, without leaving an inventory." The job of producing an inventory is a first necessity, Gramsci continued, and so it must be now, when the "inventory" of what Zionism's victims (*not* its beneficiaries) endured is rarely exposed to public view.[12]

If we have become accustomed to making fastidious distinctions between ideology (or theory) and practice, we shall be more accurate historically if we do not do so glibly in the case of the European imperialism that actually annexed most of the world during the nineteenth century. Imperialism was and still is a political philosophy whose aim and purpose for being is territorial expansion and its legitimization. A serious underestimation of imperialism, however, would be to consider territory in too literal a way. Gaining and holding an *imperium* means gaining and holding a domain, which includes a variety of operations, among them constituting an area, accumulating its inhabitants, having power over its ideas, people, and of course, its land, converting people, land, and ideas to the purposes and for the use of a hegemonic imperial design; all this as a result of being able to treat reality appropriatively. Thus the distinction between an idea that one *feels* to be one's own and a piece of land that one claims by right to be one's own (despite the presence on the land of its working native inhabitants) is really nonexistent, at least in the world of nineteenth-century culture out of which imperialism developed. Laying claim to an idea and laying claim to a territory—given the extraordinarily current idea that the non-European world was there to be claimed, occupied, and ruled by Europe—were considered to be different sides of the same, essentially constitutive activity, which had the force, the prestige, and the authority of *science.* Moreover, because in such fields as biology, philology, and geology the scientific consciousness was principally a reconstituting, restoring, and transforming activity turning old fields into new ones, the link between an outright imperialist attitude toward distant lands in the Orient and a scientific attitude to the "inequalities" of race was that both attitudes depended on the European *will*, on the determining force necessary to change confusing or useless realities into an orderly, disciplined set of new classifications useful to Europe. Thus in the works of Carolus Linnaeus, Georges Buffon, and Georges Cuvier the white races became scientifically different from reds, yellows, blacks, and browns, and, consequently, territories occupied by those races also newly became vacant, open to Western colonies, developments, plantations, and settlers. Additionally, the less equal races were made useful by being turned into what the white race studied and came to understand as a part of its racial and cultural hegemony (as in Joseph de Gobineau and Oswald Spengler); or, following the impulse of outright colonialism, these lesser races were put to direct use in the empire. When in 1918, Georges Clemenceau stated that he believed he had "an unlimited right of levying black troops to assist in the defense of French territory in Europe if France were attacked in the future by Germany," he was saying that by some scientific right France had the knowledge and the power to convert blacks into what Raymond Poincaré called an economic form of gunfodder for the white Frenchman.[13] Imperialism, of course, cannot be blamed on science, but what needs to be seen is the relative ease with which science could be deformed into a rationalization for imperial domination.

Supporting the taxonomy of a natural history deformed into a social anthropology whose real purpose was social control, was the taxonomy of linguistics. With the discovery of a structural affinity between groups or families of languages by such linguists as Franz Bopp, William Jones, and Freidrich von Schlegel, there began as well the unwarranted extension of an idea about language families into theories of human types having determined ethnocultural and racial characteristics. In 1808, as an instance, Schlegel discerned a clear rift between the Indo-Germanic (or Aryan) languages on the one hand and, on the other, the Semitic-African languages. The former he said were creative, regenerative, lively, and aesthetically pleasing; the latter were mechanical in their operations, unregenerate, passive. From this kind of distinction, Schlegel, and later Renan, went on to generalize about the great distance separating a superior Aryan and an inferior non-Aryan mind, culture, and society.

Perhaps the most effective deformation or translation of science into something more accurately resembling political administration took place in the amorphous field assembling together jurisprudence, social philosophy, and political theory. First of all, a fairly influential tradition in philosophic empiricism (recently studied by Harry Bracken)[14] seriously advocated a type of racial distinction that divided humankind into lesser and greater breeds of men. The actual problems (in England, mainly) of dealing with a 300-year-old

Indian empire, as well as numerous voyages of discovery, made it possible "scientifically" to show that some cultures were advanced and civilized, others backward and uncivilized; these ideas, plus the lasting social meaning imparted to the fact of color (and hence of race) by philosophers like John Locke and David Hume, made it axiomatic by the middle of the nineteenth century that Europeans always ought to rule non-Europeans.

This doctrine was reinforced in other ways, some of which had a direct bearing, I think, on Zionist practice and vision in Palestine. Among the supposed juridical distinctions between civilized and noncivilized peoples was an attitude toward land, almost a doxology about land, which noncivilized people supposedly lacked. A civilized man, it was believed, could cultivate the land because it meant something to him; on it, accordingly, he bred useful arts and crafts, he created, he accomplished, he built. For an uncivilized people, land was either farmed badly (i.e., inefficiently by Western standards) or it was left to rot. From this string of ideas, by which whole native societies who lived on American, African, and Asian territories for centuries were suddenly denied their right to live on that land, came the great dispossessing movements of modern European colonialism, and with them all the schemes for redeeming the land, resettling the natives, civilizing them, taming their savage customs, turning them into useful beings under European rule. Land in Asia, Africa, and the Americas was there for European exploitation, because Europe understood the value of land in a way impossible for the natives. At the end of the century, Joseph Conrad dramatized this philosophy in *Heart of Darkness,* and embodied it powerfully in the figure of Kurtz, a man whose colonial dreams for the earth's "dark places" were made by "all Europe." But what Conrad drew on, as indeed the Zionists drew on also, was the kind of philosophy set forth by Robert Knox in his work *The Races of Man,*[15] in which men were divided into white and advanced (the producers) and dark, inferior wasters. Similarly, thinkers like John Westlake and before him, Emer de Vattel divided the world's territories into empty (though inhabited by nomads, and a low kind of society) and civilized—and the former were then "revised" as being ready for takeover on the basis of a higher, civilized right to them.

I very greatly simplify the transformation in perspective by which millions of acres outside metropolitan Europe were thus declared empty, their people and societies decreed to be obstacles of progress and development, their space just as assertively declared open to European white settlers and their civilizing exploitation. During the 1870s in particular, new European geographical societies mushroomed as a sign that geography had become, according to Lord Curzon, "the most cosmopolitan of all the sciences."[16] Not for nothing in *Heart of Darkness* did Marlow admit to his

> passion for maps. I would look for hours at South America, or Africa, or Australia, and lose myself in all the glories of exploration. At that time there were many blank spaces [populated by natives, that is] on the earth, and when I saw one that looked particularly inviting on a map (but they all looked like that) I would put my finger on it and say, When I grow up I will go there.[17]

Geography and a passion for maps developed into an organized matter mainly devoted to acquiring vast overseas territories. And, Conrad also said, this

> . . . conquest of the earth, which mostly means the taking it away from those who have a different complexion or slightly flatter noses than ourselves, is not a pretty thing when you look into it too much. What redeems it is the idea only. An idea at the back of it; not a sentimental pretence but an idea—something you can set up, and bow down before, and offer a sacrifice to . . .[18]

Conrad makes the point better than anyone, I think. The power to conquer territory is only in part a matter of physical force: there is the strong moral and intellectual component making the conquest itself secondary to an idea, which dignifies (and indeed hastens) pure force with arguments drawn from science, morality, ethics, and a general philosophy. Everything in Western culture potentially capable of dignifying the acquisition of new domains—as a new science, for example, acquires new intellectual territory for itself—*could* be put at the service of colonial adventures. And *was* put, the "idea" always informing the conquest, making it entirely palatable. One example of such an idea spoken about openly as a quite normal justification for what today would be called colonial aggression, is to be found in these passages by Paul Leroy-Beaulieu, a leading French geographer in the 1870s:

> A society colonizes, when having itself reached a high degree of maturity and of strength, it procreates, it protects, it places in good condition of development, and it brings to virility a new society to which it has given birth. Colonization is one of the most complex and delicate phenomena of social physiology.

There is no question of consulting the natives of the territory where the new society is to be given birth. What counts is that a modern European society has enough vitality and intellect to be "magnified by this pouring out of its exuberant activity on the outside." Such activity must be good since it is believed in, and since it also carries within itself the healthy current of an entire advanced civilization. Therefore, Leroy-Beaulieu added,

> Colonization is the expansive force of a people; it is its power of reproduction; it is its enlargement and its multiplication through space; it is the subjugation of the universe or a vast part of it to that people's language, customs, ideas, and laws.[19]

Imperialism was the theory, colonialism the practice of changing the uselessly unoccupied territories of the world into useful new versions of the European metropolitan society. Everything in those territories that suggested waste, disorder, uncounted resources, was to be converted into productivity, order, taxable, potentially developed wealth. You get rid of most of the offending human and animal blight—whether because it simply sprawls untidily all over the place or because it roams around unproductively and uncounted—and you confine the rest to reservations, compounds, native homelands, where you can count, tax, use them profitably, and you build a new society on the vacated space. Thus was Europe reconstituted abroad, its "multiplication in space" successfully projected and managed. The result was a widely varied group of little Europes scattered throughout Asia, Africa, and the Americas, each reflecting the circumstances, the specific instrumentalities of the parent culture, its pioneers, its vanguard settlers.[20] All of them were similar in one other major respect—despite the differences, which were considerable—

and that was that their life was carried on with an air of *normality.* The most grotesque reproductions of Europe (South Africa, Rhodesia, etc.) were considered appropriate; the worst discrimination against and exclusions of the natives were thought to be normal because "scientifically" legitimate; the sheer contradiction of living a foreign life in an enclave many physical and cultural miles from Europe, in the midst of hostile and uncomprehending natives, gave rise to a sense of history, a stubborn kind of logic, a social and political state decreeing the present colonial venture as *normal,* justified, good.

With specific reference to Palestine, what were to become institutional Zionist attitudes to the Arab Palestinian natives and their supposed claims to a "normal" existence, were more than prepared for in the attitudes and the practices of British scholars, administrators, and experts who were officially involved in the exploitation and government of Palestine since the mid-nineteenth century. Consider that in 1903 the Bishop of Salisbury told members of the Palestine Exploration Fund that

> Nothing, I think, that has been discovered makes us feel any regret at the suppression of Canaanite civilisation [the euphemism for native Arab Palestinians] by Israelite civilisation. . . . [The excavations show how] the Bible has not misrepresented at all the abomination of the Canaanite culture which was superseded by the Israelite culture.

Miriam Rosen, a young American scholar, has compiled a spine-tingling collection of typical British attitudes to the Palestinians, attitudes which in extraordinary ways prepare for the *official* Zionist view, from Weizmann to Begin, of the native Palestinian. Here are some citations from Ms. Rosen's important work:

Tyrwhitt Drake, who wrote in a survey of Western Palestine:

> The fear of the *fellahin* that we have secret designs of re-conquering the country is a fruitful source of difficulty. This got over, remains the crass stupidity which cannot give a direct answer to a simple question, the exact object of which it does not understand; for why should a Frank wish to know the name of an insignificant wady or hill in their land?

> The *fellahin* are all in the worst type of humanity that I have come across in the east. . . . The *fellah* is totally destitute of all moral sense. . . .

The Dean of Westminster, on the "obstacles" before the Palestine Exploration Fund Survey:

> And these labours had to be carried out, not with the assistance of those on the spot, but in spite of the absurd obstacles thrown in the way of work by that singular union of craft, ignorance and stupidity, which can only be found in Orientals.

Lord Kitchener on the Survey of Galilee:

> We hope to rescue from the hands of that ruthless destroyer, the uneducated Arab, one of the most interesting ruins in Palestine, hallowed by footprints of our Lord. I allude to the synagogue of Capernaum, which is rapidly disappearing owing to the stones being burnt for lime.

One C. R. Conder in his "Present Condition of Palestine":

> The native peasantry are well worth a few words of description. They are brutally ignorant, fanatical, and above all, inveterate liars; yet they have qualities which would, if developed, render them a useful population. [He cites their cleverness, energy, and endurance for pain, heat, etc.]

Sir Flinders Petrie:

> The Arab has a vast balance of romance put to his credit very needlessly. He is as disgustingly incapable as most other savages, and no more worth romancing about than Red Indians or Maoris. I shall be glad to return to the comparatively shrewd and sensible Egyptians.

Charles Clermont-Ganneau's reflections on "The Arabs in Palestine":

> Arab civilization is a mere deception—it no more exists than the horrors of Arab conquest. It is but the last gleam of Greek and Roman

> civilization gradually dying out in the powerless but respectful hands of Islam.

Or Stanley Cook's view of the country:

> . . . rapid deterioration, which (it would seem) was only temporarily stopped by the energetic Crusaders. Modern travellers have often noticed the inherent weakness of the characters of the inhabitants and, like Robinson, have realized that, for the return of prosperity, "nothing is wanted but the hand of the man to till the ground."

Or, finally, R. A. S. Macalister:

> It is no exaggeration to say that throughout these long centuries the native inhabitants of Palestine do not appear to have made a single contribution of any kind whatsoever to material civilization. It was perhaps the most unprogressive country on the face of the earth. Its entire culture was derivative . . .[21]

These, then, are some of the main points that must be made about the background of Zionism in European imperialist or colonialist attitudes. For whatever it may have done for Jews, Zionism essentially saw Palestine as the European imperialist did, as an empty territory paradoxically "filled" with ignoble or perhaps even dispensable natives; it allied itself, as Chaim Weizmann quite clearly said after World War I, with the imperial powers in carrying out its plans for establishing a new Jewish state in Palestine, and it did not think except in negative terms of "the natives," who were passively supposed to accept the plans made for their land; as even Zionist historians like Yehoshua Porath and Neville Mandel have empirically shown, the ideas of Jewish colonizers in Palestine (well before World War I) always met with unmistakable native resistance, not because the natives thought that Jews were evil, but because most natives do not take kindly to having their territory settled by foreigners;[22] moreover, in formulating the concept of a Jewish nation "reclaiming" its own territory, Zionism not only accepted the generic racial concepts of European culture, it also banked on the fact that Palestine was actually peopled not by an advanced but by a backward people, over which it *ought* to be dominant. Thus that implicit *assumption* of domination led specifically in the case of Zionism to the practice of ignoring the natives for the most part as not entitled to serious consideration.[23] Zionism therefore developed with a unique consciousness of itself, but with little or nothing left over for the unfortunate natives. Maxime Rodinson is perfectly correct in saying that Zionist indifference to the Palestinian natives was

> an indifference linked to European supremacy, which benefited even Europe's proletarians and oppressed minorities. In fact, there can be no doubt that if the ancestral homeland had been occupied by one of the well-established industrialized nations that ruled the world at the time, one that had thoroughly settled down in a territory it had infused with a powerful national consciousness, then the problem of displacing German, French, or English inhabitants and introducing a new, nationally coherent element into the middle of their homeland would have been in the forefront of the consciousness of even the most ignorant and destitute Zionists.[24]

In short, all the constitutive energies of Zionism were premised on the excluded presence, that is, the functional absence of "native people" in Palestine; institutions were built deliberately shutting out the natives, laws were drafted when Israel came into being that made sure the natives would remain in their "nonplace," Jews in theirs, and so on. It is no wonder that today the one issue that electrifies Israel as a society is the problem of the Palestinians, whose negation is the most consistent thread running through Zionism. And it is this perhaps unfortunate aspect of Zionism that ties it ineluctably to imperialism—at least so far as the Palestinian is concerned. Rodinson again:

> The element that made it possible to connect these aspirations of Jewish shopkeepers, peddlers, craftsmen, and intellectuals in Russia and elsewhere to the conceptual orbit of imperialism was one small detail that seemed to be of no importance: Palestine was inhabited by another people.[25]

II

Zionist Population, Palestinian Depopulation

I have been discussing the extraordinary unevenness in Zionism between care for the Jews and an almost total disregard for the non-Jews or native Arab population in conceptual terms. Zionism and European imperialism are epistemologically, hence historically and politically, coterminous in their view of resident natives, but it is how this irreducibly imperialist view worked in the world of politics and in the lives of people for whom epistemology was irrelevant that justifies one's looking at epistemology at all. In that world and in those lives, among them several million Palestinians, the results can be detailed, not as mere theoretical visions, but as an immensely traumatic Zionist effectiveness. One general Arab Palestinian reaction toward Zionism is perfectly caught, I think, in the following sentence written by the Arab delegation's reply in 1922 to Winston Churchill's White Paper: "The intention to create the Jewish National Home is to cause the disappearance or subordination of the Arabic population, culture and language."[26] What generations of Palestinian Arabs watched therefore was an unfolding design, whose deeper roots in Jewish history and the terrible Jewish experience was necessarily obscured by what was taking place before their eyes as well as to those in Palestine. There the Arabs were able to see embodied

> a ruthless doctrine, calling for monastic self-discipline and cold detachment from environment. The Jews who gloried in the name of socialist worker interpreted brotherhood on a strictly nationalist, or racial basis, for they meant brotherhood with Jew, not with Arab. As they insisted on working the soil with their own hands, since exploitation of others was anathema to them, they excluded the Arabs from their regime. . . . They believed in equality, but for themselves. They lived on Jewish bread, raised on Jewish soil that was protected by a Jewish rifle.[27]

The "inventory" of Palestinian experience that I am trying to take here is based on the simple truth that the exultant or (later) the terrorized Jews who arrived in Palestine were seen essentially as foreigners whose proclaimed destiny was to create a state for Jews. What of the Arabs who were there? was the question we must feel ourselves asking now. What we will discover is that everything from the Zionist standpoint looked absolutely negative from the perspective of the native Arab Palestinians.

For they could never be fit into the grand vision. Not that "vision" was merely a theoretical matter; it was that and, as it was later to determine the character and even the details of Israeli government policy toward the native Arab Palestinians, "vision" was also the way Zionist leaders looked at the Arabs in order later (and certainly at that moment) to deal with them. Thus, as I said earlier, I have in mind the whole dialectic between theory and actual day-to-day effectiveness. My premise is that Israel developed as a social polity out of the Zionist thesis that Palestine's colonization was to be accomplished simultaneously for and by Jews *and* by the displacement of the Palestinians; moreover, that in its conscious and declared ideas about Palestine, Zionism attempted first to minimize, then to eliminate, and then, all else failing, finally to subjugate the natives as a way of guaranteeing that Israel would not be simply the state of its citizens (which included Arabs, of course) but the state of "the whole Jewish people," having a kind of sovereignty over land and peoples that no other state possessed or possesses. It is this anomaly that the Arab Palestinians have since been trying both to resist and provide an alternative for.

One can learn a great deal from pronouncements made by strategically important Zionist leaders whose job it was, after Herzl, to translate the design into action. Chaim Weizmann comes to mind at once, as much for his extraordinary personality as for his brilliant successes in bringing Zionism up from an idea to a conquering political institution. His thesis about the land of Palestine is revealing in the extent to which it repeats Herzl:

> It seems as if God has covered the soil of Palestine with rocks and marshes and sand, so that its beauty can only be brought out by those who love it and will devote their lives to healing its wounds.[28]

The context of this remark, however, is a sale made to the Zionists by a wealthy absentee landlord (the Lebanese Sursuk family) of unpromising marshland. Weizmann admits that this particular sale was of *some,* by no means a great deal, of Palestine, yet the impression he gives is of a *whole* territory essentially unused, unappreciated, misunderstood (if one can use such a word in this connection). Despite the people who lived on it, Palestine was therefore *to be made* useful, appreciated, understandable. The native inhabitants were believed curiously to be out of touch with history and, it seemed to follow, they were not really present. In the following passage, written by Weizmann to describe Palestine when he first visited there in 1907, notice how the contrast between past neglect and forlornness and present "tone and progressive spirit" (he was writing in 1941) is intended to justify the introduction of foreign colonies and settlements.

> A dolorous country it was on the whole, one of the most neglected corners of the miserably neglected Turkish Empire. [Here, Weizmann uses "neglect" to describe Palestine's native inhabitants, the fact of whose residence there is not a sufficient reason to characterize Palestine as anything but an essentially empty and patient territory, awaiting people who show a proper care for it.] Its total population was something above six hundred thousand, of which about eighty thousand were Jews. The latter lived mostly in the cities. . . . But neither the colonies nor the city settlements in any way resembled, as far as vigor, tone and progressive spirit are concerned, the colonies and settlements of our day.[29]

One short-term gain was that Zionism "raised the value of the . . . land," and the Arabs could reap profits even if politically the land was being cut out from underneath them.

As against native neglect and decrepitude, Weizmann preached the necessity of Jewish energy, will, and organization for reclaiming, "redeeming" the land. His language was shot through with the rhetoric of voluntarism, with an ideology of will and new blood that appropriated for Zionism a great deal of the language (and later the policies) of European colonialists attempting to deal with native backwardness. "New blood had to be brought into the country; a new spirit of enterprise had to be introduced." The Jews were to be the importers of colonies and colonists whose role was not simply to take over a territory but also to be schools for a Jewish national self-revival. Thus if in Palestine "there were great possibilities," the question became how to do something about the fact that "the will was lacking. How was that to be awakened? How was a cumulative process to be set in motion?" According to Weizmann, the Zionists were saved from ultimate discouragement only because of "our feeling that a great source of energy was waiting to be tapped—the national impulse of a people held in temporary check by a misguided interpretation of historic method."[30] The "method" referred to was the Zionist tendency hitherto to rely on great foreign benefactors like the Rothschilds and "neglect" the development of self-sustaining colonial institutions on the land itself.

To do this, it was necessary to visualize and then to implement a scheme for creating a network of realities—a language, a grid of colonies, a series of organizations—for converting Palestine from its present state of "neglect" into a Jewish state. This network would not so much attack the existing "realities" as ignore them, grow alongside them, and then finally blot them out, as a forest of large trees blots out a small patch of weeds. A main ideological necessity for such a program was acquiring legitimacy for it, giving it an archeology and a teleology that completely surrounded and, in a sense, outdated the native culture that was still firmly planted in Palestine. One of the reasons Weizmann modified the conception of the Balfour Declaration from its favoring a "reestablishment" was precisely to enclose the territory with the oldest and furthest reaching of possible "realities." The colonization of Palestine proceeded always as a fact of repetition: The Jews were not supplanting, destroying, breaking up a native society. That society was itself the oddity that had broken the pattern of a sixty-year Jewish sovereignty over Palestine which had lapsed for two millennia. In Jewish hearts, however, Israel had always been there, an actuality difficult for the natives to perceive. Zionism therefore reclaimed, redeemed, repeated, replanted, realized Palestine, and Jewish hegemony over it. Israel was a return to a previous state of affairs, even if the new facts bore a far greater resemblance to the methods and successes of nineteenth-century European colonialism than to some mysterious first-century forebears.

Here it is necessary to make something very clear. In each of the projects for "reestablishing" Jewish sovereignty over Palestine there were always two fundamental components. One was a careful determination to implement Jewish self-betterment. About this, of course, the world heard a great deal. Great steps were taken in providing Jews with a new sense of identity, in defending and giving them rights as citizens, in reviving a national "home" language (through the labors of Eliezer Ben Yehudah), in giving the whole Jewish world a vital sense of growth and historical destiny. Thus "there was an instrument [in Zionism] for them to turn to, an instrument which could absorb them into the new life."[31] For Jews, Zionism was a school—and its pedagogical philosophy was always clear, dramatic, intelligent. Yet the other, dialectically opposite component in Zionism, existing at its interior where it was never *seen* (even though directly experienced by Palestinians) was an equally firm and intelligent boundary between benefits for Jews and none (later, punishment) for non-Jews in Palestine.

The consequences of the bifurcation in the Zionist program for Palestine have been immense, especially for Arabs who have tried seriously to deal with Israel. So effective have Zionist ideas about Palestine been for Jews—in the sense of caring for Jews and ignoring non-Jews—that what these ideas expressed to Arabs was *only* a rejection of Arabs. Thus Israel itself has tended to appear as an entirely negative entity, something constructed for us for no other reason than either to keep Arabs out or to subjugate them. The internal solidity and cohesion of Israel, of Israelis as a people and as a society, have for the most part, therefore, eluded the understanding of Arabs generally. Thus to the walls constructed by Zionism have been added walls constructed by a dogmatic, almost theological brand of Arabism. Israel has seemed essentially to be a rhetorical tool provided by the West to harass the Arabs. What this perception entailed in the Arab states has been a policy of repression and a kind of thought control. For years it was forbidded even to refer to Israel in print; this sort of censorship led quite naturally to the consolidation of police states, the absence of freedom of expression, and a whole set of human rights abuses, all supposedly justified in the name of "fighting Zionist aggression," which meant that any form of oppression at home was acceptable because it served the "sacred cause" of "national security."

For Israel and Zionists everywhere, the results of Zionist apartheid have been equally disastrous. The Arabs were seen as synonymous with everything degraded, fearsome, irrational, and brutal.

Institutions whose humanistic and social (even socialist) inspiration were manifest for Jews—the kibbutz, the Law of Return, various facilities for the acculturation of immigrants—were precisely, determinedly inhuman for the Arabs. In his body and being, and in the putative emotions and psychology assigned to him, the Arab expressed whatever by definition stood *outside, beyond* Zionism.

The denial of Israel by the Arabs was, I think, a far less sophisticated and complex thing than the denial, and later the minimization, of the Arabs by Israel. Zionism was not only a reproduction of nineteenth-century European colonialism, for all the community of ideas it shared with that colonialism. Zionism aimed to create a society that could never be anything but "native" (with minimal ties to a metropolitan center) at the same time that it determined not to come to terms with the very natives it was replacing with new (but essentially European) "natives." Such a substitution was to be absolutely economical; no slippage from Arab Palestinian to Israeli societies would occur, and the Arabs would remain, if they did not flee, only as docile, subservient objects. And everything that did stay to challenge Israel was viewed not as something *there,* but as a sign of something *outside* Israel and Zionism bent on its destruction—from the outside. Here Zionism literally took over the typology employed by European culture of a fearsome Orient confronting the Occident, except that Zionism, as an avant-garde, redemptive Occidental movement, confronted the Orient *in* the Orient. To look at what "fulfilled" Zionism had to say about the Arabs generally, and Palestinians in particular, is to see something like the following, extracted from an article printed in *Ma'ariv,* October 7, 1955. Its author was a Dr. A. Carlebach, who was a distinguished citizen and not a crude demagogue. His argument is that *Islam* opposes Zionism, although he does find room in his argument for the Palestinians.

> These Arab Islamic countries do not suffer from poverty, or disease, or illiteracy, or exploitation; they only suffer from the worst of all plagues: Islam. Wherever Islamic psychology rules, there is the inevitable rule of despotism and criminal aggression. The danger lies in Islamic psychology, which cannot integrate itself into the world of efficiency and progress, that lives in a world of illusion, perturbed by attacks of inferiority complexes and megalomania, lost in dreams of

the holy sword. The danger stems from the totalitarian conception of the world, the passion for murder deeply rooted in their blood, from the lack of logic, the easily inflamed brains, the boasting, and above all: the blasphemous disregard for all that is sacred to the civilized world . . . their reactions—to anything—have nothing to do with good sense. They are all emotional, unbalanced, instantaneous, senseless. It is always the lunatic that speaks from their throat. You can talk "business" with everyone, and even with the devil. But not with Allah. . . . This is what every grain in this country shouts. There were many great cultures here, and invaders of all kinds. All of them—even the Crusaders—left signs of culture and blossoming. But on the path of Islam, even the trees have died. [This dovetails perfectly with Weizmann's observations about "neglect" in Palestine; one assumes that had Weizmann been writing later he would have said similar things to Carlebach.]

We pile sin upon crime when we distort the picture and reduce the discussion to a conflict of border between Israel and her neighbors. First of all, it is not the truth. The heart of the conflict is not the question of the borders; it is the question of Muslim psychology. . . . Moreover, to present the problem as a conflict between two similar parts is to provide the Arabs with the weapon of a claim that is not theirs. If the discussion with them is truly a political one, then it can be seen from both sides. Then we appear as those who came to a country that was entirely Arab, and we conquered and implanted ourselves as an alien body among them, and we loaded them with refugees and constitute a military danger for them, etc. etc. . . . one can justify this or that side—and such a presentation, sophisticated and political, of the problem is understandable for European minds—at our expense. The Arabs raise claims that make sense to the Western understanding of simple legal dispute. But in reality, who knows better than us that such is not the source of their hostile stand? All those political and social concepts are never theirs. Occupation by force of arms, in their own eyes, in the eyes of Islam, is not all associated with injustice. To the contrary, it constitutes a certificate and demonstration of authentic ownership. The sorrow for the refugees, for the expropriated brothers, has no room in their thinking. Allah expelled, Allah will care. Never has a Muslim politician been moved by such things (unless, indeed, the catastrophe endangered his personal status). If there were no

> refugees and no conquest, they would oppose us just the same. By discussing with them on the basis of Western concepts, we dress savages in a European robe of justice.

Israeli studies of "Arab attitudes"—such as the canonical one by General Harkabi[32]—take no notice of such analyses as this one, which is more magical and racist than anything one is likely to encounter by a Palestinian. But the dehumanization of the Arab, which began with the view that Palestinians were either not there or savages or both, saturates everything in Israeli society. It was not thought too unusual during the 1973 war for the army to issue a booklet (with a preface by General Yona Efrati of the central command) written by the central command's rabbi, Abraham Avidan, containing the following key passage:

> When our forces encounter civilians during the war or in the course of a pursuit or a raid, the encountered civilians may, and by Halachic standards even must be killed, whenever it cannot be ascertained that they are incapable of hitting us back. Under no circumstances should an Arab be trusted, even if he gives the impression of being civilized.[33]

Children's literature is made up of valiant Jews who always end up by killing low, treacherous Arabs, with names like Mastoul (crazy), Bandura (tomato), or Bukra (tomorrow). As a writer for *Ha'aretz* said (September 20, 1974), children's books "deal with our topic: the Arab who murders Jews out of pleasure, and the pure Jewish boy who defeats 'the coward swine!'" Nor are such enthusiastic ideas limited to individual authors who produce books for mass consumption; as I shall show later, these ideas derive more or less logically from the state's institutions themselves, to whose other, benevolent side falls the task of regulating Jewish life humanistically.

There are perfect illustrations of the duality in Weizmann, for whom such matters immediately found their way into policy, action, detailed results. He admires Samuel Pevsner as "a man of great ability, energetic, practical, resourceful and, like his wife, highly educated." One can have no problem with this. Then immediately comes the following, without so much as a transition. "For such people, going to Palestine was in effect going into a social wilderness—which is something to be remembered by those who, turning to Palestine today, find in it intellectual, cultural and social resources not inferior to those of the Western world."[34] Zionism was all foregrounding; everything else was background, and it had to be subdued, suppressed, lowered in order that the foreground of cultural achievement could appear as "civilizing pioneer work."[35] Above all, the native Arab had to be seen as an irremediable opposite, something like a combination of savage and superhuman, at any rate a being with whom it is impossible (and useless) to come to terms.

> The Arab is a very subtle debator and controversialist—much more so than the average educated European—and until one has acquired the technique one is at a great disadvantage. In particular, the Arab has an immense talent for expressing views diametrically opposed to yours with such exquisite and roundabout politeness that you believe him to be in complete agreement with you, and ready to join hands with you at once. Conversation and negotiations with Arabs are not unlike chasing a mirage in the desert: full of promise and good to look at, but likely to lead to death by thirst.
>
> A direct question is dangerous: it provokes in the Arab a skillful withdrawal and a complete change of subject. The problem must be approached by winding lanes, and it takes an interminable time to reach the kernel of the subject.[36]

On another occasion, he recounts an experience which in effect was the germ of Tel Aviv, whose importance as a Jewish center derives in great measure from its having neutralized the adjacent (and much older) Arab town of Jaffa. In what Weizmann tells the reader, however, there is only the slightest allusion to the fact of Arab life already existing there, on what was to be the adjacent future site of Tel Aviv. What matters is the production of a Jewish presence, whose value appears to be more or less self-evident.

> I was staying in Jaffa when Ruppin called on me, and took me out for a walk over the dunes to the north of the town. When we had got well out into the sands—I remember that it came over our ankles—he stopped, and said, very solemnly: "Here we shall create a Jewish city!" I looked at him with some dismay. Why should

> people come to live out in this wilderness where nothing would grow? I began to ply him with technical questions, and he answered me carefully and exactly. Technically, he said, everything is possible. Though in the first years communications with the new settlement would be difficult, the inhabitants would soon become self-supporting and self-sufficient. The Jews of Jaffa would move into the new, modern city, and the Jewish colonies of the neighborhood would have a concentrated market for their products. The Gymnasium would stand at the center, and would attract a great many students from other parts of Palestine and from Jews abroad, who would want their children to be educated in a Jewish high school in a Jewish city.
>
> Thus it was Ruppin who had the first vision of Tel Aviv, which was destined to outstrip, in size and in economic importance, the ancient town of Jaffa, and to become one of the metropolitan centers of the eastern Mediterranean. . . .[37]

In time, of course, the preeminence of Tel Aviv was to be buttressed by the military capture of Jaffa. The visionary project later turned into the first step of a military conquest, the idea of a colony being later fleshed out in the actual appearance of a colony, of colonizers, and of the colonized.

Weizmann and Ruppin, it is true, spoke and acted with the passionate idealism of pioneers; they also were speaking and acting with the authority of Westerners surveying fundamentally retarded non-Western territory and natives, planning the future *for them.* Weizmann himself did not just think that as a European he was better equipped to decide for the natives what their best interests were (e.g., that Jaffa *ought to be* outstripped by a modern Jewish city), he also believed he "understood" the Arab *as he really was.* In saying that the Arab's "immense talent" was "in fact" for never telling the truth, he said what other Europeans had observed about non-European natives elsewhere, for whom, like the Zionists, the problem was controlling a large native majority with a comparative handful of intrepid pioneers:

> It may well be asked how it is that we are able to control, with absurdly inadequate forces, races so virile and capable, with such mental and physical endowments. The reply is, I think, that there

> are two flaws to be found:—the mental and moral equipment of the average African. . . . I say that inherent lack of honesty is the first great flaw. . . . Comparatively rarely can one African depend upon another keeping his word. . . . Except in very rare instances it is a regrettable fact that this defect is enlarged rather than diminished by contact with European civilization. The second is lack of mental initiative. . . . Unless impelled from the outside the native seldom branches out from a recognized groove and this mental lethargy is characteristic of his mind.[38]

This is C. L. Temple's *Native Races and Their Rulers* (1918); its author was an assistant to Frederick Lugard in governing Nigeria and, like Weizmann, he was less a proto-Nazi racist than a liberal Fabian in his outlook.

For Temple as for Weizmann, the realities were that natives belonged to a stationary, stagnant culture. Incapable therefore of appreciating the land they lived on, they had to be prodded, perhaps even dislocated by the initiatives of an advanced European culture. Now certainly Weizmann had the additional rationalizations behind him of reconstituting a Jewish state, saving Jews from anti-Semitism, and so on. But so far as the natives were concerned, it could not have mattered initially whether the Europeans they faced in the colony were Englishmen or European Jews. Then too, as far as the Zionist in Palestine or the Britisher in Africa was concerned, he was realistic, he saw facts and dealt with them, he knew the value of truth. Notwithstanding the "fact" of long residence on a native territory, the non-European was always in retreat from truth. European vision meant the capacity for seeing not only what was there, but what *could* be there: hence the Weizmann-Ruppin exchange about Jaffa and Tel Aviv. The specific temptation before the Zionist in Palestine was to believe—and plan for—the possibility that the Arab natives would not *really* be there, which was doubtless a proven eventuality (a) when the natives would not acknowledge Jewish sovereignty over Palestine and (b) when after 1948 they became legal outsiders on their land.

But the success of Zionism did not derive exclusively from its bold outlining of a future state, or from its ability to see the natives for the negligible quantities they were or might become. Rather, I think, Zionism's effectiveness in making its way against Arab Palestinian resistance lay *in its being a policy of detail,* not simply a general colonial vision. Thus Palestine was not only the Promised Land, a concept as elusive and as abstract as any that one could encounter. It was a specific territory with specific characteristics, that was surveyed down to the last millimeter, settled on, planned for, built on, and so forth, *in detail.* From the beginning of the Zionist colonization this was something the Arabs had no answer to, no equally detailed counterproposal. They assumed, perhaps rightly, that since they lived on the land and legally owned it, it was therefore theirs. They did not understand that what they were encountering was a discipline of detail—indeed a very culture of discipline by detail—by which a hitherto imaginary realm could be constructed on Palestine, inch by inch and step by step, "another acre, another goat," so Weizmann once said. The Palestinian Arabs always opposed a *general* policy on general principles: Zionism, they said, was foreign colonialism (which strictly speaking it was, as the early Zionists admitted), it was unfair to the natives (as some early Zionists, like Ahad Ha'am, also admitted), and it was doomed to die of its various theoretical weaknesses. Even to this day the Palestinian political position generally clusters around these negatives, and still does not sufficiently try to meet the detail of Zionist enterprise; today there are, for example, seventy-seven "illegal" Zionist colonies on the West Bank and Israel has confiscated about 27 percent of the West Bank's Arab-owned land, yet the Palestinians seem virtually powerless physically to stop the growth or "thickening" of this new Israeli colonization.

The Palestinians have not understood that Zionism has been much more than an unfair colonialist master against whom one could appeal to all sorts of higher courts, without any avail. They have not understood the Zionist challenge as a policy of detail, of institutions, of organization, by which people (to this day) enter territory illegally, build houses on it, settle there, and call the land their own—with the whole world condemning them. The force of that drive to settle, in a sense *to produce,* a Jewish land can be glimpsed in a document that Weizmann says "seemed to have anticipated the shape of things to come" as indeed it did. This was an "Outline of Program for the Jewish Resettlement of Palestine in

Accordance with the Aspirations of the Zionist Movement"; it appeared in early 1917, and it is worth quoting from:

> The Suzerain Government [that is, any government, Allied or otherwise, in command of the territory] shall sanction a formation of a Jewish company for the colonization of Palestine by Jews. The said Company shall be under the direct protection of the Suzerain Government [that is, whatever went on in Palestine should be legitimized not by the natives but by some outside force]. The objects of the Company shall be: a) to support and foster the existing Jewish settlement in Palestine in every possible way; b) to aid, support and encourage Jews from other countries who are desirous of and suitable for settling in Palestine by organizing immigration, by providing information, and by every other form of material and moral assistance. The powers of the Company shall be such as will enable it to develop the country in every way, agricultural, cultural, commercial and industrial, and shall include full powers of land purchase and development, and especially facilities for the acquisition of the Crown lands, building rights for roads, railway harbors, power to establish shipping companies for the transport of goods and passengers to and from Palestine, and for every other power found necessary for the opening of the country.[39]

Underlying this extraordinary passage is a vision of a matrix of organizations whose functioning duplicates that of an army. For it is an army that "opens" a country to settlement, that organizes settlements in foreign territory, that aids and develops "in every possible way" such matters as immigration, shipping, and supply, that above all turns mere citizens into "suitable" disciplined agents whose job it is to be on the land and to invest it with their structures, organization, and institutions.[40] Just as an army assimilates ordinary citizens to its purposes—by dressing them in uniforms, by exercising them in tactics and maneuvers, by disciplining everyone to its purposes—so too did Zionism dress the Jewish colonists in the system of Jewish labor and Jewish land, whose uniform required that only Jews were acceptable. The power of the Zionist army did not reside in its leaders, nor in the arms it collected for its conquests and defense, but rather in the functioning of a whole system, a series of positions taken and held, as Weizmann says, in agriculture, culture, commerce, and industry. In short, Zionism's "company" was the translation of a theory and a vision into a set of instruments for holding and developing a Jewish colonial territory right in the middle of an indifferently surveyed and developed Arab territory.

The fascinating history of Zionist colonial apparatus, its "company," cannot long detain us here, but at least some things about its workings need to be noted. The Second Zionist Congress meeting in Basel, Switzerland (August 1898) created the Jewish Colonial Trust Limited, a subsidiary of which was founded in Jaffa in 1903 and called the Anglo-Palestine Company. Thus began an agency whose role in the transformation of Palestine was extraordinarily crucial. Out of the Colonial Trust in 1901 came the Jewish National Fund (JNF), empowered to buy land and hold it in trust for "the Jewish people"; the wording of the original proposal was that the JNF would be "a trust for the Jewish people, which . . . can be used exclusively for the purchase of land in Palestine and Syria." The JNF was always under the control of the World Zionist Organization, and in 1905 the first land purchases were made.

From its inception as a functioning body the JNF existed either to develop, buy, or lease land—only for Jews. As Walter Lehn convincingly shows (in a major piece of research on the JNF, on which I have relied for the details I mention here),[41] the Zionist goal was to acquire land in order to put settlers on it; thus in 1920, after the Palestinian Land Development Company had been founded as an agency of the JNF, a Palestine Foundation Fund was created to organize immigration and colonization. At the same time, emphasis was placed institutionally on acquiring and holding lands for "the Jewish people." This designation made it certain that a Zionist state would be unlike any other in that it was not to be the state of its citizens, but rather the state of a whole people most of which was in Diaspora. Aside from making the non-Jewish people of the state into second-class citizens, it made the Zionist organizations, and later the state, retain a large extraterritorial power in addition to the vital territorial possessions over which the state was to have sovereignty. Even the land acquired by the JNF was—as John Hope Simpson said in 1930—"extraterritorialized. It ceases to be land from which the Arab can gain any advantage either now or at any time in the future." There was no corresponding Arab effort to institutionalize Arab landholding in Palestine, no thought that it might be necessary to create an organization for holding lands "in perpetuity" for the "Arab people," above all, no informational, money-raising, lobbying work done—as the Zionists did in Europe and the United States to expand "Jewish" territory and, paradoxically, give it a Jewish presence and an international, almost metaphysical status as well. The Arabs mistakenly thought that owning the land and being on it were enough.

Even with all this sophisticated and farsighted effort, the JNF acquired only 936,000 dunams* of land in the almost half-century of its existence before Israel appeared as a state; the total land area of mandate Palestine was 26,323,000 dunams. Together with the small amount of land held by private Jewish owners, Zionist landholding in Palestine at the end of 1947 was 1,734,000 dunams, that is, 6.59 percent of the total area. After 1940, when the mandatory authority restricted Jewish land ownership to specific zones inside Palestine, there continued to be illegal buying (and selling) within the 65 percent of the total area restricted to Arabs. Thus when the partition plan was announced in 1947 it included land held illegally by Jews, which was incorporated as a *fait accompli* inside the borders of the Jewish state. And after Israel announced its statehood, an impressive series of laws legally assimilated huge tracts of Arab land (whose proprietors had become refugees, and were pronounced "absentee landlords" in order to expropriate their lands and prevent their return under any circumstances) to the JNF. The process of land alienation (from the Arab standpoint) had been completed.

The ideological, profoundly political meaning of the "company's" territorial achievements illuminates the post-1967 controversy over the fate of Arab land occupied by Israel. A large segment of the Israeli population seems to believe that Arab land can be converted into Jewish land (a) because the land had once been Jewish two millennia ago (a part of Eretz Israel) and (b) because there exists in the JNF a method for legally metamorphosing "neglected" land into the property of the Jewish people.[42] Once Jewish settlements are built and peopled, and once they are hooked into the state network, they

*A dunam is roughly a quarter of an acre.

become properly extraterritorial, emphatically Jewish, and non-Arab. To this new land is added as well a strategic rationale, that it is necessary for Israeli security. But were these things simply a matter of internal Israeli concern, and were they sophistic arguments intended only to appeal to an Israeli constituency, they might be analyzed dispassionately as being no more than curious. The fact is, however, that they impinge—as they always have—on the Arab residents of the territories, and then they have a distinct cutting edge to them. Both in theory and in practice their effectiveness lies in how they Judaize territory coterminously with de-Arabizing it.

There is privileged evidence of this fact, I think, in what Joseph Weitz had to say. From 1932 on, Weitz was the director of the Jewish National Land Fund; in 1965 his diaries and papers, *My Diary, and Letters to the Children,* were published in Israel. On December 19, 1940, he wrote:

> . . . after the [Second World] war the question of the land of Israel and the question of the Jews would be raised beyond the framework of "development"; amongst ourselves. *It must be clear that there is no room for both peoples in this country.* No "development" will bring us closer to our aim, to be an independent people in this small country. If the Arabs leave the country, it will be broad and wide-open for us. And if the Arabs stay, the country will remain narrow and miserable. When the War is over and the English have won, and when the judges sit on the throne of Law, our people must bring their petitions and their claims before them; and the only solution is Eretz Israel, or at least Western Eretz Israel, *without Arabs. There is no room for compromise on this point!* The Zionist enterprise so far, in terms of preparing the ground and paving the way for the creation of the Hebrew State in the land of Israel, has been fine and good in its own time, and could do with "land-buying"—but this will not bring about the State of Israel; that must come all at once, in the manner of a Salvation (this is the secret of the Messianic idea); and there is no way besides transferring the Arabs from here to the neighboring countries, *to transfer them all;* except maybe for Bethlehem, Nazareth and Old Jerusalem, *we must not leave a single village, not a single tribe.* And the transfer must be directed to Iraq, to Syria, and even to Transjordan. For that purpose we'll find money, and a lot of money. And only with such a transfer will the country be able to absorb mil-

> lions of our brothers, and the Jewish question shall be solved, once and for all. There is no other way out. [Emphases added][43]

These are not only prophetic remarks about what was going to happen; they are also policy statements, in which Weitz spoke with the voice of the Zionist consensus. There were literally hundreds of such statements made by Zionists, beginning with Herzl, and when "salvation" came it was with those ideas in mind that the conquest of Palestine, and the eviction of its Arabs, was carried out. A great deal has been written about the turmoil in Palestine from the end of World War II until the end of 1948. Despite the complexities of what may or may not have taken place, Weitz's thoughts furnish a beam of light shining through those events, pointing to a Jewish state with most of the original Arab inhabitants turned into refugees. It is true that such major events as the birth of a new state, which came about as the result of an almost unimaginably complex, many-sided struggle and a full-scale war, cannot be easily reduced to simple formulation. I have no wish to do this, but neither do I wish to evade the outcome of struggle, or the determining elements that went into the struggle, or even the policies produced in Israel ever since. The fact that matters for the Palestinian—and for the Zionist—is that a territory once full of Arabs emerged from a war (a) essentially emptied all of its original residents and (b) made impossible for Palestinians to return to. Both the ideological and organizational preparations for the Zionist efforts to win Palestine, as well as the military strategy adopted, envisioned taking over territory, and filling it with new inhabitants. Thus the Dalet Plan, as it has been described by the Zionist historians Jon and David Kimche, was "to capture strategic heights dominating the most likely lines of advance of the invading Arab armies, and to fill in the vacuum left by the departing British forces in such a way as to create a contiguous Jewish-held area extending from the north to the south."[44] In places like Galilee, the coastal area from Jaffa to Acre, parts of Jerusalem, the towns of Lydda and Ramla, to say nothing of the Arab parts of Haifa, the Zionists were not only taking over British positions; they were also filling in space lived in by Arab residents who were, in Weitz's word, being "transferred."

Against the frequently mentioned propositions—that Palestinians left because they were ordered to by their leaders, that the invading Arab armies were an unwarranted response to Israel's declaration of independence in May 1948—I must say categorically that *no one has produced any evidence of such orders sufficient to produce so vast and final an exodus.*[45] In other words, if we wish to understand why 780,000 Palestinians left in 1948, we must shift our sight to take in more than the immediate events of 1948; rather, we must see the exodus as being produced by a relative lack of Palestinian political, organizational response to Zionist effectiveness and, along with that, a psychological mood of failure and terror. Certainly atrocities, such as the Deir Yassin massacre of 250 Arab civilians by Menachem Begin and his Irgun terrorists in April 1948, had their effect. But for all its horror, even Deir Yassin was one of many such massacres which began in the immediate post–World War I period and which produced conscious Zionist equivalents of American Indian-killers.[46] What probably counted more has been the machinery for keeping the unarmed civilian Palestinians away, once they had moved (in most cases) to avoid the brutalities of war. Before as well as after they left there were specific Zionist instrumentalities for, in effect, obliterating their presence. I have already cited Weitz in 1940. Here he is on May 18, 1948, narrating a conversation with Moshe Shertok (later Sharett) of the Foreign Ministry:

> Transfer—*post factum;* should we do something so as to transform the exodus of the Arabs from the country into a fact, so that they return no more? . . . His [Shertok's] answer: he blesses any initiative in this matter. His opinion is also that we must act in such a way as to transform the exodus of the Arabs into an established fact.[47]

Later that year, Weitz visited an evacuated Arab village. He reflected as follows:

> I went to visit the village of Mu'ar. Three tractors are completing its destruction. I was surprised; nothing in me moved at the sight of the destruction. No regret and no hate, as though this was the way the world goes. So we want to feel good in this world, and not in some world to come. We simply want to live, and the inhabitants of those mud-houses did not want us to exist here. They not only aspire to

> dominate us, they also wanted to exterminate us. And what is interesting—this is the opinion of all our boys, from one end to the other.[48]

He describes something that took place everywhere in Palestine but he seems totally unable to take in the fact that the human lives—very modest and humble ones, it is true—actually lived in that wretched village meant something to the people whose lives they were. Weitz does not attempt to deny the villagers' reality; he simply admits that their destruction means only that "we" can now live there. He is completely untroubled by the thought that to the native Palestinians he, Weitz, is only a foreigner come to displace them, or that it is no more than natural to oppose such a prospect. Instead, Weitz and "the boys" take the position that the Palestinians wanted to "exterminate" them—and this therefore licenses the destruction of houses and villages. After several decades of treating the Arabs as if they were not there at all, Zionism came fully into its own by actively destroying as many Arab traces as it could. From a nonentity in theory to a nonentity in legal fact, the Palestinian Arab lived through the terrible modulation from one sorry condition to the other, fully able to witness, but not effectively to communicate, his or her own civil extinction in Palestine.

First he was an inconsequential native; then he became an absent one; then inside Israel after 1948 he acquired the juridical status of a less real person than any individual person belonging to the "Jewish people," whether that person was present in Israel or not. The ones who left the country in terror became "refugees," an abstraction faithfully taken account of in annual United Nations resolutions calling upon Israel—as Israel had promised—to take them back, or compensate them for their losses. The list of human indignities and, by any impartial standard, the record of immoral subjugation practiced by Israel against the Palestinian Arab remnant is bloodcurdling, particularly if counterpointed with that record one hears the chorus of praise to Israeli democracy. As if to pay that wretched 120,000 (now about 650,000) for its temerity in staying where it did not belong, Israel took over the Emergency Defense Regulations, used by the British to handle Jews and Arabs during the mandate period from 1922 to 1948. The regulations had been a justifiably favorite target of Zionist political agitation, but after 1948 they were used, *unchanged,* by Israel against the Arabs.

For example, in those parts of Israel that still retain an Arab majority, an anachronistic but no less effective and detailed policy of "Judaization" goes on apace. Thus just as Ruppin and Weizmann in the early days foresaw a Tel Aviv to "outstrip" Arab Jaffa, the Israeli government of today creates a new Jewish Nazareth to outstrip the old Arab town. Here is the project described by an Israeli in 1975:

> Upper Nazareth, which was created some fifteen years ago, "in order to create a counterweight to the Arab Nazareth," constitutes a cornerstone of the "Judaization of the Galilee" policy. Upper Nazareth was erected upon the hills surrounding Nazareth as a security belt surrounding it almost on all sides. It was built upon thousands of acres of lands which were expropriated high-handedly, purely and simply by force, from the Arab settlements, particularly Nazareth and Rana. The very choice of the name "upper" Nazareth, while the stress is upon *upper,* is an indicator of the attitude of the authorities, which give the new town special privileges according to their policy of discrimination and lack of attention regarding the city of Nazareth, which is, in their eyes, at the very bottom of the ladder. The visitor to Nazareth can acknowledge with his own eyes the neglect and lack of development of the city, and if from there he goes "up" to upper Nazareth, he will see over there the new buildings, the wide streets, the public lights, the steps, the many-storied buildings, the industrial and artisan enterprises, and he will be able to perceive the contrast: development up there and lack of care down there; constant government building up there, and no construction whatever down there. Since 1966 the [Israeli] Ministry of Housing has not built a single unit of habitation in old Nazareth. [Yoseph Elgazi in *Zo Hadareh,* July 30, 1975]

The drama of a ruling minority is vividly enacted in Nazareth. With all its advantages, upper—that is, Jewish—Nazareth contains 16,000 residents; below it, the Arab city has a population of 45,000. Clearly the Jewish city benefits from the network of resources for Jews. Non-Jews are surgically excluded. The rift between them and the Jews is intended by Zionism to signify a state of absolute difference between the two groups, not merely one of degree. If every Jew in Israel represents "the whole Jewish people"—which is a population made up not only of the Jews in Israel, but also of generations of Jews who existed in the past (of whom the present Israelis are the remnant) and those who exist in the future, as well as those who live elsewhere—the non-Jew in Israel represents a permanent banishment from his as well as all *other* past, present, and future benefits in Palestine. The non-Jew lives a meager existence in villages without libraries, youth centers, theaters, cultural centers; most Arab villages, according to the Arab mayor of Nazareth, who speaks with the unique authority of a non-Jew in Israel, lack electricity, telephone communications, health centers; none has any sewage systems, except Nazareth itself, which is only partly serviced by one; none has paved roads or streets. For whereas the Jew is entitled to the maximum, the non-Jew is given a bare minimum. Out of a total work force of 80,000 Arab workers, 60,000 work in Jewish enterprises. "These workers regard their town and villages as nothing but places of residence. Their only prosperous 'industry' is the creation and supply of manpower."[49] Manpower without political significance, without a territorial base, without cultural continuity; for the non-Jew in Israel, if he dared to remain after the Jewish state appeared in 1948, there was only the meager subsistence of being *there,* almost powerless except to reproduce himself and his misery more or less endlessly.

Until 1966, the Arab citizens of Israel were ruled by a military government exclusively in existence to control, bend, manipulate, terrorize, tamper with every facet of Arab life from birth virtually to death. After 1966, the situation is scarcely better, as an unstoppable series of popular riots and demonstrations testify; the Emergency Defense Regulations were used to expropriate thousands of acres of Arab lands, either by declaring Arab property to be in a security zone or by ruling lands to be absentee property (even if, in many cases, the absentees were present—a legal fiction of Kafkaesque subtlety). Any Palestinian can tell you the meaning of the Absentee's Property Law of 1950, the Land Acquitision Law of 1953, the Law for the Requisitioning of Property in Time of Emergency (1949), the Prescription Law of 1958. Moreover, Arabs were and are forbidden to travel freely, or to lease land from Jews, or ever to speak, agitate, be educated freely. There were instances when curfews were suddenly imposed on villages and then, when it was manifestly impossible for the working people to know of the curfew, the "guilty" peasants were summarily shot; the most wantonly brutal episode took place at Kafr Kassim in October 1956, during which 49 unarmed peasants were shot by the frontier guard, a particularly efficient section of the Israeli army. After a certain amount of scandal the officer in charge of the operation was brought to trial, found guilty, and then punished with a fine of one pilaster (less than one cent).

Since occupying the West Bank and Gaza in 1967, Israel has acquired approximately a million more Arab subjects. Its record has been no better, but this has not been surprising.[50] Indeed, the best introduction to what has been taking place in the Occupied Territories is the testimony of Israeli Arabs who suffered through Israeli legal brutality before 1967. See, for instance, Sabri Jiryis's *The Arabs in Israel* or Fouzi al-Asmar's *To Be an Arab in Israel* or Elia T. Zwrayk's *The Palestinians in Israel: A Study in Internal Colonialism.* Israel's political goal has been to keep the Arabs pacified, never capable of preventing their continued domination by Israel. Whenever a nationalist leader gains a little stature, he is either deported, imprisoned (without trial), or he disappears; Arab houses (approximately 17,000) are blown up by the army to make examples of nationalist offenders; censorship *on everything written by or about Arabs* prevails; every Arab is directly subject to military regulations. In order to disguise repression and to keep it from disturbing the tranquillity of Israeli consciousness, a corps of Arab experts—Israeli Jews who understand the Arab "mentality"—has grown up. One of them, Amnon Lin, wrote in 1968 that "the people trusted us and gave us a freedom of action that has not been enjoyed by any other group in the country, in any field." Consequently,

> [o]ver time we have attained a unique position in the state as experts, and no one dares to challenge our opinions or our actions. We are represented in every department of government, in the Histadrut and in the political parties; every department and office has its "Arabists" who alone act for their minister among the Arabs.[51]

This quasi government interprets, and rules the Arabs behind a facade of privileged expertise. When visiting liberals wish to find out about "the Arabs," they are given a suitably cosmetic picture.[52] Meanwhile, of course, Israeli settlements on occupied territories multiply (over ninety of them since 1967); the logic of colonization after 1967 follows the same pattern, resulting in the same displacements of Arabs as before 1948.[53]

There are Zionism and Israel for Jews, and Zionism and Israel for non-Jews. Zionism has drawn a sharp line between Jew and non-Jew; Israel built a whole system for keeping them apart, including the much admired (but completely apartheid) kibbutzim, to which no Arab has ever belonged. In effect, the Arabs are ruled by a separate government premised on the impossibility of isonomic rule for both Jews and non-Jews. Out of this radical notion it became natural for the Arab Gulag Archipelago to develop its own life, to create its own precision, its own detail. Uri Avneri put it this way to the Knesset:

> A complete government . . . was created in the Arab sector, a secret government, unsanctioned by law . . . whose members and methods are not known . . . to anyone. Its agents are scattered among the ministries of government, from the Israel Lands Administration to the ministry of education and the ministry of religions. It makes fateful decisions affecting [Arab] lives in unknown places without documents and communicates them in secret conversations or over the telephone. This is the way decisions are made about who goes to the teachers' seminar, or who will obtain a tractor, or who will be appointed to a government post, or who will receive financial subsidies, or who will be elected to the Knesset, or who will be elected to the local council—if there is one—and so on for a thousand and one reasons.[54]

But from time to time there have been inadvertent insights into government for Arabs in Israel given to watchful observers. The most unguarded example was a secret report by Israel Koenig, northern district (Galilee) commissioner of the ministry, written for the then Prime Minister Yitzhak Rabin on "handling the Arabs in Israel." (The full text was subsequently leaked to *Al-Hamishmar* on September 7, 1976.) Its contents make chilling reading, but they fulfill the assumptions of Zionism toward its victims, the non-Jews. Koenig frankly admits that Arabs present a demographic problem since unlike Jews, whose natural increase is 1.5 percent annually, the Arabs increase at a yearly rate of 5.9 percent. Moreover, he assumes that it is national policy for the Arabs to be kept inferior, although they may be naturally susceptible to nationalist restlessness. The main thing, however, is to make sure that in areas like Galilee the density of the Arab population, and consequently its potential for trouble, be reduced, contained, weakened. Therefore, he suggested that it is necessary to

> expand and deepen Jewish settlement in areas where the contiguity of the Arab population is prominent, and where they number considerably more than the Jewish population; examine the possibility of diluting existing Arab population concentrations. Special attention must be paid to border areas in the country's northwest and to the Nazareth region. The approach and exigency of performance have to deviate from the routine that has been adopted so far. Concurrently, the state law has to be enforced so as to limit "breaking of new ground" by Arab settlements in various areas of the country.

The quasi-military strategy of these suggestions is very near the surface. What we must also remark is Koenig's unquestioning view of the Zionist imperatives he is trying to implement. Nothing in his report intimates any qualms about the plainly racial end his suggestions promote; nor does he doubt that what he says is thoroughly consistent with the history of Zionist policy toward those non-Jews who have had the bad luck to be on Jewish territory, albeit in disquietingly large numbers. He goes on to argue—logically—that any Arab leaders who appear to cause trouble should be replaced, that the government should set about to "create" (the word has an almost theological tone very much in keeping with Jewish policy toward Arabs) "new [Arab] figures of high intellectual standard, figures who are equitable and charismatic," and completely acceptable to the Israeli rulers. Moreover, in "dissipating" the restless nationalist leaders, whose main sin seems to be that they encourage other natives to chafe at their enforced inferiority, the government should form a "special team . . . to examine the personal habits of . . . leaders and other negative people and this information should be made available to the electorate."

Not content then with "diluting" and manipulating the Arab citizens of Israel, Koenig goes on to suggest ways for economically "neutralizing" and "encumbering" them. Very little of this can be effective, however, unless there were some method of somehow checkmating the "large population of frustrated intelligentsia forced by a mental need to seek relief. Expressions of this are directed against the Israeli establishment of the state." Koenig appeared to think it natural enough for Arabs to be kept frustrated, for in reading his suggestions there is little to remind one that Arabs are people, or that his report was written not about Jews by a Nazi during World War II, but in 1976 by a Jew about his Arab co-citizens. The master stroke of Koenig's plan comes when he discusses the social engineering required to use the Arab's backward "Levantine character" against itself. Since Arabs in Israel are a disadvantaged community, this reality must be enhanced as follows:

> a) The reception criteria for Arab university students should be the same as for Jewish students and this must also apply to the granting of scholarships.
>
> A meticulous implementation of these rules will produce a natural selection [the Darwinian terminology speaks eloquently for itself] and will considerably reduce the number of Arab students. Accordingly, the number of low-standard graduates will also decrease, a fact that will facilitate their absorption in work after studies [the plan here is to make certain that young Arabs would easily be assimilated into menial jobs, thus ensuring their intellectual emasculation].
>
> b) Encourage the channeling of students into technical professions, the physical and natural sciences. These studies leave less time for dabbling in nationalism and the dropout rate is higher. [Koenig's ideas about the incompatibility between science and human values go C. P. Snow one better. Surely this is a sinister instance of the use of science as political punishment; it is new even to the history of colonialism.]
>
> c) Make trips abroad for studies easier, while making the return and employment more difficult—this policy is apt to encourage their emigration.
>
> d) Adopt tough measures at all levels against various agitators among college and university students.
>
> e) Prepare absorption possibilities in advance for the better part

> of the graduates, according to their qualifications. This policy can be implemented thanks to the time available (a number of years) in which the authorities may plan their steps.

Were such ideas to have been formulated by Stalinists or Orwellian socialists or even Arab nationalists, the liberal outcry would be deafening. Koenig's suggestions, however, seem universally justified by the logic of events pitting a small, valiant Western population of Jews against a vast and amorphous, metastasizing and ruinously mindless Arab population. Nothing in Koenig's report conflicts with the basic dichotomy in Zionism, that is, benevolence toward Jews and an essential but paternalistic hostility toward Arabs. Moreover, Koenig himself writes from the standpoint of an ideologist or theorist as well as from a position of authority and power within Israeli society. As a ruler of Arabs in Israel, Koenig expresses both an official attention to the well-being of Jews, whose interests he maintains and protects, and a paternalistic, managerial dominance over inferior natives. His position is therefore consecrated by the institutions of the Jewish state; licensed by them, he thinks in terms of a maximum future for Jews and a minimal one for non-Jews. All of these notions are perfectly delivered in the following paragraph from his report:

> Law enforcement in a country with a developing society like that of Israel is a problem to be solved with flexibility, care and much wisdom. At the same time, however, the administrative and executive authority in the Arab sector must be aware of the existence of the law and its enforcement so as to avoid erosion.[55]

Between Weizmann and Koenig there exists an intervening period of several decades. What was visionary projection for the former became for the latter a context of actual law. From Weizmann's epoch to Koenig's, Zionism for the native Arabs in Palestine had been converted from an advancing encroachment upon their lives to a settled reality—a nation-state—enclosing them within it. For Jews after 1948, Israel not only realized their political and spiritual hopes, it continued to be a beacon of opportunity guiding those of them still living in Diaspora, and keeping those who lived in former Palestine on the frontier of Jewish development and self-realization. For the Arab Palestinians, Israel meant one essentially hostile fact and several unpleasant corollaries. After 1948 every Palestinian disappeared nationally and legally. Some Palestinians reappeared juridically as "non-Jews" in Israel; those who left become "refugees" and later some of those acquired new Arab, European, or American identities. No Palestinian, however, lost his "old" Palestinian identity. Out of such legal fictions as the nonexistent Palestinian in Israel and elsewhere, however, the Palestinian has finally emerged—and with a considerable amount of international attention prepared at last to take critical notice of Zionist theory and praxis.

The outcry in the West after the 1975 "Zionism is racism" resolution was passed in the United Nations was doubtless a genuine one. Israel's Jewish achievements—or rather its achievements on behalf of European Jews, less so for the Sephardic (Oriental) Jewish majority—stand before the Western world; by most standards they are considerable achievements, and it is right that they not sloppily be tarnished with the sweeping rhetorical denunciation associated with "racism." For the Palestinian Arab who has lived through and who has now studied the procedures of Zionism toward him and his land, the predicament is complicated, but not finally unclear. He knows that the Law of Return allowing a Jew immediate entry into Israel just as exactly prevents him from returning to his home; he also knows that Israeli raids killed thousands of civilians, all on the acceptable pretext of fighting terrorism,[56] but in reality because Palestinians as a race have become synonymous with unregenerate, essentially unmotivated terrorism; he understands, without perhaps being able to master, the intellectual process by which his violated humanity has been transmuted, unheard and unseen, into praise for the ideology that has all but destroyed him. *Racism* is too vague a term: Zionism is Zionism. For the Arab Palestinian, this tautology has a sense that is perfectly congruent with, but exactly the opposite of, what it says to Jews.

Burdened with a military budget draining off 35 percent of its Gross National Product, isolated except for its few and increasingly critical Atlantic friends, beset with social, political, and ideological issues it can deal with only by retreating from them entirely, Israel today faces a grim future. President Sadat's mission of peace has at last occasioned the semblance of opposition to Begin's fossilized theological madness, but it is doubtful whether in the absence of a conceptual, much less institutional, apparatus for coming humanely to terms with the Palestinian actualities, any decisive change will come from that quarter. The powerfully influential American Jewish community still imposes its money and its reductive view of things on the Israeli will. Then, too, one must not overlook the even more redoubtable U.S. defense establishment, more than a match for the business sector's hunger over oil-bloated Arab markets, as it continues to heap advanced weapons on an Israel and now an Egypt primed daily to combat "radicalism," the Soviet Union, or any other of the United States' geopolitical bugbears. The net effect in unrestrained Israeli militarism is accurately indicated by a *Ha'aretz* article (March 24, 1978) celebrating the Lebanese adventure in the following terms:

> What has happened last week, has shown to everyone who has eyes in his head, that the Israeli defense force is today an American Army both in the quantity and quality of its equipment: the rifles, the troop-carriers, the F-15's, and even the KFIR planes with their American motors, are a testimony that will convince everybody.

But even this paean to what its author calls Israel's "overflowing military equipment" is equaled in pernicious influence by Western and Israeli intellectuals who have continued to celebrate Israel and Zionism unblinkingly for thirty years. They have perfectly played the role of Gramsci's "experts in legitimation," dishonest and irrational despite their protestations on behalf of wisdom and humanity. Check the disgraceful record and you will find only a small handful—among them Noam Chomsky, Israel Shahak, I. F. Stone, Elmer Berger, Judah Magnes—who have tried to see what Zionism did to the Palestinians not just once in 1948, but over the years. It is one of the most frightening cultural episodes of the century, this almost total silence about Zionism's doctrines for and treatment of the native Palestinians. Any self-respecting intellectual is willing today to say something about human rights abuses in Argentina, Chile, or South Africa, yet when irrefutable evidence of Israeli preventive detention, torture, population transfer, and deportation of Palestinian Arabs is presented, literally nothing is said. The merest assurances that democracy is being respected in Israel are enough to impress a Daniel Moynihan or a Saul Bellow, for instance, that all is well on the moral front. But perhaps the true extent of this state-worship can only be appreciated when one reads of a meeting held in 1962 between Martin Buber and Avraham Aderet, published in the December 1974 issue of *Petahim*, an Israeli religious quarterly. Aderet is extolling the army as a character-building experience for young men, and uses as an instance an episode during the 1956 war with Egypt when an officer ordered a group of soldiers simply to kill "any Egyptian prisoners of war . . . who were in our hands." A number of volunteers then step forward and the prisoners are duly shot, although one of the volunteers avers that "he closed his eyes when he shot." At this point Aderet says: "There is no doubt that this test can bring a confusion to every man of conscience and of experience of life, and even more so to young boys who stand at the beginning of their lives. The bad thing which happened is not the confusions in which those young men were during the time of the deed, but in the internal undermining which took place in them afterwards." To this edifying interpretation, Buber—moral philosopher, humane thinker, former binationalist—can say only: "This is a great and true story, you should write it down." Not one word about the story's horror, or of the situation making it possible.

But just as no Jew in the last hundred years has been untouched by Zionism, so too no Palestinian has been unmarked by it. Yet it must not be forgotten that the Palestinian was not simply a function of Zionism. His life, culture, and politics have their own dynamic and ultimately their own authenticity.

from *The Question of Palestine*

6

Islam as News

(1980)

On November 4, 1979, a group of Iranian students occupied the U.S. Embassy in Teheran. Holding fifty-two U.S. government officials hostage, the students demanded that the United States return Mohammed Reza Shah Pahlevi, whom the CIA had installed in power in 1953, to Teheran for trial. The "hostage crisis," as it came to be known to viewers of prime-time news, lasted four hundred and forty-four days, led to the defeat of Jimmy Carter, the election of Ronald Reagan, the Iran-Contra scandal, and the birth of a cottage industry of think tanks and its so-called terrorist experts who routinely decried the "revival" of the "Islamic threat." In the mainstream media, Islam became synonymous with everything irrational and anti-Western. In one editorial, for example, *The New York Times* discoursed on the contents of the "Persian psyche"; the *Atlanta Journal Constitution* declared that "new barbarians" held power in Iran. Exceptional was the reporter or commentator who viewed the events in Iran in the greater context of U.S. involvement in the overthrow of Mossedegh and the brutality of the U.S. and Israeli-trained Iranian secret police known as SAVAK.

The third and final book of the *Orientalism* trilogy, *Covering Islam* focuses on Western media's representation of Islam during the period of the "hostage crisis" and after. Islam, Said writes, "has licensed not only patent inaccuracy but also expressions of unrestrained ethnocentrism, cultural and even racial hatred, deep yet paradoxically free-floating hostility."

Fifteen years after the first edition of the book appeared, Said revisited the issue in the introduction to the book's second edition. He found that the media's portrayal of Islam had grown even more exaggerated. "Sensationalism, crude xenophobia, and insensitive belligerence are the order of the day, with results on both sides of the imaginary line between 'us' and 'them' that are extremely unedifying."[1]

In order to make a point about alternative energy sources for Americans, Consolidated Edison of New York (Con Ed) ran a striking television advertisement in the summer of 1980. Film clips of various immediately recognizable OPEC personalities—Yamani, Qaddafi, lesser-known robed Arab figures—alternated with stills as well as clips of other people associated with oil and Islam: Khomeini, Arafat, Hafez al-Assad. None of these figures was mentioned by name, but we were told ominously that "these men" control America's sources of oil. The solemn voice-over in the background made no reference to who "these men" actually are or where they come from, leaving it to be felt that this all-male cast of villains has placed Americans in the grip of an unrestrained sadism. It was enough for "these men" to appear as they have appeared in newspapers and on television for American viewers to feel a combination of anger, resentment, and fear. And it is this combination of feelings that Con Ed instantly aroused and exploited for domestic commercial reasons, just as a year earlier Stuart Eizenstat, President Carter's domestic policy adviser, had urged the president that "with strong steps we [should] mobilize the nation around a real crisis and with a clear enemy—OPEC."

There are two things about the Con Ed commercial that, taken together, form the subject of this book. One, of course, is Islam, or rather the image of Islam in the West generally and in the United States in particular. The other is the use of that image in the West and especially in the United States. As we shall see, these are connected in ways that ultimately reveal as much about the West and the United States as they do, in a far less concrete and interesting way, about Islam. But let us first consider the history of relationships between Islam and the Christian West before we go on to examine the current phase.

From at least the end of the eighteenth century until our own day, modern Occidental reactions to Islam have been dominated by a radically simplified type of thinking that may still be called Orientalist. The general basis of Orientalist thought is an imaginative and yet drastically polarized geography dividing the world into two unequal parts, the larger, "different" one called the Orient, the other, also known as "our" world, called the Occident or the West.[2] Such divisions always come about when one society or culture thinks about another one, different from it; but it is interesting that even when the Orient has uniformly been considered an inferior part of the world, it has always been endowed both with greater size and with a greater potential for power (usually destructive) than the West. Insofar as Islam has always been seen as belonging to the Orient, its particular fate within the general structure of Orientalism has been to be looked at first of all as if it were one monolithic thing, and then with a very special hostility and fear. There are, of course, many religious, psychological and political reasons for this, but all of these reasons derive from a sense that so far as the West is concerned, Islam represents not only a formidable competitor but also a latecoming challenge to Christianity.

For most of the Middle Ages and during the early part of the Renaissance in Europe, Islam was believed to be a demonic religion of apostasy, blasphemy, and obscurity.[3] It did not seem to matter that Muslims considered Mohammed a prophet and not a god; what mattered to Christians was that Mohammed was a false prophet, a sower of discord, a sensualist, a hypocrite, an agent of the devil. Nor was this view of Mohammed strictly a doctrinal one. Real events in the real world made of Islam a considerable political force. For hundreds of years great Islamic armies and navies threatened Europe, destroyed its outposts, colonized its domains. It was as if a younger, more virile and energetic version of Christianity had arisen in the East, equipped itself with the learning of the ancient Greeks, invigorated itself with a simple, fearless, and warlike creed, and set about destroying Christianity. Even when the world of Islam entered a period of decline and Europe a period of ascendancy, fear of "Mohammedanism" persisted. Closer to Europe than than any of the other non-Christian religions, the Islamic world by its very adjacency evoked memories of its encroachments on Europe, and always, of its latent power again and again to disturb the West. Other great civilizations of the East—India and China among them—could be thought of as defeated and distant and hence not a constant worry. Only Islam seemed never to have submitted completely to the West; and when, after the dramatic oil-price rises of the early 1970s, the Muslim world seemed once more on the verge of repeating its early conquests, the whole West seemed to shudder.

Then in 1978 Iran occupied center stage, causing Americans to feel increasing anxiety and passion. Few nations so distant and different from the United States have so intensely engaged Americans. Never have Americans seemed so paralyzed, so seemingly powerless to stop one dramatic event after another from happening. And never in all this could they put Iran out of mind, since on so many levels the country impinged on their lives with a defiant obtrusiveness. Iran was a major oil supplier during a period of energy scarcity. It lies in a region of the world that is commonly regarded as volatile and strategically vital. An important ally, it lost its imperial regime, it army, its value in American global calculations during a year of tumultuous revolutionary upheaval virtually unprecedented on so huge a scale since October 1917. A new order which called itself Islamic, and appeared to be popular and anti-imperialist, was struggling to be born. Ayatollah Khomeini's image and presence took over the media, which failed to make much of him except that he was obdurate, powerful, and deeply angry at the United States. Finally, as a result of the ex-shah's entry into the United States on October 22, 1979, the United States Embassy in Teheran was captured by a group of students on November 4; many American hostages were held. This crisis nears its end as I write.

Reactions to what took place in Iran did not occur in a vacuum. Further back in the public's subliminal cultural consciousness, there was the longstanding attitude to Islam, the Arabs, and the Orient in general that I have been calling Orientalism. For whether one looked at such recent, critically acclaimed fiction as V. S. Naipaul's *A Bend in the River* and John Updike's *The Coup,* or at grade-school history textbooks, comic strips, television serials, films, and cartoons, the iconography of Islam was uniform, was uniformly ubiquitous, and drew its material from the same time-honored view of Islam: hence the frequent caricatures of Muslims as oil suppliers, as terrorists, and more recently, as bloodthirsty mobs. Conversely, there has been very little place either in the culture generally or in discourse about non-Westerners in particular to speak or even to think about, much less to portray, Islam or anything Islamic sympathetically. Most people, if asked to name a *modern* Islamic writer, would probably be able to pick only Khalil Gibran (who wasn't Islamic). The academic experts whose specialty is Islam have generally treated the religion and its various cultures within an invented or culturally determined ideological framework filled with passion, defensive prejudice, sometimes even revulsion; because of this framework, *understanding* of Islam has been a very difficult thing to achieve. And to judge from the various in-depth media studies and interviews on the Iranian revolution during the spring of 1979, there has been little inclination to accept the revolution itself as much more than a defeat for the United States (which in a very specific sense, of course, it was), or a victory over dark over light.

V. S. Naipaul's role in helping to clarify this general hostility towards Islam is an interesting one. In a recent interview published in *Newsweek International* (August 18, 1980) he spoke about a book he was writing on "Islam," and then volunteered that "Muslim fundamentalism has no intellectual substance to it, therefore it must collapse." What Muslim fundamentalism he was referring to specifically, and what sort of intellectual substance he had in mind, he did not say: Iran was undoubtedly meant, but so too—in equally vague terms—was the whole postwar wave of Islamic anti-imperialism in the Third World, for which Naipaul has developed a particularly intense antipathy. In *Guerrillas* and *A Bend in the River,* Naipaul's last two novels, Islam is in question, and it is part of Naipaul's general (and with liberal Western readers, popular) indictment of the Third World that he lumps together the corrupt viciousness of a few grotesque rulers, the end of European colonialism, and postcolonial efforts at rebuilding native societies as instances of an over-all intellectual failure in Africa and Asia. "Islam" plays a major part according to Naipaul, whether it is in the use of Islamic surnames by pathetic West Indian guerrillas, or in the vestiges of the African slave trade. For Naipaul and his readers, "Islam" somehow is made to cover everything that one most disapproves of from the standpoint of civilized, and Western, rationality.[4]

It is as if discriminations between religious passion, a struggle for a just cause, ordinary human weakness, political competition, and the history of men, women, and societies seen *as* the history of men, women, and societies cannot be made when "Islam," or the Islam now at work in Iran and in other parts of the Muslim world, is dealt with by novelists, reporters, policy-makers, "experts." "Islam" seems to engulf all aspects of the diverse Muslim world, reducing them all to a special malevolent and unthinking essence. Instead of analysis and understanding as a result, there can be for the most part only the crudest form of us-versus-them. Whatever Iranians or Muslims say about their sense of justice, their history of oppression, their vision of their own societies, seems irrelevant; what counts for the United States instead is what the "Islamic revolution" is doing right now, how many people have been executed by the Komitehs, how many bizarre outrages the Ayatollah, in the name of Islam, has ordered. Of course no one has equated the Jonestown massacre or the destructive frenzy produced at the Who concern in Cincinnati or the devastation of Indochina with Christianity, or with Western or American culture at large; that sort of equation has been reserved for "Islam."

Why is it that a whole range of political, cultural, social, and even economic events has often seemed reducible in so Pavlovian a way to "Islam"? What is it about "Islam" that provokes so quick and unrestrained a response? In what way do "Islam" and the Islamic world differ for Westerners from, say, the rest of the Third World and from the Soviet Union? These are far from simple questions, and they must therefore be answered piecemeal, with many qualifications and much differentiation.

Labels purporting to name very large and complex realities are notoriously vague and at the same time unavoidable. If it is true that "Islam" is an imprecise and ideologically loaded label, it is also true that "the West" and "Christianity" are just as problematic. Yet there is no easy way of avoiding these labels, since Muslims speak of Islam, Christians of Christianity, Westerners of the West, and all of them about all the others in ways that seem to be both convincing and exact. Instead of trying to propose ways of going around the labels, I think it is more immediately useful to admit at the outset that they exist and have long been in use as an integral part of cultural history rather than as objective classifications [. . .]. We must therefore remember that "Islam," "the West," and even "Christianity" function in at least two different ways, and produce at least two meanings, each time they are used. First, they perform a simple identifying function, as when we say Khomeini is a Muslim, or Pope John Paul II is a Christian. Such statements tell us as a bare minimum what something is, as opposed to all other things. On this level we can distinguish between an orange and an apple (as we might distinguish between a Muslim and a Christian) only to the extent that we know they are different fruits, growing on different trees, and so forth.

The second function of these several labels is to produce a much more complex meaning. To speak of "Islam" in the West today is to mean a lot of the unpleasant things I have been mentioning. Moreover, "Islam" is unlikely to mean anything one knows either directly or objectively. The same is true of our use of "the West." How many people who use the labels angrily or assertively have a solid grip on all aspects of the Western tradition, or on Islamic jurisprudence, or on the actual languages of the Islamic world? Very few, obviously, but this does not prevent people from confidently characterizing "Islam" and "the West," or from believing they know exactly what it is they are talking about.

For that reason, we must take the labels seriously. To a Muslim who talks about "the West" or to an American who talks about "Islam," these enormous generalizations have behind them a whole history, enabling and disabling at the same time. Ideological and shot through with powerful emotions, the labels have survived many experiences and have been capable of adapting to new events, information, and realities. At present, "Islam" and "the West" have taken on a powerful new urgency everywhere. And we must note immediately that it is always the West, and not Christianity, that seems pitted against Islam. Why? Because the assumption is that whereas "the West" is greater than and has surpassed the stage of Christianity, its principal religion, the world of Islam—its varied societies, histories, and languages notwithstanding—is still mired in religion, primitivity, and backwardness. Therefore, the West is modern, greater than the sum of its parts, full of enriching contradictions and yet always "Western" in its cultural identity; the world of Islam, on the other hand, is no more than "Islam," reducible to a small number of unchanging characteristics despite the appearance of contradictions and experiences of variety that seem on the surface to be as plentiful as those of the West.

A recent example of what I mean is to be found in an article for the "News of the Week in Review" section of the Sunday *New York Times,* September 14, 1980. The piece in question is by John Kifner, the able *Times* correspondent in Beirut, and its subject is the extent of Soviet penetration of the Muslim world. Kifner's notion is evident enough from his article's title ("Marx and Mosque Are Less Compatible Than Ever"), but what is noteworthy is his use of Islam to make what in any other instance would be an unacceptably direct and unqualified connection between an abstraction and a vastly complex reality. Even if it is allowed that, unlike all other religions, Islam is totalistic and makes no separation between church and state or between religion and everyday life, there is something uniquely—and perhaps deliberately—uninformed and uninforming, albeit conventional enough, about such statements as the following:

> The reason for Moscow's receding influence is disarmingly simple: Marx and mosque are incompatible. [Are we to assume, then, that Marx and church, or Marx and temple, are more compatible?]
>
> For the Western mind [this is the point, obviously enough], conditioned since the Reformation to historical and intellectual developments which have steadily diminished the role of religion, it is difficult to grasp the power exerted by Islam [which, presumably, has been conditioned neither by history nor by intellect]. Yet, for centuries it has been the central force in the life of this region and, for the moment at least, its power seems on the upsurge.
>
> In Islam, there is no separation between church and state. It is a total system not only of belief but of action, with fixed rules for everyday life and a messianic drive to combat or convert the infidel. To the deeply religious, particularly to the scholars and clergy but also to the masses [in other words, no one is excluded], Marxism, with its purely secular view of man, is not only alien but heretical.

Not only does Kifner simply ignore history and such complications as the admittedly limited but interesting series of parallels between Marxism and Islam (studied by Maxime Rodinson in a book that attempts to explain why Marxism seems to have made some inroads in Islamic societies over the years[5]) but he also rests his argument on a hidden comparison between "Islam" and the West, so much more various and uncharacterizable than simple, monolithic, totalitarian Islam. The interesting thing is that Kifner can say what he says without any danger of appearing either wrong or absurd.

Islam versus the West: this is the ground bass for a staggeringly fertile set of variations. Europe versus Islam, no less than America versus Islam, is a thesis that it subsumes.[6] But quite different concrete experiences with the West as a whole play a significant role too. For there is an extremely important distinction to be made between American and European awareness of Islam. France and England, for example, until very recently possessed large Muslim empires; in both countries, and to a lesser degree in Italy and Holland, both of which had Muslim colonies too, there is a long tradition of direct experience with the Islamic world.[7] This is reflected in a distinguished European academic discipline of Orientalism, which of course existed in those countries with colonies as well as in those (Germany, Spain, prerevolutionary Russia) that either wanted them, or were close to Muslim territories, or were once Muslim states. Today the Soviet Union has a Muslim population of about 50 million, and since the last days of 1979 has been in military occupation of Muslim Afghanistan. None of these things is comparably true of the United States, even though never before have so many Americans written, thought, or spoken about Islam.

The absence in America either of a colonial past or of a longstanding cultural attention to Islam makes the current obsession all the more peculiar, more abstract, more secondhand. Very few Americans, comparatively speaking, have actually had much to do with real Muslims; by comparison, in France the country's second religion in point of numbers is Islam, which may not be more popular as a result, but is certainly more known. The modern European burst of interest in Islam was part of what was called "the Oriental renaissance," a period in the late eighteenth and early nineteenth centuries when French and British scholars discovered "the East" anew—India, China, Japan, Egypt, Mesopotamia, the Holy Land.

Islam was seen, for better or for worse, as part of the East, sharing in its mystery, exoticism, corruption, and latent power. True, Islam had been a direct military threat to Europe for centuries before; and true also that during the Middle Ages and early Renaissance, Islam was a problem for Christian thinkers, who continued for hundreds of years to see it and its prophet Mohammed as the rankest variety of apostasy. But at least Islam existed for many Europeans as a kind of standing religiocultural challenge, which did not prevent European imperialism from building its institutions on Islamic territory. And however much hostility there was between Europe and Islam, there was also direct experience, and in the case of poets, novelists, and scholars like Goethe, Gérard de Nerval, Richard Burton, Flaubert, and Louis Massignon, there was imagination and refinement.

Yet in spite of these figures and others like them, Islam has never been welcome in Europe. Most of the great philosophers of history from Hegel to Spengler have regarded Islam without much enthusiasm. In a dispassionately lucid essay, "Islam and the Philosophy of History," Albert Hourani has discussed this strikingly constant derogation of Islam as a system of faith.[8] Apart from some occasional interest in the odd Sufi writer or saint, European vogues for "the wisdom of the East" rarely included Islamic sages or poets. Omar Khayyám, Harun al-Rashid, Sindbad, Aladdin, Hajji Baba, Scheherazade, Saladin, more or less make up the entire list of Islamic figures known to modern educated Europeans. Not even Carlyle could make the Prophet widely acceptable, and as for the substance of the faith Mohammed propagated, this has long seemed to Europeans basically unacceptable on Christian grounds, although precisely for that reason not uninteresting. Towards the end of the nineteenth century, as Islamic nationalism in Asia and Africa increased, there was a widely shared view that Muslim colonies were meant to remain under European tutelage, as much because they were profitable as because they were underdeveloped and in need of Western discipline.[9] Be that as it may, and despite the frequent racism and aggression directed at the Muslim world, Europeans *did* express a fairly energetic sense of what Islam meant to them. Hence the representations of Islam—in scholarship, art, literature, music, and public discourse—all across European culture, from the end of the eighteenth century until our own day.

Little of this concreteness is to be found in America's experience of Islam. Nineteenth-century American contacts with Islam are very restricted; one thinks of occasional travelers like Mark Twain and Herman Melville, or of missionaries here and there, or of short-lived military expeditions to North Africa. Culturally there was no distinct place in America for Islam before World War II. Academic experts did their work on Islam usually in quiet corners of schools of divinity, not in the glamorous limelight of Orientalism nor in the pages of leading journals. For about a century there has existed a fascinating although quiet symbiosis between American missionary families to Islamic countries and cadres of the foreign service and the oil companies; periodically this has surfaced in the form of hostile comments about State Department and oil-company "Arabists," who are considered to harbor an especially virulent and anti-Semitic form of philo-Islamism. On the other hand, all the great figures known in the United States as important academic experts on Islam have been foreign-born: Lebanese Philip Hitti at Princeton, Austrian Gustave von Grunebaum at Chicago and UCLA, British H. A. R. Gibb at Harvard, German Joseph Schacht at Columbia. Yet none of these men has had the relative cultural prestige enjoyed by Jacques Berque in France and Albert Hourani in England.

But even men like Hitti, Gibb, von Grunebaum, and Schacht have disappeared from the American scene, as indeed it is unlikely that scholars such as Berque and Hourani will have successors in France and England. No one today has their breadth of culture, nor anything like their range of authority. Academic experts on Islam in the West today tend to know about jurisprudential schools in tenth-century Baghdad or nineteenth-century Moroccan urban patterns, but never (or almost never) about the whole civilization of Islam—literature, politics, history, sociology, and so on. This has not prevented experts from generalizing from time to time about the "Islamic mind-set" or the "Shi'a penchant for martyrdom," but such pronouncements have been confined to popular journals or to the media, which solicited these opinions in the first place. More significantly, the occasions for public discussions of Islam, by experts or by nonexperts, have almost always been provided by political crises. It is extremely rare to see informative articles on Islamic culture in the *New York Review of Books,* say, or in *Harper's.* Only when the stability of Saudi Arabia or Iran has been in question has "Islam" seemed worthy of general comment.

Consider therefore that Islam has entered the consciousness of most Americans—even of academic and general intellectuals who know a great deal about Europe and Latin America—principally if not exclusively because it has been connected to newsworthy issues like oil, Iran and Afghanistan, or terrorism.[10] And all of this by the middle of 1979 had come to be called either the Islamic revolution, or "the crescent of crisis," or "the arc of instability," or "the return of Islam." A particularly telling example was the Atlantic Council's Special Working Group on the Middle East (which included Brent Scowcroft, George Ball, Richard Helms, Lyman Lemnitzer, Walter Levy, Eugene Rostow, Kermit Roosevelt, and Joseph Sisco, among others): when this group issued its report in the fall of 1979 the title given it was "Oil and Turmoil: Western Choices in the Middle East."[11] When *Time* magazine devoted its major story to Islam on April 16, 1979, the cover was adorned with a Gérôme painting of a bearded muezzin standing in a minaret, calmly summoning the faithful to prayer; it was as florid and overstated a nineteenth-century period piece of Orientalist art as one could imagine. Anachronistically, however, this quiet scene was emblazoned with a caption that had nothing to do with it: "The Militant Revival." There could be no better way of symbolizing the difference between Europe and America on the subject of Islam. A placid and decorative painting done almost routinely in Europe as an aspect of one's general culture had been transformed by three words into a general American obsession.

But surely I am exaggerating? Wasn't *Time's* cover story on Islam simply a piece of vulgarization, catering to a supposed taste for the sensational? Does it *really* reveal anything more serious than that? And since when have the media mattered a great deal on questions of substance, or of policy, or of culture? Besides, was it *not* the case that Islam had indeed thrust itself upon the world's attention? And what had happened to the experts on Islam, and why were their contributions either bypassed entirely or submerged in the "Islam" discussed and diffused by the media?

A few simple explanations are in order first. As I said above, there has never been any American expert on the Islamic world whose audience was a wide one; moreover, with the exception of the late

Marshall Hodgson's three-volume *The Venture of Islam,* posthumously published in 1975, no general work on Islam has ever been put squarely before the literate reading public.[12] Either the experts were so specialized that they only addressed other specialists, or their work was not distinguished enough intellectually to command the kind of audience that came to books on Japan, Western Europe, or India. But these things work both ways. While it is true that one could not name an American "Orientalist" with a reputation outside Orientalism, as compared with Berque or Rodinson in France, it is also true that the study of Islam is neither truly encouraged in the American university nor sustained in the culture at large by personalities whose fame and intrinsic merit might make their experiences of Islam important on their own.[13] Who are the American equivalents of Rebecca West, Freya Stark, T. E. Lawrence, Wilfred Thesiger, Gertrude Bell, P. H. Newby, or more recently, Jonathan Raban? At best, they might be former CIA people like Miles Copeland or Kermit Roosevelt, very rarely writers or thinkers of any cultural distinction.

A second reason for the critical absence of expert opinion on Islam is the experts' marginality to what seemed to be happening in the world of Islam when it became "news" in the mid-1970s. The brutally impressive facts are, of course, that the Gulf oil-producing states suddenly appeared to be very powerful; there was an extraordinarily ferocious and seemingly unending civil war in Lebanon; Ethiopia and Somalia were involved in a long war; the Kurdish problem unexpectedly became pivotal and then, after 1975, just as unexpectedly subsided; Iran deposed its monarch in the wake of a massive, wholly surprising "Islamic" revolution; Afghanistan was gripped by a Marxist coup in 1978, then invaded by Soviet troops in late 1979; Algeria and Morocco were drawn into protracted conflict over the Southern Sahara issue; a Pakistani president was executed and a new military dictatorship set up. There were other things taking place too, most recently a war between Iran and Iraq, but let us be satisfied with these. On the whole I think it is fair to say that few of these happenings might have been illuminated by expert writing on Islam in the West; for not only had the experts not predicted them nor prepared their readers for them, they had instead provided a mass of literature that seemed, when compared with what was happening, to be about an impossibly distant region of the world, one that bore practically no relation to the turbulent and threatening confusion erupting before one's eyes in the media.

This is a central matter, which has scarcely begun to be discussed rationally even now, and so we should proceed carefully. Academic experts whose province was Islam before the seventeenth century worked in an essentially antiquarian field; moreover, like that of specialists in other fields, their work was very compartmentalized. They neither wanted nor tried in a responsible way to concern themselves with the modern consequences of Islamic history. To some extent their work was tied to notions of a "classical" Islam, or to supposedly unchanging patterns of Islamic life, or to archaic philological questions. In any event, there was no way of using it to understand the modern Islamic world, which to all intents and purposes, and depending on what part of it was of interest, had been developing along very different lines from those adumbrated in Islam's earliest centuries (that is, from the seventh to the ninth centuries).

The experts whose field was modern Islam—or to be more precise, whose field was made up of societies, people, and institutions within the Islamic world since the eighteenth century—worked within an agreed-upon framework for research formed according to notions decidedly *not* set in the Islamic world. This fact, in all its complexity and variety, cannot be overestimated. There is no denying that a scholar sitting in Oxford or Boston writes and researches principally, though not exclusively, according to standards, conventions, and expectations shaped by his or her peers, not by the Muslims being studied. This is truism, perhaps, but it needs emphasis just the same. Modern Islamic studies in the academy belong to "area programs" generally—Western Europe, the Soviet Union, Southeast Asia, and so on. They are therefore affiliated to the mechanism by which national policy is set. This is not a matter of choice for the individual scholar. If someone at Princeton happened to be studying contemporary Afghan religious schools, it would be obvious (especially during times like these) that such a study *could* have "policy implications," and whether or not the scholar wanted it he or she would be drawn into the network of government, corporate, and foreign-policy associations; funding would be affected, the kind of people met would also be affected, and in general, certain rewards and types of interaction would be offered. Willy-nilly, the scholar would be transmuted into an "area expert."

For scholars whose interests are directly connected to policy issues (political scientists, principally, but also modern historians, economists, sociologists, and anthropologists), there are sensitive, not to say dangerous, questions to be addressed. For example, how is one's status as a scholar reconciled with the demands made on one by governments? Iran is a perfect case in point. During the shah's regime, there were funds available to Iranologists from the Pahlevi Foundation, and of course from American institutions. These funds were disbursed for studies that took as their point of departure the status quo (in this case, the presence of a Pahlevi regime tied militarily and economically to the United States), which in a sense became the research paradigm for students of the country. Late in the crisis a House Permanent Select Committee on Intelligence staff study said that the United States' assessments of the regime were influenced by existing policy "not directly, through the conscious suppression of unfavorable news, but indirectly . . . policymakers were not asking whether the Shah's autocracy would survive indefinitely; policy was premised on that assumption."[14] This in turn produced only a tiny handful of studies seriously assessing the shah's regime and identifying the sources of popular opposition to him. To my knowledge only one scholar, Hamid Algar of Berkeley, was correct in estimating the contemporary political force of Iranian religious feelings, and only Algar went so far as to predict that Ayatollah Khomeini was likely to bring down the regime. Other scholars—Richard Cottam and Ervand Abrahamian among them—also departed from the status quo in what they wrote, but they were a small band indeed.[15] (In fairness we must note the European scholars on the left, who were less sanguine about the shah's survival, did not do very well either in identifying the religious sources of Iranian opposition.[16])

Even if we leave aside Iran, there were plenty of no less important intellectual failures elsewhere, all of them the result of relying uncritically on what a combination of government policy and cliché dictated. Here, the Lebanese and Palestinian cases are instructive. For years Lebanon had been regarded as a model of what a pluralistic or mosaic culture was supposed to be. Yet so reified and static had the models been which were used for the study of Lebanon that no inkling was possible of the ferocity and violence of the civil war (which ran from 1975 to 1980 at least). Expert eyes seem in the past to have been extraordinarily transfixed by images of Lebanese "stability": traditional leaders, elites, parties, national character, and successful modernization were what was studied.

Even when Lebanon's polity was described as precarious, or when its insufficient "civility" was analyzed, there was a uniform assumption that its problems were on the whole manageable and far from being radically disruptive.[17] During the sixties, Lebanon was portrayed as "stable" because, one expert tells us, the "inter-Arab" situation was stable; so long as that equation was kept up, he argued, Lebanon would be secure.[18] It was never even supposed that there could be inter-Arab stability and Lebanese *instability,* mainly because—as with most subjects in this consensus-ridden field—the conventional wisdom assigned perpetual "pluralism" and harmonious continuity to Lebanon, its internal cleavages and its Arab neighbors' irrelevance notwithstanding. Any trouble for Lebanon therefore had to come from the surrounding *Arab* environment, never from Israel or from the United States, both of which had specific but never-analyzed designs on Lebanon.[19] Then too, there was the Lebanon that embodied the modernization myth. Reading a classic of this sort of ostrich-wisdom today, one is struck by how serenely the fable could be advanced as recently as 1973, when the civil war had in fact begun. Lebanon might undergo revolutionary change, we were told, but that was a "remote" likelihood; what was much more likely was "future modernization involving the public [a sadly ironic euphemism for what was to be the bloodiest civil war in recent Arab history] within the prevailing political structure."[20] Or as a distinguished anthropologist put it, "The Lebanese 'nice piece of mosaic' remains intact. Indeed . . . Lebanon has continued to be the most effective in containing its deep primordial cleavages."[21]

As a result, in Lebanon and in other places, experts failed to understand that much of what truly mattered about postcolonial states could not easily be herded under the rubric of "stability." In Lebanon it was precisely those devastatingly mobile forces the experts had never documented or had consistently underestimated—social dislocations, demographic shifts, confessional loyalties, ideological currents—that tore the country apart so savagely.[22] Similarly, it has been conventional wisdom for years to regard the Palestinians merely as resettlable refugees, not as a political force having estimable consequences for any reasonably accurate assessment of the Near East. Yet by the mid-seventies the Palestinians were one of the major acknowledged problems for United States policy, and still they had not received the scholarly and intellectual attention their importance deserved;[23] instead, the persisting attitude was to treat them as adjuncts to United States policy toward Egypt and Israel and quite literally to ignore them in the Lebanese conflagration. There has been no important *scholarly* or expert counterweight to this policy, and the results for American national interests are likely to be disastrous, especially since the Iran-Iraq War seems, once again, to have caught the intelligence community off guard and very wrong in estimates of both countries' military capacities.

Add to this conformity between a docilely plodding scholarship and unfocused government interests the sorry truth that too many expert writers on the Islamic world did not command the relevant languages and hence had to depend on the press or other Western writers for their information. This reinforced dependence on the official or the conventional picture of things was a trap into which, in their over-all performance on prerevolutionary Iran, the media fell. There was a tendency to study and restudy, to focus resolutely on the same things: elites, modernization programs, the role of the military, greatly visible leaders, geopolitical strategy (from the American point of view), communist inroads.[24] Those things may at the time have seemed interesting to the United States as a nation, yet the fact is that in Iran they were all literally swept away by the revolution in a matter of days. The whole imperial court crumbled; the army, into which billions of dollars had been poured, disintegrated; the so-called elites either disappeared or found their way into the new state of affairs, though in neither case could it be asserted, as it had been, that they determined Iranian political behavior. One of the experts given credit for predicting what the "crisis of '78" might lead to, James Bill of the University of Texas, nevertheless recommended to American policy-makers as late as December 1978 that the United States government should encourage "the shah . . . to open the system up."[25] In other words, even a supposedly dissenting expert voice was still committed to maintaining a regime against which, at the very moment he spoke, literally millions of its people had risen in one of the most massive insurrections in modern history.

Yet Bill made important points about general United States ignorance on Iran. He was right to say that media coverage was superficial, that official information had been geared to what the Pahlevis wanted, and that the United States made no effort either to get to know the country in depth or to make contact with the opposition. Although Bill did not go on to say it, these failures were and are symptomatic of the general United States and European attitude toward the Islamic world and, as we shall see, toward most of the Third World; indeed, the fact that Bill did not connect what he was justly saying about Iran to the rest of the Islamic world was part of the attitude too. There has been no responsible grappling first of all with the central methodological question, namely, What is the value (if any) of speaking about "Islam" and the Islamic resurgence? What, secondly, is or ought to be the relationship between government policy and scholarly research? Is the expert supposed to be above politics or a political adjunct to governments? Bill and William Beeman of Brown University argued on separate occasions that a major cause of the United States–Iran crisis in 1979 was the failure to consult those academic experts who had been given expensive educations precisely to learn to know the Islamic world.[26] Yet what went unexamined by Bill and Beeman was the possibility that it was *because* scholars sought out such a role, at the same time calling themselves scholars, that they seemed ambiguous and hence not credible figures to the government as well as to the intellectual community.[27]

Besides, is there any way for an independent intellectual (which is, after all, what an academic scholar is meant to be) to maintain his or her independence and also to work directly for the state? What is the connection between frank political partisanship and good insight? Does one preclude the other, or is that true only in some cases? Why was it that the whole (but admittedly small) cadre of Islamic scholars in the country could not get a larger hearing? Why was this the case at a time when the United States seemed to be most in need of instruction? All of these questions, of course, can be answered only within the actual and largely political framework governing relationships historically between the West and the Islamic world. Let us look at this framework and see what role there is in it for the expert.

I have not been able to discover any period in European or American history since the Middle Ages in which Islam was generally discussed or thought about *outside* a framework created by passion, prejudice, or political interests. This may not seem a surprising discovery, but included in it is the entire gamut of scholarly and scientific disciplines which, since the early nineteenth century, have either called themselves collectively the discipline of Orientalism or have tried systematically to deal with the Orient. No one would disagree with the statement that early commentators on Islam like Peter the Venerable and Barthélemy d'Herbelot were passionate Christian polemicists in what they said. But it has been an unexamined assumption that since Europe and the West advanced into the modern scientific age and freed themselves of superstition and ignorance, the march must have included Orientalism. Wasn't it true that Silvestre de Sacy, Edward Lane, Ernest Renan, Hamilton Gibb, and Louis Massignon were learned, objective scholars, and isn't it true that following upon all sorts of advances in twentieth-century sociology, anthropology, linguistics, and history, American scholars who teach the Middle East and Islam in places like Princeton, Harvard, and Chicago are therefore unbiased and free of special pleading in what they do? The answer is no. Not that Orientalism is more biased than other social and humanistic sciences; it is simply as ideological and as contaminated by the world as other disciplines. The main difference is that Orientalist scholars have tended to use their standing as experts to deny—and sometimes even to cover—their deep-seated feelings about Islam with a language of authority whose purpose is to certify their "objectivity" and "scientific impartiality."

That is one point. The other distinguishes a historical pattern in what would otherwise be an undifferentiated characterization of Orientalism. Whenever in modern times an acutely political tension has been felt between the Occident and *its* Orient (or between the West and *its* Islam), there has been a tendency in the West to resort not to direct violence but first to the cool, relatively detached instruments of scientific, quasi-objective representation. In this way "Islam" is made more clear, the "true nature" of its threat appears, an implicit course of action against it is proposed. In such a context both science and direct violence come to be viewed by many Muslims, living in widely varied circumstances, as forms of aggression against Islam.

Two strikingly similar examples illustrate my thesis. We can now see retrospectively that during the nineteenth century both France and England preceded their occupations of portions of the Islamic East with a period in which the various scholarly means of characterizing and understanding the Orient underwent remarkable technical modernization and development.[28] The French occupation of Algeria in 1830 followed a period of about two decades during which French scholars literally transformed the study of the Orient from an antiquarian into a rational discipline. Of course, there had been Napoleon Bonaparte's occupation of Egypt in 1798, and of course one should remark the fact that he had prepared for his expedition by marshaling a sophisticated group of scientists to make his enterprise more efficient. My point, however, is that Napoleon's short-lived occupation of Egypt closed a chapter. A new one began with the long period during which, under Silvestre de Sacy's stewardship at French institutions of Oriental study, France became the world leader in Orientalism; this chapter climaxed a little later when French armies occupied Algiers in 1830.

I do not at all want to suggest a causal relationship between one thing and the other, nor to adopt the anti-intellectual view that all scientific learning necessarily leads to violence and suffering. All I want to say is that empires are not born instantaneously, nor during the modern period have they been run by improvisation. If the development of learning involves the redefinition and reconstitution of fields of human experience by scientists who stand above the material they study, it is not impertinent to see the same development occurring among politicians whose realm of authority is redefined to include "inferior" regions of the world where new "national" interests can be discovered—and later seen to be in need of close supervision.[29] I very much doubt that England would have occupied Egypt in so long and massively institutionalized a way had it not been for the durable investment in Oriental learning first cultivated by scholars like Edward William Lane and William Jones. Familiarity, accessibility, representability: these were what Orientalists demonstrated about the Orient. The Orient could be seen, it could be studied, it could be managed. It need not remain a distant, marvelous, incomprehensible, and yet very rich place. It could be brought home—or more simply, Europe could make itself at home there, as it subsequently did.

My second example is a contemporary one. The Islamic Orient today is clearly important for its resources or for its geopolitical location. Neither of these, however, is interchangeable with the interests, needs, or aspirations of the native Orientals. Ever since the end of World War II, the United States has been taking positions of dominance and hegemony once held in the Islamic world by Britain and France. With this replacement of one imperial system by another have gone two things: first, the moderate burgeoning of crisis-oriented academic and expert interest in Islam, and second, an extraordinary revolution in the techniques available to the largely private-sector press and electronic journalism industries. Never before has an international trouble spot like Iran been covered so instantaneously and so regularly as it has by the media: Iran has therefore seemed to be *in* American lives, and yet deeply alien from them, with an unprecedented intensity. Together these two phenomena—the second much more than the first—by which a sizable apparatus of university, government, and business experts study Islam and the Middle East and by which Islam has become a subject familiar to every consumer of news in the West, have almost entirely domesticated the Islamic world, or at least those aspects of it that are considered newsworthy. Not only has that world become the subject of the most profound cultural and economic Western saturation in history—for no non-Western realm has been so dominated by the United States as the Arabic-Islamic world is today—but the interchange between Islam and the West, in this case the United States, is profoundly one-sided and, so far as other, less newsworthy parts of the Islamic world are concerned, profoundly skewed.

It is only a slight overstatement to say that Muslims and Arabs are essentially covered, discussed, apprehended, either as oil suppliers or as potential terrorists. Very little of the detail, the human density, the passion of Arab-Muslim life has entered the awareness of even those people whose profession it is to report the Islamic world. What we have instead is a limited series of crude, essentialized caricatures of the Islamic world presented in such a way as, among other things, to make that world vulnerable to military aggression.[30]

I do not think it is an accident that recent talk of United States military intervention in the Arabian Gulf, or the Carter Doctrine, or discussions of Rapid Development Forces, has been preceded by a period of "Islam's" rational presentation through the cool medium of television and through "objective" Orientalist study (which, paradoxically, either in its "irrelevance" to modern actualities or in its propagandistic "objective" variety, has a uniformly alienating effect): in many ways our actual situation today bears a chilling resemblance to the nineteenth-century British and French examples cited previously.

There are other political and cultural reasons for this. After World War II, when the United States took over the imperial role played by France and Britain, a set of policies was devised for dealing with the world that suited the peculiarities and the problems of each region that affected (and was affected by) United States interests. Europe was designated for postwar recovery, for which the Marshall Plan, among other similar American policies, was suited. The Soviet Union of course emerged as the United States' most formidable competitor, and, so no one needs to be told, the cold war produced policies, studies, even a mentality, which still dominate relationships between one superpower and the other. That left what has come to be called the Third World, an arena of competition not only between the United States and the Soviet Union but also between the United States and various native powers only recently in possession of their independence from European colonizers.

Almost without exception, the Third World seemed to American policy-makers to be "underdeveloped," in the grip of unnecessarily archaic and static "traditional" modes of life, dangerously prone to communist subversion and internal stagnation. For the Third World "modernization" became the order of the day, so far as the United States was concerned. And, as has been suggested by James Peck, "modernization theory was the ideological answer to a world of increasing revolutionary upheaval and continued reaction among traditional political elites."[31] Huge sums were poured into Africa and Asia with the aim of stopping communism, promoting United States trade, and above all, developing a cadre of native allies whose express *raison d'être* seemed to be the transformation of backward countries into mini-Americas. In time the initial investments required additional sums and increased military support to keep them going. And this in turn produced the interventions all over Asia and Latin America which regularly pitted the United States against almost every brand of native nationalism.

The history of United States efforts on behalf of modernization and development in the Third World can never be completely understood unless it is also noted how the policy itself produced a style of thought and a habit of seeing the Third World which increased the political, emotional, and strategic investment in the very idea of modernization. Vietnam is a perfect instance of this. Once it was decided that the country was to be saved from communism and indeed from itself, a whole science of modernization for Vietnam (whose latest and most costly phase came to be known as "Vietnamization") came into being. Not only government specialists but university experts were involved. In time, the survival of pro-American and anticommunist regimes in Saigon dominated everything, even when it became clear that a huge majority of the population viewed those regimes as alien and oppressive, and even when the cost of fighting unsuccessful wars on behalf of those regimes had devastated the whole region and cost Lyndon Johnson the presidency. Still, a very great amount of writing on the virtues of modernizing traditional society had acquired an almost unquestioned social, and certainly cultural, authority in the United States, at the same time that in many parts of the Third World "modernization" was connected in the popular mind with foolish spending, unnecessary gadgetry and armaments, corrupt rulers, and brutal United States intervention in the affairs of small, weak countries.

Among the many illusions that persisted in modernization theory was one that seemed to have a special pertinence to the Islamic world: namely, that before the advent of the United States, Islam existed in a kind of timeless childhood, shielded from true development by an archaic set of superstitions, prevented by its strange priests and scribes from moving out of the Middle Ages into the modern world. At this point, Orientalism and modernization theory dovetail nicely. If, as Orientalist scholarship had traditionally taught, Muslims were no more than fatalistic children tyrannized by their mind-set, their *'ulama,* and their wild-eyed political leaders into resisting the West and progress, could not every political scientist, anthropologist, and sociologist worthy of trust show that, given a reasonable chance, something resembling the American way of life might be introduced into Islam via consumer goods, anticommunist propaganda, and "good" leaders? The main difficulty with Islam, however, was that unlike India and China, it had never really been pacified or defeated. For reasons which seemed always to defy the understanding of scholars, Islam (or some version of it) continued its sway over its adherents, who, it came regularly to be argued, were unwilling to accept reality, or at least that part of reality in which the West's superiority was demonstrable.

Efforts at modernization persisted all through the two decades that followed World War II. Iran became in effect the modernization success story and its ruler the "modernized" leader *par excellence*. As for the rest of the Islamic world, whether it was Arab nationalists, Egypt's Gamal Abdel Nasser, Indonesia's Sukarno, the Palestinian nationalists, Iranian opposition groups, or thousands of unknown Islamic teachers, brotherhoods, and orders, it was all either opposed or not covered by Western scholars with a heavy investment in modernization theory and American strategic and economic interests in the Islamic world.

During the explosive decade of the seventies, Islam gave further proof of its fundamental intransigence. There was, for example, the Iranian revolution: neither procommunist nor promodernization, the people who overthrew the shah were simply not explainable according to the canons of behavior presupposed by modernization theory. They did not seem grateful for the quotidian benefits of modernization (cars, an enormous military and security apparatus, a stable regime) and appeared indifferent to the blandishments of "Western" ideas altogether.[32] What was especially troubling about their attitude—Khomeini's in particular—was their fierce unwillingness to accept any style of politics (or for that matter, of rationality) that was not deliberately their own. Above all, it was their attachment to Islam that seemed especially defiant. Ironically, only a few commentators on "Islamic" atavism and medieval modes of logic in the West noted that a few miles to the west of Iran, in Begin's Israel, there was a regime fully willing to mandate its actions by religious authority and by a very backward-looking theological doctrine.[33] An even smaller number of commentators decrying the apparent upsurge in Islamic religiosity connected it to the upsurge in the United States of television religions numbering many millions of adherents, or to the fact that two of the three major presidential candidates in 1980 were enthusiastic born-again Christians.

Religious intensity was thus ascribed solely to Islam even when religious feeling was spreading remarkably everywhere: one need only remember the effusive treatment by the liberal press of patently illiberal religious figures like Solzhenitsyn or Pope John Paul II to see how one-sidedly hostile the attitude to Islam was.[34] A retreat into religion became the way most Islamic states could be explained, from Saudi Arabia—which, with what was supposed to be a peculiarly Islamic logic, refused to ratify the Camp David Accords—to Pakistan, Afghanistan, and Algeria. In this way, we can see how the Islamic world was differentiated, in the Western mind generally, in the United States' in particular, from regions of the world to which a cold-war analysis could be applied. There seemed to be no way, for example, in which one could speak of Saudi Arabia and Kuwait as parts of "the free world"; even Iran during the shah's regime, despite its overwhelming anti-Soviet commitment, never really belonged to "our" side the way France and Britain do. Nevertheless policy-makers in the United States persisted in speaking of the "loss" of Iran as, during the past three decades, they spoke of the "loss" of China, Vietnam, and Angola. Moreover it has been the singularly unhappy lot of the Persian Gulf's Islamic states to be considered by American crisis managers as places ready for American military occupation. Thus George Ball in the *New York Times Magazine* of June 28, 1970, warned that "the tragedy of Vietnam" might lead to "pacifism and isolation" at home, whereas United States interests in the Middle East were so great that the president ought to "educate" Americans about the possibility of military intervention there.[35]

One more thing needs mention here: the role of Israel in mediating Western and particularly American views of the Islamic world since World War II. In the first place, Israel's avowedly religious character is rarely mentioned in the Western press: only recently have there been overt references to Israeli religious fanaticism, and all of these have been to the zealots of Gush Emunim, whose principal activity has been the violent setting up of illegal settlements on the West Bank. Yet most accounts of Gush Emunim in the West simply leave out the inconvenient fact that it was "secular" labor governments that first instituted illegal settlements in occupied

Arab territory, not just the religious fanatics now stirring things up. This kind of one-sided reporting is, I think, an indication of how Israel—the Middle East's "only democracy" and "our staunch ally"—has been used as a foil for Islam.[36] Thus Israel has appeared as a bastion of Western civilization hewn (with much approbation and self-congratulation) out of the Islamic wilderness. Secondly, Israel's security in American eyes has become conveniently interchangeable with fending off Islam, perpetuating Western hegemony, and demonstrating the virtues of modernization. In these ways, three sets of illusions economically buttress and reproduce one another in the interests of shoring up the Western self-image and promoting Western power over the Orient: the view of Islam, the ideology of modernization, and the affirmations of Israel's general value to the West.

In addition, and to make "our" attitudes to Islam very clear, a whole information and policy-making apparatus in the United States depends on these illusions and diffuses them widely. Large segments of the intelligentsia allied to the community of geopolitical strategists together deliver themselves of expansive ideas about Islam, oil, the future of Western civilization, and the fight for democracy against turmoil and terrorism. For reasons that I have already discussed, the Islamic specialists feed into this great stream, despite the undeniable fact that only a relative fraction of what goes on in academic Islamic studies is directly infected with the cultural and political visions to be found in geopolitics and cold-war ideology. A little lower down come the mass media, which take from the other two units of the apparatus what is most easily compressed into images: hence the caricatures, the frightening mobs, the concentration on "Islamic" punishment, and so on. All of this is presided over by the great power establishments—the oil companies, the mammoth corporations and multinationals, the defense and intelligence communities, the executive branch of the government. When President Carter spent his first New Year in office with the shah in 1978, and said that Iran was "an island of stability," he was speaking with the mobilized force of this formidable apparatus, representing the United States interests and covering Islam at the same time.

from *Covering Islam*

7

Traveling Theory

(1982)

"Traveling Theory" is one of Said's most influential essays on literary theory. Originally appearing in *Raritan Quarterly* (1982), and later included in his book *The World, the Text, and the Critic,* it has since been widely anthologized, cited, and commented upon. Here Said investigates how ideas or theories "travel" from place to place and what happens in the process. Using the Hungarian Marxist Georg Lukács's theory of "reification" as his example, Said argues that theories develop in response to specific historical and social reasons, but when they move from their points of origin, the power and rebelliousness attached to them dissipates as they become domesticated, dehistoricized, and assimilated (often by an academic orthodoxy) into their new location. Twelve years later, Said would revise his thesis ("Traveling Theory Reconsidered") and propose that there is also the possibility that a theory can be reinterpreted, and thus reinvigorated, by a new political situation (using the work of Frantz Fanon and arguing for an influence of Lukács on Fanon).

Like people and schools of criticism, ideas and theories travel—from person to person, from situation to situation, from one period to another. Cultural and intellectual life are usually nourished and often sustained by this circulation of ideas, and whether it takes the form of acknowledged or unconscious influence, creative borrowing, or wholesale appropriation, the movement of ideas and theories from one place to another is both a fact of life and a usefully enabling condition of intellectual activity. Having said that, however, one should go on to specify the kinds of movement that are possible, in order to ask whether by virtue of having moved from one place and time to another an idea or a theory gains or loses in strength, and whether a theory in one historical period and national culture becomes altogether different for another period or situation. There are particularly interesting cases of ideas and theories that move from one culture to another, as when so-called Eastern ideas about transcendence were imported into Europe during the early nineteenth century, or when certain European ideas about society were translated into traditional Eastern societies during the later nineteenth century. Such movement into a new environment is never unimpeded. It necessarily involves processes of representation and institutionalization different from those at the point of origin. This complicates any account of the transplantation, transference, circulation, and commerce of theories and ideas.

There is, however, a discernible and recurrent pattern to the movement itself, three or four stages common to the way any theory or idea travels.

First, there is a point of origin, or what seems like one, a set of initial circumstances in which the idea came to birth or entered discourse. Second, there is a distance transversed, a passage through the pressure of various contexts as the idea moves from an earlier point to another time and place where it will come into a new prominence. Third, there is a set of conditions—call them conditions of acceptance or, as an inevitable part of acceptance, resistances—which then confronts the transplanted theory or idea, making possible its introduction or toleration, however alien it might appear to be. Fourth, the now full (or partly) accommodated (or incorporated) idea is to some extent transformed by its new uses, its new position in a new time and place.

It is obvious that any satisfactorily full account of these stages would be an enormous task. But though I have neither the intention nor the capacity to undertake it, it seemed worthwhile to describe the problem in a sketchy and general way so that I might at length and in detail address a particularly topical, highly limited aspect of it. Of course the discrepancy between the general problem and any particular analysis is itself deserving of comment. To prefer a local, detailed analysis of how one theory travels from one situation to another is also to betray some fundamental uncertainty about specifying or delimiting the field to which any one theory or idea might belong. Notice, for example, that when professional students of literature now use words like "theory" and "criticism" it is not assumed that they must or should confine their interests to literary theory or literary criticism. The distinction between one discipline and another has been blurred precisely because fields like literature and literary study are no longer considered to be as all-encompassing or as synoptic as, until recently, they once were. Although some polemical scholars of literature can still, nonetheless, attack others for not being literary enough, or for not understanding (as who should not?) that literature, unlike other forms of writing, is essentially mimetic, essentially moral, and essentially humanistic, the resultant controversies are themselves evidence of the fact that no consensus exists on how the outer limits of the word "literature" or the word "criticism" are to be determined. Several decades ago, literary history and systematic theory, of the kind pioneered by Northrop Frye, promised an orderly, inhabitable, and hospitable structure in which, for instance, it might be demonstrated that the mythos of summer could be transformed definably into the mythos of autumn. "The primal human act in Frye's system," writes Frank Lentricchia in *After the New Criticism,* quoting Frye's *The Educated Imagination,* "and a model for all human acts, is an 'informative,' creative act which transforms a world that is merely objective, set over against us, in which we 'feel lonely and frightened and unwanted' into a home."[1] But most literary scholars find themselves now, once again, out in the cold. Similarly, the history of ideas and comparative literature, two disciplines closely associated with the study of literature and literary criticism, do not routinely authorize in their practitioners quite the same Goethean sense of a concert of all literatures and ideas.

In all these instances the specific situation or locality of a particular intellectual task seems uneasily distant from, and only rhetorically assisted by, the legendary wholeness, coherence, and integrity of the general field to which one professionally belongs. There seem to be too many interruptions, too many distractions, too many irregularities interfering with the homogeneous space supposedly holding scholars together. The division of intellectual labor, which has meant increasing specialization, further erodes any direct apprehension one might have of a whole field of literature and literary study; conversely, the invasion of literary discourse by the *outré* jargons of semiotics, post-structuralism, and Lacanian psychoanalysis has distended the literary critical universe almost beyond recognition. In short, there seems nothing inherently literary about the study of what have traditionally been considered literary texts, no literariness that might prevent a contemporary literary critic from having recourse to psychoanalysis, sociology, or linguistics. Convention, historical custom, and appeals to the protocols of humanism and traditional scholarship are of course regularly introduced as evidence of the field's enduring integrity, but more and more these seem to be rhetorical strategies in a debate about what literature and literary criticisms ought to be rather than convincing definitions of what in fact they are. . . .

In the absence of an enclosing domain called literature, with clear outer boundaries, there is no longer an authorized or official position for the literary critic. But neither is there some new sovereign method, some new critical technology compelling allegiance and intellectual loyalty. Instead there is a babel of arguments for the limitlessness of all interpretation; of ideologies that proclaim the eternal yet determinate value of literature or "the humanities"; for all systems that in asserting their capacity to perform essentially self-confirming tasks allow for no counterfactual evidence. You can call such a situation pluralistic if you like or, if you have a taste for the melodramatic, you can call it desperate. For my part, I prefer to see it as an opportunity for remaining skeptical and critical, succumbing neither to dogmatism nor to sulky gloom.

Hence the specific problem of what happens to a theory when it moves from one place to another proposes itself as an interesting topic of investigation. For if fields like literature or the history of ideas have no intrinsically enclosing limits, and if, conversely, no one methodology is imposable upon what is an essentially heterogeneous and open area of activity—the writing and interpretation of texts—it is wise to raise the questions of theory and of criticism in ways suitable to the situation in which we find ourselves. At the outset, this means an historical approach. Assume therefore that, as a result of specific historical circumstances, a theory or idea pertaining to those circumstances arises. What happens to it when, in different circumstances and for new reasons, it is used again and, in still more different circumstances, again? What can this tell us about theory itself—its limits, its possibilities, its inherent problems—and what can it suggest to us about the relationship between theory and criticism, on the one hand, and society and culture on the other?

Lukács's *History and Class Consciousness* (1923) is justly famous for its analysis of the phenomenon of reification, a universal fate afflicting all aspects of life in an era dominated by commodity fetishism. Since, as Lukács argues, capitalism is the most articulated and quantitatively detailed of all economic systems, what it imposes upon human life and labor under its rule has the consequence of radically transforming everything human, flowing, processual, organic, and connected into disconnected and "alienated" objects, items, lifeless atoms. In such a situation, then, time sheds its qualitative, variable, flowing nature; it freezes into an exactly delimited, quantifiable continuum filled with quantifiable "things" (the reified, mechanically objectified "performance" of the worker, wholly separated from his total human personality): in short, it becomes space. In this environment where time is transformed into abstract, exactly measurable, physical space, an environment at once the cause and effect of the scientifically and mechanically fragmented and specialized production of the object of labor, the subjects of labor must likewise be rationally fragmented. On the one hand, the objectification of their labor-power into something opposed to their total personality (a process already accomplished with the sale of that labor-power as a commodity) is now made into the permanent ineluctable reality of their daily life. Here, too, the personality can do no more than look on helplessly while its own existence is reduced to an isolated particle and fed into an alien system. On the other hand, the mechanical disintegration of the process of production into its components also destroys those bonds that had bound individuals to a community in the days when production was still "organic." In this respect, too, mechanization makes of them isolated abstract atoms whose work no longer brings them together directly and organically; it becomes mediated to an increasing extent exclusively by the abstract laws of the mechanism which imprisons them.[2] If this picture of the public world is bleak, it is matched by Lukács's description of what happens to intellect, "the subject" as he calls it. After an astonishingly brilliant account of the antinomies of classical philosophy from Descartes to Kant to Fichte, Hegel, and Marx, in which he shows the increasing retreat of the subject into passive, privatized contemplation, gradually more and more divorced from the overwhelmingly fragmented realities of modern industrial life, Lukács then depicts modern bourgeois thought as being at an impasse, transfixed and paralyzed into terminal passivity. The science that it produces is based on mere fact gathering; the rational forms of understanding therefore cannot cope with the irrationality of physical *données*, and when efforts are made to compel "the facts" to submit to "system," their fragmentation and endlessly atomized *thereness* either destroy the system or turn the mind into a passive register of discrete objects.

There is, however, one form of experience that concretely represents the essence of reification as well as its limitation: crisis. If capitalism is the embodiment in economic terms of reification, then everything, including human beings, ought to be quantified and given a market value. This of course is what Lukács means when he speaks of articulation under capitalism, which he sometimes characterizes as if it were a gigantic itemized list. In principle nothing—no object, person, place, or time—is left out, since everything can be calculated. But there are moments when "the qualitative existence of the 'things' that lead their lives beyond the purview of economics as misunderstood and neglected things-in-themselves, as use-values [Lukács here refers to such "irrational" things as sentiment, passion, chance] suddenly becomes the decisive factor (suddenly, that is, for reified, rational thought). Or rather: these 'laws' fail to function and the reified mind is unable to perceive a pattern in this 'chaos.'"[3] At such a moment, then, mind or "subject" has its one opportunity to escape reification: by thinking through what it is that causes reality to appear to be only a collection of objects and economic *données*. And the very act of looking for process behind what appears to be eternally given and objectified, makes it possible for the mind to know itself as subject and not as a lifeless object, then to go beyond empirical reality into a putative realm of possibility. When instead of inexplicable shortage of bread you can imagine the human work and, subsequently, the human beings who produced the bread but are no longer doing so because there is a bakers' strike, you are well on your way to knowing that crisis is comprehensible because process is comprehensible; and if process is comprehensible, so too is some sense of the social whole created by human labor. Crisis, in short, is converted into criticism of the status quo: the bakers are on strike for a reason, the crisis can be explained, the system does not work infallibly, the subject has just demonstrated its victory over ossified objective forms.

Lukács puts all of this in terms of the subject-object relationship, and proper justice to his argument requires that it be followed to the point where he shows that reconciliation between subject and object will be possible. Yet even he admits that such an eventuality is very far into the future. Nevertheless, he is certain that no such future is attainable without the transformation of passive, contemplative consciousness into active, critical consciousness. In positing a world of human agency outside the reach of reification, the critical consciousness (the consciousness that is given rise to by crisis) becomes genuinely aware of its power "unceasingly to overthrow the objective forms that shape the life of man."[4] Consciousness goes beyond empirical givens and comprehends, without actually experiencing, history, totality, and society as a whole—precisely those unities that reification had both concealed and denied. At bottom, class consciousness is thought thinking its way through fragmentation to unity; it is also thought aware of its own subjectivity as something active, energetic, and, in a profound sense, poetic. . . .

Now because it rises above objects, consciousness enters a realm of potentiality, that is, of theoretical possibility. The special urgency of Lukács's account of this is that he is describing something rather far from a mere escape into fantasy. Consciousness attaining self-consciousness is no Emma Bovary pretending to be a lady in Yonville. The direct pressures of capitalist quantification, that relentless cataloguing of everything on earth, continue to be felt, according to Lukács; the only thing that changes is that the mind recognizes a class of beings like itself who have the power to think generally, to take in facts but to organize them in groups, to recognize processes and tendencies where reification only allows evidence of lifeless atoms. Class consciousness therefore begins in critical consciousness. Classes are not real the way trees and houses are real; they are imputable by consciousness, using its powers to posit ideal types in which with other beings it finds itself. Classes are the result of an insurrectionary act by which consciousness refuses to be confined to the world of objects, which is where it had been confined in the capitalist scheme of things.

Consciousness has moved from the world of objects into the world of theory. Although Lukács describes it as only a young German philosopher could describe it—in language bristling with more metaphysics and abstractions than even I have been using—we must not forget that he is performing an act of political insurgency. To attain to theory is to threaten reification, as well as the entire bourgeois system on which reification depends, with destruction. But, he assures his readers, this destruction "is no single unrepeatable tearing of the veil that masks the process [of reification] but the unbroken alternation of ossification, contradiction and movement."[5] Theory, in fine, is won as a result of a process that begins when consciousness first experiences its own terrible ossification in the general reification of all things under capitalism; then when consciousness generalizes (or classes) itself as something opposed to other objects, and feels itself as a contradiction to (or crisis within) objectification, there emerges a consciousness of change in the status quo; finally, moving toward freedom and fulfillment, consciousness looks ahead to complete self-realization, which is of course the revolutionary process stretching forward in time, perceivable now only as theory or projection. . . .

Theory for him was what consciousness produced, not as an avoidance of reality but as a revolutionary will completely committed to worldliness and change. According to Lukács, the proletariat's consciousness represented the theoretical antithesis to capitalism; as Merleau-Ponty and others have said, Lukács's proletariat can by no means be identified with a ragged collection of grimy-faced Hungarian laborers. The proletariat was his figure for consciousness defying reification, mind asserting its powers over mere matter, consciousness claiming its theoretical right to posit a better world outside the world of simple objects. And since class consciousness derives from workers working and being aware of themselves that way, theory must never lose touch with its origins in politics, society, and economics.

This, then, is Lukács describing his ideas about theory—and of course his theory of sociohistorical change—in the early twenties. Consider how Lukács's disciple and student, Lucien Goldmann, whose *Le Dieu caché* (1955) was one of the first and certainly among the most impressive attempts to put Lukács's theories to practical scholarly use. In Goldmann's study of Pascal and Racine, class consciousness has been changed to "vision du monde," something that is not an immediate, but a collective consciousness expressed in the work of certain highly gifted writers.[6] But this is not all. Goldmann says that these writers derive their world vision from determinate political and economic circumstances common to members of their group; yet the world vision itself is premised not so much on empirical detail as on a human faith that a reality exists "which goes beyond them as individuals and finds its expression in their work."[7] Writing as a politically committed scholar (and not like Lukács as a directly involved militant), Goldmann then argues that because Pascal and Racine were privileged writers, their work can be constituted into a significant whole by a process of dialectical theorizing, in which part is related to assumed whole, assumed whole verified empirically by empirical evidence. Thus individual texts are seen to express a world vision; second, the world vision constitutes the whole intellectual and social life of the group (the Port-Royal Jansenists); third, the thoughts and feelings of the group are an expression of their economic and social life.[8] In all this—and Goldmann argues with exemplary brilliance and subtlety—the theoretical enterprise, an interpretive circle, is a demonstration of coherence: between part and whole, between world vision and texts in their smallest detail, between a determinate social reality and the writings of particularly gifted members of a group. In other words, theory is the researcher's domain, the place in which disparate, apparently disconnected things are brought together in perfect correspondence: economics, political process, the individual writer, a series of texts.

Goldmann's indebtedness to Lukács is clear, although it has not been noted that what in Lukács is an ironic discrepancy between theoretical consciousness and reified reality is transformed and localized by Goldmann into a tragic correspondence between world vision and the unfortunate class situation of the *noblesse de robe* in late seventeenth-century France. Whereas Lukács's class consciousness defies, indeed is an insurgent against, the capitalist order, Goldmann's tragic vision is perfectly, absolutely expressed by the works of Pascal and Racine. True, the tragic vision is not directly expressed by those writers, and true also that it requires an extraordinarily complex dialectical style of research for the modern researcher to draw forth the correspondence between world vision and empirical detail; the fact nevertheless is that Goldmann's adaptation of Lukács removes from theory its insurrectionary role. The sheer existence of class, or theoretical, consciousness for Lukács is enough to suggest to him the projected overthrow of objective forms. For Goldmann an awareness of class or group consciousness is first of all a scholarly imperative, and then—in the works of highly privileged writers—the expression of a tragically limited social situation. Lukács's *zugerechmetes Bewusstsein* (imputed consciousness) is an unverifiable, yet absolutely prior theoretical necessity if one is to effect a change in social reality; in Goldmann's version of it, admittedly limited to an acutely circumscribed situation, theory and consciousness are expressed in the Pascalian wager upon an unseen and silent god, the *deus absconditus;* they are also expressed for Goldmann the scientific researcher, as he calls himself, in the theoretical correspondence between text and political reality. Or to put the matter in another way, for Lukács theory originates as a kind of irreducible dissonance between mind and object, whereas for Goldmann theory is the homological relationship that can be seen to exist between individual part and coherent whole.

The difference between the two versions of Lukács's theory of theory is evident enough: Lukács writes as a participant in a struggle (the Hungarian Soviet Republic of 1919), Goldmann as an expatriate historian at the Sorbonne. From one point of view we can say that Goldmann's adaptation of Lukács degrades theory, lowers it in importance, domesticates it somewhat to the exigencies of a doctoral dissertation in Paris. I do not think, however, that degradation here has a moral implication, but rather (as one of its secondary meanings suggests) that degradation conveys the lowering of color, the greater degree of distance, the loss of immediate force that occurs when Goldmann's notions of consciousness and theory are compared with the meaning and role intended by Lukács for theory. Nor do I want to suggest that there is something inherently wrong about Goldmann's conversion of insurrectionary, radically adversarial consciousness into an accommodating consciousness of correspondence and homology. It is just that the situation has changed sufficiently for the degradation to have occurred, although there is no doubt that Goldmann's reading of Lukács mutes the latter's almost apocalyptic version of consciousness.

We have become so accustomed to hearing that all borrowings, readings, and interpretations are misreadings and misinterpretations that we are likely to consider the Lukács-Goldmann episode as just another bit of evidence that everyone, even Marxists, misreads and misinterprets. I find such a conclusion completely unsatisfying. It implies, first of all, that the only possible alternative to slavish copying is creative misreading and that no intermediate possibility exists. Second, when it is elevated to a general principle, the idea that all reading is misreading is fundamentally an abrogation of the critic's responsibility. It is never enough for a critic taking the idea of criticism seriously simply to say that interpretation is misinterpretation or that borrowings inevitably involve misreadings. Quite the contrary: it seems to me perfectly possible to judge misreadings (as they occur) as part of a historical transfer of ideas and theories from one setting to another. Lukács wrote *for* as well as *in* a situation that produced ideas about consciousness and theory that are very different from the ideas produced by Goldmann in his situation. To call Goldmann's work a misreading of Lukács's, then to go on immediately to relate that misreading to a general theory of interpretation as misinterpretation, is to pay no critical attention to history and to situation, both of which play an important determining role in changing Lukács's ideas into Goldmann's. The Hungary of 1919 and post–World War II Paris are two quite different environments. To the degree that Lukács and Goldmann are read carefully, then to that precise degree we can understand the critical change—in time and in place—that occurs between one writer and another, both of whom depend on theory to accomplish a particular job of intellectual work. I see no need here to resort to the theory of limitless intertextuality as an Archimedean point outside the two situations. The particular voyage from Hungary to Paris, with all that entails, seems compelling enough, adequate enough for critical scrutiny, unless we want to give up critical consciousness for critical hermeticism.

In measuring Lukács and Goldmann against each other, then, we are also recognizing the extent to which theory is a response to a specific social and historical situation of which an intellectual occasion is a part. Thus what is insurrectionary consciousness in one instance becomes tragic vision in another, for reasons that are elucidated when the situations in Budapest and Paris are seriously compared. I do not wish to suggest that Budapest and Paris determined the kinds of theories produced by Lukács and Goldmann. I do mean that "Budapest" and "Paris" are irreducibly first conditions, and they provide limits and apply pressures to which each writer, given his own gifts, predilections, and interests, responds.

Let us now take Lukács as used by Goldmann, a step further: the use made of Goldmann by Raymond Williams. Brought up in the tradition of Cambridge English studies, trained in the techniques of Leavis and Richards, Williams was formed as a literary scholar who had no use whatever for theory. He speaks rather poignantly of how intellectuals educated as he was could use "a separate and self-defining language" that made a fetish of minute, concrete particulars; this meant that the intellectuals could approach power but speak antiseptically only of microcosm, profess not to understand reification, and to speak instead of the objective correlative, not to know mediation although they knew catharsis.[9] Williams tells us that Goldmann came to Cambridge in 1970 and gave two lectures there. This visit, according to Williams in the moving commemorative essay he wrote about Goldmann after his death, was a major event. It introduced Cambridge to theory, Williams claims, understood and employed as it had been by thinkers trained in the major Continental tradition. Goldmann induced in Williams an appreciation of Lukács's contribution to our understanding of how, in an era of "the dominance of economic activity over all other forms of human activity," reification was both a false objectivity so far as knowledge was concerned and a deformation thoroughly penetrating life and consciousness more than any other form. Williams continues:

> The idea of totality was then a critical weapon against this precise deformation; indeed, against capitalism itself. And yet this was not idealism—an assertion of the primacy of other values. On the contrary, just as the deformation could be understood, at its roots, only by historical analysis of a particular kind of economy, so the attempt to overcome and surpass it lay not in isolated witness or in separated

> activity but in practical work to find, assert and to establish more human social ends in more human and political and economic means.[10]

Once again Lukács's thought—in this instance the avowedly revolutionary idea of totality—has been tamed somewhat. Without wishing in any way to belittle the importance of what Lukács's ideas (via Goldmann) did for the moribund state of English studies in late twentieth-century Cambridge, I think it needs to be said that those ideas were originally formulated in order to do more than shake up a few professors of literature. This is an obvious, not to say easy, point. What is more interesting, however, is that because Cambridge is not revolutionary Budapest, because Williams is not the militant Lukács, because Williams is a reflective critic—this is critical—rather than a committed revolutionary, he can see the limits of a theory that begins as a liberating idea but can become a trap of its own.

> At the most practical level it was easy for me to agree [with Lukács's theory of totality as a response to reification]. But then the whole point of thinking in terms of a totality is the realization that we are part of it; that our own consciousness, our work, our methods, are then critically at stake. And in the particular field of literary analysis there was this obvious difficulty: that most of the work we had to look at was the product of just this work of reified consciousness, so that *what looked like the methodological breakthrough might become, quite quickly, the methodological trap.* I cannot yet say this finally about Lukács, since I still don't have access to all his work; but in some of it, at least, *the major insights of History and Class-Consciousness,* which he has now partly disavowed, *do not get translated into critical practice* [Williams refers here to Lukács's later, much cruder work on European realism] and certain cruder operations—essentially still those of base and superstructure—keep reappearing. *I still read Goldmann collaboratively and critically asking the same question,* for I am sure the practice of totality is still for any of us, at any time, profoundly and even obviously difficult.[11]

This is an admirable passage. Even though Williams says nothing about the lamentable repetitiveness of Goldmann's later work, it is important that as a critic who has learned from someone else's theory he should be able to see the theory's limitations, especially the fact that a breakthrough can become a trap, if it is used uncritically, repetitively, limitlessly. What he means, I think, is that once an idea gains currency because it is clearly effective and powerful, there is every likelihood that during its peregrinations it will be reduced, codified, and institutionalized. Lukács's remarkably complex exposition of the phenomenon of reification indeed did turn into a simple reflection theory; to a degree of course, and Williams is too decently elegiac to say it about a recently dead old friend, it did become this sort of idea in Goldmann's hands. Homology is, after all, a refined version of the old Second International base-and-superstructure model.

Beyond the specific reminder of what could happen to a vanguard theory, Williams's ruminations enable us to make another observation about theory as it develops out of a situation, begins to be used, travels, and gains wide acceptance. For if reification-and-totality (to turn Lukács's theory now into a shorthand phrase for easy reference) can become a reductionist implement, there is no reason why it could not become too inclusive, too ceaselessly active and expanding a habit of mind. That is, if a theory can move down, so to speak, become a dogmatic reduction of its original version, it can also move up into a sort of bad infinity, which—in the case of reification-and-totality—is the direction intended by Lukács himself. To speak of the unceasing overthrow of objective forms, and to speak as he does in the essay on class consciousness, of how the logical end of overcoming reification is the self-annihilation of the revolutionary class itself, means that Lukács had pushed his theory farther forward and upward, unacceptably (in my opinion). The contradiction inherent in this theory—and perhaps in most theories that develop as responses to the need for movement and change—is that it risks becoming a theoretical overstatement, a theoretical parody of the situation it was formulated originally to remedy or overcome. To prescribe "an *unbroken* alternation of ossification, contradiction and movement" toward totality as a theoretical remedy for reification is in a sense to substitute one unchanging formula for another. To say of theory and theoretical consciousness, as Lukács does, that they intervene in reification and introduce process is not carefully enough to calculate, and allow for, the details and the resistances offered by an intransigent, reified reality to theoretical consciousness. For all the brilliance of his account of reification, for all the care he takes with it, Lukács is unable to see how even under capitalism reification itself cannot be totally dominant—unless, of course, he is prepared to allow something that theoretical totality (his insurrectional instrument for overcoming reification) says is impossible, namely, that totality in the form of totally dominant reification is theoretically possible under capitalism. For if reification is totally dominant, how then can Lukács explain his own work as an alternative form of thought under the sway of reification?

Perhaps all this is too fussy and hermetic. Nevertheless, it seems to me that however far away in time and place Williams may be from the fiery rebelliousness of the early Lukács, there is an extraordinary virtue to the distance, even the coldness of his critical reflections on Lukács and Goldmann, to both of whom he is otherwise so intellectually cordial. He takes from both men a sophisticated theoretical awareness of the issues involved in connecting literature to society, as he puts it in his best single theoretical essay, "Base and Superstructure in Marxist Cultural Theory." The terminology provided by Marxist aesthetic theory for mapping the peculiarly uneven and complicated field lying between base and superstructure is generally inadequate, and then Williams goes on to do work that embodies *his* critical version of the original theory. He puts this version very well, I think, in *Politics and Letters:* "however dominant a social system may be, the very meaning of its domination involves a limitation or selection of the activities it covers, so that by definition it cannot exhaust all social experience, which therefore always potentially contains space for alternative acts and alternative intentions which are not yet articulated as a social institution or even project."[12] *The Country and the City* records both the limits and the reactive alternatives to dominance, as in the case of John Clare, whose work "marks the end of pastoral poetry [as a systematic convention for describing the English countryside] in the very shock of its collision with actual country experience." Clare's very existence as a poet was threatened by the removal of an acceptable social order from the customary landscape idealized by Jonson and Thomson; hence Clare's turning—as an alternative not yet fully realized and not yet completely subdued by the inhuman relationships that obtained under the system of market exploitation—to "the green language of the new Nature," that is, the Nature to be celebrated in a new way by the great Romantics.[13]

There is no minimizing the fact that Williams is an important critic because of his gifts and his insights. But I am convinced it would be wrong to underestimate the role in his mature writings played by what I have been alluding to as borrowed, or traveling, theory. For borrow we certainly must if we are to elude the constraints of our immediate intellectual environment. Theory we certainly need, for all sorts of reasons that would be too tedious to rehearse here. What we also need over and above theory, however, is the critical recognition that there is no theory capable of covering, closing off, predicting all the situations in which it might be useful. This is another way of saying, as Williams does, that no social or intellectual system can be so dominant as to be unlimited in its strength. Williams therefore has the critical recognition, and uses it consciously to qualify, shape, and refine his borrowings from Lukács and Goldmann, although we should hasten to add that it does not make him infallible or any less liable to exaggeration and error for having it. But unless theory is unanswerable, either through its successes or its failures, to the essential untidiness, the essential unmasterable presence that constitutes a large part of historical and social situations (and this applies equally to theory that derives from somewhere else or theory that is "original"), then theory becomes an ideological trap. It transfixes both its users and what it is used on. Criticism would no longer be possible.

Theory, in short, can never be complete, just as one's interest in everyday life is never exhausted by simulacra, models, or theoretical abstracts of it. Of course one derives pleasure from actually making evidence fit or work in a theoretical scheme, and of course it is ridiculously foolish to argue that "the facts" or "the great texts" do not require any theoretical framework or methodology to be appreciated or read properly. No reading is neutral or innocent, and by the same token every text and every reader is to some extent the product of a theoretical standpoint, however implicit or unconscious such a standpoint may be. I am arguing, however, that we distinguish theory from critical consciousness by saying that the latter is a sort of spatial sense, a sort of measuring faculty for locating or situating theory, and this means that theory has to be grasped in the place and the time out of which it emerges as a part of that time, working in and for it, responding to it; then, consequently, that first place can be measured against subsequent places where the theory turns up for use. The critical consciousness is awareness of the differences between situations, awareness too of the fact that no system or theory exhausts the situation out of which it emerges or to which it is transported. And, above all, critical consciousness is awareness of the resistances to the theory, reactions to it elicited by those concrete experiences or interpretations with which it is in conflict. Indeed I would go as far as saying that it is the critic's job to provide resistances to theory, to open it up toward historical reality, toward society, toward human needs and interests, to point up those concrete instances drawn from everyday reality that lie outside or just beyond the interpretive area necessarily designated in advance and thereafter circumscribed by every theory.

Much of this is illustrated if we compare Lukács and Williams on the one hand with Goldmann on the other. I have already said that Williams is conscious of what he calls a methodological trap. Lukács, for his part, shows in his career as a theorist (if not in the fully fledged theory itself) a profound awareness of the necessity to move from hermetic aestheticism (*Die Seele und die Formen, Die Theorie des Romans*) toward the actual world of power and institutions. By contrast, Goldmann is enmeshed in the homological finality that his writing, brilliantly and persuasively in the case of *Le Dieu caché,* demonstrates. Theoretical closure, like social convention or cultural dogma, is anathema to critical consciousness, which loses its profession when it loses its active sense of an open world in which its faculties must be exercised. One of the best lessons of that is to be found in Lentricchia's powerful *After the New Criticism,* a wholly persuasive account of what he calls "the currently paralyzed debates" of contemporary literary theory.[14] In instance after instance he demonstrates the impoverishment and rarefication that overtake any theory relatively untested by and unexposed to the complex enfolding of the social world, which is never a merely complaisant context to be used for the enactment of theoretical situations. (As an antidote to the bareness afflicting the American situation, there is in Fredric Jameson's *The Political Unconscious,* an extremely useful account of three "semantic horizons" to be figured in dialectically by the interpreter as parts of the decoding process, which he also calls "the cultural mode of production."[15])

Yet we must be aware that the social reality I have been alluding to is no less susceptible to theoretical overtotalization, even when, as I shall be showing in the case of Foucault, extremely powerful historical scholarship moves itself out from the archive toward the world of power and institutions, toward precisely those resistances to theory ignored and elided by most formalistic theory—deconstruction, semiotics, Lacanian psychoanalysis, the Althusserian Marxism attacked by E. P. Thompson.[16] Foucault's work is most challenging because he is rightly considered to be an exemplary opponent of ahistorical, asocial formalism. But he too, I believe, falls victim to the systematic degradation of theory in ways that his newest disciples consider to be evidence that he has not succumbed to hermeticism.

Foucault is a paradox. His career presents his contemporary audience with an extraordinarily compelling trajectory whose culmination, most recently, has been the announcement made by him, and on his behalf by his disciples, that his real theme is the relationship between knowledge and power. Thanks to the brilliance of his theoretical and practical performances, *pouvoir* and *savior* have provided his readers (it would be churlish not to mention myself; but see also Jacques Donzelot's *La Police des familles*) with a conceptual apparatus for the analysis of instrumental discourses that stands in stark contrast to the fairly arid metaphysics produced habitually by the students of his major philosophical competitors. Yet Foucault's earliest work was in many ways remarkably unconscious of its own theoretical force. Reread *Histoire de la folie* after *Surveiller et punir* and you will be struck with how uncannily prescient the early work is of the later; and yet you will also be struck that even when Foucault deals with *renfermement* (confinement), his obsessive theme, in discussing asylums and hospitals, power is never referred to explicitly. Neither for that matter is *volonté,* will. *Les Mots et les choses* might be excused for the same neglect of power, on the grounds that the subject of Foucault's inquiry was intellectual, not institutional history. In *The Archeology of Knowledge* there are intimations here and there that Foucault is beginning to approach power through a number of abstractions, surrogates for it: thus he refers to such things as acceptability, accumulation, preservation, and formation that are ascribed to the making and the functioning of statements, discourses, and archives; yet he does so without spending any time on what might be the common source of their strength within institutions or fields of knowledge or society itself.

Foucault's theory of power—to which I shall restrict myself here—derives from his attempt to analyze working systems of confinement from the inside, systems whose functioning depends equally on the continuity of institutions as on the proliferation of justifying technical ideologies for the institutions. These ideologies are his discourses and disciplines. In his concrete presentation of local situations in which such power and such knowledge are deployed, Foucault has no peer, and what he has done is remarkably interesting by any standard. As he says in *Surveiller et punir,* for power to work it must be able to manage, control, and even create detail: the more detail, the more real power, management breeding manageable units, which in turn breed a more detailed, a more finely controlling knowledge. Prisons, he says in that memorable passage, are factories for producing delinquency, and delinquency is the raw material for disciplinary discourses.

With descriptions and particularized observations of this sort I have no trouble. It is when Foucault's own language becomes general (when he moves his analyses of power from the detail to society as a whole) that the methodological breakthrough becomes the theoretical trap. Interestingly, this is slightly more evident when Foucault's theory is transported from France and planted in the work of his overseas disciples. Recently, for example, he has been celebrated by Ian Hacking as a kind of hard-headed alternative to the too backward and forward-looking "Romantic" Marxists (which Marxists? all Marxists?), and as a ruthlessly anarchistic opponent of Noam Chomsky, who is described inappropriately as "a marvelously sane liberal reformer."[17] Other writers, who quite rightly see Foucault's discussions of power as a refreshing window opened on to the real world of politics and society, uncritically misread his pronouncements as the latest thing about social reality.[18] There is no doubt that Foucault's work is indeed an important alternative to the ahistorical formalism with which he has been conducting an implicit debate, and there is a great merit to his view that as a specialized intellectual (as opposed to a universal intellectual)[19] he and others like him can wage small-scale guerrilla warfare against some repressive institutions, and against "silence" and "secrecy."

But all that is quite another thing from accepting Foucault's view in *The History of Sexuality* that "power is everywhere" along with all that such a vastly simplified view entails.[20] For one, as I have said, Foucault's eagerness not to fall into Marxist economism causes him to obliterate the role of classes, the role of economics, the role of insurgency and rebellion in the societies he discusses. Let us suppose that prisons, schools, armies, and factories were, as he says, disciplinary factories in nineteenth-century France (since he talks almost exclusively about France), and that panoptic rule dominated them all. What resistances were there to the disciplinary order and why, as Nicos Poulantzas has so trenchantly argued in *State, Power, Socialism,* does Foucault never discuss the resistances that always end up dominated by the system he describes? The facts are more complicated of course, as any good historian of the rise of the modern state can demonstrate. Moreover, Poulantzas continues, even if we accept the view that power is essentially rational, that it is not held by anyone but is strategic, dispositional, effective, that, as *Discipline and Punish* claims, it invests all areas of society, is it correct to conclude, as Foucault does, that power is exhausted in its use?[21] Is it not simply wrong, Poulantzas asks, to say that power is not *based* anywhere and that struggles and exploitation—both terms left out of Foucault's analyses—do not occur?[22] The problem is that Foucault's use of the term *pouvoir* moves around too much, swallowing up every obstacle in its path (resistances to it, the class and economic bases that refresh and fuel it, the reserves it builds up), obliterating change and mystifying its microphysical sovereignty.[23] A symptom of how overblown Foucault's conception of power can become when it travels too far is Hacking's statement that "nobody knows this knowledge; no one yields this power." Surely this is going to extremes in order to prove that Foucault is not a simple-minded follower of Marx.

In fact, Foucault's theory of power is a Spinozist conception, which has captivated not only Foucault himself but many of his readers who wish to go beyond Left optimism and Right pessimism so as to justify political quietism with sophisticated intellectualism, at the same time wishing to appear realistic, in touch with the world of power and reality, as well as historical and antiformalistic in their bias. The trouble is that Foucault's theory has drawn a circle around itself, constituting a unique territory in which Foucault has imprisoned himself and others with him. It is certainly wrong to say, with Hacking, that hope, optimism, and pessimism are shown by Foucault to be mere satellites of the idea of a transcendental, enduring subject, since empirically we experience and act according to those things daily without reference to any such irrelevant "subject." There is after all a sensible difference between Hope and hope, just as there is between Logos and words: we must not let Foucault get away with confusing them with each other, nor with letting us forget that history does not get made without work, intention, resistance, effort, or conflict, and that none of these things is silently absorbable into micronetworks of power.

There is a more important criticism to be made of Foucault's theory of power, and it has been made most tellingly by Chomsky. Unfortunately most of Foucault's new readers in the United States seem not to know of the exchange that took place between them several years ago on Dutch television,[24] nor of Chomsky's succinct critique of Foucault contained in *Language and Responsibility.* Both men agreed on the necessity of opposing repression, a position Foucault has since found it more difficult to take unequivocally. Yet for Chomsky the sociopolitical battle had to be waged with two tasks in mind: one, "to imagine a future society that conforms to the exigencies of human nature as best we understand them; the other to analyze the nature of power and oppression in our present societies."[25] Foucault assented to the second without in any way accepting the first. According to him, any future societies that we might imagine now "are only the inventions of our civilization and result from our class system." Not only would imagining a future society ruled according to justice be limited by false consciousness, it would also be too utopian to project for anyone like Foucault who believes that "the idea of justice in itself is an idea which in effect has been invented and put to work in different societies as an instrument of a certain political and economic power or as a weapon against that power."[26] This is a perfect instance of Foucault's unwillingness to take seriously his own ideas about resistances to power. If power oppresses and controls and manipulates, then everything that resists it is not morally equal to power, is not neutrally and simply a weapon against that power. Resistance cannot equally be an adversarial alternative to power and a dependent function of it, except in some metaphysical, ultimately trivial sense. Even if the distinction is hard to draw, there is a distinction to be made—as, for example, Chomsky does when he says that he would give his support to an oppressed proletariat if as a class it made justice the goal of its struggle.

The disturbing circularity of Foucault's theory of power is a form of theoretical overtotalization superficially more difficult to resist because, unlike many others, it is formulated, reformulated, and borrowed for use in what seem to be historically documented situations. But note that Foucault's history is ultimately textual, or rather textualized; its mode is one for which Borges would have an affinity. Gramsci, on the other hand, would find it uncongenial. He would certainly appreciate the fineness of Foucault's archeologies, but would find it odd that they make not even a nominal allowance for emergent movements, and none for revolutions, counterhegemony, or historical blocks. In human history there is always something beyond the reach of dominating systems, no matter how deeply they saturate society, and this is obviously what makes change possible, limits power in Foucault's sense, and hobbles the theory of that power. One could not imagine Foucault undertaking a sustained analysis of powerfully contested political issues, nor, like Chomsky himself and writers like John Berger, would Foucault commit himself to descriptions of power and oppression with some intention of alleviating human suffering, pain, or betrayed hope.

It may seem an abrupt conclusion to reach, but the kinds of theory I have been discussing can quite easily become cultural dogma. Appropriated to schools or institutions, they quickly acquire the status of authority within the cultural group, guild, or affiliative family. Though of course they are to be distinguished from grosser forms of cultural dogma like racism and nationalism, they are insidious in that their original provenance—their history of adversarial, oppositional derivation—dulls the critical consciousness, convincing it that a once insurgent theory is still insurgent, lively, responsive to history. Left to its own specialists and acolytes, so to speak, theory tends to have walls erected around itself, but this does not mean that critics should either ignore theory or look despairingly around for newer varieties. To measure the distance between theory then and now, there and here, to record the encounter of theory with resistances to it, to move skeptically in the broader political world where such things as the humanities or the great classics ought to be seen as small provinces of the human venture, to map the territory covered by all the techniques of dissemination, communication, and interpretation, to preserve some modest (perhaps shrinking) belief in noncoercive human community: if these are not imperatives, they do at least seem to be attractive alternatives. And what is critical consciousness at bottom if not an unstoppable predilection for alternatives?

from *The World, the Text, and the Critic*

8

Secular Criticism

(1983)

As the literary critic Aamir Mufti has noted, it is through the strategy of "secular criticism" that Said repeatedly identifies his critical practice, not "postcolonial criticism," the field developed out of *Orientalism* nor "contrapuntal reading," the sensibility encouraged in *Culture and Imperialism*. What exactly is secular criticism? First elaborated upon in this lead essay from *The World, the Text, and the Critic*, secular criticism should not be understood as a critical method established to debunk organized religion. Rather, it is commentary on the manner in which literary criticism is itself bound up with social realities, human experiences, and institutions of authority and power. "Criticism," Said writes, "can no longer cooperate in or pretend to ignore this enterprise. It is not practicing criticism either to validate the status quo or to join up with a priestly caste of acolytes and dogmatic metaphysicians." This stance against "priestly castes" of all structures of authority and dogma, what Said (borrowing from the Italian Marxist Antonio Gramsci) calls a "critical consciousness," is what defines "secular criticism."

"Secular Criticism" does not only self-consciously reflect on Said's own critical project. It also investigates the role of literary scholarship generally and attempts to account for the rise of increasing specialization among literary critics vis-à-vis the growth of a new academic literary industry (literary theory) with the concomitant ascendancy of Reaganism. By ignoring "the world of events and societies, which modern history, intellectuals, and critics have in fact built," this "flight into method" by literary critics can far too easily allow the critic to reinforce prevailing cultural pieties of ethnocentrism, nationalism, and "quasi-religious quietism." Said counterposes this esoteric professionalism not only with the practice of "secular criticism" but with his concept of "worldliness," a recognition that intellectual work is always situated somewhere in the world, somewhere between "culture and system."

The conceptual innovations of secular criticism and worldliness as elaborated in this essay and in the rest of *The World, the Text, and the Critic* were bold confrontations to a profession that largely wished to avoid difficult questions of its ethical practice. The impact would be long-lasting, proving what Raymond Williams wrote when reviewing the book, that Said was "beginning to substantiate, as distinct from announcing, a genuinely emergent way of thinking."

Literary criticism is practiced today in four major forms. One is the practical criticism to be found in book reviewing and literary journalism. Second is academic literary history, which is a descendant of such nineteenth-century specialties as classical scholarship, philology, and cultural history. Third is literary appreciation and interpretation, principally academic but, unlike the other two, not confined to professionals and regularly appearing authors. Appreciation is what is taught and performed by teachers of literature in the university and its beneficiaries in a literal sense are all those millions of people who have learned in a classroom how to read a poem, how to enjoy the complexity of a metaphysical conceit, how to think of literature and figurative language as having characteristics that are unique and not reducible to a simple moral or political message. And the fourth form is literary theory, a relatively new subject. It appeared as an eye-catching topic for academic and popular discussion in the United States later than it did in Europe: people like Walter Benjamin and the young Georg Lukács, for instance, did their theoretical work in the early years of this century, and they wrote in a known, if not universally uncontested, idiom. American literary theory, despite the pioneering studies of Kenneth Burke well before World War II, came of age only in the 1970s, and that because of an observably deliberate attention to prior European models (structuralism, semiotics, deconstruction). . . .

Now the prevailing situation of criticism is such that the four forms represent in each instance specialization (although literary theory is a bit eccentric) and a very precise division of intellectual labor. Moreover, it is supposed that literature and the humanities exist generally within the culture ("our" culture, as it is sometimes known), that the culture is ennobled and validated by them, and yet that in the version of culture inculcated by professional humanists and literary critics, the approved practice of high culture is marginal to the serious political concerns of society.

This has given rise to a cult of professional expertise whose effect in general is pernicious. For the intellectual class, expertise has usually been a service rendered, and sold, to the central authority of society. This is the *trahison des clercs* of which Julien Benda spoke in the 1920s. Expertise in foreign affairs, for example, has usually meant legitimization of the conduct of foreign policy and, what is more to the point, a sustained investment in revalidating the role of experts in foreign affairs.[1] The same sort of thing is true of literary critics and professional humanists, except that their expertise is based upon noninterference in what Vico grandly calls the world of nations but which prosaically might just as well be called "the world." We tell our students and our general constituency that we defend the classics, the virtues of a liberal education, and the precious pleasures of literature even as we also show ourselves to be silent (perhaps incompetent) about the historical and social world in which all these things take place.

The degree to which the cultural realm and its expertise are institutionally divorced from their real connections with power was wonderfully illustrated for me by an exchange with an old college friend who worked in the Department of Defense for a period during the Vietnam War. The bombings were in full course then, and I was naively trying to understand the kind of person who could order daily B-52 strikes over a distant Asian country in the name of the American interest in defending freedom and stopping communism. "You know," my friend said, "the Secretary is a complex human being: he doesn't fit the picture you may have formed of the cold-blooded imperialist murderer. The last time I was in his office I noticed Durrell's *Alexandria Quartet* on his desk." He paused meaningfully, as if to let Durrell's presence on that desk work its awful power alone. The further implication of my friend's story was that no one who read and presumably appreciated a novel could be the cold-blooded butcher one might suppose him to have been.[2] Many years later this whole implausible anecdote (I do not remember my response to the complex conjunction of Durrell with the ordering of bombing in the sixties) strikes me as typical of what actually obtains: humanists and intellectuals accept the idea that you can read classy fiction as well as kill and maim because the cultural world is available for that particular sort of camouflaging, and because cultural types are not supposed to interfere in matters for which the social system has not certified them. What the anecdote illustrates is the approved separation of high-level bureaucrat from the reader of novels of questionable worth and definite status.

During the late 1960s, however, literary theory presented itself with new claims. The intellectual origins of literary theory in Europe were, I think it is accurate to say, insurrectionary. . . . And yet something happened, perhaps inevitably. From being a bold interventionary movement across lines of specialization, American literary theory of the late seventies had retreated into the labyrinth of "textuality," dragging along with it the most recent apostles of European revolutionary textuality—Derrida and Foucault—whose trans-Atlantic canonization and domestication they themselves seemed sadly enough to be encouraging. It is not too much to say that American or even European literary theory now explicitly accepts the principle of noninterference, and that its peculiar mode of appropriating its subject matter (to use Althusser's formula) is *not* to appropriate anything that is worldly, circumstantial, or socially contaminated. "Textuality" is the somewhat mystical and disinfected subject matter of literary theory.

Textuality has therefore become the exact antithesis and displacement of what might be called history. Textuality is considered to take place, yes, but by the same token it does not take place anywhere or anytime in particular. It is produced, but by no one and at no time. It can be read and interpreted, although reading and interpreting are routinely understood to occur in the form of misreading and misinterpreting. The list of examples could be extended indefinitely, but the point would remain the same. As it is practiced in the American academy today, literary theory has for the most part isolated textuality from the circumstances, the events, the physical senses that made it possible and render it intelligible as the result of human work.

Even if we accept (as in the main I do) the arguments put forward by Hayden White—that there is no way to get past texts in order to apprehend "real" history directly[3]—it is still possible to say that such a claim need not also eliminate interest in the events and the circumstances entailed by and expressed in the texts themselves. Those events and circumstances are textual too (nearly all of Conrad's tales and novels present us with a situation—giving rise to the narrative that forms the text), and much that goes on in texts alludes to them, *affiliates* itself directly to them. My position is that texts are worldly, to some degree they are events, and, even when they appear to deny it, they are nevertheless a part of the social world, human life, and of course the historical moments in which they are located and interpreted.

Literary theory, whether of the Left or of the Right, has turned its back on these things. This can be considered, I think, the triumph of the ethic of professionalism. But it is no accident that the emergence of so narrowly defined a philosophy of pure textuality and critical noninterference has coincided with the ascendancy of Reaganism, or for that matter with a new cold war, increased militarism and defense spending, and a massive turn to the right on matters touching the economy, social services, and organized labor.[4] In having given up the world entirely for the aporias and unthinkable paradoxes of a text, contemporary criticism has retreated from its constituency, the citizens of modern society, who have been left to the hands of "free" market forces, multinational corporations, the manipulations of consumer appetites. A precious jargon has grown up, and its formidable complexities obscure the social realities that, strange though it may seem, encourage a scholarship of "modes of excellence" very far from daily life in the age of declining American power.

Criticism can no longer cooperate in or pretend to ignore this enterprise. It is not practicing criticism either to validate the status quo or to join up with a priestly caste of acolytes and dogmatic metaphysicians. The realities of power and authority—as well as the resistances offered by men, women, and social movements to institutions, authorities, and orthodoxies—are the realities that make texts possible, that deliver them to their readers, that solicit the attention of critics. I propose that these realities are what should be taken account of by criticism and the critical consciousness.

It should be evident by now that this sort of criticism can only be practiced outside and beyond the consensus ruling the art today in the four accepted forms I mentioned earlier. Yet if this is the function of criticism at the present time, to be between the dominant culture and the totalizing forms of critical systems, then there is some comfort in recalling that this has also been the destiny of critical consciousness in the recent past.

No reader of Erich Auerbach's *Mimesis,* one of the most admired and influential books of literary criticism ever written, has failed to be impressed by the circumstances of the book's actual writing. These are referred to almost casually by Auerbach in the last lines of his epilogue, which stands as a very brief methodological explanation for what is after all a monumental work of literary intelligence. In remarking that for so ambitious a study as "the representation of reality in Western Literature" he could not deal with everything that had been written in and about Western literature, Auerbach then adds:

> I may also mention that the book was written during the war and at Istanbul, where the libraries are not equipped for European studies. International communications were impeded; I had to dispense with almost all periodicals, with almost all the more recent investigations, and in some cases with reliable critical editions of my texts. Hence it is possible and even probable that I overlooked things which I ought to have considered and that I occasionally assert something that

> modern research has disproved or modified. . . . On the other hand, it is quite possible that the book owes its existence to just this lack of a rich and specialized library. If it had been possible for me to acquaint myself with all the work that has been done on so many subjects, I might never have reached the point of writing.[5]

The drama of this little bit of modesty is considerable, in part because Auerbach's quiet tone conceals much of the pain of his exile. He was a Jewish refugee from Nazi Europe, and he was also a European scholar in the old tradition of German Romance scholarship. Yet now in Istanbul he was hopelessly out of touch with the literary, cultural, and political bases of that formidable tradition. In writing *Mimesis,* he implies to us in a later work, he was not merely practicing his profession despite adversity: he was performing an act of cultural, even civilizational, survival of the highest importance. What he had risked was not only the possibility of appearing in his writing to be superficial, out of date, wrong, and ridiculously ambitious (who in his right mind would take on as a project so vast a subject as Western literature in its entirety?). He had also risked, on the other hand, the possibility of *not* writing and thus falling victim to the concrete dangers of exile: the loss of texts, traditions, continuities that make up the very web of a culture. And in so losing the authentic presence of the culture, as symbolized materially by libraries, research institutes, other books and scholars, the exiled European would become an exorbitantly disoriented outcast from sense, nation, and milieu.

That Auerbach should choose to mention Istanbul as the place of his exile adds yet another dose of drama to the actual fact of *Mimesis.* To any European trained principally, as Auerbach was, in medieval and renaissance Roman literatures, Istanbul does not simply connote a place outside Europe. Istanbul represents the terrible Turk, as well as Islam, the scourge of Christendom, the great Oriental apostasy incarnate. Throughout the classical period of European culture Turkey was the Orient, Islam its most redoubtable and aggressive representative.[6] This was not all, though. The Orient and Islam also stood for the ultimate alienation from and opposition to Europe, the European tradition of Christian Latinity, as well as to the putative authority of ecclesia, humanistic learning, and cultural community. For centuries Turkey and Islam hung over Europe like a gigantic composite monster, seeming to threaten Europe with destruction. To have been an exile in Istanbul at that time of fascism in Europe was a deeply resonating and intense form of exile from Europe.

Yet Auerbach explicitly makes the point that it was precisely his distance from home—in all senses of that word—that made possible the superb undertaking of *Mimesis*. How did exile become converted from a challenge or a risk, or even from an active impingement on his European selfhood, into a positive mission, whose success would be a cultural act of great importance?

The answer to this question is to be found in Auerbach's autumnal essay "Philologie der Weltliteratur." The major part of the essay elaborates on the notion first explicitly announced in *Mimesis,* but already recognizable in Auerbach's early interest in Vico, that philological work deals with humanity at large and transcends national boundaries. As he says, "our philological home is the earth: it can no longer be the nation." His essay makes clear, however, that his earthly home is European culture. But then, as if remembering the period of his extra-European exile in the Orient, he adds: "The most priceless and indispensable part of a philologist's heritage is still his own nation's culture and heritage. Only when he is first separated from this heritage, however, and then transcends it does it become truly effective."[7] In order to stress the salutary value of separation from home, Auerbach cites a passage from Hugo of St. Victor's *Didascalicon:*

> It is, therefore, a great source of virtue for the practiced mind to learn, bit by bit, first to change about in visible and transitory things, so that afterwards it may be able to leave them behind altogether. The man who finds his homeland sweet is still a tender beginner; he to whom every soil is as his native one is already strong; but he is perfect to whom the entire world is as a foreign land [the Latin text is more explicit here—*perfectus vero cui mundus totus exilium est*].

This is all that Auerbach quotes from Hugo; the rest of the passage continues along the same lines.

> The tender soul has fixed his love on one spot in the world; the strong man has extended his love to all places; the perfect man has

> extinguished his. From boyhood I have dwelt on foreign soil, and I know with what grief sometimes the mind takes leave of the narrow hearth of a peasant's hut, and I know, too, how frankly it afterwards disdains marble firesides and panelled halls.[8]

Auerbach associates Hugo's exilic credo with the notions of *paupertas* and *terra aliena,* even though in his essay's final words he maintains that the ascetic code of willed homelessness is "a good way also for one who wishes to earn a proper love for the world." At this point, then, Auerbach's epilogue to *Mimesis* suddenly becomes clear: "it is quite possible that the book owes its existence to just this lack of a rich and specialized library." In other words, the book owed its existence to the very fact of Oriental, non-Occidental exile and homelessness. And if this is so, then *Mimesis* itself is not, as it has so frequently been taken to be, only a massive reaffirmation of the Western cultural tradition, but also a work built upon a critically important alienation from it, a work whose conditions and circumstances of existence are not immediately derived from the culture it describes with such extraordinary insight and brilliance but built rather on an agonizing distance from it. Auerbach says as much when he tells us in an earlier section of *Mimesis* that, had he tried to do a thorough scholarly job in the traditional fashion, he could never have written the book: the culture itself, with its authoritative and authorizing agencies, would have prevented so audacious a one-man task. Hence the executive value of exile, which Auerbach was able to turn into effective use.

Let us look again at the notion of place, the notion by which during a period of displacement someone like Auerbach in Istanbul could feel himself to be out of place, exiled, alienated. The readiest account of place might define it as the nation, and certainly in the exaggerated boundary drawn between Europe and the Orient—a boundary with a long and often unfortunate tradition in European thought[9]—the idea of the nation, of a national-cultural community as a sovereign entity and place set against other places, has its fullest realization. But this idea of place does not cover the nuances, principally of reassurance, fitness, belonging, association, and community, entailed in the phrase *at home* or *in place.* In this book I shall use the word "culture" to suggest an environment, process, and hegemony in which individuals (in their private circumstances) and their works are embedded, as well as overseen at the top by a superstructure and at the base by a whole series of methodological attitudes. It is in culture that we can seek out the range of meanings and ideas conveyed by the phrases *belonging to* or *in a* place, being *at home in a place*.

The idea of culture of course is a vast one. As a systematic body of social and political as well as historical significance, "culture" is similarly vast; one index of it is the Kroeber-Kluckhohn thesaurus on meanings of the word "culture" in social science.[10] I shall avoid the details of these proliferating meanings, however, and go straight to what I think can best serve my purposes here. In the first place, culture is used to designate not merely something to which one belongs but something that one possesses and, along with that proprietary process, culture also designates a boundary by which the concepts of what is extrinsic or intrinsic to the culture come into forceful play. These things are not controversial: most people employing *culture* would assent to them, as Auerbach does in the epilogue when he speaks of being in Istanbul, away from his habitual cultural environment, within its research materials and familiar environment.

But, in the second place, there is a more interesting dimension to this idea of culture as possessing possession. And that is the power of culture by virtue of its elevated or superior position to authorize, to dominate, to legitimate, demote, interdict, and validate: in short, the power of culture to be an agent of, and perhaps the main agency for, powerful differentiation within its domain and beyond it too. It is this idea that is evident in French Orientalism, for example, as distinguished from English Orientalism, and this in turn plays a major role in the work of Ernest Renan, Louis Massignon, and Raymond Schwab. . . .

When Auerbach speaks of not being able to write such a book as *Mimesis* had he remained in Europe, he refers precisely to that grid of research techniques and ethics by which the prevailing culture imposes on the individual scholar its canons of how literary scholarship is to be conducted. Yet even this sort of imposition is a minor aspect of culture's power to dominate and authorize work. What is more important in culture is that it is a system of values *saturating* downward almost everything within its purview; yet, paradoxically, culture dominates from above without at the same time being available to everything and everyone it dominates. In fact, in our age of media-produced attitudes, the ideological insistence of a culture drawing attention to itself as superior has given way to a culture whose canons and standards are invisible to the degree that they are "natural," "objective," and "real."

Historically one supposes that culture has always involved hierarchies; it has separated the elite from the popular, the best from the less than best, and so forth. It has also made certain styles and modes of thought prevail over others. But its tendency has always been to move downward from the height of power and privilege in order to diffuse, disseminate, and expand itself in the widest possible range. . . .

The entire history of nineteenth-century European thought is filled with such discriminations as these, made between what is fitting for us and what is fitting for them, the former designated as inside, in place, common, belonging, in a word *above,* the latter, who are designated as outside, excluded, aberrant, inferior, in a word *below.* From these distinctions, which were given their hegemony by the culture, no one could be free, not even Marx—as a reading of his articles on India and the Orient will immediately reveal.[11] The large cultural-national designation of European culture as the privileged norm carried with it a formidable battery of other distinctions between ours and theirs, between proper and improper, European and non-European, higher and lower: they are to be found everywhere in such subjects and quasi-subjects as linguistics, history, race theory, philosophy, anthropology, and even biology. But my main reason for mentioning them here is to suggest how in the transmission and persistence of a culture there is a continual process of reinforcement, by which the hegemonic culture will add to itself the prerogatives given it by its sense of national identity, its power as an implement, ally, or branch of the state, its rightness, its exterior forms and assertions of itself: and most important, by its vindicated power as a victor over everything not itself.

There is no reason to doubt that all cultures operate in this way or to doubt that on the whole they tend to be successful in enforcing their hegemony. They do this in different ways, obviously, and I think it is true that some tend to be more efficient than others, particularly when it comes to certain kinds of police activities. But this is a topic for comparative anthropologists and not one about which broad generalizations should be risked here. I am interested, however, in noting that if culture exerts the kinds of pressure I have mentioned, and if it creates the environment and the community that allows people to feel they belong, then it must be true that resistance to the culture has always been present. Often that resistance takes the form of outright hostility for religious, social, or political reasons (one aspect of this is well described by Eric Hobsbawm in *Primitive Rebels*). Often it has come from individuals or groups declared out of bounds or inferior by the culture (here of course the range is vast, from the ritual scapegoat to the lonely prophet, from the social pariah to the visionary artist, from the working class to the alienated intellectual). But there is some very compelling truth to Julien Benda's contention that in one way or the other it has often been the intellectual, the *clerc,* who has stood for values, ideas, and activities that transcend and deliberately interfere with the collective weight imposed by the nation-state and the national culture.

Certainly what Benda says about intellectuals (who, in ways specific to the intellectual vocation itself, are responsible for defiance) resonates harmoniously with the personality of Socrates as it emerges in Plato's *Dialogues,* or with Voltaire's opposition to the Church, or more recently with Gramsci's notion of the organic intellectual allied with an emergent class against ruling-class hegemony. Even Arnold speaks of "aliens" in *Culture and Anarchy,* "persons who are mainly led, not by their class spirit, but by a general humane spirit," which he connects directly with ideal culture and not, it would appear, with that culture he was later to identify with the State. Benda is surely wrong, on the other hand, to ascribe so much social power to the solitary intellectual whose authority, according to Benda, comes from his individual voice and from his opposition to organized collective passions. Yet if we allow that it has been the historical fate of such collective sentiments as "my country right or wrong" and "we are whites and therefore belong to a higher race than blacks" and "European or Islamic or Hindu culture is superior to all others" to coarsen and brutalize the individual, then it is probably true that an isolated individual consciousness, going against the surrounding environment as well as allied to contesting classes, movements, and values, is an isolated voice out of place but very much *of* that place, standing consciously against the prevailing orthodoxy and very much for a professedly universal or humane set of values, which has provided significant local resistance to the hegemony of one culture. It is also the case, both Benda and Gramsci agree, that intellectuals are eminently useful in making hegemony work. For Benda this of course is the *trahison des clercs* in its essence; their unseemly participation in the perfection of political passions is what he thinks is dispiritingly the very essence of their contemporary mass sellout. For Gramsci's more complex mind, individual intellectuals like Croce were to be studied (perhaps even envied) for making their ideas seem as if they were expressions of a collective will.

All this, then, shows us the individual consciousness placed at a sensitive nodal point, and it is this consciousness at that critical point which this book attempts to explore in the form of what I call *criticism*. On the one hand, the individual mind registers and is very much aware of the collective whole, context, or situation in which it finds itself. On the other hand, precisely because of this awareness—a worldly self-situating, a sensitive response to the dominant culture—the individual consciousness is not naturally and easily a mere child of the culture, but a historical and social actor in it. And because of that perspective, which introduces circumstance and distinction where there had only been conformity and belonging, there is distance, or what we might also call criticism. A knowledge of history, a recognition of the importance of social circumstance, an analytical capacity for making distinctions: these trouble the quasi-religious authority of being comfortably at home among one's people, supported by known powers and acceptable values, protected against the outside world.

But to repeat: the critical consciousness is a part of its actual social world and of the literal body that the consciousness inhabits, not by any means an escape from either one or the other. Although as I characterized him, Auerbach was away from Europe, his work is steeped in the reality of Europe, just as the specific circumstances of his exile enabled a concrete critical recovery of Europe. We have in Auerbach an instance both of filiation with his natal culture and, because of exile, *affiliation* with it through critical consciousness and scholarly work. We must look more closely now at the cooperation between filiation and affiliation that is located at the heart of critical consciousness.

. . .

Relationships of filiation and affiliation are plentiful in modern cultural history. One very strong three-part pattern, for example, originates in a large group of late nineteenth- and early twentieth-century writers, in which the failure of the generative impulse—the failure of the capacity to produce or generate children—is portrayed in such a way as to stand for a general condition afflicting society and culture together, to say nothing of individual men and women. *Ulysses* and *The Waste Land* are two especially well-known instances, but there is similar evidence to be found in *Death in Venice* or *The Way of All Flesh, Jude the Obscure, À la recherche du temps perdu,* Mallarmé's and Hopkins's poetry, much of Wilde's writing, and *Nostromo.* If we add to this list the immensely authoritative weight of Freud's psychoanalytic theory, a significant and influential aspect of which posits the potentially murderous outcome of bearing children, we will have the unmistakable impression that few things are as problematic and as universally fraught as what we might have supposed to be the mere natural continuity between one generation and the next. Even in great work that belongs intellectually and politically to another universe of discourse—Lukács's *History and Class Consciousness*—there is much the same thesis being advanced about the difficulties and ultimately the impossibility of natural filiation: for, Lukács says, reification is the alienation of men from what they have produced, and it is the starkly uncompromising severity of his vision that he means by this all the products of human labor, children included, which are so completely separated from each other, atomized, and hence frozen into the category of ontological objects as to make even natural relationships virtually impossible.

Childless couples, orphaned children, aborted childbirths, and unregenerately celibate men and women populate the world of high modernism with remarkable insistence, all of them suggesting the difficulties of filiation.[12] But no less important in my opinion is the second part of the pattern, which is immediately consequent upon the first, the pressure to produce new and different ways of conceiving human relationships. For if biological reproduction is either too difficult or too unpleasant, is there some other way by which men and women can create social bonds between each other that would substitute for those ties that connect members of the same family across generations?

A typical answer is provided by T. S. Eliot during the period right after the appearance of *The Waste Land.* His model now is Lancelot Andrewes, a man whose prose and devotional style seem to Eliot to have transcended the personal manner of even so fervent and effective a Christian preacher as Donne. In the shift from Donne to Andrewes, which I believe underlies the shift in Eliot's sensibility from the world-view of *"Prufrock," Gerontion,* and *The Waste Land* to the conversion poetry of *Ash Wednesday* and the *Ariel Poems,* we have Eliot saying something like the following: the aridity, wastefulness, and sterility of modern life make filiation an unreasonable alternative at least, an unattainable one at most. One cannot think about continuity in biological terms, a proposition that may have had urgent corroboration in the recent failure of Eliot's first marriage but to which Eliot's mind gave a far wider application.[13] The only other alternatives seemed to be provided by institutions, associations, and communities whose social existence was not in fact guaranteed by biology, but by affiliation. Thus according to Eliot Lancelot Andrewes conveys in his writing the enfolding presence of the English church, "something representative of the finest spirit of England of the time [and] . . . a masterpiece of ecclesiastical statesmanship." With Hooker, then, Andrewes invoked an authority beyond simple Protestantism. Both men were

> on terms of equality with their Continental antagonists and [were able] to elevate their Church above the position of a local heretical sect. They were fathers of a national Church and they were Europeans. Compare a sermon of Andrewes with a sermon by another earlier master, Latimer. It is not merely that Andrewes knew Greek, or that Latimer was addressing a far less cultivated public, or that the sermons of Andrewes are peppered with allusion and quotation. It is rather that Latimer, the preacher of Henry VIII and Edward VI, is merely a Protestant; but the voice of Andrewes is the voice of a man who has a formed visible Church behind him, who speaks with the old authority and the new culture.[14]

Eliot's reference to Hooker and Andrewes is figurative, but it is meant with a quite literal force, just as that second "merely"

(Latimer is merely a Protestant) is an assertion by Eliot of "the old authority and the new culture." If the English church is not in a direct line of filiation stemming from the Roman church, it is nevertheless something more than a mere local heresy, more than a mere protesting orphan. Why? Because Andrewes and others like him to whose antecedent authority Eliot has now subscribed were able to harness the old paternal authority to an insurgent Protestant and national culture, thereby creating a new institution based not on direct genealogical descent but on what we may call, barbarously, *horizontal affiliation.* According to Eliot, Andrewes's language does not simply express the anguished distance from an originating but now unrecoverable father that a protesting orphan might feel; on the contrary, it converts that language into the expression of an emerging affiliative corporation—the English church—which commands the respect and the attention of its adherents.

In Eliot's poetry much the same change occurs. The speakers of *Prufrock* and *Gerontion* as well as the characters of *The Waste Land* directly express the plight of orphanhood and alienation, whereas the personae of *Ash Wednesday* and *Four Quartets* speak the common language of other communicants within the English church. For Eliot the church stands in for the lost family mourned throughout his earlier poetry. And of course the shift is publicly completed in *After Strange Gods* whose almost belligerent announcement of a credo of royalism, classicism, and catholicism form a set of affiliations achieved by Eliot outside the filial (republican, romantic, protestant) pattern given him by the facts of his American (and outlandish) birth.

The turn from filiation to affiliation is to be found elsewhere in the culture and embodies what Georg Simmel calls the modern cultural process by which life "incessantly generates forms for itself," forms that, once they appear, "demand a validity which transcends the moment, and is emancipated from the pulse of life. For this reason, life is always in a latent opposition to the form."[15] One thinks of Yeats going from the blandishments of "the honey of generation" to the Presences who are "self-born mockers of man's enterprise," which he set down in *A Vision* according to a spacious affiliative order he invented for himself and his work. Or, as Ian Watt has said about Conrad's contemporaries, writers like Lawrence, Joyce, and Pound, who present us with "the breaking of ties with family, home, class, country, and traditional beliefs as necessary stages in the achievement of spiritual and intellectual freedom": these writers "then invite us to share the larger transcendental [affiliative] or private systems of order and value which they have adopted and invented."[16] In his best work Conrad shows us the futility of such private systems of order and value (say the utopian world created by Charles and Amelia Gould in *Nostromo*), but no less than his contemporaries he too took on in his own life (as did Eliot and Henry James) the adopted identity of an emigré-turned-English-gentleman. On the other side of the spectrum we find Lukács suggesting that only class consciousness, itself an insurrectionary form of an attempt at affiliation, could possibly break through the antinomies and atomizations of reified existence in the modern capitalist world order.

What I am describing is the transition from a failed idea or possibility of filiation to a kind of compensatory order that, whether it is a party, an institution, a culture, a set of beliefs, or even a world vision, provides men and women with a new form of relationship, which I have been calling affiliation but which is also a new system. Now whether we look at this new affiliative mode of relationship as it is to be found among conservative writers like Eliot or among progressive writers like Lukács and, in his own special way, Freud, we will find the deliberately explicit goal of using that new order to reinstate vestiges of the kind of authority associated in the past with filiative order. This, finally, is the third part of the pattern. Freud's psychoanalytic guild and Lukács's notion of the vanguard party are no less providers of what we might call a restored authority. The new hierarchy or, if it is less a hierarchy than a community, the new community is greater than the individual adherent or member, just as the father is greater by virtue of seniority than the sons and daughters; the ideas, the values, and the systematic totalizing worldview validated by the new affiliative order are all bearers of authority too, with the result that something resembling a cultural system is established. Thus if a filial relationship was held together by natural bonds and natural forms of authority—involving obedience, fear, love, respect, and instinctual conflict—the new affiliative relationship changes these bonds into what seem to be transpersonal forms—such as guild consciousness, consensus, collegiality, professional respect, class, and the hegemony of a dominant culture.

The filiative scheme belongs to the realms of nature and of "life," whereas affiliation belongs exclusively to culture and society.

It is worth saying incidentally that what an estimable group of literary artists have adumbrated in the passage from filiation to affiliation parallels similar observations by sociologists and records corresponding developments in the structure of knowledge. Tönnies's notion of the shift from *Gemeinschaft* to *Gesellschaft* can easily be reconciled with the idea of filiation replaced by affiliation. Similarly, I believe, the increased dependence of the modern scholar upon the small, specialized guild of people in his or her field (as indeed the very idea of a field itself), and the notion within fields that the originating human subject is of less importance than transhuman rules and theories, accompany the transformation of naturally filiative into systematically affiliative relationships. The loss of the subject, as it has commonly been referred to, is in various ways the loss as well of the procreative, generational urge authorizing filiative relationships.

The three-part pattern I have been describing—and with it the processes of filiation and affiliation as they have been depicted—can be considered an instance of the passage from nature to culture, as well as an instance of how affiliation can easily become a system of thought no less orthodox and dominant than culture itself. What I want abruptly to talk about at this juncture are the effects of this pattern as they have affected the study of literature today, at a considerable remove from the early years of our century. The structure of literary knowledge derived from the academy is heavily imprinted with the three-part pattern I have illustrated here. This imprinting has occurred in ways that are impressive so far as critical thought (according to my notion of what it ought to be) is concerned. Let me pass directly now to concrete examples.

Ever since Eliot, and after him Richards and Leavis, there has been an almost unanimously held view that it is the duty of humanistic scholars in our culture to devote themselves to the study of the great monuments of literature. Why? So that they may be passed on to younger students, who in turn become members, by affiliation and formation of the company of educated individuals. Thus we find the university experience more or less officially consecrating the pact between a canon of works, a band of initiate instructors, a group of younger affiliates; in a socially validated manner all this reproduces the filiative discipline supposedly transcended by the educational process. This has almost always been the case historically within what might be called the cloistral world of the traditional Western, and certainly of the Eastern, university. But we are now, I think, in a period of world history when for the first time the compensatory affiliative relationships interpreted during the academic course of study in the Western university actually exclude more than they include. I mean quite simply that, for the first time in modern history, the whole imposing edifice of humanistic knowledge resting on the classics of European letters, and with it the scholarly discipline inculcated formally into students in Western universities through the forms familiar to us all, represents only a fraction of the real human relationships and interactions now taking place in the world. Certainly Auerbach was among the last great representatives of those who believed that European culture could be viewed coherently and importantly as unquestionably central to human history. There are abundant reasons for Auerbach's view being no longer tenable, not the least of which is the diminishing acquiescence and deference accorded to what has been called the Natopolitan world long dominating peripheral regions like Africa, Asia, and Latin America. New cultures, new societies, and emerging visions of social, political, and aesthetic order now lay claim to the humanist's attention, with an insistence that cannot long be denied.

But for perfectly understandable reasons they are denied. When our students are taught such things as "the humanities" they are almost always taught that these classic texts embody, express, represent what is best in our, that is, the only, tradition. Moreover they are taught that such fields as the humanities and such subfields as "literature" exist in a relatively neutral political element, that they are to be appreciated and venerated, that they define the limits of what is acceptable, appropriate, and legitimate so far as culture is concerned. In other words, the affiliative order so presented surreptitiously duplicates the closed and tightly knit family structure that secures generational hierarchical relationships to one another. Affiliation then becomes in effect a literal form of *re-presentation*, by which what is ours is good, and therefore deserves incorporation and inclusion in our programs of humanistic study, and what is not ours in this ultimately provincial sense is simply left out. And out of this representation come the systems from Northrop Frye's to Foucault's, which claim the power to show how things work, once and for all, totally and predictively. It should go without saying that this new affiliative structure and its systems of thought more or less directly reproduce the skeleton of family authority supposedly left behind when the family was left behind. The curricular structures holding European literature departments make that perfectly obvious: the great texts, as well as the great teachers and the great theories, have an authority that compels respectful attention not so much by virtue of their content but because they are either old or they have power, they have been handed on in time or seem to have no time, and they have traditionally been revered, as priests, scientists, or efficient bureaucrats have taught.

It may seem odd, but it is true, that in such matters as culture and scholarship I am often in reasonable sympathy with conservative attitudes, and what I might object to in what I have been describing does not have much to do with the activity of conserving the past, or with reading great literature, or with doing serious and perhaps even utterly conservative scholarship as such. I have no great problem with those things. What I am criticizing is two particular assumptions. There is first the almost unconsciously held ideological assumption that the Eurocentric model for the humanities actually represents a natural and proper subject matter for the humanistic scholar. Its authority comes not only from the orthodox canon of literary monuments handed down through the generations, but also from the way this continuity reproduces the filial continuity of the chain of biological procreation. What we then have is a substitution of one sort of order for another, in the process of which everything that is nonhumanistic and nonliterary and non-European is deposited outside the structure. If we consider for a minute that most of the world today is non-European, that transactions within what the UNESCO/McBride Report calls the world information order is therefore not literary, and that the social sciences and the media (to name only two modes of cultural production in ascendancy today over the classically defined humanities) dominate the diffusion of knowledge in ways that are scarcely imaginable to the traditional humanistic scholar, then we will have some idea of how ostrichlike and retrograde assertions about Eurocentric humanities really are. The process of representation, by which filiation is reproduced in the affiliative structure and made to stand for what belongs to us (as we in turn belong to the family of our language and traditions), reinforces the known at the expense of the knowable.

Second is the assumption that the principal relationships in the study of literature—those I have identified as based on representation—ought to obliterate the traces of other relationships within literary structures that are based principally upon acquisition and appropriation. This is the great lesson of Raymond Williams' *The Country and the City.* His extraordinarily illuminating discussion there of the seventeenth-century English country-house poems does not concentrate on what those poems represent, but on what they *are* as the result of contested social and political relationships. Descriptions of the rural mansion, for example, do not at bottom entail only what is to be admired by way of harmony, repose, and beauty; they should also entail for the modern reader what in fact has been excluded from the poems, the labor that created the mansions, the social processes of which they are the culmination, the dispossessions and theft they actually signified. Although he does not come out and say it, Williams' book is a remarkable attempt at a dislodgement of the very ethos of system, which has reified relationships and stripped them of their social density. What he tries to put in its place is the great dialectic of acquisition and representation, by which even realism—as it is manifest in Jane Austen's novels—has gained its durable status as the result of contests involving money and power. Williams teaches us to read in a different way and to remember that for every poem or novel in the canon there is a social fact being requisitioned for the page, a human life engaged, a class suppressed or elevated—none of which can be accounted for in the framework rigidly maintained by the processes of representation and affiliation doing above-ground work for the conservation of filiation. And for every critical system grinding on there are events, heterogeneous and unorthodox social configurations, human beings and texts disputing the possibility of a sovereign methodology of system.

Everything I have said is an extrapolation from the verbal echo we hear between the words "filiation" and "affiliation." In a certain sense, what I have been trying to show is that, as it has developed through the art and critical theories produced in complex ways by modernism, filiation gives birth to affiliation. Affiliation becomes a form of representing the filiative processes to be found in nature, although affiliation takes validated nonbiological social and cultural forms. Two alternatives propose themselves for the contemporary critic. One is organic complicity with the pattern I have described. The critic enables, indeed transacts, the transfer of legitimacy from filiation to affiliation; literally a midwife, the critic encourages reverence for the humanities and for the dominant culture served by those humanities. This keeps relationships within the narrow circle of what is natural, appropriate, and valid for "us," and thereafter excludes the nonliterary, the non-European, and above all the political dimension in which all literature, all texts, can be found. It also gives rise to a critical system or theory whose temptation for the critic is that it resolves all the problems that culture gives rise to. As John Fekete has said, this "expresses the modern disaffection for reality, but progressively incorporates and assimilates it within the categories of prevailing social (and cultural) rationality. This endows it with a double appeal, and the expanding scope of the theory, corresponding to the expanding mode of the production and reproduction of social life, gives it authority as a major ideology."[17]

The second alternative is for the critic to recognize the difference between instinctual filiation and social affiliation, and to show how affiliation sometimes reproduces filiation, sometimes makes its own forms. Immediately, then, most of the political and social world becomes available for critical and secular scrutiny, as in *Mimesis* Auerbach does not simply admire the Europe he has lost through exile but sees it anew as a composite social and historical enterprise, made and remade unceasingly by men and women in society. This secular critical consciousness can also examine those forms of writing affiliated with literature but excluded from consideration with literature as a result of the ideological capture of the literary text within the humanistic curriculum as it now stands. My analysis of recent literary theory [in *The World, the Text, and the Critic*] focuses on these themes in detail, especially in the way critical systems—even the most sophisticated kind—can succumb to the inherently representative and reproductive relationship between a dominant culture and the domains it rules.

. . .

What does it mean to have a critical consciousness if, as I have been trying to suggest, the intellectual's situation is a worldly one and yet, by virtue of that worldliness itself, the intellectual's social identity should involve something more than strengthening those aspects of the culture that require more affirmation and orthodox compliancy from its members?

My position, again, is that the contemporary critical consciousness stands between the temptations represented by two formidable and related powers engaging critical attention. One is the culture to which critics are bound filiatively (by birth, nationality, profession); the other is a method or system acquired affiliatively (by social and political conviction, economic and historical circumstances, voluntary effort and willed deliberation). Both of these powers exert pressures that have been building toward the contemporary situation for long periods of time: my interest in eighteenth-century figures like Vico and Swift, for example, is premised on their knowledge that their era also made claims on them culturally and systematically, and it was their whole enterprise therefore to resist these pressures in everything they did, albeit of course, that they were worldly writers and materially bound to their time.

As it is now practiced and as I treat it, criticism is an academic thing, located for the most part far away from the questions that trouble the reader of a daily newspaper. Up to a certain point this is as it should be. But we have reached the stage at which specialization and professionalization, allied with cultural dogma, barely sublimated ethnocentrism and nationalism, as well as a surprisingly insistent quasi-religious quietism, have transported the professional and academic critic of literature—the most focused and intensely trained interpreter of texts produced by the culture—into another world altogether. In that relatively untroubled and secluded world there seems to be no contact with the world of events and societies, which modern history, intellectuals, and critics have in fact built. Instead, contemporary criticism is an institution for publicly affirming the values of our, that is, European, dominant elite culture, and for privately setting loose the unrestrained interpretation of a universe defined in advance as the endless misreading of a misinterpretation. The result has been the regulated, not to say calculated, irrelevance of criticism, except as an adornment to what the powers of modern industrial society transact: the hegemony of militarism and a new cold war, the depoliticization of the citizenry, the overall compliance of the intellectual class to which critics belong. The situation I attempt to characterize in modern criticism (not excluding "Left" criticism) has occurred in parallel with the ascendancy of Reaganism. The role of the Left, neither repressed nor organized, has been important for its complaisance.

I do not wish to be misunderstood as saying that the flight into method and system on the part of critics who wish to avoid the ideology of humanism is altogether a bad thing. Far from it. Yet the dangers of method and system are worth noting. Insofar as they become sovereign and as their practitioners lose touch with the resistance and the heterogeneity of civil society, they risk becoming wall-to-wall discourses, blithely predetermining what they discuss, heedlessly converting everything into evidence for the efficacy of the method, carelessly ignoring the circumstances out of which all theory, system, and method ultimately derive.

Criticism in short is always situated; it is skeptical, secular, reflectively open to its own failings. This is by no means to say that it is value-free. Quite the contrary, for the inevitable trajectory of critical consciousness is to arrive at some acute sense of what political, social, and human values are entailed in the reading, production, and transmission of every text. To stand between culture and system is therefore to stand *close to*—closeness itself having a particular value for me—a concrete reality about which political, moral, and social judgments have to be made and, if not only made, then exposed and demystified. If, as we have recently been told by Stanley Fish, every act of interpretation is made possible and given force by an interpretive community, then we must go a great deal further in showing what situation, what historical and social configuration, what political interests are concretely entailed by the very existence of interpretive communities.[18] This is an especially important task when these communities have evolved camouflaging jargons.

Were I to use one word consistently along with *criticism* (not as a modification but as an emphatic) it would be *oppositional*. If criticism is reducible neither to a doctrine nor to a political position on a particular question, and if it is to be in the world and self-aware simultaneously, then its identity is its difference from other cultural activities and from systems of thought or of method. In its suspicion of totalizing concepts, in its discontent with reified objects, in its impatience with guilds, special interests, imperialized fiefdoms, and orthodox habits of mind, criticism is most itself and, if the paradox can be tolerated, most unlike itself at the moment it starts turning into organized dogma. "Ironic" is not a bad word to use along with "oppositional." For in the main—and here I shall be explicit—criticism must think of itself as life-enhancing and constitutively opposed to every form of tyranny, domination, and abuse; its social goals are noncoercive knowledge produced in the interests of human freedom. If we agree with Raymond Williams, "that however dominant a social system may be, the very meaning of its domination involves a limitation or selection of the activities it covers, so that by definition it cannot exhaust all social experience, which therefore always potentially contains space for alternative acts and alternative intentions which are not yet articulated as a social institution or even project,"[19] then criticism belongs in that potential space inside civil society, acting on behalf of those alternative acts and alternative intentions whose advancement is a fundamental human and intellectual obligation.

There is a danger that the fascination of what's difficult—criticism being one of the forms of difficulty—might take the joy out of one's heart. But there is every reason to suppose that the critic who is tired of management and the day's war is, like Yeats's narrator, quite capable at least of finding the stable, pulling out the bolt, and setting creative energies free. Normally, however, the critic can but entertain, without fully expressing, the hope. This is a poignant irony, to be recalled for the benefit of people who maintain that criticism is art, and who forget that, the moment anything acquires the status of a cultural idol or a commodity, it ceases to be interesting. That at bottom is a *critical* attitude, just as doing criticism and maintaining a critical position are critical aspects of the intellectual's life.

from *The World, the Text, and the Critic*

9

Permission to Narrate

(1984)

> [W]e're here in Beirut as names for a different homeland, where meanings will find their words again in the midst of this sea and on the edge of this desert. For here, where we are, is the tent for wandering meanings and words gone astray and the orphaned fight, scattered and banished from the center.
>
> —Mahmoud Darwish, *Memory for Forgetfulness August, Beirut, 1982*

On the night of September 16, 1982, while Israeli flares lit a dark sky, Christian Phalangist militias massacred 2,062 Palestinians and Lebanese at the Sabra and Shatila refugee camps in Lebanon.[1] The attack was a coordinated part of Israel's invasion of Lebanon that began on June 5, 1982, and involved an unrelenting siege of West Beirut that lasted for most of the summer. Without interruption, the Israeli military attacked Beirut from the air, from the sea, with cluster bombs, vacuum bombs, phosphorous rockets, mortars, all in an attempt to destroy the Beirut-based Palestinian leadership and the Palestinians themselves.[2]

In "Permission to Narrate," Said examines why Israeli brutality was received with such incredible approbation in the U.S. media. "How is it," Said asks, "that the premises on which Western support for Israel is based are still maintained even though the reality, the facts, cannot possibly bear these premises out?" In what was originally written as a *London Review of Books* essay on half a dozen books about the invasion,[3] Said argues that the Palestinian narrative of dispossession has faced a concerted and systematic tendency to deny and suppress its authority. By labeling Palestinians terrorists, by branding critics of Israel anti-Semites, and above all by denying the historical and lived reality of a Palestinian homeland, the West, Said powerfully asserts, has revoked the permission to narrate the Palestinian experience.

As a direct consequence of Israel's 1982 invasion of Lebanon, an international commission of six jurists headed by Sean MacBride undertook a mission to investigate reported Israeli violations of international law during the invasion. The commission's conclusions were published in *Israel in Lebanon* by a British publisher;[4] it is reasonably clear that no publisher could or ever will be found for the book in the United States. Anyone inclined to doubt the Israeli claim that "'purity of arms" dictated the military campaign will find support for that doubt in the report, even to the extent of finding Israel also guilty of attempted "ethnocide" and "genocide" of the Palestinian people (two members of the commission demurred at that particular conclusion, but accepted all the others). The findings are horrifying—and almost as much because they are forgotten or routinely denied in press reports as because they occurred. The commission says that Israel was indeed guilty of acts of aggression contrary to international law; it made use of forbidden weapons and methods; it deliberately, indiscriminately, and recklessly bombed civilian targets—"for example, schools, hospitals, and other nonmilitary targets"; it systematically bombed towns, cities, villages, and refugee camps; it deported, dispersed, and ill-treated civilian populations; it had no really valid reasons "under international law for its invasion of Lebanon, for the manner in which it conducted hostilities, or for its actions as an occupying force"; it was directly responsible for the Sabra and Shatila massacres.

As a record of the invasion, the MacBride Commission report is therefore a document of importance. But it has had no appreciable effect on the one outside force—America—whose indulgent support for Israel has made possible continued turbulence in Lebanon. The political question of moment is why, rather than fundamentally altering the Western view of Israel, the events of the summer of 1982 have been accommodated in all but a few places in the public realm to the view that prevailed before those events: that since Israel is in effect a civilized, democratic country constitutively incapable of barbaric practices against Palestinians and other non-Jews, its invasion of Lebanon was *ipso facto* justified.

Naturally, I refer here to official or policy-effective views and not the inchoate, unfocused feelings of the citizenry, which, to judge from several polls, is unhappy about Israeli actions. U.S. aid levels to Israel since the siege of Beirut have gone up to a point where Israel received roughly half of the entire American foreign aid budget, most of it in outright gifts and in subsidies to Israeli industries directly competitive with American counterparts. Presidential candidates, with the exception of George McGovern and Jesse Jackson, outbid each other in paeans of praise for Israel. The administration has refurbished the strategic "understanding" it made with Israel during Alexander Haig's time as Secretary of State, as if the invasion had never happened, the theory being that, given unlimited aid, Israel will be assured of its security and prove a little more flexible. This has not happened. And, of course, Israel now sits on even greater amounts of Arab land, with occupation policies that are more brutally and blatantly repressive than those of most other twentieth-century occupation regimes.

Gideon Spiro, an Israeli, testified to the MacBride Commission:

> We don't pay the price of anything that we are doing, not in the occupied territories, because Israel is in this a unique miracle. There is no country in the world which has over 100 percent inflation, which is occupying the West Bank, occupying another people, and building all those settlements with billions of dollars, and spending 30 percent of the GNP on defense—and still we can live

> here, I mean, somebody is paying for everything, so if everybody can live well and go abroad and buy cars, why not be for the occupation? So they are all luxury wars and people are very proud of the way we are fighting, the quick victories, the self-image of the brave Israeli—very flattering![5]

Yes, Israelis have fought well, and for the most part the Arabs haven't, but how is it that, as has been the case for much of this century, the premises on which Western support for Israel is based are still maintained, even though the reality, the facts, cannot possibly bear these premises out?

Look at the summer of 1982 more closely. A handful of poorly armed Palestinians and Lebanese held off a very large Israeli army, air force, and navy from June 5 till the middle of August. This was a major political achievement for the Palestinians. Something else was at stake in the invasion, however, to judge by its results a year and a half later—results which include Arab inaction, Syrian complicity in the unsuccessful PLO mutiny, and a virulent American hostility to Palestinian nationalism. That something was, I think, the inadmissible existence of the Palestinian people whose history, actuality, and aspirations, as possessed of a coherent narrative direction pointed toward self-determination, were the object of this violence. Israel's war was designed to reduce Palestinian existence as much as possible. Most Israeli leaders and newspapers admitted the war's *political* motive. In Rafael Eytan's words, to destroy Palestinian nationalism and institutions in Lebanon would make it easier to destroy them on the West Bank and in Gaza: Palestinians were to be turned into "drugged roaches in a bottle." Meanwhile the clichés advocating Israel's right to do what it wants grind on: Palestinians are rejectionists and terrorists, Israel wants peace and security, the Arabs won't accept Israel and want to destroy it, Israel is a democracy, Zionism is (or can be made consonant with) humanism, socialism, liberalism, Western civilization, the Palestinian Arabs ran away in 1948 because the other Arabs told them to, the PLO destroyed Lebanon, Israel's campaign was a model of decorum greeted warmly by "the Lebanese" and was only about the protection of the Galilee villagers.

Despite the MacBride Commission's view that "the facts speak for themselves" in the case of Zionism's war against the Palestinians, the facts have never done so, especially in America, where Israeli propaganda seems to lead a life of its own. Whereas, in 1975, Michael Adams and Christopher Mayhew were able to write about a coherent but unstated policy of unofficial British press censorship, according to which unpleasant truths about Zionism were systematically suppressed,[6] the situation is not nearly as obvious so far as the British media today are concerned. It still obtains in America, however, for reasons to do with a seemingly absolute refusal on the part of policy makers, the media, the liberal intelligentsia to make connections, draw conclusions, state the simple facts, most of which contradict the premises of declared U.S. policy. Paradoxically, never has so much been written and shown of the Palestinians, who were scarcely mentioned fifteen years ago. They are there all right, but the narrative of their present actuality—which stems directly from the story of their existence in and displacement from Palestine, later Israel—that narrative is not.

A disciplinary communications apparatus exists in the West both for overlooking most of the basic things that might present Israel in a bad light, and for punishing those who try to tell the truth. How many people know the kind of thing suggested by the following incident—namely, the maintenance in Israel of a rigid distinction between privileged Jew and underprivileged Palestinian? The example is recent, and its very triviality indicates the by-now unconscious adherence to racial classification which pervades official Israeli policy and discourse. I have this instance from Professor Israel Shahak, chairman of the Israeli League of Human Rights, who transcribed it from the Israeli journal *Kol Ha'ir.* The journal reports, with some effect of irony:

> The society of sheep raisers in Israel (an entirely Jewish body from which Arabs are totally excluded) has agreed with the Ministry of Agriculture that a special sheepfold will be built in order to check the various immunizations on sheep. Which sheep? Jewish sheep in Israel, writes Baruch Bar Shelev, secretary of the sheep raisers' society, in a circular letter to all sheep raisers. In the letter they are asked to pay, toward the cost of the sheepfold, twenty shekels for Jewish sheep. This demand was also received by Semadar Kramer of the secretariat of "Neve Shalom" near Latron.
>
> Semadar Kramer sent the society of sheep raisers only half of the

> sum requested for building the Jewish sheepfold because "Never Shalom" is a Jewish-Arab village, and therefore its sheep are also Jewish-Arab. They also claim that they have no certain knowledge about mixed marriages among the sheep, and that lately some difficulties about the conversion to Judaism were encountered in their sheepfold.

This, one might think, is either insanity or some comic fantasy produced in the imagination of a Swift or Kafka. Jewish sheep? The conversion of Arab sheep to Judaism? Surely these things cannot be real. Such distinctions, however, are part of the system of possessive exclusivism which has been imposed upon reality by central forces in Israeli society. The system is rarely discussed at all in the West, certainly not with anything resembling the intensity with which Palestinian terrorism is discussed. When an attempt is made to speak critically of Israel, the result is frightening—if the attempt succeeds in getting any diffusion at all. One small index is the fact that the Anti-Defamation League in America and the American-Israel Public Affairs Committee have each published books identifying Israel's "enemies" and employing tactics for police or vigilante action. In addition, there is the deep media compliance I have referred to—so that effective, and especially narrative, rendering of the Palestine-Israel contest are either attacked with near-unanimous force or ignored. The fortunes of Le Carré's novel *The Little Drummer Girl* and Costa-Gavras's film *Hanna K* illustrate these alternatives.

Having made a strong impression regionally and internationally during the years 1970 to 1982, the Palestinian narrative, as we shall see in a moment, is now barely in evidence. This is not an aesthetic judgment. Like Zionism itself, post-1948 Palestinian nationalism has had to achieve formal and ideological prominence well before any actual land has been gained. Strange nationalisms these, conducted for years in exile and alienation, for years protective, stubborn, passionately believed in. The major difference is that Zionism was a hothouse flower grown from European nationalism, anti-Semitism, and colonialism, while Palestinian nationalism, derived from the great wave of Arab and Islamic anticolonial sentiment, has since 1967, though tinged with retrogressive religious sentiment, been located within the mainstream of secular post-imperialist thought. Even more important, Zionism is essentially a dispossessing movement so far as non-Jews are concerned. Palestinianism since 1967 has generally been inclusive, trying (satisfactorily or not) to deal with the problem created by the presence of more than one national community in historical Palestine. And for the years between 1974 and 1982, there was a genuine international consensus underwriting the Palestinian communal narrative and restoring it as an historical story to its place of origin and future resolution in Palestine. I speak here of the idea that Israel should return the Occupied Territories and that a Palestinian state be created alongside Israel. That this went against the grain of Zionism, despite its many internal differences, was obvious: nevertheless, there were many people in the world both willing and able to contest Golda Meir's 1969 fiat that the Palestinians did not exist historically, had no communal identity, and no national rights. But when the whole force of the Palestinian national movement proposed a political resolution in Palestine based on the narrative shape of alienation, return, and partition, in order to make room for two peoples, one Jewish and the other Arab, neither Israel nor the West accepted it. Hence the bitter Arab and Palestinian infighting, which has been caused by Arafat's—i.e., the mainstream PLO's—failure to get any real response to the notion of partition from those Western nations most associated with the fate of Palestine. Bruno Kreisky puts the case forcefully in "L'Échec d'Arafat, c'est notre faute" (*Les Nouvelles,* December 1983). The symbolism of Palestinians fighting each other in the forlorn outskirts of Tripoli in North Lebanon is too stark to be misinterpreted. The course taking Palestinians, in Rosemary Sayigh's phrase, from peasants to refugees to the revolutionaries of a nation in exile has for the time being come to an abrupt stop, curling about itself violently. What was once a radical alternative to Zionism's master code of Jewish exclusivism seems reduced to mere points on the map miles away from Palestine. Lebanon, the Soviet buildup, Syria, Druze and Shia militancy, the new American-Israeli quasi-treaty—these dominate the landscape, absorb political energies.

Two anecdotes give a sense of the political and ideological problem I am trying to describe. Between August 29 and September 7, the United Nations held an international conference, mandated by the General Assembly, on the question of Palestine. The conference was to be held in Paris, but, worried by the threat of demonstrations and incidents from French Zionist organizations, the Mitterrand government requested that it be held elsewhere: France's *quid pro quo* to the UN, which was actually entitled to hold the conference in Paris at UNESCO's extraterritorial headquarters, was to be full participation by France. The conference was duly moved to Geneva, and France, just as duly, reneged on its promise and participated only as an "observer." One hundred thirty-seven nations showed up, a fact repeatedly changed to seventy-five nations by the U.S. press. The central document of the conference was to be a "Profile of the Palestinian People"—the title and the study's focus were specified by the General Assembly. With a small group of other "experts," I was engaged to produce the Profile. It went to the Secretary General's office for three months, and was returned for discussion to the Preparatory Committee of twenty-odd nations. There it sat until the beginning of June, at which point I was told that the Profile could not, and would never, be approved for use at the conference. The reasons given were, as usual, diplomatic and diverse. But, as an apologetic ambassador from a friendly Arab country made clear to me, by positing the existence—and historical narrative—of a Palestinian people, the Profile had "created" a dual-nationality problem for the Arab countries in which Palestinians had been dispersed since 1948. The same scriptures and fears applied to the proposal I made to conduct the first-ever census of refugee and expatriate Palestinians, most of whom live in the Arab world. There is an Arab context and an Israeli context, I was told: to speak of Palestinians outside the Occupied Territories was to challenge the collective Arab narrative and, in the words of a young Arab Third Secretary, to view history in too "liberal and Western" a way. Thus no Palestinian narrative, no Profile, no census: Palestine yes, Palestinians no.

The second anecdote is taken from the other side of the aisle, where, as we have seen, things are no less peculiar. The Israeli commentator Yoav Karni wrote in 1983:

> Last week I was invited to the Israeli Army Radio program *Correct Till Now* to speak about the historical backgrounds of Armenian terrorism. Against their usual custom, the editors insisted on taping the talk beforehand. Afterwards, I understood why. I was asked if the Armenian holocaust really occurred. I answered: "There is no doubt

> that genocide occurred. For thousands of years people lived on its land, and suddenly it was no more. This is genocide," or words to that effect. The Israeli Army Radio refused to broadcast the talk. They were ready to do it only on condition that I should change the text, and say, "There was a massacre, which perhaps approaches genocide."[7]

He concludes that "perhaps it was the great mistake of the last Jewish generation which caused it. It should have been forbidden to Jews to treat the concept of 'genocide' as applying to them alone. It should be told in every Israeli school that many other peoples were, and still are, expelled and massacred."

Conversely, Israelis are told by Chaim Herzog that when Israel fosters good relations with Right Wing regimes which practice racial discrimination and kill their own people, the only criterion ought to be: "Is it good for the Jews?" A related sentiment was expressed by a Jewish-Israeli resident of upper Nazareth about his Israeli-Arab neighbors: "Love is more dangerous than hate. It's dangerous to our existence."

The Palestinian narrative has never been officially admitted to Israeli history, except as that of "non-Jews," whose inert presence in Palestine was a nuisance to be ignored or expelled. With the exception of a small and marginal group of Israelis, most of Israel has as a result not found it difficult to get over the story of the Lebanese war and its subsequent horrors. Take Abba Eban—liberal, humane, judicious. In his introduction to the Israeli Kahan Commission report, published as a book in the West, he praises the "meticulous" analysis that, in a sense, exonerates Israel: yet in so doing he nowhere mentions such things as the explicitly fascist nature of Israel's chief allies, the Lebanese Phalanges, or the fact—which doesn't speak for itself—that the Palestinians in Lebanon were not *ipso facto* "terrorists," as the report has it, but were there because they had been driven out of Palestine in implementation of an admitted policy of expulsion.

Thus, as much as Begin and Sharon, Eban refuses to consider the PLO as more than a gang of terrorists. Indeed, he makes it seem that the PLO and the Phalangists, both of whom are "the chief agents of the tragedy," are equally culpable for killing the Palestinians at Sabra and Shatila. As to whether "terrorism" is adequately defined simply by ascribing it to Palestinians because of Israeli deaths (the figures are interesting—between 1967 and 1982, 290 Israelis were killed in Palestinian attacks, whereas Lebanese police, UN, and Red Cross figures put Israeli-caused Arab casualties at 20,000 deaths for July and August 1982 alone), or whether any act of Palestinian resistance is terrorism, Eban does not say. Yet the *other* Israeli report on Sabra and Shatila is perfectly clear on Israeli responsibility for, and even complicity with, what took place: I refer here to the Israeli journalist Amnon Kapeliouk's powerfully concise book, *Sabra et Chatila: Enquête sur un massacre,* which has still found no established British or American publisher.

Facts do not at all speak for themselves, but require a socially acceptable narrative to absorb, sustain, and circulate them. Such a narrative has to have a beginning and an end: in the Palestinian case, homeland for the resolution of its exiles since 1948. But, as Hayden White has noted in a seminal article, "narrative in general, from the folk tale to the novel, from annals to the fully realized 'history,' has to do with the topics of law, legality, legitimacy, or, more generally, *authority.*"[8] Now there are numerous UN resolutions certifying the Palestinians as a people, their struggle as a legitimate one, their right to have an independent state as "inalienable." Such resolutions, however, do not have the authority of which White speaks. None has drawn any acknowledgment from Israel or the United States, which have restricted themselves to such nonnarrative and indefinite formulae as—in the language of lackadaisical U.S. pronouncements—"resolution of the Palestinian problem in all its aspects."[9]

No television watcher could have had any doubts that the Israelis were savage and ruthless during the siege of Beirut. Yet a campaign has been waged in the media attacking the media for a pro-PLO slant. It got started, well before the Israeli invasion, in pro-Zionist publications like *The New Republic,* and it continues long after in *Encounter, Commentary,* and *Policy Studies,* as well as on college campuses where lectures entitled "NBC in Lebanon: A Study in Misrepresentation" are regularly given. The basic line is that the media have taken liberties with language, that analogies between Warsaw and Beirut are wrong, that any images showing Israeli troops engaged in bombing plainly civilian targets are anti-Semitic, that the millions of feet of newsreel are less trustworthy than the impressions of a supporter of Israel who spent a day in Lebanon touring the place as a guest of the Israeli army. Underlying all attacks on the media is the allegation that the PLO has intimidated or seduced journalists into partisan, anti-Semitic, and anti-Western attacks on Israel, a charge grandiloquently pronounced by Norman Podhoretz in his imitation of Zola, "J'Accuse."[10]

The repetition and accumulation of these claims amount to a virtual orthodoxy, setting limits, defining areas, asserting pressures, and the Chancellor incident of July 1982 stands as something of a monument to the process. John Chancellor is a leading American television commentator who arrived in Beirut during the siege and witnessed the destruction brought about by the indiscriminate bombing that was taking place all around him. The report he produced in full view of a vast national audience included references to "savage Israel," "an imperialist state that we never knew existed before." Yet a week later he reappeared in Jerusalem more or less retracting his remarks from Beirut: what he had seen there, he now said, was a "mistake," Israel did not intend the city's siege but had "bumbled into it." Commenting on this volte-face, Richard Poirier wrote in *Raritan Review* that "the feelings aroused in Chancellor (and in millions of viewers presumably) by the television footage simply had no place to go outside the program." Far from just changing his mind from one week to the next, Chancellor:

> unwittingly exposed the degree to which the structure of the evening news depends on ideas of reality determined by the political and social discourse already empowered outside the newsroom. Feelings about the victims of the siege could not, for example, be attached to an idea for the creation of a Palestinian homeland, since, despite the commitments, muffled as they are, of the Camp David accords, no such idea has as yet managed to find an enabling vocabulary within what is considered "reasonable" political discourse in this country.[11]

What needs to be added to Poirier's astute comments is that the "idea" of a Palestinian homeland would have to be enabled by the prior acceptance of a narrative entailing a homeland. And this has been resisted as strenuously on the imaginative and ideological level as it has been politically.

While it is true that the ideological dimension is always important in political contests, the oddity here is that the physical distance from the territory aspired to, and the heavily saturated significance of that territory, make crucial the need for antecedent ideological projection in narrative form in the West. For Palestine is a privileged site of origin and return for both Judaism and Christianity—all the more so given the fact that Palestine for one and a half millennia had been in non-Jewish and non-Christian hands. It figures prominently in such momentous events as the Crusades, the nineteenth-century imperial conflicts, in Zionism, and in a whole congerie of major cultural texts from Augustine's autobiography, to Dante's vision, to Shakespeare's dramatic geography, and Blake's apocalypse. In more material and mundane terms, Palestine has also been important to the Arab and Muslim experience: a comparative study of that experience with the Judaic and Christian would be of extraordinary interest. The point I'm trying to make is that insofar as the West has complementarily endowed Zionism with a role to play in Palestine along with its own, it has stood against the perhaps humble narrative of native Palestinians once resident there and now reconstituting themselves in exile in the Occupied Territories.

With this background in mind, the current disapproval of terrorism can more easily be understood. As first articulated during the late months of the Carter administration on, and amplified in such books as *The Terror Network* and *The Spike,* as unrestrainedly used by Israel—and now by American—officials to describe "enemies," terrorism is the biggest and yet for that reason the most precise of concepts. This is not at all to say that terrorism does not exist, but rather to suggest that its existence has occasioned a whole new signifying system as well. Terrorism signifies first, in relation to "us," the alien and gratuitously hostile force. It is destructive, systematic, and controlled. It is a web, a network, a conspiracy run from Moscow, via Bulgaria, Beirut, Libya, Tehran, and Cuba. It is capable of anything. One fervent anti-Communist Israeli has written a book revealing the Sabra and Shatila massacres to be a plot engineered by Moscow and the PLO to kill Palestinians (using Germans) in order to frame democratic Israel. Most of all, terrorism has come to signify "our" view of everything in the world that seems inimical to our interests, army, policy, or values.

As such, it can be used retrospectively (as in the cases of Iran and Lebanon) or prospectively (Grenada, Honduras, Nicaragua) to justify everything "we" do and to delegitimize as well as dehumanize everything "they" do. The very indiscriminateness of terrorism, actual and described, its tautological and circular character, is antinarrative. Sequence, the logic of cause and effect as between oppressors and victims, opposing pressures—all these vanish inside an enveloping cloud called "terrorism." Israeli commentators have remarked that the systematic use by Begin, Sharon, Eytan, and Arens of the rubric "terrorist" to describe Palestinians made it possible for them to use phrases like "terrorists' nest," "cancerous growth" and "two-legged beasts" in order to bomb refugee camps. An Israeli paratrooper said that "every Palestinian is automatically a suspected terrorist and by our definition of the term it is actually true." One should add that Likud's antiterrorist language and methods represent only an increase in intensity over previous Israeli policies, which were no less callous about Palestinians as real people with a real history.

No wonder, then, that "facts" and the truth of a consecutive historical experience stand very little chance of wide acceptance or distribution in this wilderness of mirrors. To know, for example, that Shamir's Stern Gang collaborated with the Nazis,[12] or that everything the Israelis now do to Palestinians constitutes brutality and oppression easily rivaling the deeds of the Polish or South African regimes, is also sadly to know that antiapartheid activists regularly avoid discussion of Israel when they criticize one of its chief allies, South Africa, or that American journalists do not report the details of daily life on the West Bank with the tenacity they bring to reports about daily life behind the Iron Curtain, or that leaders of the antinuclear movement have nothing to say about the Israeli nuclear threat. Worse yet, there is every chance that ignorance about Israel's attitude toward Palestinians will keep pace with sustained encomiums on Israel's pioneering spirit, democracy, and humanism. On the uprooting of Palestinian orchards in Gaza in 1972 to make way for settlements, Chomsky notes here: this is "what is called in technical terms 'making the desert bloom.'"[13]

There have been refugees before. There have been new states built on the ruins of old. The unique things about this situation is Palestine's unusual centrality, which privileges a Western master narrative, highlighting Jewish alienation and redemption—with all of it taking place as a modern spectacle before the world's eyes. So that when Palestinians are told to stop complaining and to settle elsewhere like other refugees before them, they are entitled to respond that no other refugees have been required systematically to watch an unending ceremony of public approbation for the political movement, army, or country that made them refugees and occupied their territory. Occupying armies, as Chomsky observes, do not as a rule "bask in the admiration of American intellectuals for their unique and remarkable commitment to 'purity of arms.'"[14] To top it all, Palestinians are expected to participate in the dismantling of their own history at the same time.

As long as discussions of Palestine and Israel are conducted on this level, the superior force of the ideological consensus I have been describing will prevail. Palestinians will initially have to play the major role in changing the consensus and, alas, characteristically, they have not been very successful. I recall during the siege of Beirut obsessively telling friends and family there, over the phone, that they ought to record, write down their experiences; it seemed crucial as a starting point to furnish the world some narrative evidence, over and above atomized and reified TV clips, of what it was like to be at the receiving end of Israeli "antiterrorism," also known as "Peace for Galilee." Naturally, they were all too busy surviving to take seriously the unclear theoretical imperatives being urged on them intermittently by a distant son, brother, or friend. As a result, most of the easily available written material produced since the fall of Beirut has in fact not been Palestinian and, just as significant, it has been of a fairly narrow range of types:[15] a small archive to be discussed in terms of absences and gaps—in terms either prenarrative or, in a sense, antinarrative. The archive speaks of the depressed condition of the Palestinian narrative at present.

This does not, however, make any of the works in question less valiant, less indicative of a new moral isolation enveloping Israel—for all the absence of a Palestinian narrative. Each functions on some inevitably primitive level as valuable testimonial, as raw information for a setting, Europe and America, where definitions of the Middle East serve to screen the reality of Israeli actions. Jonathan Randal—a senior American foreign correspondent, veteran of Vietnam, Cuba, and Algeria—like John Bulloch of the *Daily Telegraph*, like Kapeliouk, like Salim Nassib and Caroline Tisdall, like Tony Clifton, is a journalist writing what is in effect surplus reportage, as if the constraints of newspaper columns could not contain what was seen. This is an interesting phenomenon, perhaps a new journalistic mode. Each of these writers, except Chomsky, tells a story sympathetic to the Palestinians, if not always in political agreement with them; there is also a solidarity with those Lebanese who have suffered for decades the unmitigated stupidity of their leaders and foreign friends. All of these writers chronicle the relentless brutality of the siege, the outrage felt at the unctuous language of military communiqués glossing over massacres and heroism. Although their works overlap in many ways, each contributes a piece to the larger picture attempted in his redoubtably encyclopedic way by Chomsky.

As straight narrative of the battle culminating in Beirut between Israel and the PLO, Bulloch's book is difficult to better, though it is dotted with careless errors (Said Aql for Basil Aql). Its economy of line and unsparingly harsh perspective allow a clear but circumscribed picture to emerge of what forces were engaged together; his conclusion is that Israel lost the war. But even though he makes an effort at describing the momentum of Palestinian nationalism, its lopsided anomalous achievements in Lebanon, its inevitably messy involvement in Lebanese and Syrian politics, its better than expected efforts to cope with circumstances too complex for anyone to overcome, he writes as an outsider, and there is little in his narrative to prepare one for the continuing drama of the PLO, or for the bloody Israeli occupation of South Lebanon, or for the unfolding national catastrophe that has been Lebanon since August 1982.

Bulloch is of the school which thinks of Lebanon's history as the time-honored story of *zaims* (or semifeudal patrons), factions, and loyalties. He follows Lebanon's leading historian, Kamal Salibi, in this,[16] although unlike Elie Salem (Lebanon's current foreign minister), Bulloch hasn't concluded that Lebanon's sudden modern prosperity was ever, or could ever be, maintained without disastrous upheaval—Salem's prediction, as recently as twelve years ago.[17] It would be hard to be more unfortunately wrong. Not that anyone was more correct in predicting the two-decade cataclysm, first of wealth, then of civil war, which is tearing Lebanon apart.

David Gilmour's first chapter exposes the jungle that was "the old Lebanon" with merciless precision, and his last chapter presciently lays for the scenario now being enacted. His account of the overwhelming mess unleashed by piratical commerce, governmental incompetence, regional and ideological confusions, tremendous demographic change, and utter cynicism is unique. It gives one a compelling rationale for the emergence of the PLO inside (rather than its "invasion" of) Lebanon, where among a largely destitute and confined refugee population no one could survive at all without some form of political organization for protection. One senses in Gilmour's book, however, some frustration at the recalcitrant, non-narrative character of Lebanon's problems. No other modern society has torn itself apart with that crazy mixture of brutality and style. Few countries have concentrated within their borders so impossibly heterogeneous a collection of interests, most of them having coarse domination, profit, and manipulation as their goal. Some adumbration of this is conveyed in the American title of Randal's book—*Going All the Way*—and much of its substance similarly delivers the irrationality of Lebanon: the relentless Lebanese willingness to see yet another car bomb (surely, at this "post-political" stage, an art form), the stupid, opportunistic ideological fantasies constructed by different factions. There are cultural and intellectual roots to the things that move Maronites, Sunni, and Shia Muslim, Greek Orthodox Christians and Druze in Lebanon, and these Randal does not explore. A pity, since, as he notes, for a corps of Western journalists afflicted with too rapid and frequent a turnover in complicated places like Lebanon, there is by now a specialist literature that ought not to be ignored: the pioneering studies of Lebanon and Syria by Albert Hourani and Domnique Chevalier have been elaborated in the work of younger colleagues and students. Instead Randal relies on his instinct for relevant observation. His sketches of the checkmating, of the multiple "negations," between communities on which modern Lebanon has rested are good, as is his portrait of U.S. ignorance, bumbling, and mistimed and misplaced pressures.

There has never been an American policy on Lebanon, as anyone today can quite easily ascertain. Randal, however, takes the further step of characterizing American weakness in the face of Israeli strength as actively promoting Lebanon's destruction. At most, "Lebanon, for the United States, ended up a disposable place of unknown loyalties and complicated working, not to be entirely trusted." This by no means explains the presence of 2,000 Marines and a Navy flotilla, but it goes a long way toward telling us that no coherent mission for them will ever be found, and, unfortunately for those Lebanese who have put their trust in U. S. military policy, that the Marines are almost certain to be pulled out ungracefully fairly soon. Randal's best moments come when he narrates Bashir Gemayel's rise to power—a chilling tale that lays to rest any illusions about the Maronite-Phalange claim to be defending the values of "Western civilization." It is difficult to understand the romance that lingers about Bashir's short life, in which he was just as capable of killing as of marshaling the members of his own community. Randal also helps one to grasp the basic premises of Israeli policy on Lebanon, and Israel's only recently challenged alliance with the fascist Phalanges. (Interestingly, it was an interagency conflict that brought these matters into the open—between the Mossad, who promoted the Phalanges, and Israeli military intelligence, who felt that Mossad had lost "objectivity" by overidentfying with their Lebanese clients.)

Randal's book goes back to the period just after World War I to show how Zionists envisaged incorporating South Lebanon into the future Jewish state, but the bulk of his evidence dates from the fifties and after, when it became a matter of official Israeli policy—fascinatingly documented in Moshe Sharett's *Diaries*—to intervene directly in Lebanese affairs, sponsor militia, bribe officials, collaborate with Maronites to help maintain an imbalance between dramatic rises in the Muslim population and the increasingly unyielding Christian control which was handed to the Maronite oligarchs by French colonialism in 1943.

Two other journalists' books deserve mention. One is Tony Clifton's *God Cried,* which, with Catherine Leroy's graphic and painful photographs, narrates the agonies of conscience, sympathy, and rage felt by an Australian correspondent reporting the Palestinian and Lebanese experience that culminated in the siege. Clifton pours it out—all the anger at Israel's detailed, almost fastidious effort to humiliate and pain the very refugees it had expelled in 1948, and has been stamping on ever since. As with Randal's work, we are obliged in the end to rely on one man's sensitive and informed testimony. There is some slight resemblance between Clifton and Jacobo Timerman, whose rambling but affecting account of an Israeli's awakening of conscience has been criticized by some for unfairness to Israel, by others for reducing the whole war to a problem for one

Jewish witness.[18] In both instances, nonetheless, there is an urgency in the author's conviction that what he writes is unfairly matched against a public narrative skewed very much in Israel's favor.

It may have been with some of these problems of subjectivity in mind that Salim Nassib and Caroline Tisdall shaped their book the way they did. *Beirut: Frontline Story* has the effect of a montage sequence: interviews with a wide spectrum of political figures interspersed with vignettes of daily life, of which the best is a lively "cross section of the war—five stories of a Beirut apartment block" whose occupants are Greek Orthodox, Maronites, Sunni Muslims, Druzes, and Shia Muslims. This is the Israeli invasion seen in vivid microcosm, daily life surgically rendered, but, as in a Zola novel, there is an active sympathy at work. Nassib's pieces were his dispatches for *Libération,* and they conclude with Arafat aboard the Greek freighter *Atlantis* on his way from Beirut to Athens, speaking about the war. Caroline Tisdall's pages of eyewitness description relive the Sabra and Shatila massacres, and end with this telling Palestinian comment:

> Before the war they said we were terrorists and that we were training terrorists in our camps. Everyone who knows us knows we were fighters you could trust, and that we were trying to build a progressive mentality. Why didn't they write that every day? It's related to philosophy: when you are building something and the enemy comes and destroys this thing again and again, it means you are on the right road, however long it may be.

This comment (and especially the image of repeated destruction followed by repeated efforts to rebuild) should be kept in mind as one proceeds through Chomsky's panorama of stupidity, immorality, and corruption, *The Fateful Triangle,* which, for its documentation, may be the most ambitious book ever attempted on the conflict between Zionism and the Palestinians viewed as centrally involving the United States. But this, too, is not the narrative that is missing.

For Chomsky's book is decidedly not written from the point of view of a Palestinian trying, as it were, to give national shape to a life now dissolving into many unrelated particles. *The Fateful Triangle* is instead a dogged exposé of human corruption, greed, and intellectual dishonesty. It is also a great and important book, which must be read by anyone concerned with public affairs. The facts for Chomsky are there to be recognized, although no one else has ever recognized them so systematically. His mainly Israeli and U.S. sources are staggeringly complete, and he is capable of registering contradictions, distinctions, and lapses which occur between them. But, as we shall see, his work is not only deeply and unacceptably pessimistic; it is also a work not critical and reflective enough about its own premises, and this is partly because he does not, in a narrative way, look back to the beginning of the conflict between Zionism and the Palestinians.

These criticisms cannot be made at all lightly, or without acknowledging the unparalleled energy and honesty of his achievement. There is something deeply moving about a mind of such noble ideals repeatedly stirred on behalf of human suffering and injustice. One thinks here of Voltaire, of Benda, or Russell, although more than any of them Chomsky commands what he calls "reality"—facts—over a breathtaking range. He has two aims. One is an account of the origins of Israel's attack upon the Palestinians during its invasion of Lebanon in 1982; out of that account comes a survey of diplomatic, intellectual, economic, and political history that connects these disparate realms with each other. His major claim is that Israel and the United States—especially the latter, seen by Chomsky as the archvillain of the piece—are rejectionists opposed to peace, whereas the Arabs, including the PLO, have for years been trying to accommodate themselves to the reality of Israel.

The other aim of Chomsky's book is to compare the history—so profoundly inhuman, cynical, and deliberately cruel to the Palestinian people—with its systematically rewritten record as kept by those whom Chomsky calls "the supporters of Israel." As with another book of his, it is Chomsky's contention that the liberal intelligentsia (Irving Howe, Arthur Goldberg, Alan Dershowitz, Michael Walzer, Amos Oz, Jane Fonda, Tom Hayden, Shlomo Avineri, Martin Peretz) and even segments of the organized Left are more culpable, more given to lying, than conservatives are. The Western media come off badly in comparison with their Israeli counterparts, although Chomsky notes, shrewdly, that media accuracy is rarely a matter of goodwill or of unhypocritical journalists: it is just that "the totalitarian mentality" ruling the West since Vietnam can't always keep up with the swarming life of fact in the Western democracies.

So the book can be read as a protracted war between fact and a series of myths—Israeli democracy, Israeli purity of arms, the benign occupation, no racism against Arabs in Israel, Palestinian terrorism, peace for Galilee. Although Chomsky's model for these myths is Orwellian newspeak and doublethink (aspects, he says, of a revision of history in the post-Vietnam era), the process of dismantling to which he submits the myths is actually a form of deconstruction, since all of the material he uses against texts like *The New Republic, The New York Times,* the *Jerusalem Post* is itself textual. Nearly everywhere he looks he finds either suppression or outright apologies for gangsterism (as when The *New Republic* on July 27, 1977, prints "the first explicit defense of torture to have appeared in the West apart from the ravings of the ultra-right in France during the Algerian war"), all done in the interest of sustaining Israeli and U.S. hegemony. Having rehearsed the "official" narrative, he then blows it away with vast amounts of counterevidence, leading us to the conclusion that the Middle East, along with the rest of the world, is on the road to Armageddon.

I can give only a hint of his tremendously effective methods and recourse—his thousands of footnotes, his frequently angry irony, his compassion for the weak, the forgotten and calumniated. Thus as he tells us of older Israeli soldiers testifying that even in European service during World War II they saw nothing to compare to the destruction of Ein-el-Hilweh Camp, or that "long and repeated interrogations were accompanied by constant beating, or attacks by dogs on leashes," or that Israeli border guards force people to crawl, bark, laud Begin, or that during collective punishment in the West Bank village of Halhul "people were ordered to urinate on one another, sing 'Hativka' . . . lick the ground," or that the director-general of the Israel Broadcasting Authority in 1974 wrote an article expressing his preference for South African over black Africa, complete "with citations of research proving the genetic inferiority of blacks"—as he gives these and literally thousands more such horrifying details, he notes the silence of *The New Republic,* the praise for Israeli purity of arms, the defense of Israel's occupation (collective detention, torture, and murder) policy, the high praise for Israel's moral values, the testimony of cultural authorities such as

Saul Bellow, who sees in Israel a land "where almost everyone is reasonable and tolerant, and rancor against the Arabs is rare." Worse yet, there are the many cases where apologists for Zionism and socialism like Irving Howe ignore the killing of Jews by the Irgun, speak about the evils of Begin (although much of Chomsky's evidence is that Labour was at least as bad as Likud), and then go on to pronounce on the "habitual violence" of Arab politics. Chomsky gives much attention to the organized racial persecution of Arabs and of "Oriental" Jews, usually abetted by learned or religious authorities, or by figures like Elie Wiesel who use the Holocaust to legitimate excesses; he also notes that none of Israel's liberal supporters has anything to say about this.

Chomsky is not especially gentle to the PLO, whose "self-destructiveness" and "suicidal character" he likes no more than he approves of its program of armed struggle and erratic violence. The Arab regimes, he says, are not "decent," and, he might have added, not popular either. But this—and not incidentally—is one of the gaps in this almost preposterously complete book. I am referring to its relative inattention to the Arab world. He is certainly right to say that there exists a standard Western practice, racist in origin, of dismissing Arab sources as unreliable, and he suggests that the unavailability of written Arab work in the West is in part due to the same "democratic" censorship that promotes the image of Israel. Yes, but the dynamic of "a fateful triangle" would make more sense if, included in it, there could be some account of political, social, and economic trends in the Arab world—or if it were changed to the figure of a square or circle. Among such trends one would have to place the economic dependence of the Arab states on the United States (amounting, in some instances, to objective collaboration with Israel); the almost total absence of democratic freedoms in the Arab world; the peculiar relationships that obtain between Palestinians, or for that matter the PLO, and various Arab countries; Western cultural penetration of the Arab world and the Islamic reactions this has bred; the role of the Arab Left and the Soviet Union. Despite their stated willingness to have peace, the Arab regimes have not been able to make peace, or to mobilize their societies for war; such facts—which are not entirely a consequence of Israeli-American rejection—Chomsky does not fully consider.

There is also some confusion in the book, some inconsistency at the level of principle. The normative picture proposed by Chomsky—with which I am in agreement—is that Palestine should be partitioned into two states, and that the PLO, plus most of the Arab states, have had this end in mind at least since the early seventies. I think he is absolutely right to say that because, in the words of Israeli commentators like Yehoshua Porath and Danny Rubenstein, Israel feared moderate and responsible Palestinians more than terrorists, it was Israel, aided by the United States, which prevented any realization of this reasonable if imperfect plan. But it isn't clear to me how you can recognize that Zionism has always excluded and discriminated against Arabs—which you oppose—and yet maintain that Jews do have a communal right to settlement from abroad in Palestine. My point is that here you must more explicitly define what those rights are, and in what way your definition of those rights is not like that of those Zionists who simply disregarded the fact of Arab inhabitants already in Palestine. How can you formulate the right to move people into Palestine despite the wishes of all the already present native Palestinians, without at the same time implying and repeating the tragic cycle of violence and counterviolence between Palestinians and Jews? How do you avoid what has happened if you do not more precisely reconcile *allowable* claims?

In leaving this problem unresolved, Chomsky is led to one of the chief difficulties of his book—namely, his pessimistic view that "it is too late" for any reasonable or acceptable settlement. The facts, of course, are with him: The rate of Jewish colonization on the West Bank has passed any easily retrievable mark, and as Meron Benvenisti and other anti-Likud Israelis have said, the fight for Palestinian self-determination in the Occupied Territories is now over—good and lost. Pessimism of the intellect *and* pessimism of the will . . . But most Palestinians would say in response: If those are the facts, then so much the worse for the facts. The supervening reality is that the struggle between Zionism, in its present form, and the Palestinians is very far from over; Palestinian nationalism has had, and will continue to have, an integral reality of its own, which, in the view of many Palestinians who actually live the struggle, is not about to go away, or submit to the ravages of Zionism and its backers. And curiously this is what Chomsky does not or perhaps cannot see, although he is right to forecast a worsening of the situation, increasing levels of violence, more polarization, militarization, irrationality. In having accepted the Zionist first principle of a right to settle Jews in Palestine against the wishes of the native inhabitants, Chomsky almost unconsciously takes the next step of assuming that the Palestinian struggle is over, that the Palestinians have given up—maybe because their historical existence hasn't totally convinced him of its permanence. Perhaps giving up is the rational thing to do, yet—and here Chomsky's own fighting energies contradict him—injustice is injustice, and no one should acquiesce in it. Chomsky himself, with this massive volume, is a case in point.

That raises another problem. His isolation from the actual arena of contest, his distance from power as a fiercely uncompromising intellectual, his ability to tell the dispassionate truth (while no longer able to write in previously hospitable places like the *New York Review of Books*) have made it possible for him to avoid the ideological traps and the dishonesty he perceives in Israeli and U.S. apologists. There is, of course, no state-worship in Chomsky, nor is there any glossing over uncomfortable truths or indecent practices that exist within one's own camp. But are isolation, the concern for justice, the passion to record injustice, sufficient to ensure one's own freedom from ideology? When Chomsky claims to be dealing with facts, he does deal with more facts than his opponents. But where are facts if not embedded in history, and then reconstituted and recovered by human agents stirred by some perceived or desired or hoped-for historical narrative whose future aim is to restore justice to the dispossessed? In other words, the reporters of fact, like Chomsky, as well as the concealers of fact, like the "supporters of Israel," are acting within history, according to codifiable norms of representation, in a context of competing ideological and intellectual values. When he states the facts as widely, as clearly, as completely as any person alive, Chomsky is not merely performing a mechanical reporting chore, from some Archimedean point outside propaganda and cliché: he is doing something extremely sophisticated, underpinned by standards of argument, coherence and proof that are not derived from the merely "factual." But the irony is that Chomsky does not reflect theoretically on what he does; he just does it. So, on the one hand, he leaves us to suppose that telling the truth is a simple matter while, on the other hand, he compiles masses of evidence showing that no one can really deal with the facts. How can we then suppose that one man can tell the truth?

Does he believe that in writing this book he will lead others to tell the truth also? What makes it possible for us as human beings to face the facts, to manufacture new ones, or to ignore some and focus on others?

Answers to these questions must reside in a theory of perception, a theory of intellectual activity, and in an epistemological account of ideological structures as they pertain to specific problems as well as to concrete historical and geographical circumstances. None of these things is within the capacity of a solitary individual to produce, and none is possible without some sense of communal or collective commitment to assign them a more than personal validity. It is this commitment that national narratives authorize and represent, although Chomsky's understandable reluctance to hew to any national or state line prevents him from admitting it. But in a situation like that of the Palestinians and Israelis, hardly anyone can be expected to drop the quest for national identity and go straight to a history-transcending universal rationalism. Each of the two communities, misled though both may be, is interested in its origins, its history of suffering, its need to survive. To recognize these imperatives, as components of national identity, and to try to reconcile them rather than dismiss them as so much nonfactual ideology, strikes me as the task at hand.

from *The Politics of Dispossession*

10

Interiors

(1986)

After the Last Sky, Edward Said's most experimental book, draws its title from a poem by the Palestinian poet Mahmoud Darwish but owes its birth to two contradictions. Said had been acting as a consultant to the United Nations for its International Conference on the Question of Palestine in 1983. Having suggested that a photo essay of Palestinians be hung in the assembly hall in Geneva for the conference, Said was met with a rude surprise. Several participating nations objected to his idea. A compromise was eventually reached whereby pictures could be hung but no captions were allowed to be attached. The belligerent nations in this case were not Israel or the United States (both of whom had boycotted the conference), but principally Arab states who found Palestinians, as Said writes, "useful up to a point—for attacking Israel, for railing against Zionism, imperialism, the United States, for bewailing the settlement and expropriation of Arab land in the Occupied Territories. Beyond that point, when it came to the urgent needs of the Palestinians *as a people,* or to the deplorable conditions in which many Palestinians live in Arab countries as well as in Israel, lines had to be drawn." *After the Last Sky* is an attempt to erase such lines and fill in the spaces with subjective accounts of being Palestinian.

The second major contradiction of *After the Last Sky* rests in the fact that at the time it was being written, Said was barred from entering Israel (not until

1992 did he return) and thus had no direct access to the land of his birth and childhood. "I cannot reach the actual people who were photographed, except through a European photographer," Said writes in *After the Last Sky.* This is "an exile's book," he explains.

The work was met with overwhelming critical success. In was widely reviewed and even spawned an experimental dance piece of the same name in England in 1995. In 1999 Columbia University Press reissued the text.

Reviewing the book for the Manchester *Guardian Weekly,* Salman Rushdie called it "the most beautiful piece of prose I have read about what it means to be a Palestinian." *The New York Times* praised the work, commenting that Said has introduced new Arabic vocabularies into our discussions of the Palestinians (*manfa* for "exile," *ghurba* for "estrangement," *awdah* for "return") and noting that Said "writes not to the pictures but from them."

In fact, *After the Last Sky* is a deliberate attempt to interrogate the very tools of representation (photography, prose). The choice of Jean Mohr as photographer for the work is not accidental. Mohr had previously collaborated with the critic and novelist John Berger in two works (*Another Way of Telling* and *A Seventh Man*), where Berger was rethinking the political uses of photography. In an essay published several years before *After the Last Sky,* Said had praised Berger for his use of "the visual faculty . . . to restore the nonsequential energy of lived historical memory and subjectivity as fundamental components of meaning in representation." Said was drawn to Berger's ability to make something new out of the very tools of representation which maintain the status quo. As Berger explained in *Another Way of Telling,* "When photographs are used in control systems, their evidence is more or less limited to establishing identity and presence. But as soon as a photograph is used as a means of communication, the nature of lived experience is involved, and then the truth becomes more complex." *After the Last Sky* involves its readers, through the interplay of photography and prose, in what it means to be Palestinian.

The phrase *min al-dakhil,* "from the interior," has a special resonance to the Palestinian ear. It refers, first of all, to regions of the interior of Israel, to territories and people still Palestinian despite the interdictions of the Israeli presence. Until 1967, therefore, it meant the Palestinians who lived within Israel; after 1967 the phrase expanded to include the inhabitants of the West Bank, Gaza, and the Golan Heights, and since 1982 it has also meant the Palestinians (and Lebanese) of South Lebanon. The most striking thing about this meaning of *al-dakhil* is the change in value that has taken place in its connotation. As recently as the early 1970s, I can recall, Israeli Palestinians were considered a special breed—someone you might easily be suspicious of if you were a member of the exile or refugee Palestinian population residing outside Israel. We always felt that Israel's stamp on these people (their passports, their knowledge of Hebrew, their comparative lack of self-consciousness about living with Israeli Jews, their references to Israel as a real country, rather than "the Zionist entity") had changed them. They weren't like us in the sense that as Arabs living in the Arab world, subject to the heady triumphs and weepy sorrows of Arab nationalism, we were leading a life independent of imperialism and Zionism. They were different in a pejorative sense.

Now they are still different, but privileged. The people of the interior are cherished as Palestinians "already there," so to speak, Palestinians whose lives on the edge, under the gun, inside the barriers and *kasbahs,* entitle them to a kind of grace denied the rest of us. It is also true, alas, that since 1970 our collective history *fil-kharij* ("in the exterior") or in the *manfa* and *ghurba* ("exile" and "estrangement") has been singularly unsuccessful, progressively graceless, unblessed, more and more eccentric, de-centered, alienated. We Palestinians lost our status in Jordan, Lebanon, Syria, and Egypt. Of course, the PLO is recognized by over one hundred countries, and we have a whole sheaf of UN resolutions to our credit, but no one has any illusions about our real status as outcasts, and failures to boot. A look at our balance sheet reveals massacres, expulsions, and demotions on one side of the ledger, and practically nothing on the other, the credit side. And, to jump to another metaphor, not only is the writing on the wall ominous, but we're not sure what it is trying to tell us.

Therefore, those in Palestine, in the interior, who experience Israeli rule directly, are in a sense better off than those of us who can only *talk* about Zionism while experiencing the unlovely solicitude of our Arab brethren on the outside. Politically, it is important to note that Palestinian activity is now mainly directed toward and focused on the interior, whereas until the 1982 Israeli invasion of Lebanon, the problems and politics of the exterior were what mattered most.

The second meaning of *al-dakhil* is slightly more complicated. It refers to privacy, to that region on the inside that is protected by both the wall of solidarity formed by members of the group, and the hostile enclosure created around us by the more powerful. Two Palestinians meet for the first time, let us say in Delhi or London, and strike up a conversation. Within a minute or two, and with no explicit questions or answers, they can determine each other's original residence, their type of work, their political persuasion (even the deviation or current within that), and their value system—all of them conveyed in a set of specific words or phrases, names, inflections, and emphases, known *only* to Palestinians. But to be on the inside is also not to be yourself on the outside: You have to participate in and speak the language of the outside world, which means that you have to use "their" codes, but to mean something quite different. But the problem of the inside is that it *is* inside, private, and can never be made plain or evident to anyone, perhaps not even to one's fellow members. The world of secrecy, of private existence, of cabals and conspiracies is a fact of most societies. In Arab tradition it is almost always colored by religion, both Muslim and Christian, but in ways that, I think, are much more subtle and nuanced than most Orientalists (or outsiders) have suspected. Even when it appears that insiders or initiates know the codes, they are never sure whether these codes can in fact deliver the right answers to the important questions, can confirm the stability of what is or gain the assent of the whole group. Thus, although to Palestinians today the word *awdah* ("return") is crucial and stands at the very heart of our political quest for self-determination, to some it means return to a Palestinian state alongside Israel, yet to others it means a return to *all* of Palestine.

To be on the inside, in this sense, is to speak from, be in, a situation which, paradoxically, you do not control and cannot really be sure of even when you have evolved special languages—sometimes evasive, always idiosyncratic—that only you and others like you can understand. The structure of your situation is such that being inside is a privilege that is an affliction, like feeling hemmed in by the house you own. Yes, an open door is necessary for passing between inside and outside, but it is also an avenue used by others to enter. Even though we are inside our world, there is no preventing others from getting in, overhearing us, decoding our private messages, violating our privacy. That is how we read the history of Palestine, from the Crusades to Balfour and Weizmann: that it was entered despite us, and lived in despite us.

What do you do then? You try to get used to living alongside outsiders and endlessly attempting to define what is yours on the inside. We are a people of messages and signals, of allusions and indirect expression. We seek each other out, but because our interior is always to some extent occupied and interrupted by others—Israelis and Arabs—we have developed a technique of speaking *through* the given, expressing things obliquely and, to my mind, so mysteriously as to puzzle even ourselves.

Example: The cult of physical strength, of fascination with bodybuilding, karate, and boxing, which has been a striking fact of life among Palestinian youth for quite a while, is obviously the response of the weak to a strong, visibly dominating other. But it is also an eye-catching, almost decorative pattern woven through ordinary experience, and it means something much more than "making ourselves strong." It is an assertion of self, an insistence on details beyond any rational purpose. But what may appear to outsiders as utter stupidity for us scores a tiny, almost imperceptible point on the inside, as it were.

The following story illustrates my meaning. The wife of a distin-

In a camp north of Ramallah, 1979. A youth club where, as in prison, it is vital to keep in good physical shape.

guished European literary figure wrote me some time ago of their visit to Jerusalem; he was lecturing at the university, as was she, I think. They were there for six weeks. During that time she said they'd only met Palestinians twice, of which one meeting was the occasion for her letter. The man "in charge of a shop [selling embroidery] in David Street" engaged her in conversation, in between bargaining over some merchandise. It appeared that he was "an acquaintance and admirer" of mine: It was clear to me that he had volunteered this information in response to her telling him in a perfectly natural but quite irrelevant way that she knew Edward Said. She had undertaken then "to send on . . . the enclosed message," which was written in Arabic on a small bit of paper torn out of a spiral notebook. My friend also noted the man's wish to register

Palestinian superiority over the Arabs in all things (intelligence, martial arts, trading), a superiority expressed by him in the phrase "we are the Jews of the Arab world." In all this my correspondent accurately sensed "rhetorical nuances and complications which I [she] was too unsituated to understand," especially since she was accompanied by an Israeli friend for whose benefit much of the man's performance was carried on.

After all this, what was the message to me? I confess to a certain excitement as I unfolded the tiny bit of paper, and also to a self-congratulatory feeling about the esteem in which I was held by people who didn't know me but who nevertheless valued the contribution I was making to our cause. To begin with, the message was headed by my name in roman script. There followed five lines of Arabic, telling of the writer's great expertise in karate and of his participation in the world karate championship "under the name of Palestine." There was nothing else. But, I thought, how typical of Palestinian insiders' communications—that odd bravado, not really meant to be a joke. The exchange of messages came almost naturally to both of us, given our situations. He was inside, and using the good offices of a sympathetic outsider to contact me, an insider who was now outside Jerusalem, the place of our common origin. That he wrote my name in English was as much a sign that he too could deal with the world I lived in as it was that he followed what I did, with some pride, perhaps, but also with the wariness of one who for too long has been "represented" by Westernized intellectuals whose track record wasn't any too good. The time had come to demonstrate a healthy indication that the Edward Saids had better remember that we were being watched (by karate experts), somewhat approvingly, but also cautiously. Finally, his (to me) comic insistence on his physical skills revealed the same, often uninspired, assertion of self all of us seem to possess. He had already done his super-Palestinian routine for my friend, and probably knew that she would tell me; now he was doing it again, knowing that I would repeat the story. I have.

Such networks of witnesses, testimonials, and authorities threaded through our dispersed community amplify our assertions with such insistence as to be positively numbing. To outsiders this assertiveness is frustrating, not only because of its obduracy, but also because it seems to renew itself ceaselessly, without ever pro-

Jenin, 1984.

ducing anything new or anything outside it that might be illuminating. To me, and to others like me who live in the *manfa* ("exile") or *ghurba* ("estrangement"), there is nevertheless something reassuring (if a bit inane) about those on the inside—in Palestine or in the Arab world, which is closer than New York or Berlin to *al-dakhil*—repeating familiar patterns to the point where repetition itself becomes more important than what is being repeated. In the rigorous discipline of the repetition, as my karate expert knew perfectly, you cannot get out of it, cannot easily transform it into a symbol of something else. Karate does not stand for self-development, but only for the repeated act of being a Palestinian karate expert. A Palestinian. It is as if the activity of repeating prevents us, and others, from skipping us or overlooking us entirely.

This compulsion to repeat is evident in the interiors of Palestinian houses of all classes. The same food and eating rituals organized around a table or central space occur with maddening regularity. The rituals of offering and hospitality are designed, I think, to be excessive, to put before a guest more than is needed, more than will be consumed, more than can be afforded. Wherever there are Palestinians, the same signs of hospitality and offering keep appearing, the same expectant intimacy, the same displays of affection and of objects—replicas of the Mosque of Omar, plates inlaid with mother-of-pearl, tiny Palestinian flags—appropriated for protection as well as sociability. Naturally, they authenticate and certify the fact that you are in a Palestinian home. But it is more than that. It is part of a larger pattern of repetition in which even I, supposedly liberated and secular, participate. We keep re-creating the interior—tables are set, living rooms furnished, knick-knacks arranged, photographs set forth—but it inadvertently highlights and preserves the rift or break fundamental to our lives. You see this if you look carefully at what is before you. Something is always slightly off, something always doesn't work. Pictures in Palestinian houses are always hung too high, and in what seem to be random places. Something is always missing by virtue of the excess. I do not mean that the result is tragic or sad; to the contrary, the rift is usually expressed as a comic dislocation, the effect of too much for too little a space or for too uninteresting an occasion. Too many places at a table; too many pictures; too many objects; too much food. My own rather trivial version of this tendency toward disproportion and repetition is that I always carry too many objects—most of them unused—when I travel, which I do frequently. Every time it occurs, the repetition introduces an almost imperceptible variation. Each of us, I believe, recognizes the pattern in her- or himself, and in others.

This pattern of similarly unbalanced, but always infinitesimally varied, interiors will ultimately attract the attention of the outside observer—as it has caught Jean Mohr's eye—but I doubt that deeper reasons for it are easily explained. Yes, the oddness of these excesses, and asymmetries, their constitutively anti-aesthetic effect, their communicated insecurity seem to symbolize exile—exile from a place, from a past, from the actuality of a home. But there is yet another problem being expressed in this form of repetition.

Palestine is a small place. It is also incredibly crowded with the traces and claims of peoples. Its legacy is one not just of conquest and resettlement, but also of reexcavations and reinterpretations of history. Glenn Bowersock, the classical historian, describes this history aptly as the "deliberate fragmentation of a fundamentally unified region." The novelty of Bowersock's approach is that because of his special focus on pre-Zionist and pre-Islamic early Palestine, he is able to perceive beyond all the jostling and shoving "the fact of an Arabian state and subsequently an even more extensive Palestinian state in the Middle East" during the period from Alexander's death to the coming of Islam.

The original spaciousness of that region disappeared, alas, with the arrival of a whole army of nineteenth- and twentieth-century foreign claimants to Palestine. Instead, topographically and even bibliographically, the place is unimaginably divided, dense, and cluttered. Cover a map of Palestine with the legends, insignia, icons, and routes of all the peoples who have lived there, and you will have no space left for terrain. And the more recent the people, the more exclusive their claim, and the more vigorous the pushing out and suppressing of all others. In addition, each claim invents its own tradition, its own dynastic filiations, causing still more deflections, shoving matches, and dislocations: The already overcrowded map now seethes with violently conflicting forces, raging over the surface.

We, too, have lost the sense of space. We think of Palestine not as "an extensive Palestinian state" but as a small, extremely congested piece of land from which we have been pushed. Every effort we make to retain our Palestinian identity is also an effort to get back on the map, to help those *fil-dakhil* to keep their precarious foothold. This is a secular effort—as are most of the struggles of our own recent political history—and I would insist that religious considerations are secondary, are consequences, not causes. But the map, like the land itself, or like the walls of our houses, is already so saturated and cluttered that we have had to get used to working within an already dense and worked-over space. Far from being innovators, we are latecomers, a people in the late twentieth century trying to gain the right of self-determination that everyone else has (even the Falklanders, juridically at least, have what we still seek). We do what everyone does, therefore; there is no novelty about us. Our efforts seem like adornments to what is already adorned.

Every direct route to the interior, and consequently the interior itself, is either blocked or preempted. The most we can hope for is to find margins—normally neglected surfaces and relatively isolated, irregularly placed spots—on which to put ourselves. We can only do so through much perseverance and repetition (so many have already done this ahead of us) and in the knowledge that our distinction may well appear at the end and after much effort as a small nick, a barely perceptible variation, a small jolt. Irony. Imposition. Odd decorum.

As our situation has worsened, our closely managed acts of self-assertion have grown odder, more ironic, and darker. During the Israeli invasion of Lebanon, the conquerors would periodically put a captured Palestinian—male, able-bodied, potentially a trouble-maker—on the radio, and make him go through paces for the benefit of other Palestinians. This was a propaganda exercise to which, on the West Bank and in South Lebanon (the areas whose inhabitants were the targets of the exercise), Palestinians had no comparable response or propaganda apparatus of their own. Insofar as they could respond, they had to do so through the already ongoing discourse of the Israeli interrogation itself, as in the dialogue that follows here, translated from the colloquial Arabic. Note the deliberately stupid miming tactics of the hapless, but by no means witless, prisoner:

ISRAELI BROADCASTER: Your name?

CAPTURED PALESTINIAN *fedayi* ("GUERRILLA"): My name is Ahmed Abdel Hamid Abu Site.

I.B.: What's your movement name?

PAL.: My movement name is Abu Leil ["father of night"].

I.B.: Tell me, Mr. Abu Leil, to which terrorist organization do you belong?

PAL.: I belong to the Popular Front for the Liberation [*tahrir*]—I mean Terrorization [*takhrib*]—of Palestine.

I.B.: And when did you get involved in the terrorists' organization?

PAL.: When I first became aware of terrorism.

I.B.: And what was your mission in South Lebanon?

PAL.: My mission was terrorism . . . in other words, we would enter villages and just terrorize. And wherever there were women and children, we would terrorize. Everything and all we did was terrorism.

I.B.: And did you practice terrorism out of belief in a cause or simply for money?

PAL.: No, by God, just for money. What kind of cause is this anyway? Why? Is there still a cause? We sold out a long time ago.

I.B.: Tell me, where do the terrorist organizations get their money?

PAL.: From anyone who has spare money for terrorism; in other words, from the Arab regimes that support terrorism.

I.B.: What's your opinion of the terrorist Arafat?

PAL.: I swear that he's the greatest terrorist of all. He's the one who sold us and the cause out. His whole life is terrorism.

I.B.: What's your opinion of the way the Israel Defense Forces have conducted themselves?

PAL.: On my honor, we thank the Israel Defense Forces for their good treatment to each terrorist.

I.B.: Do you have any advice for other terrorists who are still terrorizing and attacking the IDF?

PAL.: My advice to them is to surrender their arms to the IDF and what they'll find there is the best possible treatment.

I.B.: Lastly, Mr. Terrorist: Would you like to send a message to your family?

PAL.: I'd like to assure my family and friends that I'm in good health, and I'd also like to thank the enemy broadcasting facility for letting me speak out like this.

I.B.: You mean the *Kol Israel,* the Voice of Israel?

PAL.: Yes sir, thank you sir, naturally sir.

If you want a terrorist, given that all Palestinians who opposed Israel in Lebanon are terrorists, then any Palestinian you get is a terrorist, a "terrorist" with a vengeance. The ideological mufflers of the interrogator's mind are so powerful as to shut out any alertness to the Palestinian's parody of terrorism: Each line he speaks repeats and, by rhetorical overkill, overdoes what his interrogator wants from him. Buried in the black comedy of his performance is his message, which cannot speak straight out but must lie in wait to be perceived by others. This story and several others like it circulate among Palestinians like epics; there are even cassettes of it available for an evening's entertainment.

I am reminded also of the late poet Mu'in Basisu's autobiographical *Descent into the Water,* which describes life in the Gaza Strip during the fifties, when it was ruled by Egypt. Basisu was a young militant in the Palestinian Communist Party who passed his formative years in a series of Egyptian jails. These travails took place entirely within an Arab (and not an Israeli) setting, which makes the irony of Arab "nationalists" abusing those very Palestinians whose cause is at the center of their nationalist concerns, all the more pronounced. Still more ironic for Basisu is the fact that his guards are Palestinians. When he and his companions come to the Cairo prison, "the secret police guards expressed joy at seeing us. Perhaps for one second in five years the Palestinian secret policeman pauses to remember that he is a Palestinian, but then he resumes writing his reports against Palestinians."

Palestinians are cast in the roles set for them by other Arabs. Basisu's jailers are "mimic men," although for one infrequent second their roles allow a break from the dreadful routine into which they have been fitted and to which they have become accustomed.

The dynastic sense, the feeling for one's immediate past, the effort of placing ourselves in a living continuum: there is little help to be gotten for such things. The closeness and clutter of the present force us to attend to the details of everyday life. Whenever I look at what goes on in the interior I am always surprised at how things seem to be managed normally, as if I had been expecting signs of how different "they," the people of the interior, are, and then find that they still do familiar things. We Palestinians conduct ourselves, I think, with an energetic consciousness that there are still chores to be done, children to be raised, houses to be lived in, despite our anomalous circumstances.

I am obsessed with how as a people we got here. In early 1982 I spent several weeks with a British film crew, recording life in a South Lebanon refugee camp for Palestinians. The sequences were to be part of a television documentary called "The Shadow of the West," which concerned the essentially imperialist relationship of Britain, France, and the United States to the Arabs. A central component of the film was a look at a spinoff of that relationship, the question of Palestine. Many of the Palestinians I spoke to and filmed in South Lebanon were younger than I; Lebanon was all they really knew, so they deferred to the older people on matters historical. On two occasions I became perturbed by the inadequacy of our history and the way we use it. Once an old man was prodded into reminiscences of life in Palestine by a group of his young male relatives. He spoke about it very elaborately—the village he grew up in, the family gatherings, feasts and memorable occasions, the pleasures of being at home. But when I asked how it ended, how he became a refugee, he suddenly stopped. Then he got up and left.

The second occasion concerned an old woman who, along with a group of her nieces and daughters, was cheerily regaling me with advice about what, as a Palestinian living in America, I should be doing. Make a revolution, one of them said; have more children, said another, implying that the two I had so far produced testified at best to an impaired manhood and patriotism. Then we got on to life in Qasmiyeh, the refugee camp we were in. None of the women felt they would be there for long, as, after all, they didn't belong there. Then I turned to the old woman, Um Ahmed, and said: "How did you get here?" She paused for a moment, as if such a question was a surprise, and then rather offhandedly said, "I don't really know; I just found myself here."

But for the people who live in or near the interior where it is impossible to deny their Palestinian origins, there is at least the privilege of obduracy. Here we are, unmoved by your power, proceeding with our lives and with future generations. These statements of presence are fundamentally silent, but they occur with unmistakable force. When you compare them with the cautious worried glance of Palestinians in the West you cherish them more. Recently I was driving back to New York along Route 1 in New Jersey and stopped at a filling station. The attendant's accented English spoke to me, as it did probably to no one else that day, of a Palestinian, a middle-aged, frighteningly busy man who never looked up from his pumps or his clipboard, "You're an Arab," I said in Arabic. "Yes, yes," he replied with a sudden elevation of his bent head. "Where from, what place, what town?" I pursued him. "Jordan," he quickly returned. "But you're Palestinian, aren't you?" "From Nablus," he said, and then he moved away from me, busy still. It hurt me, his apparent unwillingness to declare himself, and I wanted to resume our conversation with a few words about not being ashamed to admit our backgrounds. . . . But perhaps he suspected me of being some sort of spy. In any event, he was too far away and too preoccupied with getting things done to give me more notice.

When my thirteen-year-old, Wadie, and I were in Amman, he would ask everyone he met whether he or she was Jordanian or Palestinian. One bearded taxi driver with a strong Palestinian accent answered, "Jordanian," to which Wadie impatiently shot back, "Where in Jordan exactly?" Predictably the answer was Tull-Karm—a West Bank town—followed by a verbose disquisition on how "today"—the occasion being that famous 1984 meeting of the Palestinian National Council held in Amman, at which King Hussein spoke—there was no difference between Jordanians and Palestinians. Wadie, perhaps sensing my sullen disapproval of the driver's waffling and reacting to my unusual reluctance to press the point, insisted otherwise. "There *is* a difference," he said, only at his age he couldn't quite articulate it. For our pains the man drove us at least five miles out of our way, and then dumped us at the edge of the city. "Get someone else to take you back!"

It isn't wrong, I think, to comprehend these lapses about the past as the result of two forces. One is the bewildering and disorienting present. Look at the maze of uncertainties, conflicting predicaments, untidy overlappings of Palestinian life in Palestine. Look at it with some sense of what it means to negotiate it. You will immediately see its symbolic analogue in any panoramic overview of contested sites such as Gaza or even Amman, where the patchwork of overbuilt and structureless dwellings offers little perspective or direction. Everything seems packed in without regard to symmetry, form, or pattern. The second is that the past for all of us Arabs is so discredited as to be lost, or damned, or thought about exclusively in contrast to the present and a not too credible projection of the future. Perhaps this just amounts to the same thing, except that we tend too readily to grant the future (which is at best ambiguous) an aura of legitimacy. After all, as the Lebanese literary critic and novelist Elias Khoury has said, the legitimacy of the future is built almost solely on the illegitimacy of the past—that seemingly limitless series of failures, invasions, conspiracies, destructions, and betrayals. And after you've listed them all, there is not much more to say, so you say nothing. This in turn has allowed the entire apparatus of the modern Arab state, tyrannical and lusterless in equal parts, to propose itself as the legitimate guarantor of the future and, more important, the legitimate ruler of the present. Israel has tried to do the same thing, but for Palestinians the Jewish state has no moral legitimacy. Because they keep promising a bright future, Arab states do have some, but it is dwindling very fast.

But once another power—Arab, European, or Israeli—invades your interior, dismisses your past, and stakes its claims on your future, perhaps it does not make any difference who or what that power is. I am not a great believer in the claims of ethnos, tribe, blood, or even patria, but I must, I feel, make the distinction between the varieties of invasion. It is a matter of what, say, the Israeli does not allow us that the Arab, highly ambivalent about us, does. Maybe it is simply a matter of degrees of alienation, or of various dialects of the same language (Arabic) versus totally different languages.

The attitude expressed in the construction of settlements on the West Bank is unmistakable. Visually there is a rude interventionary power in them that, I am told, shocks even Israelis. One thinks not only of a coarse army of heedless and rough crusaders, but also—given some of the structures themselves—of a marching cancer. As for the effect on the landscape and Palestine's ecology, the offense is deep and lasting.

Palestine's Arab identity—and I am perfectly willing to grant that it has other identities too—was and is being rewritten and defaced, as when you scrawl across a perfectly legible page and turn it into something ugly and offensive. This process continues with results, at a great distance from Palestine, that hurt a great deal. One example: *New York* magazine reports cleverly in its "Intelligencer" column (by one Sharon Churcher) on a national costume show of forty nations put on by UNESCO at its Paris headquarters. Included was a display of Palestinian embroidered dresses, the kind that have always been made and worn by Palestinian women. The title of Churcher's piece, however, was "Terrorist Couture," presumably because as a member of UNESCO, the PLO was responsible for supplying the exhibit of Palestinian dresses.

Churcher implies that the PLO was hijacking Palestinian culture, and that UNESC0 fell for it. She quotes Owen Harries (the Australian who led the successful Heritage Foundation campaign to get the United States to leave UNESCO), who accuses UNESCO of using the national costume ploy "to convince the U.S. they [the PLO] are changing"—presumably from a Communist front to a legitimate cultural agency. Churcher then draws upon her large fund of knowledge for the *coup de grâce:* "UNESCO may not have that good a fix on terrorist couture: It showed the 'Sunday best' of an upper-middle-class Bethlehem lady, a Middle East expert observed."

If you sort out the plague-on-all-your-houses aspect of this item, you'll see a number of things suggested. First of all, we are led to believe that the Palestinians never had folk, popular, or authentic native costumes; the dresses exhibited are only the Sunday dress-ups of the upper middle class. Second, the PLO and UNESCO, both scoundrels, are in league, the former lying about its people, the latter either complicit or ignorant, or both. Finally, the small picture of one of these costumes is not allowed to speak for itself. It is described as "upper middle class" by an unnamed "expert," and just in case the point of the PLO-UNESCO deceit is missed, the whole discussion is herded under the rubric of "terrorist couture."

The facts are that the picture is indeed of a Palestinian woman's dress, that it is a kind made and used by all classes, and that there exists an extensive anthropological and folkloric literature on such dresses, almost any item of which would have confirmed the PLO's fulfillment of UNESCO's charge that costumes should be national, popular, genuine. In a small way, one can see the mischievous dirt-doing of the item (which is part of a much more complex and extensive pattern). Everything about Arab Palestine is rewritten. Turn it into something extremely suspect, show that it is connected to terrorism, or ridicule it and push it away derisively. There are no Arab Palestinians. The land did not exist as Palestine, and perhaps the people did not exist either. "We Palestinians" have almost imperceptibly become "they," a very doubtful lot.

A story like that always evokes a kind of tired bitterness in me. Who, in the great scheme of things, is Sharon Churcher? She produces a few lines of column in a frivolous magazine, and I feel impelled to bring logic, history, and rhetoric to my aid, at tedious length. We need to retell our story from scratch every time, or so we feel. What we are left with when we get to scratch is not very much, and memory alone will not serve. This seems to be the point from which Jabra Jabra's powerful novel, *The Search for Walid Massood*—an extraordinary work of late-blooming Palestinian sensibility—takes off: that memory is not enough. The "innocence and ambiguity" of memory, Jabra writes, require sentences that correspond to that memory exactly. But no such sentences exist, and they would take years to produce, with very doubtful results. "What has been cogently thought," Adorno says, "must be thought in some other place and by other people. This confidence accompanies even the loneliest and most impotent thought." That is another way of phrasing the Palestinian dream: the desire for a perfect congruence between memory, actuality, and language. Anything is better than what we have now—but still the road forward is blocked, the instruments of the present are insufficient, we can't get to the past.

Still, I am impressed by some of the methods used to restore Palestine in the meantime. There is the steady trickle of memoirs: the daybooks, journals, albums, diaries, and recollections of various Palestinians. All of them rely on the notion of statement—enunciations grounded in personal authority—and strive for the clarity of unquestioned evidence. The journals of Akram Zuayter; Hisham Sharabi's somber autobiography, *Al Jamr wa'l Rumad* (*Ashes and Embers*); the testimony of Zakaria al-Shaikh on resisting the Sabra and Shatila massacres in his eyewitness report, as a camp-dwelling refugee, of the 1982 inferno. Others I have read and been impressed with arise from, as it were, a scene of regular life inside Palestine (*min dakhil Filastin*)—the harrowing, episodic narrations of Raja'i Buseilah, a blind Palestinian poet and scholar, who recounts his experiences as a child in 1948 forced to leave Lydda (thanks to the prodding of the then Hagannah commander, Yitzhak Rabin); Walid Khalidi's immense compilation of largely personal photographs of Palestinians during the period between 1876 and 1948, *Before Their Diaspora*; Shafik al-Hout's memories of Jaffa, "The Bride of Palestine"; the little encyclopedia produced a couple of years before he died by Shafik's father-in-law, Ajjaj Nouweihid, *Rijal min Filastin* (*The Men of Palestine*), a work of affectionate compilation that recalls Abbasid biographical dictionaries and in which I found reference to my father's family.

And yet, I recognize in all this a fundamental problem—the crucial absence of women. With few exceptions, women seem to have played little more than the role of hyphen, connective, transition, mere incident. Unless we are able to perceive at the interior of our life the statements women make—concrete, watchful, compassionate, immensely poignant, strangely invulnerable—we will never fully understand our experience of dispossession.

I can see the women everywhere in Palestinian life, and I see how they exist between the syrupy sentimentalism of roles we ascribe to them (mothers, virgins, martyrs) and the annoyance, even dislike, that their unassimilated strength provokes in our warily politicized, automatic manhood.

When my mother speaks of her early life in Nazareth—her immensely strict father's special gentleness with her, her closeness to her mother and her subsequent alienation from her, the (to me) rural authenticity of their life there, an authenticity with which I have had no contact—I have always sensed in her an apprehension of the regretted and unbridgeable gap separating her from that life. Not that she was driven from Nazareth in 1948—she wasn't. She left with my father in 1932. But she tells this story. Immediately after she and my father were married at the mandatory government's registry office, a British official ripped up her passport. "You will now travel on your husband's passport," he said. To her remonstrations and queries he replied, in effect, "this negation of your separate identity will enable us to provide a legal place for one more Jewish immigrant from Europe."

Too symbolic, and too definitive perhaps a tale of woman's disenfranchisement in a colonial situation. I do not know how frequent such practices were, and whether there was some absolute correspondence between the disappearance of my mother's distinct legal identity and the appearance of a Jewish settler. The experience itself of the ripped-up passport is too searingly painful and graphic not to have remained vivid for over fifty years in my mother's life, and she tells the story with great reluctance, and even shame. As her son I have sympathetically preserved the episode, a tender hurt endured in consequence of her new identity as my father's wife, my mother and the closest companion of my early years. I have therefore interpreted her trauma as the sign that she passed from full immediacy of being—the fullness of being that comes from her person as a young Palestinian woman—to a mediated and perhaps subsidiary person, the wife and the mother.

Later I realized that being such a mediated person, distributed among a number of important but secondary roles, is the fate of all

Palestinian and Arab women; this is the way I encounter them, and the way they exist in our various societies. Certainly these are general social and historical facts, but their particular meaning in Palestinian life, given our special situation, is unusually intense. The question becomes how to see the woman's predicament: Is she subordinated and victimized principally because she is a woman in Arab, Muslim society, or because she is Palestinian? However the question is answered, there is an urgent need to take stock with equal precision of the woman's negation and the Palestinian's dispossession, both of which help to constitute our present situation.

The sense of my mother's story as a just representation of the Palestinian woman's plight struck me with great intensity when I saw a documentary film by the young Palestinian director Michel Khleifi. Like my mother, Khleifi was born and grew up in Nazareth. Now a resident of Brussels carrying an Israeli passport, he, too, is an exile. In a number of ways his film, *The Fertile Memory*, responded to the need I feel for restitution and recognition when I think of my mother's experience and all it implies.

Khleifi puts before us two Palestinian women who live as subjects of Israel. One of them, his aunt, Farah Hatoum, is an elderly widow who remained in Nazareth after 1948. We see her working in an Israeli bathing-suit factory, riding a bus, singing a lullaby to her grandson, cooking and washing. The sequences of her at work show a combination of very close detail and highly concentrated repetition, especially in household chores of the sort normally taken for granted by other family members. The impression one gets of this almost frighteningly concrete expenditure of energy is that it sustains life in ways that are just below the threshold of consciousness. One feels a peculiar respect for its protracted discipline, a respect that the effusively male character of Palestinian nationalism doesn't ordinarily permit. The woman's loneliness, the menial offices to which she is consigned, the essentially tending nature of her work, the fineness of her tasks (sewing among them), all suggest a truer condition of Palestinian life than our articulate discourse normally discloses.

The centerpiece of the film is a dramatization of the old woman's relationship to the land. This is done in the two connected scenes that build her into a potent symbol for what has been called "internal exile," a condition already in evidence during the period of the

British mandate, when my mother was stripped of her passport. Farah is first shown in conversation with her adult children, both of whom are trying to convince her to sell land that she owns but that in fact has been "repossessed" by Israelis. Although she still holds the title deed, she well knows it is only a piece of paper. Now her children tell her that legal advice has convinced them that despite the expropriation by the Israelis, there is an opportunity to sell the land to its present tenants: Apparently someone wants to legalize her dispossession by giving her money in return for final entitlement.

She'll have none of it. A large, jowly woman, she sits rocklike at the kitchen table, unmoved by the logic of financial well-being and peace of mind being offered her. No, no, no, she says. I want to keep the land. But you don't actually have it, is the rejoinder which makes those of us living in exile quietly feel even more sympathy for her, since she at least continues to assert the value of some, any, connection with the land. But just as quickly, the woman's stubbornness reminds us that our mementos, memories, title deeds, legal claims simply accentuate the remove at which we now live. In the various cocoons provided by exile there may be room symbolically to restore discrete parts of our heritage; and yet, the discrepancies between symbol and reality remain, as when the finest collection of Palestinian dresses is preserved, catalogued, and reproduced by Wadad Kawar in Amman, published in Japan, ignored and overlooked by American columnists who instead trade in the easy coin of "terrorist couture." Of course, the land is not truly ours.

Farah resumes her statement thoughtfully and feelingly, "I don't have the land now, but who knows what will happen? We were here first, then the Jews came, and others will come after them. I own the land. I will die. But it will stay there, despite all the comings and goings." This is a logic that defies understanding on one level; on another, it is deeply satisfying to her. Thus we also remember the many instances of a repeated stubbornness that makes no sense, such as proclaiming "here I stand" surrounded by the icons of our glorious failures (Abdel Nasser chief among them)—or that makes only enough sense to distinguish our side of the line from theirs.

Later in *The Fertile Memory* Farah is taken to see her land for the first time in her life. This is perhaps a curious thing but, as Khleifi once explained to me, not so unusual for a woman of that generation whose late husband had owned the property, cared for it, and willed it to her when he died. When she came into it she had already been dispossessed, and for all that her title deed has done for her, she might have been in Syria displaying pictures of the Hanging Gardens of Babylon.

Somehow, Khleifi has managed in his film to record Farah's first visit to her land. We see her step tentatively onto a field; then she turns around slowly with arms outstretched. A look of puzzled serenity comes over her face. There is little hint on it of pride in ownership. The film unobtrusively registers the fact that she is there on her land, which is also there; as for the circumstances intervening between these two facts, we remember the useless title deed and Israeli possession, neither of which is actually visible. Immediately then we realize that what we see on the screen, or in any picture representing the solidity of Palestinians in the interior, is only that, a utopian image making possible a connection between Palestinian individuals and Palestinian land. Farah's reconnection with her land, merely formal though it is, called up, and even calmed, the painful memory of my mother and the identity taken from her in 1932. An aesthetic experience a generation later, partially healing the wound.

The other major figure in *The Fertile Memory* is Sahar Khalifé, a successful young novelist and teacher from Nablus. Her presence is by no means nostalgic or inarticulate. Of a younger generation than Farah, she is more self-aware, both as a woman and as a Palestinian. She describes herself as a militant, though with considerable irony. But even Sahar's life is more impressive than Farah's—she too is dispossessed, her identity undercut: as a nationalist, by the structure of Israeli power holding the West Bank; as a divorced working woman, by the conventions of the predominantly Muslim and traditional community of Nablus. She expresses alienation from political and, to a degree, sexual fulfillment; both have been denied her, the first because she is a Palestinian, the second because she is an Arab woman. Nevertheless, Sahar is securely in place. One feels about her, and other Nabulsis, that—Israeli occupation, and political and social tensions notwithstanding—they are securely in place, their lives are led where such lives have always been led.

It is Khleifi's achievement to have embodied certain aspects of Palestinian women's lives in film. He is careful to let the strengths of Farah and Sahar emerge slowly, even if at a pace that risks losing the film the larger audience it deserves. He deliberately disappoints the expectations engendered in us by the commercial film (plot, suspense, drama), in favor of a representational idiom more innovative and—because of its congruence with its anomalous and eccentric material—more authentic. Each of us bears fragmented memories of the experiences of the generation whose culminating tragedy was dispossession in 1948. To these experiences Farah Hatoum is allowed to speak. Each of us senses the subtle undercutting that takes place on the shadow line between two worlds. To this, Sahar Khalifé gives expression.

But Khleifi does not give in to the editorial manipulation that, for example, Farah's real situation—and his, as her compatriot—might have provoked. Her daily existence is not portrayed as taking place directly against the standard scenes of Israeli domination. There is barely a glimpse of Israeli soldiers, none of Palestinians being rounded up by police. He even resists the temptation to italicize the significance of Sahar's more militant, if still subdued, position. No cuts to scenes of Palestinian activism, tire-burning, or rock-throwing.

Instead, Khleifi has given the women's lives an aesthetic clarity which, for me, a male Palestinian, sheds new light on our experience of dispossession. Yet because I am separated from those experiences by time, by gender, by distance—they are, after all, experiences of an interior I cannot inhabit—I am reconfirmed in my outsider's role. This in turn leads me, defensively perhaps, to protect the integrity of exile by noting the compromises of life in the Palestinian interior—the forgetfulness and carelessness that have historically characterized the losing battle with Zionism, the too close perspective that allows thoughts to be unthought, sights unrecorded, persons unmemorialized, and time thrown away.

Here is another face of a woman spun out with the familiarity of years, concealing a lifetime of episodes, splendidly recorded by a listening photographer. It is a face, I thought when I first saw it, of our life at home. Six months later I was showing the pictures casually to

Amman, 1984. Mrs. Farraj.

my sister. "There's Mrs. Farraj," she said. Indeed, it was. I first saw her in 1946 when my cousin married her daughter, who was the first beautiful woman I encountered in real life. Then I saw her in the fifties, and then again now, in Jean Mohr's picture. Connected to me, my sister, my friends, her relatives, her acquaintances, and the places she's been, her picture seems like a map pulling us all together, even down to her hair net, her ribbed sweater, the unattractive glasses, the balanced smile and strong hand. But all the connections only came to light, so to speak, some time after I had seen the photograph, after we had decided to use it, after I had placed it in sequence. As soon as I recognized Mrs. Farraj, the suggested intimacy of the photograph's surface gave way to an explicitness with few secrets. She is a real person—Palestinian—with a real history at the interior of ours. But I do not know whether the photograph can, or does, say things as they really are. Something has been lost. But the representation is all we have.

from *After the Last Sky*

11

Yeats and Decolonization

(1988)

William Butler Yeats's remark that "a poet's mouth be silent, for in truth / We have no gift to set a statesman right" has frequently led critics to regard Yeats's poetry more for its contribution to literary high modernism than for its connection to Irish nationalism. As an Irish-Protestant writing a lyric about Ireland specifically for an Irish audience, Yeats was also politically active in the Irish national movement from an early age. The literary critic Declan Kiberd has observed that for Yeats "Ireland was an 'imaginary homeland,' the sort of place endlessly invented and reinvented by exiles who fear that, if they do not give it a local habitation in words, it may entirely disappear."[1]

Said published "Yeats and Decolonization" in Ireland as a Field Day Pamphlet in 1988 (having given it as a lecture at Sligo) and also delivered the essay as a lecture at the Dia Art Foundation in New York City. The essay was originally conceived as part of Said's *Culture and Imperialism* and became a chapter in that book. It reinterprets the high modernist poetry of William Butler Yeats away from the comfortable canons of English literature and into a discourse of anticolonial nationalism. Said places Yeats within a tradition of other anti-imperialist poets, namely Pablo Neruda, Aimé Césaire, Faiz Ahmad Faiz, and Mahmoud Darwish, finding that all of them seek a cartographic sensibility with their poetry, reclaiming, renaming, and reinhabiting their colonized land with their poetry.

William Butler Yeats has now been almost completely assimilated into the canon as well as into the discourses of modern English literature and European high modernism. Both of these reckon with him as a great modern Irish poet, deeply affiliated and interacting with his native traditions, the historical and political context of his times, and the complex situation of being a poet writing in English in a turbulently nationalist Ireland. Despite Yeats's obvious and, I would say, settled presence in Ireland, in British culture and literature, and in European modernism, he does present another fascinating aspect: that of the indisputably great *national* poet who during a period of anti-imperialist resistance articulates the experiences, the aspirations, and the restorative vision of a people suffering under the dominion of an offshore power.

From this perspective Yeats is a poet who belongs in a tradition not usually considered his, that of the colonial world ruled by European imperialism during a climactic insurrectionary stage. If this is not a customary way of interpreting Yeats, then we need to say that he also belongs naturally to the cultural domain, his by virtue of Ireland's colonial status, which it shares with a host of non-European regions: cultural dependency and antagonism together.

The high age of imperialism is said to have begun in the late 1870s, but in English-speaking realms, it began well over seven hundred years before, as Angus Calder's gripping book *Revolutionary Empire* demonstrates so well. Ireland was ceded by the Pope to Henry II of England in the 1150s; he himself came to Ireland in 1171. From that time on an amazingly persistent cultural attitude existed toward Ireland as a place whose inhabitants were a barbarian and degenerate race. Recent critics and historians—Seamus Deane, Nicholas Canny, Joseph Leerson, and R. N. Lebow among others—have studied and documented this history, to whose formation such impressive figures as Edmund Spenser and David Hume contributed in very large measure.

Thus India, North Africa, the Caribbean, Central and South America, many parts of Africa, China and Japan, the Pacific archipelago, Malaysia, Australia, New Zealand, North America, and of course Ireland belong in a group together, although most of the time they are treated separately. All of them were sites of contention well before 1870, either between various local resistance groups, or between the European powers themselves; in some cases, India and Africa, for instance, the two struggles against outside domination were going on simultaneously long before 1857, and long before the various European congresses on Africa at the end of the century.

The point here is that no matter how one wishes to demarcate high imperialism—that period when nearly everyone in Europe and America believed him or herself to be serving the high civilizational and commercial cause of empire—imperialism itself had already been a continuous process for several centuries of overseas conquest, rapacity, and scientific exploration. For an Indian, or Irishman, or Algerian, the land was and had been dominated by an alien power, whether liberal, monarchical, or revolutionary.

But modern European imperialism was a constitutively, radically different type of overseas domination from all earlier forms. Scale and scope were only part of the difference, though certainly not Byzantium, or Rome, or Athens, or Baghdad, or Spain and Portugal during the fifteenth and sixteenth centuries controlled anything like the size of the territories controlled by Britain and France in the nineteenth century. The more important differences are first the sustained longevity of the disparity in power, and second, the massive organization of the power, which affected the details and not just the large outlines of life. By the early nineteenth century, Europe had begun the industrial transformation of its economies—Britain leading the way; feudal and traditional landholding structures were changing; new mercantilist patterns of overseas trade, naval power, and colonialist settlement were being established; the bourgeois revolution was entering its triumphant stage. All these developments gave Europe a further ascendancy over its offshore possessions, a profile of imposing and even daunting power. By the beginning of World War I, Europe and America held most of the earth's surface in some sort of colonial subjugation.

This came about for many reasons, which a whole library of systematic studies (beginning with those by critics of imperialism during its most aggressive phase such as Hobson, Rosa Luxemburg, and Lenin) has ascribed to largely economic and somewhat ambiguously characterized political processes (in the case of Joseph Schumpeter, psychologically aggressive ones as well). The theory I advance is that culture played a very important, indeed indispensable role. At the heart of European culture during the many decades of imperial expansion lay an undeterred and unrelenting Eurocentrism. This accumulated experiences, territories, peoples, histories; it studied them, it classified them, it verified them, and as Calder says, it allowed "European men of business" the power "to scheme grandly";[2] but above all, it subordinated them by banishing their identities, except as a lower order of being, from the culture and indeed the very idea of white Christian Europe. This cultural process has to be seen as a vital, informing, and invigorating counterpoint to the economic and political machinery at the material center of imperialism. This Eurocentric culture relentlessly codified and observed everything about the non-European or peripheral world, and so thoroughly and in so detailed a manner as to leave few items untouched, few cultures unstudied, few peoples and spots of land unclaimed.

From these views there was hardly any significant divergence from the Renaissance on, and if it is embarrassing for us to remark that those elements of a society we have long considered to be progressive were, so far as empire was concerned, uniformly retrograde, we still must not be afraid to say it. Advanced writers and artists, the working class, and women—groups marginal in the West—showed an imperialist fervor that increased in intensity and perfervid enthusiasm as the competition among various European and American powers increased in brutality and senseless, even profitless, control. Eurocentrism penetrated to the core of the workers' movement, the women's movement, the avant-garde arts movement, leaving no one of significance untouched.

As imperialism increased in scope and in depth, so too, in the colonies themselves, the resistance mounted. Just as in Europe the global accumulation that gathered the colonial domains into the world market economy was supported and enabled by a culture giving empire ideological license, so in the overseas *imperium* the massive political, economic, and military resistance was carried forward and informed by an actively provocative and challenging culture of resistance. This was a culture with a long tradition of integrity and power in its own right, not simply a belated reactive response to Western imperialism.

In Ireland, Calder says, the idea of murdering Gaels was from the start "as part of a royal army or with royal approval, [considered] patriotic, heroic and just."[3] The idea of English racial superiority became ingrained; so humane a poet and gentleman as Edmund Spenser in his *View of the Present State of Ireland* (1596) was boldly proposing that since the Irish were barbarian Scythians, most of them should be exterminated. Revolts against the English naturally began early, and by the eighteenth century under Wolfe Tone and Grattan the opposition had acquired an identity of its own, with organizations, idioms, rules. "Patriotism was coming into vogue"[4] during mid-century, Calder continues, which, with the extraordinary talents of Swift, Goldsmith, and Burke, gave Irish resistance a discourse entirely its own.

Much but by no means all the resistance to imperialism was conducted in the broad context of nationalism. "Nationalism" is a word that still signifies all sorts of undifferentiated things, but it serves me quite adequately to identify the mobilizing force that coalesced into resistance against an alien and occupying empire on the part of peoples possessing a common history, religion, and language. Yet for all its success—indeed because of its success—in ridding many territories of colonial overlords, nationalism has remained a deeply problematic enterprise. When it got people out on the streets to march against the white master, nationalism was often led by lawyers, doctors, and writers who were partly formed and to some degree produced by the colonial power. The national bourgeoisies and their specialized elites, of which Fanon speaks so ominously, in effect tended to replace the colonial force with a new class-based and ultimately exploitative one, which replicated the old colonial structures in new terms. There are states all across the formerly colonized world that have bred pathologies of power, as Eqbal Ahmad has called them.[5] Also, the cultural horizons of a nationalism may be fatally limited by the common history it presumes of colonizer and colonized. Imperialism after all was a cooperative venture, and a salient trait of its modern form is that it was (or claimed to be) an educational movement; it set out quite consciously to modernize, develop, instruct, and civilize. The annals of schools, missions, universities, scholarly societies, hospitals in Asia, Africa, Latin America, Europe, and America are filled with this history, which over time established so-called modernizing trends as much as it muted the harsher aspects of imperialist domination. But at its center it preserved the nineteenth-century divide between native and Westerner.

The great colonial schools, for example, taught generations of the native bourgeoisie important truths about history, science, culture. Out of that learning process millions grasped the fundamentals of modern life, yet remained subordinate dependents of an authority band elsewhere than in their lives. Since one of the purposes of colonial education was to promote the history of France or Britain, that same education also demoted the native history. Thus for the native, there were always the Englands, Frances, Germanys, Hollands as distant repositories of the Word, despite the affinities developed between native and "white man" during the years of productive collaboration. Joyce's Stephen Dedalus as he faces his English director of studies is a famous example of someone who discovers this with unusual force:

> The language we are speaking is his before it is mine. How different are the words *home, Christ, ale, master,* on his lips and on mine! I cannot speak or write these words without unrest of spirit. His language, so familiar and so foreign, will always be for me an acquired speech. I have not made or accepted its words. My voice holds them at bay. My soul frets in the shadow of his language.[6]

Nationalism in Ireland, India, and Egypt, for example, was rooted in the long-standing struggle for native rights and independence by nationalist parties like the Sinn Fein, Congress, and Wafd. Similar processes occurred in other parts of Africa and Asia. Nehru, Nasser, Sukarno, Nyerere, Nkrumah: the pantheon of Bandung flourished, in all its suffering and greatness, because of the nationalist dynamic, which was culturally embodied in the inspirational autobiographies, instructional manuals, and philosophical meditations of these great nationalist leaders. An unmistakable patriarchal cast can be discerned everywhere in classical nationalism, with delays and distortions in women's and minority rights (to say nothing of democratic freedoms) that are still perceptible today. Crucial works like Panikar's *Asia and Western Dominance,* George Antonius's *The Arab Awakening,* and the various works of the Irish Revival were also produced out of classical nationalism.

Within the nationalist revival, in Ireland and elsewhere, there were two distinct political moments, each with its own imaginative culture, the second unthinkable without the first. The first was a pronounced awareness of European and Western culture *as* imperialism; this reflexive moment of consciousness enabled the African, Caribbean, Irish, Latin American, or Asian citizen to assert the end of Europe's cultural claim to guide and/or instruct the non-European or non-mainland individual. Often this was first done, as Thomas Hodgkin has argued, by "prophets and priests,"[7] among them poets and visionaries, versions perhaps of Hobsbawm's "primitive rebels." The second more openly liberationist moment occurred during the dramatically prolonged Western imperial mission after World War Two in various colonial regions, principally Algeria, Vietnam, Palestine, Ireland, Guinea, and Cuba. Whether in the Indian constitution, or in statements of Pan-Arabism and Pan-Africanism, or in its particularist forms such as Pearse's Gaelic or Senghor's *négritude,* conventional nationalism was revealed to be both insufficient and crucial, but only as a first step. Out of this paradox comes the idea of liberation, a strong new post-nationalist theme that had been implicit in the works of Connolly, Garvey, Martí, Mariategi, Cabral, and Du Bois, for instance, but required the propulsive infusion of theory and even of armed, insurrectionary militancy to bring it forward clearly.

Let us look again at the literature of the first of these moments, that of anti-imperialist resistance. If there is anything that radically distinguishes the imagination of anti-imperialism, it is the primacy of the geographical element. Imperialism after all is an act of geographical violence through which virtually every space in the world is explored, charted, and finally brought under control. For the native, the history of colonial servitude is inaugurated by loss of the locality to the outsider; its geographical identity must thereafter be searched for and somehow restored. Because of the presence of the colonizing outsider, the land is recoverable at first only through the imagination.

Let me give three examples of how imperialism's complex yet firm geographical *morte main* moves from the general to the specific. The most general is presented in Crosby's *Ecological Imperialism.* Crosby says that wherever they went Europeans immediately began to change the local habitat; their conscious aim was to transform territories into images of what they had left behind. This process was never-ending, as a huge number of plants, animals, and crops as well as building methods gradually turned the colony into a new place, complete with new diseases, environmental imbalances, and traumatic dislocations for the overpowered natives.[8] A changed ecology also introduced a changed political system. In the eyes of the later nationalist poet or visionary, this alienated the people from their authentic traditions, ways of life, and political organizations. A great deal of romantic mythmaking went into these nationalist versions of how imperialism alienated the land, but we must not doubt the extent of the actual changes wrought.

A second example is the rationalizing projects of long-standing territorial possession, which seek routinely to make land profitable and at the same time to integrate it with an external rule. In his book *Uneven Development* the geographer Neil Smith brilliantly formulates how capitalism historically has produced a particular kind of nature and space, an unequally developed landscape that integrates poverty with wealth, industrial urbanization with agricultural diminishment. The culmination of this process is imperialism, which dominates, classifies, and universally commodifies all space under the aegis of the metropolitan center. Its cultural analogue is late-nineteenth-century commercial geography, whose perspectives (for example in the work of Mackinder and Chisolm) justified imperialism as the result "natural" fertility or infertility, available sea-lanes, permanently differentiated zones, territories, climates, and peoples.[9] Thus is accomplished "the universality of capitalism," which is "the differentiation of national space according to the territorial division of labor."[10]

Following Hegel, Marx, and Lukács, Smith calls the production of this scientifically "natural" world a *second* nature. To the anti-imperialist imagination, our space at home in the peripheries has been usurped and put to use by outsiders for their purpose. It is therefore necessary to seek out, to map, to invent, or to discover a *third* nature, not pristine and pre-historical ("Romantic Ireland's dead and gone," says Yeats) but deriving from the deprivations of the present. The impulse is cartographic, and among its most striking examples are Yeats's early poems collected in "The Rose," Neruda's various poems charting the Chilean landscape, Césaire on the Antilles, Faiz on Pakistan, and Darwish on Palestine—

Restore to me the color of face
And the warmth of body,
The light of heart and eye,
The salt of bread and earth . . . the Motherland.[11]

But—a third example—colonial space must be transformed sufficiently so as no longer to appear foreign to the imperial eye. More than any other of its colonies, Britain's Ireland was subjected to innumerable metamorphoses through repeated settling projects and, in culmination, its virtual incorporation in 1801 through the Act of Union. Thereafter an Ordnance Survey of Ireland was ordered in 1824 whose goal was to anglicize the names, redraw the land boundaries to permit valuation of property (and further expropriation of land in favor of English and "seignorial" families), and permanently, subjugate the population. The survey was carried out almost entirely by English personnel, which, as Mary Hamer has cogently argued, had the "immediate effect of defining the Irish as incompetent [and . . . depress[ing their] national achievement."[12] One of Brian Friel's most powerful plays, *Translations* (*1980*), deals with the shattering effect of the Ordnance Survey on the indigenous inhabitants. "In such a process," Hamer continues, "the colonized is typically [supposed to be] passive and spoken for, does not control its own representation but is represented in accordance with a hegemonic impulse by which it is constructed as a stable and unitary entity."[13] And what was done in Ireland was also done in Bengal or, by the French, in Algeria.

One of the first tasks of the culture of resistance was to reclaim, rename, and reinhabit the land. And with that came a whole set of further assertions, recoveries, and identifications, all of them quite literally grounded on this poetically projected base. The search for authenticity, for a more congenial national origin than that provided by colonial history, for a new pantheon of heroes and (occasionally) heroines, myths, and religions—these too are made possible by a sense of the land reappropriated by its people. And along with these nationalistic adumbrations of the decolonized identity, there always goes an almost magically inspired, quasi-alchemical redevelopment of the native language.

Yeats is especially interesting here. With Caribbean and some

African writers he expresses the predicament of sharing a language with the colonial overlord, and of course he belongs in many important ways to the Protestant Ascendancy, whose Irish loyalties were confused, to put it mildly, if not in his case quite contradictory. There is a fairly logical progression from Yeats's early Gaelicism, with its Celtic preoccupations and themes, to his later systematic mythologies as set down in programmatic poems like "Ego Dominus Tuus" and in the treatise *A Vision*. For Yeats the overlapping he knew existed of his Irish nationalism with the English cultural heritage, which both dominated and empowered him, was bound to cause tension, and one may speculate that it was the pressure of this urgently political and secular tension that caused him to try to resolve it on a "higher," that is, nonpolitical level. The deeply eccentric and aestheticized histories he produced in *A Vision* and the later quasi-religious poems elevate the tension to an extra-worldly level, as if Ireland were best taken over, so to speak, at a level above that of the ground.

Seamus Deane, in *Celtic Revivals,* the most interesting and brilliant account of Yeats's super-terrestrial idea of revolution, has suggested that Yeats's early and invented Ireland was "amenable to his imagination . . . [whereas] he ended by finding an Ireland recalcitrant to it." Whenever Yeats tried to reconcile his occultist views with an actual Ireland—as in "The Statues"—the results are strained, Deane says correctly.[14] Because Yeats's Ireland was a revolutionary country, he could use its backwardness as a source for a radically disturbing, disruptive return to spiritual ideals lost in an overt developed modern Europe. In such dramatic realities as the Easter 1916 uprising, Yeats also saw the breaking of a cycle of endless, perhaps finally meaningless recurrence, as symbolized by the apparently limitless travails of Cuchulain. Deane's theory is that the birth of an Irish national identity coincides for Yeats with the breaking of the cycle, although it also underscores, and reinforces in Yeats himself, the colonialist British attitude of a specific Irish national character. Thus Yeats's return to mysticism and his recourse to fascism, Deane says perceptively, underline the colonial predicament also expressed, for example, in V. S. Naipaul's representations of India, that of a culture indebted to the mother country for its own self and for a sense of "Englishness" and yet turning toward the colony: "such a search for a national signature becomes colonial, on account of the different histories of the two islands. The greatest flowering of such a search has been Yeats's poetry."[15] Far from representing an outdated nationalism, Yeats's wilful mysticism and incoherence embody a revolutionary potential, and the poet insists "that Ireland should retain its culture by keeping awake its consciousness of metaphysical questions," as Deane puts it.[16] In a world from which the harsh strains of capitalism have removed thought and reflection, a poet who can stimulate a sense of the eternal and of death into consciousness is the true rebel, a figure whose colonial diminishments spur him to a negative apprehension of his society and of "civilized" modernity.

This rather Adorno-esque formulation of Yeats's quandary is of course powerfully attractive. Yet perhaps it is weakened by its wanting to render Yeats more heroic than a crudely political reading would have suggested, and excuse his unacceptable and indigestible reactionary politics—his outright fascism, his fantasies of old homes and families, his incoherently occult divagations—by translating them into an instance of Adorno's "negative dialectic." As a small corrective, we might more accurately see Yeats as an exacerbated example of the *nativist* phenomenon which flourished elsewhere (e.g., *négritude*) as a result of the colonial encounter.

True, the physical, geographical connections are closer between England and Ireland than between England and India, or between France and Algeria or Senegal. But the imperial relationship is there in all cases. Irish people never be English any more than Cambodians or Algerians can be French. This it seems to me was always the case in every colonial relationship, because it is the first principle that a clear-cut and absolute hierarchical distinction should remain constant between ruler and ruled, whether or not the latter is white. Nativism, alas, reinforces the distinction even while revaluating the weaker or subservient partner. And it has often led to compelling but demagogic assertions about a native past, narrative or actuality that stands free from worldly time itself. One sees this in such enterprises as Senghor's *négritude,* or in the Rastafarian movement, or in the Garveyite back to Africa project for American Blacks, or in the rediscoveries of various unsullied, precolonial Muslim essences.

The tremendous *ressentiment* in nativism aside (for example, in Jalal Ali Ahmad's *Occidentosis,* an influential Iranian tract published in 1978 that blames the West for most evils in the world), there are two reasons for rejecting, or at least reconceiving, the nativist enterprise. To say, as Deane does, that it is incoherent and yet, by its negation of politics and history, also heroically revolutionary seems to me is to fall into the nativist position as if it were the only choice for a resisting, decolonizing nationalism. But we have evidence of its ravages: to accept nativism is to accept the consequences of imperialism, the racial, religious, and political divisions imposed by imperialism itself. To leave the historical world for the metaphysics of essences like *négritude*, Irishness, Islam, or Catholicism is to abandon history for essentializations that have the power to turn human beings against each other; often this abandonment of the secular world has led to a sort of millenarianism if the movement has had a mass base, or it has degenerated into small-scale private craziness, or into an unthinking acceptance of stereotypes, myths, animosities, and traditions encouraged by imperialism. Such programs are hardly what great resistance movements had imagined as their goals.

A useful way of getting a better hold of this analytically is to look at an analysis of the same problem done in the African context: Wole Soyinka's withering critique of *négritude* published in 1976. Soyinka notes that the concept of *négritude* is the second, inferior term in in opposition—European versus African—that "accepted the dialectical structure of European ideological confrontations but borrowed from the very components of its racist syllogism."[17] Thus Europeans are analytical, Africans "incapable of analytical thought. Therefore the African is not highly developed" whereas the European is. The result is, according to Soyinka, that

> *négritude* trapped itself in what was primarily a defensive role, even though its accents were strident, its syntax hyperbolic and its strategy aggressive . . . *Négritude* stayed within a pre-set system of Eurocentric intellectual analysis of both man and his society, and tried to re-define the African and his society in those externalized terms.[18]

We are left with the paradox that Soyinka himself articulates, that (he has Fanon in mind) adoring the Negro is as "sick" as abominating him. And while it is impossible to avoid the combative, assertive early stages in the nativist identity—they *always* occur: Yeats's early poetry is not only about Ireland, but about Irishness—there is a good deal of promise in getting beyond them, not remaining trapped in the emotional self-indulgence of celebrating one's own identity. There is first of all the possibility of discovering a world *not* constructed out of warring essences. Second, there is the possibility of a universalism that is not limited or coercive, which believing that all people have only one single identity is—that all the Irish are only Irish, Indians Indians, Africans Africans, and so on *ad nauseam*. Third, and most important, moving beyond nativism does not mean abandoning nationality, but it does mean thinking of local identity as not exhaustive, and therefore not being anxious to confine oneself to one's own sphere, with its ceremonies of belonging, its built-in chauvinism, and its limiting sense of security.

Nationality, nationalism, nativism: the progression is, I believe, more and more constraining. In countries like Algeria and Kenya one can watch the heroic resistance of a community partly formed out of colonial degradations, leading to a protracted armed and cultural conflict with the imperial powers, in turn giving way to a one-party state with dictatorial rule and, in the case of Algeria, an uncompromising Islamic fundamentalist opposition. The debilitating despotism of the Moi regime in Kenya can scarcely be said to complete the liberationist currents of the Mau Mau uprising. No transformation of social consciousness here, but only an appalling pathology of power duplicated elsewhere—in the Philippines, Indonesia, Pakistan, Zaire, Morocco, Iran.

In any case nativism is *not* the only alternative. There is the possibility of a more generous and pluralistic vision of the world, in which imperialism courses on, as it were, belatedly in different forms (the North-South polarity of our own time is one), and the relationship of domination continues, but the opportunities for liberation are open. Even though there was an Irish Free State by the end of his life in 1939, Yeats partially belonged to this second moment, as shown by his sustained anti-British sentiment and the anger and gaiety of his anarchically disturbing last poetry. In this phase *liberation,* and not nationalist independence, is the new alternative, liberation which by its very nature involves, in Fanon's words, a transformation of social consciousness beyond national consciousness.[19]

Looking at it from this perspective, then, Yeats's slide into incoherence and mysticism during the 1920s, his rejection of politics, and his arrogant if charming espousal of fascism (or authoritarianism of an Italian or South American kind) are not to be excused, not too quickly to be dialecticized into the negative utopian mode. For one can quite easily situate and criticize those unacceptable attitudes of Yeats without changing one's view of Yeats as a poet of decolonization.

This way beyond nativism is figured in the great turn at the climax of Césaire's *Cahier d'un retour* when the poet realizes that, after rediscovering and reexperiencing his past, after re-entering the passions, horrors, and circumstances of his history as a Black, after feeling and then emptying himself of his anger, after accepting—

J'accepte . . . j'accepte . . . entièrement, sans reserve
ma race qu'aucune ablution d'hypsope et de lys melés ne pourrait purifier
ma race rongée de macule
ma race raisin mur pour pieds ivres[20]

(I accept . . . I accept totally, without reservation
my race that no ablution of hyssop mixed with lilies could purify
my race pitted with blemishes
my race a ripe grape for drunken feet)

—after all this he is suddenly assailed by strength and life "comme un taureau," and begins to understand that

il n'est point vrai que l'oeuvre de l'homme est finie
que nous n'avons rien à faire au monde
que nous parasitons le monde
qu'il suffit que nous mettions au pas du monde
mais l'oeuvre de l'homme vient seulment de commencer
et il reste à l'homme à conquérir toute interdiction
immobilisée aux coins de sa ferveur et aucune race
ne possède le monopole de la beauté, de l'intelligence, de la force

et il est place pour tous au rendez-vous de la conquête
et nous savons maintenant que le soleil tourne
autour de notre terre éclairant la parcelle qu'a fixé

notre volonté seule et que toute étoile chute de ciel
en terre à notre commandement sans limite.[21]

(for it is not true that the work of man is done
that we have no business being on earth
that we parasite the world
that it is enough for us to heel to the world
whereas the work has only begun
and man still must overcome all the interdictions
wedged in the recesses of his fervor and no race has a
monopoly on beauty, on intelligence, on strength

and there is room for everyone at the convocation of
conquest and we know now that the sun turns around our
earth lighting the parcel designated by our will alone
and that every star falls from sky to earth at our
omnipotent command.)

The striking phrases are "à conquérir toute interdiction immobilisée aux coins de sa ferveur" and "le soleil . . . éclairant la parcelle qu'a fixé notre volonté seule." You don't give in to the rigidity and interdictions of self-imposed limitations that come with race, moment, or milieu; instead you move through them to an animated and expanded sense of "[le] rendez-vous de la conquête," which necessarily involves more than your Ireland, your Martinique, your Pakistan.

I don't mean to use Césaire *against* Yeats (or Seamus Deane's Yeats), but rather more fully to associate a major strand in Yeats's poetry both with the poetry of decolonization and resistance, and with the historical alternatives to the nativist impasse. In many other ways Yeats is like other poets resisting imperialism—in his insistence on a new narrative for his people, his anger at England's schemes for Irish partition (and enthusiasm for wholeness), the celebration and commemoration of violence in bringing about a new order, and the sinuous interweaving of loyalty and betrayal in the nationalist setting. Yeats's direct association with Parnell and O'Leary, with the Abbey Theatre, with the Easter Uprising, bring to his poetry what R. P. Blackmur, borrowing from Jung, calls "the terrible ambiguity of an immediate experience."[22] Yeats's work of the early 1920s has an uncanny resemblance to the engagement and ambiguities of Darwish's Palestinian poetry half a century later, in its renderings of violence, of the overwhelming suddenness and surprises of historical events, of politics and poetry as opposed to violence and guns (see his marvelous lyric "The Rose and the Dictionary"),[23] of the search for respites after the last border has been crossed, the last sky flown in. "The holy centaurs of the hills are vanished," says Yeats, "I have nothing but the embittered sun."

One feels in reading the great poems of that climactic period after the Easter Uprising of 1916, like "Nineteen Hundred and Nineteen" or "Easter 1916," and "September 1913," not just the disappointments of life commanded by "the greasy till" or the violence of roads and horses, of "weasels fighting in a hole," or the rituals of what has been called Blood Sacrifice poetry, but also a terrible new beauty that changes the old political and moral landscape. Like all poets of decolonization, Yeats struggles to announce the contours of an imagined or ideal community, crystallized by its sense not only of itself but also of its enemy. "Imagined community" is apt here, so long as we are not obliged also to accept Benedict Anderson's mistakenly linear periodizations. In the cultural discourses of decolonization, a great many languages, histories, forms circulate. As Barbara Harlow has shown in *Resistance Literature,* the instability of time, which has to be made and remade by the people and its leaders, is a theme one sees in all the genres—spiritual autobiographies, poems of protest, prison memoirs, didactic dramas of deliverance. The shifts in Yeats's accounts of his great cycles invoke this instability, as does the easy commerce in his poetry between popular and formal speech, folktale and learned writing. The disquiet of what T. S. Eliot calls the "cunning history [and] contrived corridors" of time—the wrong turns, the overlap, the senseless repetition, the occasionally glorious moment—furnishes Yeats, as it does all the poets and men of letters of decolonization—Tagore, Senghor, Césaire—with stern martial accents, heroism, and the grinding persistence of "the uncontrollable mystery on the bestial floor." Thus the writer rises out of his national environment and gains universal significance.

In the first volume of his memoirs, Pablo Neruda speaks of a writers' congress in Madrid held in 1937 in defense of the Republic. "Priceless replies" to the invitations "poured in from all over. One was from Yeats, Ireland's national poet; another, from Selma Lagerlöf, the notable Swedish writer. They were both too old to travel to a beleaguered city like Madrid, which was steadily being pounded by bombs, but they rallied to the defense of the Spanish Republic."[24] Just as Neruda saw no difficulty in thinking of himself as a poet who dealt both with internal colonialism in Chile and with external imperialism throughout Latin America, we should think of Yeats, I believe, as an Irish poet with more than strictly local Irish meaning and applications. Neruda accepted him as a national poet representing the Irish nation in its war against tyranny and, according to Neruda, Yeats responded positively to that unmistakably anti-fascist call, despite his frequently cited dispositions toward European fascism.

The resemblance between Neruda's justly famous poem "El Pueblo" (in the 1962 collection *Plenos Poderes,* translated by Alastair Reid, whose version I have used, as *Fully Empowered*) and Yeats's "The Fisherman" is striking: in both poems the central figure is an anonymous man of the people, who in his strength and loneliness is a mute expression *of* the people, a quality that inspires the poet in his work. Yeats:

It's long since I began
To call up to the eyes
This wise and simple man.
All day I'd look in the face
What I had hoped 'twould be
To write for my own race
And the reality.[25]

Neruda:

I knew that man, and when I could
when I still had eyes in my head,
when I still had a voice in my throat,
I sought him among the tombs and I said to him,
pressing his arm that still was not dust:
"Everything will pass, you will still be living.
You set fire to life.

You made what is yours."
So let no one be perturbed when
I seem to be alone and am not alone;
I am not without company and I speak for all.
Someone is hearing me without knowing it,
But those I sing of, those who know,
go on being born and will overlfow the world.[26]

The poetic calling develops out of a pact made between people and poet; hence the power of such invocations to an actual poem as those provided by the figures both men seem to require.

The chain does not stop there, since Neruda goes on (in "Deber del Poeta") to claim that "through me, freedom and the sea / will call in answer to the shrouded heart," and Yeats in "The Tower" speaks of sending imagnation forth "and call[ing] images and memories / From ruin or from ancient trees."[27] Because such protocols of exhortation and expansiveness are announced from under the shadow of domination, we may connect them with the narrative of liberation depicted so memorably in Fanon's *Wretched of the Earth.* For whereas the divisions and separations of the colonial order freeze the population's captivity into a sullen torpor, "new outlets . . . engender aims for the violence of colonized peoples."[28] Fanon specifies the declarations of rights, clamors for free speech and trades union demands; later, an entirely new history unfolds as a revolutionary class of militants, drawn from the ranks of the urban poor, outcasts, criminals, and *déclassés,* takes to the countryside, there slowly to form cells of armed activists, who return to the city for the final stages of the insurgency.

The extraordinary power of Fanon's writing is that it is presented as a surreptitious counter-narrative to the above-ground force of the colonial regime, which in the teleology of Fanon's narrative is certain to be defeated. The difference between Fanon and Yeats is that Fanon's theoretical and perhaps even metaphysical narrative of anti-imperialist decolonization is marked throughout with the accents and inflections of liberation: this is far more than a reactive native defensiveness, whose main problem (as Soyinka analyzed it) is that it implicitly accepts, and does not go beyond, the basic European versus non-European oppositions. Fanon's is a discourse of that anticipated triumph, liberation, that marks the second moment of decolonization. Yeats's early work, by contrast, sounds the nationalist note and stands at a threshold it cannot cross, although he sets a trajectory in common with that of other poets of decolonization, like Neruda and Darwish, which he could not complete, even though perhaps they could go further than he. One might at least give him credit for adumbrating the liberationist and utopian revolutionism in his poetry that was belied and even cancelled out by his later reactionary politics.

Yeats has often been cited in recent years as someone whose poetry warned of nationalist excesses. He is quoted without attribution, for example, in Gary Sick's book on the Carter admistration's handling of the Iranian hostage crisis 1979–1981 (*All Fall Down*);[29] and *The New York Times* correspondent in Beirut in 1975–1977, the late James Markham, quoted the same passages from "The Second Coming" in an article on the onset of the Lebanese civil war in 1976. "Things fall apart; the centre cannot hold" is one phrase. The other is "'The best lack all conviction, while the worst / Are full of passionate intensity." Sick and Markham both write as American liberals alarmed at the revolutionary tide sweeping through a Third World once contained by Western power. Their use of Yeats is minatory: remain orderly, or you're doomed to a frenzy you cannot control. As to how, in an inflamed colonial situation, the colonized are supposed to hold the center, neither Sick nor Markham tells us, but their presumption is that Yeats, in any event, would oppose the anarchy of civil war. It is as if both men had not thought to take the disorder back to the colonial intervention in the first place—which is what Chinua Achebe did in 1959 in his great novel *Things Fall Apart*.[30]

The point is that Yeats is at his most powerful precisely as he imagines and renders that very moment. It is helpful to remember that "the Anglo-Irish conflict" with which Yeats's poetic *oeuvre* is saturated was a "model of twentieth-century wars of liberation."[31] His greatest decolonizing works concern the birth of violence, or the violent birth of change, as in "Leda and the Swan," instants when a blinding flash of simultaneity is presented to his colonial eyes—the girl's rape, and alongside that, the question "Did she put on his knowledge with his power / Before the indifferent beak could let her drop?"[32] Yeats situates himself at at juncture where the violence of change is unarguable but where the results of the violence beseech necessary, if not always sufficient, reason. His greatest theme, in the poetry that culminates in *The Tower* (1928), is how to reconcile the inevitable violence of the colonial conflict with the everyday politics of an ongoing national struggle, and also how to square the power of the various parties in the conflict with the discourse of reason, persuasion, organization, and the requirements of poetry. Yeats's prophetic perception that at some point violence cannot be enough and that the strategies of politics and reason must come into play is, to my knowledge, the first important announcement in the context of decolonization of the need to balance violent force with an exigent political and organizational process. Fanon's assertion that liberation cannot be accomplished simply by seizing power (though "Even the wisest man grows tense / With some sort of violence")[33] comes almost half a century later. That neither Yeats nor Fanon offers a prescription for making a transition *after* decolonization to a period when a new political order achieves moral hegemony is symptomatic of the difficulty that millions of people live with today.

It is an amazing thing that the problem of Irish liberation not only has continued longer than other comparable struggles, but is so often not regarded as being an imperial or nationalist issue; instead it is comprehended as an aberration within the British dominions. Yet the facts conclusively reveal otherwise. Since Spenser's 1596 tract on Ireland, a whole tradition of British and European thought has considered the Irish to be a separate and inferior race, usually unregenerately barbarian, often delinquent and primitive. Irish nationalism for at least the last two hundred years is marked by internecine struggles involving the land question, the Church, the nature of parties and leaders. But dominating the movement is the attempt to regain control of the land where, in the words of the 1916 proclamation that founded the Irish Republic, "the right of the people of Ireland to the ownership of Ireland, and to the unfettered control of Irish destinies, [is] to be sovereign and indefeasible."[34]

Yeats cannot be severed from this quest. Regardless of his astounding genius, he contributed, as Thomas Flanagan puts it, "in Irish terms, and of course in a singularly powerful and compelling manner, that process of simultaneous abstraction and reification that, defiant of logic, is the heart of nationalism."[35] And to this work several generations of lesser writers also contributed, articulating the expression of Irish identity as it attaches to the land, to its Celtic origins, to a growing body of nationalist experiences and leaders (Wolfe Tone, Connolly, Mitchel, Isaac Butt, O'Connell, the United Irishmen, the Home Rule movement, and so on), and to a specifically national literature.[36] Literary nationalism also retrospectively includes many forerunners: Thomas Moore, early literary historians like the Abbe McGeoghehan and Samuel Ferguson, James Clarence Mangan, the Orange–Young Ireland movement, Standish O'Grady. In the poetic, dramatic, and scholarly work of today's Field Day Company (Seamus Heaney, Brian Friel, Seamus Deane, Tom Paulin) and of the literary historians Declan Kiberd and W. J. McCormack, these "revivals" of the Irish national experience are brilliantly reimagined and take the nationalist adventure to new forms of verbal expression.[37]

The essential Yeatsian themes sound through the earlier and later literary work: the problem of assuring the marriage of knowledge to power, of understanding violence; interestingly they are also sounded in Gramsci's roughly contemporary work, undertaken and elaborated in a different context. In the Irish colonial setting, Yeats seems best able to pose and re-pose the question provocatively, using his poetry, Blackmur says, as a technique of trouble.[38] And he goes further in the great poems of summation and vision like "Among School Children," "The Tower," "A Prayer for My Daughter," "Under Ben Bulben," and "The Circus Animals' Desertion." These are poems of genealogy and recapitulation, of course: telling and retelling the story of his life from early nationalist turbulence to the status of a senator walking through a classroom and thinking of how Leda figured in all their pasts, or a loving father thinking about his child, or a senior artist trying to achieve equanimity of vision, or finally, as a long-time craftsman somehow surviving the loss (desertion) of his powers, Yeats reconstructs his own life poetically as an epitome of the national life.

These poems reverse the reductive and slanderous encapsulation of Irish actualities which, according to Joseph Leerssen's learned book *Mere Irish and Fior-Ghael,* had been the fate of the Irish at the hands of English writers for eight centuries, displacing ahistorical rubrics like "potato-eaters," or "bog-dwellers," or "shanty people."[39] Yeats's poetry joins his people to its history, the more imperatively in that as father, or as "sixty-year-old smiling public man," or as son and husband, the poet assumes that the narrative and the density of personal experience are equivalent to the experience of his people. The references in the closing strophes of "Among School Children" suggest that Yeats was reminding his audience that history and the nation are not separable, any more than a dancer is separate from the dance.

The drama of Yeats's accomplishment in restoring a suppressed history and rejoining the nation to it is expressed well by Fanon's description of the situation Yeats had to overcome: "Colonialism is not satisfied merely with holding a people in its grip and emptying the native's brain of all form and content. By a kind of perverted logic, it turns to the past of the people, and distorts, disfigures and destroys it."[40] Yeats rises from the level of personal and folk experience to that of national archetype without losing the immediacy of the former or the stature of the latter. And his unerring choice of genealogical fables and figures speaks to another aspect of colonialism as Fanon described it: its capacity for separating the individual from his or her own instinctual life, breaking the generative lineaments of the national identity:

> On the unconscious plane, colonialism therefore did not seek to be considered by the native as a gently loving mother who protects her child from a hostile environment, but rather as a mother who unceasingly restrains her fundamentally perverse offspring from managing to commit suicide and from giving free rein to its evil instincts. The colonial mother protects her child from itself, from its ego, and from its physiology, its biology, and its own unhappiness which is its very essence.
>
> In such a situation the claims of the native intellectual [and poet] are not a luxury but a necessity in any coherent program. The native intellectual who takes up arms to defend his nation's legitimacy, who is willing to strip himself naked to study the history of his body, is obliged to dissect the heart of his people.[41]

No wonder that Yeats instructed Irish poets to

Scorn the sort now growing up
All out of shape from toe to top,

Their unremembering hearts and heads
Base-born products of base beds.[42]

That in the process Yeats ended up creating not individuals but types that "cannot quite overcome the abstractions from which they sprang," again according to Blackmur,[43] is true insofar as the decolonizing program and its background in the history of Ireland's subjugation are ignored, as Blackmur was wont to do; his interpretations are masterful yet ahistorical. When the colonial realities are taken into account, we get insight and experience, and not merely "the allegorical simulacrum churned with action."[44]

Yeats's full system of cycles, pernes, and gyres seems important only as it symbolizes his efforts to lay hold of a distant and yet orderly reality as a refuge from the turbulence of his immediate experience. When in the Byzantium poems he asks to be gathered into the artifice of eternity, the need for respite from age and from what he would later call "the struggle of the fly in marmalade" is even more starkly at work. Otherwise it is difficult to read most of his poetry and not feel that Swift's devastating anger and genius were harnessed by Yeats to lift the burdens of Ireland's colonial afflictions. True, he stopped short of imagining full political liberation, but he gave us a major international achievement in cultural decolonization nonetheless.

from *Culture and Imperialism*

PART III

Late Styles

12

Performance as an Extreme Occasion

(1989)

"Performance as an Extreme Occasion" was the first of three Wellek Library lectures that Edward Said delivered in May 1989 at the University of California at Irvine. Later published in *Musical Elaborations,* the lectures reflect Said's long-standing interest in polyphonic, Western classical music. An accomplished pianist, Said had studied piano under Ignace Tiegerman, a Polish Jew who immigrated to Cairo in 1933 where he instructed the city's *haute société.* Although Said did not pursue the piano professionally (he found practicing physically exacting and monotonous), he would go on to write about classical music with as much as passion as he would play it. In 1986 Said began writing an occasional music column for *The Nation* magazine, which was far more willing in the 1980s to publish his reviews of performances of Berlioz and Beethoven than his comments on Israel's occupation of the West Bank and Gaza.

One of the significant statements in contemporary criticism occurs at the opening of Richard Poirier's classic essay "The Performing Self." He is discussing modern writers like Yeats, Norman Mailer, and Henry James whose "powers of rendition" define the "performance that matters—pacing, economics, juxtapositions, aggregations of tone, the whole conduct of the shaping presence." And if this, says Poirier, partakes of brutality and even savagery it is because

> Performance is an exercise of power, a very anxious one. Curious because it is at first so furiously self-consultive, so even narcissistic, and later so eager for publicity, love and historical dimensions. Out of an accumulation of secretive acts emerges at last a form that presumes to complete with reality itself for control of the mind exposed to it. Performance in writing, in painting, or in dance is made of thousands of tiny movements each made with a calculation that is also its innocence. By innocence I mean that the movements have an utterly moral neutrality—they are designed to serve one another and nothing else; and they are innocent, too, because contrived with only a vague general notion of what they might ultimately be responsible for—the final thing, the accumulation called "the work."[1]

Poirier's purpose in these lines is to separate the academic, liberal, and melioristic attitudes toward literature, attitudes that serve codes, institutions, and orthodoxies, from the processes of literary performance that, he argues, are essentially "dislocating, disturbing impulses." Yet performance is not merely a happening but rather "an action which must go through passages that both impede the action and give it form." Thus, "performance comes to function at precisely the point where the potentially destructive impulse to mastery brings forth from the material its most essential irreducible, clarified, and therefore beautiful nature."[2]

Although Poirier does not discuss music here, all of his comments about rendition and enactment—except perhaps the one about innocence, to which I'd like to return later—are deeply pertinent to modern musical performance, which is also rather like an athletic event in its demand for the admiringly rapt attention of its spectators. Yet Poirier's literary examples are drawn from the work of creative artists, whereas the performances that concern me here are the essentially re-creative and interpretive reenactments of musical compositions by pianists, violinists, singers, and so forth. Indeed we should begin by noting how the extreme specialization of all aesthetic activity in the contemporary West has overtaken and been inscribed within musical performance so effectively as to screen entirely the composer from the performer. There are no major performers before the public today who are also influential composers of the first rank; even Pierre Boulez and Leonard Bernstein, to mention two immediately obvious possible exceptions, belong separately albeit simultaneously and equally to the worlds of composing and of performing, but it is not as performers of their own work that they are known principally. Beethoven, Mozart, Chopin, and Liszt were.

There is a further specialization to be noted, that of the listeners or spectators who in the aggregate make up audiences at events of musical performance. Some years ago Adorno wrote a famous and, I think, correct account of "the regression of hearing," in which he emphasized the lack of continuity, concentration, and knowledge in the listeners that has made real musical attention more or less impossible. Adorno blamed such things as radio and records for undermining and practically eliminating the possibility that the average concertgoer could play an instrument or read a score.[3] To those disabilities we can add today's complete professionalization of performance. This has widened the distance between the "artist" in evening dress or tails and, in a lesser, lower, far more secondary space, the listener who buys records, frequents concert halls, and is routinely made to feel the impossibility of attaining packaged virtuosity of a professional performer. Whether we focus on the repeatable mechanically reproduced performance available on disc, tape, or video-record, or on the alienating social ritual of the concert itself, with the scarcity of tickets and the staggeringly brilliant technique of the performer achieving roughly the same distancing effect, the listener is in a relatively weak and not entirely admirable position. Here Poirier's rather melodramatic ideas about brutality, savagery, and power can be moderated with an acknowledgment of the listener's poignant speechlessness as he/she faces an onslaught of such refinement, articulation, and technique as almost to constitute a sadomasochistic experience.[4]

Consider as an example the performance of Chopin's Etudes by Maurizio Pollini, the extraordinarily proficient and brilliant Italian pianist. His interpretation is available on disc and, since Pollini performs the works regularly in recital and was also winner of the Chopin Prize when he was only eighteen, these recorded performances of opus 10 and opus 25 stand as representative of his considerable virtuosity. Chopin wrote them originally as aids to his teaching, as explanations of various aspects of keyboard technique (octaves, thirds, left-hand and passage work, legato playing, arpeggios, etc.). In Pollini's performance the power and astonishing assertiveness of the playing, which begins in opus 10, number 1, with a massive C-major bass octave chord and is immediately followed by a burst of lightning-fast arpeggiated passage work, absolutely free of hesitation, wrong notes, or grasping, immediately establishes the distance between these performances and any amateur attempt to render Chopin's music. Moreover, the grandeur of Pollini's technique, its scale, and its dominating display and reach completely dispatch any remnant of Chopin's original intention for the music, which was to afford the pianist, any pianist, an entry into the relative seclusion and reflectiveness of problems of technique.

Evidence testifying to the performer's power, unattached to the correlative skills either of improvisation or of composing, emerges after the first third of the nineteenth century. The virtuoso singer, pianist, or violinist who is the ancestor of today's Jessye Norman, Pollini, or Menuhin comes not just with the appearance of Paganini on European stages in the late 1820s, the great archetype of the preternaturally skilled and demonic performer on endlessly fascinating display, but with the emergence of transcription as an art both of display and of encroachment, and along with transcription a relative demotion in the priority of the musical text (about which in his magisterial book *Nineteenth-Century Music* Carl Dahlhaus has interesting things to say).[5] When pianists invade the orchestral or operatic repertoire we have gone well beyond even the contests in virtuosity that engaged Bach, Handel, and Mozart, who played the music of other masters as easily as they cannibalized and plagiarized their own work. Modern performance has to do with rights asserted over music written by and for others, rights won by a rigorous, highly specialized training in interpretation most often not grounded in composition. Busoni may be the last of the major composers, transcribers, and performers to operate before a Western musical public; the line of impressive omni-competent musicians that was so boldly begun with Bach, so robustly continued with Beethoven, so colorfully overstated with Liszt and Busoni, disappears completely after Rachmaninoff, Prokofiev, Britten, and Bartok.

Performance cut off from composing therefore constitutes a special form of ownership and work. Let me return briefly to transcription, since it is in the theory and practice of transcription that the various incorporations and consolidations of monopolistic performance most strikingly take place. There is in all Western classical music from the late seventeenth century on a dynamic between performance designed for the public place secured and held by church and court, on the one hand, and, on the other hand, music whose performance is private and domestic. Orchestral and choral works of any moderate size belong principally to the public sphere, although both Bach and Handel trafficked across the lines so to speak in writing music that could be performed in either one space or the other, by one kind of instrument, solo or concerted, or another. Many of Beethoven's instrumental works and lieder were written for nonprofessionals, although they have since become standard works in the performing repertory of professional singers and instrumentalists.

The main nineteenth-century examples of transcription were (and have remained in the twentieth century) the reductions of large concerted works to the smaller resources of one instrument, most often the piano. This practice argues the steady presence of amateur musicians who could not readily obtain or decipher full scores but whose desire to play the music could be satisfied by reading and playing it in piano versions for either two or four hands. Before records and radio this in fact was the main introduction to concert music for uncounted numbers of people for whom—even after mechanical reproduction became a standard feature of modern life—the pleasure of getting control of a full score, and enacting a concert event in the home, was perhaps greater and certainly more frequent than attending concerts. The transcription for public concert purposes of operas, of music for other instruments (especially the organ) and for voice, as well as of full-scale orchestral works, is a qualitatively different thing, however. Liszt was the most famous exemplar of this practice, which at last enters the public sphere in the 1840s and makes a new kind of statement about the act of performance itself.

At the simplest level, Liszt's transcriptions are an art of sustained and extended quotation, and later of quotation prolonged elaborately into what Liszt was to call a concert paraphrase or fantasia.

The variations, paraphrases, fantasias he wrote on Bach's "Weinen, Klagen, Sorgen, Zagen" and on Verdi's *Rigoletto* are well-known examples that still turn up on contemporary recital programs. But on a second level, concert quotations that became full-fledged pieces on their own, autonomous works that leave behind the original or blot it out entirely, are assertions of the transcriber's skill and, much more important, of the performer's virtuosity. For not only does the listener marvel (as people marveled at Liszt's fastidious transcription of the Beethoven Sixth Symphony) at how only a magician could reduce and render a full score so idiomatically for the piano, but the work's formidable digital difficulty is a display of the concert musician's prerogative to help her/himself to pieces from the repertory of orchestra, organ, or opera and establish them in a new, highly specialized environment.

With his considerably advanced and almost metacritical sense of what the performer's work was really about, Glenn Gould illustrated the main features of this new environment as it had developed by the mid-twentieth century. Consider as a start that he was the first major performer to announce his retirement from the concert stage at age thirty-one; he then proceeded to spend the rest of his life publicly saying that he had done so, all the while performing around, but never again in, the concert hall. He made dozens of recordings, wrote numerous articles, lectured, did radio and television work, and acted as producer for many of his own performances. Second, no sooner had he deserted concert life than Gould's repertory suddenly departed from the mainly Baroque and contemporary works in which he excelled and for which he had become famous. He began a new career as "concert-dropout" playing not just Bach and Schoenberg but Liszt's piano transcriptions of the Beethoven Fifth and Sixth symphonies; in a later recording he delivered himself of his own transcriptions of Wagner, including "Dawn and Rhine Journey" from *Götterdämmerung* as well as the Prelude to *Die Meistersinger.* So complicated and intimidatingly difficult were these scores that Gould's point seemed to be that he wanted to reassert the pianist's prerogative to dominate over all other fields of music, and to do so completely as a function of unapproachably superior, uniquely "different" capacities for instrumental display.

There is even a dramatic point being underscored in the actual reduction of score from its full orchestral version, which is what Beethoven wrote, to its brilliant pianistic miniaturization by Liszt. To see the difference in size between the two versions is to note that the piano reduction is the metaphoric equivalent of forcing an army to walk single-file through a single turnstile, with the pianist as gatekeeper (Example 1 and Example 2).

Only a professional pianist can render such a work as this—here we must note how pianists play the preeminent role in the developments I am describing—just as the act of executing such a work is no longer an act of affection (*amateur* is a word to be taken first in its literal sense) but an act of almost institutional mastery and therefore a public occasion. Similarly the sheer length and the scope of the solo performance in the nineteenth-century transcriptions were designed for the technical virtuosity—the complex chordal and passage work, leaps, etc., that had emerged as the hallmark of piano playing after Beethoven—of the performer's actual playing. What today we experience in the concert hall is the completed relocation of the site of a score's musical realization from the amateur's home to the concert hall, from an ordinary, mainly domestic and private passage of time, to an occasional, heightened public experience of the solo or concert repertory by a professional performer.

After the middle of the nineteenth century virtuosos seem to have regarded their concerts not just as samplings of a few works (that practice continues today) but as marathon surveys of the entire musical literature. And indeed, in the legendary programs put on by Busoni in Berlin and by Anton Rubinstein in St. Petersburg, audiences got immense multi-hour traversals of the whole keyboard repertory. Attenuated versions of these recitals continue today in the all-Beethoven cycles executed by Artur Schnabel, Alfred Brendel, Daniel Barenboim, and Richard Goode, among others. The great master professionals become in fact the living embodiment of their instrument's history, their programs the narrative of that history presented didactically and integrally. The celebrated orchestral conductors attempt a similar combination of performance and history (Bernstein and the Mahler symphonies, Karajan and the Bruckner symphonies, Solti and Wagner, Toscanini and Beethoven).

Until the early twentieth century most concert performers who were not composers routinely scheduled the work of contemporary

EXAMPLE 1. *Beethoven's Symphony No. 5 in C Minor, opening of first movement*

p cresc.
f
cresc.

EXAMPLE 2. *Listz's piano transcription of Example 1*

composers on their program. Artur Rubinstein was probably the last pianist a significant portion of whose repertory until he died a few years ago was made up of works (the Stravinsky *Petrushka,* Ravel's *Valses Nobles et Sentimentales,* many pieces by Szymanowski, Albeniz, de Falla) he played as their composers' by contemporary and friend. But this practice has fallen off dramatically. Ursula Oppens, a fine New York pianist, is one of the few first-rate professionals still doing that. Otherwise the concert professional's programs are if not antiquarian, then curatorial, with occasional nods at the musician's obligation also to be instructive and acceptably contemporary.

Performances of Western classical music are therefore highly concentrated, rarified, and extreme occasions. They have a commercial rationale that is connected not just to selling tickets and booking tours but also to selling records for the benefit of large corporations. Above all, the concert occasion itself is the result of a complex historical and social process—some aspects of which I have tried to present here—that can be interpreted as a cultural occasion staked upon specialized eccentric skills, upon the performer's interpretive and histrionic personality fenced in by his or her obligatory muteness, upon the audience's receptivity, subordination, and paying patience. What competes with these occasions is not the amateur's experience but other public displays of specialized skill (sports, circus, dance contests) that, at its worst and most vulgar, the concert may attempt to match.

What interests me about the concert occasion is that there is an enduring perhaps even atavistic quality to certain aspects of the performance, interpretation, and production of Western classical music that can be studied and examined precisely because the integrity and specialization involved nevertheless converge upon other cultural and theoretical issues that are not musical, or that do not belong completely to the sphere of music. Clearly, for example, musical performance, with its narcissistic, self-referential, and, as Poirier says, self-consultive qualities, is the central and most socially stressed musical experience in modern Western society, but it is both a private musical experience for performer and listener, and a public experience too. The two experiences are interdependent and overlap with each other. But how can one understand the connection between the two and, more interestingly, how does one interpret it? Are there particularly useful ways of doing so in order that the enabling conditions of performance and their connection with the sociocultural sphere can be seen as a coherent part of the whole experience?

Now the connection between modern or new music and contemporary Western society has been the subject of Theodor Adorno's extremely influential theoretical reflections and analysis. There are three things, however, about Adorno's work that in a sense start me off here, and from which, for reasons I shall explain briefly, I necessarily depart. The first is Adorno's theory that after Beethoven (who died in 1827) music veered off from the social realm into the aesthetic almost completely. According to Adorno, Beethoven's late style gains for music a new autonomy from the world of ordinary historical reality.[6] Adorno believed that it was Arnold Schoenberg's extraordinary achievement in his theory and career a hundred years after Beethoven's death to have first comprehended and subsumed the real meaning of music's trajectory in the preceding century, and then having thoroughly incorporated it, to have derived his new rationale from a deepened, tragic intensification of the separation between music and society.[7]

The technicalization of the dodecaphonic system, its totally rationalized form and preprogrammed expressiveness, its forcefully articulated laws, are an elimination of transcendence and an affirmation and alienation as well; everything about music that had characterized it hitherto, its concepts of improvisation, creativity, composition, variation, and sociability, now come, Adorno says, to a paralyzed standstill.[8] From the time of the Baroque, music had been not only a documentation of the bourgeoisie's reality but also one of its principal art forms, since the proletariat never formulated or was permitted to constitute itself as a musical subject. By the early twentieth century, radical modern music of the kind composed by Schoenberg and his main disciples Berg and Webern has had its social substance abstracted from it by entirely musical means. New music has become isolated and hermetic not by virtue of "asocial" but rather because of social concerns.

Thus modern music expresses its social "concern through its pure quality, doing so all the more emphatically, the more purely this quality is revealed; it points out the ills of society rather than sublimating those ills into a deceptive humanitarianism which would pretend that humanitarianism had already been achieved in the present." Adorno continues: "The alienation present in the consistency of artistic technique forms the very substance of the work of art. The shocks of incomprehension, emitted by artistic technique, undergo a sudden change. They illuminate the meaningless world."[9] I take Adorno to be saying that by its very rigor and distance from the everyday world of listeners and perhaps even of performers, new music casts a devastatingly critical light upon the degraded and therefore meaningless world, precisely the world for which Georg Lukács thirty years before in *The Theory of the Novel* had designed his interpretation of the form of the novel.

"Modern music," Adorno concludes,

> sacrifices itself to this effort. It has taken upon itself all the darkness and guilt of the world. Its fortune lies in the perception of misfortune; all of its beauty is in denying itself the illusion of beauty. No one wished to become involved with art—individuals as little as collectives. It dies away unheard, without even an echo. . . . Music which has not been heard falls into empty time like an impotent bullet. Modern music spontaneously aims towards this last experience, evidenced hourly in mechanical [by which Adorno means music that is reproduced mechanically, unthinkingly, like Muzak or background

music] means. Modern music sees absolute oblivion as its goal. It is the surviving message of despair from the shipwrecked.[10]

The commanding figure of Schoenberg dominates and gloomily irradiates this description but, I believe, most of what Adorno theorizes about turns out to have little prophetic validity, aside from its rather willful avoidance of such "new" composers as Debussy, Busoni, and Janacek. (To his credit he wrote an essay years later entitled "Modem Music Is Growing Old" conceding the point.)[11] Not only did serialism become an academic, thoroughly (too) respectable technique but many of the early masterpieces of the Viennese twelve-tone method are now items of considerable prestige and frequency in the performing repertory.

Some of the alienating distance of the ascetic compositional techniques described so powerfully by Adorno nevertheless survives in the rituals of virtuoso performance that, despite the relative scarcity of virtuosity, nevertheless continue into the present. Classical music is not only not unheard but is heard in new configurations of aesthetic and social experience. Thus what furnished us with an excellent starting point—the observation that Adorno's characterization of new music is true for the period during which he wrote—is inadequate once we are past the period of the Second Viennese school's apogee in the 1920s; analysis must be extended into a present to which the application of Adorno's prescriptive admonishments appears (dare one say it?) sentimental. The fact is that music remains situated within the social context as a special variety of aesthetic and cultural experience that contributes to what, following Gramsci, we might call the elaboration or production of civil society. In Gramsci's usage elaboration equals maintenance, that is, the work done by members of a society that keeps things going; certainly musical performance fits the description, as do cultural activities like lectures, conferences, graduation ceremonies, awards banquets, etc. The problematics of great musical performance, social as well as technical, therefore provide us with a post-Adornian occasion for analysis and for reflecting on the role of classical music in contemporary Western society.

My second point about Adorno, to whose work I am profoundly indebted in all sorts of ways, is illuminated by an anecdote recounted by Pierre Boulez on the occasion of Michel Foucault's death. Although he and Foucault never spoke about their intellectual specialties to each other—Foucault about philosophy, Boulez about composition—it transpired that Foucault once noted to Boulez the remarkable ignorance of contemporary intellectuals about music, whether classical or popular.[12] Perhaps the two men had in mind the contrast with a previous generation of European intellectuals for whom reflection on music was a central part of their work. Certainly Adorno and Ernst Bloch, for example, demonstrate in their careers the striking relevance of, say, philosophy and religion to music, or the intrinsically necessary presence of musical analysis to Adorno's negative dialectics or Bloch's theses on hope and utopian thought.

As we look back to the modernist movement for which music was culturally central—Proust, Mann, Eliot, Joyce come additionally to mind—we have good reason to remark that just as Adorno was able to rationalize and ironically connect Schoenberg's work in and for modern society, we are able to demonstrate how in the general division of intellectual labor after modernism musical experience was fragmented. Historical musicology, theory, ethnomusicology, composition today furnish most academic music departments with four distinct enterprises. For its part, music criticism is now effectively the report of attendance at concerts that are really evanescent happenings, unrepeatable, usually unrecordable, nonrecuperable. And yet in the interesting recharting of intellectual undertakings, attempted by what has been called cultural studies, certain aspects of the musical experience can be understood inclusively as taking place within the cultural setting of the contemporary West.[13] The performance occasion, as I have been calling it, is one such aspect, which is why I shall be looking at it from this broad cultural perspective.

Lastly, Adorno's main argument about modern music is that its exclusivism and hermetic austerity do not constitute something new but testify rather to a quasi-neurotic insistence on music's separate, almost mute, and formally nondiscursive character as an art. Anyone who has written or thought about music has of course confronted the problem of meaning and interpretation, but must always return to a serious appraisal of how music manages in spite of everything to preserve its reticence, mystery, or allusive silence, which in turn symbolizes its autonomy as an art. The Adornian model for music history as compellingly analyzed by Rose Subotnik suggests that music eludes philosophical statement only after Beethoven, and that the "alienation present in the consistency of [Schoenberg's] musical technique" is a fulfillment of the privatization of the art begun during the early days of romanticism.[14] I do not disagree with this view, nor it would seem does Carl Dahlhaus, whose monumental study *Nineteenth-Century Music* (referred to earlier) fleshes out the same model with considerable subtlety and detail. But it is, I think, accurate to say that we can regard the public nature of musical performance today—professionalized, ritualized, specialized though it may be—as a way of bridging the gap between the social and cultural spheres on the one hand, and music's reclusiveness on the other. Performance is thus an inflected and highly determined point of convergence where the specific and the general come together, music as the most specialized of aesthetics with a discipline entirely specific to it, performance as the general, socially available form of its cultural presentation.

Yet—and here I return now to my main argument about performance as an occasion—it is appropriate to stress the social abnormality of the concert ritual itself. What attracts audiences to concerts is that what performers attempt on the concert or opera stage is exactly what most members of the audience cannot emulate or aspire to. But this unattainable actuality, so strikingly dramatic when we see it before us on a stage, depends on the existence of unseen faculties and powers that make it possible: the performers' training and gifts; cultural agencies like concert associations, managers, ticketsellers; the conjunction of various social and cultural processes (including the revolutions in capitalism and telecommunication, electronic media, jet travel) with an audience's wish or appetite for a particular musical event. The result is what can be called an extreme occasion, something beyond the everyday, something irreducibly and temporally not repeatable, something whose core is precisely what can be experienced only under relatively severe and unyielding conditions.

At no point has the extremism and severity of the contemporary performance experience been more clearly affirmed than in Arturo Toscanini's combination of scrupulously fanatic attention and supernally dominating musical technique—the fabulous memory, the total grasp of the score, the authoritative understanding of each instrument, and so on. Both during his American career and more or less uninterruptedly since his death, there has been a strenuous debate about Toscanini's achievements, his impressive legacy, his influence on conducting, and his musicianship in general, as well as his shortcomings. It is worth citing as one often quite interesting and provocative monument to the Toscanini debate Joseph Horowitz's 1987 book *Understanding Toscanini.*[15] Horowitz is steeped in the debate, even though his argument that Toscanini's style of taut, literalist objectivism coincided perfectly with the NBC corporate ethos in its ambition to create, Barnum-like, a vast popular audience for classical music is an argument that often either ignores or unjustly diminishes the genuinely electrifying—albeit exaggerated—quality of Toscanini's performances.

On the other hand, for all the generous detail he provides, as well as his admiring yet disapproving accounts of the sometimes unconscious cooperation between Toscanini's narrow aesthetic perspectives and David Sarnoff's corporate ideology, Horowitz does not go as far in severity as Adorno's characterization of Toscanini's Führer-like *Meisterschaft,* based as it is, in Adorno's words, on "iron discipline—but precisely iron." In Adorno's view Toscanini's performances, with their predetermined dynamics, their eliminated tensions, and "the protective fixation of the work," obliterate the symphonic work altogether. In Toscanini's performances, control forbids music from going where it might want to go: he is incapable of letting a phrase "play out," he foregrounds soprano parts (as in Wagner) and "cleans up" complex counterpoint, he refuses to stray from the restricted nineteenth-century repertory that imposes an avoidance either of Baroque or of advanced modern music. Because of this pretended objectivity (*sachlichkeit*) Toscanini for Adorno comes to embody "the triumph of technology and administration over music," even if in performances of Italian opera he produced a sort of exactness (without lingering or sentiment) for which there was no equivalent in the presentation of opera in Germany.[16]

One can actually accept both the Adorno and the Horowitz position—particularly as they discuss Toscanini's complicity in the creation of a basically illiterate mass-market appetite more interested in stereotypes about "the world's greatest conductor conducting the world's greatest music" than in refined and illuminating performances of the kind given by Eugen Jochum, Otto Klemperer, and

Wilhelm Furtwängler (all of whom, according to Horowitz, were defeated by Toscanini in America)—that is, one can accept the positions without altogether conceding the point that Toscanini's work clarified what is extreme about the concert occasion itself. This is something I think centrally missing in both their accounts of the Toscanini phenomenon. What stamps the still available 1938 performance by Toscanini of the *Eroica* is the absolute rigor of the logic that he lets unfold in Beethoven's music, and in so doing discloses a process, almost a narrative, that is irreducibly unique, eccentric, contrary to everyday life. So highly wrought is this that it feels like a clear aesthetic alternative to the travails of ordinary human experience.

As Toscanini characteristically takes them, the opening E-flat chords of the *Eroica* announce this process with the distinctive authority of two successive thunderclaps. Thereafter, without a whit of sentimentality or of rubato, the cellos begin the principal theme, passing it to the flutes and horns, until in measure 41 a gigantic *tutti* recaptures the theme for the full ensemble: all this occurs in a block of time that communicates the rigor and straightforward compression of a wind tunnel, stripped of any sort of palliative adornment or lingering nostalgia. It is not that Toscanini highlights only the melody (as Adorno charged) but that each of the measures of the score is realized with a taut inevitability suggesting the expressivity of pure forward movement that seems to be making only provisional or convenient use of music, rather than communicating the orchestral equivalent of shaped phrasings that derive from the human voice.

What Toscanini seems to me to be doing here is trying to force into prominence, or perhaps enforce, the utterly contrary quality of the performance occasion, its total discontinuity with the ordinary, regular, or normative processes of everyday life. No wonder that Adorno preferred a Furtwängler for whom the performance of, say, the Bruckner or Schubert Ninth symphonies was felt to derive from his private, intuitive interpretation brought out and displayed, as if by the sheerest coincidence, on a public concert platform. In the drier, more unyielding acoustical and expressive contours of a Toscanini performance the concert stage is the public occasion, and *only that;* it stands before us stripped of any vestiges of home, individual subject, family, tradition, or national style. And because it is really very difficult to prove that from a logical point of view

Toscanini is wrong, or that concerts under late capitalism are really "music-making" or "communities of interpretation" or shared "subjectivity," and that traditions of performance established in nineteenth-century Berlin and Vienna are being violated, there has been in general an unwillingness to grant that the unrelaxed emotional pressure projected on his audiences by his performances stems immediately from what is extreme in the occasion itself. Out of touch with a reflective composing tradition that was never really his, having lost contact with the vagaries and permissiveness of amateurish musical practice, specialized into the ascetic discipline of a concert repertory based entirely on masterpieces from the past, Toscanini's conducting, I believe, rarified and concentrated the whole business several steps further, and made it for a time *the* dominant musical paradigm. That the paradigm was endorsed and subsidized by a corporate patron is a precise index of business acumen, and of course of the way in which the culture industry operates.

And, I further contend, in its artificiality and restrictive boundaries, the entire mix produces a further clarification, at a notch up from Toscanini, in the career and performances of Glenn Gould. Here I should be perfectly clear about what I do and do *not* mean. I am not saying that Toscanini and Gould are the only performers who are interesting; far from it. I am also not saying that the two of them define all the options for the interpretation and reproduction of Western classical music. I am, however, saying that they elucidate and dramatize the fate of music and music-making as it gets concentrated and constricted into the performance occasion in the period after the one Adorno describes as both heroic and tragic in *Philosophy of Modern Music*. In a society with important ongoing (if perhaps only vestigial) commitments to the central classical canon of the main European tradition, we can say that the concert occasion has superseded the contemporary composer (who, with a few exceptions, has been marginalized by becoming important mainly to other professional composers) or, if the idea of a competition between performer and contemporary composer appears to be too coarse for a cultural phenomenon, we can say that the social configuration in which the concert occasion is the most important factor has provided a wholly separate alternative for the production of music. Whereas a century ago the composer occupied stage center as author and performer, now only the performer (star singer, pianist, violinist, trumpeter, or conductor) remains. There is thus a special importance to be given to a performance that emerges, as Poirier remarks, "out of an accumulation of secretive acts." This, he says, becomes "at last a form that presumes to compete with reality itself for control of the minds exposed to it."

Gould's career as a performing musician begins (almost too neatly) at just about the time of Toscanini's death in 1957. A recently published biography of Gould by Otto Friedrich provides sufficient detail for us to understand the relentless artificiality and, from the point of view of what is socially and culturally considered to be "normal," the unyieldingly abnormal contours of Gould's life. So strong are they that Gould appears not just unnatural but anti-natural, his feelings about his hands, for example, making it impossible and frightening for him as a child even to contemplate playing marbles. In addition, Gould's rather ordinary family (from which he seemed if not estranged then at least disengaged), his calculated solitude and celibacy, his unencumbered and debtless playing style (his only teacher in Toronto appears to have handed on practically none of his ideas to Gould) fostered the illusion of a self-born man, re-creating and even reinventing piano-playing as if from scratch.[17]

Gould died in 1982 at age fifty; yet, as I said earlier, he only played concerts in public for about ten years—between the mid-1950s and the mid-1960s—and after retiring from concert life permanently devoted himself to making records, TV broadcasts, films, and radio programs, most, but not all, featuring him playing the piano. In short, the phenomenally gifted Gould seemed never to have done anything that was not in some way purposefully eccentric. He claimed to avoid the romantic composers (Chopin, Schumann, Liszt, Rachmaninoff) whose work forms the core of the performing pianists' main repertory, and concentrated instead on Bach, or on twentieth-century composers like Schoenberg, Krenek, and Hindemith; in addition, he seemed inclined to an odd assortment of other composers (Beethoven, Brahms, Richard Strauss, Sibelius, Bizet, Grieg, and Wagner, for example) whose work he sometimes approached as no one else did, often playing compositions by them that no other pianist played. On occasion he played works he did not like by composers he seemed to disdain: his nearly integral recording of the Mozart piano sonatas is a case in point, and even though other musicians have also performed works they did not care for, no one except Gould advertised the fact and played accordingly.

Gould's astounding virtuosity and rhythmic grace produced a sound ideally suited to making complex music sound clearer and more intelligently understood and organized than the sound produced by other pianists. His first recording, Bach's *Goldberg* Variations, was made when he was barely out of his teens, but the work's extraordinary contrapuntal logic, its dazzlingly beautiful and yet rigorous structures, its brilliant keyboard configurations were rendered by the young pianist with a pianistic flair that was unprecedented. And that of course is the principal point to be made about Gould's sound, his style, and his entire deportment: his complete separation from the world of other pianists, of other people, of other prerogatives. His career seemed to be constructed like a self-conscious counternarrative to the careers of all other musicians. Once the initial constraints were understood and accepted by Gould the rest of what he did can be read retrospectively to have followed consequentially.

These constraints—together with the discipline they impose constituting what I have been calling "performance as an extreme occasion"—were those provided by the frame of the performance itself and, within that, by the illusion of the performer's inaccessibility to the routine demands not just of other performing styles but also of human life as lived by other human beings. Friedrich's book makes that point with almost devastating force. Gould neither ate, slept, nor behaved socially like anyone else. He kept himself alive with drugs, his musical and intellectual habits were ringed with insomnia and endless quasi-clinical self-observation, and in every way imaginable he allowed himself to be absorbed into a sort of airless but pure performance enclave that in turn paradoxically kept reminding one of the very concert platform he had deserted. Occasionally what Gould did seemed as if he was stepping past the platform into a strange world beyond it.

Gould's direct appropriation of Bach from the very outset of his career can be seen retrospectively to have been a brilliantly right, that is strategically created, beginning. Listen to the opening theme of the *Goldberg* Variations as he recorded the work in 1955: the listener will be struck by the unprotected directness of the proleptic announcement the theme makes (as if the gigantic work is somehow secreted within the theme in fragile outline), not just of the vastly proliferating variations that Bach elaborated out of it, but also of Gould's fantastically brilliant performing style, its heady brashness even in quiet moments, its unidiomatic heightening of the piano's percussive traits, its fearless negotiation of the most elaborate patterns and configurations. Gould used the *Goldberg* as a way of immediately setting himself apart from other debut recitalists (whose choice of repertory was always more predictable than his), as if instead of continuing the romantic tradition that sustained virtuoso performers, Gould was starting *his* pedigree earlier than theirs and then vaulting past them into the present.

Thereafter Gould recorded the Partitas, both books of the *Well-Tempered Clavier,* the Toccatas, the English and French suites, the inventions and short preludes and fugues, plus a major section of the *Art of Fugue*; some concerted pieces (concerti and violin and gamba sonatas) were also performed and recorded. What stands out in all this is not so much a uniform style but a clear and immediately impressive continuity of attack and rhetorical address that, during the decades he performed in public, was italicized and highlighted by a massive catalogue of mannerisms—humming, conducting, low chair, slouch, etc. Even a short series of extracts from his recordings reveals the clarity of voices, the rhythmic inventiveness, and the effortless tonal and digital logic that permits an unbroken continuity of identity and performing signature to emerge.

I suggest, for instance, a handful of preludes and fugues from the *Well-Tempered Clavier,* in which what in effect is a solemn, didactic exercise is refurbished by Gould, is transformed into a set of mood pieces, strictly delivered in correctly realized contrapuntal style, but always phrased, shaped, and rendered into a completely integrated characterization. His recording of the Toccatas, like that of the French Suites, gives the dance-inspired movements an astonishing vividness that separates them entirely from their social origins, and transfigures them into abstract typifications of particular rhythms and syncopations. Using the same technique Gould turned to a set of what are known as "little" preludes, a recording of one of which (BWV 933 in C major) delivers a fascinating study of interweaving patterns—turns with arpeggiated chords, running passages with highlighted themes—kept bright and bustling by the acutely stressed operation of Gould's rhythmical vitality.

None of the remarkable things that Gould does, however, would have been possible without a truly rare digital mechanism that easily rivals those of "legendary" technicians like Vladimir Horowitz, Jorge Bolet, Arturo Benedetti Michelangeli, and one or two others. Gould always seemed to achieve a seamless unity among his fingers, the piano, and the music he was playing, one working by extension *into* the other, the three becoming indistinguishable from start to finish. It was as if Gould's virtuosity finally derived its fluency from the piece and not from a residue of technical athleticism built up independently over the years. Pollini has some of the same quality as Gould in this respect, but it is the wonderfully intelligent exercise of his fingers in polyphonic music that separates Gould from every other pianist. Only a great Bach organist communicates in something like the same way, except that as a concert pianist Gould had an awareness of the essentially theatrical frame that calls attention to what keeps him on the distinct side of the divide between audience and performer.

But two more things about Gould distinguished him from other pianists. I have already mentioned the first. In 1964 he stopped playing concerts and, as I said, completely left public "live" performing in order to devote himself to recording, writing, and composing. Although his career on concert stages had been very successful, he said he quit "live" performances because, he now argued, they distorted the music theatrically, on the one hand, and on the other hand, concert-giving did not allow him the necessary "taketwoness" of the recording studio, the opportunity to replay sections of music requiring further elaboration and polish.

The second of Gould's fateful attributes was his exceptional—if not prodigal—verbal gift, to which he gave increasingly wider play after he was no longer performing concerts (he began by giving lectures during the 1960s). Unlike many performing musicians, he seemed to have not only ideas and a mind but the ability to apply them to music both as performer and as critic. His performances, in short, approximated to an argument, and his discursive arguments were often borne out by his pianistic feats. This was never more evident (as we shall see presently) than in the remarkable series of films made about Gould by various British, Canadian, French, and German directors, films that allowed Gould to speak, perform, illustrate his ideas with scintillating wit, and to considerable effect, in settings that were a hybrid of living-room, practice studio, and lecture hall. He was thus musician, teacher, "personality," and performer all at once.

To take from Gould one or another of these various roles is to end up with an actually *more* improbable, less interesting phenomenon. As a writer Gould, I think, requires the piano and the immediacy of his lively presence to make what he says work. The published material, collected in a one-volume potpourri of essays, articles, and record liners, is often overwritten and underargued.[18] There are garrulous displays of wit and parody that are, to my taste, both forced and insufferably tedious. Gould was neither intellectually disciplined nor a fully cultivated man, and his learning, for all the exuberance with which he deployed it, often reveals the trying awkwardness of the naive village philosopher. The paradox is that his writings are nevertheless essential as the verbal counterpoint he provided for himself as a performer. Thus quite deliberately Gould extended the limited theatrical space provided by performance as an extreme occasion to one whose scope includes speech, time as duration, an interlude from daily life that is not controlled by mere consecutiveness. Thus for Gould performance was an inclusive phenomenon but it was still kept within the bounds and the inaccessibility imposed by his studied eccentricity. In addition, his performances were unmistakably affiliated with aspects of the contemporary technological and cultural environment, especially his longtime relationships with CBS records and the Canadian Broadcasting Corporation.

There is something Jamesian about the last part of Gould's career: he can be interpreted like one of the symbolic figures appearing in Henry James's parables of the 1880s that were meditations on both the problems of the craft of writing and the personality of the artist. One can imagine James fashioning a story about an artist called Glenn Gould who after ten years of concerts at the mercy of ticket-holders, schedules, and impresarios decides to become the author of his own scripts and so forces upon the whole process of performance—which is, after all, what *he* has been condemned to in the age of specialization—his own individualistic transformation: he invites friends home to perform for them. Gould's audience nonetheless continued to hear in the records that he was to make during his post concert-giving period the same recognizable stylistic signature, although now—if we take his record of Wagner transcriptions as an instance of the new transformation—the playing has expanded from Bach into a late twentieth-century transcription of late nineteenth-century Wagnerian counterpoint and melody, conveyed in the modern idiom already pioneered by Gould for the contemporary piano.

The most typically Gouldian extracts are the *Meistersinger* prelude and his considerably edited version of the *Siegfried Idyll*. The orchestral piece that begins Wagner's only comic opera is seen by Gould as no conductor or orchestra has ever played it: it becomes a compendium of eighteenth-century contrapuntal writing displayed for an audience with a sort of anatomical glee by Gould, who plays the piece with such neat virtuosity as to make you forget that human hands are involved. Near the end, as Wagner's orchestral writing becomes too thick and the number of simultaneous themes too great even for Gould, the pianist resorts (he tells us in a liner note) to overdubbing, superimposing his recording of one part of the dense score on his recording of another part. This is as if by doubling the electronic prerogatives of the performing occasion Gould had exponentially also increased the rarity and power of the performer's hold on the duration of a concert favorite. In his transcription of the *Siegfried Idyll* Gould tampers with Wagner's notes so as somewhat to reduce the similarity between piano transcription and orchestra original in order to elevate the special character of a twentieth-century pianistic reproduction. In both instances, however, Gould's ideas of Wagner are supplementally reinforced by his prose notes for the record jacket.

As Gould seems to have suspected, his choice of Wagner itself would be most fully commented on not just by playing his ideas, so to speak, but also by his "additional" prose. Note that Gould's ideas are worth looking into not so much only because they are of inherent validity (they have, for instance a fascinating resonance in the Canadian context as shown by B. W. Powe in *The Solitary Outlaw*)[19] but because they also show us Gould grappling publicly with his predicament as a performing pianist who discursively notes everything that he can comment on as pianist and as critic along the way.

As such, then, Gould's observations furnish the most intense example of the performance occasion being forcibly pulled out of the tired routine and unthinking consensus that ordinarily support the concert performance as a relatively lifeless social form. But what I am also saying is that Gould's restless forays into writing, radio, television, and film enhanced, enlivened, and illuminated his playing itself, giving it a self-conscious aesthetic and cultural presence whose aim, while not always clear, was to enable performance to engage or to affiliate with the world itself, without compromising the essentially reinterpretive, reproductive quality of the process. This, I think, is the Adornian measure of Gould's achievement, and also its limitations, which are those of a late capitalism that has condemned classical music to an impoverished marginality and anti-intellectualism sheltered underneath the umbrella of "autonomy." Yet like Toscanini before him, Gould sets the standard by which in an art without an easily graspable ideological or social value (perhaps an aspect of what Poirier calls its moral neutrality and innocence) it could itself be interpreted.

From his writing it seems quite clear that Gould saw nothing at all exceptional about playing the piano well. What he wanted was an escape from everything that determined or conditioned his reality as a human being. Consider, for example, that his favorite state was "ecstasy," his favorite music was music ideally not written for specific instruments and hence "essentially incorporeal," and his highest words of praise were *repose, detachment, isolation.* To this, Friedrich's biography contributes the notion of *control,* which is the motif of much of Gould's life. Moreover, Gould seems to have believed that art was "mysterious," but that it allowed "the gradual, life-long construction of a state of wonder and serenity" that, when conveyed through radio and recordings, shapes "the elements of aesthetic narcissism" and responds "'to the challenge that each man contemplatively creates his own divinity.'"[20]

This is not complete metaphysical nonsense, at least not if it is read as a comment on Gould's peculiar situation. He seems to have been finally discontent both with the nonverbal, nondiscursive nature of music—its silence about itself—and with the actual physical achievement of being a performing pianist. In the amusing interviews he did with Jonathan Cott in 1974, first published in *Rolling Stone* and now done up as a little book adorned with handsome photographs,[21] Gould speaks with laughable exaggeration of being able to teach anyone the skills of pianism in half an hour. Elsewhere he says he hardly practiced or bothered with playing the piano for its own sake. He was more interested in those aspects of music and of his own talents that spilled over from musical expression into language, in how the daily reminders of his indebtedness both to composer and to audience might be transmuted into the utopia of an infinitely changeable and extendable world where time or history did not occur, and because of which all expression was transparent, logical, and not hampered by flesh-and-blood performers or people at all.

Considered as the record of Gould's lifelong struggle to be more than just a performing pianist, his prose is thus eminently worth consideration. Whether Gould's writing is a sign that he regarded his career as a luxury item to be transcended, or whether his verbal energies concealed the deeper personal crisis of someone with nowhere really to go, as afraid of maturity as of commitment to the processes of life in human society, I cannot say. But beneath the tinkle of his often cheerful words there lurks something far less assured and satisfied than Gould's tone explicitly permits: of that one can be certain.

Perhaps the most interesting thing about Gould's writing is how it seems like an attempt to extend his ideas about musical performance into other realms. And clearly his writings remind one of Gould's music, not because they refer specifically to or summarize how he plays, but in the way they touch one with their restless energy and their remorseless articulation of meanings, neither stable nor fully attainable. There is much the same play of counterpoint here between words and performance that one also hears in Gould's recordings of Bach fugues. Their sheer vitality makes such experiences rare and precious as a result.

Another dimension is added by Gould's films, the most interesting and riveting of which show Gould performing pieces either contrapuntal (fugues and canons, mainly) or variational in nature. One hour-long program is devoted to fugue, and it comprises selections from Bach's *Well-Tempered Clavier,* the last movement of Beethoven's opus 110 sonata, and a stunningly fluent and demonic rendition of the last fugal movement of Hindemith's Third Sonata, a fine piece hardly ever played in concert today for reasons that have to do with the intellectual cowardice and low aesthetic standards of a majority of today's musicians, which Gould's career as a whole so strenuously impugns.

The variations program climaxes with performances of Webern's *Variations* and Beethoven's E major Sonata, opus 109. Gould links the two by a brilliant highlighting of the structural finesse and expressive detail that is so similar in both works. This is a considerable achievement since the pieces are written out of tonal idioms with diametrically opposed consequences, one (Beethoven's) exfoliative and elaborate, the other (Webern's) concentrated and crabbed. In addition, Gould delivers a severely restrained performance of a Sweelinck Organ Fantasy on the same program. I recall hearing it during a Gould recital in 1959 or 1960, struck at the time (and again in watching the film) by how Gould could apparently disappear as a performer into the work's long complications, thereby providing an instance of the *ecstasy* he characterized as the state of standing outside time and within an integral artistic structure.

Yet by far the most moving and affecting of all of Gould's films is Bruno Monsaingeon's 1981 rendition of Gould as he first speaks about, then plays through, the *Goldberg* Variations. Gould in this film is no longer the lean and youthfully eager intellectual who has the caustic wit to say (as he does in an earlier film) of Beethoven that he was always going to meet his destiny at the next modulation. He has now become a potbellied, bald, and somewhat mournful middle-aged aesthete whose jowly face and slightly decadent lips suggest secret vices and too many rich meals. Even his fingers, which have retained their fabulously efficient elegance and economy, are now evidently older, and more worldly. Indeed, Gould's performance of these thirty extraordinary pieces has acquired layers of sophistication and cleverness in added ornaments, in oddly varied and usually slower tempi, in surprising repetitions, in more sharply inflected lines (for example, the heavily strummed bass line in Variation One, or the underlinings of the theme in Bach's unison canon in the Third Variation, etc.).

This is one of the very few films I have seen of Gould that is in color and quite obviously the work of a film-maker, not simply of a TV cameraman. Its autumnal hues are made more startling by the realization that this was to be Gould's very last performance of, fittingly enough, the work that first brought him widespread attention: it is impossible not to imagine the film as an act of closure. I was told by Professor Geoffrey Payzant of the University of Toronto (a philosopher whose excellent book on Gould is the only work on the pianist even to begin to do him some justice)[22] that Monsaingeon had a cache of 52 hour-long films of Gould performances that he was trying unsuccessfully to sell to various TV companies in Europe and the United States. But, I think, Monsaingeon was right so singlemindedly to want to film Gould at work: the man was quite literally a full-scale cultural enterprise, endlessly at work on performance.

But the most interesting thing about Gould is, as Monsaingeon saw, that he constantly oversteps boundaries and bursts confining restraints, thereby, sometimes poignantly sometimes comically, *confirming* the performance space itself. In 1987 Monsaingeon himself published a book about Gould in France whose last section is a "video montage" of Gould being interviewed by five critics *after his death*:[23] Clearly Monsaingeon saw the man as someone for whom ordinary mortality was no limit at all. Gould certainly cultivated this notion in his audience. Not only was it clear that Gould could, and in fact did (with a few puzzling omissions, noted by Friedrich), command the entire range of Western music from the Renaissance until the present—there are instances in some of the films of Gould talking away about a series of musical examples and then turning to the piano, illustrating them from memory—he also could do with it what he liked, improvise, transpose, parody, reproduce, etc.

Most good musicians do in fact have at their fingertips, or lips, or hearts, much more music than they perform in public. Memory is part of the gift every performer carries within, so to speak. Yet we see performances only on the stage, *in* a program confined by the performance occasion itself. Thus Gould went to very great lengths after he left the concert stage in 1964 to communicate his diverse talents to an audience as he spilled out his knowledge, his articulate analyses, his prodigious technical facility into other forms and styles well beyond the two-hour concert experience. Everything that Gould did was in a continuum with the original place and time that he had afforded as a performer, the concert platform. And whenever he seemed to have settled into a niche, say, as a Bach pianist, he would up and record Wagner transcriptions, or the Grieg sonata, repertory that could not have been more unexpected, or he would become a writer, or a television personality.

Most important in all this, however, was Gould's talent for doing one thing brilliantly (playing the piano well, for example) and suggesting that he was doing something else too. Hence his predilection for contrapuntal or variational forms or, on a slightly different level, his habit of playing the piano *and* conducting *and* singing, or his way of being able to quote both musically and intellectually more or less any thing at any time. In a sense then Gould was gradually moving toward a kind of nontheatrical and anti-aesthetic *Gesamstkunstwerk,* a description that sounds antiformal and contradictory at the same time. I am not sure how aware he was of this, and how conscious he was of Rimbaud's *deracinement du sens,* but it strikes me as apt since the idea seems to me to approach the unsettling and yet attractively intelligent qualities in Gould's unusual enterprise, which was at once to make the performance more—because packed, bustling, overflowing—of an occasion, and more extreme, more odd, more unlike the lived reality of humankind, and still more unlike other concerts. By its radical force Gould's career in fine has supplied us with a largely but not completely new concept of what performance is all about, which like most things in musical elaboration—because it is still ideologically and commercially linked to the past and to present society—is neither a total disruption nor a total transformation of customary practice.

The distensions and peculiarities in what Gould did may in time come to seem totally innocuous, tamed or incorporated by the ongoing culture business, of which classical musical performance is only one component. An index of this diminishment to Gould's real activity is that he is known today almost exclusively either as a curiosity or as a very gifted pianist, just as Toscanini is known entirely as a great conductor about whose interpretations one may have opinions, but the social and aesthetic meanings of whose career are now generally screened from attention or study. The critical discourse of ongoing musical performance allows itself to report on concert life only in the manner of a scoresheet. But when we look from the rigid (and rigidly enforced) habits of concert life and journalism to the more extravagant excursions of performance art or rock music, only then can we assess the resourcefulness and imagination at work in performers like Toscanini or Gould who first accepted, then elaborated the logic of what contemporary classical music offered them, and did so with at least some measure of self-consciousness and spirit.

from *Musical Elaborations*

13

Jane Austen and Empire

(1990)

Almost without exception, reviewers of *Culture and Imperialism* focused on the chapter "Jane Austen and Empire." *The New York Times, The London Review of Books, The Nation,* and *Dissent* all published articles that emphasized Said's criticism of *Mansfield Park,* Jane Austen's novel about Fanny Price, who is raised by her aunt's family on a English country estate, financed by the slave labor of her uncle's sugar plantation in Antigua. In a full-page review by Michael Gorra, *The New York Times Book Review* asked, "Who Paid the Bills at Mansfield Park?" In *The Nation,* John Leonard wrote: "See Jane sit in the poise and order of Mansfield Park, not much bothering her pretty head about the fact that harmonious 'social space,' Sir Thomas Bertram's country estate, is sustained by slave labor."[1]

By drawing connections between Mansfield Park and the slave trade in Antigua, Said's criticism was often mistaken for an attempt to diminish the literary significance of Jane Austen. Yet Said's argument was far from an attack on Austen's literary value, a fact that confounded Irving Howe in his review of *Culture and Imperialism* in *Dissent.* Instead, Said's essay was, among other things, a response to Raymond Williams's influential reading of Jane Austen in *The Country and the City.*[2] While Williams overlooked the colonial foundations upon which the immaculately groomed country estates of Austen's novels rested, Said restored *Mansfield Park* to the geographical and his-

> torical situation of colonialism to which it refers yet which it conceals: "We should . . . regard the geographical division of the world—after all significant in *Mansfield Park*—as not neutral, but as politically charged, beseeching the attention and elucidation its considerable proportions require. The question is not only how to understand and with what to connect Austen's morality and its social basis, but what to *read* of it."

We are on solid ground with V. G. Kiernan when he says that "empires must have a mould of ideas or conditioned reflexes to flow into, and youthful nations dream of a great place in the world as young men dream of fame and fortunes."[3] It is too simple and reductive to argue that everything in European or American culture therefore prepares for or consolidates the grand idea of empire. It is also, however, historically inaccurate to ignore those tendencies—whether in narrative, political theory, or pictorial technique—that enabled, encouraged, and otherwise assured the West's readiness to assume and enjoy the experience of empire. If there was cultural resistance to the notion of an imperial mission, there was not much support for that resistance in the main departments of cultural thought. Liberal though he was, John Stuart Mill—as a telling case in point—could still say, "The sacred duties which civilized nations owe to the independence and nationality of each other, are not binding towards those to whom nationality and independence are certain evil, or at best a questionable good." Ideas like this were not original with Mill; they were already current in the English subjugation of Ireland during the sixteenth century and, as Nicholas Canny has persuasively demonstrated, were equally useful in the ideology of English colonization in the Americas.[4] Almost all colonial schemes begin with an assumption of native backwardness and general inadequacy to be independent, "equal," and fit.

Why that should be so, why sacred obligation on one front should not be binding on another, why rights accepted in one may be denied in another, are questions best understood in the terms of a culture well-grounded in moral, economic, and even metaphysical norms designed to approve a satisfying local, that is European, order and to permit the abrogation of the right to a similar order abroad. Such a statement may appear preposterous or extreme. In fact, it formulates the connection between Europe's well-being and cultural identity on the one hand and, on the other, the subjugation of imperial realms overseas rather too fastidiously and circumspectly. Part of our difficulty today in accepting any connection at all is that we tend to reduce this complicated matter to an apparently simple causal one, which in turn produces a rhetoric of blame and defensiveness. I am *not* saying that the major factor in early European culture was that it *caused* late-nineteenth-century imperialism, and I am not implying that all the problems of the formerly colonial world should be blamed on Europe. I am saying, however, that European culture often, if not always, characterized itself in such a way as simultaneously to validate its own preferences while also advocating those preferences in conjunction with distant imperial rule. Mill certainly did: he always recommended that India *not* be given independence. When for various reasons imperial rule concerned Europe more intensely after 1880, this schizophrenic habit became useful.

The first thing to be done now is more or less to jettison simple causality in thinking through the relationship between Europe and the non-European world, and lessening the hold on our thought of the equally simple temporal sequence. We must not admit any notion, for instance, that proposes to show that Wordsworth, Austen, or Coleridge, because they wrote *before* 1857, actually caused the establishment of formal British government rule over India *after* 1857. We should try to discern instead a counterpoint between overt patterns in British writing about Britain and representations of the world beyond the British Isles. The inherent mode for this counterpoint is not temporal but spatial. How do writers in the period before the great age of explicit, programmatic colonial expansion—the "scramble for Africa," say—situate and see themselves and their work in the larger world? We shall find them using striking but careful strategies, many of them derived from expected sources—positive ideas of home, of a nation and its language, of proper order, good behavior, moral values.

But positive ideas of this sort do more than validate "our" world. They also tend to devalue other worlds and, perhaps more significantly from a retrospective point of view, they do not prevent or inhibit or give resistance to horrendously unattractive imperialist practices. No, cultural forms like the novel or the opera do not cause people to go out and imperialize—Carlyle did not drive Rhodes directly, and he certainly cannot be "blamed" for the problems in today's southern Africa—but it is genuinely troubling to see how little Britain's great humanistic ideas, institutions, and monuments, which we still celebrate as having the power ahistorically to command our approval, how little they stand in the way of accelerating imperial process. We are entitled to ask how this body of humanistic ideas co-existed so comfortably with imperialism, and why—until the resistance to imperialism *in the imperial domain*, among Africans, Asians, Latin Americans, developed—there was little significant opposition or deterrence to empire at home. Perhaps the custom of distinguishing "our" home and order from "theirs" grew into a harsh political rule for accumulating more of "them" to rule, study, and subordinate. In the great, humane ideas and values promulgated by mainstream European culture, we have precisely that "mould of ideas or conditioned reflexes" of which Kiernan speaks, into which the whole business of empire later flowed.

The extent to which these ideas are actually invested in geographical distinctions between real places is the subject of Raymond Williams's richest book, *The Country and the City.* His argument concerning the interplay between rural and urban places in England admits of the most extraordinary transformations—from the pastoral populism of Langland, through Ben Jonson's country-house poems and the novels of Dickens's London, right up to visions of the metropolis in twentieth-century literature. Mainly, of course, the book is about how English culture has dealt with land, its possession, imagination, and organization. And while he does address the export of England to the colonies, Williams does so, as I suggested earlier, in a less focused way and less expansively than the practice actually warrants. Near the end of *The Country and the City* he volunteers that "from at least the mid-nineteenth century, and with important instances earlier, there was this larger context [the relationship between England and the colonies, whose effects on the English imagination "have gone deeper than can be easily traced"] within which every idea and every image was consciously and unconsciously affected." He goes on quickly to cite "the idea of emigration to the colonies" as one such image prevailing in various novels by Dickens, the Brontës, Gaskell, and rightly shows that "new rural societies," all of them colonial, enter the imaginative metropolitan economy of English literature via Kipling, early Orwell, Maugham. After 1880 there comes a "dramatic extension of landscape and social relations": this corresponds more or less exactly with the great age of empire.[5]

It is dangerous to disagree with Williams, yet I would venture to say that if one began to look for something like an imperial map of the world in English literature, it would turn up with amazing insistence and frequency well before the mid–nineteenth century. And turn up not only with the inert regularity suggesting something taken for granted, but—more interestingly—threaded through, forming a vital part of the texture of linguistic and cultural practice. There were established English offshore interests in Ireland, America, the Caribbean, and Asia from the sixteenth century on, and even a quick inventory reveals poets, philosophers, historians, dramatists, statesmen, novelists, travel writers, chroniclers, soldiers, and fabulists who prized, cared for, and traced these interests with continuing concern. (Much of this is well discussed by Peter Hulme in *Colonial Encounters.*)[6] Similar points may be made for France, Spain, and Portugal, not only as overseas powers in their own right, but as competitors with the British. How can we examine these interests at work in modern England before the age of empire, i.e., during the period between 1800 and 1870?

We would do well to follow Williams's lead, and look first at that period of crisis following upon England's wide-scale land enclosure at the end of the eighteenth century. The old organic rural communities were dissolved and new ones forged under the impulse of parliamentary activity, industrialization, and demographic dislocation, but there also occurred a new process of relocating England (and in France, France) within a much larger circle of the world map. During the first half of the eighteenth century, Anglo-French competition in North America and India was intense; in the second half there were numerous violent encounters between England and France in the Americas, the Caribbean, and the Levant, and of course in Europe itself. The major pre-Romantic literature in

France and England contains a constant stream of references to the overseas dominions: one thinks not only of various Encyclopedists, the Abbé Raynal, de Brosses, and Volney, but also of Edmund Burke, Beckford, Gibbon, Johnson, and William Jones.

In 1902 J. A. Hobson described imperialism as the expansion of nationality, implying that the process was understandable mainly by considering *expansion* as the more important of the two terms, since "nationality" was a fully formed, fixed quantity,[7] whereas a century before it was still in the process of *being formed*, at home and abroad as well. In *Physics and Politics* (1887) Walter Bagehot speaks with extraordinary relevance of "nation-making." Between France and Britain in the late eighteenth century there were two contests: the battle for strategic gains abroad—in India, the Nile delta, the Western Hemisphere—and the battle for a triumphant nationality. Both battles contrast "Englishness" with "the French," and no matter how intimate and closeted the supposed English or French "essence" appears to be, it was almost always thought of as being (as opposed to already) made, and being fought out with the other great competitor. Thackeray's Becky Sharp, for example, is as much an upstart as she is because of her half-French heritage. Earlier in the century, the upright abolitionist posture of Wilberforce and his allies developed partly out of a desire to make life harder for French hegemony in the Antilles.[8]

These considerations suddenly provide a fascinatingly expanded dimension to *Mansfield Park* (1814), the most explicit in its ideological and moral affirmations of Austen's novels. Williams once again is in general dead right: Austen's novels express an "attainable quality of life," in money and property acquired, moral discriminations made, the right choices put in place, the correct "improvements" implemented, the finely nuanced language affirmed and classified. Yet, Williams continues,

> What [Cobbett] names, riding past on the road, are classes. Jane Austen, from inside the houses, can never see that, for all the intricacy of her social description. All her discrimination is, understandably, internal and exclusive. She is concerned with the conduct of people who, in the complications of improvement, are repeatedly trying to make themselves into a class. But where only one class is seen, no classes are seen.[9]

As a general description of how Austen manages to elevate certain "moral discriminations" into "an independent value," this is excellent. Where *Mansfield Park* is concerned, however, a good deal more needs to be said, giving greater explicitness and width to Williams's survey. Perhaps then Austen, and indeed, pre-imperialist novels generally, will appear to be more implicated in the rationale for imperialist expansion than at first sight they have been.

After Lukács and Proust, we have become so accustomed to thinking of the novel's plot and structure as constituted mainly by temporality that we have overlooked the function of space, geography, and location. For it is not only the very young Stephen Dedalus, but every other young protagonist before him as well, who sees himself in a widening spiral at home, in Ireland, in the world. Like many other novels, *Mansfield Park* is very precisely about a series of both small and large dislocations and relocations in space that occur before, at the end of the novel, Fanny Price, the niece, becomes the spiritual mistress of Mansfield Park. And that place itself is located by Austen at the center of an arc of interests and concerns spanning the hemisphere, two major seas, and four continents.

As in Austen's other novels, the central group that finally emerges with marriage and properly "ordained" is not based exclusively upon blood. Her novel enacts the disaffiliation (in the literal sense) of some members of a family, and the affiliation between others and one or two chosen and tested outsiders: in other words, blood relationships are not enough to assure continuity, hierarchy, authority, both domestic and international. Thus Fanny Price—the poor niece, the orphaned child from the outlying city of Portsmouth, the neglected, demure, and upright wallflower—gradually acquires a status commensurate with, even superior to, that of most of her more fortunate relatives. In this pattern of affiliation and in her assumption of authority, Fanny Price is relatively passive. She resists the misdemeanors and the importunings of others, and very occasionally she ventures actions on her own: all in all, though, one has the impression that Austen has designs for her that Fanny herself can scarcely comprehend, just as throughout the novel Fanny is thought of by everyone as "comfort" and "acquisition" despite herself. Like Kipling's Kim O'Hara, Fanny is both device and instrument in a larger pattern, as well as a fully fledged novelistic character.

Fanny, like Kim, requires direction, requires the patronage and outside authority that her own impoverished experience cannot provide. Her conscious connections are to some people and to some places, but the novel reveals other connections of which she has faint glimmerings that nevertheless demand her presence and service. She comes into a situation that opens with an intricate set of moves which, taken together, demand sorting out, adjustment, and rearrangement. Sir Thomas Bertram has been captivated by one Ward sister, the others have not done well, and "an absolute breach" opens up; their "circles were so distinct," the distances between them so great that they have been out of touch for eleven years;[10] fallen on hard times, the Prices seek out the Bertrams. Gradually, and even though she is not the eldest, Fanny becomes the focus of attention as she is sent to Mansfield Park, there to begin her new life. Similarly, the Bertrams have given up London (the result of Lady Bertram's "little ill health and a great deal of indolence") and come to reside entirely in the country.

What sustains this life materially is the Bertram estate in Antigua, which is not doing well. Austen takes pains to show us two apparently disparate but actually convergent processes: the growth of Fanny's importance to the Bertram's economy, including Antigua, and Fanny's own steadfastness in the face of numerous challenges, threats, and surprises. In both, Austen's imagination works with a steel-like rigor through a mode that we might call geographical and spatial clarification. Fanny's ignorance when she arrives at Mansfield as a frightened ten-year-old is signified by her inability to "put the map of Europe together,"[11] and for much of the first half of the novel the action is concerned with a whole range of issues whose common denominator, misused or misunderstood, is space: not only is Sir Thomas in Antigua to make things better there and at home, but at Mansfield Park, Fanny, Edmund, and her aunt Norris negotiate where she is to live, read, and work, where fires are to be lit; the friends and cousins concern themselves with the improvement of estates, and the importance of chapels (i.e., religious authority) to domesticity is envisioned and debated. When, as a device for stirring things up, the Crawfords suggest a play (the tinge of France that hangs a little suspiciously over their background is significant), Fanny's discomfiture is polarizingly acute. She cannot participate, cannot easily accept that rooms for living are turned into theatrical space, although, with all its confusion of roles and purposes, the play, Kotzebue's *Lovers' Vows,* is prepared for anyway.

We are to surmise, I think, that while Sir Thomas is away tending his colonial garden, a number of inevitable mismeasurements (explicitly associated with feminine "lawlessness") will occur. These are apparent not only in innocent strolls by the three pairs of young friends through a park, in which people lose and catch sight of one another unexpectedly, but most clearly in the various flirtations and engagements between the young men and women left without true parental authority, Lady Bertram being indifferent, Mrs. Norris unsuitable. There is sparring, innuendo, perilous taking on of roles: all of this of course crystallizes in preparations for the play, in which something dangerously close to libertinage is about to be (but never is) enacted. Fanny, whose earlier sense of alienation, distance, and fear derives from her first uprooting, now becomes a sort of surrogate conscience about what is right and how far is too much. Yet she has no power to implement her uneasy awareness, and until Sir Thomas suddenly returns from "abroad," the rudderless drift continues.

When he does appear, preparations for the play are immediately stopped, and in a passage remarkable for its executive dispatch, Austen narrates the re-establishment of Sir Thomas's local rule:

> It was a busy morning with him. Conversation with any of them occupied but a small part of it. He had to reinstate himself in all the wonted concerns of his Mansfield life, to see his steward and his bailiff—to examine and compute—and, in the intervals of business, to walk into his stables and his gardens, and nearest plantations; but active and methodical, he had not only done all this before he resumed his seat as master of the house at dinner, he had also set the carpenter to work in pulling down what had been so lately put up in the billiard room, and given the scene painter his dismissal, long enough to justify the pleasing belief of his being then at least as far off as Northampton. The scene painter was gone, having spoilt only the floor of one room, ruined all the coachman's sponges, and made five of the under-servants idle and dissatisfied; and Sir Thomas was in hopes that another day or two would suffice to wipe away every

> outward momento of what had been, even to the destruction of every unbound copy of 'Lovers' Vows' in the house, for he was burning all that met his eye.[12]

The force of this paragraph is unmistakable. Not only is this a Crusoe setting things in order: it is also an early Protestant eliminating all traces of frivolous behavior. There is nothing in *Mansfield Park* that would contradict us, however, were we to assume that Sir Thomas does exactly the same things—on a larger scale—in his Antigua "plantations." Whatever was wrong there—and the internal evidence garnered by Warren Roberts suggests that economic depression, slavery, and competition with France were at issue[13]—Sir Thomas was able to fix, thereby maintaining his control over his colonial domain. More clearly than anywhere else in her fiction, Austen here synchronizes domestic with international authority, making it plain that the values associated with such higher things as ordination, law, and propriety must be grounded firmly in actual rule over and possession of territory. She sees clearly that to hold and rule Mansfield Park is to hold and rule an imperial estate in close, not to say inevitable association with it. What assures the domestic tranquillity and attractive harmony of one is the productivity and regulated discipline of the other.

Before both can be fully secured, however, Fanny must become more actively involved in the unfolding action. From frightened and often victimized poor relation she is gradually transformed into a directly participating member of the Bertram household at Mansfield Park. For this, I believe, Austen designed the second part of the book, which contains not only the failure of the Edmund–Mary Crawford romance as well as the disgraceful profligacy of Lydia and Henry Crawford, but Fanny Price's rediscovery and rejection of her Portsmouth home, the injury and incapacitation of Tom Bertram (the eldest son), and the launching of William Price's naval career. This entire ensemble of relationships and events is finally capped with Edmund's marriage to Fanny, whose place in Lady Bertram's household is taken by Susan Price, her sister. It is no exaggeration to interpret the concluding sections of *Mansfield Park* as the coronation of an arguably unnatural (or at very least, illogical) principle at the heart of a desired English order. The audacity of Austen's vision is disguised a little by her voice, which despite its occasional archness is understated and notably modest. But we should not misconstrue the limited references to the outside world, her lightly stressed allusions to work, process, and class, her apparent ability to abstract (in Raymond Williams's phrase) "an everyday uncompromising morality which is in the end separable from its social basis." In fact Austen is far less diffident, far more severe.

The clues are to be found in Fanny, or rather in how rigorously we are able to consider her. True, her visit to her original Portsmouth home, where her immediate family still resides, upsets the aesthetic and emotional balance she has become accustomed to at Mansfield Park, and true she has begun to take its wonderful luxuries for granted, even as being essential. These are fairly routine and natural consequences of getting used to a new place. But Austen is talking about two other matters we must not mistake. One is Fanny's newly enlarged sense of what it means to be *at home;* when she takes stock of things after she gets to Portsmouth, this is not merely a matter of expanded space.

> Fanny was almost stunned. The smallness of the house, and thinness of the walls, brought every thing so close to her, that, added to the fatigue of her journey, and all her recent agitation, she hardly knew how to bear it. *Within* the room all was tranquil enough, for Susan having disappeared with the others, there were soon only her father and herself remaining; and he taking out a newspaper—the accustomary loan of a neighbour, applied himself to studying it, without seeming to recollect her existence. The solitary candle was held between himself and the paper, without any reference to her possible convenience; but she had nothing to do, and was glad to have the light screened from her aching head, as she sat in bewildered, broken, sorrowful contemplation.
>
> She was at home. But alas! it was not such a home, she had not such a welcome, as—she checked herself; she was unreasonable. . . . A day or two might shew the difference. *She* only was to blame. Yet she thought it would not have been so at Mansfield. No, in her uncle's house there would have been a consideration of times and seasons, a regulation of subject, a propriety, an attention towards every body which there was not here.[14]

In too small a space, you cannot see clearly, you cannot think clearly, you cannot have regulation or attention of the proper sort. The fineness of Austen's detail ("the solitary candle was held between himself and the paper, without any reference to her possible convenience") renders very precisely the dangers of unsociability, of lonely insularity, of diminished awareness that are rectified in larger and better administered spaces.

That such spaces are not available to Fanny by direct inheritance, legal title, by propinquity, contiguity, or adjacence (Mansfield Park and Portsmouth are separated by many hours' journey) is precisely Austen's point. To earn the right to Mansfield Park you must first leave home as a kind of indentured servant or, to put the case in extreme terms, as a kind of transported commodity—this, clearly, is the fate of Fanny and her brother William—but then you have the promise of future wealth. I think Austen sees what Fanny does as a domestic or small-scale movement in space that corresponds to the larger, more openly colonial movements of Sir Thomas, her mentor, the man whose estate she inherits. The two movements depend on each other.

The second more complex matter about which Austen speaks, albeit indirectly, raises an interesting theoretical issue. Austen's awareness of empire is obviously very different, alluded to very much more casually, than Conrad's or Kipling's. In her time the British were extremely active in the Caribbean and in South America, notably Brazil and Argentina. Austen seems only vaguely aware of the details of these activities, although the sense that extensive West Indian plantations were important was fairly widespread in metropolitan England. Antigua and Sir Thomas's trip there have a definitive function in *Mansfield Park,* which, I have been saying, is both incidental, referred to only in passing, and absolutely crucial to the action. How are we to assess Austen's few references to Antigua, and what are we to make of them interpretatively?

My contention is that by that very odd combination of casualness and stress, Austen reveals herself to be *assuming* (just as Fanny assumes, in both senses of the word) the importance of an empire to the situation at home. Let me go further. Since Austen refers to and uses Antigua as she does in *Mansfield Park,* there needs to be a commensurate effort on the part of her readers to understand concretely the historical valences in the reference; to put it differently, we should try to understand *what* she referred to, why she gave it the importance she did, and why indeed she made the choice, for she might have done something different to establish Sir Thomas's wealth. Let us now calibrate the signifying power of the references to Antigua in *Mansfield Park;* how do they occupy the place they do, what are they doing there?

According to Austen we are to conclude that no matter how isolated and insulated the English place (e.g., Mansfield Park), it requires overseas sustenance. Sir Thomas's property in the Caribbean would have had to be a sugar plantation maintained by slave labor (not abolished until the 1830s): these are not dead historical facts but, as Austen certainly knew, evident historical realities. Before the Anglo-French competition the major distinguishing characteristic of Western empires (Roman, Spanish, and Portuguese) was that the earlier empires were bent on loot, as Conrad puts it, on the transport of treasure from the colonies to Europe, with very little attention to development, organization, or system within the colonies themselves; Britain and, to a lesser degree, France both wanted to make their empires long-term, profitable, ongoing concerns, and they competed in this enterprise, nowhere more so than in the colonies of the Caribbean, where the transport of slaves, the functioning of large sugar plantations, and the development of sugar markets, which raised the issues of protectionism, monopolies, and price—all these were more or less constantly, competitively at issue.

Far from being nothing much "out there," British colonial possessions in the Antilles and Leeward Islands were during Jane Austen's time a crucial setting for Anglo-French colonial competition. Revolutionary ideas from France were being exported there, and there was a steady decline in British profits: the French sugar plantations were producing more sugar at less cost. However, slave rebellions in and out of Haiti were incapacitating France and spurring British interests to intervene more directly and to gain greater local power. Still, compared with its earlier prominence for the home market, British Caribbean sugar production in the nineteenth century had to compete with alternative sugar-cane supplies in Brazil and Mauritius, the emergence of a European beet-sugar industry, and the gradual dominance of free-trade ideology and practice.

In *Mansfield Park*—both in its formal characteristics and in its contents—a number of these currents converge. The most important is the avowedly complete subordination of colony to metropolis. Sir Thomas, absent from Mansfield Park, is never seen as *present* in Antigua, which elicits at most a half dozen references in the novel. There is a passage, a part of which I quoted earlier, from John Stuart Mill's *Principles of Political Economy* that catches the spirit of Austen's use of Antigua. I quote it here in full:

> These [outlying possessions of ours] are hardly to be looked upon as countries, carrying on an exchange of commodities with other countries, but more properly as outlying agricultural or manufacturing estates belonging to a larger community. Our West Indian colonies, for example, cannot be regarded as countries with a productive capital of their own . . . [but are rather] the place where England finds it convenient to carry on the production of sugar, coffee and a few other tropical commodities. All the capital employed is English capital; almost all the industry is carried on for English uses; there is little production of anything except for staple commodities, and these are sent to England, not to be exchanged for things exported to the colony and consumed by its inhabitants, but to be sold in England for the benefit of the proprietors there. The trade with the West Indies is hardly to be considered an external trade, but more resembles the traffic between town and country.[15]

To some extent Antigua is like London or Portsmouth, a less desirable setting than a country estate like Mansfield Park, but producing goods to be consumed by everyone (by the early nineteenth century every Britisher used sugar), although owned and maintained by a small group of aristocrats and gentry. The Bertrams and the other characters in *Mansfield Park* are a subgroup within the minority, and for them the island is wealth, which Austen regards as being converted to propriety, order, and, at the end of the novel, comfort, an added good. But why "added"? Because, Austen tells us pointedly in the final chapters, she wants to "restore every body, not greatly in fault themselves, to tolerable comfort, and to have done with all the rest."[16]

This can be interpreted to mean first that the novel has done enough in the way of destabilizing the lives of "every body" and must now set them at rest: actually Austen says this explicitly, in a bit of meta-fictional impatience, the novelist commenting on her own work as having gone on long enough and now needing to be brought to a close. Second, it can mean that "every body" may now be finally permitted to realize what it means to be properly at home, and at rest, without the need to wander about or to come and go. (This does not include young William, who, we assume, will continue to roam the seas in the British navy on whatever commercial and political missions may still be required. Such matters draw from Austen only a last brief gesture, a passing remark about William's "continuing good conduct and rising fame.") As for those finally resident in Mansfield Park itself, more in the way of domesticated advantages is given to these now fully acclimatized souls, and to none more than to Sir Thomas. He understands for the first time what has been missing in his education of his children, and he understands it in the terms paradoxically provided for him by unnamed outside forces, so to speak, the wealth of Antigua and the imported example of Fanny Price. Note here how the curious alternation of outside and inside follows the pattern identified by Mill of the outside *becoming* the inside by use and, to use Austen's word, "disposition":

> Here [in his deficiency of training, of allowing Mrs. Norris too great a role, of letting his children dissemble and repress feeling] had been grievous mismanagement; but, bad as it was, he gradually grew to feel that it had not been the most direful mistake in his plan of education. Some thing must have been wanting *within*, or time would have worn away much of its ill effect. He feared that principle, active principle, had been wanting, that they had never been properly taught to govern their inclinations and tempers, by that sense of duty which can alone suffice. They had been instructed theoretically in their religion, but never required to bring it into daily practice. To be distinguished for elegance and accomplishments—the authorized object of their youth—could have had no useful influence that way, no moral effect on the mind. He had meant them to be good, but his cares had been directed to the understanding and manners, not the disposition; and of the necessity of self-denial and humility, he feared they had never heard from any lips that could profit them.[17]

What was wanting *within* was in fact supplied by the wealth derived from a West Indian plantation and a poor provincial relative, both brought in to Mansfield Park and set to work. Yet on their own, neither the one nor the other could have sufficed; they require each other and then, more important, they need executive disposition, which in turn helps to reform the rest of the Bertram circle. All this Austen leaves to her reader to supply in the way of literal explication.

And that is what reading her entails. But all these things having to do with the outside brought in seem unmistakably *there* in the suggestiveness of her allusive and abstract language. A principle "wanting *within*" is, I believe, intended to evoke for us memories of Sir Thomas's absences in Antigua, or the sentimental and near-whimsical vagary on the part of the three variously deficient Ward sisters by which a niece is displaced from one household to another. But that the Bertrams did become better if not altogether good, that some sense of duty was imparted to them, that they learned to govern their inclinations and tempers and brought religion into daily practice, that they "directed disposition": all of this did occur because outside (or rather outlying) factors were lodged properly inward, became native to Mansfield Park, with Fanny the niece its final spiritual mistress, and Edmund the second son its spiritual master.

An additional benefit is that Mrs. Norris is dislodged; this is described as "the great supplementary comfort of Sir Thomas's life."[18] Once the principles have been interiorized, the comforts follow: Fanny is settled for the time being at Thornton Lacey "with every attention to her comfort"; her home later becomes "the home of affection and comfort"; Susan is brought in "first as a comfort to Fanny, then as an auxiliary, and at last as her substitute"[19] when the new import takes Fanny's place by Lady Bertram's side. The pattern established at the outset of the novel clearly continues, only now it has what Austen intended to give it all along, an internalized and retrospectively guaranteed rationale. This is the rationale that Raymond Williams describes as "an everyday, uncompromising morality which is in the end separable from its social basis and which, in other hands, can be turned against it."

I have tried to show that the morality in fact is not separable from its social basis: right up to the last sentence, Austen affirms and repeats the geographical process of expansion involving trade, production, and consumption that predates, underlies, and guarantees the morality. And expansion, as Gallagher reminds us, whether "through colonial rule was liked or disliked, [its] desirability through one mode or another was generally accepted. So in the event there were few domestic constraints upon expansion."[20] Most critics have tended to forget or overlook that process, which has seemed less important to critics than Austen herself seemed to think. But interpreting Jane Austen depends on *who* does the interpreting, *when* it is done, and no less important, from *where* it is done. If with feminists, with great cultural critics sensitive to history and class like Williams, with cultural and stylistic interpreters, we have been sensitized to the issues their interests raise, we should now proceed to regard the geographical division of the world—after all significant to *Mansfield Park*—as not neutral (any more than class and gender are neutral) but as politically charged, beseeching the attention and elucidation its considerable proportions require. The question is thus not only how to understand and with what to connect Austen's morality and its social basis, but also *what* to read of it.

Take once again the casual references to Antigua, the ease with which Sir Thomas's needs in England are met by a Caribbean sojourn, the uninflected, unreflective citations of Antigua (or the Mediterranean, or India, which is where Lady Bertram, in a fit of distracted impatience, requires that William should go "'that I may have a shawl. I think I will have two shawls.'")[21] They stand for a significance "out there" that frames the genuinely important action *here*, but not for a great significance. Yet these signs of "abroad" include, even as they repress, a rich and complex history, which has since achieved a status that the Bertrams, the Prices, and Austen herself would not, could not recognize. To call this "the Third World" begins to deal with the realities but by no means exhausts the political or cultural history.

We must first take stock of *Mansfield Park*'s prefigurations of a later English history as registered in fiction. The Bertrams' usable colony in *Mansfield Park* can be read as pointing forward to Charles Gould's San Tomé mine in *Nostromo*, or to the Wilcoxes' Imperial and West African Rubber Company in Forster's *Howards End*, or to any of these distant but convenient treasure spots in *Great Expectations*, Jean Rhys's *Wide Sargasso Sea*, *Heart of Darkness*—resources to be visited, talked about, described, or appreciated for domestic reasons, for local metropolitan benefit. If we think ahead to these other novels, Sir Thomas's Antigua readily acquires a slightly greater density than the discrete, reticent appearances it makes in the pages of *Mansfield Park.* And already our reading of the novel begins to open up at those points where ironically Austen was most economical and her critics most (dare one say it?) negligent. Her "Antigua" is therefore not just a slight but a definite way of marking the outer limits of what Williams calls domestic improvements, or a quick allusion to the mercantile venturesomeness of acquiring overseas dominions as a source for local fortunes, or one reference among many attesting to a historical sensibility suffused not just with manners and courtesies but with contests of ideas, struggles with Napoleonic France, awareness of seismic economic and social change during a revolutionary period in world history.

Second, we must see "Antigua" held in a precise place in Austen's moral geography, and in her prose, by historical changes that her novel rides like a vessel on a mighty sea. The Bertrams could not have been possible without the slave trade, sugar, and the colonial planter class; as a social type Sir Thomas would have been familiar to eighteenth- and nineteenth-century readers who knew the powerful influence of the class through politics, plays (like Cumberland's *The West Indian*), and many other public activities (large houses, famous parties and social rituals, well-known commercial enterprises, celebrated marriages). As the old system of protected monopoly gradually disappeared and as a new class of settler-planters displaced the old absentee system, the West Indian interest lost dominance: cotton manufacture, an even more open system of trade, and abolition of slave trade reduced the power and prestige of people like the Bertrams, whose frequency of sojourn in the Caribbean then decreased.

Thus Sir Thomas's infrequent trips to Antigua as an absentee plantation owner reflect the diminishment in his class's power, a reduction directly expressed in the title of Lowell Ragatz's classic *The Fall of the Planter Class in the British Caribbean, 1763–1833* (1928). But is what is hidden or allusive in Austen made sufficiently explicit more than one hundred years later in Ragatz? Does the aesthetic silence or discretion of a great novel in 1814 receive adequate explication in a major work of historical research a full century later? Can we assume that the process of interpretation is fulfilled, or will it continue as new material comes to light?

For all his learning Ragatz still finds it in himself to speak of "the Negro race" as having the following characteristics: "he stole, he lied, he was simple, suspicious, inefficient, irresponsible, lazy, superstitious, and loose in his sexual relations."[22] Such "history" as this therefore happily gave way to the revisionary work of Caribbean historians like Eric Williams and C. L. R. James, and more recently Robin Blackburn, in *The Overthrow of Colonial Slavery, 1776–1848;* in these works slavery and empire are shown to have fostered the rise and consolidation of capitalism well beyond the old plantation monopolies, as well as to have been a powerful ideological system whose original connection to specific economic interests may have gone, but whose effects continued for decades.

> The political and moral ideas of the age are to be examined in the very closest relation to the economic development. . . .
>
> An outworn interest, whose bankruptcy smells to heaven in historical perspective, can exercise an obstructionist and disruptive effect which can only be explained by the powerful services it had previously rendered and the entrenchment previously gained. . . .
>
> The ideas built on these interests continue long after the interests have been destroyed and work their old mischief, which is all the more mischievous because the interests to which they correspond no longer exist.[23]

Thus [wrote] Eric Williams in *Capitalism and Slavery* (1961). The question of interpretation, indeed of writing itself, is tied to the question of interests, which we have seen are at work in aesthetic as well as historical writing, then and now. We must not say that since *Mansfield Park* is a novel, its affiliations with a sordid history are irrelevant or transcended, not only because it is irresponsible to do so, but because we know too much to say so in good faith. Having read *Mansfield Park* as part of the structure of an expanding imperialist venture, one cannot simply restore it to the canon of "great literary masterpieces"—to which it most certainly belongs—and leave it at that. Rather, I think, the novel steadily, if unobtrusively, opens up a broad expanse of domestic imperialist culture without which

Britain's subsequent acquisition of territory would not have been possible.

I have spent time on *Mansfield Park* to illustrate a type of analysis infrequently encountered in mainstream interpretations, or for that matter in readings rigorously based in one or another of the advanced theoretical schools. Yet only in the global perspective implied by Jane Austen and her characters can the novel's quite astonishing general position be made clear. I think of such a reading as completing or complementing others, not discounting or displacing them. And it bears stressing that because *Mansfield Park* connects the actualities of British power overseas to the domestic imbroglio within the Bertram estate, there is no way of doing such readings as mine, no way of understanding the "structure of attitude and reference" except by working through the novel. Without reading it in full, we would fail to understand the strength of that structure and the way it was activated and maintained in literature. But in reading it carefully, we can sense how ideas about dependent races and territories were held both by foreign-office executives, colonial bureaucrats, and military strategists and by intelligent novel-readers educating themselves in the fine points of moral evaluation, literary balance, and stylistic finish.

There is a paradox here in reading Jane Austen which I have been impressed by but can in no way resolve. All the evidence says that even the most routine aspects of holding slaves on a West Indian sugar plantation were cruel stuff. And everything we know about Austen and her values is at odds with the cruelty of slavery. Fanny Price reminds her cousin that after asking Sir Thomas about the slave trade, "There was such a dead silence"[24] as to suggest that one world could not be connected with the other since there simply is no common language for both. That is true. But what stimulates the extraordinary discrepancy into life is the rise, decline, and fall of the British empire itself and, in its aftermath, the emergence of a post-colonial consciousness. In order more accurately to read works like *Mansfield Park,* we have to see them in the main as resisting or avoiding that other setting, which their formal inclusiveness, historical honesty, and prophetic suggestiveness cannot completely hide. In time there would no longer be a dead silence when slavery was spoken of, and the subject became central to a new understanding of what Europe was.

It would be silly to expect Jane Austen to treat slavery with anything like the passion of an abolitionist or a newly liberated slave. Yet what I have called the rhetoric of blame, so often now employed by subaltern, minority, or disadvantaged voices, attacks her, and others like her, retrospectively, for being white, privileged, insensitive, complicit. Yes, Austen belonged to a slave-owning society, but do we therefore jettison her novels as so many trivial exercises in aesthetic frumpery? Not at all, I would argue, if we take seriously our intellectual and interpretative vocation to make connections, to deal with as much of the evidence as possible, fully and actually, to read what is there or not there, above all, to see complementarity and interdependence instead of isolated, venerated, or formalized experience that excludes and forbids the hybridizing intrusions of human history.

Mansfield Park is a rich work in that its aesthetic intellectual complexity requires that longer and slower analysis that is also required by its geographical problematic, a novel based in an England relying for the maintenance of its style on a Caribbean island. When Sir Thomas goes to and comes from Antigua, where he has property, that is not at all the same thing as coming to and going from Mansfield Park, where his presence, arrivals, and departures have very considerable consequences. But precisely because Austen is so summary in one context, so provocatively rich in the other, precisely because of that imbalance we are able to move in on the novel, reveal and accentuate the interdependence scarcely mentioned on its brilliant pages. A lesser work wears its historical affiliation more plainly; its worldliness is simple and direct, the way a jingoistic ditty during the Mahdist uprising or the 1857 Indian Rebellion connects directly to the situation and constituency that coined it. *Mansfield Park* encodes experiences and does not simply repeat them. From our later perspective we can interpret Sir Thomas's power to come and go in Antigua as stemming from the muted national experience of individual identity, behavior, and "ordination," enacted with such irony and taste at Mansfield Park. The task is to lose neither a true historical sense of the first, nor a full enjoyment or appreciation of the second, all the while seeing both together.

from *Culture and Imperialism*

14

Intellectual Exile: Expatriates and Marginals

(1993)

In June 1993, Edward Said delivered the highly esteemed Reith Lectures on BBC radio. (The essays were later collected and published as a book.) Inaugurated by Bertrand Russell in 1948, the Reith Lectures are an important event of intellectual life in Britain and have been given by such luminaries as John Kenneth Galbraith, J. Robert Oppenheimer, and Arnold Toynbee. Under Said's direction, the lectures centered on the representations of the intellectual, a topic meant to have dual meaning: what the intellectual represents to a culture as well as how the intellectual is represented by a culture.

From the moment he was invited, opposition was raised to giving Said this honor, all of it coming from those who accuse Said of being a fanatic and a demagogue due to his Palestinian credentials. It is with some irony, then, that these lectures oppose exactly this type of narrow-minded thinking. In them, Said argues that the role of the intellectual is to raise awkward questions, reject orthodoxies of opinion, and to be "on the same side as the weak and the underrepresented." Drawing on a wide array of sources—literary, academic, political—Said explains that the true "intellectual" becomes accustomed to being "embarrassing, contrary, even unpleasant" to the powers that be.

The third of six essays delivered as the 1993 Reith Lectures on the BBC in England, "Intellectual Exile:

Expatriates and Marginals" is Said's meditation on the relationship between the life of the mind and the modern condition of exile. (It was also published in *Grand Street* and later in *Representations of the Intellectual*.) By examining the life and writings of the German philosopher T. W. Adorno and others, Said investigates the ways in which exile can be viewed as both an actual condition of banishment and a metaphorical condition of living outside of the privileges, honors, seductions, and powers of a given culture. In this sense, the intellectual as exile, like the actual exile, learns to see the world through a "double perspective." In other words, "an idea or experience is always counterposed with another, therefore making them both appear in a sometimes new and unpredictable light." This essay extends key concepts from "Secular Criticism" and "Traveling Theory" insofar as the spirit of an undomesticated critical consciousness is propagated, one that is wary of being tamed or put on loan to those who would buy it or appropriate it. "To be marginal and as undomesticated as someone who is in real exile," Said writes, "is for an intellectual to be unusually responsive to the traveler rather than to the potentate, to the provisional and risky rather than to the habitual, to innovation and experiment rather than the authoritatively given *status quo*."

Exile is one of the saddest fates. In premodern times banishment was a particularly dreadful punishment since it not only meant years of aimless wandering away from family and familiar places, but also meant being a sort of permanent outcast, someone who never felt at home, and was always at odds with the environment, inconsolable about the past, bitter about the present and the future. There has always been an association between the idea of exile and the terrors of being a leper, a social and moral untouchable. During the twentieth century, exile has been transformed from the exquisite, and sometimes exclusive, punishment of special individuals—like the great Latin poet Ovid, who was banished from Rome to a remote town on the Black Sea—into a cruel punishment of whole communities and peoples, often the inadvertent result of impersonal forces such as war, famine, and disease.

In this category are the Armenians, a gifted but frequently displaced people who lived in large numbers throughout the eastern Mediterranean (Anatolia especially) but who after genocidal attacks on them by the Turks flooded nearby Beirut, Aleppo, Jerusalem, and Cairo, only to be dislocated again during the revolutionary upheavals of the post–World War II period. I have long been deeply drawn to those large expatriate or exile communities who peopled the landscape of my youth in Palestine and Egypt. There were many Armenians of course, but also Jews, Italians, and Greeks who, once settled in the Levant, had grown productive roots there—these communities after all produced prominent writers like Edmond Jabes, Giuseppe Ungaretti, Constantine Cavafy—that were to be brutally torn up after the establishment of Israel in 1948 and after the Suez war of 1956. To new nationalist governments in Egypt and Iraq and elsewhere in the Arab world, foreigners who symbolized the new aggression of European postwar imperialism were forced to leave, and for many old communities this was a particularly nasty fate. Some of these were acclimatized to new places of residence, but many were, in a manner of speaking, re-exiled.

There is a popular but wholly mistaken assumption that being exiled is to be totally cut off, isolated, hopelessly separated from your place of origin. Would that surgically clean separation were true, because then at least you could have the consolation of knowing that what you have left behind is, in a sense, unthinkable and completely irrecoverable. The fact is that for most exiles the difficulty consists not simply in being forced to live away from home, but rather, given today's world, in living with the many reminders that you are in exile, that your home is not in fact so far away, and that the normal traffic of everyday contemporary life keeps you in constant but tantalizing and unfulfilled touch with the old place. The exile therefore exists in a median state, neither completely at one with the new setting nor fully disencumbered of the old, beset with half-involvements and half-detachments, nostalgic and sentimental on one level, an adept mimic or a secret outcast on another. Being skilled at survival becomes the main imperative, with the danger of getting too comfortable and secure constituting a threat that is constantly to be guarded against.

Salim, the main character of V. S. Naipaul's novel *A Bend in the River,* is an affecting instance of the modern intellectual in exile: an East African Muslim of Indian origin, he has left the coast and journeyed towards the African interior, where he has survived precariously in a new state modeled on Mobuto's Zaire. Naipaul's extraordinary antennae as a novelist enable him to portray Salim's life at a "bend in the river" as a sort of no-man's-land, to which come the European intellectual advisers (who succeed the idealistic missionaries of colonial times), as well as the mercenaries, profiteers, and other Third World flotsam and jetsam in whose ambiance Salim is forced to live, gradually losing his property and his integrity in the mounting confusion. By the end of the novel—and this of course is Naipaul's debatable ideological point—even the natives have become exiles in their own country, so preposterous and erratic are the whims of the ruler, Big Man, who is intended by Naipaul to be a symbol of all postcolonial regimes.

The widespread territorial rearrangements of the post–World War II period produced huge demographic movements, for example, the Indian Muslims who moved to Pakistan after the 1947 partition, or the Palestinians who were largely dispersed during Israel's establishment to accommodate incoming European and Asian Jews; and these transformations in turn gave rise to hybrid political forms. In Israel's political life there has been not only a politics of the Jewish diaspora but also an intertwining and competing politics of the Palestinian people in exile. In the newly founded countries of Pakistan and Israel the recent immigrants were seen as part of an exchange of populations, but politically they were also regarded as formerly oppressed minorities enabled to live in their new states as members of the majority. Yet far from settling sectarian issues, partition and the separatist ideology of new statehood have rekindled and often inflamed them. My concern here is more with the largely unaccommodated exiles, like Palestinians or the new Muslim immigrants in continental Europe, or the West Indian and African blacks in England, whose presence complicates the presumed homogeneity of the new societies in which they live. The intellectual who considers him- or herself to be a part of a more general condition affecting the displaced national community is therefore likely to be a source not of acculturation and adjustment, but rather of volatility and instability.

This is by no means to say that exile doesn't also produce marvels of adjustment. The United States today is in the unusual position of having two extremely high former officers in recent presidential administrations—Henry Kissinger and Zbigniew Brzezinski—who were (or still are, depending on the observer's outlook) intellectuals in exile, Kissinger from Nazi Germany, Brzezinski from Communist Poland. In addition Kissinger is Jewish, which puts him in the extraordinarily odd position of also qualifying for potential immigration to Israel, according to its Basic Law of Return. Yet both Kissinger and Brzezinski seem on the surface at least to have contributed their talents entirely to their adopted country, with results in eminence, material rewards, national, not to say worldwide, influence that are light-years away from the marginal obscurity in which Third World exile intellectuals live in Europe or the United States. Today, having served in government for several decades, the two prominent intellectuals are now consultants to corporations and other governments.

Brzezinski and Kissinger are not perhaps as socially exceptional as one would assume if it is recalled that the European theater of World War II was considered by other exiles—like Thomas Mann—as a battle for Western destiny, the Western soul. In this "good war" the United States played the role of savior, also providing refuge for a whole generation of scholars, artists and scientists who had fled Western fascism for the metropolis of the new Western *imperium.* In scholarly fields like the humanities and social sciences a large group of extremely distinguished scholars came to America. Some of them, like the great Romance philologists and scholars of comparative literature Leo Spitzer and Erich Auerbach, enriched American universities with their talents and Old World experience. Others, among them scientists like Edward Teller and Werner von Braun, entered the Cold War lists as new Americans dedicated to winning the arms and space race over the Soviet Union. So all-engrossing was this concern after the war that, as has recently been revealed, well-placed American intellectuals in the social sciences managed to recruit former Nazis known for their anti-Communist credentials to work in the United States as part of the great crusade.

Along with the rather shady art of political trimming, a technique of not taking a clear position but surviving handsomely nonetheless, how and intellectual works out an accommodation with a new or emerging dominant power is a topic I shall deal with in my next two lectures in [*Representations of the Intellectual.*] Here I want to focus on its opposite, the intellectual who because of exile cannot, or, more to the point, will not make the adjustment, preferring instead to remain outside the mainstream, unaccommodated, uncoopted, resistant: but first I need to make some preliminary points.

One is that while it is an *actual* condition, exile is also for my purposes a *metaphorical* condition. By that I mean that my diagnosis of the intellectual in exile derives from the social and political history of dislocation and migration with which I began this lecture, but is not limited to it. Even intellectuals who are lifelong members of a society can, in a manner of speaking, be divided into insiders and outsiders: those on the one hand who belong fully to the society as it is, who flourish in it without an overwhelming sense of dissonance or dissent, those who can be called yea-sayers; and on the other hand, the nay-sayers, the individuals at odds with their society and therefore outsiders and exiles so far as privileges, power, and honors are concerned. The pattern that sets the course for the intellectual as outsider is best exemplified by the condition of exile, the state of never being fully adjusted, always feeling outside the chatty, familiar world inhabited by natives, so to speak, tending to avoid and even dislike the trappings of accommodation and national well-being. Exile for the intellectual in this metaphysical sense is restlessness, movement, constantly being unsettled, and unsettling others. You cannot go back to some earlier and perhaps more stable condition of being at home; and, alas, you can never fully arrive, be at one with your new home or situation.

Secondly—and I find myself somewhat surprised by this observation even as I make it—the intellectual as exile tends to be happy with the idea of unhappiness, so that dissatisfaction bordering on dyspepsia, a kind of curmudgeonly disagreeableness, can become not only a style of thought, but also a new, if temporary, habitation.

The intellectual as ranting Thersites perhaps. A great historical prototype for what I have in mind is a powerful eighteenth-century figure, Jonathan Swift, who never got over his fall from influence and prestige in England after the Tories left office in 1714, and spent the rest of his life as an exile in Ireland. An almost legendary figure of bitterness and anger—*saeve indignatio* he said of himself in his own epitaph—Swift was furious at Ireland, and yet its defender against British tyranny, a man whose towering Irish works *Gulliver's Travels* and *The Drapier's Letters* show a mind flourishing, not to say benefiting, from such productive anguish.

To some degree the early V. S. Naipaul, the essayist and travel writer, resident off and on in England, yet always on the move, revisiting his Caribbean and Indian roots, sifting through the debris of colonialism and postcolonialism, remorselessly judging the illusions and cruelties of independent states and the new true believers, was a figure of modern intellectual exile.

Even more rigorous, more determinedly the exile than Naipaul, is Theodor Wiesengrund Adorno. He was a forbidding but endlessly fascinating man, and for me, the dominating intellectual conscience of the middle twentieth century, whose entire career skirted and fought the dangers of fascism, communism, and Western mass-consumerism. Unlike Naipaul, who has wandered in and out of former homes in the Third World, Adorno was completely European, a man entirely made up of the highest of high cultures that included astonishing professional competence in philosophy, music (he was a student and admirer of Berg and Schoenberg), sociology, literature, history, and cultural analysis. Of partially Jewish background, he left his native Germany in the mid-1930s shortly after the Nazi seizure of power: he went first to read philosophy at Oxford, which is where he wrote an extremely difficult book on Husserl. He seems to have been miserable there, surrounded as he was by ordinary language and positivist philosophers, he with his Spenglerian gloom and metaphysical dialectics in the best Hegelian manner. He returned to Germany for a while but, as a member of the University of Frankfurt Institute of Social Research, reluctantly decamped for the safety of the United States, where he lived for a time first in New York (1938–41) and then in southern California.

Although Adorno returned to Frankfurt in 1949 to take up his old professorship there, his years in America stamped him with the marks of exile forever. He detested jazz and everything about popular culture; he had no affection for the landscape at all; he seems to have remained studiously mandarin in his ways; and therefore, because he was brought up in a Marxist-Hegelian philosophical tradition, everything about the worldwide influence of American films, industry, habits of daily life, fact-based learning, and pragmatism raised his hackles. Naturally Adorno was very predisposed to being a metaphysical exile before he came to the United States: he was already extremely critical of what passed for bourgeois taste in Europe, and his standards of what, for instance, music ought to have been were set by the extraordinarily difficult works of Schoenberg, works which Adorno averred were honorably destined to remain unheard and impossible to listen to. Paradoxical, ironic, mercilessly critical: Adorno was the quintessential intellectual, hating *all* systems, whether on our side or theirs, with equal distaste. For him life was at its most false in the aggregate—the whole is always the untrue, he once said—and this, he continued, placed an even greater premium on subjectivity, on the individual's consciousness, on what could not be regimented in the totally administered society.

But it was his American exile that produced Adorno's great masterpiece, the *Minima Moralia,* a set of 153 fragments published in 1953, and subtitled "Reflections from Damaged Life." In the episodic and mystifying eccentric form of this book, which is neither sequential autobiography nor thematic musing nor even a systematic exposé of its author's worldview, we are reminded once again of the peculiarities of Bazarov's life as represented in Turgenev's novel of Russian life in the mid-1860s, *Fathers and Sons.* The prototype of the modern nihilistic intellectual, Bazarov is given no narrative context by Turgenev; he appears briefly, then he disappears. We see him briefly with his aged parents, but it is very clear that he has deliberately cut himself off from them. We deduce from this that by virtue of living a life according to different norms, the intellectual does not have a story, but only a sort of destabilizing effect; he sets off seismic shocks, he jolts people, but he can neither be explained away by his background nor his friends.

Turgenev himself actually says nothing of this at all: he lets it happen before our eyes, as if to say that the intellectual is not only a being set apart from parents and children, but that his modes of life, his procedures of engaging with it are necessarily allusive, and can only be represented realistically as a series of discontinuous performances. Adorno's *Minima Moralia* seems to follow the same logic, although after Auschwitz, Hiroshima, the onset of the Cold War, and the triumph of America, representing the intellectual honestly is a much more tortuous thing than doing what Turgenev had done for Bazarov a hundred years earlier.

The core of Adorno's representation of the intellectual as a permanent exile, dodging both the old and the new with equal dexterity, is a writing style that is mannered and worked over in the extreme. It is fragmentary first of all, jerky, discontinuous; there is no plot or predetermined order to follow. It represents the intellectual's consciousness as unable to be at rest anywhere, constantly on guard against the blandishments of success, which, for the perversely inclined Adorno, means trying consciously *not* to be understood easily and immediately. Nor is it possible to retreat into complete privacy, since as Adorno says much later in his career, the hope of the intellectual is not that he will have an effect on the world, but that someday, somewhere, someone will read what he wrote exactly as he wrote it.

One fragment, number 18 in *Minima Moralia,* captures the significance of exile quite perfectly. "Dwelling, in the proper sense," says Adorno, "is now impossible. The traditional residences we have grown up in have grown intolerable: each trait of comfort in them is paid for with a betrayal of knowledge, each vestige of shelter with the musty pact of family interests." So much for the prewar life of people who grew up before Nazism. Socialism and American consumerism are no better: there "people live if not in slums, in bungalows that by tomorrow may be leaf-huts, trailers, cars, camps, or the open air." Thus, Adorno states, "the house is past [i.e. over]. . . . The best mode of conduct, in face of all this, still seems an uncommitted, suspended one. . . . *It is part of morality not to be at home in one's home.*"

Yet no sooner has he reached an apparent conclusion than Adorno reverses it: "But the thesis of this paradox leads to destruction, a loveless disregard for things which necessarily turns against people too; and the antithesis, no sooner uttered, is an ideology for those wishing with a bad conscience to keep what they have. Wrong life cannot be lived rightly."[1]

In other words, there is no real escape, even for the exile who tries to remain suspended, since that state of inbetweenness can itself become a rigid ideological position, a sort of dwelling whose falseness is covered over in time, and to which one can all too easily become accustomed. Yet Adorno presses on. "Suspicious probing is always salutary," especially where the intellectual's writing is concerned. "For a man who no longer has a homeland, writing becomes a place to live," yet even so—and this is Adorno's final touch—there can be no slackening of rigor in self-analysis:

> The demand that one harden oneself against self-pity implies the technical necessity to counter any slackening of intellectual tension with the utmost alertness, and to eliminate anything that has begun to encrust the work [or writing] or to drift along idly, which may at an earlier stage have served, as gossip, to generate the warm atmosphere conducive to growth, but is now left behind, flat and stale. In the end, the writer is not allowed to live in his writing.[2]

This is typically gloomy and unyielding. Adorno the intellectual in exile heaping sarcasm on the idea that one's own work can provide some satisfaction, an alternative type of living that might be a slight respite from the anxiety and marginality of no "dwelling" at all. What Adorno doesn't speak about are indeed the pleasures of exile, those different arrangements of living and eccentric angles of vision that it can sometimes afford, which enliven the intellectual's vocation, without perhaps alleviating every last anxiety or feeling of bitter solitude. So while it is true to say that exile is the condition that characterizes the intellectual as someone who stands as a marginal figure outside the comforts of privilege, power, being-at-homeness (so to speak), it is also very important to stress that that condition carries with it certain rewards and, yes, even privileges. So while you are neither winning prizes nor being welcomed into all those self-congratulating honor societies that routinely exclude embarrassing troublemakers who do not toe the party line, you *are* at the same time deriving some positive things from exile and marginality.

One of course is the pleasure of being surprised, of never taking anything for granted, of learning to make do in circumstances of shaky instability that would confound or terrify most people. An intellectual is fundamentally about knowledge and freedom. Yet these acquire meaning not as abstractions—as in the rather banal statement "You must get a good education so that you can enjoy a good life"—but as experiences actually lived through. An intellectual is like a shipwrecked person who learns how to live in a certain sense *with* the land, not *on* it, not like Robinson Crusoe whose goal is to colonize his little island, but more like Marco Polo, whose sense of the marvelous never fails him, and who is always a traveler, a provisional guest, not a freeloader, conqueror, or raider.

Because the exile sees things both in terms of what has been left behind and what is actual here and now, there is a double perspective that never sees things in isolation. Every scene or situation in the new country necessarily draws on its counterpart in the old country. Intellectually this means that an idea or experience is always counterposed with another, therefore making them both appear in a sometimes new and unpredictable light: from that juxtaposition one gets a better, perhaps even more universal idea of how to think, say, about a human rights issue in one situation by comparison with another. I have felt that most of the alarmist and deeply flawed discussions of Islamic fundamentalism in the West have been intellectually invidious precisely because they have not been compared with Jewish or Christian fundamentalism, both equally prevalent and reprehensible in my own experience of the Middle East. What is usually thought of as a simple issue of judgment against an approved enemy, in double or exile perspective impels a Western intellectual to see a much wider picture, with the requirement now of taking a position as a secularist (or not) on *all* theocratic tendencies, not just against the conventionally designated ones.

A second advantage to what in effect is the exile standpoint for an intellectual is that you tend to see things not simply as they are, but as they have come to be that way. Look at situations as contingent, not as inevitable, look at them as the result of a series of historical choices made by men and women, as facts of society made by human beings, and not as natural or god-given, therefore unchangeable, permanent, irreversible.

The great prototype for this sort of intellectual position is provided by the eighteenth-century Italian philosopher Giambattista Vico, who has long been a hero of mine. Vico's great discovery, which derived in part from his loneliness as an obscure Neapolitan professor, scarcely able to survive, at odds with the Church and his immediate surroundings, is that the proper way to understand social reality is to understand it as a process generated from its point of origin, which one can always locate in extremely humble circumstances. This, he said in his great work *The New Science,* meant seeing things as having evolved from definite beginnings, as the adult human being derives from the babbling child.

Vico argues that this is the only point of view to take about the secular world, which he repeats over and over again is historical, with its own laws and processes, not divinely ordained. This entails respect, but not reverence, for human society. You look at the grandest of powers in terms of its beginnings, and where it might be headed; you are not awed by the august personality, or the magnificent institution which to a native, someone who has always seen (and therefore venerated) the grandeur but not the perforce humbler *human* origins from which it derived, often compels silence and stunned subservience. The intellectual in exile is necessarily ironic, skeptical, even playful—but not cynical.

Finally, as any real exile will confirm, once you leave your home, wherever you end up you cannot simply take up life and become just another citizen of the new place. Or if you do, there is a good deal of awkwardness involved in the effort, which scarcely seems worth it. You can spend a lot of time regretting what you lost, envying those around you who have always been at home, near their loved ones, living in the place where they were born and grew up without ever having to experience not only the loss of what was once theirs, but above all the torturing memory of a life to which they cannot return. On the other hand, as Rilke once said, you can become a beginner in your circumstances, and this allows you an unconventional style of life, and above all, a different, often very eccentric career.

For the intellectual an exilic displacement means being liberated from the usual career, in which "doing well" and following in time-honored footsteps are the main milestones. Exile means that you are always going to be marginal, and that what you do as an intellectual has to be made up because you cannot follow a prescribed path. If you can experience that fate not as a deprivation and as something to be bewailed, but as a sort of freedom, a process of discovery in which you do things according to your own pattern, as various interests seize your attention, and as the particular goal you set yourself dictates: that is a unique pleasure. You see it in the odyssey of C. L. R. James, the Trinidadian essayist and historian, who came to England as a cricket player between the two World Wars and whose intellectual autobiography, *Beyond a Boundary,* was an account of his life in cricket, and of cricket in colonialism. His other works included *The Black Jacobins,* a stirring history of the late-eighteenth-century Haitian black slave revolt led by Toussaint L'Ouverture; being an orator and political organizer in America; writing a study of Herman Melville, *Mariners, Renegades, and Castaways,* plus various works on pan-Africanism, and dozens of essays on popular culture and literature. An eccentric, unsettled course, so unlike anything we would today call a solid professional career, and yet what exuberance and unending self-discovery it contains.

Most of us may not be able to duplicate the destiny of exiles like Adorno or C. L. R. James, but their significance for the contemporary intellectual is nevertheless very pertinent. Exile is a model for the intellectual who is tempted, and even beset and overwhelmed, by the rewards of accommodation, yea-saying, settling in. Even if one is not an actual immigrant or expatriate, it is still possible to think as one, to imagine and investigate in spite of barriers, and always to move away from the centralizing authorities towards the margins, where you see things that are usually lost on minds that have never traveled beyond the conventional and the comfortable.

A condition of marginality, which might seem irresponsible or flippant, frees you from having always to proceed with caution, afraid to overturn the applecart, anxious about upsetting fellow members of the same corporation. No one is ever free of attachments and sentiments of course. Nor do I have in mind here the so-called free-floating intellectual, whose technical competence is on loan and for sale to anyone. I am saying, however, that to be as marginal and as undomesticated as someone who is in real exile is for an intellectual to be unusually responsive to the traveler rather than to the potentate, to the provisional and risky rather than to the habitual, to innovation and experiment rather than the authoritatively given *status quo*. The *exilic* intellectual does not respond to the logic of the conventional but to the audacity of daring, and to representing change, to moving on, not standing still.

from *Representations of the Intellectual*

15

The Middle East "Peace Process": Misleading Images and Brutal Actualities

(1995)

Published in an abbreviated form in *The Nation* magazine in October 1995, "The Middle East 'Peace Process'" articulates Said's objections to the Oslo accords. Ceremoniously signed by Yasir Arafat and Yitzhak Rabin on the White House lawn on September 13, 1993, the Declaration of Principles granted the Palestinians autonomy but no sovereignty over land that Israel had illegally occupied since the 1967 Arab-Israel War. Said was among the few Palestinian intellectuals to speak against what he saw as a "deeply flawed and imperfect peace." Oslo, Said has said, was a "peace of the weak," an effort by the Palestinian leadership to preserve its authority and ensure its political survival.

With the stroke of a pen, Arafat signed an agreement that made no mention of the end of the Israeli occupation. Nor did it even address the predicament of the 3.5 million Palestinian refugees outside of Gaza and the West Bank, who were driven from their homes and dispossessed of their land in 1948. According to Oslo's terms, Israel maintained control of 97 percent of the West Bank and 40 percent of Gaza; yet it left Israel in charge of borders, security, and air and water rights to such an extent that Said wrote, "even Yasir Arafat has to receive permission from the

Israelis to exit and enter Gaza." The results of the agreement were shocking. Palestinian unemployment skyrocketed to over 35 percent; the Israeli settlements continued to be built, while the demolition of Palestinian homes continued under the Israel Military Law of Occupation.

Said's criticism of Oslo not surprisingly earned him the acrimony of the PLO leadership. On August 22, 1996, officials of the Palestinian Authority raided a number of bookstores in the West Bank city of Ramallan and in Gaza and seized copies of Said's books, one of which included the Arabic translation of "The Middle East 'Peace Process.'"

Under pressure from the Palestinian residents of Hebron not to sign an agreement that would give 450 Israeli settlers encamped in the center of town separate rights and an army to guard them, Yasir Arafat theatrically pulled out of his eleventh-hour meeting with Shimon Peres. "We are not slaves!" Arafat shouted. Moments later he was reached on the telephone by Dennis Ross, the U.S. State Department's "coordinator" in charge of the Middle East peace process. "If you don't sign now," Ross was reported to have said, "you don't get the $100 million"—a reference to America's yearly pledge toward Palestinian development projects in the West Bank. Arafat signed, and the protests in Hebron continued.

As a negotiating turn, this was not unusual. Without maps of their own, without the requisite detailed knowledge of the facts or figures possessed by the Israelis, without a firm commitment to principle, the Palestinian negotiators have consistently yielded to Israeli and American pressures. What Palestinians have gotten in the latest agreement, initialed in Taba, Egypt, is a series of municipal responsibilities in Bantustans dominated from the outside by Israel. What Israel has gotten is official Palestinian consent to continued occupation.

What's astonishing is that this agreement—popularly known as

Oslo II—is now being celebrated in the West as an Israeli "withdrawal" from the Occupied Territories, as an honorable and serious move toward peace, when in fact there is neither occasion nor cause to justify such hand-clapping. Signed and saluted in the White House on September 28, almost two years to the day after the "historic handshake" that sealed Oslo I, the agreement enjoins Israel merely to redeploy its troops from the center of the main West Bank towns (excluding Hebron) to their outskirts. In this redeployment, Israel will establish sixty-two new military bases in the West Bank. As Prime Minister Yitzhak Rabin has put it, "The problem is not [the army's] permanent presence but its freedom of action." Israel will thus retain control of exits and entries to the towns, as it will control all roads on the West Bank.

Palestinians will have municipal authority over the towns and some 400 villages within the Israeli cordon, but they will have no real security responsibility, no right to resources or land outside the populated centers, and no authority at all over Israeli settlers, police, and army. Israel will continue to hold fifty or sixty Palestinian villages. The settlements will be untouched and a system of roads will connect them to one another, making it possible for settlers, like whites in the old South Africa, to avoid or never even see the people of the Bantustans, and making it impossible for Palestinians to rule over any contiguous territory.

In numerical terms, the Palestinians will at first have civil control—without sovereignty—of about 5 percent of the West Bank. Israel will have exclusive control of 8 percent (the settlements, *not counting* those around illegally annexed East Jerusalem), plus effective control—security, water, land, air space and airwaves, roads, borders, etc.—of the whole.

Politically and economically this is disastrous, and I think it is absolutely legitimate to suggest that no negotiations, and no agreement, would be better than what has so far been determined. Oslo II gives the Palestinian National Authority the appurtenances of rule without the reality—a kingdom of illusions, with Israel firmly in command. Any West Bank town, under the new agreement, can be closed at will by the Israelis, as was Jericho during the last days of August, and Gaza in September. All commercial traffic between Gaza and the West Bank autonomy zones is in Israeli hands. Thus, a truckload of tomatoes going from Gaza to the West Bank town of

Nablus must stop at the border, be unloaded onto an Israeli truck, then be reloaded onto a Palestinian truck upon entering Nablus. This takes three days, with the fruit rotting in the meantime and the costs going so high as to make such transactions prohibitive. (In the West Bank it is cheaper to import tomatoes from Spain than from Gaza.)

The idea, of course, is to impress upon Palestinians, in as humiliating a way as possible, that Israel controls their economy. Likewise, their future political process. The Legislative Council of eighty-two people is to be elected next spring, although candidates have to be approved by the Israelis. "Racists" and "terrorists" will be barred. (There is no parallel proscription on the Israeli side, where, for instance, Rafael Eitan, a war criminal of the 1982 Lebanon invasion and a man who has referred to Palestinians as "cockroaches," sits in the Knesset.) Israel may veto any piece of legislation enacted by the Council, which has no jurisdiction over or representatives from East Jerusalem. Arafat, in any case, has won for himself the privilege of being called chairman/president, although the Israelis insisted that he name a vice president/chairman. He seems to have refused, insisting that anyone inferior to him must be known only as *mutahaddith*, or spokesman.

Much of what Oslo II prescribes so disadvantageously for Palestinians—and, in the long run, for Israelis as well—was set in motion by Oslo I. You wouldn't know this from conventional "expert" opinion in the West. The prevailing belief underlying most analysis—from such dubious authorities as Bernard Lewis, Judith Miller, Steven Emerson, Daniel Pipes, and others—has been that now the only serious obstacles to peace are Islamic fundamentalism and terrorism. In this, the experts have followed the politicians. The British journalist Robert Fisk, writing in *The Independent* on October 30, 1994, noted how frequently President Clinton used the words "terrorism" and "violence" while on a trip through the Middle East:

> The use of that one corrosive word "terror" . . . crept through every speech the President made. He lectured King Hussein on "the face of terror and extremism"; he talked in Damascus of "terrorist infiltration" and "of murderous acts of terror," he spoke in the Knesset of

> "the merchants of terror," linking them in his Israeli speech with what he called "the plague of anti-Semitism."

That the "peace" under which so many Palestinians have lost hope of any real freedom might be an undesirable state, that it might drive some people to suicidal violence, is a matter almost never looked at, much less debated and admitted.

Consider the situation in the two years since Oslo I was signed. Gaza's unemployment stands at almost 60 percent. Israel continues to control about 40 percent of Gazan land. It also unilaterally controls the border with Gaza, which is now closed to all but 8,000 Gazans, who must have a pass card showing that they work in Israel. In pre-Oslo 1993, 30,000 people were allowed to cross; in 1987, 80,000. Sara Roy, who more than anyone else in America has chronicled Israel's systematic de-development of Gaza, wrote in *The Christian Science Monitor* this past April 12:

> Israel will not allow any raw materials into the Gaza Strip. At present, for example, there is no cement in Gaza. Hence, $40 million in donor aid sitting in Gazan banks cannot be spent because needed project material cannot be transported into the strip.
>
> Israel now allows only certain foodstuffs and consumer goods to enter Gaza, including benzene, cooking gas, and sand. Of the 2,000 trucks in the Gaza Strip, only 10 have permits to enter Israel.

Arafat himself still cannot enter Gaza without a permit; nor is there any free passage between Gaza and Jericho. One thousand one hundred military laws still pertain in "autonomous" Gaza; 1,400 in the West Bank. A system of fifty-eight roadblocks prevents Palestinians from going from north to south in the West Bank, especially as the "Judaization" of Jerusalem (imagine the outcry if Jews were forced to endure "Arabization"!) prohibits Arabs from entering the now greatly distended boundaries of the city. Four hundred Gazan students of Bir Zeit University and twelve professors were unable to go to school for about three months. Not only is East Jerusalem cut off from the West Bank and Gaza, which is closed to the outside world like an enormous prison, but Arab life in the Old City is being choked off. People there are being forced out of their houses, and residents of outlying areas like Beit Hanina, Shoufat, and Silwan watch powerless as settler housing projects rear their grossly out-of-proportion dimensions, ruining the city's natural contours, its air, and its environment. This year has seen a boom in such construction outside East Jerusalem: 1,126 units in the first quarter of 1995, as against 324 in the whole of 1994. All of this occurs with practically nothing being done to resist or prevent the deliberate transformation of an Arab city into a Jewish one.

The wonder of it—given twenty-eight years of military occupation, the deliberate wrecking of the economy and infrastructure, the active humiliation of an entire people, the enormous number of murdered Palestinians (more than 2,000 during the *intifada* alone, 18,000 to 20,000 during Israel's 1982 invasion of Lebanon)—is not that there is terrorism but that there isn't more of it.

The Israeli novelist David Grossman, writing in *Ha'aretz* on April 4, chastised the Jewish left for its shallowness of understanding and "almost complete paralysis" since Oslo I:

> Does our very silence constitute a dereliction of historical proportions which will have bitter consequences for Israel for generations to come? . . . I would suggest that we not despise the anxieties of the Palestinians, with whom I have talked. Perhaps they are able to feel on their skins, long before we can, what is actually happening on the ground: it may be that the "entity" that Rabin is willing to "grant" them will in fact be a weird hybrid between autonomy and confederation, crisscrossed by "Israeli" roads and fences, and spotted with numerous settlements at strategic points, in a way which will perpetuate the settlements. An as-if state.

Now with Oslo II, this "as if" status has been certified. Yet every leader responsible for its creation—whether Israeli, Palestinian, or American—as well as their intellectual adjuncts, insists publicly that a series of fractured cantons is really a governable "entity," and that subservience is self-determination. The dishonesty of it all is breathtaking.

Israel's settlement policy, for instance, is not discussed; like the question of Jerusalem, it has been placed behind a screen pending final status negotiations, supposed to begin in May of 1996. Yet it is intimately tied to the fate of the "autonomous" areas, as Hebron illustrates. There, the presence of 450 settlers occupying Arab buildings in the center of town has resulted in mass punishment—curfews (one lasting three months), killings, housing demolitions, imprisonments—of the town's 100,000 Palestinian residents. Elsewhere the situation may be less dramatic, but the pattern of land seizure through expropriation, defoliation, uprooting of trees, and refusal of permits to build or enhance existing Palestinian structures will continue to shape Palestinian life.

If one includes the area around East Jerusalem, Israel has stolen and asserted a presence upon roughly 75 percent of the land of the occupied territories. The settler population now stands at about 320,000. There were ninety-six recorded confiscations and assaults on Palestinian land between October 1993 and January 1995, and there have been more, unrecorded, since. On April 28, 1995, *The New York Times* reported the confiscation of 135 acres of land (later temporarily "frozen") in the East Jerusalem sections of Beit Safafa and Beit Hanina but characteristically failed to report what the Arab press and the *Monitor* reported: that those 135 acres were part of a bigger projected land grab of almost 450 acres. According to the Washington-based *Report on Israeli Settlements,* the authoritative non-Israeli source on these matters, Rabin has continued building and adding to settlements *as a matter of policy.*

His government's "exceptions committee," headed by Nach Kinarti, a senior official in the Defense Ministry, "has permitted housing construction in every settlement," according to the Report's Geoffrey Aronson, who states further:

> The massive construction occurring under the auspices of the Rabin government is being undertaken by private contractors, working on the basis of proposals put out for bid by the Ministry of Housing. Most of the residential construction in greater Jerusalem and in settlements along the Green Line is being executed in this manner. In Ma'ale Adumim, for example, "the Ministry of Housing is pushing the city's development with all its ability," according to a report in the Israeli daily *Yediot Aharanot.*
>
> The construction proceeds on the basis of a decision in principle made by the minister of housing or by the prime minister himself. The exceptions committee later approves formal plans along with the settlements' planning committee. The government then allo-

> cates "state land" for construction . . . [and] assists with the development of infrastructure.

In a settlement just outside Jenin, one of the towns covered by Oslo II, Israel recently approved an expansion project for five new factories, with land provided free to investors, who also got substantial tax breaks. Will this industrial zone ultimately revert to Palestine? Will it be annexed by Israel, its managers simultaneously taking advantage of cheap Palestinian labor? Will Palestinians demand reparations for this and all the land illegally appropriated by the Israeli occupiers? Reparations, a fairly common element in other international peace agreements, have never been raised as an issue for Palestine.

The Clinton Administration, meanwhile, has said or done nothing to oppose these policies, even though U.S. taxpayers are still providing about $5 billion a year to Israel, no strings attached, plus $10 billion in loan guarantees. U.S. Ambassador Martin Indyk, former American Israel Public Affairs Committee (AIPAC) lobbyist, former head of the pro-Israel Washington Institute for Near East Policy, was asked during his confirmation hearings this year whether there was any U.S. policy vis-à-vis Israeli settlement activity. He said only that he thought the settlements "complicated" the negotiations, though "terrorism has a much more complicating impact." A few moments later, when asked whether the Rabin government had added to the settlements or permitted new ones since 1993, he said "No," an outright falsehood.

At Congressional hearings in 1993, Secretary of State Warren Christopher refused even to characterize the territories as occupied. A year later his department's deputy press secretary, Christine Shelley, when asked by reporters if there was a "clear statement of policy on settlements," replied:

> It certainly comes up from time to time in the context of, you know, testimony and other things. We do—the briefers also from time to time get those questions as well. As to—you know, nothing has changed on that in terms of our position and, you know, I think it's—you know, I can refer you to, you know, to probably to previous statements by officials on that. But I don't have anything—you know, I

> mean, you know, our—I think—I don't have—you know, I—we—usually we try to have, you know, a little bit of something on that. I'm not sure that it's going to be, you know, specifically what you're looking for. You know, generally speaking, our position that on settlements that it's the Palestinians and Israelis have agreed that the final status negotiations will cover these issues and, you know, that's—that's also our view.

There is a causal relationship between this sort of talk and Israel's emboldened land expropriation. Indeed, silence and the wanton murder of language evident in the phrase "peace process" are central to the Israeli (and American) project. As Peres said in January of this year, "We will build, but without declaring it in public. . . . The Labour Party always knew how to do things quietly . . . but today, everybody announces everything they do in public." Thus, the Israeli Central Bureau of Statistics estimated in 1993 a net increase of 10,900 in the settler population; in October 1994 the settler's council claimed a larger figure (23,600 more than the CBS's) for the total settler population in the territories, excluding Jerusalem. Israel's Peace Now reported that there was an increase of 70 percent in government and private investment in settlements in the year following the famous handshake.

In Washington, no one paid attention. Indeed, in the wake of Oslo II, an Arab journalist in the capital told me it is virtually impossible to get any direct answer on U.S. policy positions regarding the occupied territories.

Where Washington has been busiest is in the enfeeblement and marginalization of the United Nations, historically a forum for Palestinian protest, from these proceedings. U.S. Ambassador to the UN Madeleine Albright has importuned member states to rescind, modify or otherwise ignore resolutions that might prejudice or in any way affect bilateral negotiations between Israel and Yasir Arafat. All of these resolutions either urged consideration of Palestinian claims for self-determination or denounced unlawful Israeli occupation practices (most of them in contravention of the Fourth Geneva Convention or of UN principles forbidding the annexation of war gains). Although these were paper resolutions, for Palestinians as a people they represented the only international guarantee that their claims would not be ignored.

Remember that over half the dispossessed Palestinian population—about 3.5 million people—does not reside in the West Bank or Gaza, and according to the peace process, these people have little hope of repatriation or compensation for what they have lost or suffered. Many are stateless refugees eking out a below-subsistence existence in camps in Lebanon, Jordan, and Syria, without the right to work or leave. (That they have no place to go is now being painfully illustrated: 35,000 Palestinians just expelled from Libya were barred from Gaza by Israel and wander homeless, rebuffed by Lebanon, as well.) It is argued that Oslo left the fate of these people to final status negotiations, but the damage has already been done. After laboriously constructing the unity of Palestinians everywhere, bringing together the Diaspora and the 800,000 Palestinian citizens of Israel, as well as the residents of the occupied territories, the PLO by a stroke of the pen split the three components apart, accepting the Israeli designation of Palestinians as only the encaged residents of the territories. No other liberation movement in the twentieth century got so little—roughly 5 percent of its territory. And no other leaders of a liberation movement accepted what in effect is permanent subordination of their people.

Although it now seems that many Palestinians have been demoralized by what faces them in reality, I believe the Palestinian people will continue to want their rights to be equal with those of their neighbors, the Israeli Jewish people. The emergence of Hamas and Islamic Jihad are part of the continuing protest and should be understood as that. Their suicide missions, bomb throwing, and provocative slogans are acts of defiance principally, refusals to accept the crippling conditions of Israeli occupation and Palestinian collaboration. No matter how much secular people like myself lament their methods and their vision (such as it is), there is no doubting the truth that for many Palestinians these people express a furious protest against the humiliations, demeanments, and denials imposed on all Palestinians as a people. It is ironic that Hamas, having been encouraged by Israel in the 1980s as a tool for breaking the PLO and the *intifada*, should now be elevated to the rank of superdevil.

. . .

Of course, the best response to terrorism is justice, not more repression. The deep tragedy of Palestine is that a whole people's history and aspirations have been under such comprehensive assault—not only by Israel (with its patron and collaborator the United States) but also by the Arab governments and, since Oslo, by the PLO under Arafat.

It is necessary here to try to describe the complicated mix of emotions and actualities that govern Palestinian life in the occupied territories today. True, Arafat's entry into Gaza on July 1, 1994, gave people there the sense that they are no longer as confined as they once were. They can go to the beaches, they do not have to be indoors after sundown, and they enjoy some rapport with a Palestinian (not an Egyptian or Israeli) police force. In every other respect life has become worse. There is a cynical Israeli policy of letting Arafat become as much a petty dictator as is consistent with their interests. Thus, the tolerance for his inflated police force and intelligence services, totaling about 19,000 (Oslo I and a subsequent Cairo agreement limited him to 9,000).

Arafat's political arm is his party, Fatah, which now plays the role of enforcer, armed by him throughout the territories. He himself governs unilaterally, in the absence of real laws or constitution. At the urging of Israel and the United States, he has instituted military courts that can arrest, detain, and sentence people without due process. (When Warren Christopher and Al Gore visited the autonomy zones in March they commended Arafat's decision to establish these courts.) Raji Sourani, the brilliant Gaza lawyer who has spent his whole life defending Palestinians against Israeli measures of this kind, protested Arafat's fiat, and was arrested and detained for a short period without trial in February. He was recently stripped of the chairmanship of his own human rights group, with the connivance of Arafat's Palestinian National Authority (PA).

Having effectively dismembered the PLO—the only organization that Palestinians throughout the Diaspora have had to represent their national aspirations—Arafat now surrounds himself with a formidable network of hangers-on, sycophants, commission agents, spies, and informers. All of his appointments to his Cabinet of eighteen ministers (seventeen of them men) are beholden to him for their budgets, and indeed for their political existence. In some ministries, whose work and authority exist mainly on paper, he continues to appoint deputies (plus about 750 "director-generals" without any known jobs to perform). The total number of people employed directly by Arafat for the PA is estimated at 48,000; this includes the 19,000 police plus about 29,000 members of the civil administration. Whatever money Arafat gets from donors (about $10 million a month), local taxes and taxes collected for him by the Israelis (a total of nearly $30 million a month) is all he has to spend. Little is left over for improving sewage, health services, or employment.

With all the Palestinian competence in economics and engineering available, Arafat instead consistently engages the services of shady figures like the Moroccan Gabriel Banon and the Lebanese Pierre Rizk, former Phalangist contact for the Mossad in Lebanon, or one Khalid Slam (aka Mohammed Rashid), a Kurd of uncertain background notoriously skilled at arranging quick deals. These are his fixers and advisers, along with a new group of American business consultants, who supposedly function as his economic counselors.

There is, moreover, no system of financial accountability. According to David Hirst, writing in *The Guardian* for April 15, Arafat's attorney general is "a man whom Fatah once sentenced to death for stealing funds destined for the *intifada*." Arafat does what he pleases, spends as he likes, disposes how he feels his interests might be served. Above all, as Julian Ozanne wrote in *The Financial Times*, his pact with Israel "keeps the Palestinian economy largely within Israel's broad macroeconomic trade and taxation policy, recognizing the dependence of the territories on their neighboring economic giant for the foreseeable future." All petroleum and petroleum products used by Palestinians come exclusively from the Israeli petroleum authority. Local Palestinians pay an excise tax, the net amount of which is held in Arafat's name in an Israel bank account. Only he can get to it, and only he can spend it. At a donors' meeting in Paris this past April, an IMF observer told me that the group voted $18.5 million to the Palestinian people: $18 million was paid directly to Arafat; $500,000 was put in the public treasury. How it shall be disbursed is at Arafat's discretion alone.

A group of wealthy Palestinian businessmen (most of whom made their fortunes in the Persian Gulf) have claimed to be fed up with Arafat's methods and have devised a series of projects for electricity, telecommunications, and the like. These are financed through what they call "public" stock offerings, though the actual public is far too poor to invest in such schemes. These men (who additionally invest in, and profit from, real estate) nevertheless also deal directly with Arafat. They meet with him secretly and are not beholden to anything like a national planning or regulatory authority. They build the way they want, responsible only to themselves.

Given such activity, Arafat is lucky that the international media have largely spared him their investigations. This comes after dozens of books and articles before Oslo on the PLO's finances, its support of terrorism, etc. At home, meanwhile, the Palestinian press is not free. Very little that is critical of Arafat appears there. On May 5, *al-Hayat* reported that the offices of *al-Ummah*, an opposition paper in Jerusalem, were deliberately burned; the paper's owner blamed Palestinian police. The opinions of opponents are severely curtailed. Hanan Ashrawi, by now internationally known, cannot be read or seen or read about in the semi-official Palestinian daily *al-Quds* because she is considered too independent.

Arafat and his Palestinian Authority have become a sort of Vichy government for Palestinians. Those of us who fought for Palestine before Oslo fought for a cause that we believed would spur the emergence of a just order. Never has this ideal been further from realization than today. Arafat is corrupt. Hamas and Islamic Jihad are no alternative. And most Palestinian intellectuals have been too anxious to bolster their own case, following Arafat and his lieutenants in the abandonment of their principles and history just to be recognized by the West, to be invited to the Brookings Institution, and to appear on U.S. television.

The Israelis have clung to their power and their old policies, the Arabs have capitulated and fawned on their victors without a trace of guts or decency. In the long run Israel is not acting wisely. As the Israeli commentator Haim Baram wrote on March 18, 1994 in *Kol Ha'ir:*

> The concept of a Golda Meir–style territorial compromise is still characteristic of Rabin. His desire to keep the settlements firmly rooted in the territories constitutes an impenetrable roadblock to peace and a prescription for political and military disaster. His desire to bring Rafael Eitan and his friends into the coalition stems directly from this as well. Rabin armed the settlers and for years allowed the Kahanists to go on their rampages in spite of warning from the

> *Shabak* (General Security Services). Rabin should retire from the political arena.
>
> The claim of the doves, that they are just using Rabin's name to implement the policies of Peres, is proving itself to be worthless for the long term. Peace can only by made openly, by demonstrating both leadership and wisdom. Rabin is simply not able to rise to the occasion. He is a small-minded person, a hawk from the Tabenken school of thought in the Labor movement, who fell into a situation bigger than himself. Everything else is worthless public relations.

In the end there will be reactions to it that it would not have foreseen, any more than the *intifada* was foreseen before it happened.

I do not pretend to have any quick solutions for the situation now referred to as "the peace process," but I do know that for the vast majority of Palestinian refugees, day laborers, peasants, and town and camp dwellers, those who cannot make a quick deal and those whose voices are never heard, for them the process has made matters far worse. Above all, they may have lost hope. And that is also true of the Palestinian political consciousness in general.

All of us know that because of its aggressive behavior, its continued policies of occupation, settlement and domination, Israel is not embarked on a course of peace with us, but of protracted hostility in which as countries, cultures, and peoples the Arabs are supposed to submit to Israel's power. Neither the United States administration, which essentially cooperates in this plan, nor the media, which with the exception of a few reports here and there, drones on about a paradigm of "peace-making" that exists only in their own irrelevant commentaries, has offered very much in the way of real peace. Forbidden to recall their history of dispossession and suffering, the Palestinians today are an orphaned people, a fact gradually being understood not only by themselves but also by the many Egyptians, Jordanians, Syrians, and Lebanese who have gradually awakened to the perfidy and indifference of their leaders. For the first time that I can remember, though, the governments no longer bother to conceal what they really are about. In early April 1995, for instance, *Al-Hayat* revealed that in 1976 Hafez al-Assad sought and received permission from Mr. Rabin, then Israeli Prime Minister, to send his troops into Lebanon; the go-between was King Hussein. All this at a time when there was supposed to be no communication between such implacable enemies. Well, the Syrian troops are still in Lebanon and, since the Syrian mission for entry into Lebanon at the time was the weakening of the Palestinians, we also know that the Palestinians as a people and leadership have indeed become weaker.

At a time when people are suffering and shabby leaders are reaping Nobel Prizes that only enable more exploitation, it is crucial to bear witness to the truth. As Palestinians we must ask whether our century of struggle should conclude not with a state and not with a democracy but with an awful caricature of both, extracted by a country that alone in the world has no officially declared borders and manipulated by a man whose methods and patrons resemble those of every other Arab tyrant.

This policy cannot be an excuse for continuing to misreport and misrepresent the realities. Were it just a matter of the mass media's laziness or ignorance that would be bad enough. But elite, knowledgeable, authoritative groups like the Council on Foreign Relations and its house organ *Foreign Affairs* connive in perpetuating the fiction that the Middle East has finally accepted the American paradigm. Consider that the journal ran three articles on "The Palestinian Future" in its July/August 1994 issue; two of them were by Israelis (neither one known for his pacific views), one by a former United States National Security Council official. Earlier (November/December 1993) it had published two pieces on "aftershocks of the peace plan"; both were by Americans one of whom (the author of the essay on Islamic militants) was a specialist on medieval Iran. Then again two issues partially devoted to "Is Islam a Threat?" and "The Islamic Cauldron" (Spring 1993 and May/June 1995), both contained not one article by a Muslim but were mostly written by poorly informed journalists, publicists, special pleaders.

Besides there is now an ample supply of alternative sources on what is happening on the ground, all of it in English, and better, more representative, more rounded in its coverage and the range of its detail. In Israel the Alternative Information Center publishes a monthly as well as a weekly bulletin: both provide excellent analysis and reporting. Israel Shahak still produces the most compelling and rigorous reports and translations (with his own trenchant commentaries) from the Hebrew press: they are easily available from the Middle East Data Center in Woodbridge, Virginia. *Middle East Mir-*

ror does a daily fax report drawn from Arab and Israeli newspapers, magazines, broadcasts. *Middle East International* is, I think, the best fortnightly magazine on the Middle East. In addition the French, British, and London-based Arab press is full of material, none of it used by the United States media to alter the misleading images attached to the peace process, and its basically retrograde designs.

The peace process has attempted first to isolate, then to pacify individual Arab states so that Israel, which has obviously figured out that it cannot forever depend on United States aid on such a lavish scale, can become the regional economic and military power, the Arabs providing what little is left of their squandered wealth, and their unlimited manpower. I have been particularly disheartened by the role played in all this by liberal Americans, Jewish and non-Jewish alike, those who have lamented the Holocaust and the massacres in Bosnia, Chechnya, and Rwanda. Silence is not a response, and neither is some fairly tepid endorsement of a Palestinian state, with Israeli settlements and army more or less still there, still in charge. I believe that Israel has no future unless its people are a real part of the Middle East, not its soldiers nor its puppetmasters. I think we have to look beyond exclusivism and separatist nationalism and see that all over the area there are in fact smaller contests for democracy and rights: there is a women's movement in every Arab country, there is a human rights movement, and most important, there is a secular actuality that willingly engages religious intolerance and extremism of every kind.* Israelis and their American supporters have a stake in those struggles, not in the distortion of hopes and rightful aspirations that has been called the peace process. And indeed, there is a secular versus religious struggle inside Israel, as well as a danger in Israel, the Occupied Territories and elsewhere, that this might become an overt civil war.

This peace process must be demystified and spoken about truthfully and plainly. Palestine/Israel is no ordinary bit of geography: it is more saturated in religious, historical, and cultural significance than any place on earth. It is also now the place where two peoples,

*I have discussed this at length in *The Politics of Dispossession* (New York and London: Pantheon, Chatto and Windus, 1994; Vintage, 1995), pp. 372–411.

whether they like it or not, live inextricably linked lives, tied together by history, war, daily contact, and suffering. To speak in grandiose geopolitical terms, or to speak mindlessly about "separating" them is nothing less than to provide prescriptions for more violence and degradation. There is simply no substitute for seeing these two communities as equal to each other in rights and expectations, then proceeding from there to do justice to their living actualities. But whatever one does there is no alternative in my opinion to recognizing that the United States–supported peace process is a process with no real and lasting peace: it has actively harmed Palestinians and Israelis who deserve better. And, in its present form, I am convinced, it will not stand the test of time: it must be completely rethought and put on a more promising course. The so-called Oslo II Agreement provides no such rethinking: it allows Israel to rule the Occupied Territories from the intact settlements and bypassing roads. I urge fellow Palestinians, Arabs, Israelis, Europeans, and Americans not to flinch from the unpalatable truth and to demand a reckoning from the unscrupulous leaders and their minions who have ignored or dismissed the facts and tampered with the lives of far too many decent people.

from *Peace and Its Discontents*

16

On Writing a Memoir

(1999)

In 1994, three years after Edward Said was diagnosed with leukemia, he began writing his memoir, *Out of Place*. A subjective account of his early life, his memoir narrates the dislocating currents that formed his experiences in British Mandate Jerusalem, in colonial Cairo, in Lebanon, and in the United States. "To me," he writes, "nothing more painful and paradoxically sought after characterizes my life than the many displacements from countries, cities, abodes, languages, environments that have kept me in motion all these years." With undertones of Proust, *Out of Place* "is a record of an essentially lost or forgotten world."

Although his memoir was received with widespread acclaim, its appearance coincided with the publication of a diatribe in *Commentary* magazine that claimed that Said had misrepresented his early life in Jerusalem and his identity as a Palestinian.[1] The article was reminiscent of other politically motivated efforts to deny the reality of the Palestinian experience of dispossession. The journalist Alexander Cockburn observed that the *Commentary* writer was a former employee of the Israeli Ministry of Justice who had used his position to deny the validity of Israeli human rights abuses in the Occupied Territories. "To show that Said somehow isn't Palestinian," Cockburn wrote, "is as weirdly audacious as Golda Meir's notorious claim many years ago that there was no such entity as the Palestinian people, only Arab transplants with no rights."[2]

The *Commentary* article was riddled with mistakes and fabrications. In *The Nation*, British journalist Christopher Hitchens outlined the "farrago of inaccuracies and incomprehension" that the *Commentary* article put forth.[3] Despite the contrived nature of the claims, the media relished the baseless charge that a prominent Palestinian intellectual had invented his past. *The Wall Street Journal*, for example, printed excerpts of the *Commentary* article without offering Said the opportunity to respond. Ironically, only the Israeli daily newspaper *Ha'aretz* printed Said's rebuttal. Said wrote, "I have always advocated the acknowledgment by each other of the Palestinian and Jewish peoples' past sufferings. Only in this way can they coexist peacefully together in the future. [*Commentary*'s writer] is more interested in using the past—either an individual or collective past—to prevent understanding and reconciliation. It is a pity that so much time, money, and venom as he has expended couldn't have been used for better purposes."

Many reviewers of the book, however, rose above the controversy and viewed the memoir as part of the long and important tradition of exilic narrative. "The experience of dispersion, exile and rootless cosmopolitan life has been the fate of almost all Arab writers and intellectuals this century," wrote Ammiel Alcalay. "While enriching the possibilities of our own cultural horizons, in retrospect, Edward Said's *Out of Place* clearly joins itself to that embattled, often heroic and altogether much-neglected tradition."[4]

All families invent their parents and children, give each of them a history, character, fate, and even a language. There was always something wrong with how I was invented and meant to fit in with the world of my parents and four sisters. Whether this was because I constantly misread my part or because of some deep flaw in my being I could not tell for most of my early life. Sometimes I was intransigent, and proud of it. At other times I seemed to myself to be nearly devoid of character, timid, uncertain, without will. Yet the overriding sensation I had was of never being quite right. As I have said before, it took me about fifty years to become accustomed to, or more exactly to feel less uncomfortable with, "Edward," a foolishly English name yoked to the unmistakably Arabic family name "Said." True, "Edward" was for the Prince of Wales who cut so fine a figure in 1935, the year of my birth, and "Said" was the name of various uncles and cousins. But the rationale of my name broke down when I discovered no grandparents called "Said," and when I tried to connect my fancy English name with its Arabic partner. For years, and depending on the exact circumstances, I would rush past "Edward" and emphasize "Said," or do the reverse, or connect the two to each other so quickly that neither would be clear. The one thing I could not tolerate, but very often would have to endure, was the disbelieving, and hence undermining, reaction: Edward? Said?

The travails of bearing such a name were compounded by an equally unsettling quandary when it came to language. I have never known what language I spoke first, Arabic or English, or which one was mine beyond any doubt. What I do know, however, is that the two have always been together in my life, one resonating in the other, sometimes ironically, sometimes nostalgically, or, more often, one correcting and commenting on the other. Each can seem like my absolutely first language, but neither is. I trace this primal instability to my mother who I remember speaking to me both in English and Arabic, although she always wrote to me in English—once a week, all her life, as did I, all of hers. Certain spoken phrases of hers, like *tislamli* or *Mish 'arfa shu biddi 'amal*? or *rouh'ha*—dozens of them—were Arabic, and I was never conscious of having to translate them or, even in cases like *tislamli*, of knowing exactly what they meant. They were a part of her infinitely maternal atmosphere, for which in moments of great stress I found myself yearning in the softly uttered phrase *ya mama*, always dreamily seductive then suddenly snatched away, with the promise of something in the end never given.

But woven into her Arabic speech were English words like *naughty boy* and of course my name, pronounced *Edwaad*. I am still haunted by the sound, at exactly the same time and place, of her voice calling me *Edwaad*, the word wafting through the dusk air at the Fish Garden's closing time, and me, undecided whether to answer or to remain in hiding for just a while longer, enjoying the pleasure of being called, being wanted, the non-Edward part of myself finding luxurious respite in not answering until the silence of my being became unendurable. Her English deployed a rhetoric of statement and norms that has never left me. Once my mother left Arabic and spoke English there was a more objective and serious tone that mostly banished the forgiving and musical intimacy of *her* first language, Arabic. At age five or six I knew that I was irremediably *naughty* and at school all manner of comparably disapproved of things like *fibber* and *loiterer*. By the time I was fully conscious of speaking English fluently, if not always correctly, I regularly referred to myself not as *me* but as *you*. "Mummy doesn't love you, naughty boy," she would say, and I would respond, half plaintive echoing, half defiant assertion: "Mummy doesn't love you, but Auntie Melia loves you." Auntie Melia was her elderly maiden aunt, who doted on me as a very young child. "No she doesn't," my mother persisted. "All right. Saleh loves you," I would conclude—Salah was Auntie Melia's driver—rescuing something from the enveloping gloom.

I hadn't then any idea where my mother's English came from or who, in the national sense of the phrase, she was: this strange state of ignorance continued until relatively late in my life, when I was in graduate school. In Cairo, one of the places where I grew up, her spoken Arabic was fluent Egyptian, but to my keener ear, and to the many Egyptians she knew, it was, if not outright *Shami*, then perceptibly inflected by it. *Shami* (Damascene) is the collective adjective and noun used by Egyptians to describe both an Arabic-speaker who is not Egyptian and someone who is from Greater Syria, i.e., Syria itself, Lebanon, Palestine, Jordan; but *Shami* is also used to designate the Arabic dialect spoken by a *Shami*. Much more than my father, whose linguistic ability was primitive compared to hers, my mother had an excellent command of the classical language as well as the demotic. Not enough of the latter to disguise her as Egyptian, however, which of course she was not. Born in Nazareth, then sent to boarding school and junior college in Beirut, she was

Palestinian, even though her mother Munira was Lebanese. I never knew her father, but he, I discovered, was the Baptist minister in Nazareth, although he originally came from Safad, via a sojourn in Texas.

Not only could I not absorb, much less master, all the meanderings and interruptions of these details as they broke up a simple dynastic sequence; I could not grasp why she was not a straight English mummy. I have retained this unsettled sense of many identities—mostly in conflict with each other—all my life, together with an acute memory of the despairing wish that we could have been all-Arab, or all-European and American, or all-Christian, or all-Muslim, or all-Egyptian, and on and on. I found I had two alternatives with which to counter the process of challenge, recognition, and exposure to which I felt subject, questions and remarks like: "What are you?" "But Said is an Arab name." "You're American?" "You're an American without an American name, and you've never been to America." "You don't look American!" "How come you were born in Jerusalem and you live *here*?" "You're an Arab after all, but what kind are you?"

I do not remember that any of the answers I gave out loud to such probings were satisfactory, or even memorable. My alternatives were hatched entirely on my own: one might work, say, in school, but would not work in church or on the street with my friends. My first approach was to adopt my father's brashly assertive tone and say to myself: "I'm an American citizen, and that's it." He was American by dint of having lived in the United States followed by service in the Army during World War One. Partly because this alternative was not only implausible but imposed on me, I found it far from convincing. To say "I am an American citizen" in the setting of an English school, with wartime Cairo dominated by British troops and what seemed to me a totally homogeneous Egyptian populace, was foolhardy, something to be risked in public only when I was challenged officially to name my citizenship; in private I could not maintain it for long, so quickly did the affirmation wither under existential scrutiny.

The second of my alternatives was even less successful. It was to open myself to the deeply disorganized state of my real history and origins as I had gleaned them and then to try to make some sort of sense of them. But I never had enough information; there was never the right number of functioning connectives between the parts I knew about or was able to somehow excavate; the total picture was never quite right. The trouble seemed to begin with my parents, their pasts and names. My father Wadie was later called William (an early discrepancy that I assumed for a long time was only an Anglicization of his Arabic name, but soon it appeared to me suspiciously like a case of assumed identity, with the name "Wadie" cast aside except by his wife and sister for not very creditable reasons). Born in Jerusalem in 1895 (my mother said it was more likely 1893), he never told me more than ten or eleven things about his past, none of which ever changed and which hardly conveyed anything except a series of portable words. He was at least forty at the time of my birth.

He hated Jerusalem, and although I was born there and we spent long periods of time there, the only thing he ever said about it was that it reminded him of death. At some point in his life his father was a dragoman and because he knew German was said to have shown Palestine to Kaiser Wilhelm. Never referred to by name except when my mother, who never knew him, called him "Abu Assad," my grandfather bore the surname "Ibrahim." In school, therefore, my father was known as Wadie Ibrahim. I still do not know where "Said" came from, and no one seems able to explain it. The only relevant detail about his father that my father thought fit to convey to me was that Abu Assad's whippings of him were much more severe than his of me. "How did you endure it?" I asked, to which he replied with a chuckle: "Most of the time I ran away." I was never able to, and never even considered it.

One day my mother announced that John Gielgud was coming to Cairo to perform *Hamlet* at the Opera House. "We must go," she said with infectious resolve, and indeed the visit was duly set up, although of course I had no idea who John Gielgud was. I was nine at the time, and had just learned a bit about the play in the volume of Shakespeare stories by Charles and Mary Lamb I had been given for Christmas a few months earlier. Mother's idea was that she and I should gradually read through the play together. For that purpose a beautiful one-volume Shakespeare was brought down from the shelf, its handsome red morocco-leather binding and its delicate onion-skin paper embodying for me all that was luxurious and exciting in a book. Its opulence was heightened by the pencil or charcoal drawings illustrating the dramas, *Hamlet*'s being an exceptionally taut tableau by Henry Fuseli of the Prince of Denmark, Horatio, and the Ghost seeming to struggle against each other as the announcement of murder and the agitated response to it gripped them.

The two of us sat in the front reception room, she in a big armchair, I on a stool next to her, with a smoky half-lit fire in the fireplace on her left, and we read *Hamlet* together. She was Gertrude and Ophelia, I Hamlet, Horatio, and Claudius. She also played Polonius, as if in solidarity with my father, who often quoted "neither a borrower nor a lender be" as a reminder of how risky it was for me to be given money to spend on my own. We skipped the whole play-within-a-play sequence as it was too bewilderingly ornate and complicated for the two of us.

There must have been at least four, and perhaps even five or six sessions when, sharing the book, we read and tried to make sense of the play, the two of us completely alone and together, with Cairo, my sisters and father shut out.

I did not understand many of the lines, though Hamlet's basic situation, his outrage at his father's murder and his mother's remarriage, his endless wordy vacillation, did come through half-consciously. I had no idea what incest and adultery were, but could not ask my mother, whose concentration on the play seemed to have drawn her in and away from me. What I remember above all was the change from her normal voice to a new stage voice as Gertrude: it went up in pitch, smoothed out, became exceptionally fluent and, most of all, acquired a bewitchingly flirtatious and calming tone. "Good Hamlet," I remember her clearly saying to me, not to Hamlet, "cast thy nighted colour off, / And let thine eye look like a friend on Denmark." I felt that she was speaking to my better, less disabled and still fresh self, hoping perhaps to lift me out of the sodden delinquency of my life, already burdened with worries and anxieties that I was now sure were to threaten my future.

Reading *Hamlet* as an affirmation of my status in her eyes, not as someone devalued, as in mine I had become, was one of the great moments in my childhood. We were two voices to each other, two happily allied spirits in language. I knew nothing consciously of the inner dynamics that link desperate prince and adulterous queen at the play's interior, nor did I really understand the fury of the scene between them when Polonius is killed and Gertrude verbally flayed by Hamlet. We read together through all that, since what mattered to me was that in a curiously un-Hamlet-like way, I could count on her to be someone whose emotions and affections engaged mine without really being more than an exquisitely maternal, protective and reassuring person. Far from feeling that she had tampered with her obligations to her son, I felt that these readings confirmed the deepness of our connection to each other; for years I kept in my mind the higher than usual pitch of her voice, the unagitated poise of her manner, the soothing, conclusively patient outline of her presence, as goods to be held onto at all costs, but rarer and rarer as my delinquencies increased in number, and her destructive and dislocating capacities threatened me more.

When I saw the play at the Opera House I was jolted out of my seat by Gielgud's declaiming "Angels and ministers of grace defend us," and the sense it conveyed of being a miraculous confirmation of what I had read privately with Mother. The trembling resonance of his voice, the darkened, windy stage, the distantly shining figure of the ghost, all seemed to have brought to life the Fuseli drawing that I had long studied, and it raised my sensuous apprehension to a pitch I do not think I have ever again experienced. But I was also disheartened by the physical incongruities between me and the men whose green and crimson tights set off fully rounded, perfectly shaped legs, that seemed to mock my awkward carriage, my unskilled movements, my spindly, shapeless legs. Everything about Gielgud and the blond man who played Laertes communicated an ease and confidence of being—they were English heroes after all—that reduced me to buglike status, curtailing my capacity for enjoying the play. A few days later, when an Anglo-American classmate called Tony Howard invited me to meet Gielgud at his house, it was all I could do to manage a feeble, silent handshake. Gielgud was in a grey suit, but said nothing; he pressed my small hand with an Olympian half-smile.

It must have been the memory of those long-ago *Hamlet* afternoons in Cairo that made my mother, during the last two or three years of her life, enthusiastic once again about us going to the theater together. The most memorable time was when—her cancer afflictions already pronounced—she arrived in London from Beirut on her way to the United States to consult a specialist; I met her at the airport and brought her to Brown's Hotel for the one night she had to spend there. With barely two hours to get ready and have an early supper, she nevertheless gave an unhesitating "yes" to my suggestion that we see Vanessa Redgrave and Timothy Dalton as Antony and Cleopatra at the Haymarket. It was an understated, unopulent production, and the long play transfixed her in a way that surprised me. After years of Lebanese war and Israeli invasion she had become distracted, often querulous, worried about her health and what she should do with herself. All of this, however, went into abeyance, as we watched and heard Shakespeare's lines ("Eternity was in our lips and eyes, / Bliss in our brows' bent") as if speaking to us in the accents of wartime Cairo, back in our little cocoon, the two of us very quiet and concentrated, savoring the language and communion with each other—despite the disparity in our ages and the fact that we were mother and son—for the very last time. Eight months later she had begun her final descent into the disease that killed her, her mind ravaged by metastases which, before striking her completely silent for the two months before she died, caused her to speak fearsomely of plots around her. The last lucidly intimate thing she ever said to me was "my poor little child," pronounced with such sad resignation, a mother taking final leave of her son. Eighteen months later I was diagnosed with the leukemia that must have already been in me when she died.

When I was growing up I always wished that she might have been the one to watch me play football or tennis, or that she alone could have talked to my teachers, relieved of her duties as my father's partner in the joint program for my reform and betterment. After she died, and I no longer wrote her my weekly letter, nor spoke directly to her in our daily phone call, I kept her as a silent companion. As a small boy to be held in her arms when she wished to cuddle and stroke me was bliss indeed, but such attention could never be sought or asked for. Her moods regulated mine, and I recall one of the most anguished states of my childhood and early adolescence was trying, with nothing to guide me and no great prospect of success, to distract her from her role as taskmaster, and to tease her into giving me approval and support. A good deed, a decent grade, a well-executed passage on the piano might bring about a sudden transfiguration of her face, a dramatic elevation in her tone, a breathtakingly wide opening of arms, as she took me in: "Bravo Edward, my darling boy, bravo, bravo. Let me kiss you."

Yet most of the time she was so driven by a sense of her duty as mother and supervisor of household life that the main voice that has stayed with me from those years is the one that called out injunctions: "Practice your piano, Edward!" "Get back to your homework." "Don't waste time: begin your composition." "Have you had your milk, your tomato juice, your cod-liver oil?" "Finish your plate." "Who ate the chocolates? A full box has disappeared. Edward!"

Time seemed forever against me, and except for a brief morning period when I sensed the day ahead as a possibility, I was boxed in by schedules, chores, assignments, with not a moment for leisurely enjoyment or reflection. I was given my first watch, an insipid-looking Tissot, at the age of eleven or twelve; for several days I spent hours staring at it, mystified by my inability to see its movement, constantly worried that it had stopped. I suspected at first that it was not entirely new since there seemed to be something suspiciously worn about it, but was assured by my parents that it was indeed new, and that its slightly yellowed (tinged with orange) face was characteristic of the model. There the discussion ended. But the watch obsessed me. I compared it first with what my schoolmates wore which, except for the Mickey Mouse and Popeye models that symbolized the America I didn't belong to, struck me as inferior to mine. There was an early period of experimenting with different ways of wearing it: the face turned inwards; on the sleeve; underneath it; fastened tightly; fastened loosely; pushed forward onto my wrist; and on the right hand. I ended up with it on my left wrist, where for a long time it gave me the decidedly positive feeling of being dressed up.

But the watch never failed to impress me with its unimpeded forward movement, which in nearly every way added to my feeling of being behind and at odds with my duties and commitments. I do not recall ever being much of a sleeper but I do remember the faultless punctuality of early-morning reveille and the sense of anxious urgency I felt the moment I got out of bed. There was never any time to dawdle or loiter, though I was inclined to both. I began a lifelong habit then of experiencing time as a wasting, while also resisting it by doing more and more (reading furtively, staring out of the window, looking for a superfluous object like a penknife or yesterday's shirt) in the few moments left before the inexorable deadline. My watch was a help when it showed me that there was time to spare, but most often it guarded my life like a sentinel, on the side of an external order of parents, teachers, and inflexible appointments.

In my early adolescence I was completely in the grip, at once pleasant and unpleasant, of time passing as a series of deadlines—an experience that has remained with me ever since. The day's milestones were set relatively early in that period and have not varied. Six-thirty (or in cases of great pressure six—I still use the phrase "I'll get up at six to finish this") was time to get up; seven-thirty started the meter running, at which point I entered the strict regime of hours and half-hours governed by classes, church, private lessons, homework, piano practice, sports, until bedtime. This sense of the day divided into periods of appointed labor has never left me, has indeed intensified. Eleven A.M. still imbues me with a guilty awareness that the morning has passed without enough being accomplished—it is 11:20 as I write these very words—and 9 P.M. still represents "lateness," that moment which connotes the end of the day, the hastening need to begin thinking about bed, the time beyond which to do work means to do it at the wrong time, fatigue and a sense of having failed all creeping up on one, time slowly getting past its proper period, lateness in all senses.

My watch furnished the basic motif underlying all this, an impersonal discipline that somehow kept the system in order. Leisure was unavailable. I recall with stunning clarity my father's early injunction against remaining in pyjamas and dressing-gown past the early morning hours; slippers in particular were objects of contempt. I still cannot spend any time at all lounging in a dressing-gown: the combined feeling of time-wasting guilt and lazy impropriety overwhelms me. As a way of getting around the discipline, illness (sometimes feigned, sometimes exaggerated) made life away from school positively acceptable. I became the family joke for being especially gratified by, even soliciting, an unnecessary bandage on my finger, knee, or arm. And now by some devilish irony I find myself with an intransigent, treacherous leukemia which, ostrich-like, I try to banish from my mind entirely, attempting with reasonable success to live in my system of time, working, sensing lateness and deadlines and that feeling of insufficient achievement I learned fifty years ago and have so remarkably internalized. But, in another odd reversal, I secretly wonder to myself whether the system of duties and deadlines may now save me, although I know that my illness creeps invisibly on, more secretly and insidiously than the time announced by my first watch, which I carried with so little awareness of how it numbered my mortality, divided it up into perfect, unchanging intervals of unfulfilled time for ever and ever.

In early September 1991, on the eve of the Madrid Peace Conference and forty years after I left the Middle East for the United States, I was in London for a seminar I had convened of Palestinian intellectuals and activists. After the Gulf War and the Palestinian leadership's fatal stand alongside Saddam Hussein, we were in a very weak negotiating position. The idea of the conference was to try to articulate a common set of themes that would assist our progress towards self-determination. We came from all over the dispersed Palestinian world—the West Bank and Gaza, the Palestinian diaspora in various Arab countries, Europe, and North America. What transpired during the seminar was a terrible disappointment: the endless repetition of well-known arguments, our inability to fix on a collective goal, the apparent desire to listen only to ourselves. In short, nothing came of it except an eerie premonition of the Palestinian failure at Oslo.

Midway through the debate, during one of the scheduled breaks, I phoned Mariam, my wife, in New York to ask her if the results of the blood test I had taken for my annual physical had been satisfactory. Cholesterol was what had concerned me and no, she said, everything was fine on that front but added with some hesitation: "Charles Hazzi"—our doctor—"would like to speak to you when you get back." Something in her voice suggested to me that all was not well, so I immediately rang Charles at his office. "Nothing to get excited about," he said, "we'll talk in New York." His repeated refusals to tell me what was wrong finally provoked me to impatience. "You must tell me, Charles. I'm not a child, and I have a right to know." With a whole set of demurrals—it's not serious, a hematologist can very easily take care of you, it's chronic after all—he told me that I had chronic lymphocytic leukemia (CLL), although it took me a week to absorb the initial impact of my diagnosis. I was asymptomatic and sophisticated diagnostic techniques were needed to confirm the original finding. It was another month before I understood how thoroughly shaken I was by this "sword of Damocles," as one doctor called it, hanging over me, and a further six months before I found the extraordinary doctor, Kanti Rai, under whose care I have been since June 1992.

A month after I was diagnosed I discovered myself in the middle of a letter to my mother, who had been dead for a year and a half. Somehow the urge to communicate with her overcame the factual reality of her death, which in mid-sentence stopped my fanciful urge, leaving me slightly disoriented, even embarrassed. A vague narrative urge seemed to be stirring inside me, but I was too caught up in the anxieties and nervousness of my life with CLL to pay it much attention. During that period in 1993 I contemplated several changes in my life which I realized without any fear would be shorter and more difficult now. I thought about moving to Boston to return to a place I had lived in and enjoyed when I was a student, but I soon admitted to myself that because it was a quiet town relative to New York I had been thinking regressively about finding a place to die in. I gave up the idea.

So many returns, attempts to go back to bits of life, or people who were no longer there: these constituted a steady response to the increasing rigors of my illness. In 1992 I went with my wife and children to Palestine for the first time in forty-five years. In July 1993 I went on my own to Cairo, making it a point in the middle of a journalistic mission to visit old haunts. All this time I was being monitored, without treatment, by Dr. Rai, who occasionally reminded me that I would at some point require chemotherapy. By the time I began treatment in March 1994 I realized that I had at least entered, if not the final phase of my life, then the period—like Adam and Eve leaving the Garden—from which there would be no return to my old life. In May 1994 I began work on the memoir I am writing.

These details are important as a way of explaining to myself and to my reader how the time of the memoir is intimately tied to the time, phases, ups and downs, variations in my illness. As I grew weaker, the more the number of infections and bouts of side effects increased, the more the memoir was my way of constructing something in prose while in my physical and emotional life I grappled with the anxieties and pains of degeneration. Both tasks resolved themselves into details: to write is to get from word to word, to suffer illness is to go through the infinitesimal steps that take you from one state to another. With other sorts of work that I did, essays, lectures, teaching, journalism, I was going across the illness, punctuating it almost forcibly with deadlines and cycles of beginning, middle, and end: with this memoir I was borne along by the episodes of treatment, hospital stay, physical pain and mental anguish, letting those dictate how and when I could write, for how long and where. Periods of travel were often productive since I carried my handwritten manuscript with me wherever I went and took advantage of every hotel room or friend's house I stayed in. I was therefore rarely in a hurry to get a section done, though I had a precise idea of what I planned to put in it. Curiously the memoir and the phases of my illness share exactly the same time, although most traces of the latter have been effaced in the story of my early life. This record of a life and the ongoing course of a disease are one and the same, it could be said; the same but deliberately different.

And the more this relationship developed the more important it became to me, the more also my memory—unaided by anything except concentrated reflection on and archaeological prying into a very distant and essentially irrecoverable past—seemed hospitable and generous to my often importunate forays. Despite the travail of disease and the restrictions imposed on me by my having left the places of my youth, I can say with the poet: "nor in this bower, / This little lime-tree bower, have I not mark'd / Much that has soothed me." There had been a time when I could not bear to think about my past, especially Cairo and Jerusalem, which for two sets of different reasons were no longer accessible. The latter had been replaced by Israel, the former, by one of those cruel coincidences, was closed to me for legal reasons. Unable to visit Egypt for the fifteen years between 1960 and 1975, I rationed early memories of my life there (considerably chopped up, full of atmospherics that conveyed a sense of warmth and comfort by contrast with the harsh alienation I felt in my New York life) as a way of falling asleep, an activity that has grown more difficult with time, time that has also dissolved the aura of happiness around my early life and let it emerge as a more complicated and difficult period. To grasp it, I realized, I would have to be sharply alert, awake, avoiding dreamy somnolence. I've thought in fact that the memoir in some fundamental way is all about sleeplessness, all about the silence of wakefulness and, in my case, the need for conscious recollection and articulation as a substitute for sleep. Not just for sleep but for holidays and relaxation, all that passes for middle- and upper-class "leisure," on which, about ten years ago, I unconsciously turned my back. As one of the main responses to my illness I found in the memoir a new kind of challenge: not just a new kind of wakefulness but a project about as far from my professional and political life as it was possible for me to go.

The underlying motifs for me have been, on the one hand, the emergence of a second self buried for a very long time beneath a surface of often expertly acquired and wielded social characteristics belonging to the self my parents tried to construct, the "Edward" I speak of intermittently, and, on the other, an understanding of the way an extraordinary number of departures have unsettled my life from its earliest beginnings. To me, nothing more painful and paradoxically sought after characterizes my life than the many displacements from countries, cities, abodes, languages, environments that have kept me in motion all these years. Twelve years ago I wrote in *After the Last Sky* that when I travel I always take too much with me, and that even a trip downtown requires the packing of a briefcase stocked with items disproportionately larger in size and number than the actual period of the trip. Analyzing that, I concluded that I had a secret but ineradicable fear of not returning. What I've since discovered is that despite this fear I fabricate occasions for departure, thus giving rise to the fear voluntarily. The two seem absolutely necessary to my rhythm of life and have intensified dramatically during the period of my illness. I say to myself: if you don't take this trip, don't prove your mobility and indulge your fear of being lost, don't override the normal rhythms of domestic life now, you certainly will not be able to do so in the near future. I also experience the anxious moodiness of travel (*la mélancholie des paquebots*, as Flaubert calls it; *bahnhofstimmung* in German), along with envy for those who stay behind, whom I see on my return, their faces unshadowed by dislocation or what seems to be enforced mobility, happy with their families, draped in a comfortable suit and raincoat, there for all to see. Something about the invisibility of the departed, being missing and perhaps missed, in addition to the intense, repetitive and predictable sense of banishment that takes you away from all you know and can take comfort in, makes you feel the need to leave out of some prior, but self-created logic, and a sense of rapture. In all cases, though, the great fear is that departure is the state of being abandoned, even though it is you who leave.

During the last few months of my mother's life she would tell me plaintively and frequently about the misery of trying to fall asleep. She was in Washington, I in New York, we would speak constantly, see each other about once a month. Her cancer was spreading, I knew. She refused to have chemotherapy: "Ma biddee at'adthab," she would say: "I don't want the torture of it." Years later I was to have four years of it with no success, but she never buckled, never gave in even to her doctor's importunings, never had chemotherapy. But she could not sleep at night. Sedatives, sleeping pills, soothing drinks, the counsel of friends and relatives, reading, praying: none, she said, did any good. "Help me to sleep, Edward," she once said to me with a piteous trembling in her voice that I can still hear as I write. But then the disease spread to her brain, and for the last six weeks she slept all the time. Sitting by her bed with my sister Grace, waiting for her to awaken, was, for me, the most anguished and paradoxical of my experiences with her.

Now I have divined that my own inability to sleep may be her last legacy to me, a counter to her struggle for sleep. For me sleep is something to get over as quickly as possible. I can only go to bed very late, but I am up, literally, at dawn. Like her, I don't possess the secret of long sleep, though unlike her I have reached the point where I do not want it. For me, sleep is death, as is any diminishment in awareness. During my last treatment—a twelve-week ordeal—I was most upset by the drugs I was given to ward off fever and shaking chills, and manifestly upset by the sense of being infantilized, the helplessness that many years ago I had conceded as that of a child to my mother and, differently, to my father. I fought the medical soporifics bitterly, as if my identity depended on that resistance.

Sleeplessness for me is a cherished state, to be desired at almost any cost; there is nothing for me as invigorating as the early-morning shedding of the shadowy half-consciousness of a night's loss, reacquainting myself with what I might have lost completely a few hours earlier. I occasionally experience myself as a cluster of flowing currents. I prefer this to the idea of a solid self, the identity to which so many attach so much significance. These currents, like the themes of one's life, are borne along during the waking hours, and at their best they require no reconciling, no harmonizing. They may be not quite right, but at least they are always in motion, in time, in place, in the form of strange combinations moving about, not necessarily forward, against each other, contraptually yet without one central theme. A form of freedom, I'd like to think, even if I am far from being totally convinced that it is. That skepticism, too, is something I particularly want to hold onto. With so many dissonances in my life I have learned to prefer being not quite right, out of place.

from *Out of Place*

PART IV

Spoken Words

17

An Interview with Edward W. Said

New York, July–August 1999

You once wrote that "a beginning methodologically unites a practical need with a theory, an intention with a method." Having completed your memoir, Out of Place, *in which you write about the need to leave behind a "subjective account" of your youth in Egypt, Palestine, Lebanon, and the United States, you chose to focus on a period of your life before the 1967 war. What is the intention behind your beginning?*

Edward Said: It is difficult to describe what you feel when you get a peculiar diagnosis, such as the one I received in September of 1991. I was told that I had a very obscure disease, though it is quite common among the leukemias. While I showed no symptoms, I was told that I had a sword of Damocles hanging over my head. It suddenly dawned on me that I was going to die.

I don't think that I was ever consciously afraid of dying, though I soon grew aware of the shortage of time. My first impulse was to go some place quieter than New York, but that idea didn't last very long. And then, from out of the blue, I think probably left over from the death of my mother, who died in July of 1990, I considered writing about my early years, most of them connected with her. Two and a half years later, in March 1994, I began the memoir.

During the treatment, writing the memoir became a kind of discipline for me. I would use the time in the mornings to write and to follow my memory to reconstruct a world that I had lost and was losing more and more of everyday. As a way of shaping the book, I tried to recall the places that had changed irrecoverably in my life: Egypt, Palestine, and Lebanon. During that period I visited those places. I went back to Palestine in 1992 for the first time in forty-five years, and I went back to Lebanon in 1992, my first visit there since the Israeli invasion of 1982.

What does it mean for you to recover loss in your own mind as opposed to responding to the objective and political experience of national loss?

With *Out of Place*, I was trying to free myself from the responsibility that, whether I liked it or not, was imposed on me whenever I wrote about the Middle East. There was always a political issue to respond to. My whole engagement after the 1967 war was predicated on that basis, and I never really had time to do much else.

Out of Place was written in a setting of a certain amount of suffering. A lot of the time I was quite ill. I would write a few sentences and then I would have to get up and take some medicine, or lie down. Writing *Out of Place* was a completely different kind of experience for me. I wasn't trying to address an audience, though I had some idea of addressing my children's generation. Neither of my children knew my father, for example, whereas both of them knew my mother. The memoir was an attempt to describe my past for them and to record events and experiences that had made a great impression on me, as is the case with both of my aunts about whom I write. My maternal great-aunt and my paternal aunt had been very important in my life and in the life of our community when I was younger. A feeling of Virgilian sadness gave a life to things that had passed. *Out of Place* is also, in a way, a Proustian meditation.

How would you compare this to your other longer autobiographical meditation, After the Last Sky?

After the Last Sky was written in response to a particular political situation. It arose from a conference at the United Nations in Geneva in 1983 and from the fact that the United Nations would not allow us to place captions beneath the photographs of Palestinians. At roughly the same time, I had met the photographer Jean Mohr and the writer John Berger, whose work together—*Another Way of Telling* and the *Seventh Man*—had greatly influenced me. *After the Last Sky* was a political occasion geared at reconstructing the experience and lives of Palestinians. In contrast, *Out of Place* had to do with my own sense of my life ebbing away.

You begin Out of Place *with the idea of the invention of families and of the self, which has echoes of your first book,* Joseph Conrad and the Fiction of Autobiography. *More than Foucault or Frantz Fanon, why has Conrad occupied such a central place in your writing?*

I first read Conrad when I was about seventeen or eighteen years old as an undergraduate at Princeton. It was my freshman year, and I was reading *Heart of Darkness*, which completely mystified me at the time. It presented a kind of writing that I had never encountered before. As a child I had read a lot—Walter Scott, Conan Doyle, Alexandre Dumas, Dickens, Thackeray—and I had acquired a very strong background in what I would call not just novels of adventure, but *novels of openness*—novels where everything seems available to you. *Heart of Darkness* had the form of an adventure story, but the more I looked at it, the more the adventure story dissolved. I remember having discussions with my friends in the dormitory trying to figure out what "the horror" meant, who Kurtz was, and so forth. Sometime later, a year before I went to graduate school, I then began to read an enormous amount of Conrad, and the more I read, the more I wanted to know about him. As a graduate student at Harvard, I looked through a volume of letters that he wrote to Cunningham Graham and I was struck that there was a certain back and forth between his letters and his fiction—many of the things that appeared in his letters would turn up in a different way in his fiction.

Conrad always seems to come back to me in one way or another. I think that his exile, the overtones of his writing, its accents, its slippages, his sense of being in and out of language, being in and out of worlds, his skepticism, his radical uncertainty, the sense that you always feel that something terribly important is going on, what Forster made fun of—a tremendous crisis happening but you can't tell what it is—has just gripped me more than any other writer has.

How did the relatively little-read Giambattista Vico come to have such marked presence in your work?

Vico was an accidental discovery through a dear friend, Arthur Gold, who was a classmate of mine at Princeton and Harvard. What interested me most about Vico was that he was self-made and self-taught. Vico represented somebody who succeeded on his own by the act and strength of his imagination. Throughout his writings, for example, there are wild and fantastic images—of giants, of men and women copulating, of ferocious settings with thunder striking, and so on. For him, imagery was inextricably related to the writing of history, and added to that was the connection between imagery and words, and how words are, at the first stage onomatopoeic—primitive imitations of emotions of fear and of disorganization. Vico completely disrupted the Cartesian paradigm.

What also attracted me to Vico was his interest in philology, and, I must say, his relative obscurity. He was a philologist, a professor of eloquence and Latin jurisprudence at the University of Naples in the early eighteenth century. The more I read about him, the more he attracted me. He led me to Erich Auerbach, since Auerbach had translated Vico into German. In addition, there was something private about Vico, just as there was something private about Conrad that neither one of them every fully disclosed. I focused on that and tried to make of it what I could, as a way of validating what I was trying to do outside the given academic track. Lastly, as with Conrad, I found the organization of Vico's work, *The New Science*, completely original, almost artistic. Vico was a great theoretician of beginnings.

Is that how you came to write Beginnings?

Beginnings is really the product of the 1967 war. I was at Columbia in the summer of 1967, and I had been awarded a fellowship at the University of Illinois, where I spent 1967 and 1968 at the Center for Advanced Study.

Around that time I was serving on a jury. The day the war began, June 5, was my first day as a juror. I listened to the reports of the war on a little transistor radio. "How were 'we' doing?" the jurors would ask. I found I wasn't able to say anything—I felt embarrassed. I was the only Arab there, and everybody was very powerfully identified with the Israelis. Also, during that summer, which I spent in New York, I became connected with the Arab political world because of the UN meetings. I started to meet diplomats, and I suddenly found myself, after sixteen years of being in this country, back in touch directly with the Middle East and the Arab world.

My project for Illinois was to be a book on Swift. But when I arrived in Illinois, I found myself in a difficult situation because of the war, I became increasingly concerned about my family still in the Middle East, and became increasingly aware of a part of the world that now had been thrust upon me. Furthermore, my marriage was coming apart. One day I found myself talking about beginnings. I began writing an essay entitled "Meditation on Beginnings," which was really an attempt to reformulate where I was. I remember the room in the Center for Advanced Study with rows of books on and by Jonathan Swift, but the question of beginnings obsessed me. I divorced the following year and began to work on a study of the relationship between beginnings and narrative, which brought me back to Vico. *Beginnings* was thus really a project of reaction to a crisis that caused me to rethink what I was doing, and try to make more connections in my life between things that had been either suppressed, or denied, or hidden.

Orientalism *also addresses this theme of denial, or suppression, through a cultural paradigm. It has been a tremendously influential book, translated into many languages, but, as you write in the afterword, it has, in a Borgesian way, become more than one book. It has been interpreted in many different ways. Why do you think this book has produced so many different reactions and readings?*

Every context produces different readers and different kinds of misinterpretations. In *Orientalism*, I begin with a notion that interpretation is misinterpretation, that there is no such thing as the correct interpretation. For instance, I recently got a letter from the publisher of the Bulgarian edition of *Orientalism*, asking if I would write a preface for it. I didn't know what to say. *Orientalism* is about to appear in Hungary, in Vietnam, and in Estonia. These are all places that I've never been to and I know very little about. So you can see how uncontrolled all these interpretations can be. In that respect, I think certain kinds of distortions and deviations are inevitable.

What you *can* control is your own ideas. If you keep repeating them, simplifying them, and making them more accessible, through disciples, through rewritings and lectures on the same subject, then you can induce the kind of Borgesian trap that you referred to. I've been very conscious about not doing that. I've always tried to develop my ideas further, in ways that paradoxically make them in a certain sense ungraspable and unparaphrasable. I've found myself, for example, being more interested in some of the inconsistencies and irreconcilabilities of historical experience, including that of *Orientalism*. There are certain contradictions, what I call antinomies, that cannot be resolved, and it's important to explore and to deepen investigation of them. I want to say, well, they're there, we can't wish them away, we can't reconcile them under duress, as Theodor Adorno says. As intellectuals, we have to be able to make them more apparent, to make their influence more profound and more felt, which requires more work and more of an understanding of different kinds of political organizations and intellectual efforts.

This notion of irreconcilable antinomies sounds very much like dissonances in music. In your essay on Jane Austen's Mansfield Park, *for example, you discuss Austen's silence around Thomas Bertram's slaveholding in the sugar plantations in Antigua. Figures of silence and sound have been very important in your literary criticism. How do you think your training as a musician has affected your reading of literature?*

That's a very interesting question. The idea that I have borrowed from R. P. Blackmur, the idea of bringing literature to performance, is certainly connected to the notion of music. The idea is that works of art place a premium on expression, articulation, clarity. All the things that we associate with writing and with performance involve a discourse that needs to be unfolded and then presented.

But at the same time, I've always been interested in what gets left out. That's why I'm interested in the figure from the "Ode on a Grecian Urn," the "silent form" that "dost tease us out of thought." That's why I'm interested in Raymond Williams's discussion of the country house poems, where the representation of the country house necessarily excludes the silence of the peasants who have been driven off the land; or the fields that have been manicured to produce the beautiful spaces that Jane Austen exploits in her novels, where livelihood is transformed into property. I'm interested in the tension between what is represented and what isn't represented, between the articulate and the silent. For me, it has a very particular background in the questioning of the document. What does the document include? What doesn't it include? That's why I have been very interested in attempts of the Subaltern Studies Collective, and others, to talk about excluded voices.

In the particular case of the Palestinians, one of our problems is that we don't have documents to substantiate what we said happened to us. Take one of the Israeli new historians, Benny Morris, for instance. He's very literal-minded, and he's done very important work, but his assumption is that he can't say anything about what happened in 1947–1948 unless there's a document to show for it. I say, well, why not try to animate that silence? Why not look at the poetry of Mahmoud Taha, who writes about *al-Nakba* in a very interesting way? Why not look at oral history? Why not look at geographical evidence? Why not look at the landscape? Why not go through the process of trying to reconstruct out of the silence what was either destroyed or excluded?

A lot of my work has this very strong geographical as opposed to Hegelian dimension. The contrast between Georg Lukács and Antonio Gramsci is very important to me here. For Gramsci (in contrast to Lukács, who is more concerned about time) there is a territorial, geographical, and material basis for art that isn't always expressed in the document. For Gramsci, territoriality is represented in many forms: the testimony of victims, the refugees who still carry keys to the houses from which they've been driven. Silence and territoriality has been crucial to a lot of the work I've been doing and the work I've done.

Is this concern with silence and sound reflected in the types of music that interest you, and what's the relationship between music and the idea of the "contrapuntal," an idea borrowed from music and elaborated in Culture and Imperialism, *where you discuss ways of reading works of literature from the First and Third Worlds as overlapping experiences?*

One of the things that has been commented on—and which I've responded to—is that I'm only interested in a particular kind of Western music. Why, for example, does the music of Bach or of Wagner interest me more than the music of Bellini, Donizetti, or Verdi, who emphasize the solo voice and the melodic *fioritura*? It's simply because I'm not interested in monophony. Polyphony, the organization of more than one voice, is what really interests me. I'm attracted to the combination of voices, the way one voice becomes subordinated by another. I'm interested in the possibilities for the interpreter to bring out voices which, to the author or to the composer, may not have been apparent. Bach, for example, had a fantastic capacity for predicting what combinations of sounds could come out of a single phrase. In the interpretation of polyphonic compositions, there is no predictability. In the case of Glenn Gould, there is no predicting which voice he wants to highlight at any given moment. There are voices that are fundamentally present, yet not always apparent in polyphony. There is therefore a certain amount of leeway given to the interpreter to highlight one voice against the other, while not eliminating voices, so that other voices can come out in a different way. The effect is of a multilevel sound.

Is there something about music itself that fosters a rupture between the artist and the world?

Absolutely. Most musicians are completely wrapped up in the world of music. First, it's incredibly demanding technically. By virtue of its language, it's non-denotative, and therefore isolated from the world of everyday intercourse. Second, it's extremely competitive, especially for performers. They have to keep up at a certain level of physical practice. The intellectual component for most performers is very small because they tend to play the same pieces over and over again.

But I'm very interested in the social component of music. For example, what is the moral problem, which Adorno posed, of music in the context of Auschwitz, where the camp commander would be killing people by day and playing Bach by night? There is a shocking contemporary example which I raised once with Daniel Barenboim and has been confirmed by several reports. One of my son's friends, who had been a member of Hamas, told me that he can't tolerate the sound of Beethoven. I asked him why. He said that in Israel, where torture is legal and euphemistically called "moderate physical pressure," the Israelis would put him in a cell at night with loudspeakers and play classical music as loud as possible just to continue the strain on him. What about that? The use of classical music by a people who have a very high level of musical culture, whose philharmonic orchestra plays Beethoven as well as any orchestra in the world—for use in interrogation centers against Palestinians, well, it's simply indefensible.

Musicians exist on the stage in an extreme position where the performance blocks everything out. What I'm interested in seeing is certain kinds of connections that might not otherwise be seen, like the connections between music and patronage, between music and culture, the connection between music and power.

This is what has attracted me to Adorno in the first place and has kept me interested in him all along. For Adorno, from the beginning of his career to the end of his life, music is in a permanent, contradictory, and dialectical tension with society. As few critics of Adorno acknowledge, music is at the core of his philosophy and understanding of culture. Whereas most intellectuals have a certain fluency with films, photography, and the figurative arts generally, most have no connection at all with music. But the more you read of Adorno, the more you realize that music is in that state of tension with everything, including itself, and including the music that matters the most to him. He isolates certain figures like Arnold Schoenberg and late Beethoven as examples of the most intransigent, the most unreconciled, the most irreconcilable music. This kind of starkness of what is unreconciled and can't be synthesized is what attracted me to Adorno. Yet he doesn't give this irreconcilability the kind of tragic dimension that for me it has always had.

For me, this concept of irreconcilability has always been essential as a way of characterizing the relationship between Israelis and Palestinians. No matter what you say or what you do, you're dealing with two totally irreconcilable experiences: one premised on the nonexistence of the other, in the case of the Israelis; and in the case of the Palestinians, they are unable to forget, or to let go of what was destroyed. That's one of the reasons why I've taken such a dim view of the whole question of peace as it is being negotiated, which for me seems to negate a quintessential and irreconcilable opposition at the very core of it.

And is this irreconcilability expressed in the putative reconcilation of the Oslo peace process?

Yes, and the fundamental denial of Palestinian rights will continue. While the Israelis continue to circumvent the Oslo agreement, they will attempt to sweeten it. Instead of five percent of the land, they will give them forty percent. There's no problem giving them more land as it gives them more municipal problems. But it is also clear that security, that borders, that real economic independence will be denied to the Palestinians. As long as the disparity of power is so great between the Israelis and the Palestinians, the Palestinians will continue to suffer, no matter what.

The situation of Palestinians inside Israel is also being exacerbated all the time. There is the problem about what do you do about these basically disenfranchised citizens. There is the problem of movement, the problem of development in the Occupied Territories, the problem of economic stagnation, the problem of unemployment, the problem with refugees. All these will remain unaddressed. No matter what is fed into the economy from the World Bank and from donor nations, the economy still isn't going to fly. We're talking about four and a half to five million refugees that the Israelis under no circumstances are going to take back. Palestinians in Lebanon are still disenfranchised. Of course, arrangements will be made as part of the final status negotiations, even to take care of a few refugees here and there. But basically the problem—an unfulfilled nationalism—will remain unsettled.

This unfulfilled nationalism is the important point, which is very much in touch with and fed to a certain degree by civil, social, and economic problems in the various Arab countries. The problems of democracy, the problems of freedom of expression, the problems of the nongovernmental organizations, which is a big issue in Egypt, the problem of press laws in Jordan and Egypt suggest to me a kind of volatility, which the peace process is simply putting off. It's like putting a finger in a dike. These problems will come back, simply because the pathologies of power, as Eqbal Ahmad called them, in these countries are being consolidated by the peace process. They are not being challenged.

Consider a country like Egypt, where the army is the largest single employer. What happens after the absorptive power of the army ends? How long can they continue to absorb arms that they don't use? How long can the army and the tiny crust at the top of the financial and economic managers contain such a situation? Huge percentages of the population in a city like Cairo, which has grown six times its original size, remain unemployed, unhoused, unprovided for with basic resources. How long can they continue to hold on? The only way to think of these issues is not piecemeal, that is to say—we'll deal with the Palestinian issue, we'll deal with the Syrian issue, we'll deal with the Lebanese issue, we'll solve that in a week—you've got to take a holistic view because they are all interconnected.

The Arab world, despite what appears to be the failure of Arab nationalism, is still a united world in many ways. They are all connected by electronic communication, by a common language, by travel, by traditions, by religion, and so forth. These are going to be affected. The current system has failed miserably. Production has declined, economic development has declined, illiteracy is stunningly on the rise. The illiteracy rate in countries like Egypt is now approaching fifty percent, a retreat from what had been the earlier achievements of the Egyptian revolution. Unemployment is going up all the time. Above all, the natural resources of the Arab world, which are principally oil, are being depleted. The price of oil has gone down to one third of what it was in the 1970s, if not more. And the spending patterns and the economic plans that have been made are so stupidly and so badly organized that these countries, including Saudi Arabia, are confronting enormous economic obstacles. That's what we're facing, not the development of the Middle Eastern common market that Clinton and Peres and others talk about. Whom would that market serve? Large numbers of people are not going to be affected by it. In Jordan, they're building fifteen new five-star hotels. But they are completely empty. Who are these for? The country is in a state of economic ruin.

Yet despite the irreconcilable nature of the conflict there has been a growing recognition by you and others that the binational solution of an Israeli-Palestinian state is the only legitimate, feasible, and above all just solution for the Palestinians and the Israelis. When and how did you arrive at this conclusion of the binational state? And how would you relate this to the other vision of the Middle East that you have been detailing?

Basically, there are two things. First, the principle of separation and partition has governed Middle Eastern politics since the end of World War II until the present and including the peace process. Largely through the work of my own students who have been interested in partition, like Joe Cleary who worked on partition in Palestine, Ireland, and the Indian subcontinent, I realized that partition hasn't worked. The problems haven't gone away in any of these places. On the ground, people are living together in unequal and unfair conditions. The existential reality is that people still live together despite the schemes of partition and separation. The question is can they live together in equality and in a system that is more acceptable than apartheid? This is the Palestinian predicament.

But elsewhere in the Arab world, the whole notion of homogeneous states—the Egyptian state, the Syrian state, the Jordanian state—is an expression of a flawed concept of nationalism. It simply doesn't answer to the realities of migrant and refugee populations, and of minorities, whether it's the Kurds, the Shias, the Christians, or the Palestinians. There are different kinds of minorities. The notion of an Egyptian state for the Egyptians, a Jewish state for the Jews, simply flies in the face of reality. What we require is a rethinking of the present in terms of coexistence and porous borders. We can find other models from the past other than the separationist, partition model. If you look at the history of Andalusia and of Palestine as multicultural histories, you'll find that the models are not simply nationalist and homogeneous, but really multicultural, pluricultural, and plurireligious. Even under the Ottoman empire, communities were allowed to live in coexistence with other communities. Of course, there were inequities. But they lived without this ridiculous notion that every *millet* has to have its own state. They lived as national communities. Israel hasn't been able to do that for the Arabs. Arabs in Israel have never been recognized as a national community. Similarly, in Egypt the Copts have never been recognized as a national community. I'm not saying that one should aggravate sectarian sentiment. I'm simply saying that the model of separation, the model of partition, isn't working.

Is there some other way that one could formulate or conceive of a future that goes beyond those kinds of aggravated sectarianisms? The Lebanese example is a perfect one: fifteen years of civil war fought on sectarian grounds. The war was concluded with the peace of Taif in 1990. Lebanon is still sectarian because the system of government hasn't evolved. There is a very important intellectual role to be played by the cultural elites, as they have done in Ireland, in Cyprus, in India, and so forth. We haven't rethought these peculiar partitions and separations in our part of the world.

There is a great reluctance in the Arab world to talk about coexistence with the Israeli Jews. There have been riots in Egypt about this subject, which I think is shameful. I'm not saying that one should normalize with the Israeli government, but there are other forms of normalization. You could have relationships with like-minded people on the basis of something other than "you're a Jew, and I'm a Palestinian" or "I'm an Arab and you're a Jew." There are political and class issues that need to be discussed and through those discussions alliances can be made. The hypocrisy of the ruling class is such that they always say that they don't condone normalization, yet they make peace with Israel. Similarly, Egyptian, Jordanian, and Palestinian intellectuals say they don't want normalization, yet they want to cooperate with Israelis on the basis of who can help them. Those positions seem to me absolutely foolish because there are other constituencies in these countries with whom they have much more in common, like university students, intellectuals, writers, musicians, labor unions, and minorities. Think of the Sephardic minority, the Mizrahim in Israel. Nobody has ever tried to deal with them. What I'm advocating is an attempt to find out about the other. Consider that in the Arab world today there isn't a single university that has a department of Israeli or Hebrew studies. It's not taught. There are about sixty research institutes on the West Bank, none of which are dedicated to the study of Israeli society. Yet how many institutes in Israel are devoted to the study of Arab society? Dozens and dozens. We keep ourselves in a state of inequality and refuse to look beyond an immediate nationalism. We say that all Israelis are really in the end extensions of Netanyahu and Barak, yet we refuse to consider the complexity of what is offered.

Rosemary Sayyigh uses a phrase "too many enemies." And we've had a lot of enemies. Despite that, we've been very poorly led, which I suppose is our fault. But we've never had the leadership that really understood what they were up against. We've never had a consistent and adequate strategy that has attracted our own people to it. We have never been able to mobilize our people properly. Even at the height of the so-called militant phase, during the *intifada* or before it, during the Amman period and up to and including 1982, only a small percentage of Palestinians was involved in the Palestinian effort. A lot of talents were and are simply untapped.

The fact that we've never really had a center, or sovereignty anyplace is part of our predicament. I don't think we've ever had, as the Zionists always did, a strategic partner. In the first place they had the British Empire; after 1948 they had the Americans. We've never had anything comparable. In today's unipolar world, it isn't as if there's a big choice. That's why the current leadership is trying to get close to the Americans. The question is how much space is there in the Israeli-American relationship for Palestinians? It's not a rhetorical question. The answer is very little. But that's what the leadership has accepted.

The other crucial point is that we've never understood the importance of the United States the way the African National Congress (ANC) did, and we've never tried to organize a human rights campaign on a mass basis. The leaders and the elites have decided that their best hope was the oligarchies. They chose to attract the interest of the business community, of the State Department, instead of a wider base. That's the vision that they have of the future, and the proof of that is the kind of state that is being set up now. It's basically a police state run by an oligarchy. The question is, where is that going to go?

I don't think we've spent enough time trying to involve segments of the Israeli public in our struggle. The ANC from the very beginning announced that it would include whites in its ranks. We've never done that. Even now, sympathetic Israelis are not welcome as equal participants in Palestinian institutions on the West Bank and Gaza. They're never invited. That doesn't mean that there isn't a form of normalization going on between Israeli academics and Palestinian academics. That's going on all the time under the auspices of the Ford Foundation. It's not the same thing, however, as being involved in a militant common front for liberation.

The nature of our enemy is a very complicated one. It's not as if we're fighting white settlers in Rhodesia, in South Africa, or in Algeria. These are people whose moral stature, especially after World War II and the Holocaust, is as victims. But I don't feel that the struggle is by any means over. We have several generations to go. This apartheid peace that they've proposed cannot possibly last. It will be conclusive, and it will end with a peace treaty. There will be a final settlement, but it will be a settlement dictated by Israeli and American power rather than by justice or by the real need for self-determination and liberation for the Palestinians. It's not a peace that will provide for a real coexistence.

Picking up about what you said about the South African struggles, we want to ask you a question about human rights. "Palestine," you have written, "is today the touchstone case of human rights, not because the argument for it can be made as elegantly simple as the case for South African liberation, but because it cannot be made simple." Such a stand relies on a recognition of the universal value of human rights, yet in the same essay you detail how Western liberalism has historically been more than willing to compromise its principles when the details become too difficult or embarrassing for the strong on how they treat the weak (de Tocqueville on Algeria, or Spencer on the Irish or Mill on India). Can we have an enforceable scheme of human rights when the powerful constantly patrol the legitimacy of human rights? Is a "new universalism," as Partha Chaterjee has called for, possible, particularly with the tainted history of the United Nations in the last few years? And can the Western tradition of human rights, based on the sovereignty of the individual before the idea of community rights, be made to respond to the kind of group abuses that we see today?

Well, I think so. The whole point of the kind of work that I try to do, and many others do it as well, is to extend the notion of human rights to cover everybody, not to restrict the notion. I have no patience at all for the argument that is frequently made in my part of the world and further east that human rights is a Western imperial concept. That's complete nonsense. Torture is torture. Pain is felt just as much in Singapore as it is in Saudi Arabia, as it is in Israel, as it is in France or the United States.

One has to be absolutely vigilant for the kinds of exceptions that you mentioned, the de Tocqueville example. There's a new book out now on human rights that was reviewed recently by Jeffrey Robinson, where he talks about every notion and every instance of human rights in the world. He doesn't mention Palestine. If you're going to talk about human rights as a universal value, then you have to apply it in all cases. That was part of what I was trying to do during the Kosovo episode, to show how inconsistent and how flawed argument was that was made there, that it wasn't adequate, either to the particular instance of Kosovo or to parallel instances in Turkey, Saudi Arabia, or Israel.

I think also that there is still a major role to be played in the whole question of *humanism*. Take the American example, historically. It's all very well to proclaim the eternal values of humanism, but those values always flounder when it comes, for example, to the treatment of Native Americans, to African Americans, to Arab Americans. The only life that is possible for humanism is if it's revived in the interest of a universal concept. This is especially needed in this country, with its own views and special history of exceptionalism, "manifest destiny," and patriotism. This notion of American goodness is the sense that "we Americans" fight altruistic wars, the sense that "we" wage campaigns for the good of the other. That has to be demythologized and replaced with a real critique of power. This is implicit in the work of a lot of dissenters in this country, in the modern period, from William Appleman Williams to Gabriel Kolko to Noam Chomsky. We need to discover a new concept of humanism based of a rejuvenated idea of it, drawing also from the older traditions, including the Islamic tradition.

Everyone thinks, for example, that the notion of humanism originated in Italy in the fifteenth century. But George Makdisi has written an important study called *The Rise of Colleges: Institutions of Learning in Islam and the West*. In it, he says that the origin of the modern system of knowledge that we call humanism did not originate as Jacob Burckhardt and many others believed it did in Italy during the fifteenth and sixteenth century Renaissance, but rather in the Arab colleges, *madrasas,* mosques and courts of Iraq, Sicily, Egypt, Andalusia, from the eighth century on. Those places formed the traditions and the curricula of legal, theological, as well as secular learning—the so-called *studia abadiya*—from which European humanists derived many of their ideas not only about learning itself, but also about the environment of learning where disputation, dissent, and argument were the order of the day. Humanism is a much less exclusive Western concept than a lot of people rather proudly think. It exists in India, in the Chinese tradition, in the Islamic tradition.

I think humanism can be squared with a more humane tradition than Western liberalism, which in my opinion is bankrupt. Look at neoliberalism today, whether of the Clinton or the Blair variety. For them, it means globalization, it means the so-called free market economy, which is deepening the socio-economic and even ethnic differences much more than even classical capitalism did. I'm interested in alternatives that take into account the facts of globalization. Today's world is smaller, and there is a kind of interdependence that really began with imperialism in the nineteenth century when, for the first time, the whole global scene was made into one economic unit. In the face of that, what kind of humanism is possible? This is the most important question to answer today, when individual instances like Palestine or Ireland still cry out for resolution.

What's the role of the university in renewing this notion of humanism?

The university, at least the American university, is a kind of utopian place, and I would like to preserve it as a place where certain kinds of things are made possible. The idea that the classroom is a place where certain subjects are studied according to prescriptions other than the investigation of knowledge or truth strikes me as a betrayal of academic freedom. With the emergence of fields like ethnic studies, gay and lesbian studies, with the rise of urgent political or identitarian political issues, this has again become an issue. I have very old-fashioned ideas about these sorts of things. I'm someone who has been very politically engaged, but I also have a quite strong belief in the mission of universities in Newman's sense of the word.

Yet at the same time you have spoken out against the corporatization of the university.

My interest in that really goes back to the 1960s, when it was revealed to me that the university was being used for projects that had to do with conquest and with the penetration of other societies. I discovered through reading that this goes back to the First World War. There's a book by Carol Gruber called *Mars and Minerva.* It describes how the university was converted into an instrument of national defense during World War I. She describes the role played by people like John Dewey and others who were getting people fired because they weren't anti-German enough. There's a long history of those abuses of the university, both by the Left and the Right. I think what is happening is that we are losing our autonomy more and more.

I'm currently reviewing a book called *Who Paid the Piper?* by Frances Stonor Saunders, which is quite extraordinary. All the academic luminaries of the 1950s and 1960s, especially on the East Coast—Robert Lowell, Elizabeth Hardwick, Sidney Hook, Irving Kristol, and Lionel Trilling—were involved in the politicization of knowledge, that is, actively involved in the Cold War with CIA money and support. It's one of the great facts of history. The question is: Can one formulate a valid humanism, one that has to do with knowledge, rigor, commitment to pedagogy, and yet remain committed to citizenship in society? How does one, as an intellectual, do that? How do we define a humanism in a situation that is very embattled, where the world is creeping in on it?

That question seems to be an elaboration of the idea of noncoercive, non-dominative knowledge that you articulated in Orientalism.

Yes, exactly. If we examine this notion of noncoercive knowledge systematically in the context of problems such as globalization, corporate intervention, violence, the politics of identity, the end of the Cold War, then is it possible to speak about a humanistic, language-based vocation? I think it is. I've never felt that my own interest in literature and literary issues has been a hindrance to me. I've never longed to have been a political scientist. Literary study entails a kind of rigor. There exists an old, interesting, and very rich tradition that doesn't have any value today. By tradition I don't mean only in the past, back in the twelfth and fifteenth centuries, but a tradition that continues through the work of the great philologists of the nineteenth century: Alexander von Humboldt, Silvestre de Sacy, Mommsen, and later, people like Curtius, Spitzer, and Auerbach, and the great French scholars like Massignon. I think that it is important to renew that tradition.

And you think that that can only take place inside the university?

It is very difficult for me to imagine it elsewhere because the university is in a sense a protected space. Without wishing to romanticize the university, the university is the last remaining protected space. Of course, the university is in cahoots with the corporate world and the military. There is no question about it. But that isn't all there is. One has to go back to Raymond Williams's saying: no matter how exhausted the social and political situation is, you can't exhaust all the alternatives. Other alternatives probably could exist outside the university for a leisured class. But where else could it exist? It could happen in seminaries, I suppose. But the university as a protected space can offer a response that is sustained by the very traditions that we are losing rapidly.

In a sense, this sounds like Adorno's distinction between autonomous art and committed art, found in his essay "Commitment," where Adorno privileges the former over the latter. Is autonomy to be preserved before commitment?

For Adorno, the power of the art—which is primarily music—lies in its dialectical opposition to the society it is in. He understands that there is a kind of standoff between the work of art and society. The role of the philosopher and the critic is to highlight this dialectical opposition between the autonomous art and society. The problem with that is that once you highlight that opposition, that irreconcilable tension, art loses its autonomy, since the critic uses art for a social purpose. The position is then a very difficult one, and I don't know if it can be sustained all the way.

Without being too metaphysical, what I find valuable in Adorno is this notion of tension, of highlighting and dramatizing what I call irreconcilabilities. These irreconcilabilities are always experiential; they are not metaphysical. For me, they go back to the contested geography of Palestine, and they refer to the whole question of partition. How, for instance, do you deal with more than one people who say that this is our land? The habitual, imperial legacy has been what they call "divide and quit." You leave a place, but then you divide it, as the English did in India, as they did in Palestine, as they did in Ireland, as they did in Cyprus, and as NATO and the United States is now doing in the Balkans. There are many examples. To my mind partition hasn't worked. What I'm proposing is to go back to these geographies and to these irreconcilabilities that they represent, and suggest that we start from there and accept them and build around them, instead of saying let's just curtain it off and say this is my part and this is your part. I'm interested in that midpoint where there is that overlap.

The nature of experience is, in fact, overlapping. There is no way, for example, of writing Israeli history without Palestinian history, and vice versa. There is no way of writing Northern Irish history without the Republican point of view. That's why I'm interested in the work of the Subaltern Studies Collective, the Field Day group, and the work of people who are trying to deal with these irreconcilabilities in imaginative ways, either by looking at precisely those things that get left out for which there is no written history or documents. That's where Ranajit Guha begins his work. The history of India is really the history of people who never wrote the history. It's not the colonial history, nor is it the history of the Gandhis or the Nehrus. It's that rather peculiar space that interests me.

So the role of the intellectual is to emphasize these irreconcilabilities?

I think that this does define the role of the intellectual. To me it is very fruitful because it enables me to see the intellectual as clarifying and dramatizing the irreconcilabilities of a particular situation, rather than trying to say, as a policy maker would or as someone like Thomas Friedman says, that globalization is the answer for everything. Adorno is a very powerful corrective to that kind of impulse.

Especially in situations that are no longer easily rectified by policy solutions, it seems to me that the role of the intellectual is to give these situations a voice, to try to articulate them, to try to clarify them so that one knows on what ground one is treading.

Yet the tension over the intellectual's role—that is to say, between autonomy and commitment—is a tension that may exist in your own specific work and experiences. In other words, has there been a shift in the way you conceive of the role of the intellectual, from commitment to a constitutency to the autonomous, exiled traveler? From the mid-1980s to perhaps the fall of 1991, you had written often about the need for intellectuals to affiliate themselves directly with political causes. Your history with the Palestinian national struggle bears this out, as well as your work with the PNC. And, also at the end of the Gulf War, you said in an interview that "there is only one way to anchor yourself, and that is by affiliation with a cause, with a political movement. . . . This seems to me to be the number one priority. There's nothing else." Yet, in Representations of the Intellectual, *you use the figure of the exiled traveler as the quintessential modern intellectual. Has your idea of the intellectual changed since Oslo?*

I don't think so. I can't be sure that there aren't inconsistencies and contradictions. But consciously at least I feel that it is the same thing. By accepting the American terms of the Madrid conference, which came after the Gulf War and after Arafat's alliance with Saddam Hussein (which, by the way, he now denies), the PNC was no longer representative of the Palestinian people.

During the summer of 1991, I was involved with a group of people including Hanan Ashrawi, Faisal Husseini, Nabil Shaath, and others, to formulate the assurances that we as Palestinians required from the Americans as our entry into the Madrid process. Our conditions were fairly stringent. We stated what our minimum requirements were; Secretary of State James Baker was to guarantee them. Baker had asked Arafat for this. We put down a reasonable set of proposals: we wouldn't accept anything less than the end of the occupation, for example; we wouldn't accept anything less than the end of the settlement and the settlement process. These were perfectly normal things. But what I also found out was that when these requirements were sent to the Americans, Arafat simply canceled them all. He more or less made it clear to the Israelis and the Americans that he had no conditions. He just wanted to be in on the process. These were all part of the reasons that I felt I had to quit the PNC. This was why I also felt that by accepting these conditions, Arafat was in effect no longer representing the Palestinian people, whom I considered to be more important than the immediate survival of the PLO under his chairmanship.

Arafat's a very shrewd, tactical politician. He had all the mechanisms of the PLO under his command, and, more importantly, in his pay. There were many people who resigned from the PLO central council and from the executive committee, like Mahmoud Darwish, Shafik Al-Hout, and Abdullah Hourani. Lots of people were in a state of acute anxiety. But I was very much in the minority when I started to write publicly against the PLO in the latter part of 1993 after Oslo was announced. Technically, I was not part of a political movement in the real sense of the word, nor was I touting myself as a real alternative to the PLO. Yet I felt I was acting in affiliation with a lot of Palestinians who were disenfranchised. For example, there were all the refugees who were simply swept out of the agreement.

Since that time, I felt that I have had an independent function, and that I do speak for a constituency. I am not officially representative of anything; I remain independent. But I still feel that my affiliation is with the majority of Palestinians who are not inside Gaza and the West Bank. For the first time in our history, there are more Palestinians outside Palestine than there are inside. Though Arafat banned my books in 1996, they're still sold, and even some of the local papers, when they feel they can get away with it, publish my articles. I have a constituency, and I feel that I am attached to a movement. The problem is that it's not a very clear movement. It's not a movement with leaders and parties. I've had to act very much from outside the official opposition that sits in Damascus, the eight or ten, whatever they're called, the Popular Front and the Popular Democratic Front, among others. I have nothing to do with them. I consider them to be as irrelevant as the man on the moon. But I feel there are efforts made, here and there, in the last two, three years, in the West Bank, in Gaza, in Lebanon, in Jordan, in the United States, with which I've been associated, and to which I have given my name. For example, there has recently been an effort in Gaza to create a popular party. Eyad Sarraj asked me if I would join; I said yes. Azmi Bishara asked me if I would affiliate myself with his campaign. I did. In that sense, I am affiliated. I am not afraid of publicly identifying myself. I think the situation is roughly the same, although the situation on the ground has changed. But I don't think I've really changed.

I am constantly asked by Palestinians who are close to Arafat, including Arab foreign ministers, to declare a truce with Arafat and to make up with him for the sake of unity. He and his people have tried several times to bring us together. I've told them that I have no interest in doing this. I think he's irrelevant because it's not as if he has a large area in which he can maneuver. He's a prisoner of the process; he's a prisoner of the Israelis; he's a prisoner of the Americans. Any rapprochement I would have with him I told him I'd be happy to do in public, on a stage where we'd debate the issues. Of course, there was no question that he would ever accept that. When the whole question of loyalty is put to me, I say, well, I think I'm more loyal to the cause than he is. Now the argument is that with the onset of Barak's premiership, these are the most important times since 1993, and maybe something will come of it since the Syrians are involved. They had asked me to moderate my critique. I didn't respond. I write what I feel like writing. I'm not going to be bound by any limitations of that sort. As the events unfold, I'll comment on them.

Never solidarity before criticism.

No, of course not. Look what it got them!

However, in our unipolar world, resistance to oppression appears more and more difficult considering the power of the United States and the clamor to belong to the world market. How does one go about theorizing power and formulating resistance today?

I think it's in the nature of power to stand its hegemony, as Gramsci said, over more and more territory. Hegemony is all about permanent contest. It's a war of position to acquire more and more territory, and part of what the United States has done has been to spread an ideological blanket over discourse everywhere. To say that you're either for "the West," "the market," or "globalization" is formulaic and has a certain instant appeal to it. One has to deconstruct that. Second, there are precedents available to us in international law, in the documents and protocols signed by nearly every country in the world since the end of World War II: the Geneva Convention, the Vienna Treaty on nonintervention, the

Declaration of Human Rights, etc. It's not as if we're sailing in a sea without a compass. There are enough of these that one has to recall. It's an effort at memory that has to be made, since hegemony effectively effaces memory and says it's all bunk. What counts is what we say. There has to be an act of resistance by recollection.

Third, you have to be able to connect the specific episodes to other episodes so that you can see, for example, that NATO's intervention in Yugoslavia exists against the background of what NATO has done historically. Ethnic cleansing has been very much within the province of NATO itself, not outside of NATO, if you consider Turkey and other places where people have been driven out. These are all within the realm of Europe and NATO, and of course the United States itself. You can't lay the blame on the non-European and the non-American. NATO itself has a fantastic load of guilt and responsibility to bear. One has to connect NATO's current action with its own past, which is obscured, and, of course, with the whole history of American behavior towards "inferior others," whether it's in Guatemala, in Colombia, or in Indonesia.

The next step has to be to attract like-minded people who are necessarily separated by geographical distance and who are operating in different environments. To find out where opposition exists and to draw attention to it. One of the important aspects of the Kosovo crisis, which was obscured by this hegemony, is that there was strong opposition to Milosevic prior to NATO's bombing campaign, which began on March 24, 1999. As a result of NATO's intervention, political opposition to Milosevic was either destroyed or voluntarily turned its support over to him because this was a war against the whole of Yugoslavia, not just the Milosevic regime. One has to talk about democratic alternatives as well as nonmilitary alternatives to the war. I think that's terribly important, and that wasn't done. That was the failure of the whole intellectual class that participated in the media. Analysts and former military people did not shed light on what was happening, but consolidated support in the mass media.

It seems to me that one of the effects of that hegemony was that a lot of people on the Left who opposed the war—

It was a neoliberal war. It was a war of the Left, of the so-called conventional Left.

Right. And there were very few numbers of the American Left intellectuals who opposed the war—

Not only in America but also in Europe. A German intellectual called what was happening a form of military humanism. What an outrage! Think of it. It wasn't just the Americans. It was the Europeans too. In *The New Yorker* (August 2, 1999) there is an article by Michael Ignatieff that says that this was a "risk-free war." There's nothing in his analysis to suggest that it was immoral and destructive and that it was waged at the expense of ordinary people, many of whom opposed Milosevic.

It was a curious moment in the United States, at least, when the Left found themselves in the company with many on the Right. Jack Kemp called the bombing of Yugoslavia "an international Waco."

Did you see the advertisement in *The New York Times* that called on the president to intensify the war in Kosovo by introducing ground troops? The ad said they weren't going far enough. It said that "we" weren't up to it. Zbigniew Brzezinski, Susan Sontag, Norman Podhoretz, David Rieff, Jeane Kirkpatrick—they all signed it. Who would have thought that Susan Sontag, Jeane Kirkpatrick, Zbigniew Brzezinski, and David Rieff would all be on the same side in the war?

What does this convergence of neoliberalism and conservatism signify?

It's what is happening in Britain and the United States, where the so-called liberal wing of the polity has become virtually identified with the conservative or centrist wing. That's been the post-Cold War policy of all neoliberal parties, so-called Left parties in the West, to transform themselves into something where ideology no longer counts, where the values of the Left, which were always based on unions and decent health and social policies for everyone and a kind of equitable as opposed to an invidious tax policy, has been transformed into a kind of consumerist ideology that says it's liberal, but, in fact, is deeply reactionary and is taking back all the advances that were made in the postwar period by the welfare state. What you're getting is the replacement of the public sector by free enterprise, which is in my opinion deeply antidemocratic, and deeply ominous to the future, because if everything is going to be left to the market and to market forces, then the deprived, the disadvantaged, and the peripheral are going to have no chances whatsoever. That is the immediate challenge. The silence of the Left, or at least the traditional Left, is very ominous. It is clear that one has to look for alternatives not in the ranks of the traditional Democratic party, but elsewhere, perhaps among immigrant populations and the feminist movement. One has to be creative and look for sustenance and support in some other places that the Left has tended to forget.

One last thing. You were talking about the importance of memory for developing a kind of resistance movement, and at the same time, your own work of late has been itself a kind of research into memory and its function. Is there a way to link these two ideas of memory? That is, the one idea of memory, which is the political idea, is the notion that we make sure we recall what is being obfuscated by power, what you called resistance by recollection. The other idea of memory is that of personal memory, private memory, as found in your memoir.

I think that's a very good question. For me, they're connected in an attempt not to just resist the amnesia induced on the public level by the official narratives and the official systems of knowledge, which are growing more and more powerful, through the media, through standardization, and through the insistence on ethnic loyalty, but also on the private level. I've tried to resist the confinements imposed by age and, in my case, by my illness. I've tried to remain within the collective experience, hoping that my personal predicament might be helpful in the public realm.

All though the period that I was writing my memoir, I was also constantly maintaining my interest in and commitment to the public realm. I've found myself more and more connected to other places. I've found that a number of places have crystallized in my mind as significant, obviously one is the Middle East, and there is also Ireland, India, South Africa, North Africa, West Africa, Korea, Japan, and selected places in Latin America. I owe a lot to friends from those parts of the world who have drawn me closer to their experiences and their literatures. For me, this has been tremendously valuable, to look at the much vaster collective experience and memory that turns into a kind of anti-provincialism, anti-isolationism, and anti-exclusivism that is almost automatically imposed on you if you are very involved in a local struggle. I've always tried to bring to bear upon what I say about the Middle East or Palestine a cosmopolitan awareness of what has taken place in

Algeria, what has taken place in Latin America, what has taken place in Ireland. That's the job. To make them aware is a service that one can do for one's own people. There isn't only one struggle. There are other struggles that you can learn from. In that respect it's been an education for me as well.

NOTES

Introduction

1. Edward W. Said, *Out of Place: A Memoir* (New York: Knopf, 1999), 216.
2. Edward W. Said, *Orientalism* (New York: Vintage, 1979), 328.
3. Edward W. Said, *The World, the Text, and the Critic* (Cambridge, Mass.: Harvard University Press, 1983), 29.
4. Edward W. Said, "Opponents, Audiences, Constituencies, and Community," in Hal Foster, ed., *The Anti-Aesthetic: Essays on Postmodern Culture* (Seattle: Bay Press, 1983), 157.
5. Edward W. Said, *Representations of the Intellectual: The 1993 Reith Lectures* (New York: Pantheon, 1994), 12.
6. Theodor Adorno, *Minima Moralia: Reflections for Damaged Life*, trans. E. F. N. Jephcott (New York: Verso, 1974), 39.
7. Edward W. Said, "The Mind of Winter: Reflections on Life in Exile," *Harpers* (September 1994): 55.
8. Mary McCarthy, "Exiles, Expatriates and Internal Émigrés," *The Listener* (November 25, 1971): 706.
9. Quoted in Maya Jaggi, "Out of the Shadows," *The Guardian* (September 11, 1999).
10. Said, *Representations of the Intellectual*, 12.
11. Said, *Out of Place*, 215.
12. Said, *Out of Place*, 12.
13. Said, *Out of Place*, 9.
14. Said, *Out of Place*, 42.
15. Said, *Out of Place*, 90.
16. Said, *Out of Place*, 115.
17. Edward W. Said, *After the Last Sky: Palestinian Lives* (1986; reprint, New York: Columbia University Press, 1999), 116.
18. Said, *Out of Place*, 120.
19. Said, *Out of Place*, 278.

20. Said, *Out of Place,* 124.
21. Said, *Out of Place,* 126.
22. Said, *Out of Place,* 293.
23. Edward Said, "The Arab Portrayed," *The Arab-Israeli Confrontation of June 1967: An Arab Perspective,* ed. Ibrahim Abu-Lughod (Evanston, Ill.: Northwestern University Press, 1970), 5.
24. *The Politics of Dispossession,* xiv.
25. Hayden White, "Beginning with a Text," *Diacritics* 6, no. 3 (Fall 1976): 19.
26. Edward W. Said, *Beginnings: Intention and Method* (New York: Columbia, 1985): 349.
27. Edward W. Said, "Vico on the Discipline of Bodies and Texts," *MLN* 91, no. 5 (October 1976): 820.
28. Edward W. Said, "Arabs and Jews," *The New York Times,* October 14, 1973.
29. "Summary of Statement," "Prepared Statement of Edward W. Said," (with Abu Lughod) "Questions and Discussion." In U.S. Congress. House. Special Subcommittee on Investigations of the Committee on International Relations. *The Palestinian Issue in Middle East Peace Efforts.* 32. 94th Cong., 1st sess. September 30, 1975.
30. Nubar Hovsepian, "Connections with Palestine," *Edward Said: A Critical Reader,* ed. Michael Sprinker (Boston: Blackwell, 1992): 13.
31. *Orientalism,* 12.
32. Leon Wieseltier. *New Republic* (April 7, 1979): 29.
33. Bernard Lewis, "The Question of Orientalism," *The New York Review of Books* (June 24, 1982): 49–55.
34. Talal Asad, *English Historical Review* 95(376): 648.
35. Edward W. Said, "Orientalism: An Exchange," *The New York Review of Books* (August 12, 1982): 44. Cf. Said, "Afterword," *Orientalism,* 341–45.
36. Edward W. Said, *The Question of Palestine* (New York: Vintage, 1992), 69.
37. Edward W. Said, "Opponents, Audiences, Constituencies and Communities," *Critical Inquiry,* 9:1 (September 1982): 25.
38. "Reflections on American 'Left' Literary Criticism," *The World, the Text, and the Critic,* 163.
39. Ibid, 159.
40. David Gilmour, *Lebanon: The Fractured Country* (New York: St. Martin's Press, 1983).
41. Tabitha Petran, *The Struggle over Lebanon* (New York: Monthly Review Press, 1987): 288.
42. Edward W. Said, *The Politics of Dispossession* (New York: Vintage, 1994): 249.
43. Quoted in *The Politics of Dispossession,* 256.

44. Edward W. Said, "The Essential Terrorist," *Blaming the Victims* (New York: Verso, 1988): 153
45. Norman Finklestein, *In These Times,* September 11, 1984. See also, Finklestein, *Image and Reality of the Israel-Palestine Conflict* (New York: Verso, 1995).
46. Edward W. Said, "Conspiracy of Praise," *Blaming the Victims,* 30.
47. Edward W. Said, *After the Last Sky,* 2d ed. (New York: Columbia University Press, 1999): 4.
48. *After the Last Sky,* 6.
49. *After the Last Sky,* 4.
50. *After the Last Sky,* 24.
51. "Reflections on Exile," *Granta* 13 (Winter 1984): 159, 172.
52. "Glenn Gould's Contrapuntal Vision," *Vanity Fair* (May 1983): 98.
53. W. J. T. Mitchell, "In the Wilderness," *The London Review of Books* (April 8, 1993): 11; Michael Wood, "Lost Paradises," *The New York Review of Books* (March 3, 1994): 44–47; Michael Gorra, "Who Paid the Bills at Mansfield Park," *The New York Times Book Review* (February 28, 1993): 11.
54. John Leonard, "Novel Colonies," *The Nation* (March 22, 1993): 383.
55. *The Politics of Dispossession,* 305.
56. *Representations of the Intellectual,* 101.
57. Edward W. Said, *The Pen and the Sword: Conversations with David Barsamian* (Monroe, Me.: Common Courage Press, 1994): 110.
58. Edward W. Said, "The One State Solution," *The New York Times Magazine* (January 10, 1999): 36.
59. We have been limited to drawing upon Said's books for the *Reader;* those interested in Said's other essays are directed to a forthcoming work (by Harvard University Press) where Said's essays will be collected.

Chapter 1: The Claims of Individuality

1. Edward Said, "Between Worlds," *London Review of Books* 20:9 (May 7, 1998): 3.
2. "Henry James to Joseph Conrad," in *Twenty Letters to Joseph Conrad,* ed. G. Jean-Aubry (London: First Edition Club, 1926).
3. Richard Curle, *The Last Twelve Years of Joseph Conrad* (London: Sampson Low, Marston, 1928), p. 25.
4. Jean-Paul Sartre, *The Emotions: Outline of a Theory* (New York: Philosophical Library, 1948), p. 48.
5. The sufferings and concerns of Conrad in the letters thus form the freely speculative and painful background of his fiction. A few sentences from Heidegger's essay on "The Essence of Truth" illuminate

this kind of connection. In what follows, "letting-be" is what I have called Conrad's suffering, and "exposition" is the result of this in his personal idiom:

"To let something be *(Seinlassen)* is in fact to have something to do with it *(sich einlassen auf)*. . . . To let what-is *be* what it is means participating in something overt and its overtness, in which everything that 'is' takes up its position and which entails such overtness. . . . 'Letting-be,' i.e. freedom, is in its own self 'ex-posing' *(aussetzend)* and 'existent' *(ek-sistent)*.

"The nature of freedom, seen from the point of view of the nature of truth, now shows itself as an 'exposition' into the revealed nature of what-is." Martin Heidegger, "The Essence of Truth" (trans. R. F. C. Hull and Alan Crick), in *Existence and Being* (Chicago: Henry Regnery Co. 1949), pp. 307–8.

6. Letters of Joseph Conrad to Marguerite Poradowska, 1890–1920 (New Haven: Yale University Press, 1940): 84.
7. Joseph Conrad, "A Personal Record," *Complete Works*, vol. VI (Garden City, New York: Doubleday, 1925): 17.
8. Joseph Conrad, "Notes on Life and Letters," *Complete Works*, vol. III (Garden City, New York: Doubleday, 1925): 13.
9. R. L. Megroz, *A Talk with Joseph Conrad: A Criticism of His Mind and Method* (London: Elkin Matthews, 1926), p. 54.
10. Johan Huizinga, "The Idea of History," in *The Varieties of History*, ed. Fritz Stern (New York, 1956), p. 292.
11. Georg Lukács, *Histoire et conscience de classe* (Paris: Le Edition de Minuit 1960). See also Lucien Goldmann, "Introduction aux prémiers écrits de Georges Lukács," *Les Temps modernes*, no. 195 (August 1962), pp. 254–80.
12. R. P. Blackmur, *The Lion and the Honeycomb* (New York: Harcourt, Brace and Company, 1955), p. 123.

Chapter 2: The Palestinian Experience

1. Edward W. Said, *The Politics of Dispossession* (New York: Pantheon, 1994): xiii.
2. Erik Erikson, *Young Man Luther* (New York: Norton, 1962): 14.

Chapter 3: Molestation and Authority in Narrative Fiction

1. J. Hillis Miller, ed., *Aspects of Narrative* (New York: Columbia University, 1971).
2. See, for example, Edward Said, "A Configuration of Themes," review of J. Hillis Miller, *Poets of Reality, The Nation* (May 30, 1966): 659–61. Miller was of the second generation of the Geneva circle.

3. *Beginnings,* 194–95.
4. *Beginnings,* 319.
5. See Levin's discussion of this throughout his *Gates of Horn: A Study of Five French Realists* (New York: Oxford University Press, 1963). See also his essay "Literature as an Institution," *Accent* 6, no. 3 (Spring 1946): 159–68.
6. In Alain Robbe-Grillet, *For a New Novel: Essays on Fiction,* trans. Richard Howard (New York: Grove Press, 1966). Originally published as *Pour un nouveau roman* (1963).
7. Eric Partridge, *Origins: A Short Etymological Dictionary of Modern English* (New York: Macmillan, 1966): 32.
8. Sören Kierkegaard, *The Point of View for My Work as an Author,* trans. Walter Lowrie (London: Oxford University Press, 1939): 17.
9. Ibid., 40.
10. Ibid., 65.
11. Kierkegaard, *Fear and Trembling: A Dialectical Lyric,* trans. Walter Lowrie (Princeton: Princeton University Press, 1941): 6.
12. Wayne Booth, *The Rhetoric of Fiction* (Chicago: University of Chicago Press, 1961).
13. Gilles Deleuze, *Différence et répétition,* (Paris: Presse Universitaires de France, 1968): 14.
14. Kierkegaard, *Repetition: An Essay in Experimental Psychology* (Princeton: Princeton University Press, 1941): 6.
15. Kierkegaard, *The Concept of Irony: With Constant Reference to Socrates,* trans. Lee M. Capel (London: William Collins, 1966): 270.
16. Ibid., 276.
17. Mark Twain, *The Adventures of Huckleberry Finn* (Hartford: American Publishing Company, 1899): 15.
18. Marx, *Capital and Other Writings,* ed. Max Eastman (New York: Modern Library, 1932): 183–84.
19. Vico, *The New Science* (Ithaca, N.Y.: Cornell University Press, 1948): 121.
20. Ibid., bk. 2, "Poetic Wisdom," 109–297.
21. See Lukács, *The Theory of the Novel,* 120 ff.; also see Paul de Man, "The Rhetoric of Temporality," in *Interpretation: Theory and Practice,* ed. Charles Singleton (Baltimore: Johns Hopkins University Press, 1969): 173–209.
22. See Lévi-Strauss, *The Savage Mind* (Chicago: University of Chicago Press, 1966): 17, for a description of Wemmick as *bricoleur.*
23. Dickens, *Great Expectations* (New York: Charles Scribner's Sons, 1902): 562.
24. Ibid., 540–41.

Chapter 4: Orientalism

1. V. G. Kiernan, *The Lords of the Human Kind: Black Man, Yellow Man, White Man in the Age of Empire* (Boston: Wiedenfeld and Nicolson, 1969).
2. Said, *Orientalism,* 12.
3. Antonio Gramsci, *The Prison Notebooks: Selections,* trans. and ed. Quintin Hoare and Geoffrey Nowell Smith (New York: International Publishers, 1971), 324.
4. "In Search of Palestine," narrated and written by Edward Said (London: British Broadcasting Company, 1998).
5. Edward Said, "The Arab Portrayed," *The Arab-Israeli Confrontation of June 1967: An Arab Perspective,* ed. Ibrahim Abu-Lughod (Evanston, Ill.: Northwestern University Press, 1970), 5.
6. "Afterword," *Orientalism,* 337.
7. "Afterword," *Orientalism,* 339.
8. Leon Wieseltier, *The New Republic* (April 7, 1979): 29.
9. Bernard Lewis, "The Question of Orientalism," *The New York Review of Books* (June 24, 1982): 49–55.
10. Talal Asad, *English Historical Review* 95(376): 648.
11. Edward Said, "Orientalism: An Exchange," *The New York Review of Books* (August 12, 1982): 44. Cf. Said, "Afterword," *Orientalism,* 341–45.
12. Gyan Prakash, "Orientalism Now," *History and Theory* (October 1995): 199.
13. Thierry Desjardins, *Le Martyre du Liban* (Paris: Plon, 1976), p. 14.
14. K. M. Panikkar, *Asia and Western Dominance* (London: George Allen & Unwin, 1959).
15. Denys Hay, *Europe: The Emergence of an Idea,* 2d ed. (Edinburgh: Edinburgh University Press, 1968).
16. Steven Marcus, *The Other Victorians: A Study of Sexuality and Pornography in Mid-Nineteenth-Century England* (1966; reprint, New York: Bantam Books, 1967), 200–19.
17. Principally in his *American Power and the New Mandarins: Historical and Political Essays* (New York: Pantheon Books, 1969); and *For Reasons of State* (New York: Pantheon Books, 1973).
18. Walter Benjamin, *Charles Baudelaire: A Lyric Poet in the Era of High Capitalism,* trans. Harry Zohn (London: New Left Books, 1973), 71.
19. Harry Bracken, "Essence, Accident and Race," *Hermathena* 116 (Winter 1973): 81–96.
20. In an interview published in *Diacritics* 6, no. 3 (Fall 1976): 38.
21. Raymond Williams, *The Long Revolution* (London: Chatto & Windus, 1961), pp. 66–67.
22. In my *Beginnings: Intention and Method* (New York: Basic Books, 1975).

23. Louis Althusser, *For Marx,* trans. Ben Brewster (New York: Pantheon Books, 1969), pp. 65–67.
24. Raymond Schwab, *La Renaissance orientale* (Paris: Payot, 1950); Johann W. Fück, *Die Arabischen Studien in Europa bis in den Anfang des 20. Jahrhunderts* (Leipzig: Otto Harrassowitz, 1955); Dorothee Metlitzki, *The Matter of Araby in Medieval England* (New Haven, Conn.: Yale University Press, 1977).
25. E. S. Shaffer, *"Kubla Khan" and The Fall of Jerusalem: The Mythological School in Biblical Criticism and Secular Literature, 1770–1880* (Cambridge: Cambridge University Press, 1975).
26. George Eliot, *Middlemarch: A Study of Provincial Life* (1872; reprint, Boston: Houghton Mifflin Co., 1956), p. 164.
27. Antonio Gramsci, *The Prison Notebooks: Selections,* trans. and ed. Quintin Hoare and Geoffrey Nowell Smith (New York: International Publishers, 1971), p. 324. The full passage, unavailable in the Hoare and Smith translation, is to be found in Gramsci, *Quaderni del Carcere,* ed. Valentino Gerratana (Turin: Einaudi Editore, 1975), 2: 1363.
28. Raymond Williams, *Culture and Society, 1780–1950* (London: Chatto & Windus, 1958), p. 376.
29. Quoted by Henri Baudet in *Paradise on Earth: Some Thoughts on European Images of Non-European Man,* trans. Elizabeth Wentholt (New Haven, Conn.: Yale University Press, 1965), p. xiii.
30. Gibbon, *Decline and Fall of the Roman Empire,* 6: 289.
31. Baudet, *Paradise on Earth,* p. 4.
32. See Fieldhouse, *Colonial Empires,* pp. 138–61.
33. Schwab, *La Renaissance orientale,* p. 30.
34. A. J. Arberry, *Oriental Essays: Portraits of Seven Scholars* (New York: Macmillan Co., 1960), pp. 30, 31.
35. Raymond Schwab, *Vie d'Anquetil-Duperron suivie des Usages civils et religieux des Perses par Anquetil-Duperron* (Paris: Ernest Leroux, 1934), pp. 10, 96, 4, 6.
36. Arberry, *Oriental Essays,* pp. 62–66.
37. Frederick Eden Pargiter, ed., *Centenary Volume of the Royal Asiatic Society of Great Britain and Ireland 1823–1923* (London: Royal Asiatic Society, 1923), p. viii.
38. Quinet, *Le Génie des religions,* p. 47.
39. Jean Thiry, *Bonaparte en Égypte décembre 1797–24 août 1799* (Paris: Berger-Levrault, 1973), p. 9.
40. Constantin-François Volney, *Voyage en Égypte et en Syrie* (Paris: Bossange, 1821), 2: 241 and passim.
41. Napoleon, *Campagnes d'Égypte et de Syrie, 1798–1799: Mémoires pour servir à l'histoire de Napoléon* (Paris: Comou, 1843), 1: 211.

42. Thiry, *Bonaparte en Égypte,* p. 126. See also Ibrahim Abu-Lughod, *Arab Rediscovery of Europe: A Study in Cultural Encounters* (Princeton, N.J.: Princeton University Press, 1963), pp. 12–20.
43. Abu-Lughod, *Arab Rediscovery of Europe,* p. 22.
44. Quoted from Arthur Helps, *The Spanish Conquest of America* (London, 1900), p. 196, by Stephen J. Greenblatt, "Learning to Curse: Aspects of Linguistic Colonialism in the Sixteenth Century," in *First Images of America: The Impact of the New World on the Old,* ed. Fredi Chiapelli (Berkeley: University of California Press, 1976), p. 573.
45. Thiry, *Bonaparte en Égypte,* p. 200. Napoleon was not just being cynical. It is reported of him that he discussed Voltaire's *Mahomet* with Goethe, and defended Islam. See Christian Cherfils, *Bonaparte et l'Islam d'après les documents français arabes* (Paris: A. Pedone, 1914), p. 249 and passim.
46. Thiry, *Bonaparte en Égypte,* p. 434.
47. Hugo, *Les Orientales,* in *Oeuvres poétiques,* 1: 684.
48. Henri Dehérain, *Silvestre de Sacy, ses contemporains et ses disciples* (Paris: Paul Geuthner, 1938), p. v.
49. *Description de l'Égypte, ou Recueil des observations et des recherches qui ont été faites in Égypte pendant l'expédition de l'armée française, publié par les ordres de sa majesté l'empereur Napoléon le grand,* 23 vols. (Paris: Imprimerie impériale, 1809–28).
50. Fourier, *Préface historique,* vol. 1 of *Description de l'Égypte,* p. 1.
51. Ibid., p. iii.
52. Ibid., p. xcii.
53. Étienne Geoffroy Saint-Hilaire, *Histoire naturelle des poissons du Nil,* vol. 17 of *Description de l'Égypte,* p. 2.
54. M. de Chabrol, *Essai sur les moeurs des habitants modernes de l'Égypte,* vol. 14 of *Description de l'Égypte,* p. 376.
55. This is evident in Baron Larrey, *Notice sur la conformation physique des égyptiens et des différentes races qui habitent en Égypte, suivie de quelques réflexions sur l'embaumement des momies,* vol. 13 of *Description de l'Égypte.*
56. Cited by John Marlowe, *The Making of the Suez Canal* (London: Cresset Press, 1964), p. 31.
57. Quoted in John Pudney, *Suez: De Lesseps' Canal* (New York: Frederick A. Praeger, 1969), pp. 141–42.
58. Marlowe, *Making of the Suez Canal,* p. 62.
59. Ferdinand de Lesseps, *Lettres, journal et documents pour servir à l'histoire du Canal de Suez* (Paris: Didier, 1881), 5: 310. For an apt characterization of de Lesseps and Cecil Rhodes as mystics, see Baudet, *Paradise on Earth,* p. 68.
60. Cited in Charles Beatty, *De Lesseps of Suez: The Man and His Times* (New York: Harper & Brothers, 1956), p. 220.

61. De Lesseps, *Lettres, journal et documents,* 5: 17.
62. Ibid., pp. 342–33.

Chapter 5: Zionism from the Standpoint of Its Victims

1. Eqbal Ahmad, "An Essay in Reconciliation," *The Nation* (March 22, 1980): 341.
2. I. F. Stone, "Confessions of a Jewish Dissident," in *Underground to Palestine, and Reflections Thirty Years Later* (New York: Pantheon Books, 1978).
3. George Eliot, *Daniel Deronda* (London: Penguin Books, 1967), p. 50.
4. Ibid., p. 592.
5. Ibid., p. 594–95.
6. Edward W. Said, *Orientalism* (New York: Pantheon Books, 1978), pp. 153–57, 214, 228.
7. Arthur Hertzberg, ed., *The Zionist Idea: A Historical Analysis and Reader* (New York: Antheneum Publishers, 1976), p. 133.
8. Ibid., p. 134
9. See Sabri Jiryis, *The Arabs of Israel* (New York: Monthly Review Press, 1976), pass.; a powerful case is made also by *The Non-Jew in the Jewish State: A Collection of Documents,* ed. Israel Shahak (privately printed by Shahak, 2 Bartenura Street, Jerusalem), 1975.
10. See *Imperialism: The Documentary History of Western Civilization,* ed. Philip D. Curtin (New York: Walker & Company, 1971), which contains a good selection from the imperialist literature of the last two hundred years. I survey the intellectual and cultural backgrounds of the period in *Orientalism,* chapters 2 and 3.
11. Quoted in Desmond Steward, *Theodor Herzl* (Garden City, N.Y.: Doubleday & Co., 1974), p. 192.
12. Antonio Gramsci, *The Prison Notebooks: Selections,* ed. and trans. Quintin Hoare and Geoffrey Nowell Smith (New York: International Publishers Co., 1971), p. 324. The full text is to be found in Antonio Gramsci, *Quaderni del Carcere,* ed. Valentino Gerratana (Turin: Einaudi Editore, 1975), vol. 2, p. 1363.
13. See Hannah Arendt, *The Origins of Totalitarianism* (New York: Harcourt Brace Jovanovich, 1973), p. 129.
14. Harry Bracken, "Essence, Accident, and Race," *Hermathena* 116 (Winter 1973): 81–96.
15. See Curtin, *Imperialism,* pp. 93–105, which contains an important extract from Knox's book.
16. George Nathaniel Curzon, *Subjects of the Day: Being a Selection of Speeches and Writings* (London: George Allen & Unwin, 1915), pp. 155–56.

17. Joseph Conrad, *Heart of Darkness,* in *Youth and Two Other Stories* (Garden City, N.Y.: Doubleday, Page, 1925), p. 52.
18. Ibid., pp. 50–51.
19. Agnes Murphy, *The Ideology of French Imperialism, 1817–1881* (Washington: The Catholic University of American Press, 1948), pp. 110, 136, 189.
20. Amos Oz, a leading Israeli novelist (also considered a "dove") puts it nicely: "For as long as I live, I shall be thrilled by all those who came to the Promised Land to turn it either into a pastoral paradise or egalitarian Tolstoyan communes, or into a well-educated, middle-class Central European enclave, a replica of Austria and Bavaria. Or those who wanted to raise a Marxist paradise, who built kibbutzim on biblical sites and secretly yearned for Stalin to come one day to admit that 'Bloody Jews, you have done it better than we did,'" *Time,* May 15, 1978, p. 61.
21. I have taken all of these quotations from an excellent, and invaluable, M.A. thesis submitted by Miriam Rosen at Hunter College in 1976, "The Last Crusade: British Archeology in Palestine, 1865–1920," pp. 18–21.
22. See Neville J. Mandel, *The Arabs and Zionism before World War I* (Berkeley: University of California Press, 1976), and Yehoshua Porath, *The Emergence of the Palestinian-Arab National Movement, Vol. 1 1918–1929* (London: Frank Cass and Company, 1974).
23. See the forthright historical account in Amos Elon, *The Israelis: Founders and Sons* (1971; reprint, New York: Bantam Books, 1972), pp. 218–24.
24. Maxime Rodinson, *Israel: A Colonial-Settler State?* trans. David Thorstad (New York: Monad Press of the Anchor Foundation, 1973), p. 39.
25. Ibid., p. 38.
26. Quoted in David Waines, "The Failure of the Nationalist Resistance," in *The Transformation of Palestine,* ed. Ibrahim Abu-Lughod (Evanston, Ill.: Northwestern University Press, 1971), p. 220.
27. Ibid., p. 213.
28. Chaim Weizmann, *Trial and Error: The Autobiography of Chaim Weizmann* (New York: Harper & Row, 1959), p. 371.
29. Ibid., p. 125.
30. Ibid., pp. 128–29, 253.
31. Ibid., p. 128.
32. Yehoshafat Harkabi, *Arab Attitudes to Israel* (Jerusalem: Keter Press, 1972). Harkabi was chief of military intelligence until he was dismissed in 1959 by Ben Gurion. He later became a professor at the Hebrew University and an expert Arabist, indeed the principal propagandist in Israel against everything Arab and/or especially Palestinian. See, for

example, his virulently anti-Palestinian book (distributed gratis in this country by the Israeli embassy) *Palestinians and Israel* (Jerusalem: Keter Press, 1974). Surprisingly, General Harkabi has recently become a "dove" and a supporter of the Peace Now Movement.

33. Reproduced in *Haolam Hazeh,* May 15, 1974. *Haolam Hazeh*'s editor, Uri Avnery, has written an interesting, somewhat demagogic book, worth looking at for the light it sheds on Israeli politics: *Israel Without Zionism: A Plea for Peace in the Middle East* (New York: Macmillan Publishing Co., 1968). It contains vitriolic attacks on people like Moshe Dayan, whom Avnery describes essentially as "an Arab-fighter" (cf. Indian-fighters in the American West).
34. Weizmann, *Trial and Error,* p. 130.
35. Ibid,. p. 188.
36. Ibid., pp. 215–16.
37. Ibid., p. 130.
38. C. L. Temple, *The Native Races and Their Rulers* (1918; reprint, London: Frank Cass and Company, 1968), p. 41.
39. *Trial and Error,* pp. 156–57.
40. On the army as a matrix for organizing society, see Michel Foucault, *"Questions à Michel Foucault sur la géographie," Hérodote,* 1, 1 (first trimester 1976), p. 85. See also Yves Lacoste, *La Géographie ca sert, d'abord, à faire la guerre* (Paris: Maspero, 1976).
41. Details taken from Walter Lehn, "The Jewish National Fund," *Journal of Palestine Studies* 3, no. 4 (Summer 1974): 74–96. It is worth noting here that during the academic year 1977–78, Lehn, a retired professor of linguistics, was visiting professor at Bir Zeit University, the only Arab institution of higher learning on the occupied West Bank. During the year he continued his research on the JNF, and also signed an open letter, on January 6, protesting (as an eyewitness) the savage beating of two young Palestinian students by Israeli soldiers (one of the two was hospitalized after he collapsed from the beating). Along with six other professors, Lehn was denied a work permit by the West Bank military authorities in early May 1978. Not one U.S. newspaper carried this news. But see also Uri Davis and Walter Lehn, "And the Fund Still Lives," *Journal of Palestine Studies* 7, no. 4 (Summer 1978): 3–33.
42. As an example, consider the fate of Umm al-Fahm, a large Arab village given to Israel by King Abdallah of Jordan in 1949 according to the Rhodes agreement. Before 1948 the village owned 140,000 dunams, with a population of 5,000. In 1978 there were about 20,000 Arab inhabitants of Umm al-Fahm, but the village's land had been reduced to 15,000 dunams, almost all of it rocky and poor for cultivation. All the best land was confiscated by various "legal" decrees, including the 1953 Law of Land, Insurance and Compensation. The greatest irony perhaps is that two socialist kibbutzim—Megiddo and Givat Oz—were

built on the confiscated Arab land. What was left was turned over to a moshav, or cooperative agricultural settlement.

43. Joseph Weitz, *My Diary and Letters to the Children* (Tel Aviv: Massada, 1965), vol. 2, pp. 181–82.
44. Jon and David Kimche, *A Clash of Destinies: The Arab-Jewish War and the Founding of the State of Israel* (New York: Praeger Publishers, 1960), p. 92. See also the two important articles by Walid Khalidi, "The Fall of Haifa," *Middle East Forum,* 35, no. 10 (December 1959): 22–32; and "Plan Dalet: The Zionist Blueprint for the Conquest of Palestine," *Middle East Forum,* 35, no. 9 (November 1961): 22–28.
45. The most thorough study ever made of the Palestinian exodus, after a combing of every Arab newspaper and broadcst of the period, revealed absolutely no evidence of "orders to leave," or of anything except urgings to Palestinians to remain in their country. Unfortunately, the terror was too great for a mostly unarmed population. See Erskine Childers, "The Wordless Wish: From Citizens to Refugees," in *The Transformation of Palestine,* ed. Ibrahim Abu-Lughod (Evanston, Ill.: Northwestern University Press, 1971), pp. 165–202. Childers, an Irishman, was a free-lance journalist when he conducted his research; his findings are devastating to the Zionist case.
46. See Avnery, *Israel Without Zionism.*
47. Weitz, *My Diary,* vol. 3, p. 293.
48. Ibid., p. 302.
49. Tawfiq Zayyad, "Fate of the Arabs in Israel," *Journal of Palestine Studies,* 6, no. 1 (Autumn 1976), 98–99.
50. Yet in its editorial of May 19, 1976, *The New York Times* called the Israeli occupation of the West Bank and Gaza "a model of future cooperation" between the two peoples. Israeli destruction of Arab houses, torture, deporation, murder, administrative detention, all have been denounced by Amnesty International, the Red Cross, even the 1978 State Department Report on human rights abuses. And still the repression continues, both in the gross and coarsely brutal ways I have mentioned and in other ways, too. Collective punishment is common: In 1969 the military governor forbade the sale of mutton as a punishment for the whole town of Ramallah; during the middle of the grape season in 1970 the sale of grapes, harvesting, and the like were all prohibited unless notables denounced PLO publicity. In April 1978 a seven-day curfew was imposed on Nablus because "the inhabitants did not collaborate with the police."
51. Quoted in Jiryis, *The Arabs in Israel,* p. 70.
52. See Saul Bellow, *To Jerusalem and Back* (New York: The Viking Press, 1976), pp. 152–61 and *passim.*
53. John Cooley, "Settlement Drive Lies Behind Latest Israeli 'No,'" *Christian Science Monitor,* July 25, 1978, makes it clear that Israeli plans offi-

cially to populate the West Bank with a Jewish majority (1.25 million) by the year 2000, and that Yamit (in the Rafah salient—occupied Sinai) is being planned as a major Israeli city, under construction now. According to Arye Duzin, Chairman of the Jewish Agency, Yamit "must always remain under Jewish sovereignty" as forecast by the Zionist Executive in 1903. Many of the settlements are to be filled with South African Jews (hence Israel's close military—indeed nuclear—cooperation with South Africa, and its particularly cordial relations with Prime Minister John Vorster, a convicted Nazi), Americans, and of course Russians.

54. Jiryis, *Arabs in Israel,* p. 70.
55. The full text of the Koenig Report was printed in an English translation in *SWASIA,* III, 41 (October 15, 1976).
56. Take as an example the raid on Maalot by Palestinians in May 1974. This event has now become synonymous with Palestinian terrorism, yet no U.S. newspaper took note of the fact that for two consecutive weeks before the incident, Israeli artillery and air power were used to bombard southern Lebanon mercilessly. Well over 200 civilians were killed by napalm and at least 10,000 were made homeless. Still, only Maalot is recalled.

Chapter 6: Islam as News

1. *Covering Islam* (New York: Vintage, 1997): xlviii.
2. See Edward W. Said, *Orientalism,* pp. 49–73.
3. See Norman Daniel, *The Arabs and Medieval Europe* (London: Longmans, Green & Co., 1975); also his earlier and very useful *Islam and the West: The Making of an Image* (Edinburgh: University Press, 1960. There is a first-rate survey of this matter, set in the political context of the 1956 Suez War, by Erskine B. Childers in *The Road to Suez: A Study of Western-Arab Relations* (London: MacGibbon & Kee, 1962), pp. 25–61.
4. I have discussed Naipaul in "Bitter Dispatches from the Third World," *The Nation,* May 3, 1980, pp. 522–25.
5. Maxime Rodinson, *Marxism and The Modern World,* trans. Michael Palis (London: Zed Press, 1979). See also Thomas Hodgkin, "The Revolutionary Tradition in Islam," *Race and Class,* 21, no. 3 (Winter 1980): 221–37.
6. There is an elegant account of this theme, done by a contemporary Tunisian intellectual: see Hichem Djaït, *L'Europe et l'Islam* (Paris: Éditions du Seuil, 1979). A brillian psychoanalytic/structuralist reading of one "Islamic" motif in European literature—the seraglio—is to be found in Alain Grosrichard, *Structure du sérail: La Fiction du despotisme asiatique dans l'Occident classique* (Paris: Éditions du Seuil, 1979).

7. See Maxime Rodinson, *La Fascination de l'Islam* (Paris: Maspéro, 1980).
8. Albert Hourani, "Islam and the Philosophy of History," in *Europe and the Middle East* (London: Macmillan & Co., 1980), pp. 19–73.
9. As an instance, see the penetrating study by Syed Hussein Alatas, *The Myth of the Lazy Native: A Study of the Image of the Malays, Filipinos, and Javanese from the 16th to the 20th Century and in the Ideology of Colonial Capitalism* (London: Frank Cass & Co., 1977).
10. Not that this has always meant poor writing and scholarship: as an informative general account which answers principally to political exigencies and not mainly to the need for new knowledge about Islam, there is Martin Kramer, *Political Islam* (Washington, D.C.: Sage Publications, 1980). This was written for the Center for Strategic and International Studies, Georgetown University, and therefore belongs to the category of policy, not of "objective" knowledge. Another instance is the January 1980 (vol. 78, no. 453) special issue on "The Middle East, 1980" of *Current History.*
11. *Atlantic Community Quarterly,* 17, no. 3 (Fall 1979): 291–305, 377–78.
12. Marshall Hodgson, *The Venture of Islam,* 3 vols. (Chicago and London: University of Chicago Press, 1974). See the important review of this by Albert Hourani, *Journal of Near Eastern Studies* 37, no. 1 (January 1978): 53–62.
13. One index of this is the report "Middle Eastern and African Studies: Developments and Needs" commissioned by the U.S. Department of Health, Education, and Welfare in 1967, written by Professor Morroe Berger of Princeton, also president of the Middle East Studies Association (MESA). In this report Berger asserts that the Middle East "is not a center of great cultural achievement . . . and therefore does not constitute its own reward so far as modern culture is concerned. . . . [It] has been receding in immediate political importance to the U.S." For a discussion of this extraordinary document and the context that produced it, see Said, *Orientalism,* pp. 287–93.
14. Quoted in Michael A. Ledeen and William H. Lewis, "Carter and the Fall of the Shah: The Inside Story," *Washington Quarterly* 3, no. 2 (Spring 1980): 11–12. Ledeen and Lewis are supplemented (and supported to a degree) by William H. Sullivan, "Dateline Iran: The Road Not Taken," *Foreign Policy* 40 (Fall 1980): 175–86; Sullivan was United States ambassador to Iran before and during the revolution. See also the six-part series by Scott Armstrong, "The Fall of the Shah," *Washington Post,* October 25, 26, 27, 28, 29, 30, 1980.
15. Hamid Algar, "The Oppositional Role of the Ulama in Twentieth Century Iran," in Nikki R. Keddie, ed., *Scholars, Saints, and Sufis: Muslim Religious Institutions since 1500* (Berkeley, Los Angeles, and London:

University of California Press, 1972), pp. 231–55. See also Ervand Abrahamian, "The Crowd in Iranian Politics, 1905–1953," *Past and Present* 41 (December 1968): 184–210; also his "Factionalism in Iran: Political Groups in the 14th Parliament (1944–46)," *Middle Eastern Studies* 14, no. 1 (January 1978): 22–25; also "The Causes of the Constitutional Revolution in Iran," *International Journal of Middle East Studies* 10, no. 3 (August 1979): 381–414; and "Structural Causes of the Iranian Revolution," *MERIP Reports* no. 87 (May 1980), pp. 21–26. See also Richard W. Cottam, *Nationalism in Iran* (Pittsburgh, Pa.: University of Pittsburgh Press, 1979).

16. This is especially true of Fred Halliday, *Iran: Dictatorship and Development* (New York: Penguin Books, 1979), which is nevertheless one of the two or three best studies of Iran done since World War II. Maxime Rodinson, in *Marxism and the Muslim World,* has nearly nothing to say about the Muslim religious opposition. Only Algar (note 15 above) seems to have been right on this point—a remarkable achievement.
17. This is the argument put forward in Edward Shils, "The Prospect for Lebanese Civility," in Leonard Binder, ed., *Politics in Lebanon* (New York: John Wiley & Sons, 1966), pp. 1–11.
18. Malcolm Kerr, "Political Decision Making in a Confessional Democracy," in Binder, ed., *Politics in Lebanon,* p. 209.
19. See the extraordinarily rich material found in the Moshe Sharett *Personal Diary* (Tel Aviv: Ma'ariv, 1979); Livia Rokach, *Israel's Sacred Terrorism: A Study Based on Moshe Sharett's Personal Diary and Other Documents,* introduction by Noam Chomsky (Belmont, Mass.: Association of Arab-American University Graduates [AAZG], 1980). See also the revelations about the CIA role in Lebanon by former CIA advisor Wilbur Crane Eveland, *Ropes of Sand: America's Failure in the Middle East* (New York: W. W. Norton & Co., 1980).
20. Élie Adib Salem, *Modernization Without Revolution: Lebanon's Experience* (Bloomington and London: Indiana University Press, 1972), p. 144. Salem is also the author of "Form and Substance: A Critical Examination of the Arabic Language," *Middle East Forum* 33 (July 1958): 17–19. The title indicates the approach.
21. Clifford Geertz, "The Integrative Revolution: Primordial Sentiments and Civil Politics in the New States," in *The Interpretation of Cultures* (New York: Basic Books, 1973), p. 296.
22. For an interesting description of "expert" illusions about Lebanon on the eve of the civil war, see Paul and Susan Starr, "Blindness in Lebanon," *Human Behavior* 6 (January 1977); 56–61.
23. I have discussed this in *The Question of Palestine,* pp. 3–53 and *passim.*
24. For a brilliant account of this collective delusion see Ali Jandaghi (pseud.), "The Present Situation in Iran," *Monthly Review,* November

1973, pp. 34–47. See also Stuart Schaar, "Orientalism at the Service of Imperialism," *Race and Class* 21, no. 1 (Summer 1979): 67–80.

25. James A. Bill, "Iran and the Crisis of '78," *Foreign Affairs* 57, no. 2 (Winter 1978–79): 341.
26. William O. Beeman, "Devaluing Experts on Iran," *New York Times,* April 11, 1980; James A. Bill, "Iran Experts: Proven Right But Not Consulted," *Christian Science Monitor,* May 6, 1980.
27. As opposed to scholars during the Vietnam War who made a stronger case for themselves as "scientists" willingly serving the state: here it would be good to know why Vietnam specialists were consulted (with no less disastrous results) and Iran experts not. See Noam Chomsky, "Objectivity and Liberal Scholarship," in *American Power and the New Mandarins: Historical and Political Essays* (New York: Pantheon Books, 1969), pp. 23–158.
28. See Said, *Orientalism*, pp. 123–66.
29. On the connection between scholarship and politics as it has affected the colonial world, see *Le Mal de voir: Ethnologie et orientalisme: politique et épistémologie, critique et autocritique,* Cahiers Jussieu no. 2 (Paris: Collections 10/18, 1976). On the way in which "fields" of study coincide with national interests see "Special Supplement: Modern China Studies," *Bulletin of Concerned Asia Scholars* 3, nos. 3–4 (Summer–Fall, 1971): 91–168.
30. See Edmund Ghareeb, ed., *Split Vision: Arab Portrayal in the American Media* (Washington, D.C.: Institute of Middle Eastern and North African Affairs, 1977). For the British counterpart see Sari Nasir, *The Arabs and the English* (London: Longmans, Green & Co., 1979), pp. 140–72.
31. James Peck, "Revolution Versus Modernization and Revisionism: A Two-Front Struggle," in Victor G. Nee and James Peck, eds., *China's Uninterrupted Revolution: From 1840 to the Present* (New York: Pantheon Books, 1975), p. 71. See also Irene L. Gendzier, "Notes Toward a Reading of *The Passing of Traditional Society,*" *Review of Middle East Studies* 3 (London: Ithaca Press, 1978), pp. 32–47.
32. An account of the Pahlevi regime's "modernization" is to be found in Robert Graham, *Iran: The Illusion of Power* (New York: St. Martin's Press, 1979). See also Thierry A. Brun, "The Failures of Western-Style Development Add to the Regime's Problems," and Eric Rouleau, "Oil Riches Underwrite Ominous Militarization in a Repressive Society," in Ali-Reza Nobari, ed., *Iran Erupts* (Stanford, Calif.: Iran-America Documentation Group, 1978). Also Claire Brière and Pierre Blanchet, *Iran: La Révolution au nom de Dieu* (Paris: Éditions du Seuil, 1979); this book has an interview with Michel Foucault appended to it.
33. There has been an extraordinary reluctance on the part of the press to say anything about the explicitly *religious* formulation of positions and poli-

cies inside Israel, especially when these are directed at non-Jews. There would be interesting material found in the Gush Emunim literature, or the pronouncements of the various rabbinic authorities, and so on.

34. See Garry Wills, "The Greatest Story Ever Told," subtitled "Blissed out by the pope's U.S. visit—'unique,' 'historic,' 'transcendant'—the breathless press produced a load of papal bull," *Columbia Journalism Review* 17, no. 5 (January–February 1980): 25–33.
35. See the excellent and exhaustive study of Marwan R. Buheiry, *U.S. Threats Against Arab Oil: 1973–1979*. IPS Papers no. 4 (Beirut: Institute for Palestine Studies, 1980).
36. This is a peculiarly American syndrome. In Europe, the situation is considerably more fair, at least as far as journalism on the whole is concerned.

Chapter 7: Traveling Theory

1. Frank Lentricchia, *After the New Criticism* (Chicago: University of Chicago Press, 1980), p. 24.
2. Georg Lukács, *History and Class Consciousness: Studies in Marxist Dialectics,* trans. Rodney Livingstone (London: Merlin Press, 1971), p. 90.
3. Ibid., p. 105.
4. Ibid., p. 186.
5. Ibid., p. 199.
6. Lucien Goldmann, *The Hidden God: A Study of Tragic Vision in the "Pensées" of Pascal and the Tragedies of Racine,* trans. Philip Thody (London: Routledge and Kegan Paul, 1964), p. 15.
7. Ibid., p. 15.
8. Ibid., p. 99.
9. Raymond Williams, *Problems in Materialism and Culture* (London: Verso, 1980), p. 13.
10. Ibid., p. 21.
11. Ibid., p. 21; emphasis added.
12. Williams, *Politics and Letters: Interviews with New Left Review* (London: New Left Books, 1979), p. 252.
13. Williams, *The Country and the City* (1973; reprints, New York: Oxford University Press, 1975), p. 141.
14. Lentricchia, *After the New Criticism,* p. 351.
15. Fredric Jameson, *The Political Unconscious: Narrative as a Socially Symbolic Act* (Ithaca: Cornell University Press, 1981), pp. 74, 102.
16. E. P. Thompson, *The Poverty of Theory and Other Essays* (London: Merlin Press, 1978).
17. Ian Hacking, "The Archaeology of Foucault," *New York Review of Books* 28 (May 14, 1981): p. 36.

18. There is much evidence of this in the Winter 1980 issue of *Humanities in Society*, vol. 3, entirely devoted to Foucault.
19. The distinction is made by Foucault in *Radical Philosophy* 17 (Summer 1977).
20 Michel Foucault, *The History of Sexuality, I: An Introduction*, trans. Robert Hurley (New York: Pantheon, 1978), p. 93.
21 Foucault, *Discipline and Punish: The Birth of the Prison*, trans. Alan Sheridan (New York: Pantheon, 1977), pp. 26–27.
22. Nicos Poulantzas, *State, Power, and Socialism*, trans. Patrick Camiller (London: Verso, 1980), p. 148.
23. Ibid., pp. 150ff.
24. A transcript is to be found in *Reflexive Water: The Basic Concerns of Mankind*, ed. Fons Elders (London: Souvenir Press, 1974). The curious thing about this book and the program—"the Basic concerns of mankind"—is that "mankind" is spoken for entirely by white European-American males. No one seems bothered by the claims for universality.
25. Noam Chomsky, *Language and Responsibility* (New York: Pantheon, 1979), p. 80.
26. *Reflexive Water*, pp. 184–85.

Chapter 8: Secular Criticism

1. There is a good graphic account of the problem in Noam Chomsky, *Language and Responsibility* (New York: Pantheon, 1977): 6. See also Edward W. Said, *Covering Islam* (New York: Pantheon, 1981): 147–64.
2. The example of the Nazi who read Rilke and then wrote out genocidal orders to his concentration-camp underlings had not yet become well known. Perhaps then the Durrell-Secretary of Defense anecdote might not have seemed so useful to my enthusiastic friend.
3. See Hayden White, *Metahistory: The Historical Imagination in Nineteenth-Century Europe* (Baltimore: Johns Hopkins University Press, 1973), and his *Tropics of Discourse: Essays in Cultural Criticism* (Baltimore: Johns Hopkins University Press, 1978).
4. See my article "Opponents, Audiences, Constituencies, and Community," *Critical Inquiry* (Fall 1982), for an analysis of the liaison between the cult of textuality and the ascendancy of Reaganism.
5. Erich Auerbach, *Mimesis: The Representation of Reality in Western Literature*, trans. Willard Trask (1953; reprint, Princeton: Princeton University Press, 1968): 557.
6. See the evidence in Samuel C. Chew, *The Crescent and the Rose: Islam and England During the Renaissance* (New York: Oxford University Press, 1937).
7. Auerbach, "Philology and *Weltliteratur*," trans. M. and E. W. Said, *Centennial Review* 13 (Winter 1969): p. 17.

8. Hugo of St. Victor, *Didascalicon,* trans. Jerome Taylor (New York: Columbia University Press, 1961): 101.
9. See *Orientalism* (New York: Pantheon, 1978), esp. chap. 1.
10. A. L. Kroeber and Clyde Kluckhohn, *Culture: A Critical Review of Concepts and Definitions* (1952; reprint, New York: Vintage Books, 1963).
11. See *Orientalism,* pp. 153–56; also the important study by Bryan Turner, *Marx and the End of Orientalism* (London: Allen and Unwin, 1978).
12. See my *Beginnings: Intention and Method* (New York: Basic Books, 1975): 81–88 and passim.
13. The information is usefully provided by Lyndall Gordon, *Eliot's Early Years* (Oxford and New York: Oxford University Press, 1977).
14. T. S. Eliot, *Selected Essays* (1932; reprint, London: Faber and Faber, 1953): 343–44.
15. Georg Simmel, *The Conflict in Modern Culture and Other Essays,* trans. and ed. K. Peter Etzkorn (New York: Teachers College Press, 1968): 12.
16. Ian Watt, *Conrad in the Nineteenth Century* (Berkeley: University of California Press, 1979): 32.
17. John Fekete, *The Critical Twilight: Explorations in the Ideology of Anglo-American Literary Theory from Eliot to McLuhan* (London: Routledge and Kegan Paul, 1977): 193–94.
18. For an extended analysis of the role of interpretive communities, see Stanley Fish, *Is There a Text in This Class?* (Cambridge: Harvard University Press, 1980).
19. Raymond Williams, *Politics and Letters: Interviews with New Left Review* (London: New Left Books, 1979): 252.

Chapter 9: Permission to Narrate

1. Tabitha Petran, *The Struggle over Lebanon* (New York: Monthly Review Press, 1987): 288.
2. David Gilmour, *Lebanon: The Fractured Country* (New York: St. Martin's Press, 1983).
3. "The Permission to Narrate: A Reconstruction of the Siege of Beirut," *London Review of Books* (February 16–29, 1984).
4. Books discussed: Sean MacBride et al., *Israel in Lebanon: The Report of the International Commission* (London: Ithaca, 1983). Amnon Kapeliouk, *Sabra et Chatila: Enquête sur un massacre* (Paris: Seuil, 1982). John Bulloch, *Final Conflict: The War in the Lebanon* (London: Century, 1983). David Gilmour, *Lebanon: The Fractured Country* (Oxford: M. Robertson, 1983). Jonathan Randal, *The Tragedy of Lebanon: Christian Warlords, Israeli Adventurers and American Bunglers* (London: Chatto, 1983). Tony Clifton and Catherine Leroy, *God Cried* (London:

Quartet, 1983). Salim Nassib and Caroline Tisdal, *Beirut: Frontline Story*, with photographs by Chris Steele-Perkins (London: Pluto, 1983). Noam Chomsky, *The Fateful Triangle: Israel, the United States and the Palestinians* (London: Pluto, 1983).

5. MacBride et al., *Israel in Lebanon*, p. 222.
6. Michael Adams and Christopher Mayhew, *Publish It Not . . . :The Middle East Cover-Up*. (London: Longman, 1975).
7. Yoav, Karni, "Dr. Shekel and Mr. Apartheid," *Yediot Ahronot*, March 13, 1983.
8. In *Critical Inquiry* (autumn 1980).
9. A persuasive study by Mark Heller, an Israeli political scientist at the Centre for Strategic Studies, Tel Aviv University: *A Palestinian State: The Implications for Israel* (Cambridge, Mass., & London: Harvard University Press, 1983), represents an exception. Heller argues that a Palestinian state on the West Bank and Gaza is in Israel's best interest, and is more desirable than either annexation or returning the territories to Jordan.
10. In *Commentary* (September 1982).
11. Richard Poirier, "Watching the Evening News: The Chancellor Incident," *Raritan* 2, no. 2 (fall 1982): p. 8.
12. The background of collaboration between Zionist groups and various European fascists is studied in Lenni Brenner's *Zionism in the Age of Dictators: A Reappraisal* (London: Croom Helm, 1983).
13. Chomsky, *The Fateful Triangle*, p. 106.
14. Ibid., p. 102.
15. There is one exception to be noted: Lina Mikdadi, *Surviving the Siege of Beirut: A Personal Account* (London: Onyx Press, 1983). This delivers a Lebanese-Palestinian woman's account of life in Beirut during the siege.
16. Kamal Salibi, *The Modern History of Lebanon* (Delmar, N.Y.: Caravan Books, 1977) and *Crossroads to Civil War: Lebanon 1975–1976* (Delmar, N.Y.: Caravan Books, 1976).
17. Elie Salem, *Modernization without Revolution: Lebanon's Experiences* (Bloomington, Ind.: Indiana University Press, 1973).
18. Jacobo Timerman, *The Longest War* (London: Chatto & Windus, 1982).

Chapter 11: Yeats and Decolonization

1. Declan Kiberd, *Inventing Ireland: The Literature of the Modern Nation* (Cambridge, Mass.: Harvard University Press, 1995): 99.
2. Angus Calder, *Revolutionary Empire: The Rise of the English-Speaking Empires from the Eighteenth Century to the 1780's* (London: Cape, 1981): 14. A philosophical and ideological accompaniment is provided

(alas, in a terrible jargon) by Samir Amin, *Eurocentrism,* trans. Russell Moore (New York: Monthly Review, 1989). By contrast, a liberationist account—also on a world scale—is in Jan Nederveen Pietersee, *Empire and Emancipation* (London: Pluto Press, 1991).

3. Calder, *Revolutionary Empire,* p. 36.
4. *Ibid.,* p. 650.
5. Eqbal Ahmad, "The Neo-Fascist State: Notes on the Pathology of Power in the Third World," *Arab Studies Quarterly* 3, no. 2 (Spring 1981): 170–80.
6. James Joyce, *A Portrait of the Artist as a Young Man* (1916; reprint, New York: Viking, 1964): 189.
7. Thomas Hodgkin, *Nationalism in Colonial Africa* (London: Muller, 1956): 93–114.
8. Alfred Crosby, *Ecological Imperialism: The Biological Expansion of Europe, 900–1900* (Cambridge: Cambridge University Press, 1986): 196–216.
9. Neil Smith, *Uneven Development: Nature, Capital, and the Production of Space* (Oxford: Blackwell, 1984): 102.
10. *Ibid.,* p. 146. Further differentiations of space, with consequences for art and leisure, occur in landscape and the project for national parks. See W. J. T. Mitchell, "Imperial Landscape," in *Landscape and Power,* ed. W. J. T. Mitchell (Chicago: University of Chicago Press, 1993), and Jane Carruthers, "Creating a National Park, 1910 to 1926," *Journal of South African Studies* 15, no. 2 (January 1989): 188–216. In a different sphere compare with Mark Bassin, "Inventing Siberia: Visions of the Russian East in the Early Nineteenth Century," *American Historical Review* 96, no. 3 (June 1991): 763–94.
11. Mahmoud Darwish, "A Lover from Palestine," in *Splinters of Bone,* trans. B. M. Bannani (Greenfield Center, N.Y.: Greenfield Review Press, 1974), p. 23.
12. Mary Hamer, "Putting Ireland on the Map," *Textual Practice* 3, no. 2 (Summer 1989): 184–201.
13. *Ibid.,* p. 195.
14. Seamus Deane, *Celtic Revivals: Essays in Modern Irish Literature* (London: Faber & Faber, 1985): 38.
15. *Ibid.,* p. 49.
16. *Ibid.*
17. Wole Soyinka, *Myth, Literature and the African World* (Cambridge: Cambridge University Press, 1976): 127. See also Mudimbe, *Invention of Africa,* pp. 83–97.
18. *Ibid.,* pp. 129, 136.
19. Fanon, *Wretched of the Earth,* p. 203.
20. Césaire, *Collected Poetry,* p. 72.

21. *Ibid.*, pp. 76 and 77.
22. R. P. Blackmur, *Eleven Essays in the European Novel* (New York: Harcourt, Brace & World, 1964): 3.
23. Mahmoud Darwish, *The Music of Human Flesh,* trans. Denys Johnson-Davies (London: Heinemann, 1980): 18.
24. Pablo Neruda, *Memoirs,* trans. Hardie St. Martin (London: Penguin, 1977): 130. This passage may come as a surprise to anyone who had once been influenced by Conor Cruise O'Brien's essay "Passion and Cunning: An Essay on the Politics of W. B. Yeats," collected in his *Passion and Cunning* (London: Weidenfeld & Nicolson, 1988). Its claims and information are inadequate, especially when compared with Elizabeth Cullingford's *Yeats, Ireland and Fascism* (London: Macmillan, 1981); Cullingford also refers to the Neruda passage.
25. W. B. Yeats, *Collected Poems* (New York: Macmillan, 1959): 146.
26. Pablo Neruda, *Fully Empowered,* trans. Alastair Reid (New York: Farrar, Straus & Giroux, 1986): 131.
27. Yeats, *Collected Poetry,* p. 193.
28. Fanon, *Wretched of the Earth,* p. 59.
29. Gary Sick, *All Fall Down: America's Tragic Encounter with Iran* (New York: Random House, 1985).
30. Chinua Achebe, *Things Fall Apart* (1959; reprint New York: Fawcett, 1969).
31. Lawrence J. McCaffrey, "Components of Irish Nationalism," in *Perspective on Irish Nationalism,* eds. Thomas E. Hachey and Lawrence J. McCaffrey (Lexington: University of Kentucky Press, 1989): 16.
32. Yeats, *Collected Poetry,* p. 212.
33. *Ibid.*, p. 342.
34. Quoted in Hachey and McCaffrey, *Perspectives on Irish Nationalism,* p. 117.
35. *Ibid.*, p. 106.
36. See David Lloyd, *Nationalism and Minor Literature: James Clarence Mangan and the Emergence of Irish Cultural Nationalism* (Berkeley: University of California Press, 1987).
37. For a collection of some of their writings see *Ireland's Field Day* (London: Hutchinson, 1985). This collection includes Paulin, Heaney, Deane, Kearney, and Kiberd. See also W. J. McCormack, *The Battle of the Books* (Gigginstown, Ireland: Lilliput Press, 1986).
38. R. P. Blackmur, *A Primer of Ignorance,* ed. Joseph Frank (New York: Harcourt, Brace & World, 1967): 21–37.
39. Joseph Leerssen, *Mere Irish and Fior-Ghael: Studies in the Idea of Irish Nationality, Its Development, and Literary Expression Prior to the Nineteenth Century* (Amsterdam and Philadelphia: Benjamins, 1986).
40. Fanon, *Wretched of the Earth,* p. 210.

41. *Ibid.*, p. 214.
42. Yeats, *Collected Poetry*, p. 343.
43. R. P. Blackmur, *Language as Gesture: Essays in Poetry* (London: Allen & Unwin, 1954): 118.
44. *Ibid.*, p. 119.

Chapter 12: Performance as an Extreme Occassion

1. Richard Poirier, *The Performing Self: Compositions and Decompositions in the Languages of Contemporary Life* (New York: Oxford University Press, 1971): 87.
2. *Ibid.*, p. xiv.
3. Theodor W. Adorno, "On the Fetish Character in Music and the Regression of Listening" (1938), in *The Essential Frankfurt School Reader*, ed. Andrew Arato and Eike Gebhardt (New York: Urizen Books, 1978), especially pp. 286–99.
4. I have discussed this in *The Nation*, December 25, 1989, pp. 802–4.
5. Carl Dahlhaus, *Nineteenth Century Music*, trans. J. Bradford Robinson (Berkeley: University of California Press, 1989), especially pp. 137–42.
6. Adorno, "Spatstil Beethovens" (1937), in *Gesammelte Schriften* 17 (Frankfurt: Suhrkamp, 1982), pp. 13–17. By far the best English-language account of the significance of Adorno's views is to be found in Rose R. Subotnik, "Adorno's Diagnosis of Beethoven's Late Style: Early Symptoms of Fatal Condition," *Journal of the American Musicological Society* 29 (Summer 1976): 251–53.
7. This is the theme of Adorno's *Philosophie der neuen Musik* (1949), whose English translation is *Philosophy of Modern Music*, trans. Anne G. Mitchell and Wesley V. Blomster (New York: Seabury Press, 1973). The book depends allusively on Adorno's conceptions of late Beethoven and Wagner.
8. Adorno, *Philosophy of Modem Music*, p. 102.
9. *Ibid.*, p. 131.
10. *Ibid.*, p. 133.
11. Adorno's thesis is that, whereas for Schoenberg the twelve-tone system was the enactment of a historical and philosophical crisis, for today's component it has lost its urgency entirely. "Modern Music Is Growing Old," *The Score* 18 (December 1956): 18–29.
12. "Quelques souvenirs de Pierre Boulez," *Critique* 471–72 (Aout–Septembre 1986): 745–47.
13. A perspicacious example is Alan Durant's *Conditions of Music* (London: Macmillan, 1984).
14. Subotnik, "The Historical Structure: Adorno's 'French' Model for the

Criticism of Nineteenth-Century Music," *19th Century Music* 2 (July 1978): 36–60.

15. The full tide is *Understanding Toscanini: How He Became an American Culture-God and Helped Create a New Audience for Old Music.* I reviewed the book in some detail in *The New York Times Book Review* (March 8, 1987).
16. Adorno, "Die Meisterschaft des Maestro," in *Gesammelte Schriften 16* (Frankfurt: Suhrkamp, 1982), p. 66, and *passim.*
17. Otto Friedrich, *Glenn Gould: A Life and Variations* (New York: Random House, 1989); see pp. 15–16 for the story about Gould's not playing marbles, his unwillingness to catch a tennis ball, etc.
18. *The Glenn Gould Reader,* ed. Tim Page (New York: Alfred A. Knopf, 1984).
19. B. W. Powe, *The Solitary Outlaw: Trudeau, Lewis, Gould, Canetti, McLuhan* (Toronto: Lester and Orpen Dennys, 1987).
20. *The Glenn Gould Reader,* pp. 331–57. See also Payzant, note 22, below.
21. Jonathan Cott, *Conversations with Glenn Gould* (New York: Little, Brown, 1984).
22. Geoffrey Payzant, *Glenn Gould, Music and Mind* (1978; reprint, Toronto: Key Porter Books, 1984).
23. *Glenn Gould: Non, je ne suis pas de tout un excentrique,* montage et presentation de Bruno Monsaingeon (Paris: Fayard, 1986).

Chapter 13: Jane Austen and Empire

1. Michael Gorra, "Who Paid the Bills at Mansfield Park?" *The New York Times Book Review* (February 28, 1993): 11; John Leonard, "Novel Colonies," *The Nation* (March 22, 1993): 383; W. J. T. Mitchell, "In the Wilderness," *The London Review of Books* (April 8, 1993): 11; Michael Wood, "Lost Paradises," *The New York Review of Books* (March 3, 1994): 44–47.
2. Raymond Williams, *The Country and the City* (New York: Oxford University Press, 1973): 112–19.
3. V. G. Kiernan, *Marxism and Imperialism* (New York: St. Martin's Press, 1974): 100.
4. John Stuart Mill, *Disquisitions and Discussions,* vol. 3 (London: Longmans, Green, Reader & Dyer, 1875): 167–68. For an earlier version of this see the discussion by Nicholas Canny, "The Ideology of English Colonization: From Ireland to America," *William and Mary Quarterly* 30 (1973): 575–98.
5. Williams, *Country and the City,* p. 281
6. Peter Hulme, *Colonial Encounters: Europe and the Native Caribbean, 1492–1797* (London: Methuen, 1986). See also his anthology with Neil

L. Whitehead, *Wild Majesty: Encounters with Caribs from Columbus to the Present Day* (Oxford: Claredon Press, 1992).

7. Hobson, *Imperialism*, p. 6.
8. This is most memorably discussed in C. L. R. James's *The Black Jacobins: Toussaint L'Ouverture and the San Domingo Revolution* (1938; reprint, New York: Vintage, 1963), especially Chapter 2, "The Owners." See also Robin Blackburn, *The Overthrow of Colonial Slavery, 1776–1848* (London: Verso, 1988): 149–53.
9. Williams, *Country and the City*, p. 117.
10. Jane Austen, *Mansfield Park*, ed. Tony Tanner (1814; reprint, Harmondsworth: Penguin, 1966): 42. The best account of the novel is in Tony Tanner's *Jane Austen* (Cambridge, Mass.: Harvard University Press, 1986).
11. *Ibid.*, p. 54.
12. *Ibid.*, p. 206.
13. Warren Roberts, *Jane Austen and the French Revolution* (London: Macmillan, 1979): 97–98. See also Avrom Fleishman, *A Reading of* Mansfield Park: *An Essay in Critical Synthesis* (Minneapolis: University of Minnesota Press, 1967): 36–39 and *passim.*
14. Austen, *Mansfield Park*, pp. 375–76.
15. John Stuart Mill, *Principles of Politcal Economy*, vol. 3, ed. J. M. Robson (Toronto: University of Toronto Press, 1965): 693. The passage is quoted in Sidney W. Mintz, *Sweetness and Power: The Place of Sugar in Modern History* (New York: Viking, 1985): 42
16. Austen, *Mansfield Park*, p. 446.
17. *Ibid.*, p. 448.
18. *Ibid.*, p. 450.
19. *Ibid.*, p. 456.
20. John Gallagher, *The Decline, Revival and Fall of the British Empire* (Cambridge: Cambridge University Press, 1982): 76.
21. Austen, *Mansfield Park*, p. 308.
22. Lowell Joseph Ragatz, *The Fall of the Planter Class in the British Caribbean, 1763–1833: A Study in Social and Economic History* (1928; reprint, New York: Octagon, 1963): 27.
23. Eric Williams, *Capitalism and Slavery* (New York: Russell & Russell, 1961): 211. See also his *From Columbus to Castro: The History of the Caribbean, 1492–1969* (London: Deutsch, 1970): 177–254.
24. Austen, *Mansfield Park*, p. 213.

Chapter 14: Intellectual Exile: Expatriates and Marginals

1. Theodor Adorno, *Minima Moralia: Reflections from Damaged Life*, trans. E. F. N. Jephcott (London: New Left Books, 1951): 38–39.
2. *Ibid.*, p. 87.

Chapter 16: On Writing a Memoir

1. Justus Reid Weiner, "My Beautiful House and Other Fabrications by Edward Said," *Commentary* (September 1999).
2. Alexander Cockburn, "The Attack on Said," *Counterpunch* (September 1, 1999).
3. Christopher Hitchens, "Whose Life Is It Anyway?" *The Nation* (October 4, 1999): 9.
4. Ammiel Alcalay, "Stop-Time in the Levant," *The Nation* (December 20, 1999).

PERMISSIONS ACKNOWLEDGMENTS

Many of the essays in this collection were originally published in the following:

"Islam as News" (1980) from *Covering Islam* by Edward W. Said (Pantheon Books, a division of Random House, Inc., 1981).

"Yeats and Decolonization" (1988) and "Jane Austen and Empire" (1990) from *Culture and Imperialism* by Edward W. Said (Alfred A. Knopf, a division of Random House, Inc., 1993).

"The Introduction" and "The Scope of Orientalism" from *Orientalism* by Edward W. Said (Pantheon Books, a division of Random House, Inc., 1978).

"On Writing a Memoir" from *Out of Place* by Edward W. Said (Alfred A. Knopf, a division of Random House, Inc., 1999).

"The Middle East 'Peace Process': Misleading Images and Brutal Actualities" from *Peace and Its Discontents* by Edward W. Said (Vintage Books, a division of Random House, Inc., 1995).

"The Palestinian Experience" (1969) and "Permission to Narrate" (1984) from *The Politics of Dispossession* by Edward W. Said (Pantheon Books, a division of Random House, Inc., 1994).

"Zionism from the Standpoint of Its Victims" from *The Question of Palestine* by Edward W. Said (Random House, Inc., 1979).

"Intellectual Exile: Expatriates and Marginals" (1993) from *Representations of the Intellectual* by Edward W. Said (Pantheon Books, a division of Random House, Inc., 1994).

Grateful acknowledgment is made to the following for permission to reprint previously published material:

Columbia University Press: "Interiors" (1986) from *After the Sky* by Edward W. Said, copyright © 1999 by Columbia University Press; "Performance as an Extreme Occasion" (1989) from *Musical Elaborations* by Edward W. Said, copyright © 1991 by Columbia University Press; and "Molestation and Authority in Narrative Fiction" (1971) from *Beginnings: Intention and Method* by Edward W. Said, copyright © 1985 by Columbia University Press. Reprinted by permission of Columbia University Press.

Harvard University Press: Excerpted text from "Secular Criticism" and "Traveling Theory" from *The World, the Text, and the Critic* by Edward W. Said (Cambridge, Mass.: Harvard University Press). Copyright © 1983 by Edward W. Said. Reprinted by permission of Harvard University Press.

ABOUT THE EDITORS

Moustafa Bayoumi received his Ph.D. from the Department of English and Comparative Literature of Columbia University. He is an Assistant Professor of English at Brooklyn College, City University of New York.

Andrew Rubin earned his M.A. from the University of Sussex and in 1995 received his M.A. from Columbia University, where he is currently a doctoral candidate in the Department of English and Comparative Literature. He is the coeditor of *Theodor W. Adorno: A Critical Reader.*